KNOWLEDGE REPRESENTATION, REASONING AND DECLARATIVE PROBLEM SOLVING

KNOWLEDGE REPRESENTATION, REASONING AND DECLARATIVE PROBLEM SOLVING

CHITTA BARAL

Arizona State University

CAMBRIDGE
UNIVERSITY PRESS

CAMBRIDGE UNIVERSITY PRESS
Cambridge, New York, Melbourne, Madrid, Cape Town, Singapore,
São Paulo, Delhi, Dubai, Tokyo, Mexico City

Cambridge University Press
The Edinburgh Building, Cambridge CB2 8RU, UK

Published in the United States of America by Cambridge University Press, New York

www.cambridge.org
Information on this title: www.cambridge.org/9780521147750

First published 2003
First paperback printing 2010

A catalogue record for this publication is available from the British Library

Library of Congress Cataloguing in Publication data
Baral, Chitta.
Knowledge representation, reasoning, and declarative problem solving / Chitta Baral.
p.   cm.
Includes bibliographical references and index.
ISBN 0 521 81802 8
1. Expert systems (Computer science)   2. Artificial intelligence.   3. Knowledge
representation (Information theory).   I. Title.
QA76.76.E95 B265   2002
006.3′3–dc21   2002025622

ISBN 978-0-521-81802-5 Hardback
ISBN 978-0-521-14775-0 Paperback

Contents

Preface

Representing knowledge and reasoning with it are important components of an intelligent system, and are two important facets of Artificial Intelligence. Another important expectation from intelligent systems is their ability to accept high level requests – as opposed to detailed step-by-step instructions, and their knowledge and reasoning ability are used to figure out the detailed steps that need to be taken. To have this ability intelligent systems must have a declarative interface whose input language must be based on logic.

Thus the author considers the all-round development of a suitable declarative knowledge representation language to be a fundamental component of knowledge based intelligence, perhaps similar to the role of the language of calculus to mathematics, and physics. Taking the calculus analogy further, it is important that a large support structure is developed around the language, similar to the integration and derivation formulas and the various theorems around calculus.

Although several languages have been proposed for knowledge representation, the language of AnsProlog* – logic programming with the answer set semantics, stands out in terms of the size and variety of the support structure developed around it. The support structure includes both implementations and use of the implementations in developing applications, and theoretical results for both analyzing and step-by-step building of theories (or programs) in this language. The support structure and the desirable properties of the language are also a testimony to the appropriateness of the language for knowledge representation, reasoning, and declarative problem solving.

This book is about AnsProlog* and compiles the various results obtained over the years about AnsProlog*. This book is expected to be useful to researchers in logic programming, declarative programming, artificial intelligence, knowledge representation, and autonomous agents; to knowledge engineers who would like to create and use large knowledge bases; to software practitioners who would like to use declarative programming for fast prototyping, and for developing critical programs that must be correct with respect to a formal specification; to programmers of autonomous agents who would like to build intelligent components such as planners, schedulers, and diagnosis and repair systems; and to students and teachers using it as a text book in undergraduate and graduate classes.

The distinguishing features of this book are: (i) It uses answer set semantics of logic programs. (ii) A big part of this book is about declarative programming and knowledge representation methodology. It presents several small and big example modules, and presents the theory that describes when modules can be combined, when a module is consistent, how to incorporate an observation, etc. (iii) Because it uses answer set semantics which allows multiple 'models' of a theory, it is able to go beyond reasoning to declarative problem solving. Thus it includes encoding of applications such as planning, diagnosis, explanation generation, scheduling, combinatorial auctions, abductive reasoning, etc. Most of these applications are related to encoding problems that are **NP**-complete or beyond. The book also explores the well-founded semantics. Since the well-founded semantics is sound with respect to answer set semantics and is easier to compute, in this book it is treated as an approximation to answer set semantics. (iv) The book discusses complexity and expressiveness issues and identifies subsets belonging to different complexity and expressiveness classes. (v) It presents algorithms to compute answer sets. Some of the algorithms it discusses use heuristics and other intelligent search ideas. (vi) Most of the programs discussed in the book can be run. It uses the smodels and the dlv interpreter for this and is supplemented by a web site containing a large subset of the example programs as smodels or dlv code. We now give a brief description of the various chapters of the book.

0.1 Brief description of the chapters

- **Chapter 1: Declarative programming in AnsProlog*: introduction and preliminaries**
  In Chapter 1 we motivate the importance of declarative languages and argue that intelligent entities must be able to comprehend and process descriptions of '*what*', rather than being told '*how*' all the time. We then make the case for AnsProlog* (programming in logic with answer set semantics) and compare it with other nonmonotonic languages, and with the PROLOG programming language. We then present the syntax and semantics of various sub-classes of AnsProlog*, and consider two views of AnsProlog* programs: stand alone programs, and functions. There are more than 30 examples illustrating the various definitions and results.
- **Chapter 2: Simple modules for declarative programming with answer sets**
  In this chapter we present several small AnsProlog* programs or modules corresponding to several problem solving or knowledge representation modules. This chapter is like a tool box of programs that can be combined for larger applications. In a sense it gives a quick glimpse of the book, and can be thought of as introducing the usefulness and applicability of AnsProlog* through examples.

- **Chapter 3: Principles and properties of declarative programming with answer sets**
  In this chapter we present several fundamental results that are useful in *analyzing* and *step-by-step building* of AnsProlog* programs, viewed both as stand alone programs and as functions. To analyze AnsProlog* programs we define and describe several properties such as categoricity (presence of unique answer sets), coherence (presence of at least one answer set), computability (answer set computation being recursive), filter-abducibility (abductive assimilation of observations using filtering), language independence (independence between answer sets of a program and the language), language tolerance (preservation of the meaning of a program with respect to the original language when the language is enlarged), strong equivalence, compilability to first-order theory, amenability to removal of **or**, and restricted monotonicity (exhibition of monotonicity with respect to a select set of literals).

  We also define several sub-classes of AnsProlog* programs such as stratified, locally stratified, acyclic, tight, signed, head cycle free and several conditions on AnsProlog* rules such as well-moded, and state results about which AnsProlog* programs have what properties. We present several results that relate answer sets of an AnsProlog* program to its rules. We develop the notion of splitting and show how the notions of stratification, local stratification, and splitting can be used in step-by-step computation of answer sets.

  For *step-by-step building* of AnsProlog* programs we develop the notion of conservative extension – where a program preserves its original meaning after additional rules are added to it, and present conditions for programs that exhibit this property. We present several operators such as incremental extension, interpolation, domain completion, input opening, and input extension, and show how they can be used for systematically building larger programs from smaller modules.

- **Chapter 4: Declarative problem solving and reasoning in AnsProlog***
  In this chapter we formulate several knowledge representation and problem solving domains using AnsProlog*. Our focus in this chapter is on program development. We start with three well-known problems from the literature of constraint satisfaction, and automated reasoning: placing queens on a chess board, determining who owns the zebra, and finding tile covering in a mutilated chess board. We present several encodings of these problems using AnsProlog* and analyze them. We then discuss a general methodology for representing constraint satisfaction problems (CSPs) and show how to extend it to dynamic CSPs. We then present encodings of several combinatorial graph problems such as k-colorability, Hamiltonian circuit, and k-clique. After discussing these problem solving examples, we present a general methodology of reasoning with prioritized defaults, and show how reasoning with inheritance hierarchies is a special case of this.

- **Chapter 5: Reasoning about actions and planning in AnsProlog***
  In this chapter we consider reasoning about actions in a dynamic world and its application to plan verification, simple planning, planning with various kinds of domain constraints, observation assimilation and explanation, and diagnosis. We make a detailed and systematic formulation – in AnsProlog* – of the above issues starting from the simplest reasoning about action scenarios and gradually increasing its expressiveness by adding features such

as causal constraints, and parallel execution of actions. We also prove properties of our AnsProlog* formulations using the results in Chapter 3.

Our motivation behind the choice of a detailed formulation of this domain is two fold. (i) Reasoning about actions captures both major issues of this book: knowledge representation and declarative problem solving. To reason about actions we need to formulate the frame problem whose intuitive meaning is that objects in the worlds do not normally change their properties. Formalizing this has been one of the benchmark problems of knowledge representation and reasoning formalisms. We show how AnsProlog* is up to this task. Reasoning about actions also forms the ground work for planning with actions, an important problem solving task. We present AnsProlog* encodings of planning such that each of the answer sets encodes a plan. (ii) Our second motivation is in regard to the demonstration of the usefulness of the results in Chapter 3. We analyze and prove properties of our AnsProlog* formulations of reasoning about actions and planning by using the various results in Chapter 3, and thus illustrate their usefulness. For this we also start with simple reasoning about action scenarios and then in latter sections we consider more expressive scenarios.

- **Chapter 6: Complexity, expressiveness and other properties of AnsProlog* programs**
In this chapter we consider some broader properties that help answer questions such as: (a) how difficult is it to compute answer sets of various sub-classes of AnsProlog*? (b) how expressive are the various sub-classes of AnsProlog*? (c) how modular is AnsProlog*? and (d) what is the relationship between AnsProlog* and other non-monotonic formalisms?

The answers to these questions are important in many ways. For example, if we know the complexity of a problem that we want to solve then the answer to (a) will tell us which particular subset of AnsProlog* will be most efficient, and the answer to (b) will tell us the most restricted subset that we can use to represent that problem. To make this chapter self complete we start with the basic notions of complexity and expressiveness, and present definitions of the polynomial, arithmetic and analytical hierarchy, and their normal forms. We later use them to show the complexity and expressiveness of AnsProlog* subclasses.

- **Chapter 7: Answer set computing algorithms**
In this chapter we present several answer set computing algorithms and compare them. The particular algorithms we present are the wfs-bb algorithm that uses branch and bound after computing the well-founded semantics, the assume-and-reduce algorithm of SLG, the smodels algorithm, and the dlv algorithm.

- **Chapter 8: Query answering and answer set computing systems**
In this chapter we explain how to program using the Smodels and dlv systems, discuss the extensions that these systems have beyond AnsProlog*, and present several programs in their syntax. We then describe when a PROLOG interpreter can be used in answering queries to AnsProlog* programs and under what conditions the PROLOG interpreter is sound and complete with respect to AnsProlog*. We present several applications developed using the Smodels and dlv systems. This includes, combinatorial auctions, planning with durative actions and resources, scheduling, and specification and verification of active databases.

- **Chapter 9: Further extensions of and alternatives to AnsProlog***
  In this chapter we discuss further extensions to AnsProlog*, such as allowing **not** in the head of rules, allowing nested expressions, allowing epistemic operators, doing abductive reasoning, allowing set constructs, and allowing specification of priorities between rules. We discuss the universal query problem and discuss an extension where domain closure can be selectively specified. We also discuss some of the alternative characterizations of programs in AnsProlog* syntax.

- **Appendices**
  There are two small appendices in the book, one about ordinals, lattices, and fixpoints, and another on Turing machines.

- **Web site**
  The web site of the book has the Smodels and dlv code of several programs discussed throughout the book, a list of pointers to resources such as home pages of active scientists and researchers in the field, implemented systems, and applications and programs written with respect to those systems. See http://www.baral.us/bookone

0.2 Using it as a textbook

The book is a systematic compilation of the available support structure around AnsProlog*. It can be used as a text book with some selection and reordering of the material by the instructor. For example, for an undergraduate (junior-senior) course it is recommended that most of Chapter 1, Chapter 2, a very small part of Chapter 3, Chapter 4, parts of Chapter 5, parts of Chapter 7, and Chapter 8 are covered. In this the Smodels and dlv system in Chapter 8 should be introduced concurrently with Chapter 1 so that as the students learn the definition, they can program it. Many of the notations in Chapter 1 should first be glanced over and students should come back to it when necessary.

For a follow-up graduate course it is recommended that the remaining material (Chapter 3, most of Chapter 5, Chapter 6, parts of Chapter 7, and Chapter 9) are covered together with a quick overview of Chapters 1, 2, 4, and 8. For a stand alone graduate course that does not have the undergraduate course as the pre-requisite it is recommended that Chapters 1–8 are covered, leaving out a few sections in some of the chapters.

0.3 Appreciation and thanks

This book came about after almost a decade of interacting with and learning from my colleague and teacher Michael Gelfond at the University of Texas at El Paso. Many ideas and perspectives behind this book that unify the different sections and chapters are due to this interaction and learning. Interactions with Vladimir Lifschitz and his feedback also had a significant influence in the various aspects of this book. Thomas Eiter helped the author to understand several aspects of the complexity and expressiveness results and gave detailed feedback on Chapter 6. Gerald Pfeifer gave detailed feedback on the dlv algorithm and the dlv system covered in Chapters 7 and 8. Mauricio Osorio gave feedback on Chapters 1–5. Jack Minker (my doctoral advisor) gave feedback on several aspects of the book. Jürgen Dix provided help in the writing of Section 6.6.9, Mauricio Osorio helped in the writing of Section 3.9.7, Kewen Wang and Torsten Schaub helped in the writing of Section 9.7, Phan Minh Dung helped in the writing of Section 9.8.5, Jia-Huai You helped in the writing of Section 9.8.6, and Mutsumi Nakamura helped in the writing of Section 8.3.5.

The author would like to acknowledge the help of his students (Nam Tran, Tran Son, Le-Chi Tuan, Viet Hung Nguyen, Cenk Uyan, Saadat Anwar and Guray Alsac), the Smodels group, the dlv group, the Texas action group (TAG), and the encouragement of his colleagues Jorge Lobo, Fang-Zhen Lin, Alessandro Provetti, Mirek Truszczyński, Jose Alferes, Vladik Kreinovich, Luís Moniz Pereira, Sheila McIlraith, Yan Zhang, Ramon Otero, Pedro Cabalar, Dan Cooke, Ken Ford, Rao Kambhampati, Huan Liu and Hudson Turner in writing this book. He would also like to acknowledge support from his start-up funds at the Arizona State University, support of his past Chair Stephen Yau, and NSF support through grants IRI-9501577 and 0070463 and NASA support through grant NCC2-1232.

The author appreciates the support of David Tranah and Cambridge University Press through the whole process of getting this book out. In particular, the copy editing significantly improved the text.

Finally, the author would like to thank his parents, extended family (siblings, in-laws, Jay, and Sabrina) and his spouse Mutsumi for their support and patience, and the loving and supporting environment they created when the book was being written.

Chapter 1

Declarative programming in AnsProlog*: introduction and preliminaries

Among other characteristics, an intelligent entity – whether an intelligent autonomous agent, or an intelligent assistant – must have the ability to go beyond just following direct instructions while in pursuit of a goal. This is necessary to be able to behave intelligently when the assumptions surrounding the direct instructions are not valid, or there are no direct instructions at all. For example even a seemingly direct instruction of 'bring me coffee' to an assistant requires the assistant to figure out what to do if the coffee pot is out of water, or if the coffee machine is broken. The assistant will definitely be referred to as lacking intelligence if he or she were to report to the boss that there is no water in the coffee pot and ask the boss what to do next. On the other hand, an assistant will be considered intelligent if he or she can take a high level request of 'make travel arrangements for my trip to International AI conference 20XX' and figure out the lecture times of the boss; take into account airline, hotel and car rental preferences; take into account the budget limitations, etc.; overcome hurdles such as the preferred flight being sold out; and make satisfactory arrangements. This example illustrates *one benchmark of intelligence – the level of request an entity can handle*. At one end of the spectrum the request is a detailed algorithm that spells out *how* to satisfy the request, which no matter how detailed it is may not be sufficient in cases where the assumptions inherent in the algorithm are violated. At the other end of the spectrum the request spells out *what* needs to be done, and the entity has the knowledge – again in the *what* form rather than the *how* form – and the knowledge processing ability to figure out the exact steps (that will satisfy the request) and execute them, and when it does not have the necessary knowledge it either knows where to obtain the necessary knowledge, or is able to gracefully get around its ignorance through its ability to reason in the presence of incomplete knowledge.

The languages for spelling out *how* are often referred to as *procedural* while the languages for spelling out *what* are referred to as *declarative*. Thus our initial thesis that intelligent entities must be able to comprehend and process descriptions of *what*

1

leads to the necessity of inventing suitable declarative languages and developing support structures around those languages to facilitate their use. We consider the development of such languages to be fundamental to knowledge based intelligence, perhaps similar to the role of the language of calculus in mathematics and physics. *This book is about such a declarative language – the language of* **AnsProlog***. We now give a brief history behind the quest for a suitable declarative language for knowledge representation, reasoning, and declarative problem solving.

Classical logic which has been used as a specification language for procedural programming languages was an obvious initial choice to represent declarative knowledge. But it was quickly realized that classical logic embodies the monotonicity property according to which the conclusion entailed by a body of knowledge stubbornly remains valid no matter what additional knowledge is added. This disallowed human like reasoning where conclusions are made with the available (often incomplete) knowledge and may be withdrawn in the presence of additional knowledge. This led to the development of the field of *nonmonotonic logic*, and several nonmonotonic logics such as circumscription, default logic, auto-epistemic logic, and nonmonotonic modal logics were proposed. The AI journal special issue of 1980 (volume 13, numbers 1 and 2) contained initial articles on some of these logics. In the last twenty years there have been several studies on these languages on issues such as representation of small common-sense reasoning examples, alternative semantics of these languages, and the relationship between the languages. But the dearth of efficient implementations, use in large applications – say of more than ten pages, and studies on building block support structures has for the time being diminished their applicability. Perhaps the above is due to some fundamental deficiency, such as: all of these languages which build on top of the classical logic syntax and allow nesting are quite complex, and all except default logic lack structure, thus making it harder to use them, analyze them, and develop interpreters for them.

An alternative nonmonotonic language paradigm with a different origin whose initial focus was to consider a subset of classical logic (rather than extending it) is the programming language PROLOG and the class of languages clubbed together as 'logic programming'. PROLOG and logic programming grew out of work on automated theorem proving and Robinson's resolution rule. One important landmark in this was the realization by Kowalski and Colmerauer that logic can be used as a programming language, and the term PROLOG was developed as an acronym from PROgramming in LOGic. A subset of first-order logic referred to as Horn clauses that allowed faster and simpler inferencing through resolution was chosen as the starting point. The notion of closed world assumption (CWA) in databases was then imported to PROLOG and logic programming and the negation as failure operator **not** was used to refer to negative information. The evolution of PROLOG was guided by concerns that it be made a full fledged programming language with efficient implementations, often at the cost of sacrificing the declarativeness of logic. Nevertheless, research also continued on logic programming languages with declarative semantics. In the late 1980s and early 1990s the focus was on finding the right semantics for agreed syntactic sub-classes. One of the two most popular semantics proposed during that time is the *answer set semantics*, also referred to as the *stable model semantics*.

This book is about the language of logic programming with respect to the answer set semantics. We refer to this language as AnsProlog*, as a short form of '**Pro**gramming in **log**ic with **Ans**wer sets'[1]. In the following section we give an overview of how AnsProlog* is different from PROLOG and also the other nonmonotonic languages, and present the case for AnsProlog* to be the most suitable declarative language for knowledge representation, reasoning, and declarative problem solving.

1.1 Motivation: Why AnsProlog*?

In this section[2], for the purpose of giving a quick overview without getting into a lot of terminology, we consider an AnsProlog* program to be a collection of rules of the form:

$$L_0 \text{ or } \cdots \text{ or } L_k \leftarrow L_{k+1}, \ldots, L_m, \textbf{not } L_{m+1}, \ldots, \textbf{not } L_n.$$

where each of the L_is is a literal in the sense of classical logic. Intuitively, the above rule means that if $L_{k+1}, \ldots, L_m$ are to be true and if $L_{m+1}, \ldots, L_n$ can be safely assumed to be false then at least one of $L_0, \ldots, L_k$ must be true.

This simple language has a lot going for it to be the leading language for knowledge representation, reasoning, and declarative problem solving. To start with, the nonclassical symbols $\leftarrow$, and **not** in AnsProlog* give it a structure and allow us to easily define syntactic sub-classes and study their properties. It so happens that these various sub-classes have a range of complexity and expressiveness thus allowing us to choose the appropriate sub-classes for particular applications. Moreover, there exists a more tractable approximate characterization which can be used – at the possible cost of completeness – when time is a concern. Unlike the other nonmonotonic logics, AnsProlog* now has efficient implementations which have been used to program large applications. In addition, the expressiveness studies show AnsProlog* to be as expressive as some of these logics, while syntactically it seems less intimidating as it does not allow arbitrary formulas. Finally, the most important reason to study and use AnsProlog* is that there is now a large body (much larger than for any other knowledge representation language) of support structure around AnsProlog*

---

[1] In the recent literature it has also been referred to as A-Prolog [BGN00, Gel01].
[2] In Section 1.2 we introduce more specific terminologies and use those in the rest of the book.

that includes the above mentioned implementations and theoretical building block results that allow systematic construction of AnsProlog* programs, and assimilation of new information. We now expand on these points in greater detail.

1.1.1 AnsProlog* vs PROLOG

Although, PROLOG grew out of programming with Horn clauses – a subset of first-order logic, several nondeclarative features were included in PROLOG to make it programmer friendly. We propose AnsProlog* as a declarative alternative to PROLOG. Besides the fact that AnsProlog* allows disjunction in the head of rules, the following are the main differences between AnsProlog* and Prolog.

- The ordering of literals in the body of a rule matters in PROLOG as it processes them from left to right. Similarly, the positioning of a rule in the program matters in PROLOG as it processes them from start to end. The ordering of rules and positioning of literals in the body of a rule do not matter in AnsProlog*. From the perspective of AnsProlog*, a program is a *set* of AnsProlog* rules, and in each AnsProlog* rule, the body is a *set* of literals and literals preceded by **not**.
- Query processing in PROLOG is top-down from query to facts. In AnsProlog* query-processing methodology is not part of the semantics. Most sound and complete interpreters with respect to AnsProlog* do bottom-up query processing from facts to conclusions or queries.
- Because of the top-down query processing, and start to end, and left to right processing of rules and literals in the body of a rule respectively, a PROLOG program may get into an infinite loop for even simple programs without negation as failure.
- The *cut* operator in PROLOG is extra-logical, although there have been some recent attempts at characterizing it. This operator is not part of AnsProlog*.
- There are certain problems, such as floundering and getting stuck in a loop, in the way PROLOG deals with negation as failure. In general, PROLOG has trouble with programs that have recursions through the negation as failure operator. AnsProlog* does not have these problems, and as its name indicates it uses the *answer set* semantics to characterize negation as failure.

In this book, besides viewing AnsProlog* as a declarative alternative to PROLOG, we also view PROLOG systems as top-down query answering systems that are correct with respect to a sub-class of AnsProlog* under certain conditions. In Section 8.4 we present these conditions and give examples that satisfy these conditions.

1.1.2 AnsProlog* vs Logic programming

AnsProlog* is a particular kind of logic programming. In AnsProlog* we fix the semantics to *answer set semantics*, and only focus on that. On the other hand logic programming refers to a broader agenda where different semantics are considered as alternatives. We now compare AnsProlog (a sub-class of AnsProlog* with only one atom in the head, and without classical negation in the body) with the alternative semantics of programs with AnsProlog syntax.

Since the early days of logic programming there have been several proposals for semantics of programs with AnsProlog syntax. We discuss some of the popular ones in greater detail in Chapter 9. Among them, the most popular ones are the *stable model semantics* and the *well-founded semantics*. The stable models are same as the answer sets of AnsProlog programs, the main focus of this book. The well-founded semantics differs from the stable model semantics in that:

- Well-founded models are three-valued, while stable models are two valued.
- Each AnsProlog program has a unique well-founded model, while some AnsProlog programs have multiple stable models and some do not have any.

  For example, the program $\{p \leftarrow \textbf{not } p.\}$ has no stable models while it has the unique well-founded model where p is assigned the truth value *unknown*.

  The program $\{b \leftarrow \textbf{not } a., a \leftarrow \textbf{not } b., p \leftarrow a., p \leftarrow b.\}$ has two stable models $\{p, a\}$ and $\{p, b\}$ while its unique well-founded model assigns the truth value *unknown* to p, a, and b.

- Computing the well-founded model or entailment with respect to it is more tractable than computing the entailment with respect to stable models. On the other hand the latter increases the expressive power of the language.

As will be clear from many of the applications that will be discussed in Chapters 4 and 5, the nondeterminism that can be expressed through multiple stable models plays an important role. In particular, they are important for enumerating choices that are used in planning and also in formalizing aggregation. On the other hand, the absence of stable models of certain programs, which was initially thought of as a drawback of the stable model semantics, is useful in formulating integrity constraints whose violation forces elimination of models.

1.1.3 AnsProlog* vs Default logic

The sub-class AnsProlog can be considered as a particular subclass of default logic that leads to a more efficient implementation. Recall that a default logic is a pair (W, D), where W is a first-order theory and D is a collection of defaults of the type $\frac{\alpha:\beta_1,...,\beta_n}{\gamma}$, where α, β, and γ are well-founded formulas. AnsProlog can be considered as a special case of a default theory where $W = \emptyset$, γ is an atom, α is a conjunction of atoms, and β_is are literals. Moreover, it has been shown that AnsProlog* and default logic have the same expressiveness. In summary, AnsProlog* is syntactically simpler than default logic and yet has the same expressiveness, thus making it more usable.

1.1.4 AnsProlog* vs Circumscription and classical logic

The connective '←' and the negation as failure operator **'not'** in AnsProlog* add structure to an AnsProlog* program. The AnsProlog* rule $a \leftarrow b$. is different from the classical logic formula $b \supset a$, and the connective '←' divides the rule of an AnsProlog* program into two parts: the head and the body.

This structure allows us to define several syntactic and semi-syntactic notions such as: *splitting, stratification, signing*, etc. Using these notions we can define several subclasses of AnsProlog* programs, and study their properties such as: *consistency, coherence, complexity, expressiveness, filter-abducibility*, and *compilability to classical logic*.

The sub-classes and their specific properties have led to several building block results and realization theorems that help in developing large AnsProlog* programs in a systematic manner. For example, suppose we have a set of rules with the predicates $p_1, \ldots, p_n$ in them. Now if we add additional rules to the program such that $p_1, \ldots, p_n$ only appear in the body of the new rules, then if the overall program is consistent the addition of the new rules does not change the meaning of the original predicates $p_1, \ldots, p_n$. Additional realization theorems deal with issues such as: When can closed world assumption (CWA) about certain predicates be explicitly stated without changing the meaning of the modified program? How to modify an AnsProlog* program which assumes CWA so that it reasons appropriately when CWA is removed for certain predicates and we have incomplete information about these predicates?

The non-classical operator ← encodes a form of directionality that makes it easier to encode causality, which can not be expressed in classical logic in a straightforward way. AnsProlog* is more expressive than propositional and first-order logic and can express transitive closure and aggregation that are not expressible in them.

1.1.5 AnsProlog* as a knowledge representation language

There has been extensive study about the suitability of AnsProlog* as a knowledge representation language. Some of the properties that have been studied are:

- When an AnsProlog* program exhibits *restricted monotonicity*. That is, it behaves monotonically with respect to addition of literals about certain predicates. This is important when developing an AnsProlog* program where we do not want future information to change the meaning of a definition.
- When is an AnsProlog* program *language independent*? When is it *language tolerant*? When is it *sort-ignorable*; i.e., when can sorts be ignored?
- When can new knowledge be added through filtering?

In addition it has been shown that AnsProlog* provides *compact representation* in certain knowledge representation problems; i.e., an equivalent representation in a tractable language would lead to an exponential blow-up in space. Similarly, it has been shown that certain representations in AnsProlog* can not be *modularly* translated into propositional logic. On the other hand problems such as constraint satisfaction problems, dynamic constraint satisfaction problems, etc. can be modularly represented in AnsProlog*. In a similar manner to its relationship with default logic, subclasses of other nonmonotonic formalisms such as auto-epistemic logic have also been shown to be equivalent to AnsProlog*.

Finally, the popular sub-class AnsProlog has a sound approximate characterization, called the well-founded semantics, which has nice properties and which is computationally more tractable.

1.1.6 AnsProlog* implementations: Both a specification and a programming language

Since AnsProlog* is fully declarative, representation (or programming) in AnsProlog* can be considered both as a specification and a program. Thus AnsProlog* representations eliminate the ubiquitous gap between specification and programming.

There are now some efficient implementations of AnsProlog* sub-classes, and many applications are built on top of these implementations. Although there are also some implementations of other nonmonotonic logics such as default logic (DeReS at the University of Kentucky) and circumscription (at the Linköping University), these implementations are very slow and very few applications have been developed based on them.

1.1.7 Applications of AnsProlog*

The following is a list of applications of AnsProlog* to database query languages, knowledge representation, reasoning, and planning.

- AnsProlog* has a greater ability than Datalog in expressing database query features. In particular, AnsProlog* can be used to give a declarative characterization of the standard *aggregate operators*, and recently it has been used to define new aggregate operators, and even data mining operators. It can also be used for querying in the presence of different kinds of incomplete information, including *null values*.
- AnsProlog* has been used in planning and allows easy expression of different kinds of (procedural, temporal, and hierarchical) domain control knowledge, ramification and qualification constraints, conditional effects, and other advanced constructs, and can be used for approximate planning in the presence of incompleteness. Unlike propositional logic, AnsProlog* can be used for conformant planning, and there are attempts to use AnsProlog* for planning with sensing and diagnostic reasoning. It has also been used for

assimilating observation of an agent and planning from the current situation by an agent in a dynamic world.

- AnsProlog* has been used in product configuration, representing constraint satisfaction problems (CSPs) and dynamic constraint satisfaction problems (DCSPs).
- AnsProlog* has been used for scheduling, supply chain planning, and in solving combinatorial auctions.
- AnsProlog* has been used in formalizing deadlock and reachability in Petri nets, in characterizing monitors, and in cryptography.
- AnsProlog* has been used in verification of contingency plans for shuttles, and also has been used in verifying correctness of circuits in the presence of delays.
- AnsProlog* has been used in benchmark knowledge representation problems such as reasoning about actions, plan verification, and the frame problem therein, in reasoning with inheritance hierarchies, and in reasoning with prioritized defaults. It has been used to formulate normative statements, exceptions, weak exceptions, and limited reasoning about what is known and what is not.
- AnsProlog* is most appropriate for reasoning with incomplete information. It allows various degrees of trade-off between computing efficiency and completeness when reasoning with incomplete information.

1.2 Answer set frameworks and programs

In this section we define the syntax of an AnsProlog* program (and its extensions and sub-classes), and the various notations that will be used in defining the syntax and semantics of these programs and in their analysis in the rest of the book.

An *answer set framework*[3] consists of two alphabets (an axiom alphabet and a query alphabet), two languages (an axiom language, and a query language) defined over the two alphabets, a set of axioms, and an entailment relation between sets of axioms and queries. The query alphabet will be closely associated with the axiom alphabet and the query language will be fairly simple and will be discussed later in Section 1.3.5. We will now focus on the axiom language.

Definition 1 The axiom alphabet (or simply the *alphabet*) of an answer set framework consists of seven classes of symbols:

(1) variables,
(2) object constants (also referred to as constants),
(3) function symbols,
(4) predicate symbols,
(5) connectives,
(6) punctuation symbols, and
(7) the special symbol ⊥;

---

[3] In contrast logical theories usually have a single alphabet, a single language, and have inference rules to derive theorems from a given set of axioms. The theorems and axioms are both in the same language.

where the connectives and punctuation symbols are fixed to the set $\{\neg,\ or,\ \leftarrow, \text{not} , \text{`,'}\}$ and $\{$ '(', ')', '.' $\}$ respectively; while the other classes vary from alphabet to alphabet. □

We now present an example to illustrate the role of the above classes of symbols. Consider a world of blocks in a table. In this world, we may have object constants such as *block*1, *block*2, . . . corresponding to the particular blocks and the object constant *table* referring to the table. We may have predicates *on_table*, and *on* that can be used to describe the various properties that hold in a particular instance of the world. For example, *on_table(block1)* means that *block1* is on the table. Similarly, *on(block2, block3)* may mean that *block2* is on top of *block3*. An example of a function symbol could be *on_top*, where *on_top(block3)* will refer to the block (if any) that is on top of block3.

Unlike the earlier prevalent view of considering logic programs as a subset of first order logic we consider answer set theories to be different from first-order theories, particularly with some different connectives. Hence, to make a clear distinction between the connectives in a first-order theory and the connectives in the axiom alphabet of an answer set framework, we use different symbols than normally used in first-order theories: *or* instead of $\vee$, and ',' instead of $\wedge$.

We use some informal notational conventions. In general, variables are arbitrary strings of English letters and numbers that start with an upper-case letter, while constants, predicate symbols and function symbols are strings that start with a lower-case letter. Sometimes – when dealing with abstractions – we use the additional convention of using letters $p, q, \ldots$ for predicate symbols, $X, Y, Z, \ldots$ for variables, $f, g, h, \ldots$ for function symbols, and $a, b, c, \ldots$ for constants.

Definition 2 A *term* is inductively defined as follows:

(1) A variable is a term.
(2) A constant is a term.
(3) If f is an n-ary function symbol and $t_1, \ldots, t_n$ are terms then $f(t_1, \ldots, t_n)$ is a term.
□

Definition 3 A term is said to be *ground*, if no variable occurs in it. □

Definition 4 Herbrand Universe and Herbrand Base

- The Herbrand Universe of a language $\mathcal{L}$, denoted by $HU_{\mathcal{L}}$, is the set of all ground terms which can be formed with the functions and constants in $\mathcal{L}$.
- An *atom* is of the form $p(t_1, \ldots, t_n)$, where p is a predicate symbol and each t_i is a term. If each of the t_is is ground then the atom is said to be ground.
- The Herbrand Base of a language $\mathcal{L}$, denoted by $HB_{\mathcal{L}}$, is the set of all ground atoms that can be formed with predicates from $\mathcal{L}$ and terms from $HU_{\mathcal{L}}$.

- A *literal* is either an atom or an atom preceded by the symbol $\neg$. The former is referred to as a positive literal, while the latter is referred to as a negative literal.

  A literal is referred to as ground if the atom in it is ground.
- A *naf-literal* is either an atom or an atom preceded by the symbol **not**.

  The former is referred to as a positive naf-literal, while the latter is referred to as a negative naf-literal.
- A *gen-literal* is either a literal or a literal preceded by the symbol **not**.   □

Example 1 Consider an alphabet with variables X and Y, object constants a, b, function symbol f of arity 1, and predicate symbols p of arity 1. Let $\mathcal{L}_1$ be the language defined by this alphabet.

Then $f(X)$ and $f(f(Y))$ are examples of terms, while $f(a)$ is an example of a ground term. Both $p(f(X))$ and $p(Y)$ are examples of atoms, while $p(a)$ and $p(f(a))$ are examples of ground atoms.

The Herbrand Universe of $\mathcal{L}_1$ is the set $\{a, b, f(a), f(b), f(f(a)), f(f(b)), f(f(f(a))), f(f(f(b))), \ldots\}$.

The Herbrand Base of $\mathcal{L}_1'$ is the set $\{p(a), p(b), p(f(a)), p(f(b)), p(f(f(a))), p(f(f(b))), p(f(f(f(a)))), p(f(f(f(b)))), \ldots\}$.   □

Definition 5 A *rule* is of the form:

$$L_0 \; or \cdots or \; L_k \leftarrow L_{k+1}, \ldots, L_m, \textbf{not } L_{m+1}, \ldots, \textbf{not } L_n. \tag{1.2.1}$$

where L_is are literals or when $k = 0$, L_0 may be the symbol $\perp$, and $k \geq 0, m \geq k$, and $n \geq m$.

A rule is said to be ground if all the literals of the rule are ground.

The parts on the left and on the right of '$\leftarrow$' are called the *head* (or *conclusion*) and the *body* (or *premise*) of the rule, respectively.

A rule with an empty body and a single disjunct in the head (i.e., $k = 0$) is called a *fact*, and then if L_0 is a ground literal we refer to it as a ground fact.

A fact can be simply written without the $\leftarrow$ as:

$$L_0. \tag{1.2.2}$$

□

When $k = 0$, and $L_0 = \perp$, we refer to the rule as a *constraint*.

The $\perp$s in the heads of constraints are often eliminated and simply written as rules with empty head, as in

$$\leftarrow L_1, \ldots, L_m, \textbf{not } L_{m+1}, \ldots, \textbf{not } L_n. \tag{1.2.3}$$

Definition 6 Let r be a rule in a language $\mathcal{L}$. The *grounding* of r in $\mathcal{L}$, denoted by $ground(r, \mathcal{L})$, is the set of all rules obtained from r by all possible substitutions of elements of $HU_{\mathcal{L}}$ for the variables in r.   □

Example 2 Consider the rule $p(f(X)) \leftarrow p(X)$. and the language $\mathcal{L}_1$ from Example 1. Then $ground(r, \mathcal{L}_1)$ will consist of the following rules:

$p(f(a)) \leftarrow p(a)$.
$p(f(b)) \leftarrow p(b)$.
$p(f(f(a))) \leftarrow p(f(a))$.
$p(f(f(b))) \leftarrow p(f(b))$.
$\vdots$
                                                              □

Definition 7 The *answer set language* given by an alphabet consists of the set of all ground rules constructed from the symbols of the alphabet.   □

It is easy to see that the language given by an alphabet is uniquely determined by its constants O, function symbols F, and predicate symbols P. This triple $\sigma = (O, F, P)$ is referred to as the *signature* of the answer set framework and often we describe a language by just giving its signature.

1.2.1 AnsProlog* programs

An AnsProlog* program is a finite set of rules of the form (1.2.1), and is used to succintly express a set of axioms of an answer set framework. 'AnsProlog' is a short form for *Answer set programming in logic*, and the '*' denotes that we do not place any restrictions on the rules.

With each AnsProlog* program Π, when its language is not otherwise specified, we associate the language $\mathcal{L}(\Pi)$ that is defined by the predicates, functions, and constants occurring in Π. If no constant occurs in Π, we add some constants to $\mathcal{L}(\Pi)$ for technical reasons. Unless stated otherwise, we use the simplified notation HU_{Π} and HB_{Π} instead of $HU_{\mathcal{L}(\Pi)}$ and $HB_{\mathcal{L}(\Pi)}$, respectively. When the context is clear we may just use HU and HB, without the subscripts.

Example 3 Consider the following AnsProlog* program Π:

$p(a)$.
$p(b)$.
$p(c)$.
$p(f(X)) \leftarrow p(X)$.

Then $\mathcal{L}(\Pi)$ is the language defined by the predicate p, function f, and constants a, b, and c.

HU_Π is the set $\{a, b, c, \; f(a), \; f(b), \; f(c), \; f(f(a)), \; f(f(b)), \; f(f(c)),$
$\quad f(f(f(a))), f(f(f(b))), f(f(f(c))), \ldots\}$.

HB_Π is the set $\{p(a), \; p(b), \; p(c), \; p(f(a)), \; p(f(b)), \; p(f(c)), \; p(f(f(a))),$
$\quad p(f(f(b))), p(f(f(c))), \; p(f(f(f(a)))), p(f(f(f(b)))), p(f(f(f(c)))), \ldots\}$.
$\hfill \square$

Throughout this book we consider several distinct sub-classes of AnsProlog* programs. The important ones are:

- AnsProlog program: A set of rules where L_is are atoms and $k = 0$. This is the most popular sub-class, and to make it easier to write and refer, it does not have a superscript.

  Such programs are syntactically[4] referred to as *general logic programs* and *normal logic programs* in the literature. The program in Example 3 is an AnsProlog program.

  Example 4 Following is an example of another AnsProlog program from which we can conclude that *tweety* flies while *skippy* is abnormal and does not fly.

  $fly(X) \leftarrow bird(X), \textbf{not } ab(X).$
  $ab(X) \leftarrow penguin(X).$
  $bird(X) \leftarrow penguin(X).$
  $bird(tweety) \leftarrow.$
  $penguin(skippy) \leftarrow.$
  $\hfill \square$

- AnsProlog$^{-\textbf{not}}$ program: A set of rules where L_is are atoms, $k = 0$, and $m = n$.

  Such programs are referred to as *definite programs* and *Horn logic programs* in the literature.

  Example 5 The following is an example of an AnsProlog$^{-\textbf{not}}$ program from which we can make conclusions about the *ancestor* relationship between the constants $a, b, c, d,$ and e, for the particular parent relationship specified in the program:

  $anc(X, Y) \leftarrow par(X, Y).$
  $anc(X, Y) \leftarrow par(X, Z), anc(Z, Y).$
  $par(a, b) \leftarrow.$
  $par(b, c) \leftarrow.$
  $par(d, e) \leftarrow.$

  The first two rules of the above program can be used to define the ancestor relationship over an arbitrary set of *parent* atoms. This is an example of 'transitive closure' and in general it cannot be specified using first-order logic.
  $\hfill \square$

---

[4] AnsProlog programs also denote a particular semantics, while several different semantics may be associated with general logic programs.

- AnsProlog¬ program: A set of rules where $k = 0$.

Such programs are syntactically referred to as *extended logic programs* in the literature.

Example 6 The following is an example of an AnsProlog¬ program from which we can conclude that *tweety* flies while *rocky* does not.

$fly(X) \leftarrow bird(X), \textbf{not} \neg fly(X).$
$\neg fly(X) \leftarrow penguin(X).$
$bird(tweety) \leftarrow.$
$bird(rocky) \leftarrow.$
$penguin(rocky) \leftarrow.$ □

- AnsProlog^{or} program: A set of rules where L_is are atoms.

Such programs are syntactically referred to as *normal disjunctive logic programs* in the literature. Sub-classes of them where $m = n$ are syntactically referred to as *disjunctive logic programs*.

Example 7 The following is an example of an AnsProlog^{or} program from which we can conclude that *slinky* is either a bird or a reptile but not both.

$bird(X) \text{ or } reptile(X) \leftarrow lays\_egg(X).$
$lays\_egg(slinky) \leftarrow.$ □

- In each of the above classes if we allow constraints (i.e., rules with ⊥ in the head) then we have AnsProlog$^⊥$, AnsProlog$^{-\textbf{not},⊥}$, AnsProlog$^{¬,⊥}$, and AnsProlog$^{or,⊥}$ programs respectively.
- AnsProlog$^{¬, or,⊥}$ program: It is the same as an AnsProlog* program.
- AnsDatalog program: An AnsProlog program, with the restriction that the underlying language does not have function symbols. The programs in Example 4 and Example 5 are also AnsDatalog programs, while the program in Example 3 is not an AnsDatalog program.
- AnsDatalog^X program, $X \in \{$ '$-\textbf{not}$', '*', '¬', 'or', '¬, or', '$-\textbf{not}, ⊥$', '¬, ⊥', '$or, ⊥$', '¬, $or, ⊥$' $\}$: An AnsProlog^X program, with the restriction that the underlying language does not have function symbols. The programs in Example 5, Example 6, and Example 7 are examples of AnsDatalog$^{-\textbf{not}}$, AnsDatalog$^¬$, and AnsDatalog^{or} programs, respectively.
- Propositional Y program, where Y is one of the above classes: A program from the class Y with the added restriction that all the predicates are of arity 0, i.e., all atoms are propositional ones. An example of a propositional AnsProlog program is the program $\{a \leftarrow \textbf{not } b.b \leftarrow \textbf{not } a.\}$.
- AnsProlog*(n) program: An AnsProlog*(n) program is an AnsProlog* program that has at most n literals in the body of its rules. We can make similar restrictions for other sub-classes of AnsProlog*.

The following table relates our terminologies to the various terminologies used in the literature.

AnsProlog terminology	Earlier terminologies
answer sets (of AnsProlog programs)	stable models
AnsProlog$^{-\textbf{not}}$	definite programs, Horn logic programs
AnsProlog	general logic programs, normal logic programs
	(with stable model semantics)
AnsProlog$^{\neg}$	extended logic programs
	(with answer set semantics)
AnsProlog^{or}	normal disjunctive logic programs
	(with stable model semantics)
AnsProlog$^{-\textbf{not},or}$	disjunctive logic programs
AnsDatalog$^{-\textbf{not}}$	Datalog
AnsDatalog	Datalog$^{\textbf{not}}$ (with stable model semantics)
AnsDatalog^{or}	Datalog$^{\textbf{not},or}$ (with stable model semantics)

1.2.2 AnsProlog notations*

In this section we will present an almost comprehensive list of additional notations that will be used in the rest of this book. The reader should not become concerned with the large range of notations, and does not need to grasp them all at the same time. Only a small subset of them will be used together in a section or a chapter. The reason we give them here together instead of distributing them over the various chapters is that some of the notations are very similar and may create confusion if presented separately. By presenting them together we can contrast them easily.

- Given a rule r of the form (1.2.1):
  $head(r) = \{L_0, \ldots, L_k\}$,
  $body(r) = \{L_{k+1}, \ldots, L_m, \textbf{not } L_{m+1}, \ldots, \textbf{not } L_n\}$,
  $pos(r) = body^+(r) = \{L_{k+1}, \ldots, L_m\}$,
  $neg(r) = body^-(r) = \{L_{m+1}, \ldots, L_n\}$,
  $lit(r) = head(r) \cup pos(r) \cup neg(r)$, and
  r is said to be *active* with respect to a pair $\langle X, Y \rangle$ of sets of literals, if $pos(r) \subseteq X$, and
    $neg(r) \cap Y = \emptyset$.
  Given a set of literals S, $\textbf{not } S$ denotes the set of naf-literals $\{\textbf{not } l : l \in S\}$. Using this notation we write $\mathcal{A} \leftarrow \mathcal{B}^+, \textbf{not } \mathcal{B}^-$ to denote the rule r where $\mathcal{A}$ is $head(r)$, $\mathcal{B}^+$ is $pos(r)$, and $\mathcal{B}^-$ is $neg(r)$.
- For any program Π, $Head(\Pi) = \bigcup_{r \in \Pi} head(r)$.
- Various notations for sets of atoms.
  For a predicate p, $atoms(p)$ will denote the subset of HB_Π formed with predicate p.
  For a set of predicates A, $atoms(A)$ will denote the subset of HB_Π formed with the predicates in A.

For a list of predicates $p_1, \ldots, p_n$, $atoms(p_1, \ldots, p_n)$ denotes the set of atoms formed with predicates $p_1, \ldots, p_n$.

For a signature σ, $atoms(\sigma)$ denotes the set of atoms over σ.

Given a set of naf-literals S, $atoms(S)$ denotes the set $\{a : a$ is an atom, and $a \in S\} \cup \{a : a$ is an atom, and **not** $a \in S\}$.

- Various notations for sets of literals.

For a program Π, $lit(\Pi) = \bigcup_{r \in \Pi} lit(r)$.

For a predicate p, $Lit(p)$ denotes the collection of ground literals formed by the predicate p.

For a language $\mathcal{L}$, $Lit(\mathcal{L})$ denotes the set of all literals in $\mathcal{L}$.

For a program Π, Lit_Π denotes the set of all literals in its associated language; and when the context is clear we may just use Lit.

For a list of predicates $p_1, \ldots, p_n$, $lit(p_1, \ldots, p_n)$ denotes the set of literals formed with predicates $p_1, \ldots, p_n$.

For a signature σ, $lit(\sigma)$ denotes the set of literals over σ.

- For any logic program Π, we define

$$ground(\Pi, \mathcal{L}) = \bigcup_{r \in \Pi} ground(r, \mathcal{L})$$

and write $ground(\Pi)$ for $ground(\Pi, \mathcal{L}(\Pi))$.

Example 8 Consider the program Π from Example 3. The program $ground(\Pi)$ consists of the following rules:

$p(a) \leftarrow$.
$p(b) \leftarrow$.
$p(c) \leftarrow$.
$p(f(a)) \leftarrow p(a)$.
$p(f(b)) \leftarrow p(b)$.
$p(f(c)) \leftarrow p(c)$.
$p(f(f(a))) \leftarrow p(f(a))$.
$p(f(f(b))) \leftarrow p(f(b))$.
$p(f(f(c))) \leftarrow p(f(c))$.
$\vdots$ □

- Signature $\sigma_1 = \{O_1, F_1, P_1\}$ is said to be a sub-signature of signature $\sigma_2 = \{O_2, F_2, P_2\}$ if $O_1 \subseteq O_2$, $F_1 \subseteq F_2$ and $P_1 \subseteq P_2$.

$\sigma_1 + \sigma_2$ denotes the signature $\{O_1 \cup O_2, F_1 \cup F_2, P_1 \cup P_2\}$.

The sets of all ground terms over signature σ are denoted by $terms(\sigma)$.

Consistent sets of ground literals over signature σ are called *states* of σ and denoted by $states(\sigma)$.

- For any literal l, the symbol $\bar{l}$ denotes the literal opposite in sign to l. That is for an atom a, if $l = \neg a$ then $\bar{l} = a$, and if $l = a$ then $\bar{l} = \neg a$. Moreover, we say l and $\bar{l}$ are *complementary* or *contrary* literals.

  Similarly for a literal l, $not(l)$ denotes the gen-literal **not** l, while $not(\textbf{not }l)$ denotes l.

- For a set of literals S, $\bar{S}$ denotes the set $HB \setminus S$.
- For a set of literals S, $\neg S$ denotes the set $\{\bar{l} \,:\, l \in S\}$.
- For a set of literals S, $Cn(S) = Lit$ if S has complementary literals; otherwise $Cn(S) = S$.
- Two sets of literals S_1 and S_2 are said to disagree if $S_1 \cap \neg S_2 \neq \emptyset$. Otherwise we say that they agree.
- Given a set of literals L and an AnsProlog* program Π, $\Pi \cup L$ means the AnsProlog* program $\Pi \cup \{l \leftarrow . \,:\, l \in L\}$.
- Let Π be an AnsProlog program, A be a set of naf-literals, and B be a set of atoms. B is said to *agree* with A, if $\{a : a$ is an atom, and $a \in A\} \subseteq B$ and $\{a : a$ is an atom, and **not** $a \in A\} \cap B = \emptyset$.
- A set S of literals is said to be *complete* with respect to a set of literals P if for any atom in P either the atom or its negation is in S. When $P = S$ or P is clear from the context, we may just say S is complete.
- A set X of literals is said to be *saturated* if every literal in X has its complement in X.
- A set X of literals is said to be *supported by* an AnsProlog$^{\neg,\perp}$ program Π, if for every literal L in X there is a rule in Π with L in its head and $L_1, \ldots, L_m$, **not** L_{m+1}, **not** L_n as its body such that $\{L_1 \ldots, L_m\} \subseteq X$ and $\{L_{m+1}, \ldots, L_n\} \cap X = \emptyset$.
- A rule is said to be *range restricted* (or *allowed*) if every variable occurring in a rule of the form 1.2.1 occurs in one of the literals $L_{k+1}, \ldots, L_m$. In the presence of built-in comparative predicates such as *equal, greater than*, etc., the variables must occur in a nonbuilt-in literal among $L_{k+1}, \ldots, L_m$. A program Π is range restricted (or allowed) if every rule in Π is range restricted.

The programs in Examples 3–7 are all range restricted. The program consisting of the following rules is not range restricted, as its first rule has the variable X in the head which does not appear in its body at all.

$p(X) \leftarrow q.$
$r(a) \leftarrow .$

The program consisting of the following rules is also not range restricted, as its first rule has the variable Y, which appears in **not** $r(X, Y)$ in the body, but does not appear in a positive naf-literal in the body.

$p(X) \leftarrow q(X), \textbf{not } r(X, Y).$
$r(a, b) \leftarrow .$
$q(c) \leftarrow .$

1.3 Semantics of AnsProlog* programs

In this section we define the semantics of AnsProlog* programs. For that we first define the notion of answer sets for the various sub-classes and then define query languages appropriate for the various sub-classes and define the entailment between programs and queries. While defining the answer sets we start with the most specific sub-class and gradually consider the more general sub-classes.

The answer sets of an AnsProlog* program Π, are defined in terms of the answer sets of the ground program *ground*(Π). Hence, in the rest of the section we can assume that we are only dealing with ground programs.

1.3.1 Answer sets of AnsProlog$^{-\mathbf{not}}$ and AnsProlog$^{-\mathbf{not},\perp}$ programs

AnsProlog$^{-\mathbf{not}}$ programs form the simplest class of declarative logic programs, and its semantics can be defined in several ways. We present two of them here, and refer to [Llo84, Llo87, LMR92] for other characterizations. In particular, we present a model theoretic characterization and a fixpoint characterization.

Model theoretic characterization

A *Herbrand interpretation* of an AnsProlog$^{\perp}$ program Π is any subset $I \subseteq HB_\Pi$ of its Herbrand base. Answer sets are defined as particular Herbrand interpretations that satisfy certain properties with respect to the program and are 'minimal'. We say an interpretation I is *minimal* among the set $\{I_1, \ldots, I_n\}$ if there does not exist a j, $1 \le j \le n$ such that I_j is a strict subset of I. We say an interpretation I is *least* among the set $\{I_1, \ldots, I_n\}$ if for all j, $1 \le j \le n$ $I \subseteq I_j$.

A *Herbrand interpretation* S of Π is said to *satisfy* the AnsProlog$^{\perp}$ rule

$$L_0 \leftarrow L_1, \ldots, L_m, \mathbf{not}\ L_{m+1}, \ldots, \mathbf{not}\ L_n.$$

if (i) $L_0 \neq \perp$: $\{L_1, \ldots, L_m\} \subseteq S$ and $\{L_{m+1}, \ldots, L_n\} \cap S = \emptyset$ implies that $L_0 \in S$.
(ii) $L_0 = \perp$: $\{L_1, \ldots, L_m\} \not\subseteq S$ or $\{L_{m+1}, \ldots, L_n\} \cap S \neq \emptyset$.

A *Herbrand model* A of an AnsProlog$^{\perp}$ program Π is a Herbrand interpretation of Π such that it satisfies all rules in Π. We also refer to this as A is closed under Π.

Definition 8 An answer set of an AnsProlog$^{-\mathbf{not},\perp}$ program Π is a Herbrand model of Π which is minimal among the Herbrand models of Π.   □

Example 9 Consider the following AnsProlog$^{-\mathbf{not}}$ program:

$p \leftarrow a.$
$q \leftarrow b.$
$a \leftarrow .$

The set $\{a, b, p, q\}$ is a model[5] of this program as it satisfies all rules of this program. The sets $\{a, p, q\}$ and $\{a, p\}$ are also models of this program. But the set $\{a, b, p\}$ is not a model of this program as it does not satisfy the second rule.

Since $\{a, p\}$ is a model of this program, the sets $\{a, b, p, q\}$ and $\{a, p, q\}$ which are strict supersets of $\{a, p\}$ are not minimal models of this program. None of the sets $\{a\}$, $\{p\}$, and $\{\}$ are models of this program as each of them does not satisfy at least one of the rules of the program. Thus since all the strict subsets of $\{a, p\}$ are not models of this program, $\{a, p\}$ is a minimal model and answer set of the program.   □

Example 10 The program Π in Example 5 has an answer set S_1 given by the set $\{par(a, b), par(b, c), par(d, e), anc(a, b), anc(b, c), anc(a, c), anc(d, e)\}$, which is also its unique minimal Herbrand model. It is easy to see that S_1 satisfies all rules of $ground(\Pi)$. Hence, it is a model of Π. We now have to show that it is a minimal model. To show that S_1 is a minimal model, we will show that none of the strict subsets of S_1 are models of $ground(\Pi)$. Suppose we were to remove one of the *par* atoms of Π. In that case it will no longer be a model of $ground(\Pi)$. Now suppose we were to remove $anc(a, b)$ from S_1. The resulting interpretation is not a model of $ground(\Pi)$ as it does not satisfy one of the ground instances of the first rule of Π. The same goes for $anc(b, c)$ and $anc(d, e)$. Hence, we cannot remove one of those three and still have a model. Now, if we remove $anc(a, c)$, it will no longer be a model as it will not satisfy one of the ground instances of the second rule of Π. Hence, S_1 is a minimal model and answer set of $ground(\Pi)$ and therefore of Π.

The set $S_2 = \{par(a, b), par(b, c), par(d, e), anc(a, b), anc(b, c), anc(a, c), anc(d, e), par(d, c), anc(d, c)\}$ is a Herbrand model of $ground(\Pi)$, as it satisfies all rules in $ground(\Pi)$. S_2 is not minimal among the models of Π, as S_1, a model of Π, is a strict subset of S_2. Hence, S_2 is also not an answer set of Π.

The set $\{par(a, b), par(b, c), par(d, e), anc(a, b), anc(b, c), anc(a, c), anc(d, e), par(d, c)\}$ is not a Herbrand model of $ground(\pi)$ as it does not satisfy the rule:

$$anc(d, c) \leftarrow par(d, c).$$

which is one of the ground instances of the first rule of Π.   □

---

[5] In the rest of this section whenever it is clear from the context we may simply say 'model' instead of 'Herbrand model.'

The notion of model although useful, is a relic from the semantics of first-order logic. So alternatively, answer sets can be defined without using the notion of a model in the following way:

Definition 9 An *answer set* of an AnsProlog$^{-\textbf{not},\perp}$ program Π is a minimal subset (with respect to subset ordering) S of HB that is closed under $ground(\Pi)$.
$\square$

Proposition 1 AnsProlog$^{-\textbf{not}}$ programs have unique answer sets. $\square$

The above is not true in general for AnsProlog$^{-\textbf{not},\perp}$ programs. For example, the program $\{p \leftarrow ., \perp \leftarrow p.\}$ does not have an answer set. We will denote the answer set of an AnsProlog$^{-\textbf{not},\perp}$ program Π, if it exists, by $\mathcal{M}_0(\Pi)$. Otherwise, $\mathcal{M}_0(\Pi)$ is undefined. For an AnsProlog$^{-\textbf{not}}$ program Π we will denote its unique minimal Herbrand model by $MM(\Pi)$.

Proposition 2 The intersection of the Herbrand models of an AnsProlog$^{-\textbf{not}}$ program is its unique minimal Herbrand model. $\square$

Exercise 1 Consider the program consisting of the following rules.

$p \leftarrow p.$

What are the models of this program? What are its answer sets? $\square$

Iterated fixpoint characterization

From a computational viewpoint, a more useful characterization is an iterated fixpoint characterization. To give such a characterization let us assume Π to be a possibly infinite set of ground AnsProlog$^{-\textbf{not}}$ rules. Let 2^{HB_Π} denote the set of all Herbrand interpretations of Π. We define an operator $T_\Pi^0 : 2^{HB_\Pi} \rightarrow 2^{HB_\Pi}$ as follows:

$$T_\Pi^0(I) = \{L_0 \in HB_\Pi \mid \Pi \text{ contains a rule } L_0 \leftarrow L_1, \ldots, L_m. \text{ such that}$$
$$\{L_1, \ldots, L_m\} \subseteq I \text{ holds}\}. \tag{1.3.4}$$

The above operator is referred to as the *immediate consequence operator*. Intuitively, $T_\Pi^0(I)$ is the set of atoms that can be derived from a single application of Π given the atoms in I.

We will now argue that T_Π^0 is monotone, i.e., $I \subseteq I' \Rightarrow T_\Pi^0(I) \subseteq T_\Pi^0(I')$. Suppose X is an arbitrary element of $T_\Pi^0(I)$. Then there must be a rule $X \leftarrow L_1, \ldots, L_m$.

in Π such that $\{L_1, \ldots, L_m\} \subseteq I$. Since $I \subseteq I'$, we have that $\{L_1, \ldots, L_m\} \subseteq I'$. Hence, X must be in $T_\Pi^0(I')$. Therefore, $T_\Pi^0(I) \subseteq T_\Pi^0(I')$.

Now, let us assign the empty set to $T_\Pi^0 \uparrow 0$. Let us also define $T_\Pi^0 \uparrow (i + 1)$ to be $T_\Pi^0(T_\Pi^0 \uparrow i)$. Clearly, $T_\Pi^0 \uparrow 0 \subseteq T_\Pi^0 \uparrow 1$; and by monotonicity of T_Π^0 and transitivity of $\subseteq$, we have $T_\Pi^0 \uparrow i \subseteq T_\Pi^0 \uparrow (i + 1)$. In the case of a finite Herbrand base it can be easily seen that repeated application of T_Π^0 starting from the empty set will take us to a fixpoint of T_Π^0. We will now argue that this fixpoint – let us refer to it as a – that is reached is the least fixpoint of T_Π^0. Suppose this is not the case. Then there must be a different fixpoint b. Since b is the least fixpoint and a is only a fixpoint, $b \subseteq a$. Since $\emptyset \subseteq b$, by using the monotonicity property of T_Π^0 and by repeatedly applying T_Π^0 to both sides we will obtain $a \subseteq b$. Thus $a = b$, contradicting our assumption that b is different from a. Hence, a must be the least fixpoint of T_Π^0.

In the case of an infinite Herbrand base, the case is similar and we refer to Appendix A. We can summarize the result from Appendix A as being that the operator T_Π^0 satisfies a property called *continuity*, and the ordering $\subseteq$ over the elements in 2^{HB_Π} is a *complete lattice*, both of which guarantee that iterative application of T_Π^0 starting from the empty set will take us to the least fixpoint of T_Π^0. More formally, $\mathrm{lfp}(T_\Pi^0) = T_\Pi^0 \uparrow \omega =$ least upper bound of the set $\{T_\Pi^0 \uparrow \beta \,:\, \beta < \omega\}$, where ω is the first limit ordinal.

An AnsProlog$^{-\mathbf{not}}$ program Π can now be characterized by its least fixpoint. Recall that we assumed Π to be a possibly infinite set of ground rules. When this is not the case, and Π is non-ground, we characterize Π by the least fixpoint of the program $ground(\Pi)$. It can be shown that $\mathrm{lfp}(T_\Pi^0)$ is also the unique minimal Herbrand model of Π.

Proposition 3 For any AnsProlog$^{-\mathbf{not}}$ program Π, $\mathrm{lfp}(T_\Pi^0) =$ the unique minimal Herbrand model of $\Pi =$ the answer set of Π. $\square$

We now give two examples showing how the answer set of AnsProlog$^{-\mathbf{not}}$ programs can be computed by the iterated fixpoint method.

Example 11 Consider the following program Π from Example 9.

$p \leftarrow a.$
$q \leftarrow b.$
$a \leftarrow .$

By definition, $T_\Pi^0 \uparrow 0 = \emptyset$.

$T_\Pi^0 \uparrow 1 = T_\Pi^0(T_\Pi^0 \uparrow 0) = \{a\}.$
$T_\Pi^0 \uparrow 2 = T_\Pi^0(T_\Pi^0 \uparrow 1) = \{a, p\}.$
$T_\Pi^0 \uparrow 3 = T_\Pi^0(T_\Pi^0 \uparrow 2) = \{a, p\} = T_\Pi^0 \uparrow 2.$

Hence $\mathrm{lfp}(T_\Pi^0) = \{a, p\}$, and therefore $\{a, p\}$ is the answer set of Π. $\square$

Example 12 Let us now consider the program Π from Example 5.

By definition, $T_\Pi^0 \uparrow 0 = \emptyset$.

$T_\Pi^0 \uparrow 1 = T_\Pi^0(T_\Pi^0 \uparrow 0) = \{par(a, b), par(b, c), par(d, e)\}$.

$T_\Pi^0 \uparrow 2 = T_\Pi^0(T_\Pi^0 \uparrow 1) = \{par(a, b), par(b, c), par(d, e), anc(a, b), anc(b, c),$
$anc(d, e)\}$.

$T_\Pi^0 \uparrow 3 = T_\Pi^0(T_\Pi^0 \uparrow 2) = \{par(a, b), par(b, c), par(d, e), anc(a, b),$
$anc(b, c), anc(d, e), anc(a, c)\}$.

$T_\Pi^0 \uparrow 4 = T_\Pi^0(T_\Pi^0 \uparrow 3) = T_\Pi^0 \uparrow 3$.

Hence $\mathrm{lfp}(T_\Pi^0) = \{par(a, b), par(b, c), par(d, e), anc(a, b), anc(b, c), anc(d, e),$
$anc(a, c)\}$, is the answer set of Π. $\qquad\square$

Exercise 2 Given an AnsProlog^{-not} program Π, using Appendix A show that 2^{HB_Π} is a complete lattice with respect to the relation $\subseteq$. Also, show that T_Π^0 is continuous. $\qquad\square$

1.3.2 Answer sets of AnsProlog and AnsProlog$^\perp$ programs

AnsProlog programs are a superclass of AnsProlog^{-not} programs in that they allow the operator **not** in the body of the rules. In the literature of logic programming there are several different semantics for programs having the same syntax as AnsProlog. In this book our focus is on one particular semantics, the *answer set semantics*. Before defining the answer sets we show why the approach of minimal models and iterated fixpoints used in defining answer sets of AnsProlog^{-not} programs cannot be directly used in defining answer sets of AnsProlog programs.

The problem is that AnsProlog programs may have multiple minimal models, and intuitively not all of them may make sense. As per the iterated fixpoint approach, the direct extension of the operator T_Π^0 is not monotone, and hence its repeated application starting from the empty set may not lead to a fixpoint. The following examples illustrate these two points.

Example 13 Consider the program Π consisting of the only rule:

$a \leftarrow \textbf{not } b$.

This program has two minimal models $\{a\}$ and $\{b\}$. But the second one is not intuitive, as there is no justification for why b should be true. $\qquad\square$

Example 14 Consider the program Π consisting of the following rules:

$a \leftarrow \textbf{not } b$.
$b \leftarrow \textbf{not } a$.

Let us now consider the obvious extension of the T_Π^0 operator to AnsProlog programs. This extension, which we will refer to as T_Π^1 is defined as follows:

$$T_\Pi^1(I) = \{L_0 \in HB_\Pi \mid \Pi \text{ contains a rule } L_0 \leftarrow L_1, \ldots, L_m, \text{ not } L_{m+1}, \ldots,$$
$$\text{not } L_n.$$

such that $\{L_1, \ldots, L_m\} \subseteq I$ holds, and $\{L_{m+1}, \ldots, L_n\} \cap I = \emptyset\}$.
Now, $T_\Pi^1 \uparrow 0 = \emptyset$.

$$T_\Pi^1 \uparrow 1 = T_\Pi^1(T_\Pi^1 \uparrow 0) = \{a, b\}.$$
$$T_\Pi^1 \uparrow 2 = T_\Pi^1(T_\Pi^1 \uparrow 1) = \emptyset.$$
$$T_\Pi^1 \uparrow 3 = T_\Pi^1(T_\Pi^1 \uparrow 2) = \{a, b\}.$$

Thus the above sequence oscillates between $\emptyset$ and $\{a, b\}$, and never reaches a fixpoint. Moreover, while $\emptyset \subseteq \{a, b\}$, $T_\Pi^1(\emptyset) \not\subseteq T_\Pi^1(\{a, b\})$. That is, T_Π^1 is not a monotone operator. $\square$

The approach to defining answer sets of AnsProlog$^\perp$ programs is to use a fixpoint definition. Given a candidate answer set S for an AnsProlog$^\perp$ program Π, we first transform Π with respect to S and obtain an AnsProlog$^{-\text{not},\perp}$ program denoted by Π^S. S is defined as an answer set of Π, if S is the answer set of the transformed AnsProlog$^{-\text{not},\perp}$ program Π^S. This transformation is referred to as the Gelfond–Lifschitz transformation (also referred to as a reduct), as it was originally defined by Gelfond and Lifschitz in [GL88], their seminal paper introducing the stable model semantics. More formally,

Definition 10 Let Π be a ground AnsProlog$^\perp$ program. For any set S of atoms, let Π^S be a program obtained from Π by deleting

 (i) each rule that has a naf-literal **not** L in its body with $L \in S$, and
(ii) naf-literals of the form **not** L in the bodies of the remaining rules.

Clearly, Π^S does not contain **not**, so it is an AnsProlog$^{-\text{not},\perp}$ program and its answer set is already defined. If this answer set exists and coincides with S, then we say that S is an *answer set* of Π. In other words, an answer set of Π is characterized by the equation

$$S = \mathcal{M}_0(\Pi^S).$$ $\square$

We now illustrate the above definition through several examples.

Example 15 Consider the following program Π:

$p \leftarrow a.$
$a \leftarrow \text{not } b.$
$b \leftarrow \text{not } a.$

We will now show that $S_1 = \{p, a\}$ and $S_2 = \{b\}$ are answer sets of Π.

$\Pi^{S_1} = \{p \leftarrow a., a \leftarrow .\}$, and the answer set of Π^{S_1} is S_1. Hence, S_1 is an answer set of Π.

$\Pi^{S_2} = \{p \leftarrow a., b \leftarrow .\}$, and the answer set of Π^{S_2} is S_2. Hence, S_2 is an answer set of Π.

To illustrate why, for example, $S = \{a, b\}$ is not an answer set of Π, let us compute Π^S. $\Pi^S = \{p \leftarrow a.\}$, and the answer set of Π^S is $\emptyset$, which is different from S. Hence, S is not an answer set of Π. □

Example 16 Consider the following program Π:

$a \leftarrow$ **not** b.
$b \leftarrow$ **not** c.
$d \leftarrow .$

We will now show that $S_1 = \{d, b\}$ is an answer set of Π.

$\Pi^{S_1} = \{b \leftarrow ., d \leftarrow .\}$, and the answer set of Π^{S_1} is S_1. Hence, S_1 is an answer set of Π.

To illustrate why, for example, $S = \{a, d\}$ is not an answer set of Π, let us compute Π^S. $\Pi^S = \{a \leftarrow ., b \leftarrow ., d \leftarrow .\}$, and the answer set of Π^S is $\{a, b, d\}$, which is different from S. Hence, S is not an answer set of Π. □

Example 17 Consider the following program Π:

$p \leftarrow p$.
$q \leftarrow .$

The only answer set of this program is $\{q\}$, which is also the unique minimal model of this AnsProlog$^{-\textbf{not}}$ program. □

Example 18 Consider the following program Π:

$p \leftarrow$ **not** p, d.
$r \leftarrow .$
$d \leftarrow .$

The above program does not have an answer set. Intuitively, since r and d must be in any answer set, the two possible choices for answer sets of this program are $S_1 = \{r, d, p\}$ and $S_2 = \{r, d\}$. The program $\Pi^{S_1} = \{r \leftarrow ., d \leftarrow\}$ and it has the answer set $\{r, d\}$, which is different from S_1. Hence, S_1 is not an answer set of Π. Similarly, the program $\Pi^{S_2} = \{p \leftarrow d., r \leftarrow ., d \leftarrow\}$ and it has the answer set $\{r, d, p\}$, which is different from S_2. Hence, S_2 is not an answer set of Π.

One of the early criticisms of the answer set semantics was about the characterization of the above program. But now it is realized that the above characterization is useful in expressing constraints. For example, consider the following program:

$p \leftarrow \mathbf{not}\ p, d.$
$r \leftarrow \mathbf{not}\ d.$
$d \leftarrow \mathbf{not}\ r.$

The only answer set of this program is $\{r\}$. The first rule acts like a constraint which eliminates any candidate answer set that has d true. Thus, even though the last two rules have two answer sets $\{r\}$ and $\{d\}$, the second one is eliminated by the constraint like behavior of the first rule.

An alternative approach is to replace the first rule above by the two rules in $\{p \leftarrow \mathbf{not}\ p., p \leftarrow \mathbf{not}\ d\}$. The resulting program is:

$p \leftarrow \mathbf{not}\ p.$
$p \leftarrow \mathbf{not}\ d.$
$r \leftarrow \mathbf{not}\ d.$
$d \leftarrow \mathbf{not}\ r.$

In the above program, any candidate answer set where d is *false*, forces p to be true by the second rule, and this makes the first rule ineffective in eliminating that answer set. On the other hand, any candidate answer set where d is *true* can no longer use the second rule to force p to be true, and thus the first rule is effective in eliminating that answer set. Thus in the above program the program consisting of the last two rules has the answer sets $\{r\}$ and $\{d\}$. The first one forces p to be true by the second rule, and thus $\{r, p\}$ is an answer set of the program. The second one, on the other hand, is eliminated by the first rule, as the second rule does not come to its rescue. Thus the above program has the only answer set $\{r, p\}$. This program has some historical significance as it was used in [VG88] and later by others to argue that the answer set semantics is unintuitive. But now that we understand the role of the rule $p \leftarrow \mathbf{not}\ p.$ in constraint enforcement, the answer set characterization of the above program is quite meaningful. $\square$

Example 19 Consider the following program Π:

$p \leftarrow \mathbf{not}\ q, r.$
$q \leftarrow \mathbf{not}\ p.$

If the above program is presented to a PROLOG interpreter and a query about p or q is asked, the PROLOG interpreter will not be able to give an answer, and may get into an infinite loop. But intuitively, since there is no rule with r in its head, there is no way that r can be proven to be true and hence r can be assumed to be *false*. That means, there is no way that p can be proven true, as the first rule is the only one which can be used to prove p true, and that rule has r in its body. Thus, p can be assumed to be *false*. That in turn means, we can infer q to be true using the second rule. The answer set semantics captures this reasoning, and the above program has the unique answer set $\{q\}$, which is the answer set of $\Pi^{\{q\}} = \{q \leftarrow .\}$. $\qquad\square$

Example 20 Consider Π, the ground version of the program from Example 4 given below:

fly(tweety) $\leftarrow$ *bird(tweety)*, **not** *ab(tweety)*.
ab(tweety) $\leftarrow$ *penguin(tweety)*.
bird(tweety) $\leftarrow$ *penguin(tweety)*.
fly(skippy) $\leftarrow$ *bird(skippy)*, **not** *ab(skippy)*.
ab(skippy) $\leftarrow$ *penguin(skippy)*.
bird(skippy) $\leftarrow$ *penguin(skippy)*.
bird(tweety) $\leftarrow$.
penguin(skippy) $\leftarrow$.

We will show that the above program has $S = \{bird(tweety), penguin(skippy), bird(skippy), ab(skippy), fly(tweety)\}$ as an answer set.

The AnsProlog$^{-\textbf{not}}$ program Π^S consists of the following rules:

fly(tweety) $\leftarrow$ *bird(tweety)*.
ab(tweety) $\leftarrow$ *penguin(tweety)*.
bird(tweety) $\leftarrow$ *penguin(tweety)*.
ab(skippy) $\leftarrow$ *penguin(skippy)*.
bird(skippy) $\leftarrow$ *penguin(skippy)*.
bird(tweety) $\leftarrow$.
penguin(skippy) $\leftarrow$.

Since Π^S is an AnsProlog$^{-\textbf{not}}$ program, we will compute its answer set using the iterated fixpoint approach.

$T^0_{\Pi^S} \uparrow 0 = \emptyset.$
$T^0_{\Pi^S} \uparrow 1 = T^0_{\Pi^S}(T^0_{\Pi^S} \uparrow 0) = \{bird(tweety), penguin(skippy)\}.$
$T^0_{\Pi^S} \uparrow 2 = T^0_{\Pi^S}(T^0_{\Pi^S} \uparrow 1) = \{bird(tweety), penguin(skippy), bird(skippy),$
$\qquad\qquad\qquad\qquad ab(skippy), fly(tweety)\}.$
$T^0_{\Pi^S} \uparrow 3 = T^0_{\Pi^S}(T^0_{\Pi^S} \uparrow 2) = T^0_{\Pi^S} \uparrow 2 = S.$

Hence $\mathrm{lfp}(T^0_{\Pi^S}) = S$, is the answer set of Π^S. Thus, S is an answer set of Π. $\qquad\square$

Definition 10 defines when an interpretation is an answer set. Hence, using it we can only verify if a particular interpretation is an answer set or not. To show that a particular answer set of a program is the only answer set of that program we have to rule out the other interpretations. In Chapter 3 we discuss certain conditions such as acyclicity, stratification, and local stratification, which guarantee that an AnsProlog program has a unique answer set. The program in Example 20 is locally stratified and hence has a unique answer set.

Theorem 1.3.1 Answer sets of AnsProlog programs are also minimal Herbrand models.   □

Proof:
Let Π be an AnsProlog program and A be an answer set of Π. To show A is a minimal model of Π, we will first show that A is a model of Π.

By definition of an answer set A is a model of Π^A. It is easy to see that the body of any rule in Π that was removed during the construction of Π^A, evaluates to false with respect to A. Hence A satisfies those rules. It is also clear that A satisfies any rule in Π that remained in Π^A with possibly some changes. Hence, A is a model of Π.

Now we will show that no subset of A is a model of Π. Suppose there is a strict subset A' of A which is a model of Π. That means A' satisfies all rules in Π. Let us now consider any rule r' in Π^A. If r' is in Π then of course A' satisfies r'. Otherwise r' must come from some r in Π, where r has negative naf-literals of the form **not** p, with $p \notin A$. Since $A' \subset A$, $p \notin A'$. Thus these negative naf-literals evaluate to true both with respect to A and A'. Thus r is satisfied by A implies r' is satisfied by A'. Therefore A' is a model of Π^A, which contradicts A being the minimal model of Π^A. Hence, A must be a minimal model of Π.   □

The following proposition gives an alternative characterization of answer sets of AnsProlog that is often useful.

Proposition 4 M is an answer set of an AnsProlog program Π iff M is a model of Π and for all M', M' is a model of Π^M implies that $M \subseteq M'$.   □

Proof:
M is an answer set of Π iff
M is the answer set of Π^M iff
M is the least model of Π^M iff
M is a model of Π^M and for all M', M' is a model of Π^M implies $M \subseteq M'$ iff
M is a model of Π and for all M', M' is a model of Π^M implies $M \subseteq M'$.   □

1.3.3 Answer sets of AnsProlog⁻ and AnsProlog⁻,⊥ programs

AnsProlog programs provide negative information implicitly, through closed-world reasoning; they do not leave the user with a choice on that matter. For example, consider the program Π from Example 4. Suppose we were to observe that *tweety* is unable to fly. *We do not have a direct way to add this information to* Π. An indirect way would be to add either *penguin(tweety)* ← . or *ab(tweety)* ← . to Π.

Since an answer set of an AnsProlog program is a subset of the Herbrand base, an atom is either *true* with respect to it (i.e., it belongs to the answer set) or *false* with respect to it (i.e., it does not belongs to the answer set). Sometimes we may not want to commit either way. For example, we may want to encode the information that 'normally we can not make a *true-false* conclusion about whether a wounded bird flies or not.' We would be hard pressed to express this in AnsProlog.

For both examples above, what we need are rules that express when a bird normally flies and when it does not, and rules that can block the application of either or both. If such rules were allowed then in the first case we would just add the direct fact that 'tweety does not fly'. The question then is how do we directly express 'tweety does not fly'. We cannot use the negation as failure operator '**not**' as it means 'false by default or by assumption'. What we need is an explicit negation, similar[6] to the one used in classical logic. In the presence of such a negation operator we would be able to express 'tweety does not fly' by ¬*fly(tweety)* ←.

To further illustrate the intuitive difference between the negation as failure operator **not** and the explicit negation operator ¬, let us try to represent the knowledge[7] that it is safe for a school bus to cross a railway intersection if there is no train coming. In the absence of the explicit negation operator, we would write this as

cross ← **not** *train*.

But this rule may be dangerous. Suppose because of fog the sensors cannot figure out if there is a train coming or not and hence the program does not have the fact *train* ← . in it. The above rule would then entail that it is safe to cross the road, and this may lead to disaster if there was actually a train coming. A safer alternative would be to use the explicit negation operator ¬ and express the rule as:

cross ← ¬*train*.

---

[6] We say 'similar' but not 'same' because we do not want to transport the other properties of classical negation, such as $p \lor \neg p$ being always true. Some papers do refer to it as 'classical' negation, and others have referred to it by 'strong' negation. Pearce and Wagner [PW89] show that this negation has close ties with the constructive negation of Nelson [Nel49].

[7] This example appears in [GL91] and is attributed to McCarthy.

In that case, the conclusion of crossing the intersection will only be made if the program can derive ¬*train*, which in the presence of a direct sensor means that the sensor has added the fact ¬*train* to the program. In this case if there is fog, and the sensor adds neither *train* ← . nor ¬*train* ← ., then the conclusion to *cross* will not be made.

These are some of the motivations behind the language AnsProlog⁻ that extends AnsProlog with the operator ¬. In addition, since an AnsProlog⁻ program can include explicit negative information, instead of the embedded 'closed world assumption' in AnsProlog programs, they have the 'open world assumption'. Thus they remove the bias towards negative information present in AnsProlog programs, and treat positive and negative information at par. Nevertheless, by using the negation-as-failure operator '**not**' a user can explicitly state – by a rule of the form ¬p ← **not** p. – if certain negative information is to be inferred through closed world reasoning. A user can also do the opposite – by a rule of the form p ← **not** ¬p., and explicitly state that for certain predicates positive information will be inferred through a form of closed world reasoning.

We now define the answer sets of AnsProlog$^{¬,⊥}$ programs. For that we first consider AnsProlog$^{¬,-\textbf{not},⊥}$ programs.

A *partial Herbrand interpretation* of an AnsProlog$^{¬,⊥}$ program Π is any subset $I ⊆ Lit$. A partial Herbrand interpretation S of Π is said to *satisfy* the AnsProlog$^{¬,⊥}$ rule

$L_0 ← L_1, \ldots, L_m, \textbf{not } L_{m+1}, \ldots, \textbf{not } L_n.$ if
(i) $L_0 ≠ ⊥: \{L_1, \ldots, L_m ⊆ S\}$ and $\{L_{m+1}, \ldots, L_n\} ∩ S = ∅$ implies that $L_0 ∈ S$.
(ii) $L_0 = ⊥: \{L_1, \ldots, L_m ⊈ S\}$ or $\{L_{m+1}, \ldots, L_n\} ∩ S ≠ ∅$.

A *partial Herbrand model* of Π is a partial Herbrand interpretation S of Π such that it satisfies all rules in Π, and if S contains a pair of complementary literals, then S must be *Lit*. We also refer to this as S is closed under Π.

Definition 11 An answer set of an AnsProlog$^{¬,-\textbf{not},⊥}$ program Π is a partial Herbrand model of Π, which is minimal among the partial Herbrand models of Π.   □

Alternatively, an *answer set* of an AnsProlog$^{¬,-\textbf{not},⊥}$ program Π can be defined as a minimal (in the sense of set-theoretic inclusion) subset S of *Lit* such that S is closed under Π.

It can be shown that every AnsProlog$^{¬,-\textbf{not}}$ program Π has a unique answer set. (Such is not the case for AnsProlog$^{¬,-\textbf{not},⊥}$ programs.) We denote this answer set, if it exists, by $\mathcal{M}^{¬,⊥}(Π)$. Otherwise we say $\mathcal{M}^{¬,⊥}(Π)$ is undefined. We now consider several simple AnsProlog$^{¬,-\textbf{not},⊥}$ programs and their answer sets.

Example 21 The following table lists AnsProlog$^{\neg,-\textbf{not}}$ programs in its left column and their answer sets in its right column.

AnsProlog$^{\neg,-\textbf{not}}$ programs	Their answer sets
$\{p \leftarrow q. \neg p \leftarrow r. q \leftarrow .\}$	$\{q, p\}$
$\{p \leftarrow q. \neg p \leftarrow r. r \leftarrow .\}$	$\{r, \neg p\}$
$\{p \leftarrow q. \neg p \leftarrow r.\}$	$\{\}$
$\{p \leftarrow q. \neg p \leftarrow r. q \leftarrow . r \leftarrow .\}$	*Lit*

The answer sets of the first two programs are quite straightforward. Notice that the answer set of the third program has neither p, nor $\neg p$. On the other hand the answer set of the fourth program has $p, \neg p, q, \neg q, r$, and $\neg r$. This is because our definition[8] of answer sets says that if an answer set contains a single pair of complementary literals, then it consists of all the literals. □

In the following example we compare the answer sets of two AnsProlog$^{\neg,-\textbf{not}}$ programs and demonstrate that the notion of answer set is not 'contrapositive' with respect to $\leftarrow$ and $\neg$.

Example 22 Consider the following two AnsProlog$^{\neg,-\textbf{not}}$ programs:

$$\neg p \leftarrow . \qquad p \leftarrow \neg q.$$

and

$$\neg p \leftarrow . \qquad q \leftarrow \neg p.$$

Let us call them Π_1 and Π_2, respectively. Each of the programs has a single answer set, but these sets are different. The answer set of Π_1 is $\{\neg p\}$; the answer set of Π_2 is $\{\neg p, q\}$. Thus, our semantics is not 'contrapositive' with respect to $\leftarrow$ and $\neg$; it assigns different meanings to the rules $p \leftarrow \neg q.$ and $q \leftarrow \neg p.$ □

We now define answer sets of AnsProlog$^{\neg,\perp}$ programs.

Definition 12 Let Π be an AnsProlog$^{\neg,\perp}$ program without variables. For any set S of literals, let Π^S be the AnsProlog$^{\neg,-\textbf{not},\perp}$ program obtained from Π by deleting

(i) each rule that has a gen-literal **not** L in its body with $L \in S$, and
(ii) all gen-literals of the form **not** L in the bodies of the remaining rules. □

---

[8] Recently, there has arisen a view (among researchers such as Lifschitz and Turner) that the notion of answer sets should be modified so as to not allow *Lit* to be an answer set of AnsProlog$^{\neg,-\textbf{not}}$ programs. Although there are some benefits to this, we stay with the original definition as the consequences of this modification on the various results are not yet well-studied.

Clearly, Π^S is an AnsProlog$^{\neg,-\mathbf{not},\perp}$ program, and hence its answer set is already defined. If its answer set exists and coincides with S, then we say that S is an *answer set* of Π. In other words, the answer sets of Π are characterized by the equation

$$S = \mathcal{M}^{\neg,\perp}(\Pi^S). \tag{1.3.5}$$

Example 23 Consider the AnsProlog$^\neg$ program Π_1 consisting of just one rule:

$$\neg q \leftarrow \mathbf{not}\ p.$$

Intuitively, this rule means: 'q is *false* if there is no evidence that p is *true*.' The only answer set of this program is $\{\neg q\}$. □

Example 24 Consider the following ground version of the program Π from Example 6.

fly(*tweety*) ← *bird*(*tweety*), **not** ¬*fly*(*tweety*).
¬*fly*(*tweety*) ← *penguin*(*tweety*).
fly(*rocky*) ← *bird*(*rocky*), **not** ¬*fly*(*rocky*).
¬*fly*(*rocky*) ← *penguin*(*rocky*).
bird(*tweety*) ←.
bird(*rocky*) ←.
penguin(*rocky*) ←.

The answer set of the above program is:
{*bird*(*tweety*), *bird*(*rocky*), *penguin*(*rocky*), *fly*(*tweety*), ¬*fly*(*rocky*)}.
  The important aspect of the program Π is that if we found out that tweety does not fly, we can directly add ¬*fly*(*tweety*) to the program Π, and the resulting program will remain consistent, but will now have the answer set {*bird*(*tweety*), *bird*(*rocky*), *penguin*(*rocky*), ¬*fly*(*tweety*), ¬*fly*(*rocky*)}. □

The following proposition states that AnsProlog$^\neg$ programs cannot have more than one answer set if one of them is *Lit*.

Proposition 5 An AnsProlog$^{\neg,\perp}$ program Π has an inconsistent answer set iff Π has the unique answer set *Lit*. □

The proof of the above proposition is based on the following lemma.

Lemma 1.3.2 An AnsProlog$^{\neg,\perp}$ program cannot have two answer sets such that one is a proper subset of the other. □

Proof: Suppose an AnsProlog$^{\neg, \perp}$ program has two answer sets A and A' such that $A \subseteq A'$. Then $\Pi^{A'} \subseteq \Pi^A$. Since $\Pi^{A'}$ and Π^A are AnsProlog$^{\neg, -\textbf{not}, \perp}$ programs (i.e., they do not have the **not** operator and hence are monotonic), $\mathcal{M}^{\neg, \perp}(\Pi^{A'}) \subseteq \mathcal{M}^{\neg, \perp}(\Pi^A)$, which means $A' \subseteq A$. Hence, A must be equal to A'. $\qquad \square$

Example 25 Consider the following program Π:

$a \leftarrow \textbf{not } b.$
$b \leftarrow \textbf{not } a.$
$q \leftarrow a.$
$\neg q \leftarrow a.$

We will show that this program has the unique answer set $\{b\}$, and in particular neither $\{a, q, \neg q\}$, nor Lit are its answer sets.

$\Pi^{\{b\}}$ is the program $\{b \leftarrow .\}$, whose answer set is $\{b\}$. Hence, b is an answer set of Π.

Now, $\Pi^{\{a, q, \neg q\}}$ is the program $\{a \leftarrow ., q \leftarrow a., \neg q \leftarrow a.\}$. But, based on the definition of answer sets, the answer set of $\Pi^{\{a, q, \neg q\}}$ is Lit, not $\{a, q \neg q\}$. Hence, $\{a, q, \neg q\}$ is not an answer set of Π.

Similarly, Π^{Lit} is the program $\{q \leftarrow a., \neg q \leftarrow a.\}$, whose answer set is $\emptyset$. Hence, Lit is not an answer set of Π. $\qquad \square$

Under rather general conditions, evaluating a query for an AnsProlog$^\neg$ program can be reduced to evaluating two queries for a program that does not contain explicit negation. Let us now show that AnsProlog$^\neg$ programs can be reduced to AnsProlog programs. We will need the following notation:

For any predicate p occurring in Π, let p' be a new predicate of the same arity. The atom $p'(X_1, \ldots, X_n)$ will be called the *positive form* of the negative literal $\neg p(X_1, \ldots, X_n)$. Every positive literal is, by definition, its own positive form. The positive form of a literal L will be denoted by L^+. Π^+ stands for the AnsProlog program obtained from Π by replacing each rule (1.2.1) (with $k = 0$) by

$$L_0^+ \leftarrow L_1^+, \ldots, L_m^+, \textbf{not } L_{m+1}^+, \ldots, \textbf{not } L_n^+.$$

For any set $S \subseteq Lit$, let S^+ stands for the set of the positive forms of the elements of S.

Proposition 6 [GL90] Let S be a consistent subset of Lit. S is an answer set of an AnsProlog$^\neg$ program Π if and only if S^+ is an answer set of Π^+. $\qquad \square$

Example 26 Consider the program Π from Example 25. The program Π^+ will then consist of the following rules:

$a \leftarrow \mathbf{not}\ b.$
$b \leftarrow \mathbf{not}\ a.$
$q \leftarrow a.$
$q' \leftarrow a.$

It is easy to see that Π^+ has two answer sets $S_1^+ = \{a, q, q'\}$ and $S_2^+ = \{b\}$. Following Proposition 6 $S_2 = \{b\}$ is an answer set of Π. But $S_1 = \{a, q, \neg q\}$ does not satisfy the assumption in Proposition 6, making it inapplicable. $\square$

The above proposition relates Π and Π^+ only when Π is consistent. The following proposition relates them when Π is inconsistent.

Proposition 7 *Lit* is an answer set of an AnsProlog$^{\neg}$ program Π if and only if $\Pi^{++} = \Pi^+ \cup \{\leftarrow p, p'. : p \in HB_\Pi\}$ has no answer sets. $\square$

Proof: Exercise. $\square$

Example 27 Consider the following program Π:

$p \leftarrow q.$
$\neg p \leftarrow r.$
$q \leftarrow .$
$r \leftarrow .$

As mentioned earlier in Example 21 it has the unique answer set *Lit*. Now let us consider Π^+ given by the following rules:

$p \leftarrow q.$
$p' \leftarrow r.$
$q \leftarrow .$
$r \leftarrow .$

Π^+ has the answer set $\{p, p', q, r\}$. But Π^{++} consisting of the following additional constraints has no answer sets.

$\leftarrow p, p'.$
$\leftarrow q, q'.$
$\leftarrow r, r'.$

    $\square$

1.3.4 Answer sets of AnsProlog$^{or,\perp}$ and AnsProlog$^{\neg,\, or,\perp}$ programs

In this section, we will discuss a further extension of the language of AnsProlog$^{\neg,\perp}$ programs by the means necessary to represent disjunctive information about the world.

Our approach to expressing disjunctive information is based on the expansion of the language of AnsProlog$^{\neg}$ programs by a new connective *or* called *epistemic disjunction* [GL91]. Notice the use of the symbol *or* instead of classical $\vee$. The meaning of *or* is given by the semantics of AnsProlog$^{\neg,\, or,\perp}$ programs and differs from that of $\vee$. The meaning of $A \vee B$ is 'A is *true* or B is *true*' while a rule A *or* $B \leftarrow$. is interpreted epistemically and means 'A is believed to be *true* or B is believed to be *true*.' While for any atom A, $A \vee \neg A$ is always *true*, it is possible that A *or* $\neg A$ may not be *true*.

The definition of an answer set of an AnsProlog$^{\neg,\, or,\perp}$ program Π [Prz91, GL91] is almost identical to that of AnsProlog$^{\neg,\perp}$ programs. Let us first consider AnsProlog$^{\neg, or,-\mathbf{not},\perp}$ programs, which do not have the **not** operator.

A *partial Herbrand interpretation* of an AnsProlog$^{\neg, or,\perp}$ program Π is any subset $I \subseteq Lit$. A partial Herbrand interpretation S of Π is said to *satisfy* the AnsProlog$^{\neg,\, or,\perp}$ rule

$$L_0 \text{ or} \cdots \text{or } L_k \leftarrow L_{k+1}, \ldots, L_m, \textbf{not } L_{m+1}, \ldots, \textbf{not } L_n.$$

if (i) $k = 0$ and $L_0 = \perp$: $\{L_{k+1}, \ldots, L_m\} \not\subseteq S$ or $\{L_{m+1}, \ldots, L_n\} \cap S \neq \emptyset$

(ii) otherwise: $\{L_{k+1}, \ldots, L_m\} \subseteq S$ and $\{L_{m+1}, \ldots, L_n\} \cap S = \emptyset$ implies that $\{L_0, \ldots, L_k\} \cap S \neq \emptyset$.

A *partial Herbrand model* A of an AnsProlog$^{\neg, or,\perp}$ program Π is a partial Herbrand interpretation S of Π such that it satisfies all rules in Π, and if S contains a pair of complementary literals, then S must be *Lit*. We also refer to this as A is closed under Π.

Definition 13 An answer set of an AnsProlog$^{\neg,\, or,-\mathbf{not},\perp}$ program Π is a partial Herbrand model of Π, which is minimal among the partial Herbrand models of Π. □

Answer sets of AnsProlog$^{or,-\mathbf{not}}$ programs are defined similarly, except that instead of partial Herbrand models, we consider the Herbrand models.

Alternatively, an *answer set* of an AnsProlog$^{\neg, or,-\mathbf{not},\perp}$ program Π can be defined as a smallest (in the sense of set-theoretic inclusion) subset S of *Lit* such that S is closed under Π.

Unlike AnsProlog$^{\neg,-\mathbf{not},\perp}$ programs, an AnsProlog$^{\neg, or,-\mathbf{not},\perp}$ program may have more than one answer set. The following example illustrates such a program.

Example 28 The following AnsProlog$^{\neg, or, -\mathbf{not}}$ program

$p(a) \; or \; \neg p(b) \leftarrow.$

has two answer sets $\{p(a)\}$ and $\{\neg p(b)\}$.   □

Although, the above program can be replaced by the AnsProlog program $\{p(a) \leftarrow$ **not** $\neg p(b)., \neg p(b) \leftarrow$ **not** $p(a).\}$; in general the disjunction *or* cannot be replaced by such transformations. The following two examples illustrate this.

Example 29 Consider the following program Π.

$a \; or \; b \leftarrow.$
$a \leftarrow b.$
$b \leftarrow a.$

It has only one answer set $S = \{a, b\}$. Now consider the program Π' obtained by transforming Π by the earlier mentioned transformation. This program will have the following rules:

$a \leftarrow \mathbf{not} \; b.$
$b \leftarrow \mathbf{not} \; a.$
$a \leftarrow b.$
$b \leftarrow a.$

The set S is not an answer set of the transformed program Π'. In fact Π' does not have any answer sets.   □

Example 30 Consider the following program Π.

$p \; or \; p' \leftarrow.$
$q \; or \; q' \leftarrow.$
$not\_sat \leftarrow p, q.$
$not\_sat \leftarrow p', q'.$
$q \leftarrow not\_sat.$
$q' \leftarrow not\_sat.$

This program has two answer sets $S_1 = \{p, q'\}$ and $S_2 = \{p', q\}$. This program has no answer sets containing p, q, as that would force that answer set also to have not_sat and q' making it a strict superset of S_1. Similarly, this program has no answer sets containing p', q', as that would force that answer set also to have not_sat and q making it a strict superset of S_2.

Now consider the program Π' obtained by adding the following rule to Π.

$not\_sat \leftarrow p', q.$

This program has two answer sets $S'_1 = \{p, q'\}$ and $S'_2 = \{p', q', q, not\_sat\}$.

Consider the program Π'' obtained from Π' by replacing disjunctions through a transformation mentioned earlier. The program Π'' would then be:

$p \leftarrow \textbf{not } p'.$

$p' \leftarrow \textbf{not } p.$

$q \leftarrow \textbf{not } q'.$

$q' \leftarrow \textbf{not } q.$

$not\_sat \leftarrow p, q.$

$not\_sat \leftarrow p', q'.$

$not\_sat \leftarrow p', q.$

$q \leftarrow not\_sat.$

$q' \leftarrow not\_sat.$

While S'_1 is still an answer set of Π'', S'_2 is no longer an answer set of Π''.   □

We denote the set of answer sets of an AnsProlog$^{\neg, or, -\textbf{not}, \perp}$ program Π by $\mathcal{M}^{\neg, or, \perp}(\Pi)$. (Similarly, we denote the set of answer sets of an AnsProlog$^{or, -\textbf{not}, \perp}$ program Π by $\mathcal{M}^{or, \perp}(\Pi)$.) We are now ready to define the answer set of an arbitrary AnsProlog$^{\neg, or, \perp}$ program.

A set S of literals is an answer set of an AnsProlog$^{\neg, or, \perp}$ program Π if $S \in \mathcal{M}^{\neg, or, \perp}(\Pi^S)$ where Π^S is as defined in Definition 12. Similarly, a set S of atoms is an answer set of an AnsProlog$^{or, \perp}$ program Π if $S \in \mathcal{M}^{or, \perp}(\Pi^S)$ where Π^S is as defined in Definition 12.

Example 31 Consider the following AnsProlog^{or} program Π.

$p \text{ or } p' \leftarrow.$

$q \text{ or } q' \leftarrow.$

$not\_sat \leftarrow p, q.$

$not\_sat \leftarrow p', q'.$

$q \leftarrow not\_sat.$

$q' \leftarrow not\_sat.$

$sat \leftarrow \textbf{not } not\_sat.$

This program has two answer sets $S_1 = \{p, q', sat\}$ and $S_2 = \{p', q, sat\}$. The reason why $S = \{p, q, q', not\_sat\}$ is not an answer set of Π, is because Π^S has an answer set $\{p, q'\}$ which is a strict subset of S. For similar reasons, the set $\{p', q', q, not\_sat\}$ is not an answer set of Π.   □

Example 32 Consider the following AnsProlog$^{\perp, or}$ program:

$a \text{ or } b \leftarrow.$

$a \text{ or } c \leftarrow.$

$\leftarrow a, \textbf{not } b, \textbf{not } c.$
$\leftarrow \textbf{not } a, b, c.$

It has no answer sets. The answer sets of the sub-program consisting of the first two rules are $\{a\}$ and $\{b, c\}$ and both violate the constraints represented by the third and fourth rules.

A wrong approach to analyzing the above program would be to compute the models of the sub-program consisting of the first two rules (which are $\{a\}$, $\{a, c\}$, $\{a, b\}$, $\{b, c\}$ and $\{a, b, c\}$), eliminating the ones which violate the constraints ($\{a\}$ and $\{b, c\}$), and selecting the minimal ones from the rest. This will lead to the models $\{a, b\}$ and $\{a, c\}$.   □

The following proposition gives an alternative characterization of answer sets of AnsProlog^{or} programs that is often useful.

Proposition 8 M is an answer set of an AnsProlog^{or} program Π iff M is a model of Π and there does not exist M' such that M' is a model of Π^M and $M' \subset M$.   □

Proof:
M is an answer set of Π iff
M is an answer set of Π^M iff
M is a minimal model of Π^M iff
M is a model of Π^M and there does not exist M' such that M' is a model of Π^M and $M' \subset M$ iff
M is a model of Π and there does not exist M' such that M' is a model of Π^M and $M' \subset M$.   □

1.3.5 Query entailment

So far we have discussed the AnsProlog* languages that represent a set of axioms of an answer set framework, and defined the notion of answer sets of programs in these languages. Our main goal is to be able to reason with and derive conclusions from a given knowledge base, expressed as an AnsProlog* program. Thus we need to define the other components of an answer set framework: (i) a language to express queries; and (ii) an entailment relation $\models$ between an AnsProlog* program and a query.

The requirements of a query language are somewhat different from the requirement of a knowledge representation language. Normally the set of people who are expected to represent knowledge in a knowledge base is a very small subset of the people who are expected to use (or query) the knowledge base. The former are often referred to as domain experts and the latter are often referred to as users. Thus the query language should be simpler than the knowledge representation language, and should have constructs that are already familiar to an average user. With these requirement in mind, the connectives of our query alphabet are the ones from classical logic: $\{\neg, \vee, \wedge\}$. All other aspects of the query alphabet coincide with our axiom alphabet. We now define queries as follows:

Definition 14 Query

(1) A ground atom is a query.
(2) If q_1 and q_2 are queries, $\neg q_1$, $q_1 \vee q_2$, and $q_1 \wedge q_2$ are queries. □

We will now define two different entailment relations between AnsProlog* programs and queries. We need two different entailment relations because AnsProlog$^{or,\perp}$ programs (and AnsProlog programs) cannot represent negative information directly, while an AnsProlog$^{\neg, or,\perp}$ program can. Moreover an answer set of an AnsProlog$^{or,\perp}$ program is a set of atoms while an answer set of an AnsProlog$^{\neg,or,\perp}$ program is a set of literals. So in the first case conclusions about negative literals have to be made indirectly, while in the second case they can be made directly. We first define when a query is true and when it is false with respect to an answer set for both cases, and then define the two entailment relations: $\models$ and $\not\models$.

(1) For AnsProlog$^{or,\perp}$ programs: Let S be an answer set of such a program.
  - A ground atom p is *true* with respect to S if $p \in S$.
  - A query $\neg p$ is true with respect to S if p is not true with respect to S. (Note that if p is an atom, this means $p \notin S$.)
  - A query $p \vee q$ is true with respect to S if p is true with respect to S or q is true with respect to S.
  - A query $p \wedge q$ is true with respect to S if p is true with respect to S and q is true with respect to S.
  - A query p is said to be *false* with respect to S, if p is not *true* with respect to S.
  Given an AnsProlog$^{or,\perp}$ program Π and a query q, we say $\Pi \models q$, if q is true in all answer sets of Π. Thus, $\Pi \models \neg q$, also means that q is false in all answer sets of Π. If $\Pi \models q$ then we say that the answer to query q is *yes*, and if $\Pi \models \neg q$ then we say that the answer to query q is *no*. If q is true with respect to some answer sets of S and false with respect to the others then we say that the answer to query q is *unknown*.
(2) For AnsProlog$^{\neg, or,\perp}$ programs: Let S be an answer set of such a program.
  - A ground atom p is *true* in S if p is in S; and is *false* in S if $\neg p$ is in S.
  - A query $f \wedge g$ is *true* in S iff f is *true* in S and g is *true* in S.
  - A query $f \wedge g$ is *false* in S iff f is *false* in S or g is *false* in S.
  - A query $f \vee g$ is *true* in S iff f is *true* in S or g is *true* in S.
  - A query $f \vee g$ is *false* in S iff f is *false* in S and g is *false* in S.

- A query $\neg f$ is *true* in S iff f is *false* in S.
- A query $\neg f$ is *false* in S iff f is *true* in S.

A query q is said to be *true* with respect to an AnsProlog$^{\neg, or, \perp}$ program Π and denoted by $\Pi \models q$ if it is *true* in all answer sets of Π; q is said to be *false* with respect to Π and denoted by $\Pi \models \neg q$ if it is *false* in all answer sets of Π. Otherwise it is said to be *unknown* with respect to Π.

By $Cn(\Pi)$ we will denote the set of ground literals that are entailed by Π with respect to the entailment relation $\models$. Intuitively, $Cn(\Pi)$ refers to the set conclusions that can be drawn from Π.

Example 33 Consider the following program Π:

$p(X) \leftarrow q(X).$
$q(a) \leftarrow .$
$r(b) \leftarrow .$

The unique answer set of Π is $\{q(a), p(a), r(b)\}$. But since we can not be sure by looking at Π whether it is an AnsProlog program or an AnsProlog$^{\neg}$ program, we can consider both entailment relations $\models$ and $\models$ with respect to Π.

We can reason $\Pi \models p(a)$ and $\Pi \models \neg p(b)$; but when we consider $\models$, we have $\Pi \models p(a)$ but we do not have $\Pi \models \neg p(b)$.   □

Example 34 Consider the following AnsProlog$^{\neg}$ program Π:

$p(X) \leftarrow q(X).$
$q(a) \leftarrow .$
$\neg r(b) \leftarrow .$

The unique answer set of Π is $\{q(a), p(a), \neg r(b)\}$. Thus $\Pi \models \quad p(a)$. But $\Pi \models \neg p(b)$.   □

The reader might wonder if it is worth sacrificing the expressiveness by having such a simple query language. Actually, we are not sacrificing expressiveness. An unusual user who needs added expressiveness and who either knows or is willing to learn AnsProlog* can always represent a sophisticated query which may not be easily expressible by the above simple query language, by adding an appropriate set of AnsProlog* rules to the original program and asking a simple query to the resulting program. The following examples express this technique, which we elaborate further in Section 2.1.7.

Example 35 Suppose a user wants to find out if the knowledge base entails that at least one object in the Herbrand universe has the property p. This query can be asked by adding the following rules to the original program and asking the query q with respect to the new program, where q does not appear in the original program.

$q \leftarrow p(X)$.

Suppose a user wants to find out if the knowledge base entails that all objects in the Herbrand universe have the property p. This query can be asked by adding the following rules to the original program and asking the query q with respect to the new program, where q and not_q do not appear in the original program.

$not\_q \leftarrow \textbf{not } p(X)$.
$q \leftarrow \textbf{not } not\_q$.

Suppose a user wants to find out if the knowledge base entails that all objects in the Herbrand universe may have the property p without resulting in contradiction. This query can be asked by adding the following rules to the original program and asking the query q with respect to the new program, where q and not_q do not appear in the original program.

$not\_q \leftarrow \neg p(X)$.
$q \leftarrow \textbf{not } not\_q$. $\qquad\qquad\qquad\qquad\qquad\qquad\qquad\qquad\qquad\quad$ □

Proposition 6 suggests a simple way of evaluating queries in consistent AnsProlog⁻ programs by just using an AnsProlog interpreter. To obtain an answer for query p with respect to a consistent AnsProlog⁻ program Π we will need to run queries p and p' on the AnsProlog program Π^+. If Π^+'s answer to p is yes then Π's answer to p will be yes; if Π^+'s answer to p' is yes then Π's answer to p will be no; Otherwise Π's answer to p will be unknown.

1.3.6 A sound approximation: the well-founded semantics

In Chapter 9 we will discuss several alternative semantics of programs with AnsProlog* syntax. Among those, the well-founded semantics of AnsProlog programs is often considered as an alternative to the answer set semantics that we prefer. We view the well-founded semantics to be an approximation of the answer set semantics that has a lower time complexity. We now briefly expand on this.

In Section 1.3.2 we defined the answer set of an AnsProlog program Π as the set S of atoms that satisfy the equation $S = \mathcal{M}_0(\Pi^S)$. Let us represent the function $\mathcal{M}_0(\Pi^S)$ as $\Gamma_\Pi(S)$. Now we can say that answer sets of a program Π are the fixpoint of Γ_Π.

In Section 9.8.4 we will show that the well-founded semantics of AnsProlog programs is given by $\{\mathrm{lfp}(\Gamma_\Pi^2), \mathrm{gfp}(\Gamma_\Pi^2)\}$; according to which, for an atom p we have $\Pi \models_{wf} p$ iff $p \in \mathrm{lfp}(\Gamma_\Pi^2)$ and $\Pi \models_{wf} \neg p$ iff $p \notin \mathrm{gfp}(\Gamma_\Pi^2)$. For an AnsProlog program Π, we will denote the set $\{l \ : \ l \in \mathrm{lfp}(\Gamma_\Pi^2)\} \cup \{\neg l \ : \ l \notin \mathrm{gfp}(\Gamma_\Pi^2)\}$ by $WFS(\Pi)$.

Since fixpoints of Γ_Π are also fixpoints of Γ_Π^2, we can easily show that the well-founded semantics is an approximation of the answer set semantics for AnsProlog programs. The following proposition formally states this.

Proposition 9 [BS91] Let Π be an AnsProlog program and A be an atom.

(i) $A \in \mathrm{lfp}(\Gamma_\Pi^2)$ implies $\Pi \models A$.
(ii) $A \notin \mathrm{gfp}(\Gamma_\Pi^2)$ implies $\Pi \models \neg A$. □

Example 36 Consider the following program Π.

$p \leftarrow a.$
$p \leftarrow b.$
$a \leftarrow \textbf{not } b.$
$b \leftarrow \textbf{not } a.$

The sets $\emptyset$, and $\{p, a, b\}$ are fixpoints of Γ_Π^2 and since the Herbrand base is $\{p.a.b\}$, we have $\mathrm{lfp}(\Gamma_\Pi^2) = \emptyset$ and $\mathrm{gfp}(\Gamma_\Pi^2) = \{p, a, b\}$. Thus according to the well founded semantics a, b, and p are unknown with respect to this program. These conclusions are sound with respect to the answer set semantics, according to which a and b are unknown and p is *true*. □

1.4 Database queries and AnsProlog* functions

Often we are not merely interested in the semantics of a stand alone AnsProlog* program, but more interested in the semantics of the program when additional facts (rules with empty body) are added to it. In this context AnsProlog* programs can also be thought of as functions. Viewing an AnsProlog* program as a specification of a theory about the world does not contradict with viewing it as a function; it is then a function with no inputs.

In this section we discuss several different formulations of viewing AnsProlog* programs as functions. The formulations vary by how the domain and co-domain of the function is defined, and whether the domain, co-domain, or both are extracted from the program, or given separately. Based on these criteria we will elaborate on the following notions:

(1) Datalog and i-functions:
In the case of the 'i-function' or *inherent function* corresponding to a Datalog or AnsProlog* program, the domain and co-domain are extracted from the program. Normally, predicates in the left hand side of non-fact rules are referred to as IDB (intensional

database) or output predicates, and the other predicates are referred to as the EDB (extensional database) or input predicates.

(2) l-functions:

An l-function or *literal function* is a three-tuple $\langle \Pi, \mathcal{P}, \mathcal{V} \rangle$, where Π is an AnsProlog* program, $\mathcal{P}$ and $\mathcal{V}$ are sets of literals referred to as parameters and values, and the domain is extracted from Π and $\mathcal{P}$.

(3) s-functions:

An s-function or *signature function* is a four-tuple $\langle \Pi, \sigma_i, \sigma_o, Dom \rangle$, where Π is an AnsProlog* program, σ_i is an input signature, σ_o is an output signature, and *Dom* is the domain. Following [GG99] we also refer to s-functions as lp-functions, meaning logic programming functions.

(4) An AnsProlog* program being functional:

An AnsProlog* program Π is said to be functional from a set X to 2^Y, if for any $x \in X$, the answer sets of $\Pi \cup x$ agree on Y.

1.4.1 Queries and inherent functions

The queries in Section 1.3.5 are basically yes-no queries, where we want to find out if a query is true or false with respect to a knowledge base. Often, for example in databases, we need a more general notion of queries. In these queries we look for tuples of objects that satisfy certain properties. For example, we may need to query an employee database about the name, employee id, and salary of employees who have a Masters degree. Another example is to query a genealogy database about listing all ancestors of John. While the first query can be expressed by generalizing the query language in Section 1.3.5 by allowing non-ground atoms and quantifiers (thus having the query as first-order theory), the second query involving transitive closure cannot be expressed using first-order logic, but can be expressed by an AnsProlog* program where we have a new predicate of arity same as the arity of the tuples of objects that we are looking for, and rules about that predicate. For example, given a genealogy database, the query to list all ancestors of John can be expressed by the following AnsProlog program Π:

$anc\_of\_john(X) \leftarrow parent(john, X).$
$anc\_of\_john(X) \leftarrow anc\_of\_john(Y), parent(Y, X).$

If we just consider the above program by itself, it has $\emptyset$ as its unique answer set. That is not the right way to look at this program. The right way to look at the above program is to consider the above two rules together with a genealogy database consisting of facts of the form $parent(a, b)$. Now all the anc_of_john atoms entailed by the resulting program will answer our query about who the ancestors of John are. The answer will vary depending on the genealogy database that is used. Thus the AnsProlog program Π (and the query it represents) can be thought of as a function that maps *parent* atoms to *anc_of_john* atoms. To make this view of AnsProlog* programs more precise, we first recall some standard relational database notions.

A *relation schema* R_i has a name N_i and a finite list of attributes $L_i = \langle A_1, \ldots, A_{l_i} \rangle$, where l_i is the arity of the relation schema R_i. It will sometimes be denoted as $R_i(A_1, \ldots, A_{l_i})$. A *database schema* [Ull88a] R is a finite set $\{R_1, \ldots, R_n\}$ of relation schemata. $\mathcal{U}$ is an arbitrarily large but finite set of objects that can be used in the relations and is referred to as the *domain*. Given a relation schema R_i, a *relation instance* is a set of tuples of the form $\langle a_1, \ldots, a_{l_i} \rangle$, where $\{a_1, \ldots, a_{l_i}\} \subset \mathcal{U}$. This tuple may also be denoted by the atom $R_i(a_1, \ldots, a_{l_i})$. A *database instance* W is a set of relation instances. A *query* from a database schema R (called an input database schema) to a database schema S (called the output database schema) is a partial mapping from instances of R to (incomplete) instances of S.

In the context of AnsProlog* programs, relations in the previous paragraph correspond to a predicate, and relation instances correspond to ground facts. Given an AnsProlog* program, such as this Π, it can be viewed as a query (or i-function or inherent function) with the output database schema as the set of predicates that appear in the head of the rules of the program and the input database schema as the remaining set of predicates in the program. Thus this program Π is a query from the input database schema {*parent*} to the output database schema {*anc_of_john*}.

1.4.2 Parameters, values and literal functions

Traditionally, the intuitive meaning of a database instance W is based on the closed world assumption (CWA). That is if $R_i(a_1, \ldots, a_{l_i}) \in W$ then we say that $R_i(a_1, \ldots, a_{l_i})$ is *true* with respect to W, otherwise we say that $R_i(a_1, \ldots, a_{l_i})$ is *false* with respect to W. In the presence of incompleteness the notion of relation instance can be extended to *incomplete relation instances* which consist of positive literals (or atoms) of the form $R_i(a_1, \ldots, a_{l_i})$ and negative literals of the form $\neg R_j(a_1, \ldots, a_{l_j})$. An *incomplete database instance* is a set of incomplete relation instances. When dealing with incomplete database instances CWA is no longer assumed. Given a relation schema R_k and an incomplete database instance W, we say $R_k(a_1, \ldots, a_{l_k})$ is *true* with respect to W if $R_k(a_1, \ldots, a_{l_k}) \in W$, we say $R_k(a_1, \ldots, a_{l_k})$ is *false* with respect to W if $\neg R_k(a_1, \ldots, a_{l_k}) \in W$; otherwise we say $R_k(a_1, \ldots, a_{l_k})$ is *unknown* with respect to W. We can now define the notion of an *extended query* from a database schema R to a database schema S as a partial mapping from incomplete instances of R to incomplete instances of S.

An AnsProlog¬ program Π can be viewed as an extended query (or i-function or inherent function) with the output database schema as the set of predicates that appear in the head of the rules in Π and the input database schema as the remaining set of predicates from Π.

Example 37 Consider an instance of a genealogy database of dinosaurs obtained from a particular archaeological site. It is very likely that we will have an incomplete instance where we have facts such as *parent*(*a*, *b*) and also facts such as ¬*parent*(*c*, *d*). In that case the following AnsProlog⁻ program expresses the extended query from the input database schema {*parent*} to the output database schema {*anc_of_john*}.

maybe_parent(*Y*, *X*) ← **not** ¬*parent*(*Y*, *X*).
maybe_anc_of_john(*X*) ← *maybe_parent*(*john*, *X*).
maybe_anc_of_john(*X*) ← *maybe_anc_of_john*(*Y*), *maybe_parent*(*Y*, *X*).
anc_of_john(*X*) ← *parent*(*john*, *X*).
anc_of_john(*X*) ← *anc_of_john*(*Y*), *parent*(*Y*, *X*).
¬*anc_of_john*(*X*) ← **not** *maybe_anc_of_john*(*X*).   □

Often, instead of viewing an AnsProlog* program as an i-function where the input and output are derived from the program, we may want to explicitly specify them. In addition we may want to relax the criteria that the input and output be disjoint and that input and output be defined in terms of predicates.

Thus an AnsProlog* program Π and two sets of literals $\mathcal{P}_\Pi$ and $\mathcal{V}_\Pi$, define an *l-function (literal function)* whose domain consists of subsets of $\mathcal{P}_\Pi$ with certain restrictions that depend on the particular sub-class of AnsProlog* program we are interested in, and co-domain consists of subsets of $\mathcal{V}_\Pi$. Given a valid input X, $\Pi(X)$ is defined as the set $\{l : l \in \mathcal{V}_\Pi$ and $\Pi \cup X \models l\}$. Since it is not required that $\mathcal{P}_\Pi$ and $\mathcal{V}_\Pi$ be disjoint they are referred to as *parameters* and *values* instead of input and output. In Section 3.6 we use l-functions to represent queries and extended queries, and define the notion of expansion of queries and the corresponding interpolation of l-functions.

1.4.3 The signature functions

Recall that the language associated with an AnsProlog* program is determined by its signature consisting of the constants, function symbols, and predicate symbols. In signature functions (or s-functions) the input and output are specified through signatures. Thus an s-function has four parts: an AnsProlog* program, an input signature, an output signature, and a domain. An s-function differs from an l-function in two main aspects:

- The domain in s-functions is specified, instead of being derived as in l-functions.
- Unlike the parameters and values of l-functions which are sets of literals, inputs and outputs in s-functions are specified through input and output signatures. In both cases, they are directly specified, and are not derived from the AnsProlog* program.

The s-functions are used in formulating building block results whereby we can formally discuss composition and other operations on AnsProlog* programs viewed as s-functions.

1.4.4 An AnsProlog program being functional*

In i-functions, l-functions, and s-functions we consider the entailment relation of AnsProlog* programs and associate functions with them. A different perspective is to consider the various answer sets and analyze the mapping between the input (literals or predicates) and the output (literals or predicates) in each of the answer sets. This leads to the following definition of when an AnsProlog* program encodes a function.

Definition 15 An AnsProlog* program T is said to encode a function (or is functional) from a set of literals, called *input*, to a set of literals called *output* if for any complete subset E of input such that $T \cup E$ is consistent, all answer sets of $T \cup E$ agree on the literals from output. □

The above definition of an AnsProlog* program being functional is used in Section 3.8 as one of the sufficiency conditions for determining when an observation can be directly added to a program, and when it needs to be assimilated through abduction or conditioning.

1.5 Notes and references

Logic programming and the programming language PROLOG started off as programming with Horn clauses, a subset of first order logic formulas. The first book on logic programming and PROLOG was by Kowalski [Kow79]. Lloyd's books [Llo84, Llo87] have various formal characterizations of AnsProlog$^{-\textbf{not}}$ programs (called definite programs) and their equivalence results. A similar book on AnsProlog$^{-\textbf{not},or}$ (called disjunctive logic programs) is [LMR92] which is partly based on Rajasekar's thesis. Minker's workshop and his edited book [Min88] presents several papers on characterizing various subclasses – such as stratification and local stratification – of AnsProlog programs. The stable model semantics of AnsProlog programs was first proposed in [GL88] and then extended to AnsProlog^{-} programs in [GL90, GL91]. An equivalent characterization to stable models was independently developed in [BF91]. The notion of answer sets was first introduced in [GL90]. It was extended to AnsProlog$^{-,or}$ programs and programs with epistemic operators in [Gel91b, Gel91a, Gel94]. The survey paper [BG94] discussed and cataloged various knowledge representation possibilities using the answer set semantics of AnsProlog* programs and their extensions. The survey paper [AB94] focused on semantics of negation in logic programs. Two other more recent surveys on logic programming that have significant material on the answer set semantics are [Lif96] and [DEGV97]. The former has a good discussion on query answering methods for AnsProlog programs, while the latter has a good summary on the complexity and expressiveness of AnsProlog* languages. The paper [Gel01] is a recent survey on knowledge representation using AnsProlog*.

Chapter 2
Simple modules for declarative programming
with answer sets

In this chapter we present several small AnsProlog* programs corresponding to several declarative problem solving modules or knowledge representation and reasoning aspects. Although in general we may have intermingling of the declarative problem solving, and the knowledge representation and reasoning aspects, they can be differentiated as follows.

Normally a problem solving task is to find solutions of a problem. A declarative way to do that is to declaratively enumerate the possible solutions and the tests such that the answer sets of the resulting program correspond to the solutions of the problem. The declarative problem solving modules that we consider in this chapter include modules that enforce simple constraints, modules that enumerate interpretations with respect to a set of atoms, modules that uniquely choose from a set of possibilities, modules that encode propositional satisfiability, modules that represent closed first-order queries, modules that check satisfiability of quantified boolean formulas with up to two quantifiers, modules that assign a linear ordering between a set of objects, modules that can represent various aggregations of facts (such as minimization, maximization, sum and average), modules that encode classical disjunction conclusions, modules that encode exclusive-or conclusions, and modules that encode cardinality and weight constraints.

By knowledge representation and reasoning aspects we mean representing particular benchmark aspects of nonmonotonic and common-sense reasoning that we want to be encoded by AnsProlog* programs. The knowledge representation and reasoning modules that we consider in this chapter include: modules for representing normative statements, exceptions, weak exceptions, and direct contradictions; modules for representing the frame problem, and reasoning with incomplete information; transformations necessary for removing closed world assumption; and modules for reasoning about what is known to an agent and what is not known, as opposed to what is true or false in the world.

Although we individually examine and analyze each of these modules in this chapter, we do not discuss *general properties and principles* of these modules. We explore the latter in Chapter 3 and discuss how modules can be systematically analyzed to identify their properties, how modules can be combined or put on top of others to develop larger and more involved programs, and how answer sets of a program can be constructed by decomposing the program into smaller programs, and composing the answer sets of the smaller programs.

2.1 Declarative problem solving modules

2.1.1 Integrity constraints

Integrity constraints are written as rules with an empty head. Intuitively, an integrity constraint r written as $\leftarrow l_1, \ldots, l_m, \textbf{not } l_{m+1}, \ldots, \textbf{not } l_n$, where l_is are literals, *forbids* answer sets which contain the literals $l_1, \ldots, l_m$ and do not contain the literals $l_{m+1}, \ldots, l_n$. Sets of literals that are forbidden by r are said to violate r.

Since many of the results throughout the book are about AnsProlog* programs that do not allow constraints, we show here how constraints can be alternatively represented using rules with non-empty heads by introducing a new atom, which we will refer to as *inconsistent*, and adding the following rule $c_1(r)$ to the program.

$$inconsistent \leftarrow \textbf{not } inconsistent, l_1, \ldots, l_m, \textbf{not } l_{m+1}, \ldots, \textbf{not } l_n.$$

Proposition 10 Let Π be an AnsProlog* program that does not contain the atom *inconsistent*. Let $\{r_1, \ldots, r_n\}$ be a set of integrity constraints that does not contain the atom *inconsistent*. A is an answer set of Π that does not violate the constraints $r_1, \ldots, r_n$ iff A is an answer set of $\Pi \cup \{c_1(r_1), \ldots, c_1(r_n)\}$. $\qquad \square$

Proof: Exercise.

Example 38 Let Π be an AnsProlog program consisting of the rules:

$a \leftarrow \textbf{not } b.$
$b \leftarrow \textbf{not } a.$

It is easy to see that Π has two answer sets $\{a\}$ and $\{b\}$. Now suppose we would like to incorporate the constraint r:

$\leftarrow a.$

to prune any answer set where a is true. To achieve this we will add the following rule $c_1(r)$.

$p \leftarrow \textbf{not } p, a.$

to Π.

It is easy to see that $\Pi \cup \{c_1(r)\}$ has only one answer set, $\{b\}$ and the set $\{a\}$ which was an answer set of Π is no longer an answer set of $\Pi \cup \{c_1(r)\}$. $\square$

An alternative way to encode the integrity constraint r is to add the following – which we will refer to as $c_2(r)$ – to a program Π with the stipulation that p and q are not in the language of Π.

$p \leftarrow l_1, \ldots, l_m, \textbf{not } l_{m+1}, \ldots, \textbf{not } l_n.$
$q \leftarrow \textbf{not } p.$
$q \leftarrow \textbf{not } q.$

Proposition 11 Let Π be an AnsProlog* program that does not contain the atoms p and q. Let $\{r_1, \ldots, r_n\}$ be a set of integrity constraints that does not contain the atoms p and q. $A \setminus \{q\}$ is an answer set of Π that does not violate $r_1, \ldots, r_n$ iff A is an answer set of $\Pi \cup c_2(r_1) \cup \cdots \cup c_2(r_n)$. $\square$

Proof: Exercise.

2.1.2 Finite enumeration

Suppose we have propositions $p_1, \ldots, p_n$ and we would like to construct a program where for each interpretation of the propositions we have an answer set, and each answer set encodes a particular interpretation. An AnsProlog program that achieves this is as follows:

$p_1 \leftarrow \textbf{not } n\_p_1.$
$n\_p_1 \leftarrow \textbf{not } p_1.$
$\vdots$
$p_n \leftarrow \textbf{not } n\_p_n.$
$n\_p_n \leftarrow \textbf{not } p_n.$

An AnsProlog$^{\neg, or}$ program that achieves this is as follows:

$p_1 \text{ } or \text{ } \neg p_1 \leftarrow.$
$\vdots$
$p_n \text{ } or \text{ } \neg p_n \leftarrow.$

It should be noted that if we add the above programs to another program, then the resulting program will not necessarily preserve[1] the properties that we started with. Nevertheless, the encodings above are often useful in enumerating the interpretations and allowing other parts of the resulting program to prune out interpretations that do not satisfy certain properties.

For example, the p_is may denote action occurrences and we may want to enforce that at least one action occurs at each time point. This can be achieved by the following encoding.

p_1 *or* $\neg p_1 \leftarrow$.

$\vdots$

p_n *or* $\neg p_n \leftarrow$.
none $\leftarrow \neg p_1, \neg p_2, \ldots, \neg p_n$.
inconsistent $\leftarrow$ **not** *inconsistent*, *none*.

In Section 2.1.6 we show how enumeration is used in encoding propositional satisfiability in AnsProlog.

2.1.3 General enumeration but at least one

In the previous section we enumerated among a set of propositions. In the presence of variables and predicate symbols, we may want to enumerate a set of terms that satisfy some particular criteria. Let us assume that rules with *possible*(X) encode when X is possible, and our goal is to enumerate the various terms that are possible, with the added stipulation that in each answer set at least one term should be chosen. The following AnsProlog program achieves our purpose.

chosen$(X) \leftarrow$ *possible*(X), **not** *not_chosen*(X).
not_chosen$(X) \leftarrow$ *possible*(X), **not** *chosen*(X).
some $\leftarrow$ *chosen*(X).
inconsistent $\leftarrow$ **not** *inconsistent*, **not** *some*.

Example 39 The following AnsProlog$^{\neg, or}$ program also achieves the purpose of general enumeration but at least one.

chosen(X) *or* $\neg$*chosen*$(X) \leftarrow$ *possible*(X).
some $\leftarrow$ *chosen*(X).
inconsistent $\leftarrow$ **not** *inconsistent*, **not** *some*.

---

[1] This is true for most modules in this chapter. In Chapter 3 we study notions such as conservative extension and strong equivalence, which formalize such preservation; and also study conditions that guarantee such preservation.

Let us consider the program obtained by adding the following set of facts to the above AnsProlog$^{\neg, or}$ program.

$possible(a) \leftarrow$.
$possible(b) \leftarrow$.
$possible(c) \leftarrow$.

The resulting program has the following answer sets:

$\{possible(a), possible(b), possible(c), chosen(a), \neg chosen(b), \neg chosen(c), some\}$
$\{possible(a), possible(b), possible(c), chosen(b), \neg chosen(c), \neg chosen(a), some\}$
$\{possible(a), possible(b), possible(c), chosen(c), \neg chosen(a), \neg chosen(b), some\}$
$\{possible(a), possible(b), possible(c), chosen(a), chosen(b), \neg chosen(c), some\}$
$\{possible(a), possible(b), possible(c), chosen(a), chosen(c), \neg chosen(b), some\}$
$\{possible(a), possible(b), possible(c), chosen(b), chosen(c), \neg chosen(a), some\}$
$\{possible(a), possible(b), possible(c), chosen(a), chosen(b), chosen(c), some\}$

Note that neither $\{possible(a), possible(b), possible(c), \neg chosen(a), \neg chosen(b),$ $\neg chosen(c)\}$ nor $\{possible(a), possible(b), possible(c), \neg chosen(a), \neg chosen(b),$ $\neg chosen(c), inconsistent\}$ are answer sets of the above program.   □

2.1.4 Choice: general enumeration with exactly one

Let us continue with the assumption in the previous subsection that we have rules with $possible(X)$ in their head that encode when X is possible. Now we would like to write a program whose answer sets are such that in each answer set exactly one of the possible Xs is chosen, and there is exactly one answer set for each X that is possible. As an example, consider that we have $P = \{possible(a) \leftarrow .,$ $possible(b) \leftarrow ., possible(c) \leftarrow .\}$. Then our goal is to have a program which has answer sets with the following as subsets.

$S_1 = \{chosen(a), \neg chosen(b), \neg chosen(c)\}$
$S_2 = \{\neg chosen(a), chosen(b), \neg chosen(c)\}$
$S_3 = \{\neg chosen(a), \neg chosen(b), chosen(c)\}$

An AnsProlog$^\neg$ program Π with such answer sets can be written as follows:

$\neg chosen(X) \leftarrow chosen(Y), X \neq Y$.
$chosen(X) \leftarrow possible(X), \textbf{not } \neg chosen(X)$.

It is easy to see that $\Pi \cup P$ has three answer sets, corresponding to S_1, S_2 and S_3, respectively.

Recall that by using the Proposition 6 we can replace the above AnsProlog⁻ program by an AnsProlog program. The following is such an AnsProlog program

$diff\_chosen\_than(X) \leftarrow chosen(Y), X \neq Y.$
$chosen(X) \leftarrow possible(X), \textbf{not } diff\_chosen\_than(X).$

These constructs are widely used in applications such as encoding the linear planning condition that only one action occurs at each time point, and labeling each tuple of a database with a unique number during aggregate computation. In the Smodels logic programming system the above can be achieved by the following rules that uses cardinality constraints with variables.

$1\{chosen(X) : possible(X)\}1.$

We discuss the Smodels system in greater detail in Chapter 8.

2.1.5 Constrained enumeration

The module in the previous section can be thought of as a specific case of the more general notion of constrained enumeration where we need to obey certain constraints while enumerating. For example let us consider placing objects in a rectangular board so that no two objects are in the same row or in the same column, and at least one object is in each row and each column. Although the problem solving task may involve additional constraints, we can encode the above enumeration by the following AnsProlog program:

$not\_chosen(X, Y) \leftarrow chosen(X', Y), X' \neq X.$
$not\_chosen(X, Y) \leftarrow chosen(X, Y'), Y' \neq Y.$
$chosen(X, Y) \leftarrow row(X), column(Y), \textbf{not } not\_chosen(X, Y).$

We can also achieve the above enumeration using the general enumeration of Section 2.1.3 together with additional constraints. For example, the following will also achieve our goal.

$chosen(X, Y) \leftarrow row(X), column(Y), \textbf{not } not\_chosen(X, Y).$
$not\_chosen(X, Y) \leftarrow row(X), column(Y), \textbf{not } chosen(X, Y).$
$filled\_row(X) \leftarrow chosen(X, Y).$
$filled\_column(Y) \leftarrow chosen(X, Y).$
$missing\_row \leftarrow row(X), \textbf{not } filled\_row(X).$
$missing\_column \leftarrow column(X), \textbf{not } filled\_column(X).$
$inconsistent \leftarrow \textbf{not } inconsistent, missing\_row.$
$inconsistent \leftarrow \textbf{not } inconsistent, missing\_column.$
$inconsistent \leftarrow \textbf{not } inconsistent, chosen(X, Y), chosen(X, Z), Y \neq Z.$
$inconsistent \leftarrow \textbf{not } inconsistent, chosen(X, Y), chosen(Z, Y), X \neq Z.$

In the above program the first two rules enumerate that any pair of row X and column Y must either be chosen or not; the next six rules enforce that at least one object is in each row and each column; and the last two rules enforce that no more than one object is in each row and no more than one object is in each column.

As evident from the above two programs the constrained enumeration approach results in a smaller program than that obtained using general enumeration together with constraints. Constrained enumeration is a key component of declarative problem solving tasks. The particular constrained enumeration that we discussed in this section is useful in tasks such as the Nqueens problem; tournament scheduling problems, where rows could correspond to teams, and columns to dates; and seat assignment problems.

2.1.6 Propositional satisfiability

Propositional logic was one of the first languages used for declarative problem solving, and [KS92] reported one of the early successes of doing the problem solving task of planning by mapping a planning problem to a propositional theory, and extracting plans from the models of the propositional theory. In this subsection we show how we can map a propositional theory to an AnsProlog program so that there is a one-to-one correspondence between the models of the propositional theory and the answer sets of the AnsProlog program.

Given a set S of propositional clauses (where each clause is a disjunction of literals), we construct the AnsProlog program $\Pi(S)$, such that there is a one-to-one correspondence between models of S and answer sets of $\Pi(S)$, as follows:

- For each proposition p in S we introduce a new atom n_p and have the following two rules in $\Pi(S)$.

$p \leftarrow$ **not** n_p.
$n\_p \leftarrow$ **not** p.

- For each clause in S, we introduce a new atom c and include one rule for each literal l in S in the following way:
  - If l is a positive atom then we have the rule $c \leftarrow l$.
  - If l is a negation of an atom a then we have the rule $c \leftarrow n\_a$.
  Then we include the constraint $\leftarrow$ **not** c.

Example 40 Let $S = \{p_1 \vee p_2 \vee p_3,\ p_1 \vee \neg p_3,\ \neg p_2 \vee \neg p_4\}$. The AnsProlog program $\Pi(S)$ consists of the following:

$p_1 \leftarrow$ **not** n_p_1.
$n\_p_1 \leftarrow$ **not** p_1.
$p_2 \leftarrow$ **not** n_p_2.

$n\_p_2 \leftarrow \textbf{not } p_2$.
$p_3 \leftarrow \textbf{not } n\_p_3$.
$n\_p_3 \leftarrow \textbf{not } p_3$.
$p_4 \leftarrow \textbf{not } n\_p_4$.
$n\_p_4 \leftarrow \textbf{not } p_4$.

$c_1 \leftarrow p_1$.
$c_1 \leftarrow p_2$.
$c_1 \leftarrow p_3$.
$\leftarrow \textbf{not } c_1$.

$c_2 \leftarrow p_1$.
$c_2 \leftarrow n\_p_3$.
$\leftarrow \textbf{not } c_2$.

$c_3 \leftarrow n\_p_2$.
$c_3 \leftarrow n\_p_4$.
$\leftarrow \textbf{not } c_3$.

The models of S are $\{\{p_1, p_2, p_3\}, \{p_1, p_2\}, \{p_1, p_3, p_4\}, \{p_1, p_3\}, \{p_1, p_4\}, \{p_1\},$ $\{p_2\}\}$ and the answer sets of $\Pi(S)$ are $\{\{p_1, p_2, p_3, n\_p_4, c_1, c_2, c_3\}, \{p_1, p_2, n\_p_3,$ $n\_p_4, c_1, c_2, c_3\}, \{p_1, n\_p_2, p_3, p_4, c_1, c_2, c_3\}, \{p_1, n\_p_2, p_3, n\_p_4, c_1, c_2, c_3\}, \{p_1,$ $n\_p_2, n\_p_3, p_4, c_1, c_2, c_3\}, \{p_1, n\_p_2, n\_p_3, n\_p_4, c_1, c_2, c_3\}, \{n\_p_1, p_2, n\_p_3,$ $n\_p_4, c_1, c_2, c_3\}\}$. □

Proposition 12 [Nie99] A set of propositional clauses S is satisfiable iff $\Pi(S)$ has an answer set. □

Exercise 3 Formulate and prove the one-to-one correspondence between models of S and answer sets of $\Pi(S)$. □

2.1.7 Closed first-order queries in AnsProlog and AnsProlog¬

In Section 1.3.5 we discussed a simple query language for querying AnsProlog* programs and hinted in Example 35 how some more complex queries can be expressed by AnsProlog* programs. In this subsection we generalize Example 35 and give a methodology to express queries that can be otherwise expressed as a closed first-order theory.

Let Π be an AnsProlog program and F be a closed first-order query. To compute if $\Pi \models F$ we can systematically break down F to a set of AnsProlog rules $c(F)$ and ask if $\Pi \cup c(F) \models p\_F$, where p_F is the atom corresponding to the whole formula F. In the following we show how $c(F)$ is constructed bottom-up.

Let F_1 and F_2 be closed formulas and p_F_1 and p_F_2 be the atoms corresponding to F_1 and F_2 respectively. The following describes the rules we need to add when F is $F_1 \wedge F_2$, $F_1 \vee F_2$, $\neg F_1$, $\forall X.F_1(X)$, $\forall X.[in\_class(X) \rightarrow F_1(X)]$, $\exists X.F_1(X)$, and $\exists X.[in\_class(X) \rightarrow F_1(X)]$ respectively.

(1) **And**: The formula $F_1 \wedge F_2$ is translated to the following rule:

$p\_F \leftarrow p\_F_1, p\_F_2.$

(2) **Or**: The formula $F_1 \vee F_2$ is translated to the following rules:

$p\_F \leftarrow p\_F_1.$
$p\_F \leftarrow p\_F_2.$

(3) **Not**: The formula $\neg F_1$ is translated to the following rule:

$p\_F \leftarrow \mathbf{not}\ p\_F_1.$

(4) **Existential quantifier**: The formula $\exists X.F_1(X)$ is translated to the following rule:

$p\_F \leftarrow p\_F_1(X).$

(5) **Bounded existential quantifier**: The formula $\exists X.(in\_class(X) \rightarrow F_1(X))$ is translated to the following rule:

$p\_F \leftarrow in\_class(X), p\_F_1(X).$

(6) **Universal quantifier**: The formula $\forall X.F_1(X)$ is translated to the following rules:

$n\_p\_F \leftarrow \mathbf{not}\ p\_F_1(X).$

$p\_F \leftarrow \mathbf{not}\ n\_p\_F.$

(7) **Bounded universal quantifier**: The formula $\forall X.(in\_class(X) \rightarrow F_1(X))$ is translated to the following rules:

$n\_p\_F \leftarrow in\_class(X), \mathbf{not}\ p\_F_1(X).$

$p\_F \leftarrow \mathbf{not}\ n\_p\_F.$

If instead of AnsProlog we use AnsProlog$^\neg$ then the encodings of $F_1 \wedge F_2$, $F_1 \vee F_2$, $\exists X.F_1(X)$, and $\exists X.[in\_class(X) \rightarrow F_1(X)]$ remain unchanged while the other formulas are encoded as follows:

• **Not**: The formula $\neg F_1$ is translated to the following rule:

$p\_F \leftarrow \neg p\_F_1.$

• **Universal quantifier**: The formula $\forall X.F_1(X)$ is translated to the following rules:

$\neg p\_F \leftarrow \mathbf{not}\ p\_F_1(X).$

$p\_F \leftarrow \mathbf{not}\ \neg p\_F.$

- **Bounded universal quantifier**: The formula $\forall X.(in\_class(X) \rightarrow F_1(X))$ is translated to the following rules:

$\neg p\_F \leftarrow in\_class(X), \textbf{not } p\_F_1(X).$
$p\_F \leftarrow \textbf{not } \neg p\_F.$

Example 41 Consider an admission process in a college where admission is refused to an applicant if he or she has not taken any honors classes. The following encoding of this information is erroneous.

$refuse\_admission(X) \leftarrow applicant(X), \textbf{not } taken\_honors\_class(X, Y).$

Suppose we have an applicant John who has taken the honors class in physics and has not taken the honors class in chemistry. Since he has taken some honors classes he should not be refused admission. But the above rule will have one instantiation where Y will be instantiated to 'chemistry' and X to 'john', and due to that instantiation, it will entail *refuse_admission (john)*. An alternative explanation of the inappropriateness of the above rule is that it encodes the classical formula:

$refuse\_admission(X) \subset \exists X \exists Y.[applicant(X) \wedge \neg taken\_honors\_class(X, Y)]$

which is equivalent to

$refuse\_admission(X) \subset \exists X.[applicant(X) \wedge \exists Y.[\neg taken\_honors\_class(X, Y)]]$

which is equivalent to

$refuse\_admission(X) \subset \exists X.[applicant(X) \wedge \neg \forall Y.[taken\_honors\_class(X, Y)]].$

This is different from the information that was supposed to be encoded, which expressed in classical logic is:

$refuse\_admission(X) \subset \exists X.[applicant(X) \wedge \neg \exists Y.[taken\_honors\_class(X, Y)]].$

A correct encoding of the above information in AnsProlog is as follows:

$has\_taken\_a\_honors\_class(X) \leftarrow taken\_honors\_class(X, Y).$
$refuse\_admission(X) \leftarrow applicant(X), \textbf{not } has\_taken\_a\_honors\_class(X).$ $\square$

2.1.8 Checking satisfiability of universal quantified boolean formulas (QBFs)

Quantified boolean formulas (QBFs) are propositional formulas with quantifiers that range over the propositions. For example, if $F(p_1, p_2)$ is a propositional formula then the satisfiability of the QBF $\exists p_1 \forall p_2 F(p_1, p_2)$ means that there exists a truth value of the proposition p_1 such that for all truth values of p_2, the formula $F(p_1, p_2)$ evaluates to true. The importance of QBFs comes from the fact that they are often used as canonical examples of various complexity classes in the polynomial hierarchy. We use them in Chapter 6 when showing the complexity of various AnsProlog* classes. In this and several subsequent subsections we give examples of how QBF formulas are encoded in AnsProlog*. We start with encoding universal QBFs, which are of the form $\forall q_1, \ldots, q_l.\ F(q_1, \ldots, q_l)$, where $\{q_1, \ldots, q_l\}$ is a set of propositions, and $F(q_1, \ldots, q_l)$ is a propositional formula of the form $\theta_1 \vee \cdots \vee \theta_n$, where each θ_i is a conjunction of propositional literals (a proposition, or a proposition preceded by $\neg$). We first construct an AnsProlog$^{\neg, or}$ program which allows us to verify the satisfiability of the universal QBF $\forall q_1, \ldots, q_l.\ F(q_1, \ldots, q_l)$.

Proposition 13 The QBF $\forall q_1, \ldots, q_l.\ F(q_1, \ldots, q_l)$ is satisfiable iff *exist_satisfied* is true in all answer sets of the following program.

$q_1\ or\ \neg q_1 \leftarrow .$
$\vdots$
$q_l\ or\ \neg q_l \leftarrow .$
exist_satisfied $\leftarrow \theta_1.$
$\vdots$
exist_satisfied $\leftarrow \theta_n.$ □

Proof: Exercise.

The use of *or* in the above program is not essential. The following proposition gives us another alternative.

Proposition 14 The QBF $\forall q_1, \ldots, q_l.\ F(q_1, \ldots, q_l)$ is satisfiable iff *exist_satisfied* is true in all answer sets of the following program.

$q_1 \leftarrow \textbf{not}\ \neg q_1.$
$\neg q_1 \leftarrow \textbf{not}\ q_1.$
$\vdots$
$q_l \leftarrow \textbf{not}\ \neg q_l.$
$\neg q_l \leftarrow \textbf{not}\ q_l.$
exist_satisfied $\leftarrow \theta_1.$
$\vdots$
exist_satisfied $\leftarrow \theta_n.$ □

Proof: Exercise.

The use of $\neg$ in the above two programs is also not essential. It can be replaced by replacing each $\neg p$ by p' in all of the rules. Let θ_i' denote the transformation of θ_i, where all negative propositional literals of the form $\neg p$ are replaced by a proposition of the form p'. For example, if $\theta_i = p_1 \wedge \neg p_2 \wedge \neg p_3 \wedge p_4$ then $\theta_i' = p_1 \wedge p_2' \wedge p_3' \wedge p_4$. Besides replacing the $\neg p$ by p' in the enumeration rules, we will need to replace θ_i by θ_i' in the other rules. We use the above methodology in the following alternative encoding of a universal QBF in AnsProlog^{or}.

Proposition 15 The QBF $\forall q_1, \ldots, q_l. F(q_1, \ldots, q_l)$ is satisfiable iff *exist_satisfied* is true in the unique answer set of the following program:

q_1 *or* $q_1' \leftarrow$.

$\vdots$

q_l *or* $q_l' \leftarrow$.
exist_satisfied $\leftarrow \theta_1'$.

$\vdots$

exist_satisfied $\leftarrow \theta_n'$.
$q_1 \leftarrow$ *exist_satisfied*.
$q_1' \leftarrow$ *exist_satisfied*.

$\vdots$

$q_l \leftarrow$ *exist_satisfied*.
$q_l' \leftarrow$ *exist_satisfied*. □

Proof: Exercise.

Exercise 4 Explain why if we replace the rules of the form

q_i *or* $q_i' \leftarrow$.

by the rules

$q_i \leftarrow$ **not** q_i'.
$q_i' \leftarrow$ **not** q_i.

in the above program the answer sets will not be the same. (Hint: Consider the QBF $\forall p.(p \vee \neg p)$. The program with *or* will have an answer set, but the other program will have no answer sets.) □

2.1.9 Checking satisfiability of existential QBFs

In this subsection we construct AnsProlog^{or} programs which allows us to verify the satisfiability of the existential QBFs of the form $\exists q_1, \ldots, q_l.F(q_1, \ldots, q_l)$.

Proposition 16 The QBF $\exists q_1, \ldots, q_l.(\theta_1(q_1, \ldots, q_l) \vee \cdots \vee \theta_n(q_1, \ldots, q_l))$ is satisfiable iff *exist_satisfied* is true in at least one answer set of the following program.

q_1 *or* $q_1' \leftarrow.$
$\vdots$
q_l *or* $q_l' \leftarrow.$
exist_satisfied $\leftarrow \theta_1'.$
$\vdots$
exist_satisfied $\leftarrow \theta_n'.$ □

Proof: Exercise.

In the previous encoding, we can replace each of the rules q_i *or* q_i' by the two AnsProlog rules, $q_i \leftarrow$ **not** $q_1'.$ and $q_i' \leftarrow$ **not** $q_1.$ This is not the case in the following encoding. In this alternative encoding, let ϕ_i denote a disjunction of propositional literals and let $\hat{\phi}_i$ denote the negation of ϕ_i with literals of the form $\neg p$ replaced by propositions of the form p'. For example, if ϕ is the disjunction $p \vee q \vee \neg r$, then $\hat{\phi}$ is the conjunction $p' \wedge q' \wedge r$.

Proposition 17 The QBF $\exists q_1, \ldots, q_l.(\phi_1(q_1, \ldots, q_l) \wedge \cdots \wedge \phi_n(q_1, \ldots, q_l))$, where ϕ_is are disjunctions of propositional literals, is satisfiable iff *not_satisfied* is false in all answer sets of the following program:

q_1 *or* $q_1' \leftarrow.$
$\vdots$
q_l *or* $q_l' \leftarrow.$
not_satisfied $\leftarrow \hat{\phi}_1.$
$\vdots$
not_satisfied $\leftarrow \hat{\phi}_n.$
$q_1 \leftarrow$ *not_satisfied.*
$q_1' \leftarrow$ *not_satisfied.*
$\vdots$
$q_l \leftarrow$ *not_satisfied.*
$q_l' \leftarrow$ *not_satisfied.*   □

Proof: Exercise.

2.1.10 Checking satisfiability of Universal-existential QBFs

We now consider encoding the satisfiability of Universal-existential QBFs using AnsProlog^{or} programs. The use of *or* in these encodings is essential and cannot be eliminated, and this explains the added expressiveness of AnsProlog^{or} programs over AnsProlog programs.

Proposition 18 The QBF $\forall p_1, \ldots, p_k. \exists q_1, \ldots, q_l.(\phi_1(p_1, \ldots, p_k, q_1, \ldots, q_l) \wedge \cdots \wedge \phi_n(p_1, \ldots, p_k, q_1, \ldots, q_l))$, where ϕ_is are disjunctions of propositional literals, is satisfiable iff *not_satisfied* is false in all answer sets of the following program:

$p_1 \text{ or } p_1' \leftarrow.$
$\vdots$
$p_k \text{ or } p_k' \leftarrow.$
$q_1 \text{ or } q_1' \leftarrow.$
$\vdots$
$q_l \text{ or } q_l' \leftarrow.$
$not\_satisfied \leftarrow \hat{\phi}_1.$
$\vdots$
$not\_satisfied \leftarrow \hat{\phi}_n.$
$q_1 \leftarrow not\_satisfied.$
$q_1' \leftarrow not\_satisfied.$
$\vdots$
$q_l \leftarrow not\_satisfied.$
$q_l' \leftarrow not\_satisfied.$ $\qquad\qquad\square$

Proof: Exercise.

Exercise 5 Prove that the QBF $\forall p_1, \ldots, p_k. \exists q_1, \ldots, q_l.(\phi_1(p_1, \ldots, p_k, q_1, \ldots, q_l) \wedge \cdots \wedge \phi_n(p_1, \ldots, p_k, q_1, \ldots, q_l)$, where ϕ_is are disjunctions of propositional literals, is satisfiable iff *sat* is true in all answer sets of the following program:

$p_1 \text{ or } p_1' \leftarrow.$
$\vdots$
$p_k \text{ or } p_k' \leftarrow.$

q_1 *or* q'_1 ←.

⋮

q_l *or* q'_l ←.
not_satisfied ← $\hat{\phi}_1$.

⋮

not_satisfied ← $\hat{\phi}_n$.
q_1 ← *not_satisfied*.
q'_1 ← *not_satisfied*.

⋮

q_l ← *not_satisfied*.
q'_l ← *not_satisfied*.
sat ← **not** *not_satisfied*.   □

Example 42 Let $F(p_1, p_2, q_1, q_2)$ be the formula $(p_1 \vee p_2 \vee q_1) \wedge (q_1 \vee q_2)$. Consider the QBF

$\forall p_1, p_2. \exists q_1, q_2. F(p_1, p_2, q_1, q_2).$

It is easy to see that this QBF is satisfiable as $F(p_1, p_2, q_1, q_2)$ evaluates to *true* for the following interpretations:

$\{p_1, p_2, q_1, q_2\}$, $\{p_1, p_2, q_1, \neg q_2\}$, $\{p_1, p_2, \neg q_1, q_2\}$,
$\{p_1, \neg p_2, q_1, q_2\}$, $\{p_1, \neg p_2, q_1, \neg q_2\}$, $\{p_1, \neg p_2, \neg q_1, q_2\}$,
$\{\neg p_1, p_2, q_1, q_2\}$, $\{\neg p_1, p_2, q_1, \neg q_2\}$, $\{\neg p_1, p_2, \neg q_1, q_2\}$,
$\{\neg p_1, \neg p_2, q_1, q_2\}$, and $\{\neg p_1, \neg p_2, q_1, \neg q_2\}$.

Now let us consider the following program based on the construction in Proposition 18.

p_1 *or* p'_1 ←.
p_2 *or* p'_2 ←.
q_1 *or* q'_1 ←.
q_2 *or* q'_2 ←.
not_satisfied ← p'_1, p'_2, q'_1.
not_satisfied ← q'_1, q'_2.
q_1 ← *not_satisfied*.
q'_1 ← *not_satisfied*.
q_2 ← *not_satisfied*.
q'_2 ← *not_satisfied*.

We will now argue that the only answer sets of the above programs are as follows:

$\{p_1, p_2, q_1, q_2\}$, $\{p_1, p_2, q_1, q_2'\}$, $\{p_1, p_2, q_1', q_2\}$,
$\{p_1, p_2', q_1, q_2\}$, $\{p_1, p_2', q_1, q_2'\}$, $\{p_1, p_2', q_1', q_2\}$,
$\{p_1', p_2, q_1, q_2\}$, $\{p_1', p_2, q_1, q_2'\}$, $\{p_1', p_2, q_1', q_2\}$,
$\{p_1', p_2', q_1, q_2\}$, and $\{p_1', p_2', q_1, q_2'\}$.

It is easy to check that each of the above is closed under the above rules, and each of them is minimal because removing any element from any of the above will not make it closed with respect to one of the first four rules of the program. Thus they are all answer sets of the above programs. Now we have to argue why there are no other answer sets.

First, it is easy to show that we cannot have an answer set with both p_1 and p_1' as a subset of it will always be closed under the program rules. Similarly, we cannot have an answer set with both p_2 and p_2'.

Now let us consider the possible answer sets that contain p_1 and p_2. In the above list of answer sets we do not have an answer set that contains $\{p_1, p_2, q_1', q_2'\}$. We will now argue that no answer set can contain $\{p_1, p_2, q_1', q_2'\}$. Intuitively, any answer set that contains $\{p_1, p_2, q_1', q_2'\}$ must also contain $\{not\_satisfied, q_1, q_1', q_2, q_2'\}$. (This intuition is formalized in Proposition 22 of Chapter 3.) But then there are proper subsets of this set which are answer sets. Hence, no answer set can contain $\{p_1, p_2, q_1', q_2'\}$.

Now let us enumerate the 16 possible combinations of q_1, q_2, q_1' and q_2' and their interactions with p_1 and p_2. The sixteen combinations and whether they are part of an answer set are listed below with explanations:

(i) $\{p_1, p_2\}$ (No, not closed under 3rd and 4th rules of the program)
(ii) $\{p_1, p_2, q_1\}$ (No, not closed under 3rd and 4th rules of the program)
(iii) $\{p_1, p_2, q_2\}$ (No, not closed under 3rd and 4th rules of the program)
(iv) $\{p_1, p_2, q_1'\}$ (No, not closed under 3rd and 4th rules of the program)
(v) $\{p_1, p_2, q_2'\}$ (No, not closed under 3rd and 4th rules of the program)
(vi) $\{p_1, p_2, q_1, q_2\}$ (Yes, is an answer set)
(vii) $\{p_1, p_2, q_1, q_1'\}$ (No, not closed under 3rd and 4th rules of the program)
(viii) $\{p_1, p_2, q_1, q_2'\}$ (Yes, is an answer set)
(ix) $\{p_1, p_2, q_2, q_1'\}$ (Yes, is an answer set)
(x) $\{p_1, p_2, q_2, q_2'\}$ (No, not closed under 3rd and 4th rules of the program)
(xi) $\{p_1, p_2, q_1', q_2'\}$ (No, no answer set can contain $\{p_1, p_2, q_1', q_2'\}$)
(xii) $\{p_1, p_2, q_1, q_2, q_1'\}$ (No, its proper subset is an answer set)
(xiii) $\{p_1, p_2, q_1, q_2, q_2'\}$ (No, its proper subset is an answer set)
(xiv) $\{p_1, p_2, q_1, q_1', q_2'\}$ (No, no answer set can contain $\{p_1, p_2, q_1', q_2'\}$)

(xv) $\{p_1, p_2, q_2, q_1', q_2'\}$　　　　(No, no answer set can contain $\{p_1, p_2, q_1', q_2'\}$)

(xvi) $\{p_1, p_2, q_1, q_2, q_1', q_2'\}$　　　　(No, no answer set can contain $\{p_1, p_2, q_1', q_2'\}$)

Similarly, we can argue about the other combinations of p_1, p_2, p_1' and p_2' in terms of why there are no answer sets other than the ones we listed at the beginning.　　　　□

Example 43 Let $F(p_1, p_2, q_1, q_2)$ be the formula $(p_1 \vee p_2) \wedge (q_1 \vee q_2)$. Consider the QBF $\forall p_1, p_2. \exists q_1, q_2. F(p_1, p_2, q_1, q_2)$. It is easy to see that this QBF is not satisfiable as there is no assignment to q_1 and q_2 that will make $F(p_1, p_2, q_1, q_2)$ satisfiable when p_1 and p_2 are both assigned *false*.

Now let us consider the following program based on the construction in Proposition 18.

$p_1 \; or \; p_1' \leftarrow .$

$p_2 \; or \; p_2' \leftarrow .$

$q_1 \; or \; q_1' \leftarrow .$

$q_2 \; or \; q_2' \leftarrow .$

$not\_satisfied \leftarrow p_1', p_2'.$

$not\_satisfied \leftarrow q_1', q_2'.$

$q_1 \leftarrow not\_satisfied.$

$q_1' \leftarrow not\_satisfied.$

$q_2 \leftarrow not\_satisfied.$

$q_2' \leftarrow not\_satisfied.$

The above logic program has $S = \{p_1', p_2', q_1, q_2, q_1', q_2', not\_satisfied\}$ as one of the answer sets. It is easy to see that S is a model of the above program. We now argue why no subset of S is an answer set of the program. We cannot remove either p_1' or p_2' from S as it will no longer be a model by virtue of the first and the second rules. By virtue of the fifth rule, we cannot remove $not\_satisfied$ from S. Then by virtue of the last four rules we cannot remove any of q_1, q_2, q_1', and q_2' from S. Hence, S is an answer set of the above program.　　　　□

2.1.11 Checking satisfiability of Existential-universal QBFs

We now consider encoding the satisfiability of Existential-universal QBFs using AnsProlog^{or} programs. The use of *or* in these encodings is also essential and cannot be eliminated. This also explains the added expressiveness of AnsProlog^{or} programs over AnsProlog programs.

Proposition 19 The QBF $\exists p_1, \ldots, p_k. \; \forall q_1, \ldots, q_l. \; (\theta_1(p_1, \ldots, p_k, q_1, \ldots, q_l) \vee \cdots \vee \theta_n(p_1, \ldots, p_k, q_1, \ldots, q_l))$ is satisfiable iff *exist_satisfied* is true in at least one answer set of the following program.

p_1 *or* $p_1' \leftarrow$.
$\vdots$

p_k *or* $p_k' \leftarrow$.
q_1 *or* $q_1' \leftarrow$.
$\vdots$

q_l *or* $q_l' \leftarrow$.
exist_satisfied $\leftarrow \theta_1'$.
$\vdots$

exist_satisfied $\leftarrow \theta_n'$.
$q_1 \leftarrow$ *exist_satisfied*.
$q_1' \leftarrow$ *exist_satisfied*.
$\vdots$

$q_k \leftarrow$ *exist_satisfied*.
$q_k' \leftarrow$ *exist_satisfied*. $\qquad\qquad\qquad\qquad\qquad\qquad\qquad$ $\square$

Proof: Exercise.

Example 44 Let $F(p_1, p_2, q_1, q_2)$ be the formula $(p_1 \wedge q_1) \vee (p_2 \wedge q_2) \vee (\neg q_1 \wedge \neg q_2)$. Consider the QBF $\exists p_1, p_2.\ \forall q_1, q_2.F(p_1, p_2, q_1, q_2)$. It is easy to see that this QBF is satisfiable as $F(p_1, p_2, q_1, q_2)$ evaluates to *true* for the following interpretations:

$\{p_1, p_2, q_1, q_2\}, \{p_1, p_2, q_1, \neg q_2\}, \{p_1, p_2, \neg q_1, q_2\},$ and $\{p_1, p_2, \neg q_1, \neg q_2\}$.

Consider the following program:

p_1 *or* $p_1' \leftarrow$.
p_2 *or* $p_2' \leftarrow$.
q_1 *or* $q_1' \leftarrow$.
q_2 *or* $q_2' \leftarrow$.
exist_satisfied $\leftarrow p_1, q_1$.
exist_satisfied $\leftarrow p_2, q_2$.
exist_satisfied $\leftarrow q_1', q_2'$.
$q_1 \leftarrow$ *exist_satisfied*.
$q_1' \leftarrow$ *exist_satisfied*.
$q_2 \leftarrow$ *exist_satisfied*.
$q_2' \leftarrow$ *exist_satisfied*.

The above program has one of its answer sets as $S = \{p_1, p_2, q_1, q_2, q_1', q_2',$ *exist_satisfied* $\}$.

We will now argue that the only other answer sets of the above program are:

$S_1 = \{p_1, p'_2, q'_1, q_2\}$,
$S_2 = \{p'_1, p_2, q_1, q'_2\}$,
$S_3 = \{p'_1, p'_2, q_1, q_2\}$, $S_4 = \{p'_1, p'_2, q_1, q'_2\}$,   and $S_5 = \{p'_1, p'_2, q'_1, q_2\}$.

First we will argue why no answer set of the above program can contain $S_6 = \{p_1, p'_2, q_1, q_2\}$. Any answer set S' that contains $\{p_1, p'_2, q_1, q_2\}$ must also contain $\{exist\_satisfied, q_1, q_2, q'_1, q'_2 \}$. But then this set will be a proper superset of the answer set $\{p_1, p'_2, q'_1, q_2\}$, and hence S' cannot be an answer set. We can similarly argue that no answer set of the above program can contain any of the following sets.

$S_7 = \{p_1, p'_2, q_1, q'_2\}$, $S_8 = \{p_1, p'_2, q'_1, q'_2\}$,
$S_9 = \{p'_1, p_2, q_1, q_2\}$, $S_{10} = \{p'_1, p_2, q'_1, q_2\}$, $S_{11} = \{p'_1, p_2, q'_1, q'_2\}$,   and
$S_{12} = \{p'_1, p'_2, q'_1, q'_2\}$.

Any other set containing any other combinations of $p_1, p'_1, p_2, p'_2, q_1, q'_1, q_2$ and q'_2 which is closed under the rules of the program will be a superset of one of the sets S or $S_1, \ldots, S_{12}$, and hence will not be an answer set.

Thus it is interesting to note that S is the only answer set of the above program that contains *exist_satisfied*.   □

Example 45 Let $F(p_1, p_2, q_1, q_2)$ be the formula $(p_1 \wedge q_1) \vee (p_2 \wedge q_2)$. Consider the QBF $\exists p_1, p_2. \forall q_1, q_2. F(p_1, p_2, q_1, q_2)$. This QBF is not satisfiable as for each interpretation of p_1 and p_2 there is an interpretation of q_1 and q_2 where $F(p_1, p_2, q_1, q_2)$ evaluates to *false*. Some of these interpretations are as follows:

$\{p_1, p_2, \neg q_1, \neg q_2\}$, $\{p_1, \neg p_2, \neg q_1, q_2\}$, $\{\neg p_1, p_2, q_1, \neg q_2\}$,
    and $\{\neg p_1, \neg p_2, q_1, q_2\}$.

Consider the following program:

p_1 *or* p'_1 ←.
p_2 *or* p'_2 ←.
q_1 *or* q'_1 ←.
q_2 *or* q'_2 ←.
exist_satisfied ← p_1, q_1.
exist_satisfied ← p_2, q_2.
q_1 ← *exist_satisfied*.
q'_1 ← *exist_satisfied*.
q_2 ← *exist_satisfied*.
q'_2 ← *exist_satisfied*.

It is easy to show that the following are answer sets of the above program:

$S_1 = \{p_1, p_2, q'_1, q'_2\}$,
$S_2 = \{p_1, p'_2, q'_1, q_2\}$, $\quad S_3 = \{p_1, p'_2, q'_1, q'_2\}$,
$S_4 = \{p'_1, p_2, q_1, q'_2\}$, $\quad S_5 = \{p'_1, p_2, q'_1, q'_2\}$,
$S_6 = \{p'_1, p'_2, q_1, q_2\}$, $\quad S_7 = \{p'_1, p'_2, q_1, q'_2\}$, $\quad S_8 = \{p'_1, p'_2, q'_1, q_2\}$, and
$S_9 = \{p'_1, p'_2, q'_1, q'_2\}$.

It can now be argued (similarly to the arguments in Example 42) that there are no other answer sets of the above program. □

2.1.12 Smallest, largest, and next in a linear ordering

Suppose we are given a set of distinct objects and a linear ordering among the objects. We assume that the ordering is defined using a predicate *less_than* between the objects. We now write an AnsProlog program which defines the smallest and the largest objects (with respect to the given ordering) in that set and also the *next* object (if any) for each of the objects in the set. The first two rules define *smallest*, the next two rules define *largest*, and the last four rules define *next*.

$not\_smallest(X) \leftarrow object(X), object(Y), less\_than(Y, X).$
$smallest(X) \leftarrow object(X), \textbf{not } not\_smallest(X).$

$not\_largest(X) \leftarrow object(X), object(Y), less\_than(X, Y).$
$largest(X) \leftarrow object(X), \textbf{not } not\_largest(X).$

$not\_next(X, Y) \leftarrow X = Y.$
$not\_next(X, Y) \leftarrow less\_than(Y, X).$
$not\_next(X, Y) \leftarrow object(X), object(Y), object(Z), less\_than(X, Z), less\_than(Z, Y).$
$next(X, Y) \leftarrow object(X), object(Y), \textbf{not } not\_next(X, Y).$

Exercise 6 Suppose that the predicate *less_than* in the above program specifies a partial order instead of a linear order. Write an AnsProlog program for determining minimal elements and the least element (if any) with respect to *less_than*. □

2.1.13 Establishing linear ordering among a set of objects

In the previous section we were given a linear ordering and we only needed to define *smallest*, *largest*, and *next*. Now suppose we are only given a set of objects and our goal is to establish a linear ordering among them. Since we do not have reasons to prefer one linear ordering over the other, the following program generates answer sets such that each answer set corresponds to a particular linear ordering among the objects and each linear ordering is captured by exactly one answer set.

The program is divided into two parts. The first part enumerates an ordering *prec* between each pair of objects. The second part tests if *prec* is a linear ordering or not by trying to define the *smallest*, *largest*, and *next* with respect to *prec* and checking if the largest element can be reached from the smallest through the next operator. If that is the case then *prec* is a linear ordering; otherwise if either of the three conditions is not satisfied (no largest element, or no smallest element, or not reachable) it is not a linear ordering. The following is the program where we use the predicates *first* and *last* instead of *smallest* and *largest*, and *succ* instead of *next*.

(1) Defining *prec*: The first rule says that between any two objects one must precede the other. The second makes *prec* a transitive relation.

$prec(X, Y) \leftarrow$ **not** $prec(Y, X), X \neq Y$.
$prec(X, Z) \leftarrow prec(X, Y), prec(Y, Z)$.

(2) Defining *succ*: The following rules define when an object is a successor of another object based on the precedence ordering.

$not\_succ(X, Z) \leftarrow prec(Z, X)$.
$not\_succ(X, Z) \leftarrow prec(X, Y), prec(Y, Z)$.
$not\_succ(X, X) \leftarrow$.
$succ(X, Y) \leftarrow$ **not** $not\_succ(X, Y)$.

(3) Defining *first*: The following rules define when an object is first with respect to the precedence ordering.

$not\_first(X) \leftarrow prec(Y, X)$.
$first(X) \leftarrow$ **not** $not\_first(X)$.

(4) Defining *last*: The following rules define when an object is last with respect to the precedence ordering.

$not\_last(X) \leftarrow prec(X, Y)$.
$last(X) \leftarrow$ **not** $not\_last(X)$.

(5) Defining reachability: The following rules define which objects are reachable from the first object using the successor relationship.

$reachable(X) \leftarrow first(X)$.
$reachable(Y) \leftarrow reachable(X), succ(X, Y)$.

(6) Defining linear orderings and eliminating models that do not have a linear ordering.

An ordering is tested for linearity by checking if the last element (as defined before) is reachable from the first element through the successor relationship.

linear ← *reachable*(*X*), *last*(*X*).
inconsistent ← **not** *inconsistent*, **not** *linear*.

2.1.14 Representing aggregates

In this subsection we show how aggregate computation can be done using AnsProlog. We demonstrate our program with respect to a small example. Consider the following database, where *sold*(*a*, 10, *Jan*1) means that 10 units of item *a* was sold on Jan 1.

sold(*a*, 10, *Jan*1) ←.
sold(*a*, 21, *Jan*5) ←.
sold(*a*, 15, *Jan*16) ←.
sold(*b*, 16, *Jan*4) ←.
sold(*b*, 31, *Jan*21) ←.
sold(*b*, 15, *Jan*26) ←.
sold(*c*, 24, *Jan*8) ←.

We would like to answer queries such as: 'List all items of which more than 50 units (total) were sold, and the total quantity sold for each.' Our goal is to develop an AnsProlog program for this. For simplicity, we assume that the same item has not been sold for the same unit more than once.

(1) The first step is to assign numbers to each tuple of *sold* while grouping them based on their item. In other words we would like the answer sets to contain the following facts (or similar ones with a different numbering).

assigned(*a*, 10, 1) ←.
assigned(*a*, 21, 2) ←.
assigned(*a*, 15, 3) ←.
assigned(*b*, 16, 1) ←.
assigned(*b*, 31, 2) ←.
assigned(*b*, 15, 3) ←.
assigned(*c*, 24, 1) ←.

An AnsProlog program with such answer sets has the following three groups of rules:
(a) The following three rules make sure that numbers are uniquely assigned to each pair of items and units.

assigned(*X*, *Y*, *J*) ← *sold*(*X*, *Y*, *D*), **not** ¬assigned(*X*, *Y*, *J*).
¬assigned(*X*, *Y*, *J*) ← assigned(*X*, *Y'*, *J*), *Y* ≠ *Y'*.
¬assigned(*X*, *Y*, *J*) ← assigned(*X*, *Y*, *J'*), *J* ≠ *J'*.

(b) The following rules ensure that among the tuples corresponding to each item there is no gap in the number assignment.

$numbered(X, J) \leftarrow assigned(X, Y, J).$
$\leftarrow numbered(X, J + 1), \textbf{not } numbered(X, J), J \geq 1.$

(c) The following rules ensure that for each item, there is a tuple that is assigned the number 1.

$one\_is\_assigned(X) \leftarrow assigned(X, Y, 1).$
$\leftarrow sold(X, Y, D), \textbf{not } one\_is\_assigned(X).$

An alternative set of rules that can achieve the same purpose is as follows:

$assign\_one(X, Y, 1) \leftarrow sold(X, Y, D), \textbf{not } \neg assign\_one(X, Y, 1).$
$\neg assign\_one(X, Y, 1) \leftarrow assign\_one(X, Y', 1), Y \neq Y'.$
$assigned(X, Y, 1) \leftarrow assign\_one(X, Y, 1).$

(2) Initializing and updating the aggregate operations. Depending on the aggregate operators the *initialize* and *update* facts describe how to start the aggregation process, when the first tuple in each grouping is encountered, and how the aggregate value is updated when additional tuples are encountered. We now write several such facts for a few different aggregate operators:

(a) Sum:

$initialize(sum, Y, Y) \leftarrow.$
$update(sum, W, Y, W + Y) \leftarrow.$

Intuitively, *initialize*(*sum, Y, Y*) means that for the aggregate *sum*, during the aggregation process when the tuple (_, Y) that is assigned the initial number (which is 1) is considered, Y is the value from which the aggregation starts. The aggregation starts from the tuple assigned 1, and runs though the other tuples in the linear order of their assignment. The fact, *update*(*sum, W, Y, W + Y*) is used in that process and intuitively means that while doing the aggregation *sum*, if the next tuple (based on the ordering of its assignment) is (_,Y), and the current accumulated value is W, then after considering this tuple the accumulated value is to be updated to W + Y.

(b) Count:

$initialize(count, Y, 1) \leftarrow.$
$update(count, W, Y, W + 1) \leftarrow.$

(c) Min:

$initialize(min, Y, Y) \leftarrow.$
$update(min, W, Y, W) \leftarrow W \leq Y.$
$update(min, W, Y, Y) \leftarrow Y \leq W.$

Using the predicates *initialize* and *update* we can define other aggregate operators of our choice. Thus, AnsProlog allows us to express user-defined aggregates.

(3) The following three rules describe how the *initialize* and *update* predicates are used in computing the aggregation. The first rule uses *initialize* to account for the tuple that is assigned the number 1, and the second rule encodes the aggregate computation when we already have computed the aggregate up to the Jth tuple, and we encounter the $J + 1$th tuple.

$aggr(Aggr\_name, 1, X, Z) \leftarrow assigned(X, Y, 1), initialize(Aggr\_name, Y, Z).$
$aggr(Aggr\_name, J + 1, X, Z) \leftarrow J > 0, aggr(Aggr\_name, J, X, W), assigned$
$\quad (X, Y, J + 1), update(Aggr\_name, W, Y, Z).$

(4) Computing new aggregate predicates: Once the aggregation is done, we can define new predicates for the particular aggregation that we need. The following are some examples of the encoding of such predicates.

(a) Total sold per item:

$total\_sold\_per\_item(X, Q) \leftarrow aggr(sum, J, X, Q), \textbf{not } aggr(sum, J + 1, X, Y).$

(b) Number of transactions per item:

$number\_of\_transactions\_per\_item(X, Q) \leftarrow aggr(count, J, X, Q),$
$\quad\quad\quad\quad\quad\quad\quad\quad\quad\quad\quad\quad\quad \textbf{not } aggr(count, J + 1, X, Y).$

Here we will need an additional rule if we want to display that for some items the number of transactions is zero. One such rule could be:

$number\_of\_transactions\_per\_item(X, 0) \leftarrow \textbf{not } has\_sold(X).$
$has\_sold(X) \leftarrow sold(X, Y, Z).$

(c) Minimum amount (other than zero) sold per item:

$min\_sold\_per\_item(X, Q) \leftarrow aggr(min, J, X, Q), \textbf{not } aggr(min, J + 1, X, Y).$

Using the above program the answer sets we will obtain will contain the following:

$total\_sold\_per\_item(a, 46)$
$total\_sold\_per\_item(b, 62)$
$total\_sold\_per\_item(c, 24)$

2.1.15 Representing classical disjunction conclusions using AnsProlog

Suppose we would like to represent classical disjunction in the head of the rules. That is, suppose we would like to express rules of the following form which are not part of the AnsProlog* syntax.

$a_1 \vee \cdots \vee a_l \leftarrow a_{l+1}, \ldots, a_m, \textbf{not } a_{m+1}, \ldots, \textbf{not } a_n.$

Here $\vee$ is the classical disjunction. Intuitively, the above rule means that in every answer set where the right hand side is true we would like the left hand side to be true, and unlike when we use *or*, we do not minimize truth. That is, the program:

$$a \vee b \leftarrow p.$$
$$p \leftarrow.$$

will have three answer sets, $\{a, p\}$, $\{b, p\}$, and $\{a, b, p\}$; whereas the program

$$a \text{ or } b \leftarrow p.$$
$$p \leftarrow.$$

will have only two answer sets, $\{a, p\}$, and $\{b, p\}$.

This can be achieved by the following translation to AnsProlog.

(1) $f' \leftarrow f, \textbf{not } f'.$
(2) $f \leftarrow a'_1, \ldots, a'_l, a_{l+1}, \ldots, a_m, \textbf{not } a_{m+1}, \ldots, \textbf{not } a_n.$
(3) For $i = 1, \ldots, l$ we have
    (a) $a_i \leftarrow \textbf{not } a'_i, a_{l+1}, \ldots, a_m, \textbf{not } a_{m+1}, \ldots, \textbf{not } a_n.$
    (b) $a'_i \leftarrow \textbf{not } a_i, a_{l+1}, \ldots, a_m, \textbf{not } a_{m+1}, \ldots, \textbf{not } a_n.$

Example 46 Consider the following program with classical disjunction in its head.

$$a \vee b \leftarrow q$$
$$q \leftarrow \textbf{not } r.$$
$$r \leftarrow \textbf{not } q.$$

Our intention is that the AnsProlog program obtained by translating the above program should have the answer sets $\{q, a\}$, $\{q, b\}$, $\{q, a, b\}$, and $\{r\}$.

The translated AnsProlog program is:

$$q \leftarrow \textbf{not } r.$$
$$r \leftarrow \textbf{not } q.$$
$$f' \leftarrow f, \textbf{not } f'.$$
$$f \leftarrow q, a', b'.$$
$$a \leftarrow \textbf{not } a', q.$$
$$a' \leftarrow \textbf{not } a, q.$$
$$b \leftarrow \textbf{not } b', q.$$
$$b' \leftarrow \textbf{not } b, q.$$

and it indeed has the desired answer sets.   □

One implication of the existence of the above encoding is that adding classical disjunction to the head of the rules without any minimization requirement does not increase the expressiveness of the language. In fact the same is also true if we allow exclusive-or in the head of rules. The following subsection gives an AnsProlog encoding for such rules.

2.1.16 Representing exclusive-or conclusions using AnsProlog

Suppose we would like to represent

$$a_1 \oplus \cdots \oplus a_l \leftarrow a_{l+1}, \ldots, a_m, \textbf{not } a_{m+1}, \ldots, \textbf{not } a_n.$$

where $\oplus$ is exclusive-or. Here we require that if the right hand side is true then exactly one atom in the head should be true.

This can be achieved by the following translation to AnsProlog:

(1) $f' \leftarrow f, \textbf{not } f'.$
(2) $f \leftarrow a'_1, \ldots, a'_l, a_{l+1}, \ldots, a_m, \textbf{not } a_{m+1}, \ldots, \textbf{not } a_n.$
(3) For $i = 1, \ldots, l$ we have
    (a) $a_i \leftarrow \textbf{not } a'_i, a_{l+1}, \ldots, a_m, \textbf{not } a_{m+1}, \ldots, \textbf{not } a_n.$
    (b) $a'_i \leftarrow \textbf{not } a_i.$
(4) For each i, j such that $1 \le i < j \le l$ we have the rule:

$$f \leftarrow a_{l+1}, \ldots, a_m, \textbf{not } a_{m+1}, \ldots, \textbf{not } a_n, a_i, a_j.$$

Exercise 7 Explain the difference between the programs: $\Pi_1 = \{a \text{ } or \text{ } b \leftarrow ., a \leftarrow b., b \leftarrow a.\}$ and $\Pi_2 = \{a \oplus b \leftarrow ., a \leftarrow b., b \leftarrow a.\}$ □

2.1.17 Cardinality constraints

Cardinality and weight constraints are introduced in the logic programming implementation Smodels as an extension of AnsProlog and are given a new semantics and the complexity of the new language is analyzed to be the same as the complexity of AnsProlog. In this section and the next we show how such constraints can be expressed in AnsProlog, without any extensions.

Consider the following cardinality constraint in an example dealing with graph coloring:

$$1\{colored(V, C) : color(C)\} 1 \leftarrow vertex(V).$$

The intuitive meaning of the above cardinality constraint is that, for each vertex v, exactly one instance of $colored(v, c)$ should be chosen such that $color(c)$ holds.

The above constraint can be expressed through the following AnsProlog rules:

(1) Enumerating the possibilities:

$colored(V, C) \leftarrow vertex(V), color(C), \textbf{not } not\_colored(V, C).$
$not\_colored(V, C) \leftarrow vertex(V), color(C), \textbf{not } colored(V, C).$

(2) Rules that define *count_color*(V, N), where for any vertex *v*, *count_color*(*v*, *n*) is true in an answer set *A* if there are *n* different facts of the form *colored*(*v*, *c*) with distinct *c*s in *A*. These aggregate rules are given in Section 2.1.14.

(3) The constraint:

$\leftarrow vertex(V), number(N), count\_color(V, N), N \neq 1.$

Now consider the cardinality constraint

$l_1\{colored(V, C) : color(C)\}\, l_2 \leftarrow vertex(V).$

Intuitively, it means that for every vertex *v*, *colored*(*v*, *c*) should be true for *k* distinct *c*s, where $l_1 \leq k \leq l_2$

To encode such a cardinality constraint we proceed as above except that we have the following constraints instead of the one we had before.

(1) $\leftarrow color(V), number(N), count\_color(V, N), n < l_1.$
(2) $\leftarrow color(V), number(N), count\_color(V, N), n > l_2.$

Cardinality constraints in the body can be encoded by using the aggregate and then converting the constraints in the previous section into rules. For example if we want to define a predicate *three_six*(V) on vertices which are assigned between 3 to 6 colors we have the following rule:

(1) $three\_six(V) \leftarrow color(V), number(N), count\_color(V, N), 3 \leq N \leq 6.$

together with rules that define *count_color*(V, N).

2.1.18 Weight constraints

Cardinality constraints can be generalized to weight constraints. When cardinality constraints in the head are generalized to weight constraints, instead of count, we can use other aggregates such as '*sum*'. For example, consider the following weight constraint:

$w\ [l_1 : w_1, \ldots, l_m : w_m, \textbf{not}\ l_{m+1} : w_{m+1}, \ldots, \textbf{not}\ l_n : w_n]w' \leftarrow p.$

We can encode it in AnsProlog as follows:

(1) We give a name to the above rule, say *r*.
(2) We represent the weights of the literals as follows:

$weight(r, l_1, w_1) \leftarrow.$
$\vdots$
$weight(r, l_m, w_m) \leftarrow.$

$weight(r, l'_{m+1}, w_{m+1}) \leftarrow .$

$\vdots$

$weight(r, l'_n, w_n) \leftarrow .$

(3) We enumerate the literals in the head of the rule by having the following: We use the predicate *holds* so as to be able to compute the sum of the weights of the literals (in the head of r) that hold.

$holds(R, L) \leftarrow holds(p), weight(R, L, X), contrary(L, L'), \textbf{not } holds(R, L').$
$holds(R, L) \leftarrow holds(p), weight(R, L', X), contrary(L, L'), \textbf{not } holds(R, L').$

In addition we have the definition of *contrary*.

$contrary(l_i, l'_i) \leftarrow .$
$contrary(l'_i, l_i) \leftarrow .$

(4) We define $sum\_holds(R, Wt)$ which sums the weight of all literals in R that hold, following the approach in Section 2.1.14.

(5) To eliminate candidate answer sets whose aggregate weight do not satisfy the weight conditions in the head of r we have the following constraints:

$\leftarrow sum\_holds(r, Wt), Wt < w.$
$\leftarrow sum\_holds(r, Wt), Wt > w'.$

(6) Finally we define which literals hold.

$holds(L) \leftarrow atom(L), holds(R, L).$

2.2 Knowledge representation and reasoning modules

In this section we show how we can use AnsProlog* programs to represent various knowledge representation and reasoning modules. We start with the representation of normative statements, exceptions, weak exceptions, and direct contradictions to those statements.

2.2.1 Normative statements, exceptions, weak exceptions, and direct contradictions: the tweety flies story

Normative statements are statements of the form 'normally elements belonging to a class c have the property p.' A good representation of normative statements should at least allow us to easily 'incorporate' information about exceptional elements of c with respect to the property c. A good hallmark of incorporation of such additional information is the property of elaboration tolerance. The measure of elaboration tolerance of a representation is determined by the classes of new information that can be incorporated through local changes to the original representation. We now discuss this issue with respect to one of the oldest examples in nonmonotonic reasoning – 'Normally birds fly. Penguins are exceptional birds that do not fly.'

(1) We start with a representation in AnsProlog where the 'Closed World Assumption' about all predicates is part of the semantics. In this representation the AnsProlog program defines when positive literals are true, and negative literals are assumed (by the CWA) to hold if the corresponding positive literals are not forced to be true by the definitions.

A representation of the knowledge that 'Normally birds Fly. Tweety is a bird' that is elaboration tolerant to new knowledge of the kind 'Penguins are exceptional birds that do not fly.' is as follows:

The original representation is:

$flies(X) \leftarrow bird(X),$ **not** $ab(X).$
$bird(tweety) \leftarrow.$
$bird(sam) \leftarrow.$

From the above we can conclude that *tweety* and *sam* fly. Next when we are told that *sam* is a penguin, and penguins are exceptional birds that do not fly, we can incorporate this additional knowledge by just adding the following to our original representation.

$bird(X) \leftarrow penguin(X).$
$ab(X) \leftarrow penguin(X).$
$penguin(sam) \leftarrow.$

From the resulting program we can conclude that *tweety* flies, but now we change our earlier conclusion about *sam* and conclude that *sam* does not fly.

Now suppose we get additional knowledge of another class of birds, the ostriches, that are also exceptions. Again, this can be incorporated by simply adding the following rules:

$bird(X) \leftarrow ostrich(X).$
$ab(X) \leftarrow ostrich(X).$

(2) Now suppose we want to represent the above information in AnsProlog¬, where CWA is not hard coded in the semantics. In that case we can write explicit CWA rules about each predicate. The overall representation will then be as follows.

$flies(X) \leftarrow bird(X),$ **not** $ab(X).$
$bird(X) \leftarrow penguin(X).$
$ab(X) \leftarrow penguin(X).$
$bird(tweety) \leftarrow.$
$penguin(sam) \leftarrow.$

$\neg bird(X) \leftarrow$ **not** $bird(X).$
$\neg penguin(X) \leftarrow$ **not** $penguin(X).$
$\neg ab(X) \leftarrow$ **not** $ab(X).$
$\neg flies(X) \leftarrow$ **not** $flies(X).$

The main advantage of having explicit CWA rules is that if for a particular predicate we do not want to have CWA, then we can simply remove the corresponding explicit CWA rule. This cannot be done in an AnsProlog representation.

(3) Now let us consider a different kind of elaboration. We would like to add information about *john* who is a wounded bird, and wounded birds are a subset of birds and are *weakly exceptional* with respect to the property of flying. By this we mean that for wounded birds we cannot make a definite conclusion about whether they can fly or not.

To represent the above elaboration the first step is to remove the CWA rule about *flies* so that we are not forced to conclude one way or the other about the flying ability of wounded birds. But we do need to make conclusions about the flying ability of penguins and non-birds. For this we need to add explicit rules that state when certain objects do not fly. The following program makes these changes to our previous formulation.

$flies(X) \leftarrow bird(X),$ **not** $ab(X).$
$bird(X) \leftarrow penguin(X).$
$ab(X) \leftarrow penguin(X).$
$bird(tweety) \leftarrow.$
$penguin(sam) \leftarrow.$

$\neg bird(X) \leftarrow$ **not** $bird(X).$
$\neg penguin(X) \leftarrow$ **not** $penguin(X).$
$\neg ab(X) \leftarrow$ **not** $ab(X).$

$\neg flies(X) \leftarrow penguin(X).$
$\neg flies(X) \leftarrow \neg bird(X).$

Now we can incorporate the new knowledge about the wounded birds by adding the following rules.

$wounded\_bird(john) \leftarrow.$
$\neg wounded\_bird(X) \leftarrow$ **not** $wounded\_bird(X).$
$bird(X) \leftarrow wounded\_bird(X).$
$ab(X) \leftarrow wounded\_bird(X).$

It is easy to see that we still conclude *tweety* flies and *sam* does not fly from the resulting program, and about *john* our program does not entail *john* flies, and nor does it entail *john* does not fly.

(4) In the previous three representations we had closed world assumption – whether explicit or implicit – about *birds* and *penguins*, and had explicit CWA with respect to *wounded_bird* in the last representation. Now consider the case when our information about *birds*, *penguins*, and *wounded_birds* is *incomplete*. By this we mean that we may know that *tweety* is a bird, and know that *swa*-21 is not a bird (despite SouthWest Airlines' claim that it is the state bird of Texas), and for some other objects we may not know whether it is a bird or not. By having CWA we will be forced to conclude that these other objects are not birds. Since we do not want that we will remove the explicit CWA rule about *birds*, *penguins*, and *wounded_birds*. The resulting program is

as follows:

$flies(X) \leftarrow bird(X), \textbf{not } ab(X).$
$bird(X) \leftarrow penguin(X).$
$ab(X) \leftarrow penguin(X).$
$bird(tweety) \leftarrow.$
$penguin(sam) \leftarrow.$

$\neg flies(X) \leftarrow penguin(X).$
$\neg flies(X) \leftarrow \neg bird(X).$

$wounded\_bird(john) \leftarrow.$
$bird(X) \leftarrow wounded\_bird(X).$
$ab(X) \leftarrow wounded\_bird(X).$

Now suppose we want to reason about the object *et*, which we know to be a bird. Since *et* is not known to be a penguin or a wounded bird, the above program will not entail *ab(et)*, and hence will entail *flies(et)*. In the absence of CWA about penguins and wounded birds, it is possible that *et* is a penguin, and in that case our conclusion would be wrong. To avoid such possibly wrong conclusions, we can make some changes to our program so that it is *conservative* in making conclusions about what flies and what does not. The main change we make is in the rules that define *ab*; while before one of our rules was that *penguins* are abnormal, now we change the rule so that any object that can possibly be a penguin (i.e., we do not know for sure that it is not a penguin) is abnormal. Similarly, we change the *ab* rule about wounded birds to: any object that can possibly be a wounded bird (i.e., we do not know for sure that it is not a wounded bird) is abnormal. In addition, since we remove the explicit CWA rules about penguins and wounded birds, we must add rules that define when an object is not a penguin and when an object is not a wounded bird. The resulting program is as follows, with the changed rules underlined.

$flies(X) \leftarrow bird(X), \textbf{not } ab(X).$
$bird(X) \leftarrow penguin(X).$
$\underline{ab(X) \leftarrow \textbf{not } \neg penguin(X).}$
$bird(tweety) \leftarrow.$
$penguin(sam) \leftarrow.$

$\underline{\neg penguin(X) \leftarrow \neg bird(X).}$

$\neg flies(X) \leftarrow penguin(X).$
$\neg flies(X) \leftarrow \neg bird(X).$

$wounded\_bird(john) \leftarrow.$
$\underline{\neg wounded\_bird(X) \leftarrow \neg bird(X).}$
$bird(X) \leftarrow wounded\_bird(X).$
$\underline{ab(X) \leftarrow \textbf{not } \neg wounded\_bird(X).}$

(5) Let us now consider the case where we may have explicit information about the nonflying ability of certain birds. We would like our representation to gracefully allow such additions. The last program is not adequate to this task because if we were to add new facts $\{\neg fly(tweety), \neg penguin(tweety), \neg wounded\_bird(tweety)\}$ to it the resulting program will not have a consistent answer set, while intuitively no such breakdown in reasoning is warranted.

Such a breakdown can be avoided by replacing the rule:

$flies(X) \leftarrow bird(X), \textbf{not } ab(X).$

by the rule:

$flies(X) \leftarrow bird(X), \textbf{not } ab(X), \textbf{not } \neg flies(X).$

In addition, for *exceptions* we only need to have the rule:

$\neg flies(X) \leftarrow exceptional\_bird(X).$

and no longer need a rule of the form:

$ab(X) \leftarrow \textbf{not } \neg exceptional\_bird(X).$

For *weak exceptions* we will need the rule:

$ab(X) \leftarrow \textbf{not } \neg weakly\_exceptional\_bird(X).$

2.2.2 The frame problem and the Yale Turkey shoot

Another important benchmark in the history of knowledge representation and nonmonotonic reasoning is the 'frame problem'. The original frame problem was about succinctly representing and reasoning about what does not change in a world due to an action. The problem arises in avoiding writing explicit axioms for each object that does not change its value due to a particular axiom.

To demonstrate how AnsProlog and its extensions represent the frame problem we consider the Yale Turkey shoot from the literature. In this example, there are two actions: *load* and *shoot*. There are also two fluents – objects that may change their value due to an action: *alive* and *loaded*. In our representation we follow the notation of situation calculus from the literature.

In situation calculus the initial situation is represented by a constant s_0, and the situation arising after executing an action A in a situation S is denoted by $res(A, S)$. The truth value of fluents in a situation is described using the predicate *holds*, where $holds(F, S)$ means that the fluent F holds in the situation S.

(1) With CWA about each situation:

In our first representation we want to represent the information that initially the turkey is alive and the gun is not loaded, and the effect of the actions *load* and *shoot*. Our goal is that our representation should allow us to make conclusions about situations that may arise (i.e., about hypothetical future worlds) if we perform a particular sequence of actions. Such a reasoning mechanism can be used for verifying plans and planning.

Since *loaded* and *alive* are the only fluents, we have complete information about these fluents with respect to the initial situation, and our actions *shoot* and *load* are deterministic; in our first representation using AnsProlog we will assume CWA and only focus on the truth with the intention that conclusions about falsity can be reasoned using CWA.

We start by representing what is known about the initial situation. This can be accomplished by the following rule:

$holds(alive, s_0) \leftarrow.$

Since we are using CWA, by not having any explicit information about the fluent *load* in s_0 we can conclude using CWA that $\neg holds(loaded, s_0)$.

To represent that the fluent *loaded* will be true after executing the action *load* in any arbitrary situation S, we have the following rule, which we refer to as an *effect rule*.

$holds(loaded, res(load, S)) \leftarrow.$

To represent the frame axiom (which is a normative statement and says that fluents which are true normally preserve their value after an action) we have the following rule, which we call the *frame rule* or *inertia rule*.

$holds(F, res(A, S)) \leftarrow holds(F, S),$ **not** $ab(F, A, S).$

The atom $ab(F, A, S)$ in the above rule encodes when a fluent F is abnormal with respect to an action A and S. The intention is to use it in encoding exceptions to the normative statement. We now define particular instances when $ab(F, A, S)$ is true.

One instance is when the action *shoot* is executed in a situation where *loaded* is true. In this case the fluent *alive* will not remain true after the action. Thus it gives rise to an exception to the inertia rule. This exception is encoded by the following:

$ab(alive, shoot, S) \leftarrow holds(loaded, S).$

Note that in the above formulation we do not have an effect rule for the action *shoot*. This is because among the two fluents *loaded* and *alive*, shoot does not affect the first one, and its effect on the second one is indirectly encoded by the *exception* to the *inertia rule*. This is different from the encoding of the effect of the action *load* on the fluent *loaded* using *effect rules*. This difference is due to our use of CWA to infer $\neg holds(alive, res(shoot, S))$ by not being able to infer $holds(alive, res(shoot, S))$; thus the use of an exception instead of an effect rule.

(2) To allow incomplete information about the initial situation:

Let us now consider the case when we may have incomplete information about the initial situation. In that case we would have to explicitly represent both what we know to be true in the initial situation and what we know to be false in the initial

situation. Thus we can no longer use CWA, and we use AnsProlog⁻ as our representation
language.

Let us consider the scenario when we know that the turkey is initially alive, but
have no idea whether the gun is loaded or not. In this case the initial situation can be
represented by the following rule:

$holds(alive, s_0) \leftarrow.$

Note that since we are using AnsProlog⁻ we can no longer infer $\neg holds(loaded, s_0)$
using CWA. That is of course what we want. For the same reason we now need two
explicit inertia rules, one about the inertia of the truth of fluents and another about the
inertia of the falsity of fluents. These two rules are:

$holds(F, res(A, S)) \leftarrow holds(F, S), \textbf{not } ab(F, A, S).$
$\neg holds(F, res(A, S)) \leftarrow \neg holds(F, S), \textbf{not } ab(F, A, S).$

The effect rules due to the actions *load* and *shoot* are respectively encoded by the
following rules:

$holds(loaded, res(load, S)) \leftarrow.$
$\neg holds(alive, res(shoot, S)) \leftarrow holds(loaded, S).$

Since we have explicit effect rules for both truth and falsity we will also need exceptions
for the blocking of the opposite. In other words if A makes F true then we have to block
the inference of $\neg holds(F, res(A, S))$. (This was not necessary when we used the CWA
in our AnsProlog encoding.) The two exception rules corresponding to the above two
effect rules are as follows:

$ab(loaded, load, S) \leftarrow.$
$ab(alive, shoot, S) \leftarrow \textbf{not } \neg holds(loaded, S).$

The use of **not** $\neg holds(loaded, S)$ instead of the simpler $holds(loaded, S)$ in the body of
the last rule is because of the possibility that we may have incompleteness about the situations. In that case we want to reason *conservatively*. This can be explained in terms of
our particular scenario. Recall that we know that initially *alive* is true and we have no idea
if *loaded* is true or not. Now suppose we want to reason about the situation $res(shoot, s_0)$.
Since we have $holds(alive, s_0)$ we will conclude $holds(alive, res(shoot, s_0))$ using the
first inertia rule unless it is blocked by the derivation of $ab(alive, shoot, s_0)$. If we have
only $holds(loaded, S)$ in the body of the last exception rule, we will not be able to
derive $ab(alive, shoot, s_0)$ and hence conclude $holds(alive, res(shoot, s_0))$. Our conclusion would not be correct if in the real world *loaded* is true in s_0. The use of
not $\neg holds(loaded, S)$ instead of the simpler $holds(loaded, S)$ prevents us from making this possibly wrong conclusion. With the above formulation we neither conclude
$holds(alive, res(shoot, s_0))$, nor do we conclude $\neg holds(alive, res(shoot, s_0))$, as either
would be wrong in one of the possible scenarios: the first when *loaded* is *true* in s_0,
and the second when *loaded* is *false* in s_0.

Finally, the above encoding also works fine when there is complete information about the initial situation.

(3) Allowing backward reasoning:

In the previous two formulations our goal was to hypothetically reason about future situations. Now consider the case when in the beginning we do not know whether *loaded* is true in s_0 or not. Then we are given the oracle *holds(alive, res(shoot, s_0))*, and from this added information we would like to conclude that *loaded* must be false in s_0.

One way to be able to do such reasoning is to enumerate the possible worlds in the initial situation using AnsProlog⁻. In our example we can add the following four rules to our previous formulation.

$holds(alive, s_0) \leftarrow$ **not** $\neg holds(alive, s_0)$.
$\neg holds(alive, s_0) \leftarrow$ **not** $holds(alive, s_0)$.
$holds(loaded, s_0) \leftarrow$ **not** $\neg holds(loaded, s_0)$.
$\neg holds(loaded, s_0) \leftarrow$ **not** $holds(loaded, s_0)$.

The above four rules lead to multiple answer sets each corresponding to one of the possible worlds about the initial situation. Now we can prune out the worlds that do not lead to the oracle by having the oracle as the following integrity constraint.

$\leftarrow$ **not** $holds(alive, res(shoot, s_0))$.

The above integrity constraint will eliminate the answer sets (of the rest of the program) that do not entail the oracle *holds(alive, res(shoot, s_0))*. Since reducing the number of answer sets means we can make more conclusions, the oracle leads us to additional conclusions. In our particular scenario the integrity constraint will eliminate answer sets where *holds(loaded, s_0)* is true and in the remaining answer sets we will have $\neg holds(loaded, s_0)$. Thus the additional information provided by the oracle will lead us to the conclusion that $\neg holds(loaded, s_0)$.

2.2.3 Systematic removal of Close World Assumption: an example

Consider the following program that defines the transitive closure notion of ancestors given facts about parents.

$anc(X, Y) \leftarrow parent(X, Y)$.
$anc(X, Y) \leftarrow parent(X, Z), anc(Z, Y)$.

The above program assumes complete information about parents and gives a complete definition of ancestors. That is, using the above program together with a set of facts about *parent*, we can completely determine about any arbitrary pair (a, b), whether $anc(a, b)$ is true or false.

Now consider the case where the objects are fossils of dinosaurs dug at an archaeological site, and for pairs of objects (a, b) we can sometimes determine $par(a, b)$ through tests, sometimes determine $\neg par(a, b)$, and sometimes neither. This means our knowledge about *par* is not complete. Now the question is how do we define when *anc* is true and when it is false.

To define when *anc* is true we keep the old rules.

$anc(X, Y) \leftarrow parent(X, Y).$
$anc(X, Y) \leftarrow parent(X, Z), anc(Z, Y).$

Next we define a predicate $m\_par(X, Y)$ which encodes when X may be a parent of Y. We do this through the following rule.

$m\_par(X, Y) \leftarrow \textbf{not} \ \neg par(X, Y).$

Using m_par we now define $m\_anc(X, Y)$ which encodes when X may be an ancestor of Y. We do this through the following rule.

$m\_anc(X, Y) \leftarrow m\_par(X, Y).$
$m\_anc(X, Y) \leftarrow m\_par(X, Z), m\_anc(Z, Y).$

Now we use m_anc to define when $\neg anc(X, Y)$ is true through the following rule.

$\neg anc(X, Y) \leftarrow \textbf{not} \ m\_anc(X, Y).$

2.2.4 Reasoning about what is known and what is not

Recall that an AnsProlog$^{\neg}$ program may have an answer set with respect to which we can neither conclude an atom to be true, nor conclude it to be false. This happens if for atom f, and answer set S, neither f nor $\neg f$ is in S. In this case we can say that the truth value of f is unknown in the answer set S. We can write the following rule to make such a conclusion and reason with it further.

$unknown(f) \leftarrow \textbf{not} \ f, \textbf{not} \ \neg f.$

The following program Π_{gpa} encodes the eligibility condition of a particular fellowship and the rule (4) below deals with the case when the reasoner is not sure whether a particular applicant is eligible or not. In that case rule (4) forces the reasoner to conduct an interview for the applicant whose eligibility is unknown.

(1) $eligible(X) \leftarrow highGPA(X).$
(2) $eligible(X) \leftarrow special(X), fairGPA(X).$
(3) $\neg eligible(X) \leftarrow \neg special(X), \neg highGPA(X).$
(4) $interview(X) \leftarrow \textbf{not} \ eligible(X), \textbf{not} \ \neg eligible(X).$
(5) $fairGPA(john) \leftarrow.$
(6) $\neg highGPA(john) \leftarrow.$

2.3 Notes and references

Many of the encoding techniques discussed in this chapter are folklore in logic programming. We point out here some of the sources that we are aware of. The notion of 'choice' was first presented by Saccà and Zaniolo in [SZ90]. The encodings of quantified boolean formulas with two quantifiers and also the encoding of the linear ordering are due to Eiter and Gottlob [EG93a, EGM94] where they use such encodings to prove the complexity and expressiveness of AnsProlog^{or} programs. The encodings for aggregates are based on work by Zaniolo and his colleagues [ZAO93, GSZ93, Sac93]. The use of the '$p \leftarrow$ **not** p.' construct to encode integrity constraints, the representation of ex-or and classical disjunction in AnsProlog, and the expression of first-order queries are based on the papers by Niemelä, Simons and Soininen [Nie99, NSS99, Sim99]. Most of the knowledge representation and reasoning modules are from Gelfond's papers [GL90, GL91, Gel94] on AnsProlog and AnsProlog$^-$, and also appear in the survey paper [BG94]. The recent survey papers [MT99, Gel01] also have many small AnsProlog* modules. In Chapter 5 we consider many more examples and larger AnsProlog* programs.

Chapter 3

Principles and properties of declarative programming with answer sets

In this chapter we present several fundamental results that are useful in *analyzing* and *step-by-step building* of AnsProlog* programs, viewed both as stand alone programs and as functions. To analyze AnsProlog* programs we define and describe several properties such as categoricity (presence of unique answer sets), coherence (presence of at least one answer set), computability (answer set computation being recursive), filter-abducibility (abductive assimilation of observations using filtering), language independence (independence between answer sets of a program and the language), language tolerance (preservation of the meaning of a program with respect to the original language when the language is enlarged), compilability to first-order theory, amenability to removal of *or*, and restricted monotonicity (exhibition of monotonicity with respect to a select set of literals).

We also define several subclasses of AnsProlog* programs such as stratified, locally stratified, acyclic, tight, signed, head cycle free and several conditions on AnsProlog* rules such as well-moded and state results about which AnsProlog* programs have what properties. We present several results that relate answer sets of an AnsProlog* program to its rules. We develop the notion of splitting and show how the notions of stratification, local stratification, and splitting can be used in step-by-step computation of answer sets.

For *step-by-step building* of AnsProlog* programs we develop the notion of conservative extension – where a program preserves its original meaning after additional rules are added to it, and present conditions for programs that exhibit this property. We present several operators such as incremental extension, interpolation, domain completion, input opening, and input extension, and show how they can be used to systematically build larger programs from smaller modules.

The rest of the chapter is organized as follows. We first define some of the basic notions and properties and then enumerate many of the sub-classes and their properties. We then consider the more involved properties one-by-one and discuss conditions under which they hold.

3.1 Basic notions and basic properties

3.1.1 Categorical and coherent programs

Uniqueness of answer sets is an important property of a program. Programs which have a unique answer set are called *categorical*. Not all programs are categorical. There are programs with multiple answer sets and with no answer sets at all. The latter will be called *incoherent*. Programs with at least one answer set are called *coherent*. A program Π is said to be *consistent* if $Cn(\Pi)$ – the set of literals entailed by Π – is consistent; Otherwise Π is said to be *inconsistent*. Since programs that are not coherent do not have any answer sets, they entail *Lit*; hence those programs are also inconsistent. Coherence, categoricity, and consistency are important properties of logic programs. In Section 3.2 we consider several sub-classes of AnsProlog* programs and categorize them in terms of which ones exhibit the properties of coherence, categoricity, and consistency.

Example 47 The AnsProlog program $\{p \leftarrow \mathbf{not}\ p.\}$ is incoherent as it does not have an answer set.

The AnsProlog program $\{a \leftarrow \mathbf{not}\ b., b \leftarrow \mathbf{not}\ a.\}$, although coherent has two answer sets $\{a\}$ and $\{b\}$ and hence is not categorical.

The AnsProlog¬ program $\Pi = \{p \leftarrow \mathbf{not}\ b., \neg p \leftarrow \mathbf{not}\ b.\}$ is categorical and coherent as it has *Lit* as its unique answer set; but it is not consistent as $Cn(\Pi)$ – which contains both p and $\neg p$ – is not consistent. $\square$

3.1.2 Relating answer sets and the program rules

Suppose we are given an AnsProlog program Π and are told that an atom A belongs to one of its answer sets S. What can we infer about the relation between A and Π? An intuitive answer is that there must be at least one rule in Π with A in its head such that its body evaluates to *true* with respect to S. We refer to such a rule as *a support for the atom A with respect to S in Π*.

Similarly, given a rule r of an AnsProlog¬,^{or} program Π if we are told that its body evaluates to *true* with respect to an answer set S of Π, what can we say about the head of r? An intuitive answer in this case is that one of the literals in the head must be in S. We now formalize these intuitions as propositions. These propositions are very useful when trying to show that a given set of literals is an answer set of a program Π.

Proposition 20 [MS89] (a) **Forced atom proposition**: Let S be an answer set of an AnsProlog program Π. For any ground instance of a rule in Π of the type $A_0 \leftarrow A_1, \ldots, A_m, \mathbf{not}\ A_{m+1}, \ldots, \mathbf{not}\ A_n$. If $\{A_1, \ldots, A_m\} \subseteq S$ and $\{A_{m+1}, \ldots, A_n\} \cap S = \emptyset$ then $A_0 \in S$.

(b) **Supporting rule proposition**: If S is an answer set of an AnsProlog program Π then S is supported by Π. That is, if $A_0 \in S$, then there exists a ground instance of a rule in Π of the type $A_0 \leftarrow A_1, \ldots, A_m, \textbf{not } A_{m+1}, \ldots, \textbf{not } A_n$. Such that $\{A_1, \ldots, A_m\} \subseteq S$ and $\{A_{m+1}, \ldots, A_n\} \cap S = \emptyset$. $\qquad\square$

We now enlarge the notion of support for an atom to support for a whole set of atoms and introduce the notion of well-supportedness and relate well-supported models to answer sets.

Definition 16 A Herbrand interpretation S is said to be *well-supported* in an AnsProlog program Π iff there exists a strict well-founded partial order $\prec$ on S such that for any atom $A \in S$, there exists a rule $A \leftarrow A_1, \ldots, A_m,$ $\textbf{not } A_{m+1}, \ldots, \textbf{not } A_n$ in $ground(\Pi)$, such that $\{A_1, \ldots, A_m\} \subseteq S$ and $\{A_{m+1}, \ldots, A_n\} \cap S = \emptyset$ and for $1 \leq i \leq m$, $A_i \prec A$. $\qquad\square$

Proposition 21 [Fag90] For any AnsProlog program Π, the well-supported models of Π are exactly the answer sets of Π. $\qquad\square$

We now consider AnsProlog$^{\neg, or}$ programs and expand the forced atom proposition and supporting rule proposition for such programs.

Proposition 22 [BG94] (a) **Forced disjunct proposition**: Let S be an answer set of an AnsProlog$^{\neg, or}$ program Π. For any ground instance of a rule in Π of the type (1.2.1) if $\{L_{k+1}, \ldots, L_m\} \subseteq S$ and $\{L_{m+1}, \ldots, L_n\} \cap S = \emptyset$ then there exists an i, $0 \leq i \leq k$ such that $L_i \in S$.
(b) **Exclusive supporting rule proposition**: If S is a consistent answer set of an AnsProlog$^{\neg, or}$ program Π and $L \in S$ then there exists a ground instance of a rule in Π of the type (1.2.1) such that $\{L_{k+1}, \ldots, L_m\} \subseteq S$, and $\{L_{m+1}, \ldots, L_n\} \cap S = \emptyset$, and $\{L_0, \ldots, L_k\} \cap S = \{L\}$. $\qquad\square$

Example 48 Consider the following AnsProlog$^{\neg, or}$ program:

$a \; or \; b \leftarrow .$
$b \; or \; c \leftarrow .$
$c \; or \; a \leftarrow .$

The above program has three answer sets $S_1 = \{a, b\}$, $S_2 = \{a, c\}$, and $S_3 = \{b, c\}$. For the atom a in answer set S_1, the third rule, but not the first rule, of the above program satisfies the conditions of the exclusive supporting rule proposition. For atom b in S_1, it is the second rule. Similarly, it is easy to verify the exclusive supporting rule proposition for the atoms in the other answer sets. $\qquad\square$

3.1.3 Conservative extension

When programming in AnsProlog, we would often like to enhance a program Π with additional rules. An important question is under what conditions does the new program *preserve* the meaning of the original program? Answers to this and similar questions are very important and useful in systematically developing a large program. We now formally define the notion of conservative extension and present certain conditions under which it holds. We discuss additional aspects of systematically developing large programs in Section 3.7.

Definition 17 Let Π and Π' be ground AnsProlog* programs such that $\Pi \subseteq \Pi'$. We say that Π' is a *conservative extension* for Π if the following condition holds: A is a consistent answer set for Π iff there is a consistent answer set A' for Π' such that $A = A' \cap Lit(\mathcal{L}_\Pi)$. $\square$

The following proposition directly follows from the above definition.

Proposition 23 If a program Π' is a conservative extension of a program Π, then $Cn(\Pi) = Cn(\Pi') \cap Lit(\mathcal{L}_\Pi)$. $\square$

We now present syntactic conditions on AnsProlog$^\neg$ programs Π and D such that $\Pi \cup D$ is a conservative extension of Π.

Theorem 3.1.1 [GP91] Let $\mathcal{L}_0$ be a language and $\mathcal{L}_1$ be its extension by a set of new predicates. Let Π and D be AnsProlog$^\neg$ programs in $\mathcal{L}_0$ and $\mathcal{L}_1$ respectively. If for any rule of the type $L_0 \leftarrow L_1, \ldots, L_m, \textbf{not } L_{m+1}, \ldots, \textbf{not } L_n$ from D, $L_0 \in \mathcal{L}_1 - \mathcal{L}_0$ and for all $i, i > 0, L_i \in \mathcal{L}_0$ then if no answer set of Π satisfies the premises of contrary rules (i.e. rules with contrary literals in the head) from D then for all $L \in \mathcal{L}_0, \Pi \models L$ iff $\Pi \cup D \models L$. $\square$

The syntactic conditions in the above theorem are very restrictive. The following proposition has broader but semantic conditions and allows Π and D to be AnsProlog$^{\neg,or}$ programs.

Theorem 3.1.2 [GP96] Let D and Π be AnsProlog$^{\neg,or}$ programs such that $head(D) \cap lit(\Pi) = \emptyset$ and for any consistent answer set A of Π the program $D \cup (A \cap lit(D))$ is consistent. Then $D \cup \Pi$ is a conservative extension of the program Π. $\square$

Since semantic conditions are difficult to check, in the following proposition we present syntactic conditions but restrict D to be an AnsProlog$^\neg$ program.

Proposition 24 [LT94] If Π is an AnsProlog$^{\neg,or}$ program, C is a consistent set of literals that does not occur in Π, and D is an AnsProlog$^\neg$ program such that for every rule $r \in D$, $head(r) \subseteq C$, and $neg(r) \subseteq lit(\Pi)$ then $D \cup \Pi$ is a conservative extension of Π. □

Example 49 Let Π be the following program:

$p \leftarrow \mathbf{not}\ q.$
$q \leftarrow \mathbf{not}\ p.$

and D be the following program.

$r \leftarrow \mathbf{not}\ r, q.$
$r \leftarrow p.$

The program Π has two answer sets $\{p\}$ and $\{q\}$ and $\Pi \not\models p$. On the other hand $\Pi \cup D$ has a single answer set $\{p, r\}$ and entails p. Hence, $\Pi \cup D$ is not a conservative extension of Π. We now show that none of the conditions of Theorems 3.1.1 and 3.1.2 and Proposition 24 are satisfied with respect to this Π and D.

The first rule of D has in its body r, which belongs to the language $\mathcal{L}_1$ of D but is not in $\mathcal{L}_0$, the language of Π. Hence, the conditions of Theorem 3.1.1 are not satisfied.

Although $\{q\}$ is an answer set of Π, the program $D \cup (\{q\} \cap lit(D)) = D \cup \{q\}$ is inconsistent as it does not have any answer set. Hence, the conditions of Theorem 3.1.2 are not satisfied.

With respect to the conditions of Proposition 24 we have $C = \{r\}$. But for the first rule r_1 of D, we have $neg(r_1) = \{r\} \not\subseteq lit(\Pi)$. Hence, the conditions of Proposition 24 are not satisfied. □

3.1.4 I/O specification of a program

In this subsection we define the notion of a mode (or I/O specification) of a predicate and use it to define the notion of well-moded programs and stable programs. The notion of well-moded programs is useful in identifying for which programs the top-down query answering approach of PROLOG is correct (discussed in Section 8.4), while the notion of stable programs is one of the conditions for language tolerance in Theorem 3.5.3.

By a *mode* for an n-ary predicate symbol p in an AnsProlog we mean a function Σ_p from $\{1, \ldots, n\}$ to the set $\{+, -\}$. In an AnsProlog$^{\neg,or}$ program the mode for p also includes a function $\Sigma_{\neg p}$. If $\Sigma_p(i) = \ '+'$ the i is called an *input* position of p and if $\Sigma_p(i) = \ '-'$ the i is called an *output* position of p. We write Σ_p in the form $p(\Sigma_p(1), \ldots, \Sigma_p(n))$. Intuitively, queries formed by p will be expected to have input positions occupied by ground terms. To simplify the notation, when writing an atom as $p(u, v)$, we assume that u is the sequence of terms filling in the input positions of p and that v is the sequence of terms filling in the output positions. By $l(u, v)$ we denote expressions of the form $p(u, v)$ or **not** $p(u, v)$, and $var(s)$ denotes the set of all variables occurring in s. An assignment of modes to the predicate symbols of a program Π is called an *input-output specification*.

Definition 18 An AnsProlog rule $p_0(t_0, s_{m+1}) \leftarrow l_1(s_1, t_1), \ldots, l_m(s_m, t_m)$ is called *well-moded* with respect to an input-output specification if for $i \in [1, m + 1]$, $var(s_i) \subseteq \bigcup_{j=0}^{i-1} var(t_j)$.

An AnsProlog program is called well-moded with respect to an input-output specification if all of its rules are well-moded.   □

In other words, an AnsProlog rule is well-moded with respect to an input-output specification if

(i) every variable occurring in an input position of a body goal[1] occurs either in an input position of the head or in an output position of an earlier body goal;
(ii) every variable occurring in an output position of the head occurs in an input position of the head, or in an output position of a body goal.

Example 50 Consider the following program Π_1:

$anc(X, Y) \leftarrow par(X, Y).$
$anc(X, Y) \leftarrow par(X, Z), anc(Z, Y).$

with the input-output specification $\Sigma_{anc} = (+, +)$ and $\Sigma_{par} = (-, -)$.

We now verify that Π_1 is well-moded with respect to Σ. We first check condition (i) above, and find that Z and Y in the second rule of Π_1 occur in an input position of the body goal $anc(Z, Y)$. The variable Y occurs in an input position in the head, and the variable Z occurs in an output position of the earlier body goal $par(X, Z)$. Thus condition (i) holds. Condition (ii) holds vacuously as no variable occurs in an output position of the head of either of the rules of Π_1.

Now let us consider the following program Π_2 which is obtained from Π_1 by switching the order of the literals in the body of the second rule.

$anc(X, Y) \leftarrow par(X, Y).$
$anc(X, Y) \leftarrow anc(X, Z), par(Z, Y).$

We will show that Π_2 is not well-moded with respect to Σ. We check condition (i) above, and find that Z and Y in the second rule of Π_1 occur in an input position of

---

[1] The term 'body goal' is a held over terminology from PROLOG. By it we refer to a naf-literal in the body of a rule.

the body goal $anc(X, Z)$. The variable X occurs in an input position in the head, but the variable Z occurs neither in an input position in the head nor in an output position of an earlier body goal, as there is no earlier body goal. Thus condition (i) is violated.

From the answer set semantics point of view Π_1 and Π_2 are equivalent. The syntactic difference between them comes to the forefront when we view them as PROLOG programs, in which case the ordering of the literals in the body of rules matters and a PROLOG interpreter differentiates between Π_1 and Π_2. □

We need the following notations to define stable programs. For any term E, by *FreeVar*(E) we designate the set of free variables that occur in E. Given a mode Σ, for any literal L, *FreeVar*$^+(L)$ and *FreeVar*$^-(L)$ are the sets of free variables in the various terms in L, that are moded as $+$ and $-$ respectively.

Definition 19 (Stable programs) Let Π be an AnsProlog$^{\neg, or}$ program. A rule $R \in \Pi$ is *stable* with respect to a mode Σ if there exists an ordering $L_1, \ldots, L_k$ of $pos(R)$ such that at least one of the following conditions is satisfied for every variable X that occurs in R.

(1) for all $L \in head(R).X \in FreeVar^+(L)$. (i.e., X occurs in the input position of one of the literals in the head.)
(2) there exists $i \in \{1, \ldots, k\}$ such that $X \in FreeVar^-(L_i)$ and for all $j \in \{1, \ldots, i\}.X \notin FreeVar^+(L_j)$. (i.e., X occurs in the output position of some positive naf-literal L_i in the body, and does not occur in the input position of any positive naf-literal in the body that comes before L_i.)

An AnsProlog$^{\neg, or}$ program Π is stable with respect to Σ if every rule in Π is stable with respect to Σ, and Π is *stable* if for some Σ, Π is stable with respect to Σ. □

Example 51 Consider the program Π_1 and input-output specification Σ from Example 50. We now argue that Π_1 is stable with respect to Σ.

Let us consider the first rule. The variables X and Y occur in it. Both occur in the input position of the literal $anc(X, Y)$ in the head of the first rule, thus satisfying condition (1). Hence, the first rule is stable with respect to Σ.

Now let us consider the second rule. The variables X, Y, and Z occur in it. The variables X and Y occur in the input position of the literal $anc(X, Y)$ in the head of the first rule, thus satisfying condition (1). The variable Z does not occur in the head of the second rule, thus violating condition (1). But it occurs in the output position of the literal $par(X, Z)$ in the body of the second rule and does not occur in the input position of any positive naf-literal in the body that comes before $par(X, Z)$, as no literal comes before $par(X, Z)$ in the body. Hence, Z satisfies condition (2).

Since the three variables X, Y, and Z occurring in the second rule satisfy at least one of the two conditions we have that the second rule is stable with respect to Σ. Therefore, Π is a stable. $\qquad\square$

3.1.5 Compiling AnsProlog programs to classical logic: Clark's completion

In this section we present methods to compile AnsProlog programs to theories in classical logic. In Section 3.2 we present conditions when the answer sets of AnsProlog programs have a one-to-one correspondence with the models of the compiled theory and thus can be obtained using classical model generator systems. We first present a simple compilation of propositional AnsProlog programs to propositional theories.

Definition 20 Given a propositional AnsProlog program Π consisting of rules of the form:

$$Q \leftarrow P_1, \ldots, P_n, \textbf{not } R_1, \ldots, \textbf{not } R_m.$$

its completion $Comp(\Pi)$ is obtained in two steps:

- Step 1: Replace each rule of the above mentioned form with the formula:

  $$Q \Leftarrow P_1 \wedge \cdots \wedge P_n \wedge \neg R_1 \wedge \cdots \wedge \neg R_m$$

- Step 2: For each symbol Q, let $Support(Q)$ denote the set of all clauses with Q in the head. Suppose $Support(Q)$ is the set:

  $$Q \Leftarrow Body_1$$
  $$\vdots$$
  $$Q \Leftarrow Body_k$$

  Replace this set with the single formula,

  $$Q \Leftrightarrow Body_1 \vee \cdots \vee Body_k.$$

  If $Support(Q) = \emptyset$ then replace it by $\neg Q$. $\qquad\square$

Example 52 Consider the following program Π:

$$p \leftarrow a.$$
$$p \leftarrow b.$$
$$a \leftarrow \textbf{not } b.$$
$$b \leftarrow \textbf{not } a.$$

$Comp(\Pi) = \{p \Leftrightarrow a \vee b, a \Leftrightarrow \neg b, b \Leftrightarrow \neg a\}$, and its models are $\{a, p\}$ and $\{b, p\}$. $\qquad\square$

The above definition of completion of propositional AnsProlog programs can also be used for AnsProlog programs – such as programs Π without function symbols – whose grounding $ground(\Pi)$ is finite. In that case we compile $ground(\Pi)$. In the presence of function symbols we need the following more elaborate definition of Clark, which can also be used in the absence of function symbols.

Definition 21 Given an AnsProlog program Π consisting of rules of the form:

$$Q(Z_1, \ldots, Z_n) \leftarrow P_1, \ldots, P_n, \textbf{not } R_1, \ldots, \textbf{not } R_m.$$

with variables $Y_1, \ldots, Y_d$, where $\{Z_1, \ldots, Z_n\} \subseteq \{Y_1, \ldots, Y_d\}$,

its completion $Comp(\Pi)$ is obtained in three steps:

- Step 1: Replace each rule of the above mentioned form with the formula:

  $$Q(X_1, \ldots, X_n) \Leftarrow \exists Y_1, \ldots, Y_d((X_1 = Z_1) \wedge \cdots \wedge (X_n = Z_n)) \wedge P_1 \wedge \cdots \wedge$$
  $$P_n \wedge \neg R_1 \wedge \cdots \wedge \neg R_m.$$

- Step 2: For each predicate Q, let $Support(Q)$ denote the set of all clauses with Q in the head. Suppose $Support(Q)$ is the set:

  $$Q(X_1, \ldots, X_n) \Leftarrow Body_1$$
  $$\vdots$$
  $$Q(X_1, \ldots, X_n) \Leftarrow Body_k$$

  Replace this set with the single formula,

  $$\forall X_1, \ldots, X_n.(Q(X_1, \ldots, X_n) \Leftrightarrow Body_1 \vee \cdots \vee Body_k).$$

  If $Support(Q) = \emptyset$ then replace it by $\forall X_1, \ldots, X_n. \neg Q(X_1, \ldots, X_n)$. □

- Step 3: Add the following equality theory[2].

  (1) $a \neq b$, for all pairs a, b of distinct constants in the language.
  (2) $\forall. f(X_1, \ldots, X_n) \neq g(Y_1, \ldots, Y_m)$, for all pairs f, g of distinct function symbols.
  (3) $\forall. f(X_1, \ldots, X_n) \neq a$, for each constant a, and function symbol f.
  (4) $\forall. t[X] \neq X$, for each term $t[X]$ containing X and different from X.
  (5) $\forall.((X_1 \neq Y_1) \vee \cdots \vee (X_n \neq Y_n)) \Rightarrow f(X_1, \ldots, X_n) \neq f(Y_1, \ldots, Y_n)$, for each function symbol f.
  (6) $\forall.(X = X)$.
  (7) $\forall.((X_1 = Y_1) \wedge \cdots \wedge (X_n = Y_n)) \Rightarrow f(X_1, \ldots, X_n) = f(Y_1, \ldots, Y_n)$, for each function symbol f.
  (8) $\forall.((X_1 = Y_1) \wedge \cdots \wedge (X_n = Y_n)) \Rightarrow (p(X_1, \ldots, X_n) \Rightarrow p(Y_1, \ldots, Y_n))$, for each predicate symbol p, including $=$.

---

[2] Often in first order logic with equality '=' is interpreted as the identity relation. In that case we need not axiomatize '=' as a congruent relation and only need the axiom schemata 2, 4, and 7.

Given an AnsProlog program Π, if its completion has a Herbrand model then we say that its completion is consistent. If the Herbrand models of $Comp(\Pi)$ coincide with the answer sets of Π then we say that Π is equivalent to its completion. We use these terminologies in the summary table in Section 3.2.8. We now illustrate the above definition using an example.

Example 53 Consider the following program Π, a slight modification of the program in Example 4.

$fly(X) \leftarrow bird(X),$ **not** $ab(X).$
$ab(X) \leftarrow penguin(X).$
$ab(X) \leftarrow ostrich(X).$
$bird(X) \leftarrow penguin(X).$
$bird(X) \leftarrow ostrich(X).$
$bird(tweety) \leftarrow.$
$penguin(skippy) \leftarrow.$

$Comp(\Pi)$ consists of the equality theory plus the following:

$\forall X.fly(X) \Leftrightarrow (bird(X) \wedge \neg ab(X))$
$\forall X.ab(X) \Leftrightarrow (penguin(X) \vee ostrich(X))$
$\forall X.bird(X) \Leftrightarrow (penguin(X) \vee ostrich(X) \vee X = tweety)$
$\forall X.penguin(X) \Leftrightarrow (X = skippy)$
$\forall X.\neg ostrich(X)$ $\square$

The following example shows that for some AnsProlog$^{-\textbf{not}}$ programs the models of their completion are not necessarily the answer sets of those programs.

Example 54 Suppose that we are given a graph specified as follows:

$edge(a, b) \leftarrow.$
$edge(c, d) \leftarrow.$
$edge(d, c) \leftarrow.$

and want to describe which vertices of the graph are reachable from a given vertex a. The following rules seem to be natural candidates for such a description:

$reachable(a) \leftarrow.$
$reachable(X) \leftarrow edge(Y, X), reachable(Y).$

We clearly expect vertices c and d not to be reachable and this is manifested by the unique answer set $S = \{edge(a, b), edge(c, d), edge(d, c), reachable(a), reachable(b)\}$ of the AnsProlog$^{-\textbf{not}}$ program Π_1 consisting of the above five rules.

Its Clark's completion $Comp(\Pi_1)$ consists of the equality theory plus the following:

$$\forall X, Y.edge(X, Y) \equiv ((X = a \wedge Y = b) \vee (X = c \wedge Y = d) \vee (X = d \wedge Y = c))$$
$$\forall X. reachable(X) \equiv (X = a \vee \exists Y (reachable(Y) \wedge edge(Y, X)))$$

It is easy to see that while $S = \{edge(a, b), edge(c, d), edge(d, c), reachable(a), reachable(b)\}$ is a model of $Comp(\Pi_1)$, $S' = \{edge(a, b), edge(c, d), edge(d, c), reachable(a), reachable(b), reachable(c), reachable(d)\}$ is also a model of $Comp(\Pi_1)$.

But S' is not an answer set of Π_1. Thus while $\Pi_1 \models \neg reachable(c)$ and $\Pi_1 \models \neg reachable(d)$, $Comp(\Pi_1)$ does not entail $\neg reachable(c)$ and also does not entail $\neg reachable(d)$. $\square$

We have the following general result about completion of AnsProlog programs:

Proposition 25 [GL88] Let Π be an AnsProlog program. If M is an answer set of P then M is a minimal model of $Comp(P)$. $\square$

3.2 Some AnsProlog* sub-classes and their basic properties

In this section we exploit the structure of AnsProlog* programs to define several sub-classes and analyze their basic properties, in particular, coherence, categoricity, computability of answer set computation, relationship with completion, and computability of determining if a program belongs to that sub-class. We focus mostly on AnsProlog programs, as they have been analyzed in more detail in the literature.

3.2.1 Stratification of AnsProlog programs

In the quest for characterizing the **not** operator of AnsProlog programs, and identifying a sub-class for which the semantics was non-controversial and computable through an iteration process, one of the early notions was the notion of stratification. It was realized early that recursion through the **not** operator was troublesome in PROLOG, and in logic programming it often led to programs without a unique 2-valued semantics. Thus stratification was defined as a notion which forced stratified programs to not have recursion through **not**. There are two equivalent definitions of stratification. We start with the first one.

Definition 22 A partition $\pi_0, \ldots, \pi_k$ of the set of all predicate symbols of an AnsProlog program Π is *a stratification* of Π, if for any rule of the type

$A_0 \leftarrow A_1, \ldots, A_m, \textbf{not } A_{m+1}, \ldots, \textbf{not } A_n$, and for any $p \in \pi_s, 0 \leq s \leq k$ if $A_0 \in atoms(p)$, then:

(a) for every $1 \leq i \leq m$ there is q and $j \leq s$ such that $q \in \pi_j$ and $A_i \in atoms(q)$, and

(b) for every $m + 1 \leq i \leq n$ there is q and $j < s$ such that $q \in \pi_j$ and $A_i \in atoms(q)$.

A program is called *stratified* if it has a stratification.   □

In other words, $\pi_0, \ldots, \pi_k$ is a stratification of Π if, for all rules in Π, the predicates that appear only positively in the body of a rule are in a strata lower than or equal to the stratum of the predicate in the head of the rule, and the predicates that appear under negation as failure (**not**) are in a strata lower than the stratum of the predicate in the head of the rule.

This stratification of the predicates defines a stratification of the rules to strata $\Pi_0, \ldots, \Pi_k$ where a strata Π_i contains rules whose heads are formed by predicates from π_i. Π_i can be viewed as a definition of relations from π_i. The above condition allows definitions which are mutually recursive but prohibits the use of negation as failure for the yet undefined predicates.

Example 55 An AnsProlog program Π consisting of rules

$p(f(X)) \leftarrow p(X), \textbf{not } q(X).$
$p(a) \leftarrow.$
$q(X) \leftarrow \textbf{not } r(X).$
$r(a) \leftarrow.$

is stratified with a stratification $\{r\}, \{q\}, \{p\}$.   □

Given a program Π, the *dependency graph* D_Π of Π consists of the predicate names as the vertices and $\langle P_i, P_j, s \rangle$ is a labeled edge in D_Π iff there is a rule r in Π with P_i in its head and P_j in its body and the label $s \in \{+, -\}$ denoting whether P_j appears in a positive or a negative literal in the body of r. Note that an edge may be labeled both by $+$ and $-$. A cycle in the dependency graph of a program is said to be a negative cycle if it contains at least one edge with a negative label.

Proposition 26 [ABW88] An AnsProlog program Π is stratified iff its dependency graph D_Π does not contain any negative cycles.   □

As in the case of AnsProlog$^{-\textbf{not}}$ programs, answer sets of stratified AnsProlog programs can be computed in an iterated fashion. Recall that the operator used in the iterative characterization of AnsProlog$^{-\text{not}}$ programs in (1.3.4) was as follows:

$$T_{\Pi}^0(I) = \{L_0 \in HB_{\Pi} \mid \Pi \text{ contains a rule } L_0 \leftarrow L_1, \ldots, L_m \text{ such that } \{L_1, \ldots, L_m\} \subseteq I \text{ holds } \}.$$

We mentioned in Section 1.3.2 that this operator[3] can be extended to AnsProlog programs in the following way:

$$T_{\Pi}(I) = \{L_0 \in HB_{\Pi} \mid \Pi \text{ contains a rule } L_0 \leftarrow L_1, \ldots, L_m, \textbf{not } L_{m+1}, \ldots, \textbf{not } L_n \text{ such that } \{L_1, \ldots, L_m\} \subseteq I \text{ holds and } \{L_{m+1}, \ldots, L_n\} \cap I = \emptyset\}.$$

But unlike T_{Π}^0, the operator T_{Π} is not monotone. Consider the program $\{a \leftarrow \textbf{not } b\}$, and let $I = \emptyset$, and $I' = \{b\}$. It is easy to see that $T_{\Pi}(I) = \{a\}$ while $T_{\Pi}(I') = \emptyset$. Thus, even though $I \subset I'$, $T_{\Pi}(I) \not\subseteq T_{\Pi}(I')$. Since T_{Π} is not monotone, the Knaster–Tarski theorem is no longer applicable and the equation that the least Herbrand model is equal to $T_{\Pi} \uparrow \omega$ which is equal to the least fixpoint of T_{Π} is no longer true.

Nevertheless, for a stratified AnsProlog program Π that can be stratified to strata $\Pi_0, \ldots, \Pi_k$, the answer set A of Π can be obtained as follows:

For any stratified AnsProlog program Π we define:

$$T_{\Pi} \uparrow 0(I) = I$$
$$T_{\Pi} \uparrow (n+1)(I) = T_{\Pi}(T_{\Pi} \uparrow n(I)) \cup T_{\Pi} \uparrow n(I)$$
$$T_{\Pi} \uparrow \omega(I) = \bigcup_{n=0}^{\infty} n(I)$$

and then we define

$$M_0 = T_{\Pi_0} \uparrow \omega(\emptyset)$$
$$M_1 = T_{\Pi_1} \uparrow \omega(M_0)$$
$$\vdots$$
$$M_k = T_{\Pi_k} \uparrow \omega(M_{k-1})$$
$$A = M_k$$

The above construction leads to the following theorem describing an important property of stratified programs.

Proposition 27 [GL88] Any stratified AnsProlog program is categorical and A as defined above is its unique answer set. □

The following example illustrates the multi-strata iterated fixpoint computation of the unique answer set of AnsProlog programs.

---

[3] In Section 1.3.2 we referred to this operator as T_{Π}^1. In this section we will refer to it simply as T_{Π}.

Example 56 Consider the program Π consisting of the following rules:

$a(1) \leftarrow \textbf{not } b(1).$
$b(1) \leftarrow \textbf{not } c(1).$
$d(1) \leftarrow.$

Its predicates can be stratified to the strata: $\pi_0 = \{c, d\}$, $\pi_1 = \{b\}$, and $\pi_2 = \{a\}$. This leads to the following strata of programs. $\Pi_0 = \{d(1) \leftarrow .\}$, $\Pi_1 = \{b(1) \leftarrow \textbf{not } c(1).\}$, and $\Pi_2 = \{a(1) \leftarrow \textbf{not } b(1).\}$. We now use the iteration method to compute the answer set of Π.

$M_0 = T_{\Pi_0} \uparrow \omega(\emptyset)$ is computed as follows:
$T_{\Pi_0} \uparrow 0(\emptyset) = \emptyset$
$T_{\Pi_0} \uparrow 1(\emptyset) = T_{\Pi_0}(T_{\Pi_0} \uparrow 0(\emptyset)) \cup T_{\Pi_0} \uparrow 0(\emptyset) = T_{\Pi_0}(\emptyset) \cup \emptyset = \{d(1)\}$
$T_{\Pi_0} \uparrow 2(\emptyset) = T_{\Pi_0}(T_{\Pi_0} \uparrow 1(\emptyset)) \cup T_{\Pi_0} \uparrow 1(\emptyset) = T_{\Pi_0}(\{d(1)\}) \cup \{d(1)\}$
$\qquad\qquad = \{d(1)\} = T_{\Pi_0} \uparrow 1(\emptyset)$
Hence, $M_0 = T_{\Pi_0} \uparrow \omega(\emptyset) = \{d(1)\}$.

$M_1 = T_{\Pi_1} \uparrow \omega(M_0)$ is computed as follows:
$T_{\Pi_1} \uparrow 0(M_0) = M_0$
$T_{\Pi_1} \uparrow 1(M_0) = T_{\Pi_1}(T_{\Pi_1} \uparrow 0(M_0)) \cup T_{\Pi_1} \uparrow 0(M_0) = T_{\Pi_1}(M_0) \cup M_0$
$\qquad\qquad = \{b(1)\} \cup \{d(1)\} = \{b(1), d(1)\}$
$T_{\Pi_1} \uparrow 2(M_0) = T_{\Pi_1}(T_{\Pi_1} \uparrow 1(M_0)) \cup T_{\Pi_1} \uparrow 1(M_0) = T_{\Pi_1}(\{b(1), d(1)\})$
$\qquad \cup \{b(1), d(1)\} = \{b(1), d(1)\} = T_{\Pi_1} \uparrow 1(M_0)$
Hence, $M_1 = T_{\Pi_1} \uparrow \omega(M_0) = \{b(1), d(1)\}$.

$M_2 = T_{\Pi_2} \uparrow \omega(M_1)$ is computed as follows:
$T_{\Pi_2} \uparrow 0(M_1) = M_1$
$T_{\Pi_2} \uparrow 1(M_1) = T_{\Pi_2}(T_{\Pi_2} \uparrow 0(M_1)) \cup T_{\Pi_2} \uparrow 0(M_1) = T_{\Pi_2}(M_1) \cup M_1 =$
$\qquad\qquad \{\} \cup \{b(1), d(1)\} = \{b(1), d(1)\} = T_{\Pi_2} \uparrow 0(M_1)$
Hence, $A = M_2 = T_{\Pi_2} \uparrow \omega(M_1) = \{b(1), d(1)\}$ is the answer set of Π. $\square$

The following proposition uses the notion of stratification of AnsProlog programs to give sufficiency conditions for the categoricity of AnsProlog$^\neg$ programs.

Proposition 28 [GL90] An AnsProlog$^\neg$ program Π is categorical if

(a) Π^+, the AnsProlog program obtained by transforming Π to eliminate $\neg$ (see Section 1.3.3), is stratified, and
(b) The answer set of Π^+ does not contain atoms of the form $p(t)$, $p'(t)$. $\square$

3.2.2 Stratification of AnsProlog^{or} programs

The definition of stratification can be extended to AnsProlog^{or} programs in a straightforward way by requiring that the dependency graph – whose definition is directly applicable to AnsProlog^{or} programs – does not contain any negative cycles. The following proposition guarantees existence of answer sets for stratified AnsProlog^{or} programs.

Proposition 29 Any stratified AnsProlog^{or} program has an answer set.   □

Let us look at a few simple examples of AnsProlog^{or} programs, and their answer sets.

Let $\Pi_0 = \{p(a)\, or\ p(b) \leftarrow\}$.

It is easy to see that $\{p(a)\}$ and $\{p(b)\}$ are the only answer sets of Π_0 since they are the only minimal sets closed under its rule.

Let $\Pi_1 = \Pi_0 \cup \{r(X) \leftarrow \mathbf{not}\ p(X).\}$.

Obviously, this program is stratified and hence by Proposition 29 has an answer set S. By part (a) of the Proposition 22, S must either contain $p(a)$ or contain $p(b)$. Part (b) of the Proposition 22 guarantees that S does not contain both. Suppose S contains $p(a)$. Then, by part (a), S contains $r(b)$, and by part (b), it contains nothing else, and hence, $\{p(a), r(b)\}$ is an answer set of Π_1. Similarly, we can show that $\{p(b), r(a)\}$ is an answer set of Π_1 and that there are no other answer sets.

3.2.3 Call-consistency

Earlier we stated the result that stratified AnsProlog programs have a unique answer set. In this subsection we introduce a sub-class of AnsProlog which contains many non-stratified programs but guarantees coherence – the existence of at least one answer set.

Definition 23 An AnsProlog program is said to be *call-consistent* if its dependency graph does not have a cycle with an odd number of negative edges.   □

Call-consistent AnsProlog programs are a superset of stratified AnsProlog programs. An example of a call-consistent program which is not stratified is as follows:

$p(a) \leftarrow \mathbf{not}\ q(a).$
$q(a) \leftarrow \mathbf{not}\ p(a).$

The following two propositions describe a property of call-consistent AnsProlog programs and a property of a more restricted class of call-consistent AnsProlog programs.

Proposition 30 If Π is a call-consistent AnsProlog program then $comp(\Pi)$ has Herbrand models.   □

Proposition 31 [Fag90] A call-consistent AnsProlog program whose dependency graph does not have a cycle with only positive edges has at least one answer set.
                                                                                □

3.2.4 Local stratification and perfect model semantics

The notion of stratification partitions predicates to strata. The following more general notion of local stratification partitions the HB to strata and leads to the result that locally stratified AnsProlog programs preserve the categoricity property of stratified AnsProlog programs.

Definition 24 An AnsProlog program Π is *locally stratified* if there exists a mapping λ from HB_Π to the countable ordinal such that for every $A_0 \leftarrow A_1, \ldots, A_m, \textbf{not } A_{m+1}, \ldots, \textbf{not } A_n$ in $ground(\Pi)$, the following conditions hold for every $1 \leq i \leq n$:

- $1 \leq i \leq m$: $\lambda(A_0) \geq \lambda(A_i)$.
- $m + 1 \leq i \leq n$: $\lambda(A_0) > \lambda(A_i)$.   □

Note that the following program

$p(X) \leftarrow \textbf{not } p(f(X))$.
$q(a) \leftarrow$.

is not locally stratified as there does not exist a mapping that satisfies the condition in Definition 24. Unlike the definition of stratification in terms of the dependency graph, we cannot define local stratification in terms of not having a loop with negative edges in a more general dependency graph with atoms as nodes. (Such a definition would label the above program as locally stratified.) This is because while the dependency graph has a finite number of nodes, a more general atom dependency graph with atoms as nodes may have an infinite number of nodes. In a later section (Section 3.2.6) we give an alternative definition of local stratification using the atom dependency graph.

The following program

$p(f(X)) \leftarrow \textbf{not } p(X)$.
$q(a) \leftarrow$.

is locally stratified and the mapping $\lambda(q(a)) = 0$, and $\lambda(p(f^n(a))) = n$ satisfies the condition in Definition 24. Its unique answer set is $\{q(a), p(f(a)), p(f(f(f(a)))), \ldots\}$.

Proposition 32 [Prz88b, Prz88a, GL88] Locally stratified AnsProlog programs are categorical. □

Proposition 33 [Prz88b, Prz88a] The unique answer set of locally stratified AnsProlog programs, referred to as the *perfect model* is its least Herbrand model with respect to the following ordering $(\leq_\lambda)$ that incorporates a mapping λ satisfying the conditions of Definition 24.

For an interpretation $I \subset HB_\Pi$ and an integer j, let $I[[j]] = \{a : a \in I$ such that $\lambda(a) = n\}$.

$I \leq_\lambda I'$ if there exists an integer k such that, for all $i \leq k$, $I[[i]] = I'[[i]]$ and $I[[k]] \subseteq I'[[k]]$. □

Example 57 Consider the program consisting of the following rule:

$a \leftarrow \textbf{not } b.$

It has three models $I = \{a\}$, $I' = \{b\}$, and $J = \{a, b\}$, out of which $I = \{a\}$ and $I' = \{b\}$ are minimal models. We will now show that it has a unique perfect model $\{a\}$ which is its answer set.

The above program is locally stratified and the mapping $\lambda(b) = 1$, $\lambda(a) = 2$ satisfies the conditions of Definition 24. It is easy to see that $I <_\lambda J$ and $I' <_\lambda J$. Now let us compare I and I'. We have $I[[1]] = \{\}$, $I[[2]] = \{a\}$, $I'[[1]] = \{b\}$, and $I'[[2]] = \{\}$. Since, $I[[1]] \subseteq I'[[1]]$ we have $I \leq_\lambda I'$. But since, $I'[[1]] \nsubseteq I[[1]]$ we have $I' \nleq_\lambda I$. Hence, $I <_\lambda I'$ and I is the least among the three models. Therefore I is the perfect model of the above program. The reader can easily verify that I is also the unique answer set of this program. □

3.2.5 Acyclicity and tightness

All the sub-classes of AnsProlog that we have considered so far do not guarantee that in the presence of function symbols determining an answer set or determining entailment is Turing computable. In this subsection we present such a sub-class: acyclic AnsProlog programs, which is a sub-class of locally stratified programs. Such programs not only have unique answer sets but their unique answer set is Turing computable.

Definition 25 An AnsProlog program Π is *acyclic* if there exists a mapping λ from HB_Π to the set of natural numbers such that for every $A_0 \leftarrow A_1, \ldots,$

A_m, **not** $A_{m+1}, \ldots,$ **not** A_n in $ground(\Pi)$, and for every $1 \leq i \leq n$: $\lambda(A_0) > \lambda(A_i)$. □

Note that the program consisting of the single rule

$$p(X) \leftarrow p(f(X)).$$

is not acyclic. It is, however, locally stratified. Similarly the program consisting of the single rule

$$p \leftarrow p.$$

is also not acyclic but is locally stratified. Another historical fact about properties of acyclic programs is that when they were discovered, most alternative semantics proposed for programs with AnsProlog syntax agreed with each other with respect to acyclic programs. From that perspective, while the answer set of the non-acyclic program $\Pi = \{p \leftarrow p.\}$ is $\{\}$, and $\Pi \models \neg p$, some researchers argued that p should have the truth value *unknown* with respect to Π. We further discuss some of the alternative semantics of programs with AnsProlog syntax in Chapter 9.

The following are some results about acyclic AnsProlog programs. In Section 8.4 we present additional results (Propositions 109 and 110) about acyclic programs.

Proposition 34 [AB90] Let Π be an acyclic AnsProlog program. Then we have:

 (i) Π has a unique Turing computable answer set;
(ii) The unique answer set of Π is the unique Herbrand model of $Comp(\Pi)$;   □

Although at first glance, acyclic programs may seem to be too restrictive, many useful AnsProlog programs such as the one in part (1) of Section 2.2.2 are acyclic. Moreover, in Section 8.4.4 we show several AnsProlog programs to be acyclic and analyze them using Propositions 34, 109, and 110.

Recently, in the presence of several fast propositional solvers, one of the computation methods that has been used to compute answer sets of function-free AnsProlog programs is by computing the models of $Comp(\Pi)$. This has motivated identification of more general classes than acyclic programs that guarantee a one-to-one correspondence between answer sets and models of the completion. We now present two such generalizations.

Definition 26 (Tight programs) An AnsProlog program Π is said to be *tight* (or *positive order consistent*), if there exists a function λ from HB_Π to the set of natural numbers such that for every $A_0 \leftarrow A_1, \ldots, A_m,$ **not** $A_{m+1}, \ldots,$ **not** A_n in $ground(\Pi)$, and for every $1 \leq i \leq m$: $\lambda(A_0) > \lambda(A_i)$.   □

Proposition 35 [Fag94] For any propositional AnsProlog program, if Π is tight then X is an answer set of Π iff X is a model of $Comp(\Pi)$. □

Example 58 Consider the following program:

$p(a) \leftarrow \mathbf{not}\ p(b)$.
$p(b) \leftarrow \mathbf{not}\ p(a)$.

The above program is neither acyclic, not locally stratified. But it is tight. It has two answer sets $\{p(a)\}$ and $\{p(b)\}$, which are the two models of its completion consisting of the equality theory and the formula for all $X. p(X) \Leftrightarrow (X = a \wedge \neg p(b)) \vee (X = b \wedge \neg p(a))$. □

The notion of tight programs was further generalized in two respects, to AnsProlog$^{\neg,\perp}$ programs and with respect to a set of literals, by the following definition.

Definition 27 (Tightness on a set of literals) An AnsProlog$^{\neg,\perp}$ program Π is said to be *tight on a set X of literals*, if there exists a partial mapping λ with domain X from literals to the set of natural numbers such that for every rule $L_0 \leftarrow L_1, \dots, L_m, \mathbf{not}\ L_{m+1}, \dots, \mathbf{not}\ L_n$. In $ground(\Pi)$, if $L_0, \dots, L_m \in X$, then for every $1 \leq i \leq m$: $\lambda(L_0) > \lambda(L_i)$. □

In the above definition it should be noted that $\perp$ is not considered a literal. The following example illustrates the difference between the original notion of tightness and the notion of tightness with respect to a set of literals.

Example 59 Consider the program consisting of the only rule

$p \leftarrow p$.

This program is obviously not tight. But it is tight on the set of literals $\{\}$. □

Proposition 36 [BEL00] For any AnsProlog$^{\neg,\perp}$ program Π and any consistent set X of literals such that Π is tight on X, X is an answer set of Π iff X is closed under and supported by Π. □

Proposition 37 [BEL00] For any propositional AnsProlog program and any set X of atoms such that Π is tight on X, X is an answer set of Π iff X is a model of $Comp(\Pi)$. □

Example 60 Let us reconsider the program Π consisting of the only rule

$p \leftarrow p$.

This program is tight on the set of literals $S = \{\}$, and is not tight on the set of literals $S' = \{p\}$.

The completion of this program is $p \Leftrightarrow p$ and has the models S and S'. As suggested by Proposition 37 since Π is tight on S, S is an answer set of Π iff S is a model of $Comp(\Pi)$. Since Π is not tight on S', S' being a model of $Comp(\Pi)$ has no consequences.   □

3.2.6 Atom dependency graph and order-consistency

One of the maximal sub-classes of AnsProlog programs that guarantee an answer set is the class of *order-consistent* (or local call-consistent) programs. To define this class of program we need to introduce the following notions.

- The *atom dependency graph* AD_Π of a program Π: The nodes are elements of HB_Π. $\langle A_i, A_j, s \rangle$ is a labeled edge in AD_Π iff there is a rule r in $ground(\Pi)$ with A_i in its head, and A_j in its body, and the label $s \in \{+, -\}$, denoting whether A_j appears in a positive or a negative literal in the body of r.
- We say q *depends evenly on* p denoted by $p \leq_+ q$ if there is a path from p to q in AD_Π with an even number of negative edges.
- We say q *depends oddly on* p denoted by $p \leq_- q$ if there is a path from p to q in AD_Π with an odd number of negative edges.
- We say q *depends on* p denoted by $p \leq q$ if $p \leq_+ q$ or $p \leq_- q$.
- We say q *depends even-oddly on* p denoted by $p \leq_{+-} q$ if $p \leq_+ q$ and $p \leq_- q$.
- We say q *depends positively on* p denoted by $p \leq_0 q$ if there is a non-empty path from p to q with all edges labeled as positive.
- A binary relation (not necessarily a partial order) is *well-founded* if there is no infinite decreasing chain $x_0 \geq x_1 \geq \cdots$. (Note: well-founded implies acyclic but not vice-versa.)

We are now ready to define order-consistency.

Definition 28 An AnsProlog program Π is said to be *order consistent* if the relation $\leq_{+-}$ in AD_Π is well-founded.   □

The following two propositions define useful properties of order-consistent AnsProlog programs.

Proposition 38 [Sat90, CF90] If Π is an order-consistent AnsProlog program then $Comp(\Pi)$ has a Herbrand model.   □

Proposition 39 [Fag90] An order-consistent AnsProlog program has an answer set.   □

A superclass of order-consistent programs which also has useful properties under certain restrictions is the class of negative cycle free programs defined as follows.

Definition 29 An AnsProlog program Π is said to be *negative cycle free* if $\leq_-$ is irreflexive in AD_Π. $\square$

The following two propositions define useful properties of negative cycle free AnsProlog programs under certain restrictions.

Proposition 40 [Sat90] If Π is a negative cycle free AnsProlog program and is either function free or internal variable free (i.e., for any rule the variables in the premise appear in the conclusion) then $Comp(\Pi)$ has a Herbrand model. $\square$

Proposition 41 [Fag90] If Π is a negative cycle free and tight AnsProlog program and is either function free or internal variable free (i.e., for any rule the variables in the premise appear in the conclusion) then Π has an answer set. $\square$

Similarly to order consistency, we can define the notion of *predicate-order-consistency* for AnsProlog programs by defining the relation $\leq_{+-}$ among predicates in the dependency graph D_Π. This notion is used in Section 3.5.3 as a condition for language tolerance.

Definition 30 An AnsProlog program Π is said to be *predicate-order-consistent* if the relation $\leq_{+-}$ in D_Π is well-founded. $\square$

The various orderings defined in this section can be used to give alternative definitions for local stratified programs and tight programs.

Proposition 42 An AnsProlog program Π is locally stratified iff the relation of dependency through at least one negative edge in AD_Π is well-founded. $\square$

Proposition 43 An AnsProlog program is tight (or positive-order consistent) iff $\leq_0$ is well-founded. $\square$

Example 61 Consider the following AnsProlog program:

$p(X) \leftarrow p(s(X))$.
$p(X) \leftarrow \textbf{not } p(s(X))$.

The above program is negative cycle free, but not order consistent, nor tight because of the first rule, nor locally stratified because of the second rule.

Since the above program is internal variable free, its completion has a model. In fact in the only model of its completion p is true everywhere. However, this model is not well-supported, and hence is not an answer set. Therefore this program does not have an answer set.   □

3.2.7 Signing

One of the motivations behind studying signed programs was to find conditions on programs and their predicates such that adding new facts about certain predicates only increased the set of ground atoms that could be concluded from the program. This property is a special case of the notion 'restricted monotonicity.' Besides that, signed AnsProlog programs are coherent and some of their answer sets are related to the well-founded semantics. In this subsection we briefly discuss the last two properties and consider the restricted monotonicity aspect in a later section (Section 3.3).

Intuitively, a signed AnsProlog program is a program whose Herbrand base can be partitioned into two sets such that for any rule the atom in the head and the atoms in the body that are not preceded by **not** belong to the same partition and the atom in the head and the atoms in the body that are preceded by **not** belong to the opposite partitions. More formally,

Definition 31 An AnsProlog program is said to be signed if there is a set S (called signing) of ground atoms such that, for any ground instance of a rule of the type (1.2.1) with $k = 0$, either

$$\{L_0, L_1, \ldots, L_m\} \subseteq S \text{ and } \{L_{m+1}, \ldots, L_n\} \cap S = \emptyset$$

or

$$\{L_0, L_1, \ldots, L_m\} \cap S = \emptyset \text{ and } \{L_{m+1}, \ldots, L_n\} \subseteq S.$$ □

We now present a result which shows how to obtain one (or possibly two) answer set(s) of a signed AnsProlog program using $\mathrm{lfp}(\Gamma_\Pi^2)$ and $\mathrm{gfp}(\Gamma_\Pi^2)$ from Section 1.3.6; and since $\mathrm{lfp}(\Gamma_\Pi^2)$ and $\mathrm{gfp}(\Gamma_\Pi^2)$ always exist, we have the corollary that signed AnsProlog programs are coherent.

Proposition 44 For an AnsProlog program Π with signing S, the following are among the answer sets of Π:

(1) $\mathrm{lfp}(\Gamma_\Pi^2) \cup \left(\mathrm{gfp}(\Gamma_\Pi^2) \cap \bar{S}\right)$
(2) $\mathrm{lfp}(\Gamma_\Pi^2) \cup \left(\mathrm{gfp}(\Gamma_\Pi^2) \cap S\right)$ □

Note that the above two sets may be the same, and the signed AnsProlog program may just have a single answer set. On the other hand a signed AnsProlog program may have additional answer sets beyond the ones described by the above theorem. For example, the following AnsProlog program has $\{a, d\}$ as one of its answer sets, which is not dictated by the above theorem.

$a \leftarrow \mathbf{not}\ b$.
$b \leftarrow \mathbf{not}\ a$.
$c \leftarrow \mathbf{not}\ b, \mathbf{not}\ d$.
$d \leftarrow \mathbf{not}\ c$.

An additional connection between the answer set semantics of signed AnsProlog programs and the well-founded semantics of these programs is as follows:

Proposition 45 [Dun92] For a ground atom p, and a signed AnsProlog program Π, $\Pi \models p$ iff p is true with respect to the well-founded semantics of Π. $\qquad\square$

3.2.8 The relation between the AnsProlog sub-classes: a summary

In this section we have discussed several sub-classes of AnsProlog programs including stratified, acyclic, call-consistent, locally stratified, tight, signed, order-consistent, and negative cycle free. We now give some examples that further illustrate the differences and relationship between these classes, show in Figure 3.1 the relationship between the classes and summarize the properties of these classes in Table 3.1. (The symbol '?' in the table means that the result is an unproven conjecture.)

(1) AnsProlog$^{-\mathbf{not}}$ programs, also referred to as definite programs are a sub-class of signed programs, as for any definite program Π its Herbrand base is one of its signings.
(2) The class of stratified programs is a sub-class of the class of call-consistent programs. Checking whether a program is stratified and checking whether it is call-consistent are decidable problems. The program:

$p(a) \leftarrow \mathbf{not}\ q(a)$.
$q(a) \leftarrow \mathbf{not}\ p(a)$.

is call-consistent, but not stratified.
(3) The class of acyclic programs is a sub-class of the class of locally stratified programs, and also a sub-class of the class of tight programs. The class of tight programs and the class of locally stratified programs are not related. The program:

$p(a) \leftarrow p(a)$.

is locally stratified, but not acyclic and not tight. The program:

$p(a) \leftarrow \mathbf{not}\ p(b)$.
$p(b) \leftarrow \mathbf{not}\ p(a)$.

Table 3.1. *Properties of AnsProlog sub-classes – a summary*

Properties Sub-classes	Coherence (has ans set)	Categorical (one ans set)	Computing answer set	Relation with completion	Sub-class determination
neg. cycle free (Defn 29)	under cond. (Prop 41)	not nec.	nonrecursive	cons. under cond. (Prop 40)	nonrecursive
order-consistent (Defn 28)	yes (Prop 39)	not nec.	nonrecursive	consistent (Prop 38)	nonrecursive
call-consistent (Defn 23)	under cond. (Prop 31)	not nec.	nonrecursive	consistent (Prop 30)	recursive
locally stratified (Defn 24)	yes	yes (Prop 32)	nonrecursive	consistent	nonrecursive
stratified (Defn 22)	yes	yes (Prop 27)	nonrecursive	consistent	recursive
signed (Defn 31)	yes (Prop 44)	not nec.	nonrecursive	consistent	nonrecursive?
tight (Defn 26)	under cond. (Prop 41)	not nec.	nonrecursive	equivalent (Prop 35)	nonrecursive
acyclic (Defn 25)	yes	yes (Prop 34)	recursive (Prop 34)	equivalent (Prop 34)	nonrecursive
definite (AnsProlog−**not**)	yes	yes	nonrecursive	cons., subset	recursive

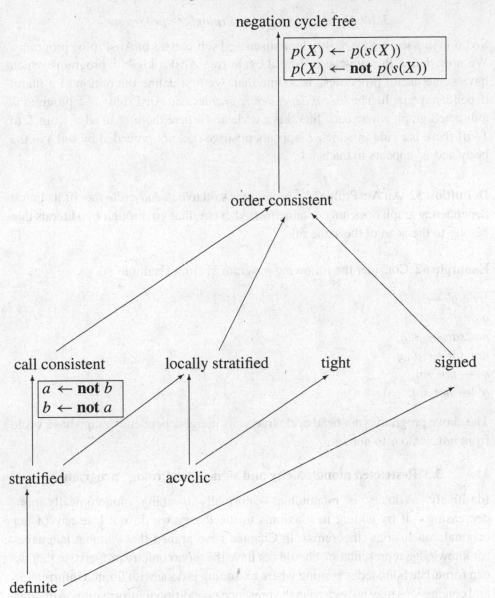

Figure 3.1: The ordering between AnsProlog sub-classes

is tight, but not locally stratified and not acyclic. The program:

$p(a) \leftarrow$ **not** $p(a).$

is tight, but not locally stratified and not acyclic.

3.2.9 Head cycle free AnsProlog$^{\neg,or}$ programs

So far in this section we mostly have discussed sub-classes of AnsProlog programs. We now define the sub-class of head cycle free AnsProlog$^{\neg,or}$ programs which have some useful properties. To define that, we first define the notion of a literal dependency graph. The *literal dependency graph* of an AnsProlog$^{\neg,or}$ program is a directed graph where each literal is a node and where there is an edge from L to L' iff there is a rule in which L appears positive (i.e, not preceded by **not**) in the body and L' appears in the head.

Definition 32 An AnsProlog$^{\neg,or}$ program is said to be *head cycle free* iff its literal dependency graph does not contain directed cycles that go through two literals that belong to the head of the same rule.   □

Example 62 Consider the following program Π from Example 30:

p *or* p' ←.
q *or* q' ←.
not_sat ← p, q.
not_sat ← p', q'.
q ← not_sat.
q' ← not_sat.

The above program is not head cycle free as its literal dependency graph has a cycle from not_sat to q to not_sat.

3.3 Restricted monotonicity and signed AnsProlog* programs

Intuitively, a theory is monotonic – normally meaning monotonically non-decreasing – if by adding new axioms to the theory we do not lose any of our original conclusions (theorems). In Chapter 1 we argued that suitable languages for knowledge representation should not have the monotonicity property so that we can formulate bounded reasoning where reasoning is done with limited information and conclusions may be revised in the presence of additional information. Although blanket monotonicity is not a desirable property, often we may want our theory to have a restricted kind of monotonicity. For example, we may not want a definition of a particular concept in our theory to change in the presence of additional information. Thus we need a notion of 'restricted monotonicity' and need to study when AnsProlog* programs have such properties.

3.3.1 Restricted monotonicity

We start with a notion of restricted monotonicity for general declarative formalisms. We will later tailor the definition to particular classes of AnsProlog* programs.

Definition 33 A *declarative formalism* is defined by a set S of symbolic expressions called *sentences*, a set P of symbolic expressions called *postulates*, and a map Cn from sets of postulates to sets of sentences.

A set of postulates is referred to as a *theory*; and a sentence A is a consequence of a theory T if $A \in Cn(T)$. □

Definition 34 Let $\langle S, P, Cn \rangle$ be a declarative formalism; and let a subset S_0 of S be designated as the set of assertions (inputs), and a set P_0 of P as the set of parameters (outputs). A theory T is said to satisfy the restricted monotonicity condition with respect to S_0 and P_0 if, for any sets $p, q \subseteq P_0$,

$$p \subseteq q \Rightarrow Cn(T \cup p) \cap S_0 \subseteq Cn(T \cup q) \cap S_0.$$ □

3.3.2 Signed AnsProlog$^{\neg,or}$ programs and their properties

Earlier in Section 3.2.7 we introduced the notion of signed AnsProlog programs. In this section we generalize the notion of signing to AnsProlog$^{\neg,or}$ programs and study properties of such programs, in particular the property of restricted monotonicity. We start with the generalized notion of signing.

Definition 35 Let Π be an AnsProlog$^{\neg,or}$ program, and S be a subset of Lit_Π, such that no literal in $S \cap Head(\Pi)$ appears in complemented form in $Head(\Pi)$. We say that S is a *signing* for Π if each rule $r \in \Pi$ satisfies the following two conditions:

- *head* $(r) \cup pos(r) \subseteq S$ and $neg(r) \subseteq \bar{S}$, or
  $head(r) \cup pos(r) \subseteq \bar{S}$ and $neg(r) \subseteq S$,
- if $head(r) \subseteq S$, then $head(r)$ is a singleton,

where $\bar{S} = Lit_\Pi \setminus S$. If a program has a signing then we say that it is *signed*. □

Example 63 Consider the following program Π_1.

$a \leftarrow \textbf{not } b.$
$b \leftarrow \textbf{not } a.$
$\neg a \leftarrow .$

Program Π_1 has a signing $S = \{b\}$. Note that neither $\{a, \neg a\}$ nor $\{a\}$ is a signing. So the definition of signing for AnsProlog$^{\neg,or}$ programs in general is asymmetric.
□

We now define an ordering between rules and programs which we will later use in defining sufficiency conditions for having the restricted monotonicity property.

Definition 36 Given rules r and r', we say that r *is subsumed by* r', and we write $r \preceq r'$, if the following three conditions hold:

(1) $neg(r') \subseteq neg(r)$,
(2) $pos(r') \subseteq pos(r)$, and
(3) every literal in $head(r') \setminus head(r)$ appears complemented in $pos(r)$. ☐

Note that $\preceq$ is reflexive and transitive but not anti-symmetric. When dealing with AnsProlog⁻ programs we replace the third condition in the above definition by $head(r) = head(r')$. In the following we define $h_S(\Pi)$, the reduction of a program Π with respect to a set S of literals.

Definition 37 Given programs Π and Π', we say Π is subsumed by Π', and we write $\Pi \preceq \Pi'$, if for each rule r in Π there is a rule r' in Π' such that $r \preceq r'$. ☐

Definition 38 Let Π be an AnsProlog$^{\neg, or}$ program. If S is a signing for Π, then

• $h_S(\Pi) = \{r \in \Pi \ : \ head(r) \subseteq S\}$, and
• $h_{\bar{S}}(\Pi) = \{r \in \Pi \ : \ head(r) \subseteq \bar{S}\}$. ☐

For AnsProlog⁻ programs Π with signing S, $h_S(\Pi)$ is alternatively denoted by Π_S and $h_{\bar{S}}(\Pi)$ is alternatively denoted by $\Pi_{\bar{S}}$. We now present two restricted monotonicity results about signed AnsProlog⁻ programs.

Proposition 46 [Tur93] For AnsProlog programs P and Q with common signing S, if $P_{\bar{S}} \preceq Q_{\bar{S}}$ and $Q_S \preceq P_S$ then P entails every ground atom in S that is entailed by Q, and Q entails every ground atom in $\bar{S}$ that is entailed by P. ☐

The above proposition implies the following two simple restricted monotonicity properties with S and P as a sets of ground atoms, and Cn as the consequence relation between AnsProlog programs and ground atoms that are entailed by it. (i) S_0, and P_0 are equal to $\bar{S}$. In this case the above proposition implies that if we start with a program P and add facts about $\bar{S}$ and obtain a new program Q, then Q still entails every ground atom in $\bar{S}$ that was entailed by P. (ii) S_0, and P_0 are equal to S. In this case the above proposition implies that if we start with a program Q and add facts about S and obtain a new program P, then P still entails every ground atom in S that was entailed by Q.

Proposition 47 [Tur93] For AnsProlog⁻ programs P and Q with common signing S, if $P_{\bar{S}} \preceq Q_{\bar{S}}$ and $Q_S \preceq P_S$ and $literals(P) \cap \bar{S} \subseteq literals(Q) \cap \bar{S}$, then Q entails every ground literal in $\bar{S}$ that is entailed by P. ☐

The above proposition implies the following simple restricted monotonicity property with S and P as sets of ground literals, and Cn as the consequence relation between AnsProlog$^-$ programs and ground literals that are entailed (through $\models^\pm$) by it. Suppose S_0 and P_0 are equal to $\bar{S}$. In this case the above proposition implies that if we start with a program P and add facts about $\bar{S}$ and obtain a new program Q, then Q still entails every ground literal in $\bar{S}$ that was entailed by P.

We now discuss an application of the above proposition. Let us consider a simpler form of the Yale Turkey shoot problem from Section 2.2.2 where the only action we have is *shoot*. Then a formulation to reason about hypothetical situations in the presence of incomplete information about the initial situation is given as follows:

r_1: *holds*(*alive*, s_0) $\leftarrow$.
r_2: *holds*(F, *res*(A, S)) $\leftarrow$ *holds*(F, S), **not** *ab*(F, A, S).
r_3: $\neg$*holds*(F, *res*(A, S)) $\leftarrow$ $\neg$*holds*(F, S), **not** *ab*(F, A, S).
r_4: $\neg$*holds*(*alive*, *res*(*shoot*, S)) $\leftarrow$ *holds*(*loaded*, S).
r_5: *ab*(*alive*, *shoot*, S) $\leftarrow$ **not** $\neg$*holds*(*loaded*, S).

As in Section 2.2.2, let us consider the case when we are given the additional oracle:

r_6: *holds*(*alive*, *res*(*shoot*, s_0)) $\leftarrow$.

Intuitively, we should now be able to conclude that the gun is not loaded in s_0. But $\Pi = \{r_1, r_2, r_3, r_4, r_5, r_6\}$ does not entail $\neg$ *holds*(*loaded*, s_0). In Section 2.2.2 we suggested using integrity constraints and enumeration with respect to the initial situation to be able to do such backward reasoning. Another alternative would be to add the following explicit rules for backward reasoning:

r_7: *holds*(*loaded*, S) $\leftarrow$ *holds*(*alive*, S), $\neg$*holds*(*alive*, *res*(*shoot*, S)).
r_8: $\neg$*holds*(*loaded*, S) $\leftarrow$ *holds*(*alive*, *res*(*shoot*, S)).
r_9: $\neg$*holds*(F, S) $\leftarrow$ $\neg$*holds*(F, *res*(A, S)), **not** *ab*(F, A, S).
r_{10}: *holds*(F, S) $\leftarrow$ *holds*(F, *res*(A, S)), **not** *ab*(F, A, S).

It can now be shown that $\Pi' = \Pi \cup \{r_7, r_8, r_9, r_{10}\}$ entails $\neg$*holds*(*loaded*, s_0). Moreover, we can use Proposition 47 to show that Π' makes all the conclusions about *holds* and $\neg$*holds* that are made by Π and possibly more. More formally,

Proposition 48 The program Π' entails every *holds* and $\neg$*holds* ground literal that is entailed by the program Π. $\qquad\qquad\square$

Proof: Let $S = \{a : a$ is an *ab* atom in our language$\}$. It is easy to see that S is a common signing for Π and Π'. It is also easy to see that $\Pi'_S = \Pi_S$ and $\Pi_{\bar{S}} \subseteq \Pi'_{\bar{S}}$. Hence, $\Pi_{\bar{S}} \preceq \Pi'_{\bar{S}}$ and $\Pi'_S \preceq \Pi_S$. Since *literals*$(\Pi) = $ *literals*(Π'), it is clear that *literals*$(\Pi) \cap \bar{S} \subseteq$ *literals*$(\Pi') \cap \bar{S}$.

Thus using Proposition 47 we have that Π' entails every ground literal in $\bar{S}$ that is entailed by the program Π. Since the *holds* and $\neg holds$ ground literals are part of $\bar{S}$, our proposition holds. $\square$

Now let us explore results about the answer sets of signed AnsProlog⁻ programs. Recall that answer sets of AnsProlog⁻ programs are defined as sets of literals S, such that $S = \mathcal{M}^\neg(\Pi^S)$. Let us denote $\mathcal{M}^\neg(\Pi^S)$ as $\Gamma^\neg_\Pi(S)$.

Theorem 3.3.1 [Tur94] Let Π be an AnsProlog⁻ program with signing S. Then Π is consistent iff $\text{lfp}(\Gamma^{\neg 2}_\Pi) \cup (\text{gfp}(\Gamma^{\neg 2}_\Pi) \cap S)$ is a consistent answer set for Π. $\square$

Definition 39 We say that an AnsProlog⁻^{,or} program Π is *head-consistent* if $Head(\Pi)$ is a consistent set. $\square$

Proposition 49 [Tur94] Let Π be a head-consistent AnsProlog⁻ program with signing S. The following three conditions hold.

(1) Π is a consistent program.
(2) $\text{lfp}(\Gamma^{\neg 2}_\Pi) \cup (\text{gfp}(\Gamma^{\neg 2}_\Pi) \cap S)$ and $\text{lfp}(\Gamma^{\neg 2}_\Pi) \cup (\text{gfp}(\Gamma^{\neg 2}_\Pi) \cap \bar{S})$ are consistent answer sets of Π.
(3) $Cn(\Pi) = \text{lfp}(\Gamma^{\neg 2}_\Pi)$. $\square$

We will now define the notion of a cover of an AnsProlog⁻^{,or} program and present a property of programs that have at least one head-consistent cover.

Definition 40 Let Π be an AnsProlog⁻^{,or} program. An AnsProlog⁻ program Π' is a cover of Π if Π' can be obtained from Π by replacing each rule $r \in \Pi$ with a rule r' such that $head(r')$ is a singleton, $head(r') \subseteq head(r)$, $pos(r') = pos(r)$, and $neg(r') = neg(r)$. $\square$

Proposition 50 [Tur94] Every signed AnsProlog⁻^{,or} program with at least one head-consistent cover is consistent. $\square$

We now present two properties of AnsProlog⁻^{,or} programs which imply several specific restricted monotonicity properties.

Theorem 3.3.2 [Tur94] Let Π and Π' be AnsProlog⁻^{,or} programs in the same language, both with signing S. If $h_{\bar{S}}(\Pi) \preceq h_{\bar{S}}(\Pi')$ and $h_S(\Pi') \preceq h_S(\Pi)$, then $Cn(\Pi) \cap \bar{S} \subseteq Cn(\Pi') \cap \bar{S}$. $\square$

The above proposition implies the following simple restricted monotonicity property with S and P as sets of ground literals, and Cn as the consequence relation between AnsProlog$^{\neg, or}$ programs and ground literals that are entailed (through $\models$) by it. Suppose S_0 and P_0 are each equal to $\bar{S}$. In this case the above proposition implies that if we start with a program Π and add facts about $\bar{S}$ and obtain a new program Π', then Π' still entails every ground literal in $\bar{S}$ that was entailed by Π. We now give a stronger result than Theorem 3.3.2 stated in terms of the answer sets of a program instead of consequences of a program.

Theorem 3.3.3 [Tur94] Let Π and Π' be AnsProlog$^{\neg, or}$ programs in the same language, both with signing S. If $h_{\bar{S}}(\Pi) \preceq h_{\bar{S}}(\Pi')$ and $h_S(\Pi') \preceq h_S(\Pi)$, then for every consistent answer set A' for program Π', there is a consistent answer set A for Π such that $A \cap \bar{S} \subseteq A' \cap \bar{S}$. $\qquad\qquad\square$

3.4 Analyzing AnsProlog* programs using 'splitting'

To be able to analyze large AnsProlog* programs we need a way to break down an AnsProlog* program to smaller components in such a way that the analysis of the components can be carried over to the whole program. In this section we introduce such a notion which is called 'splitting', and use it not only to analyze AnsProlog* programs but also to construct answer sets of the whole program by computing answer sets of the smaller components. This provides us with an alternative way to compute answer sets for many programs beyond the general tedious guess-and-test approach that follows from the definition of answer sets, when we do not have an AnsProlog^{-not} program or a stratified AnsProlog program for which we have a constructive iterative fixpoint approach to compute answer sets.

The idea of splitting a program into sequences is a generalization of the idea of local stratification. Similarly to local stratification, the ground program and the literals in the language are divided into strata such that the literals in the body of a rule in any stratum either belong to that stratum or a lower stratum, and the literals in the head of a rule belong to that stratum. But unlike local stratification there is no prohibition of recursion through negation. Thus while the program

$p \leftarrow a.$
$p \leftarrow b.$
$a \leftarrow \textbf{not } b.$
$b \leftarrow \textbf{not } a.$

is not locally stratified, it can be split into two strata, the top stratum consisting of the first two rules and the bottom stratum consisting of the other two rules. Unlike local stratification, splitting does not guarantee us a unique answer set, but it is useful in computing the answer sets of the program by computing the answer sets layer by layer. For example, for the above program, we can first compute the answer sets of the bottom layer, which are $\{a\}$ and $\{b\}$, and then use each of those answer sets to partially evaluate the top layer and compute the answer set of the partially evaluated rules. Besides helping us in computing answer sets, we can use the notion of splitting to generalize many of the sub-classes of AnsProlog programs in Section 3.2 by requiring that each stratum after partial evaluation with respect to an answer set of the subprogram consisting of all strata below that, belong to that sub-class. In the rest of this section we will formalize and illustrate the above notions.

3.4.1 Splitting sets

We start with the notion of splitting sets that is used to split a program into two layers. Later we will generalize this to splitting a program into a sequence.

Definition 41 (Splitting set) A *splitting set* for an AnsProlog$^{\neg, or}$ program Π is any set U of literals such that, for every rule $r \in \Pi$, if $head(r) \cap U \neq \emptyset$ then $lit(r) \subseteq U$. If U is a splitting set for Π, we also say that U splits Π. The set of rules $r \in \Pi$ such that $lit(r) \subseteq U$ is called the *bottom* of Π relative to the splitting set U and denoted by $bot_U(\Pi)$. The subprogram $\Pi \setminus bot_U(\Pi)$ is called *the top of* Π relative to U and denoted $top_U(\Pi)$. $\qquad\Box$

Consider the following program Π_1:

$a \leftarrow b, \textbf{not } c.$
$b \leftarrow c, \textbf{not } a.$
$c \leftarrow.$

The set $U = \{c\}$ splits Π_1 such that the last rule constitutes $bot_U(\Pi_1)$ and the first two rules form $top_U(\Pi_1)$.

Once a program is split into top and bottom with respect to a splitting set, we can compute the answer sets of the bottom part and for each of these answer sets, we can further simplify the top part by partial evaluation before analyzing it further. We now present the formal definition of partial evaluation and then define how to compute the answers set of the original program using the partial evaluation of the top part with respect to answer sets of the bottom part.

Definition 42 (Partial evaluation) The partial evaluation of a program Π with splitting set U with respect to a set of literals X is the program $eval_U(\Pi, X)$ defined as follows.

$eval_U(\Pi, X) = \{r' \mid$ there exists a rule r in Π such that $(pos(r) \cap U) \subseteq X$ and $(neg(r) \cap U) \cap X = \emptyset$, and $head(r') = head(r)$, $pos(r') = pos(r) \setminus U$, $neg(r') = neg(r) \setminus U. \}$. $\qquad\qquad\square$

For the program Π_1 mentioned above $eval_{\{c\}}(top_{\{c\}}(\Pi_1), \{c\}) = \{b \leftarrow \mathbf{not}\ a\}$.

Definition 43 (Solution) Let U be a splitting set for a program Π. A solution to Π with respect to U is a pair $\langle X, Y \rangle$ of literals such that:

- X is an answer set for $bot_U(\Pi)$;
- Y is an answer set for $eval_U(top_U(\Pi), X)$; and
- $X \cup Y$ is consistent. $\qquad\qquad\square$

Continuing with Π_1 and $U = \{c\}$, the only answer set of $bot_U(\Pi_1)$ is $\{c\}$. Now the only answer set of $eval_U(top_U(\Pi_1), \{c\})$ is $\{b\}$. Hence, $\langle\{c\}, \{b\}\rangle$ is the only solution to Π_1 with respect to $\{c\}$.

Theorem 3.4.1 (Splitting theorem) [LT94] Let U be a splitting set for a program Π. A set S of literals is a consistent answer set for Π if and only if $S = X \cup Y$ for some solution $\langle X, Y \rangle$ to Π with respect to U. $\qquad\qquad\square$

Continuing with Π_1 and $U = \{c\}$, we have that $\{c, b\}$ is the only answer set of Π_1.

Example 64 Consider the following program Π_2:

$\neg b \leftarrow.$
$a\ or\ b \leftarrow.$

Let $U = \{a, b\}$. We have $bot_U(\Pi_2) = \{a\ or\ b \leftarrow .\}$ and $top_U(\Pi_2) = \{\neg b \leftarrow .\}$. The two answer sets of $bot_U(\Pi_2)$ are $A_1 = \{a\}$ and $A_2 = \{b\}$. Now the answer set of $eval_U(top_U(\Pi_2), A_1)$ is $\{\neg b\}$, and the answer set of $eval_U(top_U(\Pi_2), A_2)$ is $\{\neg b\}$. Since $\{b, \neg b\}$ is inconsistent, the only solution to Π_2 with respect to U is $\langle\{a\}, \{\neg b\}\rangle$. $\qquad\qquad\square$

Exercise 8 Consider the following program:

$p \leftarrow \mathbf{not}\ q.$
$p \leftarrow \mathbf{not}\ p.$
$q \leftarrow \mathbf{not}\ r.$
$r \leftarrow \mathbf{not}\ q.$

Using $\{q, r\}$ as a splitting set shows that the only answer set of the above program is $\{r, p\}$.   □

Exercise 9 Consider the following program:

$c \leftarrow \textbf{not } b.$
$a \leftarrow b.$
$a \text{ or } b \leftarrow .$

Compute the answer sets of the program by using $\{a, b\}$ as a splitting set. Explain why $\{a, b\}$ is not an answer set of this program.   □

3.4.2 Application of splitting

In this subsection we illustrate a couple of applications of the notion of splitting to results about conservative extension and about adding CWA rules to a program.

Conservative extension

We first show how the notion of splitting can be used to prove one of the conservative extension propositions (Proposition 24). First let us recall the statement of Proposition 24.

Let Π be an AnsProlog$^{\neg, or}$ program, and let C be a consistent set of literals that do not occur in Π and whose complements also do not occur in Π. Let Π' be an AnsProlog$^{\neg}$ program such that for every rule $r \in \Pi'$, $head(r) \subseteq C$, and $neg(r) \subseteq lit(\Pi)$. For any literal $L \notin C$, L is a consequence of $\Pi \cup \Pi'$ iff L is a consequence of Π.   □

Proof of Proposition 24: Consider the program $\Pi \cup \Pi'$. It is easy to see that $U = lit(\Pi)$ splits $\Pi \cup \Pi'$ with Π as $bot_U(\Pi \cup \Pi')$ and Π' as $top_U(\Pi \cup \Pi')$. Let A be any consistent answer set of Π. The program $eval_U(\Pi', A)$ is an AnsProlog$^{\neg, -\textbf{not}}$ program. From this, and since the head of the rules of $eval_U(\Pi', A)$ is from C and since C is consistent, we see that $eval_U(\Pi', A)$ has a unique consistent answer set B which is a subset of C. Since neither the literals in C nor its complement appear in Π, the answer set A of Π has neither any literal from C nor any literal from the complement of C. Hence, $A \cup B$ is consistent, and $\langle A, B \rangle$ is a solution to $\Pi \cup \Pi'$ with respect to U. Thus, for every consistent answer set A of Π, there exists a $B \subseteq C$ such that $\langle A, B \rangle$ is a solution to $\Pi \cup \Pi'$ with respect to U. Now if $\langle A, B \rangle$ is a solution to $\Pi \cup \Pi'$ with respect to U then B must be a subset of C. It now follows from the splitting set theorem that a literal $L \notin C$ is a consequence of $\Pi \cup \Pi'$ iff it is a consequence of Π.   □

Adding CWA rules

We now state a proposition about the relation between the answer sets of a program with the answer sets of a second program that is obtained by adding CWA rules to the first program.

Proposition 51 (Adding CWA rules) Let Π be an AnsProlog$^{\neg, or}$ program, and let C be a consistent set of literals that do not occur in Π and let Π' be the program given by $\Pi \cup \{L \leftarrow \textbf{not } \bar{L}. \mid L \in C\}$. If X is a consistent answer set for Π, then

$$X \cup \{L \in C \mid \bar{L} \notin X\} \tag{3.4.1}$$

is a consistent answer set for Π'. Moreover, every consistent answer set for Π' can be represented in the form (3.4.1) for some consistent answer set X for Π. $\qquad\square$

Proof: Let $U = lit(\Pi)$. Since by definition $U \cap C = \emptyset$, U splits Π' with Π as its bottom. Let A be a consistent answer set of Π. The program $eval_U(\Pi' \setminus \Pi, A)$ is the set $\{L \leftarrow . : \bar{L} \notin A\}$. The only answer set of $eval_U(\Pi' \setminus \Pi, A)$ is then $\{L : \bar{L} \notin A\}$. Since A and C are both consistent and $lit(\Pi) \cap C = \emptyset$, $A \cup C$ is consistent. Thus in general for any X, $\langle X, \{L : \bar{L} \notin X\}\rangle$ is a solution to Π' with respect to U if X is an answer set of Π. The proof then follows from the splitting set theorem. $\qquad\square$

Example 65 Let Π_4 be the program

$p(1) \leftarrow .$
$\neg q(2) \leftarrow .$

Let $C = \{\neg p(1), \neg p(2), q(1), q(2)\}$. We can now obtain Π_4' as the program $\Pi_4 \cup \{\neg p(1) \leftarrow \textbf{not } p(1)., \neg p(2) \leftarrow \textbf{not } p(2)., q(1) \leftarrow \textbf{not } \neg q(1)., q(2) \leftarrow \textbf{not } \neg q(2).\}$.

Using Proposition 51 we can easily compute the answer set of Π' as $\{p(1), \neg q(2), \neg p(2), q(1)\}$. $\qquad\square$

3.4.3 Splitting sequences

We now generalize the notion of splitting a program into top and bottom, to splitting it into a sequence of smaller programs.

Definition 44 A *splitting sequence* for an AnsProlog$^{\neg, or}$ program Π is a monotone, continuous sequence[4] $\langle U_\alpha \rangle_{\alpha < \mu}$ of splitting sets for Π such that $\bigcup_{\alpha < \mu} U_\mu = lit(\Pi)$. $\qquad\square$

---

[4] See Appendix A for the definition.

Example 66 Consider the following program Π_4 that defines even numbers.

$e(0) \leftarrow.$
$e(s(X)) \leftarrow \textbf{not } e(X).$

The following sequence of length ω is a splitting sequence for Π_4:

$$\langle \{e(0)\}, \{e(0), e(s(0))\}, \{e(0), e(s(0)), e(s(s(0)))\}, \ldots \rangle \qquad (3.4.2)$$

□

As before, we define solutions to a program Π with respect to U, and then relate it to the answer sets of Π.

Definition 45 Let $U = \langle U_\alpha \rangle_{\alpha < \mu}$ be a splitting sequence for an AnsProlog$^{\neg,or}$ program Π. A *solution* to Π with respect to U is a sequence $\langle X_\alpha \rangle_{\alpha < \mu}$ of sets of literals such that:

• X_0 is an answer set for $bot_{U_0}(\Pi)$,
• for any ordinal α such that $\alpha + 1 < \mu$, $X_{\alpha+1}$ is an answer set of the program:

$$eval_{U_\alpha}(bot_{U_{\alpha+1}}(\Pi) \setminus bot_{U_\alpha}(\Pi), \bigcup_{\nu \leq \alpha} X_\nu),$$

• for any limit ordinal $\alpha < \mu$, $X_\alpha = \emptyset$, and
• $\bigcup_{\alpha \leq \mu} X_\alpha$ is consistent.

□

The only solution $\langle X_0, X_1, \ldots \rangle$ to Π_4 with respect to the splitting sequence (3.4.2) can be given by the following:

$$X_n = \begin{cases} \{p(S^n(0))\}, & \text{if } n \text{ is even} \\ \emptyset, & \text{otherwise.} \end{cases}$$

Theorem 3.4.2 (Splitting sequence theorem) [LT94]   Let $U = \langle U_\alpha \rangle_{\alpha < \mu}$ be a splitting sequence for an AnsProlog$^{\neg,or}$ program Π. A set S of literals is a consistent answer set for Π iff $S = \bigcup_{\alpha < \mu} X_\alpha$ for some solution $\langle X_\alpha \rangle_{\alpha < \mu}$ to Π with respect to U.

□

Example 67 Consider the following program Π:

$r_1: e \leftarrow c, b.$
$r_2: f \leftarrow d.$
$r_3: c \leftarrow \textbf{not } d.$
$r_4: d \leftarrow \textbf{not } c, \textbf{not } b.$
$r_5: a \leftarrow \textbf{not } b.$
$r_6: b \leftarrow \textbf{not } a.$

This program has a splitting sequence $U_0 = \{a, b\}$, $U_1 = \{a, b, c, d\}$, and $U_2 = \{a, b, c, d, e, f\}$. It is easy to see that $bot_{U_0}(\Pi) = \{r_5, r_6\}$, $bot_{U_1}(\Pi) = \{r_3, r_4, r_5, r_6\}$, and $bot_{U_2}(\Pi) = \{r_1, r_2, r_3, r_4, r_5, r_6\}$.

The answer sets of $bot_{U_0}(\Pi)$ are $X_{0.0} = \{a\}$ and $X_{0.1} = \{b\}$.

$eval_{U_0}(bot_{U_1}(\Pi) \setminus bot_{U_0}(\Pi), X_{0.0}) = eval_{U_0}(\{r_3, r_4\}, \{a\}) = \{c \leftarrow \textbf{not } d., d \leftarrow \textbf{not } c.\}$.

It has two answer sets $X_{1.0} = \{c\}$ and $X_{1.1} = \{d\}$.

$eval_{U_0}(bot_{U_1}(\Pi) \setminus bot_{U_0}(\Pi), X_{0.1}) = eval_{U_0}(\{r_3, r_4\}, \{b\}) = \{c \leftarrow \textbf{not } d.\}$.

It has one answer set $X_{1.2} = \{c\}$.

$eval_{U_1}(bot_{U_2}(\Pi) \setminus bot_{U_1}(\Pi), X_{0.0} \cup X_{1.0}) = eval_{U_1}(\{r_1, r_2\}, \{a, c\}) = \{\}$.

It has one answer set $X_{2.0} = \{\}$.

$eval_{U_1}(bot_{U_2}(\Pi) \setminus bot_{U_1}(\Pi), X_{0.0} \cup X_{1.1}) = eval_{U_1}(\{r_1, r_2\}, \{a, d\}) = \{f \leftarrow .\}$.

It has one answer set $X_{2.1} = \{f\}$.

$eval_{U_1}(bot_{U_2}(\Pi) \setminus bot_{U_1}(\Pi), X_{0.1} \cup X_{1.2}) = eval_{U_1}(\{r_1, r_2\}, \{b, c\}) = \{e \leftarrow .\}$.

It has one answer set $X_{2.2} = \{e\}$.

From the above analysis, Π has three solutions $\langle X_{0.0}, X_{1.0}, X_{2.0} \rangle$, $\langle X_{0.0}, X_{1.1}, X_{2.1} \rangle$, and $\langle X_{0.1}, X_{1.2}, X_{2.2} \rangle$. Thus, using Theorem 3.4.2 Π has three answer sets: $\{a, c\}$, $\{a, d, f\}$, and $\{b, c, e\}$. $\square$

3.4.4 Applications of the splitting sequence theorem

In this subsection we show that the notion of order consistency can be defined in terms of splitting the program into components which are signed. This leads to a different proof of coherence of order-consistent AnsProlog programs by using the proof of coherence of signed AnsProlog programs and the properties of a splitting sequence. We now formally define the notion of components.

Given a program Π and a set of literals X, $rem(\Pi, X)$ is the set of rules obtained by taking each of the rules in Π and removing from its body any literal in X, regardless of whether it is preceded by **not** or not. For any program Π and any splitting sequence $U = \langle U_\alpha \rangle_{\alpha < \mu}$ for P, the programs:

$bot_{U_0}(\Pi)$,
$rem(bot_{U_{\alpha+1}}(\Pi) \setminus bot_{U_\alpha}(\Pi), U_\alpha)$, for all $\alpha + 1 < \mu$

are called the U-components of Π.

For example, the U-components of Π_4 are the programs $\{p(S^n(0)) \leftarrow .\}$ for all n.

Exercise 10 Using the notions of components and splitting sequences prove that every stratified AnsProlog program has a unique answer set. $\square$

Earlier the notion of order-consistency was only defined for AnsProlog programs. Here we extend that definition to AnsProlog$^{\neg,or}$ programs and relate order-consistent AnsProlog$^\neg$ programs with signed AnsProlog$^\neg$ programs. We first have the following notations:

For any atom A, let P_A^+ and P_A^- be the smallest sets that satisfy the following conditions:

- $A \in P_A^+$,
- for every rule r: if $head(r) \subseteq P_A^+$ then $pos(r) \subseteq P_A^+$ and $neg(r) \subseteq P_A^-$, and
- for every rule r: if $head(r) \subseteq P_A^-$ then $pos(r) \subseteq P_A^-$ and $neg(r) \subseteq P_A^+$.

An AnsProlog$^{\neg,or}$ program P is called *order-consistent* if there exists a level mapping f such that $f(B) < f(A)$ whenever $B \in P_A^+ \cap P_A^-$.

Proposition 52 [LT94] An AnsProlog$^\neg$ program Π is order-consistent iff it has a splitting sequence U such that all U-components of Π are signed. $\square$

Exercise 11 Generalize the notion of splitting sequences to splitting into a partial order of components. Formulate and prove the theorem about computing the answer set in this case.

Discuss the advantage of this notion over the notion of splitting sequences. $\square$

3.5 Language independence and language tolerance

Recall from Section 1.2 that the answer set language given by an alphabet is uniquely determined by its constants, function symbols, and predicate symbols. The consequences of an AnsProlog* program not only depend on the rules of the program, but, because of the presence of variables in those rules, may also depend on the language. For example, consider the program Π consisting of the following two rules:

$p(a) \leftarrow \mathbf{not}\ q(X).$
$q(a) \leftarrow .$

Consider two different languages $\mathcal{L}_1$ and $\mathcal{L}_2$ of the above program, where both $\mathcal{L}_1$ and $\mathcal{L}_2$ have p and q as the predicate symbols, both have no function symbols, and

$\mathcal{L}_1$ has the constant a, while $\mathcal{L}_2$ has the constants a and b. We can now give the grounding of Π with respect to $\mathcal{L}_1$ and $\mathcal{L}_2$ as follows:

$$ground(\Pi, \mathcal{L}_1) = \begin{cases} p(a) \leftarrow \mathbf{not}\ q(a). \\ q(a) \leftarrow . \end{cases}$$

$$ground(\Pi, \mathcal{L}_2) = \begin{cases} p(a) \leftarrow \mathbf{not}\ q(a). \\ p(a) \leftarrow \mathbf{not}\ q(b). \\ q(a) \leftarrow . \end{cases}$$

It is easy to see that $p(a)$ is not a consequence of $ground(\Pi, \mathcal{L}_1)$, while it is a consequence of $ground(\Pi, \mathcal{L}_2)$. This illustrates that the consequences of an AnsProlog* program not only depend on the rules of the program, but may also depend on the language.

This raises the following question. Can we identify sufficiency conditions when the consequences of an AnsProlog* program only depend on the rules of the program, and not on the language? We will call such programs *language independent*.

We are also interested in a weaker notion which we will call *language tolerant*. Intuitively, in language tolerant programs we allow the possibility that the conclusions may be different when the languages are different, but require the condition that they have the same conclusions about literals that are in the common language. For example, consider the program Π' consisting of the only rule:

$p(X) \leftarrow .$

It is clear that the above program is not language independent as the conclusions of this program with respect to two different languages $\mathcal{L}_3$ and $\mathcal{L}_4$, where the constants in $\mathcal{L}_3$ are a and c and in $\mathcal{L}_4$ are a and b, are different. But both make the same conclusion about the atom $p(a)$ which is in both languages. In fact, we can generalize and show that the above program is language tolerant.

One of the main reasons we would like to develop the notions of language tolerance and language independence is the fact that often in AnsProlog programs we envision the terms in the different position of an atom to be of particular types. For example, in situation calculus, in the atom $holds(F, S)$, we expect F to be a fluent while S is expected to be a situation. Now consider an AnsProlog* program formulating certain aspects of situation calculus. If we do the grounding of this program using the function $ground(\Pi, \mathcal{L})$, then F and S in $holds(F, S)$ can be grounded with any of the ground terms in $\mathcal{L}$. What we would like, however, is to ground F with fluent terms and S with situation terms. To achieve that we need to expand our notion of language by allowing sorts.

This leads to the question that under what restrictions (on the program) the conclusions of an AnsProlog* program made in the presence of a many sorted language is the same as the conclusion made in the absence of multiple sorts. The notions of language tolerance and language independence come in handy in answering this question. The usefulness of the above is that many query evaluation procedures do not take sorts into account, while programmers often write programs with sorts in mind. Before proceeding further we need a definition of a language with sorts.

3.5.1 Adding sorts to answer set frameworks

To specify the axiom language $\mathcal{L}$ of a *sorted answer set framework*, in addition to variables, connectives, punctuation symbols, and a signature $\sigma_{\mathcal{L}}$, we have a nonempty set $I_{\mathcal{L}}$, whose members are called *sorts*, and a *sort specification* for each symbol of $\sigma_{\mathcal{L}}$ and the variables. When the language is clear from the context, we may drop the subscript writing just σ and I.

The sort specification assigns each variable and constant to a sort in I. Each n-ary function symbol is assigned an $n + 1$-tuple $\langle s_1, \ldots, s_n, s_{n+1} \rangle$, where for each i, $1 \le i \le n + 1$, $s_i \in I$. Each n-ary predicate symbol is assigned an n-tuple $\langle s_1, \ldots, s_n \rangle$, where for each i, $1 \le i \le n$, $s_i \in I$. In addition it is stipulated that there must be at least one constant symbol of each sort in I. The terms, atoms, and literals are defined as before except that they must respect the sort specifications. In the rest of this subsection the atoms and literals in an AnsProlog* program are either from a one-sorted language (i.e., multiple sorts) or a many-sorted language.

Example 68 Consider the following program Π in a many-sorted language $\mathcal{L}$.

$p(X, Y) \leftarrow r(X), \textbf{not } q(X, Y).$
$r(a) \leftarrow .$
$q(a, 0) \leftarrow .$

The language $\mathcal{L}$ has variables X and Y and has the signature $\sigma_{\mathcal{L}} = (\{a, 0, 1, 2\}, \{\}, \{p/2, r/1, q/2\})$. The set of sorts $I_{\mathcal{L}}$ is $\{letter, number\}$. The sort specifications are as follows:

- $sort(X) = letter$; $sort(Y) = number$;
- $sort(a) = letter$; $sort(0) = sort(1) = sort(2) = number$; and
- $sort(p) = sort(q) = \langle letter, number \rangle$; $sort(r) = \langle letter \rangle$.

The ground program *ground*$(\Pi, \mathcal{L})$ is

$p(a, 0) \leftarrow r(a), \textbf{not } q(a, 0).$
$p(a, 1) \leftarrow r(a), \textbf{not } q(a, 1).$

$p(a, 2) \leftarrow r(a), \textbf{not } q(a, 2).$
$r(a) \leftarrow .$
$q(a, 0) \leftarrow .$

The above program has the unique answer set $\{r(a), q(a, 0), p(a, 1), p(a, 2)\}$. □

We now define a notion of when a language is permissible for a program.

Definition 46 Let $\mathcal{L}$ be an arbitrary (one-sorted or many-sorted) language, and let Π be an AnsProlog* program. If every rule in Π is a rule in $\mathcal{L}$, we say that $\mathcal{L}$ is *permissible* for Π. □

3.5.2 Language independence

Definition 47 An AnsProlog* program Π is *language independent* if, for two languages $\mathcal{L}_1$ and $\mathcal{L}_2$ that are permissible for Π, the ground programs $ground(\Pi, \mathcal{L}_1)$ and $ground(\Pi, \mathcal{L}_2)$ have the same consistent answer sets. □

Proposition 53 [MT94b] Let Π be a language independent AnsProlog$^{\neg, or}$ program, and let $\mathcal{L}_1$ and $\mathcal{L}_2$ be permissible languages for Π. Then $Cn(ground(\Pi, \mathcal{L}_1)) = Cn(ground(\Pi, \mathcal{L}_2))$. □

Ground programs are trivially language independent. The following is a result about an additional class of language independent programs whose grounding depends on the language, and hence does not lead to the same grounding regardless of the language.

Theorem 3.5.1 [MT94b] Every range-restricted AnsProlog$^{\neg, or}$ program is language independent. □

Consider the program $\{p(a) \leftarrow \textbf{not } q(X)., q(a) \leftarrow .\}$ in the beginning of this subsection. It is not range-restricted as the variable in the first rule does not appear in a positive literal in the body. In the beginning of the subsection we argued why this program is not language independent. Now consider the following range-restricted program Π:

$p(X) \leftarrow r(X), \textbf{not } q(X).$
$r(a) \leftarrow .$

Its grounding with respect to $\mathcal{L}_1$ and $\mathcal{L}_2$ is as follows:

$$ground(\Pi, \mathcal{L}_1) = \begin{cases} p(a) \leftarrow r(a), \textbf{not } q(a). \\ r(a) \leftarrow . \end{cases}$$

$$ground(\Pi, \mathcal{L}_2) = \begin{cases} p(a) \leftarrow r(a), \textbf{not } q(a). \\ p(a) \leftarrow r(b), \textbf{not } q(b). \\ r(a) \leftarrow. \end{cases}$$

Both programs have the unique answer set $\{r(a), p(a)\}$.

3.5.3 Language tolerance

Definition 48 An AnsProlog* program Π is *language tolerant* if, for any two languages $\mathcal{L}_1$, $\mathcal{L}_2$ that are permissible for Π, the following holds: If A_1 is a consistent answer set for the ground program $ground(\Pi, \mathcal{L}_1)$, then there is a consistent answer set A_2 for the ground program $ground(\Pi, \mathcal{L}_2)$ such that $A_1 \cap Lit(\mathcal{L}_2) = A_2 \cap Lit(\mathcal{L}_1)$. □

Proposition 54 [MT94b] Let Π be a language tolerant AnsProlog$^{\neg, or}$ program, and let $\mathcal{L}_1$ and $\mathcal{L}_2$ be permissible languages for Π. Then $Cn(ground(\Pi, \mathcal{L}_1)) \cap Lit(\mathcal{L}_2) = Cn(ground(\Pi, \mathcal{L}_2)) \cap Lit(\mathcal{L}_1)$. □

Example 69 Let us reconsider the program Π from Example 68. Let us have a different language $\mathcal{L}'$ that differs from $\mathcal{L}$ by having an additional constant b of sort *letter* and replacing the constant 1 by 4.

The ground program $ground(\Pi, \mathcal{L}')$ is

$p(a, 0) \leftarrow r(a), \textbf{not } q(a, 0).$
$p(a, 4) \leftarrow r(a), \textbf{not } q(a, 4).$
$p(a, 2) \leftarrow r(a), \textbf{not } q(a, 2).$
$p(b, 0) \leftarrow r(b), \textbf{not } q(b, 0).$
$p(b, 4) \leftarrow r(b), \textbf{not } q(b, 4).$
$p(b, 2) \leftarrow r(b), \textbf{not } q(b, 2).$
$r(a) \leftarrow.$
$q(a, 0) \leftarrow.$

The above program has the unique answer set $S' = \{r(a), q(a, 0), p(a, 4), p(a, 2)\}$. Although this is different from the answer set S of $ground(\Pi, \mathcal{L}')$, we have that $S \cap Lit(\mathcal{L}) = S' \cap Lit(\mathcal{L}') = \{r(a), q(a, 0), p(a, 2)\}$. Thus Π is not language independent. Our goal now is to show that it is language tolerant. □

Our next goal is to identify sub-classes of AnsProlog* programs which are language tolerant. We first give a semantic condition. For that we need the following definition.

Definition 49 An AnsProlog* program Π' is a *part* of a program Π if Π' can be obtained from Π by (i) selecting a subset of the rules in Π, and (ii) deleting zero or more naf-literals from the body of each selected rule. □

Theorem 3.5.2 [MT94b] If an AnsProlog$^{\neg,or}$ program Π is stable and, for every permissible language $\mathcal{L}$ for Π, every part of *ground*$(\Pi, \mathcal{L})$ has a consistent answer set, then Π is language tolerant. □

The second condition of the above theorem needs exhaustive computation of answer sets of every part of Π. We now present a sufficiency condition that can be checked more easily.

Proposition 55 [MT94b] If Π is a predicate-order-consistent AnsProlog program, then for every permissible language $\mathcal{L}$ for Π, every part of *ground*$(\Pi, \mathcal{L})$ has a consistent answer set. □

The above sufficiency condition leads to the following theorem for language tolerance.

Theorem 3.5.3 [MT94b] If an AnsProlog program Π is stable ad predicate-order-consistent, then it is language tolerant. □

Example 70 The program Π from Example 68 is stable with respect to the modes $\Sigma_p = (-, +)$, $\Sigma_q = (-, -)$, and $\Sigma_r = (-)$. It is also predicate-order-consistent. Hence, it is language tolerant. □

Exercise 12 Show that the program $\{p(X) \leftarrow .\}$ is language tolerant. □

3.5.4 When sorts can be ignored

One of the most important applications of the notion of language tolerance is that it leads us to conditions under which we can judiciously ignore the sorts.

Definition 50 Let $\mathcal{L}$ and $\mathcal{L}'$ be languages. We say that $\mathcal{L}'$ is obtained from $\mathcal{L}$ by ignoring sorts if $\sigma_{\mathcal{L}} = \sigma_{\mathcal{L}'}$, $\mathcal{L}$ and $\mathcal{L}'$ have the same variables and $\mathcal{L}'$ does not have multiple sorts. □

Proposition 56 [MT94b] Let Π be a language tolerant AnsProlog$^{\neg,or}$ program in a language (possible with multiple sorts) $\mathcal{L}_{\Pi}$. If $\mathcal{L}$ is obtained from $\mathcal{L}_{\Pi}$ by ignoring sorts, then *ground*$(\Pi, \mathcal{L})$ is a conservative extension of *ground*$(\Pi, \mathcal{L}_{\Pi})$. □

Example 71 Consider the program Π from Example 68. Let us now consider the language $\mathcal{L}''$ obtained from $\mathcal{L}$ by having the same variables and signature but without any sorts. That means while grounding Π with respect to $\mathcal{L}''$, X and Y can take any value from $\{a, 0, 1, 2\}$. Thus $ground(\Pi, \mathcal{L}'')$ is the program:

$p(a, 0) \leftarrow r(a),$ **not** $q(a, 0).$
$p(a, 1) \leftarrow r(a),$ **not** $q(a, 1).$
$p(a, 2) \leftarrow r(a),$ **not** $q(a, 2).$
$p(a, a) \leftarrow r(a),$ **not** $q(a, a).$

$p(0, 0) \leftarrow r(0),$ **not** $q(0, 0).$
$p(0, 1) \leftarrow r(0),$ **not** $q(0, 1).$
$p(0, 2) \leftarrow r(0),$ **not** $q(0, 2).$
$p(0, a) \leftarrow r(0),$ **not** $q(0, a).$

$p(1, 0) \leftarrow r(1),$ **not** $q(1, 0).$
$p(1, 1) \leftarrow r(1),$ **not** $q(1, 1).$
$p(1, 2) \leftarrow r(1),$ **not** $q(1, 2).$
$p(1, a) \leftarrow r(1),$ **not** $q(1, a).$

$p(2, 0) \leftarrow r(2),$ **not** $q(2, 0).$
$p(2, 1) \leftarrow r(2),$ **not** $q(2, 1).$
$p(2, 2) \leftarrow r(2),$ **not** $q(2, 2).$
$p(2, a) \leftarrow r(2),$ **not** $q(2, a).$

$r(a) \leftarrow .$
$q(a, 0) \leftarrow .$

The above program has the answer set $S'' = \{r(a), q(a, 0), p(a, 1), p(a, 2), p(a, a)\}$. The answer set S'' differs from the answer set S of $ground(\Pi, \mathcal{L})$ by having the extra atom $p(a, a)$. But since $p(a, a) \notin Lit(\mathcal{L})$, $ground(\Pi, \mathcal{L}'')$ and $ground(\Pi, \mathcal{L})$ agree on $Lit(\mathcal{L})$. Thus $ground(\Pi, \mathcal{L}'')$ is a conservative extension of $ground(\Pi, \mathcal{L})$.

Intuitively the above means that by ignoring the sort we preserve the conclusions that would have been made if we considered sorts, and if we make any new conclusions then those literals are not part of the sorted language – i.e., they violate the sort conditions.   □

3.6 Interpolating an AnsProlog program

So far in this chapter we have analyzed stand alone AnsProlog* programs. As motivated in Section 1.4 AnsProlog* programs are often used to encode a function. This is particularly the case when AnsProlog* programs are used to express database queries and views. To date, most research in using AnsProlog* programs to express database queries has been with respect to AnsProlog programs. Considering that, our goal in this section is to develop techniques to transform AnsProlog programs so that they behave 'reasonably' when the CWA that is inherent in AnsProlog is removed. Currently there are a large number of queries that are expressed by AnsProlog programs, and at times there is a need to expand these queries so that they can accept incomplete inputs. The techniques of this section will be very useful for the above task.

To formulate the notions of 'reasonable behavior' in the presence of incomplete input, in expanding the query so that it accepts incomplete input, and in transforming an AnsProlog program so that it interpolates the function represented by the original program, we will use many of the database notions such as *database, database instance*, and *query*, which we introduced in Sections 1.4.1 and 1.4.2. We now start with a motivating scenario.

Consider a domain U of individuals, Sam, John, Peter, Mary, and Alberto. Now consider a database instance D consisting of the facts

par(sam, john), par(john, peter), and par(mary, alberto);

where $par(X, Y)$ means that Y is a parent of X.

Now if we would like to ask a *query* Q about the ancestor and non-ancestor pairs in D, we can express it using the AnsProlog program Π_0:

$$\left.\begin{array}{l} anc(X, Y) \leftarrow par(X, Y). \\ anc(X, Y) \leftarrow par(X, Z), anc(Z, Y). \end{array}\right\} \Pi_0$$

The above representation of the *query* assumes the Close World Assumption (CWA) [Rei78] about the database instance D, which says that an atom f will be inferred to be *false* with respect to D if it is not entailed by D. We also refer to D as a *complete database*. By $CWA(D)$ we denote the set $\{f : f$ is an atom in the language and $f \notin D\}$, and the meaning of a complete database D is expressed by the set $D \cup \neg CWA(D)$, where for any set S of atoms $\neg S$ denotes the set $\{\neg f : f \in S\}$.

The *query* Q represented by the AnsProlog program Π_0 can be considered as a function from instances of the relation *par* to instances of the relation *anc*. For example,

$Q(\{par(sam, john), par(john, peter), par(mary, alberto)\})$
$= \{anc(sam, john), anc(john, peter), anc(sam, peter), anc(mary,alberto)\}$.

The function Q can be expressed by the AnsProlog program Π_0 in the following way:

$$Q(D) = \{anc(X, Y) : \Pi_0 \cup D \models anc(X, Y)\} \qquad (3.6.3)$$

Now, let us consider the domain $\{a, b, c, d, e\}$, where a, b, c, d, and e denote the remains of five different individuals found from an archaeological site. Using sophisticated tests, scientists are able to determine that b is a parent of a and c is a parent of b, and neither is e a parent of any of a, b, c and d nor is any of them the parent of e. This information can be represented by the following set S of literals:

$$S = \{par(a, b), par(b, c), \neg par(a, e), \neg par(b, e), \neg par(c, e), \neg par(d, e),$$
$$\neg par(e, a), \neg par(e, b), \neg par(e, c), \neg par(e, d), \neg par(a, d)\}.$$

The set S is not a database instance because it contains negative literals. Recall from Section 1.4.2 that sets of both positive and negative literals are referred to as *incomplete database instances* or simply incomplete databases, in database terminology. Hence, S is an incomplete database instance.

As before we are interested in ancestor and non-ancestor pairs. But this time with respect to the incomplete database S. The function Q and our earlier concept of *query* are no longer appropriate as they require database instances as input. To define ancestor and non-ancestor pairs using the information in S, we need to consider the notion of *extended query* – from Section 1.4.2 – which allows input to be incomplete databases. In this we cannot ignore the negative literals in S and compute Q with respect to the database consisting of the positive literals in S. If we do that we will be able to infer $\neg anc(a, d)$. This is not correct intuitively, because it is possible that with further tests the scientist may determine $par(c, d)$, which will be consistent with the current determination and which will force us to infer $anc(a, d)$.

Since we cannot ignore the negative literals in S, and AnsProlog programs such as $\Pi_0 \cup D$ do not allow rules with negative literals in their head, we will use AnsProlog$^-$ programs to represent the query that determines ancestor and non-ancestor pairs from S. Let us denote this query by Q'. The next question is how are Q and Q' related?

While Q' allows incomplete databases as inputs, Q only allows complete databases. But they must coincide when the inputs are complete databases. Moreover, for any incomplete database X', $Q'(X')$ must not disagree with $Q(X)$, for any complete database X that extends X'. The intuition behind it is that if currently we have the incomplete database X' then our partial conclusion about ancestors and non-ancestors should be such that in the presence of additional information we do not retract our earlier conclusion. Also, given an incomplete database X', the extended query Q' should be such that $Q'(X')$ contains all the information about ancestors and non-ancestors that 'critically depends' on X'. In other words for any X', if for all complete databases X that agree with X' an ancestor pair is true in $Q(X)$, then that ancestor pair must be true in $Q'(X')$. Similarly, this applies to non-ancestor pairs. In general, given a query Q an extended query Q' that satisfies the above properties is referred to as its *expansion*. We formally define *expansion* of a query by an extended query and will relate it to the above described properties in Definition 54 and Proposition 57 respectively.

Now that we have an intuitive idea about Q', the next question is how to express it using an AnsProlog¬ program.

Let us start with the AnsProlog program Π that expresses the query Q. Since we would like to allow incomplete databases as inputs, let us consider Π as an AnsProlog¬ program. But then we no longer have the CWA about ancestors. The next step would be to consider the AnsProlog¬ program obtained by adding explicit CWA about ancestors to the AnsProlog program Π representing Q. The resulting AnsProlog¬ program is given as follows:

$\neg anc(X, Y) \leftarrow \textbf{not}\ anc(X, Y)$.
$anc(X, Y) \leftarrow par(x, Y)$.
$anc(X, Y) \leftarrow par(X, Z), anc(Z, Y)$.

But the resulting AnsProlog¬ program is not an adequate expression of Q'. It only works when the input database instance is complete and does not work for S, as it incorrectly infers $\neg anc(a, d)$.

In this section we adequately express this extended query through an AnsProlog¬ program and argue that it expands the query expressed by Π. The more general question we answer in this section is how to expand arbitrary queries from complete databases that are expressed by AnsProlog programs so that they are applicable to incomplete databases. We use the term 'expand' because our goal is to expand the domain of the queries from only complete databases to databases that may be incomplete. We also refer to the AnsProlog¬ program T that expands Q as the *interpolation* of Π, or say T *interpolates* Π. The intuition behind the term 'interpolation' is that T agrees with Π on all inputs where Π is defined, and for inputs where Π is not defined T interpolates to a value based on the mappings of Π on the neighboring (complete) inputs.

With this motivation we first formulate the l-functions that are encoded by AnsProlog and AnsProlog¬ programs.

3.6.1 The l-functions of AnsProlog and AnsProlog¬ programs

Recall – from Section 1.4.2 – that an AnsProlog* program and two sets of literals $\mathcal{P}$ (called *parameters*) and $\mathcal{V}$ (called *values*) partially define an l-function. We need the following notation before presenting the complete definition of the l-function of our interest.

Definition 51 Let R and S be sets of ground literals over a language $\mathcal{L}$ of an AnsProlog$^\neg$ program Π. $\Pi_R \mid S$ the S-consequences of Π and R, is defined as follows:

$$\Pi_R \mid S = \{s : s \in S \text{ and } \Pi \cup R \models s\} \qquad \square$$

Using the above notation we now precisely define an AnsProlog program that represents a query Q to be a (partial) function from complete sets of literals from the parameter (of Q) to sets of literals from the value (of Q). But, since both parameters and values may have literals, we will have to be careful about the domain of the query specified by an AnsProlog program.

- The *first* requirement is that the elements of the domain must be *complete* with respect to $\mathcal{P}$. But not all complete sets of literals from the parameter will be in the domain.
- We will *additionally require* that each element X of the domain should be a valid input in the sense that when added to Π the resulting AnsProlog program should not entail different literals from the parameter than from those in X.

The following definition makes the above ideas precise.

Definition 52 Let X be an arbitrary set from $2^{\mathcal{P}}$ and let $Y = \Pi_{atoms(X)}|\mathcal{V}$. We will say that X is a *valid input* of Π ($X \in Dom(\Pi)$) and Y is the value of Π at X (i.e. $Y = \Pi(X)$) if the following hold:

(1) $X = \Pi_{atoms(X)} \mid \mathcal{P}$, and
(2) X is complete with respect to $\mathcal{P}$. $\qquad \square$

Definition 53 For any set $X \in 2^{\mathcal{P}}$, a superset $\hat{X}$ of X is said to be a Π-*extension of* X if $\hat{X} \in Dom(\Pi)$. We denote the set of all Π-extensions of X by $S_{\Pi}(X)$. We omit Π from $S_{\Pi}(X)$ when it is clear from the context. $\qquad \square$

Intuitively, given a set $X \in 2^{\mathcal{P}}$, $S_{\Pi}(X)$ denotes the different ways in which X can be completed with additional consistent information, and still be a valid input for Π.

We are now almost ready to precisely define the interpolation of an AnsProlog program which we will specify through an AnsProlog$^\neg$ program.

We view an AnsProlog$^\neg$ program T to be a function from $2^{\mathcal{P}}$ to $2^{\mathcal{V}}$ such that $T(X) = T_X \mid \mathcal{V} = \{s : s \in \mathcal{V} \text{ and } T \cup X \models s\}$. Since we are only interested in AnsProlog$^\neg$ programs that are interpolations, we do not restrict the domain of T.

3.6.2 Interpolation of an AnsProlog program and its properties

Definition 54 (Interpolation) Let Π be an AnsProlog program representing a query Q, with parameters $\mathcal{P}$ and values $\mathcal{V}$. We say that an AnsProlog$^-$ program T *interpolates* Π, with respect to $\mathcal{P}$ and $\mathcal{V}$ if for every $X \in 2^{\mathcal{P}}$

$$T(X) = \bigcap_{\hat{X} \in S(X)} \Pi(\hat{X}) \qquad (3.6.4)$$

Moreover, we also say that the extended query represented by (the AnsProlog$^-$ program) T expands the query represented by (the AnsProlog program) Π. $\square$

For convenience, we will just say that T interpolates Π without mentioning the query Q, the parameters $\mathcal{P}$, and the values $\mathcal{V}$, whenever they are clear from the context. But it should be noted that T interpolates Π with respect to $\mathcal{P}$ and $\mathcal{V}$ does not necessarily mean that T will also be an interpolation of Π for a different query with a different pair of parameter and value. The choice of Q, $\mathcal{P}$, and $\mathcal{V}$ is an integral part of the program. The programmer designs the program with that choice in mind. This is similar to the choices and assumptions a PROLOG programmer makes about whether a particular attribute of a predicate in the head of a rule will be ground or not when that predicate is invoked.

The following proposition breaks down the definition of interpolation into three different intuitive properties: equivalence, monotonicity, and maximal informativeness. The equivalence property states that Π and T must be equivalent with respect to complete inputs. The monotonicity property states that a T which accepts incomplete inputs should be monotonic, i.e. in the presence of additional consistent information it should not retract any of its earlier conclusions. The maximal informativeness property states that given an incomplete input X, the interpolation T should entail all literals that are entailed by Π with respect to all the complete extensions of X that are in the domain of Π. Intuitively, it means that if Π entails l regardless of what complete extension of X is given to Π as an input then X has enough information to make a decision on l and hence the interpolation T should entail l with X as the input.

Proposition 57 An AnsProlog$^-$ program T interpolates an AnsProlog program Π iff the following conditions are satisfied:

(1) (**Equivalence**) For every $X \in Dom(\Pi)$, $\Pi(X) = T(X)$.
(2) (**Monotonicity**) T is monotonic, i.e. for every $X_1, X_2 \subseteq \mathcal{P}$, if $X_1 \subseteq X_2$ then $T(X_1) \subseteq T(X_2)$.

(3) (**Maximal Informativeness**) For every $v \in \mathcal{V}$ and every $X \subseteq \mathcal{P}$, if for all $\hat{X} \in S(X)$ and $v \in \Pi(\hat{X})$ then $v \in T(X)$. $\qquad\square$

Proof '$\Longrightarrow$'

Since every $X \in Dom(\Pi)$ is complete $S(X) = X$. Hence, condition 1 holds. It is obvious that condition 3 holds. Condition 2 holds because $X_2 \subseteq X_1 \Rightarrow S(X_1) \subseteq S(X_2)$.

'$\Longleftarrow$'

Condition 3 implies $T(X) \supseteq \bigcap_{\hat{X} \in S(X)} \Pi(\hat{X})$.

We now only need to show that for all $X \subseteq \mathcal{P}$, $T(X) \subseteq \bigcap_{\hat{X} \in S(X)} \Pi(\hat{X})$.

(case 1) $S(X) = \emptyset$

$\Rightarrow \bigcap_{\hat{X} \in S(X)} \Pi(\hat{X}) = Lit(\mathcal{P})$

$\Rightarrow T(X) \subseteq \bigcap_{\hat{X} \in S(X)} \Pi(\hat{X})$

(case 2) $S(X) \neq \emptyset$

Let $s \in T(X)$. Since, for all $\hat{X} \in S(X)$, $X \subseteq \hat{X}$, by monotonicity (2) we have $s \in T(\hat{X})$. But using equivalence (1) we have $s \in \Pi(\hat{X})$. Hence,

$$\text{for all } X \subseteq \mathcal{P}, T(X) \subseteq \bigcap_{\hat{X} \in S(X)} \Pi(\hat{X}) \qquad\square$$

In the following we discuss the interpolation of a non-stratified AnsProlog program.

Consider the following AnsProlog program Π_2:

$$\left.\begin{array}{l} c(X) \leftarrow p(X). \\ c(X) \leftarrow q(X). \\ p(X) \leftarrow \textbf{not } q(X), r(X). \\ q(X) \leftarrow \textbf{not } p(X), r(X). \end{array}\right\} \Pi_2$$

Here $\mathcal{P} = Lit(r)$ and $\mathcal{V} = Lit(c)$. It is easy to see that for every $X \in 2^{\mathcal{P}}$, $\Pi_2 \cup X$ is call-consistent.

Let $X \subseteq \mathcal{P}$. The program $\Pi_2 \cup X$ can be split into three layers, the bottom layer consisting of X, the next layer consisting of the rules with either p or q in the head, and the top layer consisting of the rules with c in the head. The answer sets of $\Pi_2 \cup X$ can then be computed bottom-up starting from the bottom layer. Therefore Π_2 is defined for any complete and consistent X, $X \subseteq \mathcal{P}$.

Consider T_2 obtained from Π_2 by adding to it the rule

$\neg c(X) \leftarrow \neg r(X).$

Proposition 58 [BGK98] T_2 is an interpolation of Π_2. $\qquad\square$

So far in this section we have made precise the notion of interpolation (and query expansion) and proved the interpolation results for two particular AnsProlog programs. But we still do not know which program interpolates the program Π_0 that represents the ancestor query. Our goal now is to come up with a precise algorithm that constructs interpolations of AnsProlog programs.

3.6.3 An algorithm for interpolating AnsProlog programs

In this subsection we present an algorithm which constructs an interpolation of a large class of AnsProlog programs with some restrictions on its parameter and value. We now make these restrictions precise.

Let Π be an AnsProlog program in language $\mathcal{L}$. We only consider the query Q with values $\mathcal{V}$ consisting of all ground literals formed with predicates in the heads of the rules in Π (called IDB predicates), and parameters $\mathcal{P}$ consisting of all other ground literals in *Lit* (called EDB predicates). An AnsProlog program Π representing a query Q that satisfies the above property is called a *natural representation* of Q.

Before we give the algorithm we demonstrate the intuition behind the algorithm by using the ancestor query as an example.

Interpolation of the Transitive Closure Program

Recall the ancestor query represented as an AnsProlog program was:

$$\left.\begin{aligned} anc(X, Y) &\leftarrow par(X, Y). \\ anc(X, Y) &\leftarrow par(X, Z), anc(Z, Y). \end{aligned}\right\} \Pi_0$$

where *par* is the EDB predicate and *anc* is the IDB predicate.

Our goal is to construct an interpolation of this program. We refer to our interpolation program as $\mathcal{A}(\Pi_0)$.

The main idea behind our construction is to have a program which coincides with Π_0 on atoms of the form $anc(a, b)$ and derives $\neg anc(a, b)$ when no consistent extension of the original EDB may derive $anc(a, b)$. To achieve this we introduce a new predicate m_{anc}, where $m_{anc}(c, d)$ intuitively means that 'c may be an ancestor of d'. Our information about m_{anc} is complete hence $\neg m_{anc}$ coincides with **not** m_{anc} and hence we define $\neg anc$ using the rule:

$\neg anc(X, Y) \leftarrow \textbf{not } m_{anc}(X, Y).$

Next we modify the original rules to define m_{anc} and use another new predicate m_{par}, where $m_{par}(c, d)$ means that 'c may be a parent of d'. We now define m_{anc} using the rules:

$m_{anc}(X, Y) \leftarrow m_{par}(X, Y).$
$m_{anc}(X, Y) \leftarrow m_{par}(X, Z), m_{anc}(Z, Y).$

We now need to define m_{par}. Intuitively, in the presence of incomplete information about parents we can say 'e may be a parent of f if we do not know for sure that e is not a parent of f.' This can be written as the rule:

$$m_{par}(X, Y) \leftarrow \textbf{not } \neg par(X, Y).$$

Putting all the above rules together we have an interpolation of Π_0 denoted by $\mathcal{I}(\Pi_0)$.

$$\left.\begin{array}{l}
m_{par}(X, Y) \leftarrow \textbf{not } \neg par(X, Y). \\
m_{anc}(X, Y) \leftarrow m_{par}(X, Y). \\
m_{anc}(X, Y) \leftarrow m_{par}(X, Z), m_{anc}(Z, Y). \\
\neg anc(X, Y) \leftarrow \textbf{not } m_{anc}(X, Y). \\
anc(X, Y) \leftarrow par(X, Y). \\
anc(X, Y) \leftarrow par(X, Z), anc(Z, Y).
\end{array}\right\} \mathcal{I}(\Pi_0)$$

where $\mathcal{P}$ and $\mathcal{V}$ are the same as for the program Π_0.

Theorem 3.6.1 (Interpolation)[BGK98] The interpolation $\mathcal{I}(\Pi_0)$ interpolates Π_0 with $\mathcal{P} = Lit(par)$ and $\mathcal{V} = Lit(anc)$. $\square$

Since we were using the ancestor query as an example, the above theorem is a special case of a more general theorem (Theorem 3.6.2) to be stated later.

The Interpolation Algorithm

Now we apply the idea from the previous section to arbitrary AnsProlog programs. We expand the language of such a program Π by introducing intermediate predicate m_p for every predicate p in Π. Intuitively $m_p(\bar{t})$ means that $p(\bar{t})$ may be true.

To define these predicates we consider two cases. Since negative information about EDB predicates is explicitly given, this intuition is captured by the rule:

$$m_q(\bar{t}) \leftarrow \textbf{not } \neg q(\bar{t}). \tag{v1}$$

The definition of m_a for an IDB predicate a cannot rely on negative information about a. Instead it uses the corresponding definition of a from Π. More precisely, $\mathcal{I}(\Pi)$ contains the rule

$$m_a(\bar{t}) \leftarrow m_{b_1}(\bar{t}), \ldots, m_{b_n}(\bar{t}), \textbf{not } c_1(\bar{t}), \ldots, \textbf{not } c_n(\bar{t}). \tag{v2}$$

for every rule

$$a(\bar{t}) \leftarrow b_1(\bar{t}), \ldots, b_m(\bar{t}), \textbf{not } c_1(\bar{t}), \ldots, \textbf{not } c_n(\bar{t}). \tag{v3}$$

in Π.

For any program Π, the program $\mathcal{I}(\Pi)$ contains the rule

$$a(\bar{t}) \leftarrow b_1(\bar{t}), \ldots, b_m(\bar{t}), \neg c_1(\bar{t}), \ldots, \neg c_n(\bar{t}). \qquad (v4)$$

for every rule (v3) in Π. Rule (v4) is intended to be a monotonic and weakened version of rule (v2). The intuition is that we no longer want to make hasty (revisable) conclusions using the negation as failure operator (**not**) in the body. The negation as failure operator is therefore replaced by $\neg$ in (v4). On the other hand we would like $m_a(\bar{t})$ to be true if there is any possibility that $a(\bar{t})$ is true. Hence, in the body of (v2) we still have the negation as failure operator. Once the truth of $a(\bar{t})$ is established by $\mathcal{I}(\Pi)$ through the rule (v4) it will never be retracted in the presence of additional consistent information about the EDB predicates.

The above definitions ensure that the interpolation does not entail $m_p(\bar{t})$ for an input X iff it does not entail $p(\bar{t})$ for any consistent extension Y of X. Hence it is safe to infer $\neg p(\bar{t})$ when the interpolation does not entail $m_p(\bar{t})$. This observation leads to the following definition of falsity of IDB predicates

$$\neg p(\bar{t}) \leftarrow \mathbf{not}\ m_p(\bar{t}). \qquad (v5)$$

The above intuitions can be summarized into the following algorithm that constructs the interpolations of a large class of AnsProlog programs.

Algorithm 1 *For any AnsProlog program Π the AnsProlog$^\neg$ program $\mathcal{I}(\Pi)$ contains the following rules:*

(1) If q is an EDB in the program Π, $\mathcal{I}(\Pi)$ contains the rule:

$m_q(\bar{t}) \leftarrow \mathbf{not}\ \neg q(\bar{t}).$

(2) For any rule $a(\bar{t}) \leftarrow b_1(\bar{t}), \ldots, b_m(\bar{t}), \mathbf{not}\ c_1(\bar{t}), \ldots, \mathbf{not}\ c_n(\bar{t}).$ in Π, $\mathcal{I}(\Pi)$ contains the rules:
  (a) $m_a(\bar{t}) \leftarrow m_{b_1}(\bar{t}), \ldots, m_{b_m}(\bar{t}), \mathbf{not}\ c_1(\bar{t}), \ldots, \mathbf{not}\ c_n(\bar{t}).$
  (b) $a(\bar{t}) \leftarrow b_1(\bar{t}), \ldots, b_m(\bar{t}), \neg c_1(\bar{t}), \ldots, \neg c_n(\bar{t}).$

(3) If p is an IDB in the program Π, $\mathcal{I}(\Pi)$ contains the rule:

$\neg p(\bar{t}) \leftarrow \mathbf{not}\ m_p(\bar{t}).$ $\qquad\qquad\qquad$ $\square$

Example 72 (Transitive closure) Consider Π_0 from the previous subsection:

$anc(X, Y) \leftarrow par(X, Y).$
$anc(X, Y) \leftarrow par(X, Z), anc(Z, Y).$

Then the transformation $\mathcal{I}(\Pi)$ based on the above algorithm is exactly the AnsProlog$^\neg$ program $\mathcal{I}(\Pi_0)$ obtained in Section 3.6.3. $\qquad\qquad$ $\square$

3.6.4 Properties of the transformation $\mathcal{I}$

In this subsection we formalize several properties of the transformation $\mathcal{I}$. We show that for a large class of AnsProlog programs it constructs an interpolation and for all AnsProlog programs the transformed program satisfies weaker versions of interpolation.

Theorem 3.6.2 (Properties of $\mathcal{I}(\Pi)$ for a signed program Π)[BGK98] For any signed AnsProlog program Π that is a natural representation of a query Q, $\mathcal{I}(\Pi)$ is an interpolation of Π.   □

The following example shows an unsigned but stratified AnsProlog program for which Algorithm 1 does not construct an interpolation.

Example 73 Consider the program Π_6:

$$\left.\begin{array}{l} p \leftarrow q. \\ p \leftarrow \mathbf{not}\ q. \end{array}\right\} \Pi_6$$

Here $\mathcal{V} = \{p, \neg p\}$, $\mathcal{P} = \{q, \neg q\}$. It is easy to see that for any $X \subseteq \mathcal{P}$ we have $p \in \Pi(X)$.
Program $\mathcal{I}(\Pi_6)$ consists of the following rules:

$$\left.\begin{array}{l} m_q \leftarrow \mathbf{not}\ \neg q. \\ m_p \leftarrow m_q \\ m_p \leftarrow \mathbf{not}\ q. \\ p \leftarrow q. \\ p \leftarrow \neg q. \\ \neg p \leftarrow \mathbf{not}\ m_p. \end{array}\right\} \mathcal{I}(\Pi_6) = T$$

Consider $X = \emptyset$ and the AnsProlog$^{\neg}$ program $T \cup X = T$. It is easy to see that T^+ is a stratified program, therefore T has only one answer set A. Evidently, $A = \{m_p, m_q\}$ and $p \notin A$. Therefore

$$\mathcal{I}(\Pi)(X) \neq \bigcap_{\hat{X} \in S(X)} \Pi(\hat{X})$$

□

The following theorem states that the transformation $\mathcal{I}$ preserves categoricity for signed AnsProlog programs.

Theorem 3.6.3 (Categoricity) [BGK98] Let Π be a signed AnsProlog program with signing R, and a natural representation of a query Q, and $X \subseteq \mathcal{P}$. The program $\Pi \cup atoms(X)$ is categorical if and only if the program $\mathcal{I}(\Pi) \cup X$ is categorical.   □

We now introduce some weaker notions of interpolation which will be satisfied by a larger class than the class of signed AnsProlog programs.

Definition 55 (Weak and sound interpolation) Let Π be an AnsProlog program, with parameter $\mathcal{P}$ and value $\mathcal{V}$. We say an AnsProlog$^-$ program T is a *weak interpolation* of Π with respect to $\mathcal{P}$ and $\mathcal{V}$ if the following three conditions are satisfied.

(1) (**Monotonicity**) For every $X_1, X_2 \subseteq \mathcal{P}$, if $X_1 \subseteq X_2$ then $T(X_1) \subseteq T(X_2)$.
(2) (**Equivalence**) For every $X \in Dom(\Pi)$, $\Pi(X) = T(X)$.
(3) For any $X \subseteq \mathcal{P}$

$$T(X) \subseteq \bigcap_{\hat{X} \in S(X)} \Pi(\hat{X})$$

If only the first and the third conditions are satisfied then we say T is a *sound interpolation* of Π with respect to $\mathcal{P}$ and $\mathcal{V}$. $\square$

From the third condition above it is clear that if T is a sound interpolation of Π then it satisfies the weak equivalence property defined as:

For every $X \in Dom(\Pi)$, $T(X) \subseteq \Pi(X)$.

We now state two more results about the properties of the transformation $\mathcal{I}(\Pi)$.

Theorem 3.6.4 (Properties of $\mathcal{I}(\Pi)$ for stratified AnsProlog programs) [BGK98] Let Π be a stratified AnsProlog program and a natural representation of a query Q, then $\mathcal{I}(\Pi)$ is a weak interpolation of Π. $\square$

Theorem 3.6.5 (Properties of $\mathcal{I}(\Pi)$ for arbitrary AnsProlog programs) [BGK98] Let Π be an AnsProlog program and a natural representation of a query Q, then $\mathcal{I}(\Pi)$ is a sound interpolation of Π. $\square$

In summary, the transformation $\mathcal{I}$ constructs interpolations for signed AnsProlog programs, weak interpolations for stratified AnsProlog programs, and sound interpolations for all programs. Moreover, the transformation preserves categoricity for signed programs and preserves stratification (i.e. if Π is stratified then $\mathcal{I}(\Pi)^+$ is stratified) for stratified programs.

3.7 Building and refining programs from components: functional specifications and realization theorems

In Section 3.1.3 we presented results about when a program Π enhanced with additional rules preserves the meaning of the original program. These results are part of a larger theme that will allow us to modularly build larger and more refined programs from smaller components. In this section we continue with this theme. We follow Section 1.4.3 in viewing programs (together with a domain and an input and an output signature) as s-functions – which we also refer to as lp-functions, and define operators to compose and refine these functions and present results that state when such composition and refinement can be realized when using AnsProlog* programs.

3.7.1 Functional specifications and lp-functions

To validate lp-functions with respect to an independent specification, we first introduce the notion of a functional specification.

Definition 56 A four-tuple $f = \{f, \sigma_i(f), \sigma_o(f), \mathrm{dom}(f)\}$ where

(1) $\sigma_i(f)$ and $\sigma_o(f)$ are signatures;
(2) $\mathrm{dom}(f) \subseteq states(\sigma_i(f))$;
(3) f is a function which maps $\mathrm{dom}(f)$ into $states(\sigma_o(f))$

is called an *f-specification (or functional specification)* with input signature $\sigma_i(f)$, output signature $\sigma_o(f)$ and domain $\mathrm{dom}(f)$. States over $\sigma_i(f)$ and $\sigma_o(f)$ are called input and output states respectively.   □

We now formally define lp-functions.

Definition 57 A four-tuple $\pi = \{\pi, \sigma_i(\pi), \sigma_o(\pi), \mathrm{dom}(\pi)\}$ where

(1) π is an AnsProlog¬ program (with some signature $\sigma(\pi)$);
(2) $\sigma_i(\pi)$, $\sigma_o(\pi)$ are sub-signatures of $\sigma(\pi)$ called input and output signatures of π respectively;
(3) $\mathrm{dom}(\pi) \subseteq states(\sigma_i(\pi))$

is called an lp-*function* if for any $X \in \mathrm{dom}(\pi)$ program $\pi \cup X$ is consistent, i.e., has a consistent answer set. For any $X \in \mathrm{dom}(\pi)$,

$$\pi(X) = \{l : l \in lit(\sigma_o(\pi)), \pi \cup X \models l\}.$$

   □

Definition 58 We say that an lp-function π *represents* an f-specification f if π and f have the same input and output signatures and domains and for any $X \in \mathrm{dom}(f)$, $f(X) = \pi(X)$.   □

3.7.2 *The compositional and refinement operators*

In this section we discuss four operators on functional specifications that will allow us to compose and refine them. The four operators are *incremental extension, interpolation, input opening,* and *input extension.* Among these the first one is a binary compositional operator that defines a particular composition of functional specifications. The remaining three are unary refinement operators that refine a functional specification. All three of them focus on the input domain of the function. The interpolation operator refines a functional specification so that its domain is unchanged but for certain elements in the domain the function follows the notion of interpolation in Section 3.6. The input opening operator is a further refinement of the interpolation operator where, besides interpolation, the enhanced function also reasons about the input itself and expands it to the maximum extent possible. The input extension operator refines a functional specification for particular enlargement of its domain. We now formally define these operators.

- **Incremental extension**
  Specifications f and g such that $\sigma_o(f) = \sigma_i(g)$ and $lit(\sigma_i(g)) \cap lit(\sigma_o(g)) = \emptyset$ can be combined into a new f-specification $g \circ f$ by a specification constructor $\circ$ called *incremental extension.* Function $g \circ f$ with domain $dom(f)$, $\sigma_i(g \circ f) = \sigma_i(f)$, $\sigma_o(g \circ f) = \sigma_o(f) + \sigma_o(g)$ is called the *incremental extension* of f by g if for any $X \in dom(g \circ f)$, $g \circ f(X) = f(X) \cup g(f(X))$.

  An example of incremental extension is as follows. Let f be a functional specification whose input signature consists of disjoint predicates corresponding to sub-classes of birds such as eagles, canaries, pigeons, penguins, etc., and output signature consists of the predicate 'fly'. Let g be a functional specification with input signature consisting of the predicate 'fly' and the output signature consisting of the predicate *cage_needs_top.* The incremental extension of f by g can then be used to make an inference about whether a particular bird's cage needs a top or not.

- **Interpolation and domain completion**
  Let D be a collection of states over some signature σ. A set $X \in states(\sigma)$ is called D-*consistent* if there is $\hat{X} \in D$ such that $X \subseteq \hat{X}$; $\hat{X}$ is called a D-*cover* of X. The set of all D-covers of X is denoted by $c(D, X)$.

Definition 59 (Interpolation) Let f be a closed domain f-specification with domain D. Then the F-specification $\tilde{f}$ with the same signatures as f and the domain $\tilde{D}$ is called the *interpolation* of f if

$$\tilde{f}(X) = \bigcap_{\hat{X} \in c(D,X)} f(\hat{X}) \qquad (3.7.5)$$

$\square$

This is a slight generalization of the notion of interpolation of Section 3.6 where we only considered interpolations of functions defined by AnsProlog programs.

An example of interpolation is when we have a functional specification f that maps complete initial states to the value of fluents in the future states, and to be able to reason in the presence of incomplete initial states we need an interpolation of the functional specification f.

Definition 60 A set $X \in states(\sigma)$ is called *maximally informative* with respect to a set $D \subseteq states(\sigma)$ if X is D-consistent and

$$X = \bigcap_{\hat{X} \in \cdot c(D,X)} \hat{X}. \tag{3.7.6}$$

By $\tilde{D}$ we denote the set of states of σ maximally informative with respect to D.   □

Definition 61 (Domain completion) Let D be a collection of complete states over signature σ. The *domain completion* of D is a function h_D which maps D-consistent states of σ into their maximally informative supersets.   □

We have a particular interest in domain completion when dealing with the interpolation $\tilde{f}$ of a closed domain f-specification f with domain D. In that case we refer to the *domain completion* of D as the function $\tilde{f}_D$.

- **Input opening**

The set of all D-consistent states of σ is called the *interior* of D and is denoted by D°. An f-specification f defined on a collection of complete states of $\sigma_i(f)$ is called a *closed domain specification*.

Definition 62 (Input opening) Let f be a closed domain specification with domain D. An f-specification f° is called the *input opening* of f if

$$\sigma_i(f^\circ) = \sigma_i(f), \quad \sigma_o(f^\circ) = \sigma_i(f) + \sigma_o(f), \tag{3.7.7}$$

$$dom(f^\circ) = D^\circ, \text{ and} \tag{3.7.8}$$

$$f^\circ(X) = \bigcap_{\hat{X} \in c(D,X)} f(\hat{X}) \cup \bigcap_{\hat{X} \in c(D,X)} \hat{X}. \tag{3.7.9}$$

□

The following proposition follows immediately from the definitions.

Proposition 59 [GG99, GG97] For any closed domain f-specification f with domain D

$$f^\circ = \tilde{f} \circ \tilde{f}_D. \tag{3.7.10}$$

□

- **Input extension**

Definition 63 Let f be a functional specification with disjoint sets of input and output predicates. An f-specification f^* with input signature $\sigma_i(f) + \sigma_o(f)$ and output signature $\sigma_o(f)$ is called an *input extension* of f if

(1) f^* is defined on elements of $\text{dom}(f)$ possibly expanded by consistent sets of literals from $\sigma_o(f)$,
(2) for every $X \in \text{dom}(f)$, $f^*(X) = f(X)$,
(3) for any $Y \in \text{dom}(f^*)$ and any $l \in lit(\sigma_o(f))$,
   (i) if $l \in Y$ then $l \in f^*(Y)$, and
   (ii) if $l \notin Y$ and $\bar{l} \notin Y$ then $l \in f^*(Y)$ iff $l \in f(Y \cap lit(\sigma_i(f)))$. $\qquad\square$

An example of a situation where input extension is necessary is when we have a functional specification f that maps possibly incomplete initial states to the value of fluents in the future states. Now suppose we would like to enhance our representation such that we can also have oracles about the value of fluents in the future states as input. In this case we will need the input extension of f.

Now that we have defined several operators on f-specifications, we proceed to realize these operators when dealing with lp-functions. We start with a realization theorem for incremental extension which states how to build and when we can build an lp-function representing $g \circ f$ from lp-functions that represent f and g. Similarly, the realization theorems for the other unary operators (say, o) state how to build and when we can build an lp-function representing $o(f)$ from an lp-function that represent f.

3.7.3 Realization theorem for incremental extension

Definition 64 An lp-function $\{\pi, \sigma_i(\pi), \sigma_o(\pi), \text{dom}(\pi)\}$ is said to be *output-functional* if for any $X \in \text{dom}(\pi)$ and any answer sets A_1 and A_2 of $\pi \cup X$ we have $A_1 \cap lit(\sigma_o) = A_2 \cap lit(\sigma_o)$. $\qquad\square$

Definition 65 We say that lp-functions $\{\pi_F, \sigma_i(\pi_F), \sigma_o(\pi_F), \text{dom}(\pi_F)\}$ and $\{\pi_G, \sigma_i(\pi_G), \sigma_o(\pi_G), \text{dom}(\pi_G)\}$ are *upward compatible* if

- $\sigma_o(\pi_F) = \sigma_i(\pi_G)$,
- $head(\pi_G) \cap (lit(\pi_F) \cup lit(\sigma_i(\pi_F)) \cup lit(\sigma_o(\pi_F))) = \emptyset$, and
- $(lit(\pi_G) \cup lit(\sigma_i(\pi_G)) \cup lit(\sigma_o(\pi_G))) \cap (lit(\pi_F) \cup lit(\sigma_i(\pi_F)) \cup lit(\sigma_o(\pi_F))) \subseteq lit(\sigma_o(\pi_F))$. $\qquad\square$

Theorem 3.7.1 [GG99, GG97] Let f and g be functional specifications represented by output functional lp-functions π_F and π_G, and let $g \circ f$ be the *incremental* *extension of f by g.* If π_F is upward compatible with π_G, then the lp-function $\pi_{G \circ F} = \{\pi_G \cup \pi_F, \sigma_i(\pi_F), \sigma_o(\pi_F) \cup \sigma_o(\pi_G), \mathrm{dom}(\pi_F)\}$ represents $g \circ f$. $\square$

3.7.4 Realization theorem for interpolation

To give a realization theorem for the interpolation we need the following auxiliary notions.

Let D be a collection of complete states over a signature σ. Function f defined on the interior of D is called *separable* if

$$\bigcap_{\hat{X} \in c(D,X)} f(\hat{X}) \subseteq f(X)$$

or, equivalently, if for any $X \in \mathrm{dom}(f)$ and any output literal l such that $l \notin f(X)$ there is $\hat{X} \in c(D, X)$ such that $l \notin f(\hat{X})$.

The following lemma and examples help to better understand this notion.

Lemma 3.7.2 [GG99, GG97] Let D be the set of complete states over some signature σ_i and let π be an lp-function defined on $D^\circ = states(\sigma_i)$, such that

(1) the sets of input and output predicates of π are disjoint and input literals do not belong to the heads of π; and
(2) for any $l \in \sigma_i$, $l \notin lit(\pi)$ or $\bar{l} \notin lit(\pi)$. (By $lit(\pi)$ we mean the collection of all literals which occur in the rules of the ground instantiation of π.)

Then π is separable. $\square$

The following example shows that the last condition is essential.

Example 74 Let $D = \{\{p(a)\}, \{\neg p(a)\}\}$ and consider a function f_1 defined on D° by the program

$q(a) \leftarrow p(a).$
$q(a) \leftarrow \neg p(a).$

Let $X = \emptyset$. Obviously, $f_1(X) = \emptyset$ while $\bigcap_{\hat{X} \in c(D,X)} f_1(\hat{X}) = \{q(a)\}$ and hence f_1 is not separable. $\square$

In some cases to establish separability of an lp-function π it is useful to represent π as the union of its independent components and to reduce the question of separability of π to separability of these components. Let π be an lp-function with input signature σ_i and output signature σ_o. We assume that the input literals of π do not belong to the heads of rules of π. We say that π is decomposable into independent components $\pi_0, \ldots, \pi_n$ if $\pi = \pi_0 \cup \cdots \cup \pi_n$ and $lit(\pi_k) \cap lit(\pi_l) \subseteq lit(\sigma_i)$ for any $k \neq l$. It is easy to check that, for any $0 \leq k \leq n$, four-tuple $\{\pi_k, \sigma_i, \sigma_o, \mathrm{dom}(\pi)\}$ is an lp-function, and that if all these functions are separable then so is π. This observation can be used for instance to establish separability of function f_2 defined on the interior of the set D from the previous example by the program

$q_1(a) \leftarrow p(a).$
$q_2(a) \leftarrow \neg p(a).$

(The output signature of f_2 consists of a, q_1, and q_2).

Now we are ready to formulate our realization theorem for interpolation.

Theorem 3.7.3 (Realization theorem for interpolation) [GG99, GG97] Let f be a closed domain specification with domain D represented by an lp-function π and let $\tilde{\pi}$ be the program obtained from π by replacing some occurrences of input literals l in $pos(\pi)$ by **not** $\bar{l}$. Then $\{\tilde{\pi}, \sigma_i(f), \sigma_o(f), \mathrm{dom}(\tilde{f})\}$ is an lp-function and if $\tilde{\pi}$ is separable and monotonic then $\tilde{\pi}$ represents $\tilde{f}$. □

3.7.5 Representing domain completion and realization of input opening

Let C be a collection of constraints of the form $\leftarrow \Delta$ where $\Delta \subset lit(\sigma)$. A constraint is called *binary* if Δ consists of two literals. We say that a domain D is defined by C if D consists of complete sets from $states(\sigma)$ satisfying C.

Theorem 3.7.4 [GG99, GG97] Let C be a set of binary constraints and D be the closed domain defined by C. Let $\tilde{\pi}_D$ be a program obtained from C by replacing each rule $\leftarrow l_1, l_2$ by the rules $\neg l_1 \leftarrow l_2$ and $\neg l_2 \leftarrow l_1$.

If for every $l \in lit(\sigma)$ there is a set $Z \in D$ not containing l then the lp-function $\{\tilde{\pi}_D, \sigma, \sigma, D^\circ\}$ represents domain completion of D. □

By virtue of Proposition 59 we can realize input opening by composing – through incremental extension – interpolation with domain completion.

3.7.6 Realization theorem for input extension

Definition 66 Let π be an lp-function. The result of replacing every rule

$$l_0 \leftarrow l_1, \ldots, l_m, \textbf{not } l_{m+1}, \ldots, \textbf{not } l_n.$$

of π with $l_0 \in lit(\sigma_\circ(f))$ by the rule

$$l_0 \leftarrow l_1, \ldots, l_m, \textbf{not } l_{m+1}, \ldots, \textbf{not } l_n, \textbf{not } \bar{l}_0.$$

is called the *guarded version* of π and is denoted by $\hat{\pi}$. □

Theorem 3.7.5 (Realization theorem for input extension) [GP96] Let f be a specification represented by lp-function π with signature σ. If the set $U = lit(\sigma) \setminus lit(\sigma_\circ)$ is a splitting set of π dividing π into two components $\pi_2 = top_U(\pi)$ and $\pi_1 = bot_U(\pi)$ then the lp-function $\pi^* = \pi_1 \cup \hat{\pi}_2$ represents the input extension f^* of f.   □

3.8 Filter-abducible AnsProlog$^{\neg, or}$ programs

Our concern in this section is to explore when an AnsProlog$^{\neg, or}$ program can incorporate abductive reasoning. Such reasoning is necessary to assimilate observations to a given knowledge base and is a richer notion than the notion of input extension in Section 3.7.2 and 3.7.6 where we discussed the refinement of an lp-function so that the refined function allowed input – without being inconsistent – that was only part of the output of the original lp-function.

Consider the following AnsProlog program Π_1:

$p \leftarrow a.$
$p \leftarrow b.$

Suppose we would like to assimilate our observation that p is true with respect to the knowledge encoded in Π_1. Then our intuitive conclusion would be that $a \vee b$ must be true. A reasoning mechanism that leads to such conclusions is called abductive reasoning and in this particular example, we cannot make the intended conclusion by just adding p to the program Π_1. Nor can we make the intended conclusion by adding the constraint $\leftarrow$ **not** p to Π_1. The latter is referred to as *filtering* program Π_1 with the observation p.

Let us now consider the following program Π'_1 that includes Π_1.

$p \leftarrow a.$
$p \leftarrow b.$
$a \leftarrow$ **not** $\neg a.$
$\neg a \leftarrow$ **not** $a.$
$b \leftarrow$ **not** $\neg b.$
$\neg b \leftarrow$ **not** $b.$

In this case, we can make the intended conclusion $(a \vee b)$ by adding the constraint $\leftarrow$ **not** p to Π'_1. Our goal in this section is to develop conditions when the intended abductive conclusions due to observations can be made by filtering a program with the observations. We refer to such programs as *filter-abducible*. We start by formalizing the notion of abduction in AnsProlog$^{\neg, or}$ programs.

3.8.1 Basic definitions: simple abduction and filtering

When formulating abduction in AnsProlog¬, or programs we designate a complete subset *Abd* of *Lit* as abducible literals. The set of atoms in *Abd* is denoted by Abd_a. Similarly, we designate a complete subset Obs_l of *Lit* as observable literals. The set of atoms in Obs_l is denoted by Obs_a and the set of formulas made up of literals in Obs_l and classical connectives will be denoted by the set *Obs*. We will often refer to *Obs* as *the set of observables*, and a subset *Q* of *Obs* as an *observation*. *Q* may be represented by a set of formulas with variables, where the variables serve as schema variables and are substituted with ground terms in the language to obtain *Q*.

Definition 67 (Explanation) Let Π be an AnsProlog¬, or program and *Q* be an observation. A complete set of abducibles *E* (from *Abd*) is said to be an explanation of *Q* with respect to Π if $\Pi \cup E \models Q$ and $\Pi \cup E$ is consistent (that is, it has a consistent answer set). □

We would now like to define abductive entailment ($\models_{abd}$) with respect to the pair $\langle \Pi, Q \rangle$, which we refer to as an *abductive program*. Reasoning using this abductive entailment relation will be our formulation of *abductive reasoning*.

Definition 68 (Abductive entailment) Let Π be an AnsProlog¬, or program and *Q* be an observation.

 (i) *M* is an answer set of $\langle \Pi, Q \rangle$ if there exists an explanation *E* of *Q* with respect to Π such that *M* is an answer set of $\Pi \cup E$.
 (ii) For any formula *f*, $\langle \Pi, Q \rangle \models_{abd} f$ if *f* is true in all answer sets of $\langle \Pi, Q \rangle$. □

Proposition 60 Abductive theories are monotonic with respect to the addition of observations. □

Proof: Suppose we have $Q_1 \subseteq Q_2$. Then any explanation of Q_2 with respect to *T* is an explanation of Q_1 with respect to *T*. Thus answer sets of $\langle \Pi, Q_2 \rangle$ are answer sets of $\langle \Pi, Q_1 \rangle$ and hence, $\models_{abd}$ is monotonic with respect to *Q*. □

Definition 69 Let Π be an AnsProlog¬, or program and *Q* be an observation. By *Filter*(Π, Q), we refer to the subset of answer sets of Π which entail *Q*. □

Proposition 61 Entailment with respect to *Filter*(Π, Q) is monotonic with respect to *Q*. □

Proof: Follows directly from the definition of $Filter(\Pi, Q)$.

3.8.2 Abductive reasoning through filtering: semantic conditions

We now present semantic conditions on AnsProlog$^{\neg, or}$ programs, abducibles, and observables such that abductive reasoning can be done through filtering. We now formally define such triplets.

Definition 70 (Filter-abducible) An AnsProlog$^{\neg, or}$ program Π, a set *Abd*, and a set *Obs* are said to be *filter-abducible* if for all possible observations $Q \in Obs$; $Filter(\Pi, Q)$ is the set of answer sets of $\langle \Pi, Q \rangle$.   □

Before we define conditions for filter-abducibility, we first work out the filter-abducibility of the programs Π_1 and Π'_1.

Example 75 Consider the AnsProlog$^\neg$ program Π_1:

$p \leftarrow a$.
$p \leftarrow b$.
Let $Abd = \{a, b, \neg a, \neg b\}$, and $Obs_a = \{p\}$.

Let $Q = \{p\}$. It is easy to see that the answer sets of $\langle \Pi_1, Q \rangle$ are $\{\{p, a, \neg b\}, \{p, b, \neg a\}, \{p, a, b\}\}$, while $Filter(\Pi_1, Q) = \emptyset$.

Now consider Π'_1 to be the following AnsProlog$^\neg$ program, where we have added four new rules to Π_1.

$p \leftarrow a$.
$p \leftarrow b$.
$a \leftarrow \textbf{not } \neg a$.
$\neg a \leftarrow \textbf{not } a$.
$b \leftarrow \textbf{not } \neg b$.
$\neg b \leftarrow \textbf{not } b$.

It is easy to see that the set of answer sets of $\langle \Pi'_1, Q \rangle$ is $\{\{p, a, \neg b\}, \{p, b, \neg a\}, \{p, a, b\}\}$ which is the same as $Filter(\Pi'_1, Q)$.

Note that the set of answer sets of $\Pi'_1 \cup Q$ is $\{\{p, a, \neg b\}, \{p, b, \neg a\}, \{p, a, b\}, \{p, \neg b, \neg a\}\}$ and is different from $Filter(\Pi'_1, Q)$.   □

Now let us compare Π_1 and Π'_1 and analyze the differences. Syntactically, the difference between them is the last four rules of Π'_1. These four rules guarantee that Π'_1 has at least one answer set corresponding to each potential explanation (i.e., interpretation of the abducibles). During filtering there is no scope to try each potential explanation so as not to miss any explanation, as there is during abductive reasoning, and thus the answer sets of the program should enumerate the potential explanations. This is missing in Π_1 and therefore Π_1 is not filter-abducible with respect to the above mentioned *Abd* and *Obs*. On the other hand, Π_1' satisfies this criteria and it is filter-abducible with respect to the same *Abd* and *Obs*. In the following paragraphs, we precisely state the above mentioned property as condition B. We now discuss additional conditions that may be important.

For filtering to be equivalent to abductive reasoning, each one of the answer sets obtained by filtering a program Π with an observation Q should contain an explanation of the observation. In that case the abducibles in those answer sets consist of an explanation. For that to happen, the program must be such that the abducibles uniquely determine the observables. If we want to avoid making any restrictions on the observables then the program must be such that the abducibles uniquely determine the answer set. These two conditions are precisely stated below as Condition A' and Condition A, respectively.

We now formally state the above mentioned conditions.

Condition A

If M is an answer set of a program Π then M is the unique answer set of the program $\Pi \cup (M \cap Abd)$.

Intuitively, Condition A means that the answer sets of a program Π can be characterized by just the abducible literals in that answer set. It requires that if M is an answer set of a program Π then M should be the only answer set of the program $\Pi \cup (M \cap Abd)$. This is a strong condition, as in many cases $\Pi \cup (M \cap Abd)$ may have multiple answer sets. To take into account such cases, we can weaken condition A by the following condition. But we will need to use *Obs* as part of our condition.

Condition A'

If M is an answer set of program Π then:

 (i) M is an answer set of $\Pi \cup (M \cap Abd)$;

 (ii) all answer sets of $\Pi \cup (M \cap Abd)$ are also answer sets of Π; and

(iii) all answer sets of $\Pi \cup (M \cap Abd)$ agree on *Obs*; where two answer sets M_1 and M_2 of a program are said to agree on *Obs* if for all $Q \in Obs$, we have $M_1 \models Obs$ iff $M_2 \models Obs$.

Condition B

For any complete subset E of *Abd* if $\Pi \cup E$ is consistent then there exists an answer set M of Π such that $M \cap Abd = E$.

Intuitively, Condition B means that the program Π has answer sets corresponding to each possible interpretation of the abducibles. That is, the answer sets of the program Π enumerate the possible explanations.

Lemma 3.8.1 Let Π be a program satisfying Conditions A and B. Let E be any complete subset of *Abd*. If M is an answer set of $\Pi \cup E$, then $M \cap Abd = E$. $\square$

Proof:
Let E be any complete subset of *Abd*.
From Condition B we have that there exists an answer set M' of Π such that
  $M' \cap Abd = E$.
But from Condition A, we have that M' is the unique answer set of $\Pi \cup E$.
Thus if M is an answer set of $\Pi \cup E$, then $M = M'$ and thus $M \cap Abd = E$. $\square$

Theorem 3.8.2 If Π, *Obs*, and *Abd* satisfy Conditions A' and B then they are filter-abducible; that is, they satisfy the following:
'for all observations $Q \in Obs$, *Filter*(Π, Q) is the set of answer sets of $\langle \Pi, Q \rangle$.' $\square$

Proof:
(a) We first show that if Π, *Obs*, and *Abd* satisfy Conditions A' and B then all elements of *Filter*(Π, Q) are answer sets of $\langle \Pi, Q \rangle$.

Let M be an element of *Filter*(Π, Q).
$\Rightarrow M$ is an answer set of Π and M entails Q.
From A' we have $\Pi \cup (M \cap Abd)$ is consistent and all answer sets of $\Pi \cup (M \cap Abd)$ are also answer sets of Π and agree on the observables.
Let $E = M \cap Abd$.
We then have $\Pi \cup E \models Q$ and $\Pi \cup E$ is consistent.
$\Rightarrow$ There exists an explanation E of Q with respect to Π such that M is an answer set of $\Pi \cup E$.
$\Rightarrow M$ is an answer set of $\langle \Pi, Q \rangle$.

(b) We will now show that if Π, *Obs*, and *Abd* satisfy Conditions A' and B then all answer sets of $\langle \Pi, Q \rangle$ are in *Filter*(Π, Q).

Let M be an answer set of $\langle \Pi, Q \rangle$.
$\Rightarrow$ There exists an explanation E of Q with respect to Π such that M is an answer set of $\Pi \cup E$.
$\Rightarrow$ There exists a complete set of abducibles E such that $\Pi \cup E \models Q$ and $\Pi \cup E$ is consistent and M is an answer set of $\Pi \cup E$.
From Condition B we have that there exists an answer set M' of Π such that $M' \cap Abd = E$. But from Condition A' all answer sets of $\Pi \cup E$ are also answer sets of Π and agree on Q.

Thus M is an answer set of Π. Since M is also an answer set of $\Pi \cup E$ and $\Pi \cup E \not\models Q$, we have M entails Q.

Thus $M \in \mathit{Filter}(\Pi, Q)$. □

Lemma 3.8.3 If Π, *Obs*, and *Abd* satisfy condition A then they also satisfy Condition A'. □

Proof: Straightforward.

Corollary 1 If an AnsProlog$^{\neg, or}$ program Π, and abducibles *Abd* satisfy Conditions A and B then for any set of Obs_l in the language of Π, the program Π, and the sets *Abd* and *Obs* are filter-abducible. □

Proof: Follows directly from Lemma 3.8.3 and Theorem 3.8.2.

The main significance of the above corollary is that by requiring the more restrictive Condition A we have more flexibility with the observables.

We now give an example where we can verify filter-abducibility by verifying the above mentioned conditions.

Example 76 The following AnsProlog$^{\neg, or}$ program Π_2'

$q \; or \; r \leftarrow a.$
$p \leftarrow a.$
$p \leftarrow b.$
$a \; or \; \neg a \leftarrow.$
$b \; or \; \neg b \leftarrow.$

with abducibles $\{a, b, \neg a, \neg b\}$ and $\mathit{Obs}_a = \{p\}$ satisfies Conditions A' and B.

This can be verified as follows. The program Π_2' has six answer sets, which are: $\{a, b, p, q\}, \{a, b, p, r\}, \{a, \neg b, p, q\}, \{a, \neg b, p, r\}, \{\neg a, b, p\}$, and $\{\neg a, \neg b\}$. Let us refer to them as M_1, M_2, M_3, M_4, M_5 and M_6 respectively. Consider the answer set M_1. Let us verify that it satisfies Condition A'. It is easy to see that M_1 is an answer set of $\Pi_2' \cup (M_1 \cap \mathit{Abd}) = \Pi_2' \cup \{a, b\}$, and all answer sets of $\Pi_2' \cup \{a, b\}$ are answer sets of Π_2' and they agree on *Obs*. We can similarly verify that the other answer sets of Π_2' satisfy the conditions of A'. (Note that if we include either q or r in Obs_a, Condition A' will no longer be satisfied.)

In this example there are four complete subsets of *Abd*. These are: $\{a, b\}$, $\{a, \neg b\}, \{\neg a, b\}, \{\neg a, \neg b\}$. Consider $E = \{a, b\}$. Since $\Pi_2' \cup E$ is consistent, we need to verify that there exists an answer set M of Π_2' such that $M \cap \mathit{Abd} = E$. M_1 is such an answer set of Π_2'. We can similarly verify that the other complete subsets of *Abd* satisfy Condition B. □

3.8.3 Sufficiency conditions for filter-abducibility
of AnsProlog$^{\neg, or}$ programs

In this subsection we will we will give some sufficiency conditions that guarantee that Conditions A' and B of the previous subsection hold. That will guarantee the filter-abducibility of AnsProlog$^{\neg, or}$ programs. The conditions involve the notion of splitting from Section 3.4 and the notion of an AnsProlog$^{\neg, or}$ program being functional from Section 1.4.4.

Proposition 62 An AnsProlog$^{\neg, or}$ program Π is filter-abducible with respect to abducibles *Abd* and observables *Obs* if

  (i) Π is functional from *Abd* to Obs_l,
 (ii) for all $l, \neg l \in Abd, l$ or $\neg l \leftarrow.$ is in Π, and
(iii) *Abd* is a splitting set for Π.   □

Proof: We prove this by showing that the Conditions (i)–(ii) above imply the Conditions A' and B which in turn guarantee filter abducibility of a program.

(a) **Showing** $A'(i)$
We now show that the Conditions (i)–(ii) imply $A'(i)$.
When Π is inconsistent this result trivially holds. Let us consider the case when Π is consistent.
Let M be a consistent answer set of Π.
$\Rightarrow M$ is an answer set of Π^M.
$\Rightarrow M$ is an answer set of $\Pi^M \cup (M \cap Abd)$.
$\Rightarrow M$ is an answer set of $(T \cup (M \cap Abd))^M$.
$\Rightarrow M$ is an answer set of $\Pi \cup (M \cap Abd)$.
$\Rightarrow$ Condition $A'(i)$ holds.
(b) **Showing** $A'(ii)$
Let M be an answer set of Π. It is clear that $M \cap Abd$ is a complete set of abducible literals and is an answer set of $bot_{Abd}(T)$. Thus by Theorem 3.4.1, all answer sets of $\Pi \cup (M \cap Abd)$ are answer sets of Π. Thus Condition $A'(ii)$ holds.
(c) **Showing** $A'(iii)$
Since Π is functional from *Abd* to *Obs* and $M \cap Abd$ is a complete set of abducible literals, it is clear that Condition $A'(iii)$ holds.
(d) **Showing B**
Let E be any arbitrary complete subset of *Abd*. From Condition (ii) of the proposition, E is an answer set of $bot_{Abd}(T)$. Hence by Theorem 3.4.1, there exists an answer set M of Π, such that $M \cap Abd = E$. Thus Condition B is satisfied.   □

In Section 3.8.2 we showed that the Conditions A' and B are sufficient for filter-abducibility. We now show that they are also necessary.

3.8.4 Necessary conditions for filter-abducibility

Theorem 3.8.4 Let Π be a program, and *Obs* and *Abd* be observables and abducibles such that, for all $Q \in Obs$, *Filter*(Π, Q) is equivalent to the set of answer sets of $\langle \Pi, Q \rangle$. Then Π, *Obs*, and *Abd* satisfy the Conditions B, $A'(i)$, $A'(ii)$, and $A'(iii)$. $\qquad\Box$

Proof:

(i) Suppose Π, *Obs*, and *Abd* do not satisfy Condition B. That means there exists an $E \subseteq Abd$, such that $\Pi \cup E$ is consistent, but there does not exist an answer set M of Π such that $M \cap Abd = E$.

Since $\Pi \cup E$ is consistent it has at least one answer set. Let M^* be an answer set of $\Pi \cup E$. Let Q be the conjunction of the literals in $M^* \cap Obs_l$. Obviously M^* is an answer set of $\langle \Pi, Q \rangle$. Since M^* is an answer set of $\Pi \cup E$, $M^* \cap Abd = E$. But then from our initial assumption, M^* cannot be an answer set of Π. Hence M^* is not in *Filter*(Π, Q). This contradicts the assumption in the theorem that *Filter*(Π, Q) is equivalent to the set of answer sets of $\langle \Pi, Q \rangle$. Hence Π must satisfy Condition B.

(ii) Suppose Π, *Obs*, and *Abd* do not satisfy Condition $A'(i)$. That means there is an answer set M of Π which is not an answer set of $T \cup (M \cap Abd)$. Let $Q = M \cap Abd$. Obviously, M is in *Filter*(Π, Q). We will now show that M is not an answer set of $\langle \Pi, Q \rangle$. Suppose M is an answer set of $\langle \Pi, Q \rangle$. That means there is an $E \subseteq Abd$, such that M is an answer set of $\Pi \cup E$ and $M \models Q$. But then $M \cap Abd = E$, and this contradicts our initial assumption that M is not an answer set of $T \cup (M \cap Abd)$. Hence M is not an answer set of $\langle \Pi, Q \rangle$. But this contradicts the assumption in the theorem that *Filter*(Π, Q) is equivalent to the set of answer sets of $\langle \Pi, Q \rangle$. Hence Π must satisfy Condition $A'(i)$.

(iii) Suppose Π, *Obs*, and *Abd* do not satisfy Condition $A'(ii)$. That means there is an answer set M of Π such that all answer sets of $T \cup (M \cap Abd)$ are not answer sets of Π. Let $Q = M \cap Abd$. Let M' be an answer set of $T \cup (M \cap Abd)$ which is not an answer set of Π. Obviously, M' is an answer set of $\langle \Pi, Q \rangle$. But it is not an element of *Filter*(Π, Q). This contradicts the assumption in the theorem that *Filter*(Π, Q) is equivalent to the set of answer sets of $\langle \Pi, Q \rangle$. Hence Π must satisfy Condition $A'(ii)$.

(iv) Suppose Π, *Obs*, and *Abd* do not satisfy Condition $A'(iii)$. That means there is an answer set M of Π such that all answer sets of $T \cup (M \cap Abd)$ do not agree on the observables. This means $Obs_l \setminus Abd \neq \emptyset$. Let $Q = (M \cap Obs_l) \cup (M \cap Abd)$. Obviously, M is in *Filter*(Π, Q). We will now show that M is not an answer set of $\langle \Pi, Q \rangle$. Suppose M is an answer set of $\langle T, Q \rangle$. That means there is a complete subset E of *Abd*, such that M is an answer set of $\Pi \cup E$ and $\Pi \cup E \models Q$. Since E is a complete subset of *Abd*, $E = M \cap Abd$. Since all answer sets of $T \cup (M \cap Abd)$ do not agree on observables $\Pi \cup E \not\models Q$. This contradicts our assumption and hence M is not an answer set of $\langle \Pi, Q \rangle$. But then, we have a contradiction to the assumption in the theorem that *Filter*(Π, Q) is equivalent to the set of answer sets of $\langle \Pi, Q \rangle$. Hence Π must satisfy Condition A'(iii). $\qquad \square$

We would like to mention that the known ways to satisfy Condition B in logic programs are to have rules of the form $l \, or \, \neg l$ (or have two rules of the form $l \leftarrow \mathbf{not} \, \neg l., \neg l \leftarrow \mathbf{not} \, l.$) for all abducible atoms l in logic programs. The former was first used in [Ino91] to relate semantics of abductive logic programs – based on the generalized stable models [KM90], and AnsProlog¬ programs. Hence the necessity of Condition B for filter-abducibility makes it necessary (to the best of our knowledge) to have such rules in filter-abducible logic programs.

3.8.5 *Weak abductive reasoning vs filtering*

Several instances of filtering used in the literature that define an intuitively meaningful entailment relation do not satisfy the conditions described earlier in this paper. In particular, when actions have non-deterministic effects (as in [Tur97]) filtering may still make intuitive sense, but our current definition of abductive reasoning is too strong to match the entailment defined through filtering. The following example illustrates our point.

Consider the AnsProlog¬, ^{or} program: Π

$a \, or \, b \leftarrow p.$
$p \, or \, \neg p \leftarrow.$

where $Abd = \{p, \neg p\}$, and $Obs_a = \{a, b\}$. Suppose we observe a. Using filtering we would be able to conclude (in this case, intuitively explain our observation by) p. That is, p will be true for all answer sets of *Filter*$(\Pi, \{a\})$. But the current definition of abductive reasoning is too strong to explain this observation by p. (Note that the above program will violate our Condition A'(iii).) This rigidity of abductive reasoning has been noticed earlier and several suggestions for weaker versions have been made; for example in [Gel90, Rei87, Sha97]. In this section we define a weaker notion of abductive reasoning and show that it is equivalent to filtering under less restrictive conditions than given in the earlier sections; in particular, we no longer need Condition A'(iii). As a result we can also weaken the sufficiency conditions in Propositions 62. We now formally define *weak abductive entailment* and state theorems and propositions similar to the ones in the previous sections.

Definition 71 (Weak abductive entailment) Let Π be an AnsProlog⁻, ᵒʳ program, and Q be an observation.

(i) M is a weak answer set of $\langle \Pi, Q \rangle$ if there exists a complete subset E of abducibles such that M is an answer set of $\Pi \cup E$ and $M \not\models Q$.

(ii) For any formula f, $\langle \Pi, Q \rangle \models_{wabd} f$ if f is true in all weak answer sets of $\langle T, Q \rangle$. □

Definition 72 (Weak-filter-abducible) An AnsProlog⁻, ᵒʳ program Π, a set Abd, and a set Obs are said to be *weak-filter-abducible* if for all possible observations $Q \in Obs$ we have $Filter(\Pi, Q)$ as the set of weak answer sets of $\langle T, Q \rangle$. □

Theorem 3.8.5 (Sufficiency) [Bar00] Let Π be an AnsProlog⁻, ᵒʳ program, and Obs and Abd be observables. If Π, Obs, and Abd satisfy Conditions $A'(i)$, $A'(ii)$, and B then they are weak-filter-abducible. □

Theorem 3.8.6 (Necessity) [Bar00] Let Π be an AnsProlog⁻, ᵒʳ program, and Obs and Abd be observables and abducibles such that, for all $Q \in Obs$, $Filter(\Pi, Q)$ is equivalent to the set of weak-answer sets of $\langle \Pi, Q \rangle$. Then Π, Obs, and Abd satisfy the Conditions B, $A'(i)$, and $A'(ii)$. □

Proposition 63 [Bar00] An AnsProlog⁻, ᵒʳ program Π is weak-filter-abducible with respect to abducibles Abd and observables Obs if

(i) for all $l, \neg l \in Abd$, l or $\neg l \leftarrow.$ is in Π, and
(ii) Abd is a splitting set for Π. □

Exercise 13 Formulate a broader notion of abductive reasoning in AnsProlog⁻, ᵒʳ programs by expanding the notion of explanations, to allow incomplete subsets of the abducibles. Such a notion of abductive reasoning in default theories is defined in [EGL97].

Hint: To do abductive reasoning using filtering in this case, the formulation should again be such that its answer sets enumerate the various possible explanations. Suppose $Abd = \{p, \neg p\}$. Now that we intend to allow explanations to be incomplete subsets of the abducibles, the set of possible explanations will be $\{\{p\}, \{\neg p\}, \{\}\}$. Since answer sets are minimal sets, there does not exist a logic program whose answer sets will be these three possible explanations. The minimality condition will eliminate the first two, in the presence of the third. One way to overcome this would be to use a special fluent u_p (meaning *uncommitted about p*) to represent the third explanation. Then we can have AnsProlog$^{\neg,\, or}$ programming rules of the form:

$$p \; or \; \neg p \; or \; u\_p \; \leftarrow \; .$$ □

3.9 Equivalence of programs and semantics preserving transformations

In this section we explore the circumstances governing when two AnsProlog* program are 'equivalent'. There are several notions of equivalence, starting from the simple notion that they have the same answer sets to the more rigorous notion that they encode the same function. Having such notions of equivalence is very useful. We can use them to transform a program to an equivalent program that eliminates certain syntactic features so that they are suitable for a more restricted interpreter. In this respect we discuss conditions when transformations that eliminate the **not** operator, rules with empty heads, and disjunctions (*or*) respectively, result in an equivalent program.

3.9.1 Fold/Unfold transformations

Among the earliest transformations are notions of folding and unfolding. The following example illustrates both of these transformations.

Consider a program Π containing the following three rules and no other rules with p and q in its head.

$r_1: p \leftarrow q, r.$
$r_2: q \leftarrow s.$
$r_3: q \leftarrow t.$

The first rule r_1 can be *unfolded* with respect to the other two rules r_2 and r_3 and we will have the following two rules:

$r_4: p \leftarrow s, r.$
$r_5: p \leftarrow t, r.$

which can replace the rule r_1 in Π without affecting the meaning of the program.

Similarly, consider a program Π' consisting of r_2–r_5. In that case we can replace r_4 and r_5 in Π' by the single rule r_1 without affecting the meaning of Π'. Replacing r_4 and r_5 by r_1 in the presence of r_2 corresponds to *folding*.

To formalize the above intuitive notions of folding and unfolding with respect to rules with variables, we need the notion of substitutions, unifiers, and most general unifiers.

Substitutions and unifiers

A substitution is a finite mapping from variables to terms, and is written as

$$\theta = \{X_1/t_1, \ldots, X_n/t_n\}$$

The notation implies that $X_1, \ldots, X_n$ are distinct, and we assume that for $i = 1, \ldots, n$, X_i is different from t_i. Substitutions operate on terms, a sequence of gen-literals, or a rule as a whole. Substitutions can be composed. Given substitutions $\theta = \{X_1/t_1, \ldots, X_n/t_n\}$ and $\eta = \{Y_1/s_1, \ldots, Y_m/s_m\}$ their composition $\theta\eta$ is defined by removing from the set $\theta = \{X_1/t_1\eta, \ldots, X_n/t_n\eta, Y_1/s_1, \ldots, Y_m/s_m\}$ those pairs $X_i/t_i\eta$, where $X_i \equiv t_i\eta$ as well as those pairs Y_i/s_i for which $Y_i \in \{X_1, \ldots, X_n\}$.

For example if $\theta = \{X/3, Y/f(X, a)\}$ and $\eta = \{X/4, Y/5, Z/a\}$ then $\theta\eta = \{X/3, Y/f(4, a), Z/a\}$.

A substitution θ is said to be *more general* than a substitution η, if for some substitution γ we have $\eta = \theta\gamma$.

We say θ is a *unifier* for two atoms A and B if $A\theta \equiv B\theta$. A unifier θ of two atoms A and B is said to be the *most general unifier (or mgu)* of A and B if it is more general than any other unifier of A and B. Robinson in [Rob65] showed that if two atoms are unifiable then they have a most general unifier. The notion of unifiers and mgu is directly extendable to gen-literals, terms, and rules.

Folding and unfolding

Definition 73 (Initial program) An *initial program* Π_0 is an AnsProlog$^-$ program satisfying the following condition:

Π_0 can be partitioned into two programs Π_{new} and Π_{old} such that the set of predicates in the head of the rules of Π_{new} – referred to as the *new* predicates, neither appear in the body of the rules in Π_{new} nor appear in Π_{old}. The set of predicates in the head of the rules of Π_{old} are referred to as the *old* predicates   □

Note that the partition of an initial program is slightly different from the notion of splitting. When splitting a program into a top part and a bottom part the predicates in the head of rules of the top part can be in the body of the rules in the top part. Such is not the case with respect to Π_{new}.

Definition 74 (Unfolding) Let Π_i be an AnsProlog$^-$ program and C be a rule in Π_i of the form: $H \leftarrow A, L.$, where A is a literal, and L is a sequence of gen-literals. Suppose that $C_1, \ldots, C_k$ are all the rules in Π_i such that C_j is of the form $A_j \leftarrow K_j.$, where K_j is a sequence of gen-literals, and A_j is unifiable with A, by an mgu θ_j for each j ($1 \le j \le k$). Then $\Pi_{i+1} = (\Pi_i \setminus \{C\}) \cup \{H\theta_j \leftarrow K_j\theta_j, L\theta_j. : 1 \le j \le k\}$, is a program obtained by unfolding Π, whose selected atom is A. C is called the *unfolded rule* and $C_1, \ldots, C_k$ are called the *unfolding rules*.   □

We now discuss two different notions of folding: TSS-folding is due to Tamaki, Seki, and Satoh and is defined in [TS84, Sek91, Sek93]; and MGS-folding is due to Maher, Gardner, and Shepherdson and is defined in [GS91, Mah87, Mah90, Mah93b].

Definition 75 (TSS-Folding) Let Π be an AnsProlog$^\neg$ program that has a partition Π_{new} and Π_{old}. Let Π_i be a subset of Π, C be a rule in Π_{new} (not necessarily in Π_i) of the form $A \leftarrow K, L.$, where K and L are sequences of gen-literals, and D be a rule of the form $B \leftarrow K'.$, where K' is a sequence of gen-literals. Suppose there exists a substitution θ satisfying the following conditions:

(1) $K'\theta = K$.
(2) Let $X_1, \ldots, X_j, \ldots, X_m$ be variables that appear only in the body K' of D but not in B. Then, each $X_j\theta$ is a variable in C such that it appears in none of A, L, and $B\theta$. Furthermore, $X_j\theta \neq X_{j'}\theta$ if $j \neq j'$.
(3) D is the only clause in Π_i whose head is unifiable with $B\theta$.
(4) Either the predicate of A is an old predicate, or C is the result of applying unfolding at least once to a clause in Π_0.

Then $\Pi_{i+1} = (\Pi_i \setminus C) \cup \{A \leftarrow B\theta, L.\}$ is called a TSS-folding of Π_i, the rule C is called the folded rule and the rule D is called the folding rule. $\square$

Definition 76 (MGS-Folding) Let Π_i be an AnsProlog$^\neg$ program, C be a rule in Π_i of the form $A \leftarrow K, L.$, where K and L are sequences of gen-literals, and D be a rule of the form $B \leftarrow K'.$, where K' is a sequence of gen-literals. Suppose there exists a substitution θ satisfying the following conditions:

(1) $K'\theta = K$.
(2) Let $X_1, \ldots, X_j, \ldots, X_m$ be variables that appear only in the body K' of D but not in B. Then, each $X_j\theta$ is a variable in C such that it appears in none of A, L, and $B\theta$. Furthermore, $X_j\theta \neq X_{j'}\theta$ if $j \neq j'$.
(3) D is the only clause in Π_i whose head is unifiable with $B\theta$.
(4) C is different from D.

Then $\Pi_{i+1} = (\Pi_i \setminus C) \cup \{A \leftarrow B\theta, L.\}$ is called an MGS-folding of Π_i, the rule C is called the folded rule, and the rule D is called the folding rule. $\square$

Definition 77 Let Π_0 be an initial AnsProlog$^\neg$ program and Π_{i+1} ($i \geq 0$) be obtained from Π_i by applying either unfolding, TSS-folding, or MGS-folding. Then the sequence of programs $\Pi_0, \ldots, \Pi_N$ is called a transformation sequence starting from Π_0. $\square$

Proposition 64 [AD95] The answer sets of any program Π_i in a transformation sequence starting from an initial AnsProlog$^\neg$ program Π_0 are the same as the answer sets of Π_0. $\qquad\square$

3.9.2 Replacing disjunctions in the head of rules

In this section we discuss two conditions which allow us to replace disjunctions in the head of rules by constraints, and AnsProlog$^\neg$ rules respectively. The motivation behind replacing disjunctions is that some interpreters either allow only AnsProlog$^\neg$ programs or are optimized for such programs. Moreover, as we will show in Chapter 6, in general AnsProlog$^{\neg, or}$ programs have a higher expressiveness and complexity than AnsProlog$^\neg$ programs. Thus an interpreter for AnsProlog$^{\neg, or}$ programs may not be efficient for AnsProlog$^\neg$ programs, and therefore if efficiency is a concern we should eliminate the disjunctions if possible. Also, even when efficiency is not a concern, it is useful to find out while using disjunctions, whether the disjunction is mandatory – that is, the problem needs the higher expressiveness, or whether it is for convenience and ease of representation.

We now present the two transformations. Given a rule r of the form (1.2.1)

- *constraint*(r) denotes the constraint:

  $\leftarrow$ **not** $L_0, \ldots,$ **not** $L_k, L_{k+1}, \ldots, L_m,$ **not** $L_{m+1}, \ldots,$ **not** L_n.

- and *disj_to_normal*(r) denotes the following $k + 1$ rules:

  $L_i \leftarrow$ **not** $L_0, \ldots$ **not** $L_{i-1},$ **not** $L_{i+1}, \ldots,$ **not** $L_k, L_{k+1}, \ldots, L_m,$
  not $L_{m+1}, \ldots,$ **not** L_n.

  where $0 \le i \le k$.

We now present the result that governs when AnsProlog$^{\neg, or}$ rules in a program can be replaced by AnsProlog$^\neg$ rules, while keeping the answer sets unchanged.

Theorem 3.9.1 [BED92] Let Π be an AnsProlog$^{\neg, or}$ program. Let Π' be the program obtained by replacing each rule r in Π with disjunctions in its head by the set of rules *disj_to_normal*(r). If Π is head cycle free then Π and Π' have the same consistent answer sets. $\qquad\square$

Example 77 Consider the following AnsProlog$^{\neg, or}$ program Π.

a or b or c $\leftarrow$.

It has three answer sets, $\{a\}$, $\{b\}$, and $\{c\}$. It is easy to check that Π is a head cycle free program. Let us consider the AnsProlog$^\neg$ obtained by replacing each rule r in

Π by the set *disj_to_normal*(r). We then obtain the following program.

$a \leftarrow \mathbf{not}\ b, \mathbf{not}\ c.$
$b \leftarrow \mathbf{not}\ c, \mathbf{not}\ a.$
$c \leftarrow \mathbf{not}\ a, \mathbf{not}\ b.$

It is easy to check that it also has only three answer sets, the same as the answer sets of Π. $\square$

Also recall that the program Π from Example 62 is not head cycle free and thus the above theorem is not applicable to it. This conforms with our discussion in Example 30 where we showed that if we replace the rules r from Π with disjunctions in their head by the set of rules *disj_to_normal*(r) then we do not have a program with the same answer sets as before.

We now present the result that determines when an AnsProlog$^{\neg,\mathit{or}}$ rule can be replaced by a constraint while keeping the answer sets unchanged.

Theorem 3.9.2 [LT95] Let Π and Π' be AnsProlog$^{\neg,\mathit{or}}$ programs, and let Γ be a saturated set of literals such that $Lit \setminus \Gamma$ is a signing for the program $\Pi \cup \Pi'$. If every answer set for Π is complete in Γ and if the head of every rule in Π' is a subset of Γ, then programs $\Pi \cup \Pi'$ and $\Pi \cup constraint(\Pi')$ have the same consistent answer sets. $\square$

3.9.3 From AnsProlog to AnsProlog$^{\mathit{or},-\mathbf{not}}$ and constraints

Any AnsProlog program P can be transformed to an AnsProlog$^{\mathit{or},-\mathbf{not}}$ program P' and a set of constraints IC_P such that the answer sets of P can be obtained by filtering the minimal models of P' by IC_P. The transformation is given as follows:

(1) The AnsProlog$^{\mathit{or},-\mathbf{not}}$ program P' consists of the following:
   (a) Replace each rule of the form $A_0 \leftarrow A_1, \ldots, A_m, \mathbf{not}\ A_{m+1}, \ldots, \mathbf{not}\ A_n.$ in P by the following rule:

   $$A_0\ or\ A'_{m+1}\ or\ A'_n \leftarrow A_1, \ldots, A_m.$$

   where if $A_i = p(\bar{X})$ then A'_i is obtained by replacing p by a new predicate symbol p' of the same arity as p.
   (b) For each predicate symbol p in P, the rule

   $$p'(\bar{X}) \leftarrow p(\bar{X}).$$

   is in P'.
(2) The constraints IC_P consist of the following rules for each symbol p in P:

   $$\leftarrow p'(\bar{X}), \mathbf{not}\ p(\bar{X}).$$

Theorem 3.9.3 [FLMS93] Let P be an AnsProlog program and P' and IC_P be as obtained above.

(i) M is an answer set of P iff $M' = M \cup \{p'(\bar{t}) : p(\bar{t}) \in M\}$ is an answer set of $P' \cup IC_P$.

(ii) M is an answer set of P iff $M' = M \cup \{p'(\bar{t}) : p(\bar{t}) \in M\}$ is a minimal model of P' and M' satisfies IC_P. $\qquad\square$

The following example illustrates the above.

Example 78 Consider the following AnsProlog program P:

$a \leftarrow \textbf{not } b.$

The program P' consists of

$a \text{ or } b' \leftarrow.$
$a' \leftarrow a.$
$b' \leftarrow b.$

and IC_P consists of

$\leftarrow a', \textbf{not } a.$
$\leftarrow b', \textbf{not } b.$

There are two answer sets of P': $\{a, a'\}$ and $\{b'\}$, out of which the second one violates IC_P, while the first one does not.

Indeed $\{a\}$ is the answer set of P. $\qquad\square$

Part (ii) of the above theorem is useful in computing answer sets of AnsProlog programs when there are methods available to compute minimal models of programs without **not**. In the following subsection we describe one such method.

3.9.4 AnsProlog and mixed integer programming

It is well known that models of propositional theories can be obtained by transforming the propositional theory to a set of integer linear constraints involving binary variables and solving these constraints. The transformation is quite straightforward and is given as follows:

For each proposition p, we have a binary variable X_p that can only take values 1 or 0. Without loss of generality, we assume that our propositional theory is of the form

$$(l_{11} \vee \cdots \vee l_{1i_1}) \wedge \cdots \wedge (l_{m1} \vee \cdots \vee l_{mi_m})$$

where l_{jk}s are propositional literals. For a negative literal $l = \neg p$, by X_l we denote $(1 - X_p)$ and for a positive literal $l = p$, by X_l we denote X_p.

The above propositional theory is then transformed to the following set of integer linear constraints:

$$X_{l_{11}} + \cdots + X_{l_{1i_1}} \geq 1$$
$$\vdots$$
$$X_{l_{m1}} + \cdots + X_{l_{mi_m}} \geq 1$$

The models of the propositional theory then correspond to the solution of the above constraints together with the restriction that each variable can only take the value 0 or 1. The latter can be expressed as $0 \leq X_p \leq 1$, for all propositions p. Given a propositional theory P, we refer to the above constraints as ilp(P).

Now if we have the following minimization criteria

$$min \quad \Sigma_{p \text{ is a proposition}} X_p$$

then the solution of the resulting integer linear program (ILP) will correspond to the *cardinality minimal models* (i.e., minimal models based on the ordering $M_1 \leq M_2$ iff $|M_1| \leq |M_2|$) of the propositional theory.

The minimal models of a propositional theory can then be obtained by using an iterative procedure which computes one of the cardinality minimal models and updates the theory so as to eliminate that model in the next iteration. The algorithm is formally described as follows:

Algorithm 2 (Computing minimal models)
(1) *min_model_set* := $\emptyset$ and *Constraints* := $\emptyset$.
(2) Solve the ILP
$$min \quad \Sigma_{p \text{ is a proposition}} X_p$$
subject to ilp(P) $\cup$ *Constraints*.
(3) If no (optimal) solution can be found, halt and return *min_model_set* as the set of minimal models of P.
(4) Otherwise, let M be the model corresponding to the optimal solution found in Step (2). Add M to *min_model_set*.
(5) Add the constraint $\Sigma_{A \in M} X_A \leq (k - 1)$ to *Constraints*, where k is the cardinality of M. Go to Step (2). $\qquad\qquad\square$

Example 79 Consider the propositional theory P given as $(a \vee b) \wedge (a \vee c)$. The constraints ilp($P$) then consists of the following:

$$0 \leq X_a \leq 1$$
$$0 \leq X_b \leq 1$$
$$0 \leq X_c \leq 1$$
$$X_a + X_b \geq 1$$
$$X_a + X_c \geq 1$$

Initially *Constraints* = ∅. Solving the ILP

$$min \ X_a + X_b + X_c$$

subject to ilp(P) ∪ *Constraints* will give us the solution $X_a = 1$ and $X_b = X_c = 0$. The corresponding model M is $\{a\}$. After adding M to *min_model_set* in Step (4) of the above algorithm in Step (5) we will add $X_a \leq 0$ to *Constraints*. Now solving the ILP

$$min \ X_a + X_b + X_c$$

subject to ilp(P) ∪ *Constraints* will give us the solution $X_a = 0$ and $X_b = X_c = 1$.

The corresponding model M' is $\{b, c\}$. After adding M' to *min_model_set* in Step (4) of the above algorithm in Step (5) we will add $X_b + X_c \leq 1$ to *Constraints*. Now solving the ILP

$$min \ X_a + X_b + X_c$$

subject to ilp(P) ∪ *Constraints* will not give us any solution.   □

The above method for computing minimal models of propositional theories can be used for computing minimal models of ground AnsProlog^{or} programs. Using part (ii) of Theorem 3.9.3 we can then compute answer sets of AnsProlog programs by transforming them to an AnsProlog^{or} program and a set of constraints; computing the minimal models of the AnsProlog^{or} program; and checking if the minimal models violate the constraints. An alternative way to compute answer sets of AnsProlog programs is to compute the minimal models of the program or its completion using the above mentioned technique and verifying if they are answer sets.

For AnsProlog^{-not} programs instead of solving the ILP, we can consider real values of the variables and still obtain the unique answer set. More formally,

Theorem 3.9.4 [BNNS94] Let P be an AnsProlog^{-not} program. Then:

(i) There is exactly one integer solution of ilp(P) that minimizes $\Sigma_{p \text{ is a proposition}} X_p$. And this solution corresponds to the unique minimal model of P.
(ii) Suppose the ILP constraints are relaxed such that the variables range over all real values in [0,1] instead of the integers 0, 1. Then there is exactly one solution to this problem, which is identical to the initial integer solution.   □

Since it is well known that solving linear programming problems over real numbers is significantly easier than solving them over integers, the above theorem is significant.

3.9.5 Strongly equivalent AnsProlog* programs and the logic of here-and-there

The simple notion of equivalence that we discussed so far is not adequate if we were to treat AnsProlog* programs as functions. For example the two programs $\{p(X) \leftarrow q(X)., r(X) \leftarrow s(X).\}$ and $\{r(X) \leftarrow s(X).\}$ have the same answer sets, but definitely do not encode the same information. That is because the meaning of the two programs together with a new fact $q(a)$ would be different. Similarly, the programs $\{p(X) \leftarrow q(X)., q(a) \leftarrow ., r(b) \leftarrow .\}$ and $\{p(a) \leftarrow ., q(a) \leftarrow ., r(b) \leftarrow .\}$ also have the same answer sets, but rarely will we consider replacing one with the other. The only time the simpler notion of equivalence is useful is when we are computing answer sets of the programs. If we were to treat programs as representing knowledge, or as encoding functions, we need a stronger notion of equivalence. Such a notion is defined below.

Definition 78 Two AnsProlog* programs Π_1 and Π_2 are said to be *strongly equivalent* if for every Π, $\Pi_1 \cup \Pi$ and $\Pi_2 \cup \Pi$ have the same answer sets.   □

One of the reasons behind the difference between the notions of equivalence and strong equivalence of AnsProlog* programs is due to the non-monotonicity of AnsProlog*. In a monotonic language if T_1 and T_2 have the same 'models' then for any T, $T_1 \cup T$ and $T_2 \cup T$ will have the same models. This implies that the strong equivalence of AnsProlog* programs can be inferred by transforming these programs to theories in a *suitable* monotonic logic and showing the equivalence of those theories.

In the rest of this subsection we will pursue this with respect to propositional AnsProlog*. In this quest we rule out the possibility of using classical proposition logic with the straightforward transformation of replacing **not** by $\neg$ and $\leftarrow$ by $\Leftarrow$ as being the *suitable* approach. This is because the two programs $\{a \leftarrow \textbf{not } b.\}$ and $\{b \leftarrow \textbf{not } a.\}$ are transformed to equivalent propositional theories and yet the programs themselves are not even equivalent.

A logic that serves our purpose is the 'logic of here-and-there' (*HT*), a stronger subsystem of classical propositional logic. We now describe this logic.

In *HT* formulas are built from propositional atoms and the 0-place connective $\bot$, using the binary connectives $\wedge$, $\vee$, and $\rightarrow$. The symbol $\top$ is written as a short-hand for $\bot \rightarrow \bot$, and $\neg F$ for $F \rightarrow \bot$. A theory in *HT* is a set of such formulas. A theory in *HT* can also be considered as a theory in classical propositional logic where the satisfaction relation between an interpretation I – thought of as a set of atoms, and a formula F can be defined as follows:

- If p is an atom, then $I \models p$ if $p \in I$,
- $I \not\models \bot$,

- $I \models F \wedge G$ if $I \models F$ and $I \models G$,
- $I \models F \vee G$ if $I \models F$ or $I \models G$, and
- $I \models F \rightarrow G$ if $I \not\models F$ or $I \models G$.

In HT, interpretations (referred to as HT-interpretations) are a pair (I^H, I^T) of sets of atoms such that $I^H \subseteq I^T$. Intuitively, H and T correspond to two worlds: *here* and *there*, and I^H and I^T correspond to the interpretations in the worlds H and T respectively. The satisfiability relations between HT-interpretation and formulas are defined in terms of the satisfiability relations between triplets (I^H, I^T, w) – where $w \in \{H, T\}$ is one of the two worlds, and formulas. We now define these relations.

- For any atom F, and $w \in \{H, T\}$, $(I^H, I^T, w) \models F$ if $F \in I^w$,
- $(I^H, I^T, w) \not\models \bot$,
- $(I^H, I^T, w) \models F \wedge G$ if $(I^H, I^T, w) \models F$ and $(I^H, I^T, w) \models G$,
- $(I^H, I^T, w) \models F \vee G$ if $(I^H, I^T, w) \models F$ or $(I^H, I^T, w) \models G$,
- $(I^H, I^T, H) \models F \rightarrow G$ if
  - $(I^H, I^T, H) \not\models F$ or $(I^H, I^T, H) \models G$, and
  - $(I^H, I^T, T) \not\models F$ or $(I^H, I^T, T) \models G$, and
- $(I^H, I^T, T) \models F \rightarrow G$ if $(I^H, I^T, T) \not\models F$ or $(I^H, I^T, T) \models G$.

An HT-interpretation (I^H, I^T) is said to satisfy a formula F if (I^H, I^T, H) satisfies F. An HT-model of a theory Γ is an HT-interpretation that satisfies every formula in Γ. A formula F is a consequence of a set Γ of formulas in logic HT, denoted by $\Gamma \models_{HT} F$, if every HT-model of Γ satisfies F. Two theories are said to be HT-*equivalent* (or equivalent in the logic of here-and-there) if they have the same HT-models.

Note that for a theory Γ, M is a model of Γ iff (M, M) is an HT-model of Γ. Hence, every consequence of Γ in the logic of here-and-there is a consequence of Γ in the sense of classical propositional logic. However the converse is not true.

We now present a deduction system for the logic of HT using the symbol $\vdash_{HT}$, where $\Gamma \vdash_{HT} F$ means that ϕ can be deduced from Γ in the deduction system of HT; when Γ is the empty set then it is written as $\vdash_{HT} F$.

- **(As)** If $F \in \Gamma$ then $\Gamma \vdash_{HT} F$.
- **(EFQ)** If $\Gamma \vdash_{HT} \bot$ then $\Gamma \vdash_{HT} F$.
- **($\neg$-I)** If $\Gamma, H \vdash_{HT} \bot$ then $\Gamma \vdash_{HT} \neg H$.
- **($\neg$-E)** If $\Gamma \vdash_{HT} F$ and $\Gamma \vdash_{HT} \neg F$ then $\Gamma \vdash_{HT} \bot$.
- **($\wedge$-I)** If $\Gamma_1 \vdash_{HT} F$ and $\Gamma_2 \vdash_{HT} G$ then $\Gamma_1, \Gamma_2 \vdash_{HT} F \wedge G$.
- **($\wedge$-E)** If $\Gamma \vdash_{HT} F \wedge G$ then $\Gamma \vdash_{HT} F$; if $\Gamma \vdash_{HT} F \wedge G$ then $\Gamma \vdash_{HT} G$.
- **($\vee$-I)** If $\Gamma \vdash_{HT} F$ then $\Gamma \vdash_{HT} F \vee G$; if $\Gamma \vdash_{HT} G$ then $\Gamma \vdash_{HT} F \vee G$.
- **($\vee$-E)** If $\Gamma_1 \vdash_{HT} F \vee G$; $\Gamma_2, F \vdash_{HT} H$; and $\Gamma_3, G \vdash_{HT} H$ then $\Gamma_1, \Gamma_2, \Gamma_3 \vdash_{HT} H$.
- **($\rightarrow$-I)** If $\Gamma, H \vdash_{HT} F$ then $\Gamma \vdash_{HT} (H \rightarrow F)$.
- **($\rightarrow$-E)** If $\Gamma_1 \vdash_{HT} (H \rightarrow F)$ and $\Gamma_2 \vdash_{HT} H$ then $\Gamma_1, \Gamma_2 \vdash_{HT} F$.
- **(HTA)** $\vdash_{HT} F \vee (F \rightarrow G) \vee \neg G$.

Theorem 3.9.5 $\Gamma \models_{HT} F$ iff $\Gamma \vdash_{HT} F$.   □

Note that the deduction system of classical propositional logic consists of all the above deduction rules – with the notation $\vdash_{HT}$ replaced by $\vdash$, except that (HTA) is replaced by $\vdash F \vee \neg F$, the law of the excluded middle; and a natural system of intuitionistic logic is obtained by removing (HTA) from the deduction system for HT. Moreover, in both HT and intuitionistic logic F and $\neg\neg F$ are not equivalent, while they are equivalent is classical propositional logic. We now list some consequences and equivalences that can be derived in the deduction system for HT and that are useful for our purpose of showing strong equivalence of AnsProlog^{or} programs.

Proposition 65 (i) $\vdash_{HT} \neg H \vee \neg\neg H$.
(ii) $\neg(F \vee G)$ and $\neg F \wedge \neg G$ are HT-equivalent.
(iii) $\neg(F \wedge G)$ and $\neg F \vee \neg G$ are HT-equivalent.
(iv) $\neg F \vee G$ and $\neg\neg F \to G$ are HT-equivalent.   □

Proof:
To show the HT-equivalences of two theories T and T' we can use $\vdash_{HT}$ and show that for all formulas F in T, $T' \vdash_{HT} F$, and for all formulas G in T', $T \vdash_{HT} G$. The rest of the proof is left as an exercise.   □

Note that the classical versions of (ii) and (iii) are the well-known De Morgan's laws.

Theorem 3.9.6 [LPV01] Two propositional AnsProlog^{or} programs are strongly equivalent iff the theory obtained by replacing or by $\vee$, **not** by $\neg$ and *Head* ← *Body.* by *Body* → *Head* are equivalent in the logic of here-and-there.   □

We now use the above theorem to show strong equivalence of some AnsProlog^{or} programs.

Example 80 Consider the program Π consisting of the following rules:

$p \; or \; q \; \leftarrow.$
$\bot \leftarrow p, q.$

and the program Π' consisting of the following rules:

$p \leftarrow \textbf{not} \; q.$
$q \leftarrow \textbf{not} \; p.$
$\bot \leftarrow p, q.$

The *HT*-theories obtained from Π and Π' are $\{p \vee q, \neg(p \wedge q)\}$ and $\{\neg p \rightarrow q, \neg q \rightarrow p, \neg(p \wedge q)\}$, respectively, which can be re-written using Proposition 65 as $T = \{p \vee q, \neg p \vee \neg q\}$ and $T' = \{\neg p \rightarrow q, \neg q \rightarrow p, \neg p \vee \neg q\}$. We now argue that these two theories are *HT*-equivalent.

To show T and T' are *HT*-equivalent we show that (i) for all formulas F in T, $T' \vdash_{HT} F$, and (ii) for all formulas G in T', $T \vdash_{HT} G$.

- (i) There are two formulas in T. $T' \vdash_{HT} \neg p \vee \neg q$ because of (As). We will now show that $T' \vdash_{HT} p \vee q$.
  - (a) $T' \vdash_{HT} \neg p \vee \neg q$ Using (As).
  - (b) $\{\neg p\} \vdash_{HT} \neg p$ Using (As).
  - (c) $T' \vdash_{HT} \neg p \rightarrow q$ Using (As).
  - (d) $T', \neg p \vdash_{HT} q$ Using (b), (c) and $\rightarrow$-E.
  - (e) $T', \neg p \vdash_{HT} p \vee q$ Using (d) and $\vee$-I.
  - (f) $\{\neg q\} \vdash_{HT} \neg q$ Using (As).
  - (g) $T' \vdash_{HT} \neg q \rightarrow p$ Using (As).
  - (h) $T', \neg q \vdash_{HT} p$ Using (f), (g) and $\rightarrow$-E.
  - (i) $T', \neg q \vdash_{HT} p \vee q$ Using (h) and $\vee$-I.
  - (j) $T' \vdash_{HT} p \vee q$ Using (a), (e), (i), and $\vee$-E, by having $\Gamma_1 = \Gamma_2 = \Gamma_3 = T'$.
- (ii) There are three formulas in T'. $T \vdash_{HT} \neg p \vee \neg q$ because of (As). We will now show that $T \vdash_{HT} \neg p \rightarrow q$.
  - (k) $T \vdash_{HT} p \vee q$ Using (As).
  - (l) $\neg p, p \vdash_{HT} q$ Using (EFQ) and $\neg$-E.
  - (m) $T, q \vdash_{HT} q$ Using (As).
  - (n) $T, \neg p \vdash_{HT} q$.   Using (k), (l), (m), and $\vee$-E, by having $\Gamma_1 = \Gamma_3 = T$, and $\Gamma_2 = \{\neg p\}$.
  - (o) $T \vdash_{HT} \neg p \rightarrow q$.   From (n) and $\rightarrow$-I.

$T \vdash_{HT} \neg q \rightarrow p$, can be shown in a similar way. $\qquad\qquad\square$

3.9.6 Strong equivalence using propositional logic

A new result that reduces strong equivalence of propositional AnsProlog^{or} programs to entailment in classical propositional logic has very recently been discovered by Lin [Lin02]. Given a propositional AnsProlog^{or} program Π, all of whose atoms are from a set L of propositions, let *strong_prop*(Π) be the propositional theory obtained by the following:

- For each rule of the form (1.2.1) in Π, *strong_prop*(Π) contains the following two propositional formulas.

  (1) $L_{k+1} \wedge \cdots \wedge L_m \wedge \neg L'_{m+1} \wedge \cdots \wedge \neg L'_n \supset L_0 \vee \cdots \vee L_k$
  (2) $L'_{k+1} \wedge \cdots \wedge L'_m \wedge \neg L'_{m+1} \wedge \cdots \wedge \neg L'_n \supset L'_0 \vee \cdots \vee L'_k$

  where, the L_is are new atoms not in the set L.

Theorem 3.9.7 [Lin02] Let Π_1 and Π_2 be two AnsProlog^{or} programs such that the set of atoms in Π_1 and Π_2 are from a set L of propositions. Π_1 and Π_2 are strong equivalent iff the following two assertions hold.

(1) $\{p \supset p' \mid p \in L\} \cup strong\_prop(\Pi_1)$ propositionally entails $strong\_prop(\Pi_2)$, and
(2) $\{p \supset p' \mid p \in L\} \cup strong\_prop(\Pi_2)$ propositionally entails $strong\_prop(\Pi_1)$. □

3.9.7 Additional transformations and preservation of strong equivalence

In this section we present several additional transformations of ground AnsProlog* programs all of which preserve the answer sets of ground AnsDatalog^{or} programs and some of which preserve strong equivalence of ground AnsDatalog programs.

RED$^+$: Replace a rule $\mathcal{A} \leftarrow \mathcal{B}^+, \textbf{not } \mathcal{B}^-$. by $\mathcal{A} \leftarrow \mathcal{B}^+, \textbf{not } (\mathcal{B}^- \cap head(\Pi))$.
In words, if a ground atom A is not in the head of any rules of a program Π then the transformed program Π' is obtained by removing $\textbf{not } A$ in the body of any rules in Π.

RED$^-$: Delete a rule $\mathcal{A} \leftarrow \mathcal{B}^+, \textbf{not } \mathcal{B}^-$. if there is another rule $\mathcal{A}' \leftarrow$. in Π such that $\mathcal{A}' \subseteq \mathcal{B}^-$.

SUB: Delete a rule $\mathcal{A} \leftarrow \mathcal{B}^+, \textbf{not } \mathcal{B}^-$. if there is another rule $\mathcal{A}_1 \leftarrow \mathcal{B}_1^+, \textbf{not } \mathcal{B}_1^-$. such that $\mathcal{A}_1 \subseteq \mathcal{A}, \mathcal{B}_1^+ \subseteq \mathcal{B}^+, \mathcal{B}_1^- \subseteq \mathcal{B}^-$.

GPPE: *(Generalized Principle of Partial Evaluation)* Suppose Π contains $\mathcal{A} \leftarrow \mathcal{B}^+, \textbf{not } \mathcal{B}^-$ and we fix an occurrence of an atom $g \in \mathcal{B}^+$. Then replace $\mathcal{A} \leftarrow \mathcal{B}^+, \textbf{not } \mathcal{B}^-$ by the n rules $(i = 1, \ldots, n)$

$$\mathcal{A} \cup (\mathcal{A}_i \setminus \{g\}) \leftarrow (\mathcal{B}^+ \setminus \{g\}) \cup B_i{}^+, \textbf{not } \mathcal{B}^- \cup \textbf{not } B_i{}^-.$$

where $\mathcal{A}_i \leftarrow B_i{}^+, \textbf{not } B_i{}^- \in \Pi, (\text{for } i = 1, \ldots, n)$ are all clauses with $g \in \mathcal{A}_i$. If no such rules exist, simply delete the former rule.

TAUT: Suppose that Π includes a rule $\mathcal{A} \leftarrow \mathcal{B}^+, \textbf{not } \mathcal{B}^-$. such that there exists an atom $a \in \mathcal{A} \cap \mathcal{B}^+$, then delete the rule.

CONTRA: Suppose that Π includes a rule $\mathcal{A} \leftarrow \mathcal{B}^+, \textbf{not } \mathcal{B}^-$. such that there exists an atom a and $\{a, \textbf{not } a\} \subseteq \mathcal{B}^+ \cup \textbf{not } \mathcal{B}^-$, then remove that rule.

DSUC: Suppose that Π includes a fact $a \leftarrow$. and a clause $\mathcal{A} \leftarrow \mathcal{B}^+, \textbf{not } \mathcal{B}^-$. such that $a \in \mathcal{B}^+ \cup \textbf{not } \mathcal{B}^-$. Then replace this rule by the rule $\mathcal{A} \leftarrow (\mathcal{B}^+ \cup \textbf{not } \mathcal{B}^-) \setminus \{a\}$.

FAILURE: Suppose that Π includes a rule $\mathcal{A} \leftarrow \mathcal{B}^+, \textbf{not } \mathcal{B}^-$. such that there exists an atom $a \in \mathcal{B}^+$, but $a \notin head(\Pi)$, then remove that rule.

DLOOP: Let Π be an AnsProlog program, then let *normal_to_definite*(Π) denote the program $\{\mathcal{A} \leftarrow \mathcal{B}^+. : \mathcal{A} \leftarrow \mathcal{B}^+, \textbf{not } \mathcal{B}^-. \in \Pi\}$. Recall from Section 1.3.1

that for an AnsProlog$^{-\textbf{not}}$ program Π we denote its unique minimal Herbrand model by $MM(\Pi)$.

Let $unf(\Pi) := HB_{\mathcal{L}(\Pi)} \setminus MM(normal\_to\_definite(disj\_to\_normal(\Pi)))$. The transformation **DLOOP** reduces a program Π to $\Pi_1 := \{\mathcal{A} \leftarrow \mathcal{B}^+, \textbf{not } \mathcal{B}^- . :$ $\mathcal{B}^+ \cap unf(\Pi) = \emptyset\}$.

Note that GPPE is the generalization of the unfolding transformations to AnsProlog^{or} programs. We now give some examples illustrating some of the above transformations.   □

Example 81
The following transformation involves application of RED$^+$ twice followed by an application of *SUB*.

$$
\begin{array}{ll}
a \text{ or } b \leftarrow c, \textbf{not } c, \textbf{not } d. & \\
a \text{ or } c \leftarrow b. & a \text{ or } c \leftarrow b. \\
c \text{ or } d \leftarrow \textbf{not } e. \qquad \Longrightarrow & c \text{ or } d \leftarrow . \\
b \leftarrow \textbf{not } c, \textbf{not } d, \textbf{not } e. & b \leftarrow \textbf{not } c, \textbf{not } d. \\
\end{array}
$$

□

Example 82 The following illustrates the DLOOP transformation.

$$
\begin{array}{ll}
f \text{ or } g \leftarrow . & \\
f \leftarrow g. & f \text{ or } g \leftarrow . \\
g \leftarrow f. & f \leftarrow g. \\
p \leftarrow . \qquad \Longrightarrow & g \leftarrow f. \\
a \text{ or } b \leftarrow c, \textbf{not } d. & p \leftarrow . \\
c \leftarrow a. & h \text{ or } e \leftarrow \textbf{not } a, p. \\
h \text{ or } e \leftarrow \textbf{not } a, p. & \\
\end{array}
$$

□

We now have the following results about the transformations mentioned in this section.

Proposition 66 Let Π be a ground AnsDatalog^{or} program and Π' be the program obtained by an arbitrary sequence of transformations of this section. Then Π and Π' have the same answer sets.   □

Proposition 67 [ONA01] The transformations *TAUT, CONTRA, SUB, FAILURE, RED$^-$*, and *DSUC* preserve strong equivalence of AnsDatalog^{or} programs.   □

Exercise 14 Find counterexamples for the transformations *GPPE, DLOOP* and *RED$^+$* with respect to Proposition 67.   □

Proposition 68 [ONG01] The transformations *DLOOP, RED⁻, RED⁺, TAUT, SUB, DSUC,* and *FAILURE* always reduce the size of the program and are quadratic time computable.   □

3.10 Notes and references

Among the early results about coherence and categoricity of AnsProlog programs was the result about stratified and locally stratified programs. Stratification was defined and its properties were studied in [CH85, ABW88]. The notion of stratification was extended to local stratification in [Prz88b, Prz88a, Prz89b] and further extended to weak stratification in [PP90]. Acyclic programs were originally introduced by Cavedon [Cav89] and were called locally hierarchical programs. Their properties were extensively explored in [AB90, AB91], and the properties of well-moded programs were explored in [AP91, AP94]. Existence of answer sets and various sub-classes of AnsProlog programs and their properties were further studied in [Fag90, CF90, Dun92, Sat90]. The notion of call-consistency was defined in [Kun89, Sat87]. The papers [Fag90, Fag94] present a nice summary of these results. Fages in [Fag94] used the term 'positive-order-consistency' which was later referred to as 'tight' in [Lif96] and the notion was further extended in [BEL00]. The notion of stable programs was originally defined in [Str93], and extended by McCain and Turner in [MT94b] where they discuss language independence and language tolerance. The ideas of language independence and language tolerance had their origin in the earlier deductive database research on domain independent databases [TS88]. Head cycle free programs and their properties were studied in [BED92]. One of the main properties studied in that paper concerned when disjunctions can be eliminated. Another result on eliminating disjunctions was presented in [LT95].

Marek and Subrahmanian's result [MS89] relating answer sets and AnsProlog program rules was one of the results most widely used to analyze AnsProlog programs. Its extension to AnsProlog$^{\neg, or}$ programs is reported in [BG94]. Restricted monotonicity was first studied in [Lif93b]. The notion of signing was introduced in [Kun89] and its properties were studied in [Dun92, Tur93, Tur94]. The notion of splitting was introduced in [LT94]. A similar notion was independently developed in [EGM97].

The notion of conservative extension was first studied in [GP91] and further generalized in [GP96]. The notion of interpolation of AnsProlog programs was presented in [BGK93, BGK98]. Conservative extension and interpolation were both generalized as operations on functional specifications and results about realizing functional specifications using AnsProlog* programs were presented in [GG97, GG99].

The notion of filter-abducibility and assimilation of observations was explored in [Bar00]. An alternative analysis of the relation between disjunction and abduction is presented in [LT95]. Abduction with respect to logic programming is also studied in [LY01, KM90]. We briefly discuss the abductive formulation of [KM90] in Chapter 9.

Various fold/unfold transformations were described in [GS91, Mah87, Mah90, Mah93b, Sek91, Sek93, TS84]. Their properties with respect to AnsProlog⁻ programs were compiled and extended in [AD95]. The paper [Mah88] discusses several different kinds of equivalences between logic programs. The paper [FLMS93] presents the transformation from AnsProlog programs to AnsProlog$^{or,-}$**not** programs and constraints. The use of integer linear programming and mixed integer programming in computing answer sets of AnsProlog programs is discussed in [BNNS94].

The notion of strong equivalence is an extrapolation of the earlier notion of 'uniformly equivalent' introduced in the context of Datalog in [Sag88, Mah88]. Conditions for strong equivalence of AnsProlog* programs were presented in [LPV01]. Turner simplifies this result in [Tur01]. The result in Section 3.9.6 is from [Lin02] and the proof of the theorem in that section is based on a result in [Tur01].

The results in Section 3.9.7 are based on [BD97, ADO99]. All the transformations in that section are from [BD97] except for DLOOP which is from [ADO99]. In Section 6.6.9 we look at these transformations from a different angle. Additional results about these transformations are also discussed in [ONG01, BDFZ01, DOZ01].

Chapter 4

Declarative problem solving and reasoning
in AnsProlog*

In this chapter we formulate several knowledge representation and problem solving domains using AnsProlog*. Our focus in this chapter is on program development. We start with three well known problems from the literature of constraint satisfaction, and automated reasoning: placing queens on a chess board, determining who owns the zebra, and finding tile covering in a mutilated chess board. We show several encodings of these problems using AnsProlog*. We then discuss a general methodology for representing constraint satisfaction problems (CSPs) and show how to extend it to dynamic CSPs. We then present encodings of several combinatorial graph problems such as k-colorability, Hamiltonian circuit, and k-clique. After discussing these problem solving examples, we present a general methodology of reasoning with prioritized defaults, and show how reasoning with inheritance hierarchies is a special case of this.

4.1 Three well-known problem solving tasks

A well-known methodology for declarative problem solving is the *generate and test* methodology whereby possible solutions to the problem are generated and non-solutions are eliminated by testing. This is similar to the common way of showing that a problem is in the class NP, where it is shown that after the non-deterministic choice the testing can be done in polynomial time. The 'generate' part in an AnsProlog* formulation of a problem solving task is achieved by enumerating the possibilities, and the 'test' part is achieved by having constraints that eliminate the possibilities that violate the test conditions. Thus the answer sets of the resulting program correspond to solutions of the given problem. We refer to the AnsProlog* implementation of generate and test as the *enumerate and eliminate* approach.

Given a problem solving task its AnsProlog* formulation primarily depends on how the possibilities are enumerated. That is, what variables are used and what values these variables can take. Often explicit or implicit knowledge about the domain can be used to reduce the size of the possibility space (or state space). Also, often some of the test conditions can be pushed inside the generate phase. One needs to be very careful about this though, as sometimes the pushing of the test conditions may be done wrongly although at first glance it may appear to be right. We give such an example for the n-queens problem in Section 4.1.1. In representing the constraints, one also needs to be careful about whether to represent the constraint as a fact or as a rule with empty head. For example, consider the following program Π, where the possibility space is $\{a, p\}$ and $\{b, q\}$.

$p \leftarrow a.$
$q \leftarrow b.$
$a \leftarrow$ **not** $b.$
$b \leftarrow$ **not** $a.$

Now, suppose our constraint is 'p must be true'. That is, we would like to eliminate the possibilities where p is not true. If we try to do this by adding the fact $p \leftarrow .$ to Π, then the resulting program will have the answer sets $\{a, p\}$, and $\{b, q, p\}$, which is not what we want. What we want is to eliminate $\{b, q\}$ from the possibility space and have $\{a, p\}$ as the answer. The right way to achieve this is to add $\leftarrow$ **not** $p.$ to Π.

4.1.1 n-queens

In the n-queens problem we have an $n \times n$ board and we have to place n queens such that no two queens attack each other. That is, there is exactly one queen in each row and column and no two queens are along the same diagonal line.

Following the enumerate and eliminate approach we first need to enumerate the placing of n queens in the $n \times n$ board and then eliminate those possibilities or configurations where two queens may attack each other. We now present several different encodings of this. These encodings differ in their formulation of the 'enumerate' and 'eliminate' parts. In some the 'enumerate' part itself consists of a weaker enumeration and elimination; in others parts of the 'eliminate' conditions are pushed into the 'enumerate' part.

(1) Placing queens one by one with possibility space based on the squares: In this formulation we name the queens from 1 to n and use the predicate $at(I, X, Y)$ to mean that queen I is in location (X, Y). The 'enumerate' part in this formulation consists of a weaker enumeration of the possibility space which specifies that each location may or may not have queen I, and then has elimination constraints to force each queen to be in exactly one location, and no two queens in the same location. The 'elimination' part is the usual one. The formulation is as follows:

  (a) Declarations: We have the following domain specifications.

$$queen(1) \leftarrow . \qquad \ldots \qquad queen(n) \leftarrow .$$
$$row(1) \leftarrow . \qquad \ldots \qquad row(n) \leftarrow .$$
$$col(1) \leftarrow . \qquad \ldots \qquad col(n) \leftarrow .$$

(b) Enumeration: The enumeration rules create the possibility space such that the n different queens are placed in the $n \times n$ board in different locations. The rules with their intuitive meaning are as follows:

  (i) For each locations (X, Y) and each queen I, either I is in location (X, Y) or not.

$$at(I, X, Y) \leftarrow queen(I), row(X), col(Y), \textbf{not } not\_at(I, X, Y).$$
$$not\_at(I, X, Y) \leftarrow queen(I), row(X), col(Y), \textbf{not } at(I, X, Y).$$

  (ii) For each queen I it is placed in at most one location.

$$\leftarrow queen(I), row(X), col(Y), row(U), col(Z), at(I, X, Y), at(I, U, Z),$$
$$\quad Y \neq Z.$$
$$\leftarrow queen(I), row(X), col(Y), row(Z), col(V), at(I, X, Y), at(I, Z, V),$$
$$\quad X \neq Z.$$

  (iii) For each queen I it is placed in at least one location.

$$placed(I) \leftarrow queen(I), row(X), col(Y), at(I, X, Y).$$
$$\leftarrow queen(I), \textbf{not } placed(I).$$

  (iv) No two queens are placed in the same location.

$$\leftarrow queen(I), row(X), col(Y), queen(J), at(I, X, Y), at(J, X, Y), I \neq J.$$

(c) Elimination:

  (i) No two distinct queens in the same row.

$$\leftarrow queen(I), row(X), col(Y), col(V), queen(J), at(I, X, Y), at(J, X, V),$$
$$\quad I \neq J.$$

  (ii) No two distinct queens in the same column.

$$\leftarrow queen(I), row(X), col(Y), row(U), queen(J), at(I, X, Y), at(J, U, Y),$$
$$\quad I \neq J.$$

  (iii) No two distinct queens attack each other diagonally.

$$\leftarrow row(X), col(Y), row(U), col(V), queen(I), queen(J), at(I, X, Y),$$
$$\quad at(J, U, V), I \neq J, abs(X - U) = abs(Y - V).$$

Note that the rule (1)(b)(iv) is subsumed by both (1)(c)(i) and (1)(c)(ii). In other words, in the presence of (1)(c)(i) or (1)(c)(ii) we do not need (1)(b)(iv). It is needed in (1)(b) if our only goal is enumeration.

Exercise 15 Explain why replacing the second rule of (1)(b)(iii) by the following rule makes the program incorrect.

$$placed(I) \leftarrow queen(I). \qquad \qquad \Box$$

(2) Placing queens one by one in unique locations: We now present a formulation where while enumerating the possibility space, care is taken such that queens are placed in unique locations.

(a) Declarations: As in the previous formulation.

(b) Enumeration:

(i) The combined effect of (1)(b)(i)–(iii) is achieved by the following rules which ensure that each queen is uniquely placed. The first two rules define $other\_at(I, X, Y)$ which intuitively means that the queen I has been placed in a location other than (X, Y). The third rule enforces the condition that if queen I has not been placed in a location different from (X, Y), then it must be placed in (X, Y).

$$other\_at(I, X, Y) \leftarrow queen(I), row(X), col(Y), row(U), col(Z), at(I, U, Z),$$
$$Y \neq Z.$$
$$other\_at(I, X, Y) \leftarrow queen(I), row(X), col(Y), row(Z), col(V), at(I, Z, V),$$
$$X \neq Z.$$
$$at(I, X, Y) \leftarrow queen(I), row(X), col(Y), \textbf{not } other\_at(I, X, Y).$$

(ii) The following rule is same as in (1)(b)(iv) and it forces two distinct queens to be placed in different locations.

$$\leftarrow queen(I), row(X), col(Y), queen(J), at(I, X, Y), at(J, X, Y), I \neq J.$$

(c) Elimination: As in the previous formulation.

(3) Placing queens one by one in unique locations so that they do not attack each other horizontally or vertically: In this formulation we push two of the elimination constraints into the enumeration phase. Thus while enumerating the possibility space we ensure that no two queens are in the same row or same column.

(a) Declarations: As in the previous formulation.

(b) Enumeration:

(i) As in (2)(b)(i)

$$other\_at(I, X, Y) \leftarrow queen(I), row(X), col(Y), row(U), col(Z), at(I, U, Z),$$
$$Y \neq Z.$$
$$other\_at(I, X, Y) \leftarrow queen(I), row(X), col(Y), row(Z), col(V), at(I, Z, V),$$
$$X \neq Z.$$
$$at(I, X, Y) \leftarrow queen(I), row(X), col(Y), \textbf{not } other\_at(I, X, Y).$$

(ii) The first two constraints in (2)(c) – the same as (1)(c)(i) and (1)(c)(ii) – are replaced by the following. We also no longer need (2)(b)(ii) which is subsumed by the following.

$$other\_at(I, X, Y) \leftarrow queen(I), row(X), col(Y), col(V), queen(J),$$
$$at(J, X, V), I \neq J.$$
$$other\_at(I, X, Y) \leftarrow queen(I), row(X), col(Y), row(U), queen(J),$$
$$at(J, U, Y), I \neq J.$$

(c) Elimination: We now need only one elimination rule, the same one as (1)(c)(iii).

$$\leftarrow row(X), col(Y), row(U), col(V), queen(I), queen(J), at(I, X, Y), at(J, U, V),$$
$$I \neq J, abs(X - U) = abs(Y - V).$$

(4) Placing queens with possibility space based on the squares: In the last three formulations we named the queens and placed them one by one. We can get both computational efficiency and a smaller encoding by not naming the queens. For example, when queens are numbered the 4-queens problem has 48 solutions while if we do not distinguish the queens, it has only 2 solutions. In the following we simplify the formulation in (1) by not distinguishing the queens. We use the predicate $in(X, Y)$ to mean that a queen is placed in location (X, Y).

(a) Declarations: The simpler domain specification is as follows:

$$row(1) \leftarrow . \qquad \ldots \qquad row(n) \leftarrow.$$
$$col(1) \leftarrow . \qquad \ldots \qquad col(n) \leftarrow.$$

(b) Enumeration: The enumeration now has two parts. Since we do not distinguish between the queens we no longer need (1)(b)(ii)–(iv).

  (i) The following is the simplification of (1)(b)(i) which specifies that each square either has a queen or has not.

  $$not\_in(X, Y) \leftarrow row(X), col(Y), \textbf{not } in(X, Y).$$
  $$in(X, Y) \leftarrow row(X), col(Y), \textbf{not } not\_in(X, Y).$$

  (ii) To make sure that we placed all the n queens, instead of counting, we use the knowledge that for the queens to not attack each other they must be in different rows, and hence to place all the n queens we must have a queen in each row. We specify this using the following:

  $$has\_queen(X) \leftarrow row(X), col(Y), in(X, Y).$$
  $$\leftarrow row(X), \textbf{not } has\_queen(X).$$

Note that we did not need rules similar to the above in (1)(b) as there we numbered the queens and by ensuring that each queen was in at least one location, we made sure that all the queens were placed.

(c) Elimination: The elimination rules below are simplified versions of (1)(c).

  (i) Two queens cannot be placed in the same column.

  $$\leftarrow row(X), col(Y), col(YY), Y \neq YY, in(X, Y), in(X, YY).$$

  (ii) Two queens cannot be placed in the same row.

  $$\leftarrow row(X), col(Y), row(XX), X \neq XX, in(X, Y), in(XX, Y).$$

  (iii) Two queens cannot be placed so that they attack each other diagonally.

  $$\leftarrow row(X), col(Y), row(XX), col(YY), X \neq XX, Y \neq YY,$$
  $$in(X, Y), in(XX, YY), abs(X - XX) = abs(Y - YY).$$

Exercise 16 Explain why we cannot replace the rules in (4)(b)(ii) by the following:

$\leftarrow row(X), col(Y), \mathbf{not}\ in(X, Y).$ □

(5) Placing queens so that they do not attack each other horizontally or vertically: Similarly to the formulation in (3) we now push the constraints that no two queens are in the same row or same column into the enumeration phase.

(a) Declarations: As in the previous formulation.

(b) Enumeration: We now push the constraints in (4)(c)(i) and (ii) into the enumeration phase, and generate possibilities of queen placement such that no two queens are in the same column or row, and at least one is in each row and column. We do this by using an auxiliary predicate $not\_in(X, Y)$ which intuitively means that a queen should not be placed in location (X, Y).

(i) A queen should not be placed in (X, Y) if there is a queen placed in the same row.

$not\_in(X, Y) \leftarrow row(X), col(Y), col(YY), Y \neq YY, in(X, YY).$

(ii) A queen should not be placed in (X, Y) if there is a queen placed in the same column.

$not\_in(X, Y) \leftarrow row(X), col(Y), row(XX), X \neq XX, in(XX, Y).$

(iii) A queen must be placed in (X, Y) if it is not otherwise prevented.

$in(X, Y) \leftarrow row(X), col(Y), \mathbf{not}\ not\_in(X, Y).$

(c) Elimination: We now need only one elimination constraint, the same one as in (4)(c)(iii) which prevents placements where queens can attack each other diagonally.

$\leftarrow row(X), col(Y), row(XX), col(YY), X \neq XX, Y \neq YY,$
$in(X, Y), in(XX, YY), abs(X - XX) = abs(Y - YY).$

(6) A non-solution: Let us continue the process of pushing the elimination phase into the enumeration phase one more step by removing (5)(c) and adding the following rule:

$not\_in(X, Y) \leftarrow row(X), col(Y), row(XX), col(YY), X \neq XX, Y \neq YY,$
$in(X, Y), in(XX, YY), abs(X - XX) = abs(Y - YY).$

This will result in the following overall formulation.

$row(1) \leftarrow .$ $\quad\quad\quad\cdots\quad\quad\quad row(n) \leftarrow .$
$col(1) \leftarrow .$ $\quad\quad\quad\cdots\quad\quad\quad col(n) \leftarrow .$

$not\_in(X, Y) \leftarrow row(X), col(Y), col(YY), Y \neq YY, in(X, YY).$
$not\_in(X, Y) \leftarrow row(X), col(Y), row(XX), X \neq XX, in(XX, Y).$
$not\_in(X, Y) \leftarrow row(X), col(Y), row(XX), col(YY), X \neq XX, Y \neq YY,$
$\quad\quad\quad\quad\quad in(X, Y), in(XX, YY), abs(X - XX) = abs(Y - YY).$
$in(X, Y) \leftarrow dim(X), dim(Y), \mathbf{not}\ not\_in(X, Y).$

Unfortunately the above formulation is *not correct* in the sense that it has answer sets where not all the n queens are placed. For example, if $n = 4$, then one of the answer sets encodes the following placement: $\{in(1, 1), in(3, 2), in(2, 4)\}$, where only three queens are placed, instead of four.

Further reasoning reveals that the above encoding places queens into a valid configuration, where a valid configuration is a configuration of queens that do not attack each other and to which additional queens cannot be added without that queen attacking one or more of the already placed queens. The configuration $\{in(1, 1), in(3, 2), in(2, 4)\}$ is valid in that sense, as we cannot add a new queen to it in such a way that it does not attack the already placed ones. Hence, we need to be careful in pushing elimination constraints into the enumeration phase.

Exercise 17 Add additional rules to the formulation in (6) to make it work.   □

4.1.2 Tile covering of boards with missing squares

Consider covering slightly broken $n \times n$ checker boards with tiles of size 1 by 2. We need to find a covering of the board, if it exists, using 1×2 tiles so that all the good squares are covered. Otherwise we need to report that no covering exists. A particular case is a 6×6 board. We need to show that if the board is missing squares (1,6) and (1,5) then there is a covering; and if the board is missing squares (1,6) and (6,1) then there is no covering.

(1) A formulation using two squares to denote a tile: In this formulation we use the predicate $rt\_top(X, Y)$ meaning that Y is an adjacent square to X, either on the right of X or on the top of X. The enumeration phase involves selecting pairs (X, Y) to cover with a tile so that $rt\_top(X, Y)$ is true. In the elimination phase we make sure that two different tiles do not cover the same square, and all squares are covered.

(a) We have the following domain specification.

$row(1) \leftarrow.$ ... $row(6) \leftarrow.$
$col(1) \leftarrow.$ ... $col(6) \leftarrow.$

(b) We use the predicate sq to define when a square is not missing, and the predicate *missing* to denote that the square is missing in the board.

$sq(X, Y) \leftarrow row(X), col(Y), \textbf{not } missing(X, Y).$

(c) The two particular instances in a 6×6 board are expressed by specifying the missing squares as given below:

(i) $missing(1, 6) \leftarrow.$ $missing(6, 1) \leftarrow.$
(ii) $missing(1, 6) \leftarrow.$ $missing(1, 5) \leftarrow.$

(d) The following two rules define when two squares are adjacent with the second square to the right or top of the first one.

$rt\_top(X, Y, XX, Y) \leftarrow sq(X, Y), sq(XX, Y), XX = X + 1,$
$rt\_top(X, Y, X, YY) \leftarrow sq(X, Y), sq(X, YY), YY = Y + 1.$

(e) Enumeration: Given two right-top adjacent squares the following rules either select the two squares together to be covered by a tile or leave them out as a pair. (Each individual square in that pair together with another square may be selected for covering by a tile.)

$$sel\_rt\_top(X, Y, XX, YY) \leftarrow rt\_top(X, Y, XX, YY),$$
$$\textbf{not } n\_sel\_rt\_top(X, Y, XX, YY).$$
$$n\_sel\_rt\_top(X, Y, XX, YY) \leftarrow rt\_top(X, Y, XX, YY),$$
$$\textbf{not } sel\_rt\_top(X, Y, XX, YY).$$

(f) Generalizing *sel_rt_top* to *sel*: To simplify the elimination rules we define the predicate *sel* which holds for a pair of adjacent squares if the right-top representation of the two squares is selected.

$$sel(X, Y, XX, YY) \leftarrow sq(X, Y), sq(XX, YY), sel\_rt\_top(X, Y, XX, YY),$$
$$sel(X, Y, XX, YY) \leftarrow sq(X, Y), sq(XX, YY), sel\_rt\_top(XX, YY, X, Y).$$

(g) Elimination of selections that conflict: We eliminate possibilities where a square (X, Y) is covered by two different tiles. We represent (U, V) as being different from (W, Z) by encoding it as $U \neq W$ or $V \neq Z$.

$$\leftarrow sel(X, Y, U, V), sel(X, Y, W, Z), sq(X, Y), sq(U, V), sq(W, Z), U \neq W,$$
$$\leftarrow sel(X, Y, U, V), sel(X, Y, W, Z), sq(X, Y), sq(U, V), sq(W, Z), V \neq Z.$$

(h) Finally, we eliminate selections where some squares are left uncovered.

$$covered(X, Y) \leftarrow sq(X, Y), sq(XX, YY), sel(X, Y, XX, YY).$$
$$\leftarrow sq(X, Y), not\ covered(X, Y).$$

The above formulation is not very efficient when it is run through the Smodels system. We believe the reason is that the ground version of the above program is quite large. For example, the constraints in part (g) have 6 variables and each of them can take n values; thus a naive grounding of those constraints results in 6^n ground rules. We found that for $n = 8$, the above program did not return an answer within 2 minutes when we ran it in a WinTel 400 MHz laptop with 64 MB of RAM using lparse version 0.99.52 and smodels 2.25. (The lparse grounding took 30 seconds, the smodels reading took another 60 seconds, and there was no answer for the next 60 seconds.)

(2) An efficient formulation with tiles represented by a single co-ordinate: To decrease the size of the grounding we present a formulation where tiles are represented only by their left or bottom co-ordinate. To distinguish between horizontal and vertical coverings we now have two – instead of the one in the previous formulation – predicates.

(a)–(c) are as before.

(d) Selecting horizontal coverings: For each square (X, Y) the following two rules enumerate the possibilities that there either is a horizontal tile with its left end at (X, Y) or is not.

$$sel\_rt(X, Y) \leftarrow sq(X, Y), sq(X + 1, Y), \textbf{not } n\_sel\_rt(X, Y),$$
$$n\_sel\_rt(X, Y) \leftarrow sq(X, Y), sq(X + 1, Y), \textbf{not } sel\_rt(X, Y).$$

(e) Selecting vertical coverings: For each square (X, Y) the following two rules enumerate the possibilities that there either is a vertical tile with its bottom end at (X, Y) or is not.

$sel\_top(X, Y) \leftarrow sq(X, Y), sq(X, Y + 1), \textbf{not } n\_sel\_top(X, Y),$
$n\_sel\_top(X, Y) \leftarrow sq(X, Y), sq(X, Y + 1), \textbf{not } sel\_top(X, Y).$

(f) Elimination of coverings that conflict: The following rules eliminate the possibility where a square (X, Y) is covered by two different tiles.

$\leftarrow sq(X, Y), sel\_rt(X, Y), sel\_rt(X + 1, Y).$
$\leftarrow sq(X, Y), sel\_top(X, Y), sel\_top(X, Y + 1).$
$\leftarrow sq(X, Y), sel\_rt(X, Y), sel\_top(X, Y).$
$\leftarrow sq(X, Y), sel\_rt(X, Y), sel\_top(X + 1, Y).$
$\leftarrow sq(X, Y), sel\_rt(X, Y), sel\_top(X, Y - 1).$
$\leftarrow sq(X, Y), sel\_rt(X, Y), sel\_top(X + 1, Y - 1).$

(g) Elimination of selections that do not cover some square: The following rule eliminates the possible selections where some square (X, Y) is left uncovered. A square (X, Y) can be covered in four different ways: a horizontal tile with its left end in $(X - 1, Y)$ or in (X, Y) and a vertical tile with its bottom end in $(X, Y - 1)$ or in (X, Y). If not one of these four cases holds then we reason that (X, Y) is left uncovered.

$\leftarrow sq(X, Y), \textbf{not } sel\_rt(X, Y), \textbf{not } sel\_rt(X - 1, Y),$
      $\textbf{not } sel\_top(X, Y), \textbf{not } sel\_top(X, Y - 1).$

The above formulation leads to a small number of groundings, when compared to the previous formulation. To be specific, it leads to $12 \times n^2$ ground rules beyond the domain representation. For $n = 8$, when we ran it through the Smodels system in a WinTel 400 MHz laptop with 64 MB of RAM using lparse version 0.99.52 and smodels 2.25., it took 0.87 seconds.

4.1.3 Who let the zebra out?

In this well-known problem, there are five houses each of a different color (red, green, ivory, blue, or yellow) and inhabited by a person of a particular nationality (Japanese, Englishman, Norwegian, Ukrainian, or Spaniard), with a particular pet (horse, snail, zebra, fox, or dog), drink (water, coffee, tea, milk, or orange juice) and brand of cigarette (Lucky Strike, Winston, Chesterfields, Kools, or Parliaments).
  It is given that

(1) The Englishman lives in the red house.
(2) The Spaniard owns the dog.
(3) The Norwegian lives in the first house on the left.
(4) Kools are smoked in the yellow house.

(5) The man who smokes Chesterfields lives in the house next to the man with the fox.

(6) The Norwegian lives next to the blue house.

(7) The Winston smoker owns snails.

(8) The Lucky Strike smoker drinks orange juice (oj).

(9) The Ukrainian drinks tea.

(10) The Japanese smokes Parliaments.

(11) Kools are smoked in the house next to the house where the horse is kept.

(12) Coffee is drunk in the green house.

(13) The green house is immediately to the right (your right) of the ivory house.

(14) Milk is drunk in the middle house.

A zebra is found wandering in the streets and the animal shelter wants to find out who let the zebra out. That is, which house the zebra belongs to. The solution of this problem is given by the following table:

number	cigarette brand	country	color	pet	drink
1	Kools	Norway	yellow	fox	water
2	Chesterfields	Ukraine	blue	horse	tea
3	Winston	UK	red	snails	milk
4	Lucky Strike	Spain	ivory	dog	oj
5	Parliaments	Japan	green	zebra	coffee

Our goal is to come up with an AnsProlog encoding of the above problem solving task. We rule out an encoding based on a predicate *together*(U, V, W, X, Y, Z) meaning that the house number U is together with the cigarette brand V, country W, color X, pet Y, and drink Z. The reason behind ruling out such an encoding is to limit the number of variables in rules. Also, the use of *together*(U, V, W, X, Y, Z) leads to some rules – where we want to say that no two *together* atoms can have one of their parameters the same and another parameter different – with at least seven variables. Such a rule instantiates to $5^7 = 78125$ instances. We now present two different encodings for this problem where instead of using *together* we use the house number as an anchor and associate the other features with the house number.

(1) An encoding with house number as anchor and separate predicates for each association: In the following encoding we use house number as the anchor, and have binary predicates *has_color*, *has_drink*, *has_animal*, *has_country*, and *has_brand* where the first parameter is the house number and the second parameters are color, drink, pet, country, and cigarette brand respectively.

(a) We have the following domain specification:

$$house(1) \leftarrow. \qquad \ldots \qquad house(5) \leftarrow.$$

$$right(X, X + 1) \leftarrow house(X), house(X + 1).$$

$left(X + 1, X) \leftarrow house(X), house(X + 1).$

$next(X, Y) \leftarrow right(X, Y).$
$next(X, Y) \leftarrow left(X, Y).$

$color(red) \leftarrow.$ $\qquad$ $color(green) \leftarrow.$ $\qquad$ $color(blue) \leftarrow.$
$color(ivory) \leftarrow.$ $\qquad$ $color(yellow) \leftarrow.$

$country(norway) \leftarrow.$ $\qquad$ $country(japan) \leftarrow.$ $\qquad$ $country(uk) \leftarrow.$
$country(spain) \leftarrow.$ $\qquad$ $country(ukraine) \leftarrow.$

$brand(parliaments) \leftarrow.$ $\qquad$ $brand(lucky\_strike) \leftarrow.$ $\qquad$ $brand(kools) \leftarrow.$
$brand(chester field) \leftarrow.$ $\qquad$ $brand(winston) \leftarrow.$

$drink(coffee) \leftarrow.$ $\qquad$ $drink(tea) \leftarrow.$ $\qquad$ $drink(oj) \leftarrow.$
$drink(milk) \leftarrow.$ $\qquad$ $drink(water) \leftarrow.$

$animal(dog) \leftarrow.$ $\qquad$ $animal(snails) \leftarrow.$ $\qquad$ $animal(horse) \leftarrow.$
$animal(fox) \leftarrow.$ $\qquad$ $animal(zebra) \leftarrow.$

(b) The enumerations: We now enumerate the predicates *has_color*, *has_drink*, *has_animal*, *has_country*, and *has_brand*. For the predicate *has_color*, we make sure that every house has a unique color assigned to it, and every color corresponds to a unique house. This is achieved by the following three rules:

$other\_color(H, C) \leftarrow house(H), color(C), color(CC), has\_color(H, CC),$
$$C \neq CC.$$
$other\_color(H, C) \leftarrow house(H), color(C), house(HH), has\_color(HH, C),$
$$H \neq HH.$$
$has\_color(H, C) \leftarrow house(H), color(C), \textbf{not } other\_color(H, C).$

The enumeration rules for the predicates *has_drink*, *has_animal*, *has_country*, and *has_brand* are similar to that of the enumeration rules for *has_color* and are given below:

$other\_drink(H, C) \leftarrow house(H), drink(C), drink(CC), has\_drink(H, CC),$
$$C \neq CC.$$
$other\_drink(H, C) \leftarrow house(H), drink(C), house(HH), has\_drink(HH, C),$
$$H \neq HH.$$
$has\_drink(H, C) \leftarrow house(H), drink(C), \textbf{not } other\_drink(H, C).$
$other\_animal(H, C) \leftarrow house(H), animal(C), animal(CC),$
$$has\_animal(H, CC), C \neq CC.$$
$other\_animal(H, C) \leftarrow house(H), animal(C), house(HH),$
$$has\_animal(HH, C), H \neq HH.$$
$has\_animal(H, C) \leftarrow house(H), animal(C), \textbf{not } other\_animal(H, C).$

$other\_country(H, C) \leftarrow house(H), country(C), country(CC),$
$$has\_country(H, CC), C \neq CC.$$

$other\_country(H, C) \leftarrow house(H), country(C), house(HH),$
$\qquad has\_country(HH, C), H \neq HH.$
$has\_country(H, C) \leftarrow house(H), country(C), \textbf{not } other\_country(H, C).$

$other\_brand(H, C) \leftarrow house(H), brand(C), brand(CC), has\_brand$
$\qquad (H, CC), C \neq CC.$
$other\_brand(H, C) \leftarrow house(H), brand(C), house(HH), has\_brand$
$\qquad (HH, C), H \neq HH.$
$has\_brand(H, C) \leftarrow house(H), brand(C), \textbf{not } other\_brand(H, C).$

(c) The elimination constraints: The fourteen given facts (or observations) are each encoded by the following 14 rules. If the fact i is satisfied then it forces s_i to be true.

$s_1 \leftarrow house(H), has\_country(H, uk), has\_color(H, red).$

$s_2 \leftarrow house(H), has\_animal(H, dog), has\_country(H, spain).$

$s_3 \leftarrow has\_country(1, norway).$

$s_4 \leftarrow house(H), has\_brand(H, kools), has\_color(H, yellow).$

$s_5 \leftarrow house(H), house(HH), has\_brand(H, chesterfield), has\_animal(HH, fox),$
$\qquad next(H, HH).$

$s_6 \leftarrow house(H), house(HH), has\_color(H, blue), has\_country(HH, norway),$
$\qquad next(H, HH).$

$s_7 \leftarrow house(H), has\_brand(H, winston), has\_animal(H, snails).$

$s_8 \leftarrow house(H), has\_brand(H, lucky\_strike), has\_drink(H, oj).$

$s_9 \leftarrow house(H), has\_country(H, ukraine), has\_drink(H, tea).$

$s_{10} \leftarrow house(H), has\_brand(H, parliaments), has\_country(H, japan).$

$s_{11} \leftarrow house(H), house(HH), has\_brand(H, kools), has\_animal(HH, horse),$
$\qquad next(H, HH).$

$s_{12} \leftarrow house(H), has\_color(H, green), has\_drink(H, coffee).$

$s_{13} \leftarrow house(H), house(HH), has\_color(HH, ivory), has\_color(H, green),$
$\qquad right(HH, H).$

$s_{14} \leftarrow has\_drink(3, milk).$

The following rule encodes that *satisfied* is true iff all the 14 constraints are individually satisfied.

satisfied $\leftarrow s_1, s_2, s_3, s_4, s_5, s_6, s_7, s_8, s_9, s_{10}, s_{11}, s_{12}, s_{13}, s_{14}.$

The following rule eliminates those possibilities where *satisfied* is not true. That is, when one of the 14 conditions does not hold.

$\leftarrow \textbf{not } satisfied.$

The above encoding finds the unique solution. We now present another encoding which instead of using the five association predicates: *has_color*, *has_drink*, *has_animal*, *has_country*, and *has_brand*; uses only a single association predicate.

(2) An encoding with house number as anchor and a single association predicate: In the following encoding we use a single association predicate, and use two new predicates

object and *same_type* to distinguish the association of a house number with objects of different types. The main advantage of using a single association predicate is that it makes it easier to express the observations as we do not have to remember the particular association predicate for the object being described.

(a) Besides the domain specification in (1)(a) we have the following additional rules.

$object(X) \leftarrow color(X).$
$object(X) \leftarrow drink(X).$
$object(X) \leftarrow animal(X).$
$object(X) \leftarrow country(X).$
$object(X) \leftarrow brand(X).$

$same\_type(X, Y) \leftarrow color(X), color(Y).$
$same\_type(X, Y) \leftarrow drink(X), drink(Y).$
$same\_type(X, Y) \leftarrow animal(X), animal(Y).$
$same\_type(X, Y) \leftarrow country(X), country(Y).$
$same\_type(X, Y) \leftarrow brand(X), brand(Y).$

(b) We have a single association predicate $has(X, Y)$ which intuitively means that house number X is associated with object Y. The following three enumeration rules ensure that each house number is associated with a unique object of a particular type, and each object of a particular type is associated with only a particular house number.

$other\_has(X, Y) \leftarrow house(X), object(Y), house(Z), Z \neq X, has(Z, Y).$
$other\_has(X, Y) \leftarrow house(X), object(Y), object(Z), Z \neq Y,$
$\qquad\qquad\qquad\qquad same\_type(Y, Z), has(X, Z).$
$has(X, Y) \leftarrow house(X), object(Y), \textbf{not } other\_has(X, Y).$

(c) The elimination constraints: The fourteen given facts (or observations) are each encoded by the following 14 rules. If the fact i is satisfied then it forces s_i to be true. The following rules are simplified versions of the rules in (1)(c). The simplification is that we no longer have to use different association predicates for objects of different types.

$s_1 \leftarrow house(H), has(H, uk), has(H, red).$
$s_2 \leftarrow house(H), has(H, dog), has(H, spain).$
$s_3 \leftarrow has(1, norway).$
$s_4 \leftarrow house(H), has(H, kools), has(H, yellow).$
$s_5 \leftarrow house(H), house(HH), has(H, chesterfield), has(HH, fox),$
$\qquad next(H, HH).$
$s_6 \leftarrow house(H), house(HH), has(H, blue), has(HH, norway), next(H, HH).$
$s_7 \leftarrow house(H), has(H, winston), has(H, snails).$
$s_8 \leftarrow house(H), has(H, lucky\_strike), has(H, oj).$
$s_9 \leftarrow house(H), has(H, ukraine), has(H, tea).$
$s_{10} \leftarrow house(H), has(H, parliaments), has(H, japan).$
$s_{11} \leftarrow house(H), house(HH), has(H, kools), has(HH, horse), next(H, HH).$

$s_{12} \leftarrow house(H), has(H, green), has(H, coffee).$

$s_{13} \leftarrow house(H), house(HH), has(H, green), has(HH, ivory),$
$\qquad right(HH, H).$

$s_{14} \leftarrow has(3, milk).$

The following rules are the same as in (1)(c).

$satisfied \leftarrow s_1, s_2, s_3, s_4, s_5, s_6, s_7, s_8, s_9, s_{10}, s_{11}, s_{12}, s_{13}, s_{14}.$

$\leftarrow \textbf{not } satisfied.$

4.2 Constraint satisfaction problems (CSPs)

Many problem solving tasks can be cast as a constraint satisfaction problem (CSP) solving which then leads to the solution of the original problem. In this section we formally define a CSP, and show how to encode it in AnsProlog and show that there is a one-to-one correspondence between the solutions to the CSP and the answer sets of the AnsProlog encoding. We then demonstrate this technique with respect to two problem solving tasks. We now formally define a CSP.

A constraint satisfaction problem (CSP) consists of

* a set of *variables*;
* a set of possible values for each variable, called the *domain* of the variable;
* and a set of two kinds of *constraints*: namely allowed and forbidden combinations of variables and values.

A solution to a CSP is an assignment to the variables (among the possible values) such that the constraints are satisfied.

We now give an encoding of a CSP problem P using AnsProlog such that there is a one-to-one correspondence between solutions of the CSP and answer sets of the encoded AnsProlog program $\Pi(P)$.

(1) For each domain value c in the CSP we include the constant C in the language of $\Pi(P)$.
(2) For each domain d in the CSP the program $\Pi(P)$ has a unary predicate d and the following set of facts

$d(c_1) \leftarrow.$
$\vdots$
$d(c_n) \leftarrow.$

where $c_1, \ldots, c_n$ are the possible values of domain d.
(3) For each variable v with the domain d in the CSP the program $\Pi(P)$ has the unary predicates v and $other\_v$ and the rules:

$v(X) \leftarrow d(X), \textbf{not } other\_v(X).$

$other\_v(X) \leftarrow d(X), d(Y), v(Y), X \neq Y.$

(4) For each constraint co giving a set of allowed value combinations for a set of variables $v_1, \ldots, v_j$, $\Pi(P)$ has the fact

$constraint(co) \leftarrow.$

and for each allowed value combination $v_1 = c_1, \ldots, v_j = c_j$, $\Pi(P)$ has the rule

$sat(co) \leftarrow v_1(c_1), \ldots, v_j(c_j).$

and finally $\Pi(P)$ has the rule:

$\leftarrow constraint(C),$ **not** $sat(C).$

(5) For each constraint that disallows combinations $v_1 = c_1, \ldots, v_j = c_j$, the program $\Pi(P)$ has the rule:

$\leftarrow v_1(c_1), \ldots, v_j(c_j).$

Although many problem solving tasks can be formulated as CSPs, often the CSP encoding is more cumbersome and results in a larger encoding than if we were to encode the problem directly in AnsProlog. This happens because the constraints can often be expressed more succinctly by exploiting the relationship between the variables. This relationship is not encoded in a CSP and hence the number of constraints becomes larger. We illustrate this with respect to the n-queens example.

4.2.1 n-queens as a CSP instance

The n-queens problem can be cast as a CSP instance as follows:

- We have n variables which we denote by $r[1], \ldots, r[n]$.
- Each of these variables can take a value between 1 and n. Intuitively, $r[i] = j$ means that in the ith row the queen is placed in the jth column.
- The constraints are: (a) no two rows can have a queen in the same column, that is for $X \neq Y$, the value of $r[X]$ must be different from $r[Y]$; and (b) there should not be two queens that attack each other diagonally. That is, if $r[X] = Y$ and $r[XX] = YY$ and $X \neq XX$ and $Y \neq YY$ then $abs(X - XX) \neq abs(Y - YY)$.

  To conform with the CSP notation we need either a preprocessor or multiple explicit rules to express the above constraints. For example, the constraint (a) is expressible through the following $\frac{n \times (n-1)}{2}$ explicit constraints:

  $r[1] = r[2],\ r[1] = r[3], \ldots,\ r[1] = r[n],\ r[2] = r[3], \ldots,\ r[2] = r[n], \ldots,\ r[n-1]$
  $= r[n]$ are not allowed.

In contrast a direct representation in AnsProlog allows us to treat the X in $r[X]$ as a variable, and thus we can represent the constraints much more succinctly. For example, we can view the predicate $in(X, Y)$ in the encoding (4) of Section 4.1.1 to mean that in row X, the queen is in column Y. Since $in(X, Y)$ is a relation that encodes a function we need the following:

$\leftarrow in(X, Y), in(X, YY), Y \neq YY.$

Now we can write the constraints simply as:

$\leftarrow in(X, Y), in(XX, Y), X \neq XX.$
$\leftarrow in(X, Y), in(XX, YY), abs(X - XX) = abs(Y - YY).$

4.2.2 Schur as a CSP instance

In this problem we are required to assign a set $N = \{1, 2, \ldots, n\}$ of integers into b boxes such that for any $x, y \in N$: (a) x and $2x$ are in different boxes; and (b) if x and y are in the same box, then $x + y$ is in a different box. We can cast this problem as a CSP in the following way:

- We have n variables denoted by $assign[1], \ldots, assign[n]$.
- Each of these variables can take a value between 1 and b.
- To represent the constraint 'x and $2x$ are in different boxes' we need the following explicit disallowed combinations in the CSP notation:

  $assign[1] = assign[2], \; assign[2] = assign[4], \; assign[3] = assign[6], \ldots, \; assign[\lfloor \frac{n}{2} \rfloor]$
  $= assign[2 \times \lfloor \frac{n}{2} \rfloor]$ are not allowed combinations.

  Similarly, to represent the other constraint 'if x and y are in the same box, then $x + y$ is in a different box' we need multiple explicit disallowed combinations in CSP notation.

We now present an AnsProlog$^\perp$ encoding of the above problem that exploits the relationship between the variables. In the following program $in(X, B)$ means that the integer X is assigned to box B.

(1) The domain specifications:

$num(1) \leftarrow .$ $\ldots$ $num(n) \leftarrow .$
$box(1) \leftarrow .$ $\ldots$ $box(b) \leftarrow .$

(2) Assigning integers to boxes:

$not\_in(X, B) \leftarrow num(X), box(B), box(BB), B \neq BB, in(X, BB).$
$in(X, B) \leftarrow num(X), box(B), \textbf{not } not\_in(X, B).$

(3) Constraints:
   (a) The first constraint: x and $2x$ are in different boxes.

      $\leftarrow num(X), box(B), in(X, B), in(X + X, B).$

(b) The second constraint: if x and y are in the same box, then $x + y$ is in a different box.

$$\leftarrow num(X), num(Y), box(B), in(X, B), in(Y, B), in(X + Y, B).$$

Although in the above two examples, the direct encoding in AnsProlog$^{\perp}$ was more succinct than representing it in a CSP and then translating it to an AnsProlog program, there are many problems with good CSP representations and they are good candidates for using the translation method.

4.3 Dynamic constraint satisfaction problems (DCSPs)

A dynamic constraint satisfaction problem (DCSP) is an extension of a CSP and consists of:

(1) a set $V = \{v_1, \ldots, v_n\}$ of variables;
(2) a set $\mathcal{D} = \{D_1, \ldots, D_n\}$ of domains of the variables, each domain consisting of a finite set of values that the corresponding variable can take;
(3) a set $V_I \subseteq V$ of initial variables;
(4) a set of *compatibility constraints* each of which specifies the set of allowed combinations of values for a set of variables $v_1, \ldots, v_j$; and
(5) a set of *activity constraints* that prescribes conditions when a variable must have an assigned value (i.e., be active) and when it must not be active. An activity constraint that activates a variable v is of the form **if** c **then** v, where c is of the form of a compatibility constraint. Similarly, an activity constraint that deactivates a variable v is of the form **if** c **then** **not** v. The former is referred to as a *require activity constraint* and the latter is referred to as a *not-require activity constraint*.

Unlike a CSP, all the variables in a DCSP need not be active, but the set of *initial variables* must be active in every solution. A solution to a DCSP problem is an assignment A of values to variables such that it

(1) satisfies the compatibility constraints (i.e., for all compatibility constraints c either some variable in c is inactive or A satisfies c);
(2) satisfies the activity constraints (i.e., for all activity constraints of the form **if** c **then** v, if A satisfies c then v is active in A);
(3) contains assignments for the initial variables; and
(4) is subset minimal.

4.3.1 Encoding DCSPs in AnsProlog

In this section we only give an encoding of DCSP in AnsProlog$_\oplus$, where $\oplus$ denotes the ex-or operator. The resulting AnsProlog$_\oplus$ program can be translated to an AnsProlog program using the translation described in Section 2.1.16. The mapping of a DCSP to an AnsProlog$_\oplus$ program is as follows:

(1) The language:
   (a) a new distinct atom for each variable v_i to encode its activity,
   (b) a new distinct atom $sat(c_i)$ for each compatibility constraint c_i, and
   (c) a new distinct atom $v_i(val_{i,j})$ for each variable v_i and value $val_{i,j}$ in the domain of v_i.

(2) The rules:
   (a) Each initially active variable is mapped to a fact

   $v_i \leftarrow$.

   (b) Each variable v_i and its domain $\{val_{i,1}, \ldots, val_{i,n}\}$ is mapped to the following rule:

   $v_i(val_{i,1}) \oplus \cdots \oplus v_i(val_{i,n}) \leftarrow v_i$.

   (c) A compatibility constraint on variables $v_1, \ldots, v_n$ is represented using a set of rules of the form:

   $sat(c_i) \leftarrow v_1(val_{1,j}), v_2(val_{2,k}), \ldots, v_n(val_{n,l})$.

   for each allowed value combination $val_{1,j}, val_{2,k}, \ldots, val_{n,l}$.

   In addition we have the following rule that forces each answer set to satisfy the compatibility constraints.

   $\leftarrow v_1, \ldots, v_n, \textbf{not } sat(c_i)$.

   (d) A require activity constraint of the form **if** c **then** v is represented by a set of rules of the form

   $v \leftarrow v_1(val_{1,j}), \ldots, v_n(val_{n,k})$.

   for each allowed combination (as per c) $val_{1,j}, \ldots, val_{n,k}$ of the variables $v_1, \ldots v_n$.

   (e) A not-require activity constraint of the form **if** c **then not** v is represented by a set of rules of the form

   $\leftarrow v, v_1(val_{1,j}), \ldots, v_n(val_{n,k})$.

   for each allowed combination (as per c) $val_{1,j}, \ldots, val_{n,k}$ of the variables $v_1, \ldots v_n$.

Example 83 [SN99] Consider a DCSP with two variables, *package* and *sunroof*, whose domains are $\{luxury, deluxe, standard\}$ and $\{sr_1, sr_2\}$, respectively, a set of initial variables $\{package\}$ and a require activity constraint **if** *package* has value *luxury* **then** *sunroof*. Mapping it to AnsProlog$_\oplus$ results in the following program:

package $\leftarrow$.
package(luxury) $\oplus$ *package(deluxe)* $\oplus$ *package(standard)* $\leftarrow$ *package*.
sunroof(sr$_1$) $\oplus$ *sunroof(sr$_2$)* $\leftarrow$ *sunroof*.
sunroof $\leftarrow$ *package(luxury)*. $\qquad\qquad\qquad\qquad\qquad\qquad\qquad\qquad$ $\square$

4.4 Combinatorial graph problems

In this section we consider several combinatorial graph problems and encode them in AnsProlog$^\perp$.

4.4.1 K-colorability

The first problem that we consider is the k-colorability problem. Given a positive integer k, and a graph G, we say G is k-colorable if each vertex can be assigned one of the k colors so that no two vertices connected by an edge are assigned the same color. The decision problem is to find if a graph is k-colorable. We encode this problem by the following AnsProlog$^\perp$ program:

(1) vertices: Each vertex v of the graph is denoted by the fact

   $vertex(v) \leftarrow$.

(2) edges: Each edge u, v of the graph is denoted by the fact

   $edge(u, v) \leftarrow$.

(3) colors: Each of the k colors are denoted by facts

   $col(c_1) \leftarrow$.   ... $col(c_k) \leftarrow$.

(4) Assigning colors to vertices: The following two rules assign a color to each vertex.

   $another\_color(V, C) \leftarrow vertex(V), col(C), col(D), color\_of(V, D), C \neq D.$

   $color\_of(V, C) \leftarrow vertex(V), col(C), \mathbf{not}\ another\_color(V, C).$

(5) Constraint: The following constraint eliminates the color assignments that violate the rule 'no two vertices connected by an edge have the same color'.

   $\leftarrow col(C), vertex(U), vertex(V), edge(U, V), color\_of(U, C), color\_of(V, C).$

The answer sets of the above program have a one-to-one correspondence with valid color assignments.

4.4.2 Hamiltonian circuit

A Hamiltonian circuit is a path in a graph that visits each vertex of the graph exactly once and returns to the starting vertex. The decision problem is to find if a graph has a Hamiltonian circuit. We encode this problem by the following AnsProlog$^\perp$ program:

(1) vertices: Each vertex v of the graph is denoted by the fact

   $vertex(v) \leftarrow$.

(2) edges: Each edge u, v of the graph is denoted by the fact

$edge(u, v) \leftarrow .$

(3) An initial node: We arbitrarily pick one of the nodes u as the initial node and label it as reachable.

$reachable(u) \leftarrow .$

(4) For each node u of the graph we pick exactly one outgoing edge from that node and label it as *chosen*.

$other(U, V) \leftarrow vertex(U), vertex(V), vertex(W), V \neq W, chosen(U, W).$

$chosen(U, V) \leftarrow vertex(U), vertex(V), edge(U, V), \textbf{not } other(U, V).$

(5) Using the following constraint we enforce that there is only one incoming edge to each vertex.

$\leftarrow chosen(U, W), chosen(V, W), U \neq V.$

(6) We define the vertices that are reachable from our initial vertex and enforce that all vertices be reachable.

$reachable(V) \leftarrow reachable(U), chosen(U, V).$

$\leftarrow vertex(U), \textbf{not } reachable(U).$

Each answer set of the above program encodes a Hamiltonian circuit of the graph and for each Hamiltonian circuit of the graph there is at least one answer set that encodes it.

4.4.3 k-clique

Given a number k and a graph G, we say G has a clique of size k, if there is a set of k different vertices in G such that each pair of vertices from this set is connected through an edge. The decision problem is to find if a graph has a clique of size k. We encode this problem by the following AnsProlog$^\perp$ program:

(1) vertices: Each vertex v of the graph is denoted by the fact

$vertex(v).$

(2) edges: Each edge u, v of the graph is denoted by the fact

$edge(u, v).$

(3) labels: We define $k + 1$ labels $(0, l_1, \ldots, l_k)$ with the intention of labeling each vertex using one of the labels with the restriction that each vertex has a unique label and each

nonzero label is assigned to only one vertex. The k vertices with the k nonzero labels will be our candidates for constituting the clique.

$label(0)$.
$label(l_1)$. $\ldots$ $label(l_k)$.

(4) The following two rules make sure that each vertex is assigned a unique label.

$label\_of(V, L) \leftarrow vertex(V), label(L), \textbf{not } other\_label(V, L)$.

$other\_label(V, L) \leftarrow vertex(V), label(LL), label(L), label\_of(V, LL), L \neq LL$.

(5) To enforce that no two vertices have the same nonzero label we have the following constraint.

$\leftarrow label\_of(V, L), label\_of(VV, L), V \neq VV, L \neq 0$.

(6) The following enforce that each nonzero label is assigned to some vertex.

$assigned(L) \leftarrow label\_of(V, L)$.

$\leftarrow label(L), L \neq 0, \textbf{not } assigned(L)$.

(7) We now test if the chosen k vertices – the ones with nonzero labels – form a clique. If two of the chosen vertices do not have an edge between them, then the set of chosen vertices do not form a clique.

$\leftarrow label\_of(V, L), label\_of(VV, LL), L \neq 0, LL \neq 0, V \neq VV, \textbf{not } edge(V, VV)$.

Each answer set of the above program encodes a clique of size k of the graph and for each clique of size k of the graph there is at least one answer set that encodes it.

4.4.4 Vertex cover

Given a positive integer k and a graph G, we say G has a vertex cover of size k, if there is a set of k different vertices in the graph such that at least one end point of each edge is among these vertices. The decision problem is to find if a graph has a vertex cover of size k. This problem is encoded in AnsProlog by using the rules (1)–(6) of Section 4.4.3 and the following, which tests if the chosen vertices form a vertex cover.

$\leftarrow edge(V, VV), label\_of(V, L), label\_of(VV, LL), L = 0, LL = 0$.

If there is an edge such that both its vertices are not chosen (i.e., are labeled as 0), then the chosen vertices do not form a vertex cover.

4.4.5 Feedback vertex set

Given a positive integer k and a graph G we say that G has a feedback vertex cover of size k, if there is a set S of k different vertices in G such that every cycle of G contains a vertex in S. The decision problem is to find if G has a feedback vertex set of size k. This problem is encoded in AnsProlog$^\perp$ by using the rules (1)–(6) of Section 4.4.3 and the following additional rules.

(1) Defining edges of a new graph (obtained from the original graph) where we eliminate the edges that meet at vertices that have a nonzero label.

$new\_edge(X, Y) \leftarrow edge(X, Y), label\_of(Y) = 0.$

(2) Defining the transitive closure of the new graph.

$trans(X, Y) \leftarrow new\_edge(X, Y).$
$trans(X, Y) \leftarrow new\_edge(X, Z), trans(Z, Y).$

(3) Checking if the new graph has a cycle or not.

$\leftarrow trans(X, X).$

4.4.6 Kernel

Given a directed graph $G = (V, A)$ does there exist a subset $V' \subseteq V$ such that no two vertices are joined by an arc in A and such that for every vertex $v \in V - V'$ there is a vertex $u \in V'$, for which $(u, v) \in A$?

(1) vertices: Each vertex v of the graph is denoted by the fact

$vertex(v).$

(2) edges: Each edge u, v of the graph is denoted by the fact

$edge(u, v).$

(3) Choosing a subset of the vertices.

$chosen(X) \leftarrow \textbf{not } not\_chosen(X).$
$not\_chosen(X) \leftarrow \textbf{not } chosen(X).$

(4) No two chosen vertices are joined by an edge.

$\leftarrow chosen(X), chosen(Y), X \neq Y, edge(X, Y).$

(5) For all nonchosen vertices there is an edge connecting them to a chosen vertex.

$supported(X) \leftarrow not\_chosen(X), edge(X, Y), chosen(Y).$
$\leftarrow not\_chosen(X), \textbf{not } supported(X).$

Each answer set of the above program encodes a kernel of the graph and for each kernel of the graph there is at least one answer set that encodes it.

4.4.7 Exercise

Represent the following combinatorial graph problems in AnsProlog.

(1) Independent Set
Given a graph $G = (V, E)$ and a positive integer $k \leq |V|$, does there exist a subset $V' \subseteq V$ such that $|V'| \geq k$ and such that no two vertices in V' are joined by an edge in E?
(2) Maximal Matching
Given a graph $G = (V, E)$ and a positive integer $k \leq |E|$, does there exists a subset $E' \subseteq E$ with $|E'| \leq k$ such that no two edges in E' share a common endpoint and every edge in $E - E'$ shares a common endpoint with some edge in E'?

4.5 Prioritized defaults and inheritance hierarchies

In Section 2.2.1 we considered AnsProlog* representation of normative statements of the form 'normally elements belonging to class c have the property p' and exceptions to such statements. Often we may need more than that. When we might have contradictory normative statements in which case we may need some rules specifying when one of them should be preferred over the others. We may also have sub-class information and need to encode inheritance together with ways to avoid contradictory inheritances. The early approach to such formalizations was based on directly translating such statements to AnsProlog* rules. One of the limitations of this approach was that to include preferences between possibly contradictory normative statements, the language of AnsProlog* had to be extended to allow specification of such preferences. (We discuss such languages in Section 9.7.) In the absence of that the preferences had to be hard-coded to the rules violating the elaboration tolerance principles.

In this section we discuss an approach where normative statements, exceptions, preferences, etc. are represented as facts, and there are general purpose rules that take these facts and reason with them. (This is similar to our planning modules in Chapter 5 where we separate the domain dependent part and the domain independent part.) The facts encode a particular domain, while the general purpose rules encode particular kinds of reasoning, such as cautious or brave reasoning. An additional advantage of this approach is that we can write rules for the kind of reasoning that we want rather than arguing about which is the right semantics for prioritized defaults.

4.5.1 The language of prioritized defaults

The language consists of four kinds of fact.

(1) $rule(r, l_0, [l_1, \ldots, l_m])$
(2) $default(d, l_0, [l_1, \ldots, l_m])$
(3) $conflict(d_1, d_2)$
(4) $prefer(d_1, d_2)$

where l_is are literals, d and d_is are default names, and r is a rule name.

Intuitively, (1) means that if $l_1, \ldots, l_m$ (the body) are true then l_0 (the head) must also be true, and r is the label (or name) of this rule. (Readers unfamiliar with lists are referred to any PROLOG book and readers using the Smodels or dlv systems are referred to Section 8.3.1.) Similarly, (2) means that *normally* if $l_1, \ldots, l_m$ are true then l_0 should be true, and d is the label (or name) of this default. The facts (3) and (4) mean that d_1 and d_2 are in conflict, and d_1 is to be preferred over d_2, respectively.

A description D of a prioritized default theory is a set of facts of the types (1) and (2). Literals made up of the predicates *conflict* and *prefer* in (3) and (4) can appear in facts of the types (1) and (2). If we simply want to say $conflict(d_1, d_2)$ we may say it by having the following rule of the type (1):

$rule(con(d_1, d_2), conflict(d_1, d_2), [])$.

Similarly, the fact $prefer(d_1, d_2)$ is expressed by the following rule of type (1):

$rule(pref(d_1, d_2), prefer(d_1, d_2), [])$.

4.5.2 The axioms for reasoning with prioritized defaults

Given a description D of a prioritized default theory we have additional domain independent axioms that allow us to reason with D. In these axioms we have two distinct predicates *holds* and *holds_by_default* which define when a literal holds for sure and when it holds by default, respectively. The latter is a weaker conclusion than the former and may be superseded under certain conditions.

(1) Axioms for non-defeasible inference: The following rules define when a literal *holds* and when a set of literals *holds*. Sets are implemented using the list construct. Intuitively, a set of literals holds if each of them holds, and a particular literal l holds if there is a rule with l in its head such that each literal in the body of the rule holds.
   (a) $holds\_list([]) \leftarrow$.
   (b) $holds\_list([H \mid T]) \leftarrow holds(H), holds\_list(T)$.
   (c) $holds(L) \leftarrow rule(R, L, Body), holds\_list(Body)$.

(2) Axioms for defeasible inference: The following rules define when a literal *holds_by_default* and when a set of literals *holds_by_default*. A literal that holds is also assumed to hold by default. A set of literals also holds by default if each literal in the set holds by default, and a particular literal *l* holds by default if there is a default with *l* in its head such that each literal in the body of the rule holds by default, and the rule is not defeated, and the complement of *l* does not hold by default.

   (a) *holds_by_default(L)* ← *holds(L)*.
   (b) *holds_by_default(L)* ← *rule(R, L, Body)*, *holds_list_by_default(Body)*.
   (c) *holds_by_default(L)* ← *default(D, L, Body)*, *holds_list_by_default(Body)*,
   $$\textbf{not } defeated(D), \textbf{not } holds\_by\_default(neg(L)).$$
   (d) *holds_list_by_default([])* ←.
   (e) *holds_list_by_default([H | T])* ← *holds_by_default(H)*, *holds_list_by_default(T)*.

   The third rule above will lead to multiple answer sets if there is a chance that both *l* and its complement may hold by default. In one set of answer sets *l* will hold by default while in the other set of answer sets the complement of *l* will hold by default.

(3) Asymmetry of the preference relation: The following rules make sure that we do not have contradictory preferences. If we do then the following rules will make our theory inconsistent.

   (a) $\neg holds(prefer(D_1, D_2))$ ← $holds(prefer(D_2, D_2)), D_1 \neq D_2$.
   (b) $\neg holds\_by\_default(prefer(D_1, D_2))$ ← $holds\_by\_default(prefer(D_2, D_1))$,
   $$D_1 \neq D_2.$$

(4) Defining conflict between defaults: The following rules define when conflicts between two defaults hold.

   (a) $holds(conflict(d, d'))$ ← $default(d, l_0, B), default(d', l_0', B'), contrary(l_0, l_0')$,
   $$d \neq d'.$$
   (b) $holds(conflict(d, d'))$ ← $prefer(d, d'), prefer(d', d), d \neq d'$.
   (c) $\neg holds(conflict(d, d))$ ←.
   (d) $holds(conflict(d, d'))$ ← $holds(conflict(D', d))$.

(5) Axioms that defeat defaults: We are now ready to define the notion of when a default is defeated. Different definitions of this notion lead to different kinds of reasoning.

   (a) The brave approach: In the brave approach if we have two conflicting defaults one will be considered defeated if the other is preferred over it and the other is not itself defeated. Thus if we have two conflicting defaults such that neither is preferred over the other, then neither will be defeated (in the same answer set), and we can apply both defaults in answer sets corresponding to each. The rule (2)(c) may then lead to two sets of answer sets each reflecting the application of one of the defaults.

      (i) $defeated(D)$ ← $default(D, L, Body), holds(neg(L))$.
      (ii) $defeated(D)$ ← $default(D, L, Body), default(D', L', Body')$,
      $$holds(conflict(D', D)), holds\_by\_default(prefer(D', D)),$$
      $$holds\_list\_by\_default(Body'), \textbf{not } defeated(D').$$

   (b) The cautious approach: In the cautious approach if we have two conflicting defaults such that neither is preferred over the other, then both will be defeated. Thus we cannot use (2)(c) with respect to either of the defaults.

(i) *defeated*(*D*) ← *default*(*D*, *L*, *Body*), *default*(*D'*, *L'*, *Body'*),

$\quad\quad\quad$ *holds*(*conflict*(*D'*, *D*)),

$\quad\quad\quad$ **not** *holds_by_default*(*prefer*(*D'*, *D*)),

$\quad\quad\quad$ **not** *holds_by_default*(*prefer*(*D*, *D'*)),

$\quad\quad\quad$ *holds_list_by_default*(*Body*), *holds_list_by_default*(*Body'*).

(6) Uniqueness of names for defaults and rules: The following constraints make sure that rules and defaults have unique names.

(a) ← *rule*(*R*, *F*, *B*), *default*(*R*, *F'*, *B'*).

(b) ← *rule*(*R*, *F*, *B*), *rule*(*R'*, *F'*, *B'*), *F* ≠ *F'*.

(c) ← *rule*(*R*, *F*, *B*), *rule*(*R'*, *F'*, *B'*), *B* ≠ *B'*.

(d) ← *default*(*R*, *F*, *B*), *default*(*R'*, *F'*, *B'*), *F* ≠ *F'*.

(e) ← *default*(*R*, *F*, *B*), *default*(*R'*, *F'*, *B'*), *B* ≠ *B'*.

(7) Auxiliary rules: We need the following self-explanatory additional rules.

(a) *contrary*(*l*, *neg*(*l*)) ←.

(b) *contrary*(*neg*(*l*), *l*) ←.

(c) ¬*holds*(*L*) ← *holds*(*neg*(*L*)).

(d) ¬*holds_by_default*(*L*) ← *holds_by_default*(*neg*(*L*)).

We will refer to the set of rules consisting of rules (1)–(4), (5)(a), (6) and (7) as $\pi_{pd}^{indep.brave}$ and the set of rules (1)–(4), (5)(b), (6) and (7) as $\pi_{pd}^{indep.cautious}$.

Example 84 (Legal reasoning) [Bre94, GS97a] Consider the following legal rules and facts about a particular case.

(1) Uniform commercial code (UCC): A security interest in goods may be perfected by taking possession of the collateral.

(2) Ship Mortgage Act (SMA): A security interest in a ship may only be perfected by filing a financial statement.

(3) Principle of *Lex Posterior*: A newer law has preference over an older law.

(4) Principle of *Lex Posterior* gives precedence to laws supported by the higher authority. Federal laws have a higher authority than state laws.

(5) A financial statement has not been filed.

(6) John has possession of the ship *johns_ship*.

(7) UCC is more recent than SMA.

(8) SMA is a federal law.

(9) UCC is a state law.

From the above we would like to find out if John's security interest in *johns_ship* is perfected.

The legal rules and the facts of the case can be represented by the following set $\pi_{pd.1}^{dep}$ of prioritized default facts.

(1) *default*(*d*₁, *perfected*, [*possession*]) ←.

(2) $default(d_2, \neg perfected, [\neg filed]) \leftarrow$.
(3) $default(d_3(D_1, D_2), prefer(D_1, D_2), [more\_recent(D_1, D_2)]) \leftarrow$.
(4) $default(d_4(D_1, D_2), prefer(D_1, D_2), [federal(D_1), state(D_2)]) \leftarrow$.
(5) $\neg filed \leftarrow$.
(6) $possession \leftarrow$.
(7) $more\_recent(d_1, d_2) \leftarrow$.
(8) $federal(d_2) \leftarrow$.
(9) $state(d_1) \leftarrow$.

The program $\pi_{pd}^{indep.brave} \cup \pi_{pd.1}^{dep}$ has two answer sets one containing $holds\_by\_default(perfected)$ and another containing $\neg holds\_by\_default(perfected)$.

But if we add the fact $rule(r, prefer(d4(D_1, D_2), d3(D_2, D_1)), [])$ to $\pi_{pd}^{indep.brave} \cup \pi_{pd.1}^{dep}$, then the resulting program has only one answer set that contains $\neg holds\_by\_default(perfected)$. $\square$

4.5.3 Modeling inheritance hierarchies using prioritized defaults

In this section we show how general principles about reasoning with inheritance hierarchies can be expressed using prioritized defaults. An inheritance hierarchy contains information about *subclass* relationships between classes, membership information about classes, and when elements of a class normally have or normally do not have a particular property. An example of a particular inheritance hierarchy $\pi_{pd.ih1}^{dep}$ is as follows:

(1) $subclass(a, b \leftarrow)$.
(2) $subclass(c, b) \leftarrow$.
(3) $is\_in(x_1, a) \leftarrow$.
(4) $is\_in(x_2, c) \leftarrow$.
(5) $default(d_1(X), has\_prop(X, p), [is\_in(X, b)]) \leftarrow$.
(6) $default(d_2(X), \neg has\_prop(X, p), [is\_in(X, c)]) \leftarrow$.

To reason with inheritance hierarchies we have three basic rules: (i) transitivity about the sub-class relationship, (ii) inheritance due to the sub-class relationship, and (iii) the preference principle based on specificity which says that the default property of a more specific class should be preferred over the default property of a less specific class. These three rules can be expressed by the following rules in the prioritized default language.

(1) $rule(trans(C_0, C_2), subclass(C_0, C_2), [subclass(C_0, C_1), subclass(C_1, C_2) \leftarrow$.
(2) $rule(inh(X, C_1), is\_in(X, C_1), [subclass(C_0, C_1), is\_in(X, C_0)]) \leftarrow$.
(3) $rule(pref(D_1(X), D_2(X)), prefer(D_1(X), D_2(X)),$
    $[default(D_1(X), \_, [is\_in(X, A)]), default(D_2(X), \_, [is\_in(X, B)]),$
    $subclass(A, B)]) \leftarrow$.

In addition we may have the following two defaults which play the role of closed world assumption (CWA) with respect to the predicates *is_in* and *subclass*. These defaults can be expressed by the following defaults from the prioritized default language.

(4) $default(d_3(X), \neg is\_in(X), []) \leftarrow$.
(5) $default(d_4, \neg subclass(A, B), []) \leftarrow$.

We refer to the last five rules as the domain independent formulation to reason with inheritance hierarchies, and denote them by $\pi^{dep}_{pd.ih.indep}$. The *indep* in the subscript refers to this independence. The *dep* in the superscript refers to the fact that inheritance hierarchies are a particular case of prioritized defaults. It is easy to check that the program $\pi^{dep}_{pd.ih.indep} \cup \pi^{dep}_{pd.ih1} \cup \pi^{indep.brave}_{pd}$ has a unique answer set containing $holds\_by\_default(has(x_1, p))$ and $holds\_by\_default(has(x_2, p))$.

4.5.4 Exercise

(1) Consider the bird flying example from Section 2.2.1 and express it using the approach in the previous section.
(2) Consider extended defaults of the form $default(d, l_0, [l_1, \ldots, l_m], [l_{m+1}, \ldots, l_n])$ whose intuitive meaning is that *normally* if $l_1, \ldots, l_m$ are true and there is no reason to believe $l_{m+1}, \ldots, l_n$, then l_0 can be assumed to be true by default.
    Define AnsProlog* rules for *defeated* and *holds_by_default* for reasoning with such extended defaults.
(3) Consider weak exceptions to defaults which are of the form $exception(d, l_0, [l_1, \ldots, l_m], [l_{m+1}, \ldots, l_n])$ and which intuitively mean that default d is not applicable to an object about which $l_1, \ldots, l_m$ are true and there is no reason to believe $l_{m+1}, \ldots, l_n$ to be true.
    Define AnsProlog* rules for *defeated* for reasoning with prioritized defaults in the presence of such weak exceptions.
(4) Define conditions that guarantee consistency of descriptions in the language of prioritized defaults and the above mentioned extensions. Prove your claims.

4.6 Notes and references

The n-queens problem is found in most PROLOG books. The zebra puzzle is also found in many PROLOG books and puzzle sites on the web. The tile covering problem is considered in automated reasoning books (such as [WBOL92]), and has elegant automated reasoning solutions about the nonexistence of a covering given a mutilated tile with a square missing in two diagonal corners. Many of those solutions are superior to our formulation in that they do not enumerate the various possibilities.

Representing constraint satisfaction problems is studied in [Nie99] and extended to dynamic constraint satisfaction problems in [SGN99]. Representation of graph problems in nonmonotonic languages was first done in [CMMT95]. Reasoning about prioritized defaults is studied in [GS97a]. Some of the other knowledge representation examples that we did not explore in this chapter include representation of null values [GT93] and representation of aggregates [WZ00b, WZ00c, WZ98].

Chapter 5

Reasoning about actions and planning in AnsProlog*

In Chapter 4 we formulated several knowledge representation and problem solving domains using AnsProlog* and focused on the program development aspect. In this chapter we consider reasoning about actions in a dynamic world and its application to plan verification, simple planning, planning with various kinds of domain constraints, observation assimilation and explanation, and diagnosis. We do a detailed and systematic formulation – in AnsProlog* – of the above issues starting from the simplest reasoning about action scenarios and gradually increasing its expressiveness by adding features such as causal constraints, and parallel execution of actions. We also prove properties of our AnsProlog* formulations using the results in Chapter 3.

Our motivation behind the choice of a detailed formulation of this domain is twofold. (i) Reasoning about actions captures both major issues of this book: knowledge representation and declarative problem solving. To reason about actions we need to formulate the frame problem whose intuitive meaning is that objects in the worlds do not normally change their properties. Formalizing this has been one of the benchmark problems of knowledge representation and reasoning formalisms. We show how AnsProlog* is up to this task. Reasoning about actions also forms the ground work for planning with actions, an important problem solving task. We present AnsProlog encodings of planning such that the answer sets each encode a plan. (ii) Our second motivation is in regard to the demonstration of the usefulness of the results in Chapter 3. We analyze and prove properties of our AnsProlog* formulations of reasoning about actions and planning by using the various results in Chapter 3, and thus illustrate their usefulness. For this reason we start with a simple reasoning about action scenario and gradually move into more expressive scenarios.

5.1 Reasoning in the action description language $\mathcal{A}$

To systematically reason about actions, we follow the dual characterization approach where there are two separate formalizations, one in a high level English-like language with its own intuitive semantics, and the other in a logical language which in this book is AnsProlog*; so that the second one can be validated with respect to the first one.

We choose the language $\mathcal{A}$, proposed by Gelfond and Lifschitz in [GL92], as the starting point of our high level language. This language has a simple English-like syntax to express the effects of actions on a world and the initial state of the world, and an automata based semantics to reason about the effects of a sequence of actions on the world. Historically, $\mathcal{A}$ is remarkable for its simplicity and has been later extended in several directions to incorporate additional features of dynamic worlds and to facilitate elaboration tolerance. We now present the language $\mathcal{A}$. Our presentation of $\mathcal{A}$ will be slightly different from [GL92] and will follow the current practices of presenting action languages through three distinct sub-languages: *domain description language*, *observation language*, and *query language*.

5.1.1 The language $\mathcal{A}$

The alphabet of the language $\mathcal{A}$ consists of two nonempty disjoint sets of symbols **F** and **A**. They are called the set of fluents, and the set of actions. Intuitively, a fluent expresses the property of an object in a world, and forms part of the description of states of the world. A *fluent literal* is a fluent or a fluent preceded by $\neg$. A *state* σ is a collection of fluents. We say a fluent f holds in a state σ if $f \in \sigma$. We say a fluent literal $\neg f$ holds in σ if $f \notin \sigma$.

For example, in the blocks world domain where there are many blocks on a table, some of the fluents are: *ontable(a)*, meaning that block a is on the table; *on(a, b)*, meaning that block a is on block b; *clear(a)*, meaning that the top of block a is clear; *handempty*, meaning that the hand is empty. These fluents are also fluent literals, and some other examples of fluent literals are: $\neg on(a, b)$, meaning that block a is not on top of block b; $\neg clear(b)$, meaning that the top of block b is not clear. An example of a state where we have only two blocks a and b is $\sigma = \{ontable(b), on(a, b), clear(a), handempty\}$. Besides the fluent literals that are in σ, we also have that $\neg ontable(a)$, $\neg on(b, a)$, and $\neg clear(b)$ hold in σ. Examples of actions in this domain are: *pickup(a)*, which picks up block a from the table; *putdown(b)*, which puts down block b on the table; *stack(a, b)*, which stacks block a on top of block b; and *unstack(a, b)*, which unstacks block a from the top of block b. Actions when successfully executed change the state of the world. For example, the action *unstack(a, b)* when performed in the state σ results in the state $\sigma' = \{ontable(b), clear(b)\}$.

Situations are representations of the history of action execution. In the initial situation no action has been executed: we represent this by the empty list [ ]. The situation $[a_n, \ldots, a_1]$ corresponds to the history where action a_1 is executed in the initial situation, followed by a_2, and so on until a_n. There is a simple relation between situations and states. In each situation s certain fluents are true and certain others are false, and this 'state of the world' is the state corresponding to s. In the above example if the situation [ ] corresponds to the state σ, then the situation $[unstack(a, b)]$ corresponds to the state σ'. Since the state of the world could be the same for different histories, different situations may correspond to the same state. Thus the situations [ ], $[stack(a, b), unstack(a, b)]$, $[stack(a, b), unstack(a, b),$ $stack(a, b), unstack(a, b)]$, ... correspond to σ, and the situations $[unstack(a, b)]$, $[unstack(a, b), stack(a, b), unstack(a, b)]$, ... correspond to σ'.

We now present the three sub-languages of $\mathcal{A}$.

(1) Domain description language: The domain description language is used to succinctly express the transition between states due to actions. A straightforward representation of this transition would be a 3-dimensional table of the size mn^2 where m is the number of actions and n is the number of states. Since the number of states can be of the order of $2^{|\mathbf{F}|}$, such a representation is often shunned. In addition to the space concerns, another concern is the issue of elaboration tolerance: how easy it is to update the representation in case we have elaborations, such as a few more fluents or a few more actions. The domain description sub-language of $\mathcal{A}$ is concerned with both issues.

A domain description D consists of effect propositions of the following form:

$$a \textbf{ causes } f \textbf{ if } p_1, \ldots, p_n, \neg q_1, \ldots, \neg q_r \qquad (5.1.1)$$

where a is an action, f is a fluent literal, and $p_1, \ldots, p_n, q_1, \ldots, q_r$ are fluents. Intuitively, the above effect proposition means that if the fluent literals $p_1, \ldots, p_n$, $\neg q_1, \ldots, \neg q_r$ hold in the state corresponding to a situation s then in the state corresponding to the situation reached by executing a in s (denoted by $[a|s]$) the fluent literal f must hold. If both n and r are equal to 0 in (5.1.1) then we simply write:

$$a \textbf{ causes } f \qquad (5.1.2)$$

Moreover, we often condense a set of effect propositions $\{a \textbf{ causes } f_1, \ldots, a$ $\textbf{causes } f_m\}$ by

$$a \textbf{ causes } f_1, \ldots, f_m \qquad (5.1.3)$$

We also allow as, fs and p_is in (5.1.1) to have schema variables. Such an effect proposition with schema variables is a shorthand for the set of ground effect propositions obtained by substituting the variables with objects in the domain.

Example 85 Consider the blocks world domain. Let us assume that we have three blocks a, b, and c and a table. The effect of the action $pickup(X)$ can be expressed by the following effect propositions with schema variables:

$pickup(X) \textbf{ causes } \neg ontable(X), \neg handempty, \neg clear(X), holding(X)$

For this domain with three blocks a, b, and c, the above is a shorthand for the following three effect propositions without any schema variables.

pickup(*a*) **causes** ¬*ontable*(*a*), ¬*handempty*, ¬*clear*(*a*), *holding*(*a*)
pickup(*b*) **causes** ¬*ontable*(*b*), ¬*handempty*, ¬*clear*(*b*), *holding*(*b*)
pickup(*c*) **causes** ¬*ontable*(*c*), ¬*handempty*, ¬*clear*(*c*), *holding*(*c*)   □

As mentioned earlier, the role of effect propositions is to define a transition function from states and actions to states. Given a domain description D, such a transition function Φ should satisfy the following properties. For all actions a, fluents g, and states σ:

- if D includes an effect proposition of the form (5.1.1) where f is the fluent g and $p_1, \ldots, p_n, \neg q_1, \ldots, \neg q_r$ hold in σ then $g \in \Phi(a, \sigma)$;
- if D includes an effect proposition of the form (5.1.1) where f is a negative fluent literal $\neg g$ and $p_1, \ldots, p_n, \neg q_1, \ldots, \neg q_r$ hold in σ then $g \notin \Phi(a, \sigma)$; and
- if D does not include such effect propositions, then $g \in \Phi(a, \sigma)$ iff $g \in \sigma$.

For a given domain description D, there is at most one transition function that satisfies the above properties. If such a transition function exists, then we say D is consistent, and refer to its transition function by Φ_D.

An example of an inconsistent domain description D_1 consists of the following.

a **causes** f
a **causes** $\neg f$

In the rest of this section, we only consider consistent domain descriptions.

(2) Observation language: A set[1] of observations O consists of value propositions of the following form:

$$f \textbf{ after } a_1, \ldots, a_m \tag{5.1.4}$$

where f is a fluent literal and $a_1, \ldots, a_m$ are actions. Intuitively, the above value proposition means that if $a_1, \ldots, a_m$ would be executed in the initial situation then in the state corresponding to the situation $[a_m, \ldots, a_1]$, f would hold.

When $a_1, \ldots, a_m$ is an empty sequence, we write the above as follows:

$$\textbf{initially } f \tag{5.1.5}$$

In this case the intuitive meaning is that f holds in the state corresponding to the initial situation. Here we also condense a set of value propositions of the form {**initially** $f_1, \ldots,$ **initially** f_k} by

$$\textbf{initially } f_1, \ldots, f_k \tag{5.1.6}$$

Given a consistent domain description D the set of observations O is used to determine the states corresponding to the initial situation, referred to as the *initial states* and

---

[1] In this chapter when listing a set of value propositions or effect propositions we use ';' between two propositions.

denoted by σ_0. While D determines a unique transition function, an O may not always lead to a unique initial state.

We say σ_0 is an initial state corresponding to a consistent domain description D and a set of observations O, if for all observations of the form (5.1.4) in O, the fluent literal f holds in the state $\Phi(a_m, \Phi(a_{m-1}, \ldots \Phi(a_1, \sigma_0) \ldots))$. (We will denote this state by $[a_m, \ldots, a_1]\sigma_0$.) We then say that (σ_0, Φ_D) *satisfies* O.

Given a consistent domain description D and a set of observations O, we refer to the pair (Φ_D, σ_0), where Φ_D is the transition function of D and σ_0 is an initial state corresponding to (D, O), as a *model* of (D, O). We say (D, O) is *consistent* if it has a model and say it is *complete* if it has a unique model.

Example 86 Consider the Yale turkey shooting domain where we have the fluents *alive* and *loaded*, and actions *load* and *shoot*. The effect of the actions can be expressed by the following domain description D:

load **causes** *loaded*
shoot **causes** ¬*alive* **if** *loaded*

Suppose we have the set of observations $O = \{$**initially** *alive*$\}$. There are two initial states corresponding to (D, O): $\sigma_0 = \{alive\}$ and $\sigma_0' = \{alive, loaded\}$.   □

(3) Query language: Queries also consist of value propositions of the form (5.1.4).

We say a consistent domain description D in the presence of a set of observations O entails a query Q of the form (5.1.4) if for all initial states σ_0 corresponding to (D, O), the fluent literal f holds in the state $[a_m, \ldots, a_1]\sigma_0$. We denote this as $D \models_O Q$.

Example 87 Consider D and O from Example 86. An example of a query Q in this domain is ¬*alive* **after** *shoot*. Since there are two initial states, σ_0 and σ_0', corresponding to (D, O), and while ¬*alive* holds in $[shoot]\sigma_0'$, it does not hold in $[shoot]\sigma_0$. Hence, $D \not\models_O Q$.

On the other hand $D \models_O$ ¬*alive* **after** *load, shoot* and also if $O' = \{$**initially** *alive*; **initially** *loaded*$\}$, then $D \models_{O'} Q$.   □

We can use the above formulation to enable several different kinds of reasoning about actions such as predicting the future from information about the initial state, assimilating observations to deduce about the initial state, a combination of both, and planning.

- **Temporal projection**: In temporal projection, the observations are only of the form (5.1.5) and the only interest is to make conclusions about the (hypothetical) future. There are two particular cases of temporal projection: when the observations give us a complete picture of the initial state, and when they do not. The former is referred to as the initial state being complete, and is formally defined below.

A set of observations O is said to be *initial state complete*, if O only consists of propositions of the form (5.1.5) and for all fluents f, either **initially** f is in O, or **initially** $\neg f$ is in O, but not both. For example, the set of observations O' in Example 87 is initial state complete.

In the latter case we say an initial state complete set of observations $\hat{O}$ extends O if $O \subseteq \hat{O}$. For example, the set of observations O' in Example 87 extends the set of observations O in Example 86. Moreover, the entailments in Examples 86 and 87 are examples of temporal projection.

• **Reasoning about the initial situation**: In reasoning about the initial situation, the observations can be about any situation, but the queries are only about the initial state. The following example illustrates this.

Example 88 Let $O_1 = \{$**initially** *alive*; $\neg$*alive* **after** *shoot*$\}$ and D be the domain description from Example 86. In this case there is exactly one initial state, $\{$*alive, loaded*$\}$, corresponding to (D, O_1) and we have $D \models_{O_1}$ **initially** *loaded*. Hence, from the observations O_1 we can reason backwards and conclude that the gun was initially loaded. □

• **Observation assimilation**: This generalizes temporal projection and reasoning about the initial situation. In this case both the observations and the queries can be about any situation.

Example 89 Let $O_2 = \{$**initially** *alive; loaded* **after** *shoot*$\}$ and D be the domain description from Example 86. In this case there also is exactly one initial state, $\{$*alive, loaded*$\}$, corresponding to (D, O_2) and we have $D \models_{O_2} \neg$*alive* **after** *shoot*. Hence, assimilating the observations O_2, we can conclude that if shooting happens in the initial situation then after that the turkey will not be alive. □

• **Planning**: In the case of planning we are given a domain description D, a set of observations about the initial state O, and a collection of fluent literals $G = \{g_1, \ldots, g_l\}$, which we will refer to as a goal. We are required to find a sequence of actions $a_1, \ldots, a_n$ such that for all $1 \le i \le l$, $D \models_O g_i$ **after** $a_1, \ldots, a_n$. We then say that $a_1, \ldots, a_n$ is a plan for goal G (or achieves goal G) with respect to (D, O).

If (D, O) have multiple models each with a different initial state then if we are able to find a sequence of actions $a_1, \ldots, a_n$ such that for all $1 \le i \le l$, $D \models_O g_i$ **after** $a_1, \ldots, a_n$, the sequence $a_1, \ldots, a_n$ is referred to as a conformant plan.

Example 90 Recall that $O = \{$**initially** *alive*$\}$ and $O' = \{$**initially** *alive*; **initially** *loaded*$\}$ in Examples 86 and 87. Let D be the domain description from Example 86. Now suppose $G = \{\neg$*alive*$\}$. In that case *shoot* is a plan for G with respect to (D, O'); *shoot* is not a plan for G with respect to (D, O). Moreover *load; shoot* is a plan for G with respect to (D, O). □

We now present several simple results relating models of domain descriptions and observations. These results will later be used in analyzing the correctness of AnsProlog* encodings of the various kinds of reasoning about actions.

Lemma 5.1.1 Let D be a consistent domain description and O be an initial state complete set of observations such that (D, O) is consistent. Then (D, O) has a unique model (σ_0, Φ_D), where $\sigma_0 = \{f \; : \; \textbf{initially} \; f \in O\}$.   □

Lemma 5.1.2 Let D be a consistent domain description and O be a set of observations about the initial state such that (D, O) is consistent. Then (σ_0, Φ_D) is a model of (D, O) iff $\{f \; : \; \textbf{initially} \; f \in O\} \subseteq \sigma_0$ and $\sigma_0 \cap \{f \; : \; \textbf{initially} \; \neg f \in O\} = \emptyset$.   □

Corollary 2 Let D be a consistent domain description and O be a set of observations about the initial state such that (D, O) is consistent. Then (σ_0, Φ_D) is a model of (D, O) iff there exists an extension $\hat{O}$ of O such that (σ_0, Φ_D) is the unique model of $(D, \hat{O})$.   □

Corollary 3 Let D be a consistent domain description and O be a set of observations about the initial state such that (D, O) is consistent. For any fluent f and a sequence of actions $a_1, \ldots, a_n$, $D \models_O (\neg)f$ **after** $a_1, \ldots, a_n$ iff for all $\hat{O}$ such that $\hat{O}$ extends O, $D \models_{\hat{O}} (\neg)f$ **after** $a_1, \ldots, a_n$.   □

Lemma 5.1.3 Let D be a consistent domain description and O be a set of observations. Then $M = (\sigma_0, \Phi_D)$ is a model of (D, O) iff M is the model of (D, O_M), where $O_M = \{\textbf{initially} \; f \; : \; f \in \sigma_0\} \cup \{\textbf{initially} \; \neg f \; : \; f \notin \sigma_0\}$.   □

In Sections 5.1.2–5.1.6 we give AnsProlog* formulations that (partially) compute the entailment relation $\models_O$, given a domain description D and a set of observations O. The programs that we present $(\pi_1(D, O)-\pi_6(D, O))$ are all sorted programs as introduced in Section 3.5.1, which means that variables in these programs are grounded based on their sorts. We have three sorts: *situations, fluents*, and *actions*, and variables of these sorts are denoted by $S, S' \ldots$; $F, F', \ldots$; and $A, A', \ldots$, respectively. The sorts of the arguments of the function symbols and predicates in the programs $\pi_1(D, O)-\pi_6(D, O)$ are clear from the context. In these formulations we use the notation $[a_n, \ldots, a_1]$ to denote the situation $res(a_n \ldots res(a_1, s_0) \ldots)$. Table 5.1 gives a summary of which AnsProlog* subclass the programs $\pi_1(D, O)-\pi_6(D, O)$ belong to and what kind of reasoning they make about actions.

Table 5.1. *Applicability of programs π_1–π_6*

Programs	Class	Applicability
π_1	AnsProlog	temporal projection from a complete initial state
π_2	AnsProlog$^\neg$	temporal projection from a complete initial state
π_3	AnsProlog$^\neg$	temporal projection from a (possibly incomplete) initial state
π_4	AnsProlog$^\neg$	temporal projection, backward reasoning
π_5	AnsProlog$^\neg$	temporal projection, assimilation of observations
π_6	AnsProlog$^{\neg,\,or}$	temporal projection, assimilation of observations

5.1.2 Temporal projection and its acyclicity in an AnsProlog formulation: π_1

In this section we give an AnsProlog formulation of temporal projection. In particular, given a domain description D and a set of observations O which is initial state complete, we construct an AnsProlog program $\pi_1(D, O)$ and show the correspondence between query entailment from (D, O) and entailment in $\pi_1(D, O)$. The AnsProlog program $\pi_1(D, O)$ consists of three parts π_1^{ef}, π_1^{obs}, and π_1^{in} as defined below.

(1) Translating effect propositions: The effect propositions in D are translated as follows and are collectively referred to as π_1^{ef}.

For every effect proposition of the form (5.1.1) if f is a fluent then π_1^{ef} contains the following rule:

$$holds(f, res(a, S)) \leftarrow holds(p_1, S), \ldots, holds(p_n, S),$$
$$\textbf{not } holds(q_1, S), \ldots, \textbf{not } holds(q_r, S).$$

else, if f is the negative fluent literal $\neg g$ then π_1^{ef} contains the following rule:

$$ab(g, a, S) \leftarrow holds(p_1, S), \ldots, holds(p_n, S), \textbf{not } holds(q_1, S), \ldots, \textbf{not } holds(q_r, S).$$

(2) Translating observations: The value propositions in O are translated as follows and are collectively referred to as π_1^{obs}.

For every value proposition of the form (5.1.5) if f is a fluent then π_1^{obs} contains the following rule:

$$holds(f, s_0) \leftarrow.$$

Note that if f is a negative fluent literal, we do not add any rule corresponding to it to π_1^{obs}.

(3) Inertia rules: Besides the above we have the following inertia rule referred to by π_1^{in}.

$$holds(F, res(A, S)) \leftarrow holds(F, S), \textbf{not } ab(F, A, S).$$

Example 91 Consider D from Example 86, and let $O_3 = \{$ **initially** *alive*; **initially** $\neg$ *loaded*$\}$. The program $\pi_1(D, O_3)$, which is the same as the program in part (1) of Section 2.2.2, consists of the following:

holds(loaded, res(load, S)) $\leftarrow$.
ab(alive, shoot, S) $\leftarrow$ *holds(loaded, S)*.

holds(alive, s_0) $\leftarrow$.

holds(F, res(A, S)) $\leftarrow$ *holds(F, S)*, **not** *ab(F, A, S)*.

It is easy to see that $\pi_1(D, O_3) \models holds(alive, [load])$, $\pi_1(D, O_3) \models holds(loaded, [load])$, and $\pi_1(D, O_3) \models \neg holds(alive, [shoot, load])$.

Note that $\pi_1(D, O_3) \not\models \neg holds(alive, [shoot, load])$. Thus, we must treat $\pi_1(D, O_3)$ as an AnsProlog program, not as an AnsProlog$^\neg$ program. $\qquad\square$

We now analyze $\pi_1(D, O)$ and relate entailments with respect to $\pi_1(D, O)$ with queries entailed by (D, O).

Proposition 69 Let D be a consistent domain description and O be an initial state complete set of observations. Then $\pi_1(D, O)$ is acyclic. $\qquad\square$

Proof: To show $\pi_1(D, O)$ is acyclic we need to give a level mapping λ to atoms in the language of $\pi_1(D, O)$ so that the acyclicity condition holds. To facilitate that we first give a level mapping to terms.

We assign $\lambda(s_0) = 1$, and for any action a and situation s, $\lambda(res(a, s)) = \lambda(s) + 1$. For any fluent f, action a, and situation s, we assign $\lambda(holds(f, s)) = 2 \times \lambda(s)$ and $\lambda(ab(f, a, s)) = 2 \times \lambda(s) + 1$. It is easy to see that this level assignment satisfies the acyclicity condition for the AnsProlog program $\pi_1(D, O)$. $\qquad\square$

The following corollary follows from the above proposition and Proposition 34.

Corollary 4 Let D be a consistent domain description and O be an initial state complete set of observations. Then $\pi_1(D, O)$ has the following properties.

(1) It has a unique answer set. (Let us call it M.)

(2) $A \in M$ iff $Comp(\pi_1(D, O)) \models A$. $\qquad\square$

Lemma 5.1.4 Let D be a consistent domain description and O be an initial state complete set of observations such that (D, O) is consistent. Let (σ_0, Φ_D) be the unique model of (D, O) and M be the answer set of $\pi_1(D, O)$. Let f be a fluent.

$f \in \Phi_D(a_n, \dots, \Phi_D(a_1, \sigma_0) \dots)$ iff $holds(f, [a_n, \dots, a_1]) \in M$. $\qquad\square$

Proof: We prove this by induction on the length of the action sequence.

Base case: $n = 0$.

$\implies f \in \sigma_0$ implies that **initially** $f \in D$ which implies that $holds(f, s_0) \leftarrow . \in \pi_1(D, O)$. This implies $holds(f, s_0) \in M$.

$\impliedby holds(f, s_0) \in M$ implies that $holds(f, s_0) \leftarrow . \in \pi_1(D, O)$, as no other rule in $\pi_1(D, O)$ has $holds(f, s_0)$ in its head. This implies that **initially** $f \in D$ which implies that $f \in \sigma_0$.

Inductive case: Assuming that the lemma holds for all $i < n$, let us show that it holds for $i = n$. Let us denote $\Phi_D(a_i, \ldots, \Phi_D(a_1, \sigma_0) \ldots)$ by σ_i.

($\implies$) $f \in \sigma_n$ implies two cases:

(i) $f \in \sigma_{n-1}$ and there does not exist an effect proposition of the form a **causes** $\neg f$
   if $p_1, \ldots, p_k, \neg q_1, \ldots, \neg q_r$ such that $p_1, \ldots, p_k, \neg q_1, \ldots, \neg q_r$ hold in σ_{n-1}.
(ii) there exists an effect proposition of the form a **causes** f **if** $p_1, \ldots, p_k, \neg q_1, \ldots, \neg q_r$
   such that $p_1, \ldots, p_k, \neg q_1, \ldots, \neg q_r$ hold in σ_{n-1}.

Case (i) : By induction hypothesis, $f \in \sigma_{n-1}$ implies $holds(f, [a_{n-1}, \ldots, a_1]) \in M$. We will now argue that the second part of (i) implies that $ab(f, a_n, [a_{n-1}, \ldots, a_1]) \notin M$. Let us assume the contrary. That is, $ab(f, a_n, [a_{n-1}, \ldots, a_1]) \in M$. Then by part (b) of Proposition 20 there must be a rule in $\pi_1(D, O)$ whose head is $ab(f, a_n, [a_{n-1}, \ldots, a_1])$ and whose body evaluates to true with respect to M. That means there must be an effect proposition of the form a **causes** $\neg f$ **if** $p_1, \ldots, p_k, \neg q_1, \ldots, \neg q_r$ such that $\{holds(p_1, [a_{n-1}, \ldots, a_1]), \ldots, holds(p_k, [a_{n-1}, \ldots, a_1])\} \subseteq M$ and $\{holds(q_1, [a_{n-1}, \ldots, a_1]), \ldots, holds(q_r, [a_{n-1}, \ldots, a_1])\} \cap M = \emptyset$. By induction hypothesis, this means there exists an effect proposition of the form a **causes** $\neg f$ **if** $p_1, \ldots, p_k, \neg q_1, \ldots, \neg q_r$ such that $p_1, \ldots, p_k, \neg q_1, \ldots, \neg q_r$ hold in σ_{n-1}. This contradicts the second part of (i). Hence our assumption that $ab(f, a_n, [a_{n-1}, \ldots, a_1]) \in M$ must be wrong. Therefore, $ab(f, a_n, [a_{n-1}, \ldots, a_1]) \notin M$. Now using this, the earlier conclusion that $holds(f, [a_{n-1}, \ldots, a_1]) \in M$, the inertia rule of the program $\pi_1(D, O)$, and part (a) of Proposition 20 we can conclude that $holds(f, [a_n, \ldots, a_1]) \in M$.

Case (ii) : Using the induction hypothesis, the first rule of of the program π_1^{ef} and part (a) of Proposition 20 we can conclude that $holds(f, [a_n, \ldots, a_1]) \in M$.

($\impliedby$) From $holds(f, [a_n, \ldots, a_1]) \in M$, using part (b) of Proposition 20 there are two possibilities:

(a) $holds(f, [a_{n-1}, \ldots, a_1]) \in M$ and $ab(f, a_n, [a_{n-1}, \ldots, a_1]) \notin M$.

(b) there exists an effect proposition of the form a **causes** f **if** $p_1, \ldots, p_k, \neg q_1, \ldots,$ $\neg q_r$ such that $\{holds(p_1, [a_{n-1}, \ldots, a_1]), \ldots, holds(p_k, [a_{n-1}, \ldots, a_1])\} \subseteq M$ and $\{holds(q_1, [a_{n-1}, \ldots, a_1]), \ldots, holds(q_r, [a_{n-1}, \ldots, a_1])\} \cap M = \emptyset$.

(case a): By induction hypothesis, $holds(f, [a_{n-1}, \ldots, a_1]) \in M$ implies that $f \in \sigma_{n-1}$. We will now argue that $ab(f, a_n, [a_{n-1}, \ldots, a_1]) \notin M$ implies that there does not exist an effect proposition of the form a **causes** $\neg f$ **if** $p_1, \ldots, p_k,$ $\neg q_1, \ldots, \neg q_r$ such that $p_1, \ldots, p_k, \neg q_1, \ldots, \neg q_r$ hold in σ_{n-1}. Suppose the contrary holds. In that case using induction hypothesis we will have

$\{holds(p_1, [a_{n-1}, \ldots, a_1]), \ldots, holds(p_k, [a_{n-1}, \ldots, a_1])\} \subseteq M$ and
$\{holds(q_1, [a_{n-1}, \ldots, a_1]), \ldots, holds(q_r, [a_{n-1}, \ldots, a_1])\} \cap M = \emptyset$.

Now using part (a) of Proposition 20 we will be forced to conclude $ab(f, a_n, [a_{n-1}, \ldots, a_1]) \in M$, which results in a contradiction. Hence, there does not exist an effect proposition of the form a **causes** $\neg f$ **if** $p_1, \ldots, p_k, \neg q_1, \ldots, \neg q_r$ such that $p_1, \ldots, p_k, \neg q_1, \ldots, \neg q_r$ hold in σ_{n-1}. This together with the fact that $f \in \sigma_{n-1}$ implies that $f \in \sigma_n$.

(case b): By using the induction hypothesis we can conclude that there exists an effect proposition of the form a **causes** f **if** $p_1, \ldots, p_k, \neg q_1, \ldots, \neg q_r$ such that $p_1, \ldots, p_k, \neg q_1, \ldots, \neg q_r$ hold in σ_{n-1}. This implies that $f \in \sigma_n$.

The proof is complete. $\qquad\qquad\qquad\qquad\qquad\qquad\qquad\qquad\qquad\qquad\qquad$ $\square$

Proposition 70 Let D be a consistent domain description and O be an initial state complete set of observations such that (D, O) is consistent. Let f be a fluent.

(i) $D \models_O f$ **after** $a_1, \ldots, a_n$ iff $\pi_1(D, O) \models holds(f, [a_n, \ldots, a_1])$.
(ii) $D \models_O \neg f$ **after** $a_1, \ldots, a_n$ iff $\pi_1(D, O) \not\models holds(f, [a_n, \ldots, a_1])$. $\qquad$ $\square$

Proof: Follows from Proposition 69, and Lemmas 5.1.1 and 5.1.4. $\qquad\qquad\qquad$ $\square$

5.1.3 Temporal projection in an AnsProlog¬ formulation: π_2

In this section we give an AnsProlog¬ formulation of temporal projection in the presence of a complete initial state which can also be used with additional rules to perform temporal projection when the initial state is incomplete. Given a domain description D and a set of observations O which is initial state complete, we construct an AnsProlog¬ program $\pi_2(D, O)$ consisting of three parts π_2^{ef}, π_2^{obs}, and π_2^{in} as defined below.

(1) Translating effect propositions: The effect propositions in D are translated as follows and are collectively referred to as π_2^{ef}.

For every effect proposition of the form (5.1.1) if f is a fluent then π_2^{ef} contains the following rules:

$$holds(f, res(a, S)) \leftarrow holds(p_1, S), \ldots, holds(p_n, S), \neg holds(q_1, S), \ldots,$$
$$\neg holds(q_r, S).$$

$$ab(f, a, S) \leftarrow holds(p_1, S), \ldots, holds(p_n, S), \neg holds(q_1, S), \ldots, \neg holds(q_r, S).$$

else, if f is the negative fluent literal $\neg g$ then π_2^{ef} contains the following rules:

$$\neg holds(g, res(a, S)) \leftarrow holds(p_1, S), \ldots, holds(p_n, S), \neg holds(q_1, S), \ldots,$$
$$\neg holds(q_r, S).$$

$$ab(g, a, S) \leftarrow holds(p_1, S), \ldots, holds(p_n, S), \neg holds(q_1, S), \ldots, \neg holds(q_r, S).$$

(2) Translating observations: The value propositions in O are translated as follows and are collectively referred to as π_2^{obs}.

For every value proposition of the form (5.1.5) if f is a fluent then π_2^{obs} contains the following rule:

$$holds(f, s_0) \leftarrow.$$

else, if f is the negative fluent literal $\neg g$ then π_2^{obs} contains the following rule:

$$\neg holds(g, s_0) \leftarrow.$$

(3) Inertia rules: Besides the above we have the following inertia rules referred to as π_2^{in}.

$$holds(F, res(A, S)) \leftarrow holds(F, S), \textbf{not } ab(F, A, S).$$

$$\neg holds(F, res(A, S)) \leftarrow \neg holds(F, S), \textbf{not } ab(F, A, S).$$

Example 92 Consider D from Example 86, and $O_3 = \{\textbf{initially } alive; \textbf{ initially } \neg loaded\}$ from Example 91. The program $\pi_2(D, O_3)$ consists of the following:

$$holds(loaded, res(load, S)) \leftarrow.$$
$$ab(loaded, load, S) \leftarrow.$$
$$\neg holds(alive, res(shoot, S)) \leftarrow holds(loaded, S).$$
$$ab(alive, shoot, S) \leftarrow holds(loaded, S).$$

$$holds(alive, s_0) \leftarrow.$$
$$\neg holds(loaded, s_0) \leftarrow.$$

$$holds(F, res(A, S)) \leftarrow holds(F, S), \textbf{not } ab(F, A, S).$$
$$\neg holds(F, res(A, S)) \leftarrow \neg holds(F, S), \textbf{not } ab(F, A, S).$$

It is easy to see that $\pi_2(D, O_3) \models holds(alive, [load])$, $\pi_2(D, O_3) \models holds(loaded, [load])$, and $\pi_2(D, O_3) \models \neg holds(alive, [shoot, load])$.

(Recall from Example 91 that $\pi_1(D, O_3) \not\models \neg holds(alive, [shoot, load])$.)   □

We now analyze $\pi_2(D, O)$ and relate entailments with respect to $\pi_2(D, O)$ with queries entailed by (D, O).

Lemma 5.1.5 Let D be a consistent domain description and O be an initial state complete set of observations. Then $\pi_2(D, O)^+$ is acyclic.   □

Proof: To show $\pi_2(D, O)^+$ to be acyclic we need to give a level mapping λ, to atoms in the language of $\pi_2(D, O)^+$ so that the acyclicity condition holds. To facilitate that we first give a level mapping to terms.

We assign $\lambda(s_0) = 1$, and for any action a and situation s, $\lambda(res(a, s)) = \lambda(s) + 1$. For any fluent f, action a, and situation s, we assign $\lambda(holds(f, s)) = 2 \times \lambda(s)$, $\lambda(holds'(f, s)) = 2 \times \lambda(s)$ and $\lambda(ab(f, a, s)) = 2 \times \lambda(s) + 1$. It is easy to see that this level assignment satisfies the acyclicity condition for the AnsProlog program $\pi_2(D, O)^+$.   □

From the above lemma and Proposition 34 it follows that $\pi_2(D, O)^+$ has a unique answer set.

Lemma 5.1.6 Let D be a consistent domain description and O be an initial state complete set of observations. Let M be the answer set of $\pi_2(D, O)^+$.

For any fluent f, and a sequence of actions $a_1, \ldots, a_n$, at least one, but not both of $holds(f, [a_n, \ldots, a_1])$ and $holds'(f, [a_n, \ldots, a_1])$ belongs to M.   □

Proof: (sketch) This can be proved by induction on n. The base case ($n = 0$) holds because of the translation π_2 and the assumption that O is an initial state complete set of observations. Assuming that the conclusion of the lemma holds for all $i < n$, we will argue that it holds for n. To show that at least one of $holds(f, [a_n, \ldots, a_1])$ and $holds'(f, [a_n, \ldots, a_1])$ belongs to M we can use the induction hypothesis and consider the two cases: (i) $holds(f, [a_{n-1}, \ldots, a_1]) \in M$; (ii) $holds'(f, [a_{n-1}, \ldots, a_1]) \in M$ and argue that in either case our desired conclusion holds. The argument is that if we are unable to use the inertia rules, then $ab(f, a_n, [a_{n-1}, \ldots, a_1]) \notin M$, and that means there must be an effect axiom which either causes f or causes $\neg f$ and whose preconditions hold in the situation $[a_{n-1}, \ldots, a_1]$.

Next we need to show that only one of $holds(f, [a_n, \ldots, a_1])$ and $holds'(f, [a_n, \ldots, a_1])$ belongs to M. By the induction hypothesis we can show that they do not both hold because of two inertia rules. Because of the consistency of D, they cannot both hold because of two effect axioms. Finally, they cannot both hold because of one effect axiom and one inertia rule as the presence of $ab(f, a_n, [a_{n-1}, \ldots, a_1])$ will block the inertia rule.   □

Proposition 71 Let D be a consistent domain description and O be an initial state complete set of observations such that (D, O) is consistent. Then $\pi_2(D, O)$ has a unique answer set which is consistent. $\qquad\square$

Proof: Follows from Lemma 5.1.6 and Proposition 6. If M is the answer set of $\pi_2(D, O)^+$, then the answer set of $\pi_2(D, O)$ is the following:

$$M \setminus \{holds'(f, s) \; : \; holds'(f, s) \in M\} \cup \{\neg holds(f, s) \; : \; holds'(f, s) \in M\} \qquad\square$$

Lemma 5.1.7 Let D be a consistent domain description and O be an initial state complete set of observations such that (D, O) is consistent. Let (σ_0, Φ_D) be the unique model of (D, O) and M be the answer set of $\pi_2(D, O)$. Let f be a fluent.

$f \in \Phi_D(a_n, \ldots, \Phi_D(a_1, \sigma_0) \ldots)$ iff $holds(f, [a_n, \ldots, a_1]) \in M$. $\qquad\square$

Proof: (sketch) The proof is similar to the proof of Lemma 5.1.4. $\qquad\square$

Proposition 72 Let D be a consistent domain description and O be an initial state complete set of observations such that (D, O) is consistent. Let f be a fluent.

(i) $D \models_O f$ **after** $a_1, \ldots, a_n$ iff $\pi_2(D, O) \models holds(f, [a_n, \ldots, a_1])$.
(ii) $D \models_O \neg f$ **after** $a_1, \ldots, a_n$ iff $\pi_2(D, O) \models \neg holds(f, [a_n, \ldots, a_1])$. $\qquad\square$

Proof: Follows from Lemma 5.1.7, Proposition 71, and Lemma 5.1.1. $\qquad\square$

5.1.4 Temporal projection in AnsProlog¬ in the presence of incompleteness: π_3

We now present a modification of $\pi_2(D, O)$ from the previous section so that we can reason correctly with it when the initial state is incomplete. To show what goes wrong if we reason with $\pi_2(D, O)$, when O is not initial state complete, consider the following example.

Example 93 Let D consist of the following two propositions:

a **causes** f **if** p
a **causes** f **if** $\neg p$
and $O = \{$**initially** $\neg f\}$.

The program $\pi_2(D, O)$ consists of the following:

$holds(f, res(a, S)) \leftarrow holds(p, S).$
$ab(f, a, S) \leftarrow holds(p, S).$
$holds(f, res(a, S)) \leftarrow \neg holds(p, S).$
$ab(f, a, S) \leftarrow \neg holds(p, S).$

$\neg holds(f, s_0) \leftarrow$.

$holds(F, res(A, S)) \leftarrow holds(F, S), \textbf{not } ab(F, A, S).$
$\neg holds(F, res(A, S)) \leftarrow \neg holds(F, S), \textbf{not } ab(F, A, S).$

It is easy to see that $\pi_2(D, O) \not\models \neg holds(f, [a])$, while $D \models_O f$ **after** a. Thus $\pi_2(D, O)$ makes a wrong conclusion. $\qquad\square$

Example 94 Consider D from Example 86, and $O_4 = \{\textbf{initially } alive\}$. The program $\pi_2(D, O_4)$ consists of the following:

$holds(loaded, res(load, S)) \leftarrow .$
$ab(loaded, load, S) \leftarrow .$
$\neg holds(alive, res(shoot, S)) \leftarrow holds(loaded, S).$
$ab(alive, shoot, S) \leftarrow holds(loaded, S).$

$holds(alive, s_0) \leftarrow$.

$holds(F, res(A, S)) \leftarrow holds(F, S), \textbf{not } ab(F, A, S).$
$\neg holds(F, res(A, S)) \leftarrow \neg holds(F, S), \textbf{not } ab(F, A, S).$

It is easy to see that $\pi_2(D, O_4) \not\models holds(alive, [shoot])$, while $D \not\models_{O_4} alive$ **after** *shoot*. $\qquad\square$

In both of the above examples the fault lies in not being able to block the inertia rules. The new program $\pi_3(D, O)$ consists of π_2^{obs} and π_2^{in} from the previous section and π_3^{ef} as defined below, where we modify the definition of ab so that it can block the inertia in cases such as the above examples.

Translating effect propositions: The effect propositions in D are translated as follows and are collectively referred to as π_3^{ef}.

For every effect proposition of the form (5.1.1) if f is a fluent then π_3^{ef} contains the following rules:

$holds(f, res(a, S)) \leftarrow holds(p_1, S), \dots, holds(p_n, S), \neg holds(q_1, S), \dots,$
$$\neg holds(q_r, S).$$

$ab(f, a, S) \leftarrow \textbf{not } \neg holds(p_1, S), \dots, \textbf{not } \neg holds(p_n, S), \textbf{not } holds(q_1, S), \dots,$
$$\textbf{not } holds(q_r, S).$$

else, if f is the negative fluent literal $\neg g$ then π_3^{ef} contains the following rules:

$\neg holds(g, res(a, S)) \leftarrow holds(p_1, S), \dots, holds(p_n, S), \neg holds(q_1, S), \dots,$
$$\neg holds(q_r, S).$$

$ab(g, a, S) \leftarrow \textbf{not } \neg holds(p_1, S), \dots, \textbf{not } \neg holds(p_n, S), \textbf{not } holds(q_1, S), \dots,$
$$\textbf{not } holds(q_r, S).$$

Example 95 Let D and O be as in Example 93. The program $\pi_3(D, O)$ consists of the following:

$holds(f, res(a, S)) \leftarrow holds(p, S).$
$ab(f, a, S) \leftarrow \textbf{not } \neg holds(p, S).$
$holds(f, res(a, S)) \leftarrow \neg holds(p, S).$
$ab(f, a, S) \leftarrow \textbf{not } holds(p, S).$

$\neg holds(f, s_0) \leftarrow .$

$holds(F, res(A, S)) \leftarrow holds(F, S), \textbf{not } ab(F, A, S).$
$\neg holds(F, res(A, S)) \leftarrow \neg holds(F, S), \textbf{not } ab(F, A, S).$

It is easy to see that $\pi_3(D, O) \not\models holds(f, [a])$, and also $\pi_3(D, O) \not\models \neg holds(f, [a])$; even though $D \models_O f \textbf{ after } a$.

Thus $\pi_3(D, O)$ does not make a wrong conclusion as $\pi_2(D, O)$ in Example 93. On the other hand it is not able to completely capture $\models_O$. Hence, although it is sound, it is not complete with respect to $\models_O$. □

Example 96 Consider D from Example 86, and $O_4 = \{\textbf{initially } alive\}$. The program $\pi_3(D, O_4)$, which is the same as the program in part (2) of Section 2.2.2, consists of the following:

$holds(loaded, res(load, S)) \leftarrow.$
$ab(loaded, load, S) \leftarrow.$
$\neg holds(alive, res(shoot, S)) \leftarrow holds(loaded, S).$
$ab(alive, shoot, S) \leftarrow \textbf{not } \neg holds(loaded, S).$

$holds(alive, s_0) \leftarrow .$

$holds(F, res(A, S)) \leftarrow holds(F, S), \textbf{not } ab(F, A, S).$
$\neg holds(F, res(A, S)) \leftarrow \neg holds(F, S), \textbf{not } ab(F, A, S).$

Now we have $\pi_3(D, O_4) \not\models ab(alive, shoot, s_0)$ and $\pi_3(D, O_4) \not\models holds(alive, [shoot])$. The latter agrees with $D \not\models_{O_4} alive \textbf{ after } shoot$. □

We now analyze $\pi_3(D, O)$ and relate entailments with respect to $\pi_3(D, O)$ with queries entailed by (D, O).

Proposition 73 Let D be a consistent domain description and O be an initial state complete set of observations such that (D, O) is consistent. Let f be a fluent.

  (i) $D \models_O f \textbf{ after } a_1, \ldots, a_n$ iff $\pi_3(D, O) \models holds(f, [a_n, \ldots, a_1])$.
  (ii) $D \models_O \neg f \textbf{ after } a_1, \ldots, a_n$ iff $\pi_3(D, O) \models \neg holds(f, [a_n, \ldots, a_1])$. □

Proof: (sketch) Similar to the proof of Proposition 72 and uses lemmas similar to the lemmas in Section 5.1.3.

Lemma 5.1.8 Let D be a consistent domain description and O be a (possibly incomplete) set of observations about the initial state such that (D, O) is consistent. Then,

if $\pi_3(D, O) \models (\neg)holds(f, [a_n, \ldots, a_1)$ then for all extensions $\hat{O}$ of O, $\pi_3(D, \hat{O}) \models (\neg)holds(f, [a_n, \ldots, a_1)$. $\qquad\square$

Proof: Given (D, O) satisfying the conditions of the statement of the lemma, let $\hat{O}$ be an arbitrary extension of O. Let us now consider the two programs $\pi_3(D, \hat{O})$ and $\pi_3(D, O)$. It is easy to see that both of them have the signing S, where S is the set of all ground atoms about the predicate ab. Then, $\bar{S}$ is the set of all ground literals about the predicate $holds$. Next, since $\pi_3(D, \hat{O})$ has more ground atoms about the predicate $holds$ than $\pi_3(D, O)$, it follows that $\pi_3(D, O)_{\bar{S}} \preceq \pi_3(D, \hat{O})_{\bar{S}}$. Furthermore, $\pi_3(D, \hat{O})_S = \pi_3(D, O)_S$, which implies, $\pi_3(D, \hat{O})_S \preceq \pi_3(D, O)_S$. Thus by Proposition 47, $\pi_3(D, \hat{O})$ entails every ground literal in $\bar{S}$ that is entailed by $\pi_3(D, O)$. The statement of the lemma follows from this. $\qquad\square$

Proposition 74 Let D be a consistent domain description, and O be a (possibly incomplete) set of observations about the initial state such that (D, O) is consistent. Let f be a fluent.

(i) If $\pi_3(D, O) \models holds(f, [a_n, \ldots, a_1])$ then $D \models_O f$ **after** $a_1, \ldots, a_n$.
(ii) If $\pi_3(D, O) \models \neg holds(f, [a_n, \ldots, a_1])$ then $D \models_O \neg f$ **after** $a_1, \ldots, a_n$. $\qquad\square$

Proof: Follows from Lemma 5.1.8, Proposition 73, and Corollary 3. $\qquad\square$

In the following section we give examples which show that $\pi_3(D, O)$ is not complete in the sense that $D \models_O (\neg)f$ **after** $a_1, \ldots, a_n$ but $\pi_3(D, O) \not\models (\neg)holds(f, [a_n, \ldots, a_1])$.

5.1.5 Sound reasoning with noninitial observations in AnsProlog$^-$: π_3 and π_4

In all of the previous formulations we had assumed that observations were only about the initial state. We now lift that assumption and present the first two of four sound formulations that can reason with general observations. The first two formulations are weaker than the other two but computationally more efficient.

Given a domain description D and a set of observations O, the program $\pi_3(D, O)$ is the same as in the previous section except that noninitial observations of the form $(\neg)f$ **after** $a_1, \ldots, a_n$ which were not allowed previously are now represented as $(\neg)holds(f, [a_n, \ldots, a_1])$.

Example 97 Consider D from Example 86, and $O_1 = \{$**initially** $alive; \neg alive$ **after** $shoot\}$ from Example 88. The program $\pi_3(D, O_1)$ consists of the following:

$holds(loaded, res(load, S)) \leftarrow .$
$ab(loaded, load, S) \leftarrow .$
$\neg holds(alive, res(shoot, S)) \leftarrow holds(loaded, S).$
$ab(alive, shoot, S) \leftarrow$ **not** $\neg holds(loaded, S).$

$holds(alive, s_0) \leftarrow .$
$\neg holds(alive, res(shoot, s_0)) \leftarrow .$

$holds(F, res(A, S)) \leftarrow holds(F, S),$ **not** $ab(F, A, S).$
$\neg holds(F, res(A, S)) \leftarrow \neg holds(F, S),$ **not** $ab(F, A, S).$

Now although $D \models_{O_1}$ **initially** $loaded$, we have $\pi_3(D, O_1) \not\models holds(loaded, s_0)$. Hence, $\pi_3(D, O_1)$ is not complete with respect to (D, O_1). However, it is sound, as we will formally prove later. □

Example 98 Consider D from Example 86, and $O_2 = \{$**initially** $alive; loaded$ **after** $shoot\}$ from Example 89. The program $\pi_3(D, O_2)$ consists of the following:

$holds(loaded, res(load, S)) \leftarrow .$
$ab(loaded, load, S) \leftarrow .$
$\neg holds(alive, res(shoot, S)) \leftarrow holds(loaded, S).$
$ab(alive, shoot, S) \leftarrow$ **not** $\neg holds(loaded, S).$

$holds(alive, s_0) \leftarrow .$
$holds(loaded, res(shoot, s_0)) \leftarrow .$

$holds(F, res(A, S)) \leftarrow holds(F, S),$ **not** $ab(F, A, S).$
$\neg holds(F, res(A, S)) \leftarrow \neg holds(F, S),$ **not** $ab(F, A, S).$

Now although $D \models_{O_2}$ **initially** $loaded$, and $D \models_{O_2} \neg alive$ **after** $shoot$, we have $\pi_3(D, O_2) \not\models holds(loaded, s_0)$, and $\pi_3(D, O_2) \not\models \neg holds(alive, res(shoot, s_0))$. Hence, $\pi_3(D, O_2)$ is not complete with respect to (D, O_2). However, it is sound, as we will formally prove later. □

We now present another formulation $\pi_4(D, O)$ that is sound with respect to (D, O) and show that it extends $\pi_3(D, O)$. The program $\pi_4(D, O)$ consists of five parts π_3^{ef}, and π_2^{in} from the previous sections and π_4^{obs}, π_4^{-in}, and π_4^{back}, as defined below.

(1) Backward reasoning rules: The backward reasoning rules are rules that can reason from observations about noninitial situations and make conclusions about their past up to the initial situation. They are collectively denoted by π_4^{back} and consist of the following rules.

For every effect proposition of the form (5.1.1), if f is a fluent then π_4^{back} contains the following rules:

(a) For each i, $1 \le i \le n$

$$holds(p_i, S) \leftarrow holds(f, res(a, S)), \neg holds(f, S).$$

$$\begin{aligned} \neg holds(p_i, S) \leftarrow & \neg holds(f, res(a, S)), holds(p_1, S), \ldots, holds(p_{i-1}, S), \\ & holds(p_{i+1}, S), \ldots, holds(p_n, S), \neg holds(q_1, S), \ldots, \\ & \neg holds(q_r, S). \end{aligned}$$

(b) For each j, $1 \le j \le r$

$$\neg holds(q_j, S) \leftarrow holds(f, res(a, S)), \neg holds(f, S).$$

$$\begin{aligned} holds(q_j, S) \leftarrow & \neg holds(f, res(a, S)), \neg holds(q_1, S), \ldots, \neg holds(q_{j-1}, S), \\ & \neg holds(q_{j+1}, S), \ldots, \neg holds(q_r, S), holds(p_1, S), \ldots, \\ & holds(p_n, S). \end{aligned}$$

For every effect proposition of the form (5.1.1), if f is the negative fluent literal $\neg g$ then π_4^{back} contains the following rules:

(a) For each i, $1 \le i \le n$

$$holds(p_i, S) \leftarrow \neg holds(g, res(a, S)), holds(g, S).$$

$$\begin{aligned} \neg holds(p_i, S) \leftarrow & holds(g, res(a, S)), holds(p_1, S), \ldots, holds(p_{i-1}, S), \\ & holds(p_{i+1}, S), \ldots, holds(p_n, S), \neg holds(q_1, S), \ldots, \\ & \neg holds(q_r, S). \end{aligned}$$

(b) For each j, $1 \le j \le r$

$$\neg holds(q_j, S) \leftarrow \neg holds(g, res(a, S)), holds(g, S).$$

$$\begin{aligned} holds(q_j, S) \leftarrow & holds(g, res(a, S)), \neg holds(q_1, S), \ldots, \neg holds(q_{j-1}, S), \\ & \neg holds(q_{j+1}, S), \ldots, \neg holds(q_r, S), holds(p_1, S), \ldots, \\ & holds(p_n, S). \end{aligned}$$

(2) Backward inertia: The backward inertia rules are similar to the original inertia rules, except that they are in the backward direction. They are collectively denoted by π_4^{-in} and consist of the following:

$$holds(F, S) \leftarrow holds(F, res(A, S)), \textbf{not } ab(F, A, S).$$
$$\neg holds(F, S) \leftarrow \neg holds(F, res(A, S)), \textbf{not } ab(F, A, S).$$

(3) Translating observations: The value propositions in O of the form (5.1.4) are translated as follows and are collectively referred to as π_4^{obs}.

For every value proposition of the form (5.1.4) if f is a fluent then π_4^{obs} contains the following rule:

$holds(f, [a_m, \ldots, a_1]) \leftarrow.$

else, if f is the negative fluent literal $\neg g$ then π_4^{obs} contains the following rule:

$\neg holds(g, [u_m, \ldots, u_1]) \leftarrow.$

Example 99 Consider D from Example 86, and $O_1 = \{$**initially** $alive; \neg alive$ **after** $shoot\}$ from Example 97. The program $\pi_4(D, O_1)$ consists of $\pi_3(D, O_1)$ from Example 97 and the following rules. (Recall that we analyzed this program earlier in Section 3.3.2 to demonstrate the impact of the notion of signing on restricted monotonicity.)

$holds(loaded, S) \leftarrow holds(alive, S), \neg holds(alive, res(shoot, S)).$
$\neg holds(loaded, S) \leftarrow holds(alive, res(shoot, S)).$

$holds(F, S) \leftarrow holds(F, res(A, S)), \textbf{not } ab(F, A, S).$
$\neg holds(F, S) \leftarrow \neg holds(F, res(A, S)), \textbf{not } ab(F, A, S).$

Now although $\pi_3(D, O_1) \not\models holds(loaded, s_0)$, we have $\pi_4(D, O_1) \models holds(loaded, s_0)$ which agrees with $D \models_{O_1}$ **initially** $loaded$. $\square$

Example 100 Consider D from Example 86, and $O_2 = \{$**initially** $alive; loaded$ **after** $shoot\}$ from Example 98. The program $\pi_4(D, O_2)$ consists of $\pi_3(D, O_2)$ from Example 98 and the following rules.

$holds(loaded, S) \leftarrow holds(alive, S), \neg holds(alive, res(shoot, S)).$
$\neg holds(loaded, S) \leftarrow holds(alive, res(shoot, S)).$

$holds(F, S) \leftarrow holds(F, res(A, S)), \textbf{not } ab(F, A, S).$
$\neg holds(F, S) \leftarrow \neg holds(F, res(A, S)), \textbf{not } ab(F, A, S).$

Now although $\pi_3(D, O_2) \not\models holds(loaded, s_0)$, and $\pi_3(D, O_2) \not\models \neg holds(alive, res(shoot, s_0))$ we have $\pi_4(D, O_2) \models holds(loaded, s_0)$, and $\pi_4(D, O_2) \models \neg holds(alive, res(shoot, s_0))$. $\square$

We now show the soundness of entailments of $\pi_3(D, O)$ and $\pi_4(D, O)$ with respect to queries entailed by (D, O). We also relate the entailments of $\pi_3(D, O)$ with those of $\pi_4(D, O)$.

Proposition 75 Let D be a consistent domain description, and O be a set of observations such that (D, O) is consistent. Let f be a fluent.

(i) If $\pi_3(D, O) \models holds(f, [a_n, \ldots, a_1])$ then $D \models_O f$ **after** $a_1, \ldots, a_n$.
(ii) If $\pi_3(D, O) \models \neg holds(f, [a_n, \ldots, a_1])$ then $D \models_O \neg f$ **after** $a_1, \ldots, a_n$. □

Note that the difference between the above proposition and Proposition 74 is that in the latter O is a set of observations about the initial state.

Proposition 76 Let D be a consistent domain description and O be a set of observations such that (D, O) is consistent. Let f be a fluent.

(i) If $\pi_3(D, O) \models holds(f, [a_n, \ldots, a_1])$ then $\pi_4(D, O) \models holds(f, [a_m, \ldots, a_1])$.
(ii) If $\pi_3(D, O) \models \neg holds(f, [a_n, \ldots, a_1])$ then $\pi_4(D, O) \models \neg holds(f, [a_m, \ldots, a_1])$. □

Proof: Let (D, O) satisfy the conditions of the statement of the proposition. Consider the two programs $\pi_4(D, O)$ and $\pi_3(D, O)$. It is easy to see that both of them have the signing S, where S is the set of all ground atoms about the predicate ab. Then, $\bar{S}$ is the set of all ground literals about the predicate *holds*. Next, since $\pi_4(D, O)$ has some extra ground rules with *holds* in their head than has $\pi_3(D, O)$, it follows that $\pi_3(D, O)_{\bar{S}} \preceq \pi_4(D, \hat{O})_{\bar{S}}$. Furthermore, $\pi_4(D, O)_S = \pi_3(D, O)_S$, which implies $\pi_4(D, O)_S \preceq \pi_3(D, O)_S$. Thus by Proposition 47, $\pi_4(D, O)$ entails every ground literal in $\bar{S}$ that is entailed by $\pi_3(D, O)$. The statement of the proposition follows from this. □

The program $\pi_4(D, O)$ is not always sound with respect to the queries entailed by (D, O). For example, for the domain description $D = \{a$ **causes** f **if** $p; a$ **causes** f **if** $\neg p\}$, and for the observation $O = \{f$ **after** $a\}, \pi_4(D, O)$ entails both $holds(p, s_0)$ and $\neg holds(p, s_0)$ and hence is inconsistent. For this reason the soundness of $\pi_4(D, O)$ with respect to the queries entailed by (D, O) is conditional. The following proposition states this.

Proposition 77 Let D be a consistent domain description such that for every action we only have one effect axiom, and O be a set of observations such that (D, O) is consistent. Let f be a fluent.

(i) If $\pi_4(D, O) \models holds(f, [a_n, \ldots, a_1])$ then $D \models_O f$ **after** $a_1, \ldots, a_n$.
(ii) If $\pi_4(D, O) \models \neg holds(f, [a_n, \ldots, a_1])$ then $D \models_O \neg f$ **after** $a_1, \ldots, a_n$. □

5.1.6 Assimilating observations using enumeration and constraints: π_5 and π_6

The incompleteness of $\pi_3(D, O)$ pointed out in Example 95 also plagues $\pi_4(D, O)$. We now present two formulations $\pi_5(D, O)$ and $\pi_6(D, O)$ which overcome this limitation and can reason in the presence of general observations and incomplete knowledge about the initial state. They are sound and complete with respect to the entailment relation of (D, O). The first, $\pi_5(D, O)$ is an AnsProlog$^{\neg, \perp}$ program consisting of π_2^{ef}, and π_2^{in} from Sections 5.1.3 and π_5^{obs}, and π_5^{en} as described below. The second, $\pi_6(D, O)$ is an AnsProlog$^{\neg, or, \perp}$ program consisting of π_2^{ef}, and π_2^{in} from Sections 5.1.3 and π_5^{obs}, and π_6^{en} as described below. The role of π_5^{en} in $\pi_5(D, O)$ is to enumerate the various possible values a fluent can have in the initial state. The role of π_6^{en} in $\pi_6(D, O)$ is similar.

- Enumeration in $\pi_5(D, O)$: The enumeration rules in $\pi_5(D, O)$ collectively denoted by π_5^{en} consists of the following rules:

  $holds(F, s_0) \leftarrow \textbf{not } \neg holds(F, s_0).$

  $\neg holds(F, s_0) \leftarrow \textbf{not } holds(F, s_0).$

- Enumeration in $\pi_6(D, O)$: The enumeration rules in $\pi_6(D, O)$ collectively denoted by π_6^{en} consists of the following rule:

  $holds(F, s_0) \textit{ or } \neg holds(F, s_0).$

- Observations as constraints: The value propositions in O are translated as follows and are collectively referred to as π_5^{obs}.

  For an observation of the form (5.1.4) if f is a fluent then π_5^{obs} contains the following rule:

  $\leftarrow \textbf{not } holds(f, [a_m, \ldots, a_1]).$

  else if f is the fluent literal $\neg g$, then π_5^{obs} contains the following rule:

  $\leftarrow \textbf{not } \neg holds(g, [a_m, \ldots, a_1]).$

Example 101 Let D and O be as in Example 93. The program $\pi_5(D, O)$ consists of the following:

$holds(f, s_0) \leftarrow \textbf{not } \neg holds(f, s_0).$
$\neg holds(f, s_0) \leftarrow \textbf{not } holds(f, s_0).$
$holds(p, s_0) \leftarrow \textbf{not } \neg holds(p, s_0).$
$\neg holds(p, s_0) \leftarrow \textbf{not } holds(p, s_0).$

$\leftarrow \textbf{not } \neg holds(f, s_0).$

$holds(f, res(a, S)) \leftarrow holds(p, S).$
$ab(f, a, S) \leftarrow holds(p, S).$

$holds(f, res(a, S)) \leftarrow \neg holds(p, S).$
$ab(f, a, S) \leftarrow \neg holds(p, S).$

$holds(F, res(A, S)) \leftarrow holds(F, S), \textbf{not } ab(F, A, S).$
$\neg holds(F, res(A, S)) \leftarrow \neg holds(F, S), \textbf{not } ab(F, A, S).$

The program $\pi_5(D, O)$ has two answer sets $\{\neg holds(f, s_0), holds(p, s_0),$ $ab(f, a, s_0), holds(f, [a]), holds(p, [a]), ab(f, a, [a]), holds(f, [a, a]), holds(p,$ $[a, a]), ab(f, a, [a, a]), \ldots\}$ and $\{\neg holds(f, s_0), \neg holds(p, s_0), ab(f, a, s_0),$ $holds(f, [a]), \neg holds(p, [a]), ab(f, a, [a]), holds(f, [a, a]), \neg holds(p, [a, a]),$ $ab(f, a, [a, a]), \ldots\}$. Thus, $\pi_5(D, O) \not\models holds(f, [a])$, which agrees with $D \models_O$ f **after** a. (Recall that $\pi_3(D, O) \not\models holds(f, [a])$.)

The program $\pi_5(D, O)$ is exactly the same as $\pi_4(D, O)$ except that the first two rules of $\pi_5(D, O)$ are replaced by the following two rules:

$holds(f, s_0) \, or \, \neg holds(f, s_0) \leftarrow .$
$holds(p, s_0) \, or \, \neg holds(p, s_0) \leftarrow .$

The programs $\pi_5(D, O)$ and $\pi_6(D, O)$ have the same answer sets and thus $\pi_6(D, O) \not\models holds(f, [a])$. $\qquad\square$

Lemma 5.1.9 Let D be a consistent domain description, and O be a set of observations such that (D, O) is consistent. Let (σ_0, Φ_D) be a model of (D, O) and M be a consistent answer set of $\pi_5(D, O)$ such that $\sigma_0 = \{f : holds(f, s_0) \in M\}$. Let f be a fluent and $a_1, \ldots, a_n$ be a sequence of actions.

(i) $f \in \Phi_D(a_n, \ldots, \Phi_D(a_1, \sigma_0) \ldots)$ iff $holds(f, [a_n, \ldots, a_1]) \in M$.
(ii) $f \notin \Phi_D(a_n, \ldots, \Phi_D(a_1, \sigma_0) \ldots)$ iff $\neg holds(f, [a_n, \ldots, a_1]) \in M$ $\qquad\square$

Proof: (sketch) By induction on n. $\qquad\square$

Lemma 5.1.10 Let D be a consistent domain description, and O be a set of observations such that (D, O) is consistent. For every model $M = (\sigma_0, \Phi_D)$ of (D, O) there exists a consistent answer set A of $\pi_5(D, O)$ such that $\sigma_0 = \{f : holds(f, s_0) \in A\}$. $\qquad\square$

Proof: Using Lemma 5.1.3 we have that M is a model of (D, O_M), where $O_M = \{\textbf{initially } f : f \in \sigma_0\} \cup \{\textbf{initially } \neg f : f \notin \sigma_0\}$. Consider $\pi_5(D, O_M)$.

Let $U = \{holds(f, s_0) : f \text{ is a fluent}\} \cup \{\neg holds(f, s_0) : f \text{ is a fluent }\}$. It is easy to see that U splits $\pi_5(D, O_M)$ such that $bot_U(\pi_5(D, O_M)) = \pi_5^{en}(D, O_M)$ and $top_U(\pi_5(D, O_M)) = \pi_2^{ef}(D, O_M) \cup \pi_2^{in}(D, O_M) \cup \pi_5^{obs}(D, O_M)$. It is easy to see that $A_0 = \{holds(f, s_0) : f \in \sigma_0\} \cup \{\neg holds(f, s_0) : f \notin \sigma_0\}$ is an answer set of $bot_U(\pi_5(D, O_M))$. From Theorem 3.4.1, an answer set of $top_U(\pi_5(D, O_M)) \cup A_0$ is an answer set of $\pi_5(D, O_M)$. Notice that $top_U(\pi_5(D, O_M)) \cup A_0$ is the same as $\pi_2(D, O_M) \cup \pi_5^{obs}(D, O_M)$, and $\pi_5^{obs}(D, O_M)$ is a set of constraints. Thus answer sets of $top_U(\pi_5(D, O_M)) \cup A_0$ and answer sets of $\pi_2(D, O_M)$ that satisfy the constraints $\pi_5^{obs}(D, O_M)$ coincide. Since $A_0 \subseteq \pi_2(D, O_M)$, all answer sets of $\pi_2(D, O_M)$ satisfy the constraints $\pi_5^{obs}(D, O_M)$. Thus answer sets of $top_U(\pi_5(D, O_M)) \cup A_0$ and answer sets of $\pi_2(D, O_M)$ coincide. Since from Proposition 71 the program $\pi_2(D, O_M)$ has a unique consistent answer set, $top_U(\pi_5(D, O_M)) \cup A_0$ has a unique consistent answer set. Let us refer to this answer set as A. We will show that A is a consistent answer set A of $\pi_5(D, O)$.

It is clear that A_0 is an answer set of $bot_U(\pi_5(D, O))$. We will now argue that A is an answer set of $top_U(\pi_5(D, O)) \cup A_0$, and hence by Theorem 3.4.1 is an answer set of $\pi_5(D, O)$.

It is easy to see that the answer sets of $top_U(\pi_5(D, O)) \cup A_0$ and $top_U(\pi_5(D, O_M)) \cup A_0 \cup \pi_5^{obs}(D, O)$ coincide, as the only difference between them is that the latter contains the additional constraints $\pi_5^{obs}(D, O_M)$, which are satisfied by the answer sets of both programs because of the presence of A_0.

By definition, A is the answer set of $top_U(\pi_5(D, O_M)) \cup A_0$. Using Lemma 5.1.9 with respect to (D, O_M), and the fact that M, the model of (D, O_M), is a model of (D, O), it is easy to see that A satisfies the constraints $\pi_5^{obs}(D, O)$. Hence, A is the answer set of $top_U(\pi_5(D, O_M)) \cup A_0 \cup \pi_5^{obs}(D, O)$, and therefore the answer set of $top_U(\pi_5(D, O)) \cup A_0$. Thus A is an answer set of $\pi_5(D, O)$. □

Lemma 5.1.11 Let D be a consistent domain description, and O be a set of observations such that (D, O) is consistent. For every consistent answer set A of $\pi_5(D, O)$ there exists a model $M = (\sigma_0, \Phi_D)$ of (D, O) such that $\sigma_0 = \{f : holds(f, s_0) \in A\}$. □

Proof: (sketch) Consider (D, O_A), where, $O_A = \{$**initially** $f : holds(f, s_0) \in A\} \cup \{$**initially** $\neg f : \neg holds(f, s_0) \in A\}$. Let M, be the model of (D, O_A). We then show that A is an answer set of $\pi_5(D, O_A)$. Using Lemma 5.1.9 with respect to (D, O_A), M, and A we show that M satisfies O, and hence conclude that M is a model of $\pi_5(D, O)$. □

Proposition 78 Let D be a consistent domain description, and O be a set of observations such that (D, O) is consistent. Let f be a fluent.

(i) $\pi_5(D, O) \models holds(f, [a_n, \ldots, a_1])$ iff $D \models_O f$ **after** $a_1, \ldots, a_n$.
(ii) $\pi_5(D, O) \models \neg holds(f, [a_n, \ldots, a_1])$ iff $D \models_O \neg f$ **after** $a_1, \ldots, a_n$. □

Proof: Follows from Lemmas 5.1.9, 5.1.10, and 5.1.11. $\qquad\square$

Proposition 79 Let D be a consistent domain description, and O be a set of observations such that (D, O) is consistent. Let f be a fluent.

(i) $\pi_6(D, O) \models holds(f, [a_n, \ldots, a_1])$ iff $D \models_O f$ **after** $a_1, \ldots, a_n$.
(ii) $\pi_6(D, O) \models \neg holds(f, [a_n, \ldots, a_1])$ iff $D \models_O \neg f$ **after** $a_1, \ldots, a_n$. $\qquad\square$

Proof: Similar to the proof of Proposition 78 using lemmas similar to the ones used there. $\qquad\square$

Note that the equivalence of $\pi_5(D, O)$ and $\pi_6(D, O)$ in terms of both having the same answer sets follows from the fact that $\pi_6(D, O)$ is head cycle free. This can be easily verified by observing that the only literals that appear as disjuncts in the heads of rules are of the form $holds(F, s_0)$, and these literals do not appear in the head of any other rule. So there cannot be a cycle involving these literals in the literal dependency graph of $\pi_6(D, O)$. Now since, by applying *disj_to_normal* to the rule in π_6^{en} we obtain π_5^{en}, using Theorem 3.9.1 we have that $\pi_5(D, O)$ and $\pi_6(D, O)$ have the same answer sets.

5.1.7 Ignoring sorts through language tolerance

Recall that the programs $\pi_1(D, O)$–$\pi_6(D, O)$ in the previous sections are with respect to a sorted theory. We now use the formulation of 'language tolerance' from Section 3.5.3 to show that the AnsProlog programs $\pi_2^+(D, O)$–$\pi_5^+(D, O)$ are language tolerant, and thus if we ignore the sorts of these programs we will still make the same conclusions that we would have made if we had respected the sorts. To show language tolerance, we will use the conditions in Theorem 3.5.3 which are applicable only to AnsProlog programs. Thus we consider the programs $\pi_1(D, O)$, and $\pi_2^+(D, O)$ to $\pi_5^+(D, O)$. The AnsProlog program, $\pi_1(D, O)$ is not predicate-order-consistent as $holds \leq_{+-} holds$ is true in its dependency graph. Thus we cannot use Theorem 3.5.3 to show that $\pi_1(D, O)$ is language tolerant. It is easy to see that the AnsProlog programs $\pi_2^+(D, O)$–$\pi_5^+(D, O)$ are predicate-order-consistent as the relation $\leq_{+-}$ in the dependency graph of those programs is empty.

The second condition in Theorem 3.5.3 for showing language tolerance is that the AnsProlog program must be stable. We will now argue that the AnsProlog programs $\pi_1(D, O)$, and $\pi_2^+(D, O)$ to $\pi_5^+(D, O)$ are all stable with respect to the following mode m:

$holds(-, +)$
$holds'(-, +)$
$ab(+, +, +)$

Table 5.2. *Language tolerance of programs*

program	predicate-order-consistent	stable	language tolerant
$\pi_1(D, O)$	no	yes	?
$\pi_2^+(D, O)$	yes	yes	yes
$\pi_3^+(D, O)$	yes	yes	yes
$\pi_4^+(D, O)$	yes	yes	yes
$\pi_5^+(D, O)$	yes	no	?
$\pi_{5.1}^+(D, O)$	yes	yes	yes

Consider $\pi_1(D, O)$. Both rules in π_1^{ef} are stable because S, the only variable that occurs in them, occurs in the input position (marked by $+$) in the literal in the head. The rules in π_1^{obs} are stable as they do not have variables. The rule in π_1^{in} has three variables: F, A, and S. The variables A and S occur in the input position in the literal in the head. The variable F is in the output position of the positive naf-literal $holds(F, S)$ in the body, and since there is no other naf-literal before it in the body, it satisfies the second condition of Definition 19. Hence, $\pi_1(D, O)$ is a stable program with respect to m. Similarly, we can show that $\pi_2^+(D, O)$–$\pi_4^+(D, O)$ are stable with respect to the mode m.

But the program $\pi_5^+(D, O)$ is not stable with respect to m. This is because the rules π_5^{en} are not stable with respect to m. The following changes will make it stable.

(1) Introduce a predicate *fluent*, and for all the fluents $f_1, \ldots, f_n$, add the following rules to the program.

$fluent(f_1) \leftarrow.$

$\vdots$

$fluent(f_n) \leftarrow.$

(2) Replace π_5^{en} by the following rules

$holds(F, s_0) \leftarrow fluent(F),$ **not** $\neg holds(F, s_0).$
$\neg holds(F, s_0) \leftarrow fluent(F),$ **not** $holds(F, s_0).$

(3) Enhance m by adding the Input/Output specification $fluent(-)$. Let us refer to this enhanced mode by m'.

We refer to the modified program by $\pi_{5.1}$. It is easy to see that $\pi_{5.1}^+$ is stable with respect to m' and is also predicate-order-consistent and hence language tolerant.

Table 5.2 summarizes our result about the language tolerance of the various programs. The '?' in the table denotes that we do not know if $\pi_1(D, O)$ and $\pi_5^+(D, O)$ are language tolerant or not. We only know that they do not satisfy a particular set of sufficiency conditions (being predicate-order-consistent and stable) for language tolerance.

In Section 8.4.3 we further study the properties of $\pi_1(D, O)$, $\pi_2^+(D, O)$, and $\pi_3^+(D, O)$ and show the correctness of the PROLOG interpreter and its LDNF-resolution with respect to these AnsProlog programs.

5.1.8 Filter-abducibility of π_5 and π_6

In Section 3.8 we presented conditions on AnsProlog$^{\neg, or}$ programs so that abductive reasoning with respect to such programs and particular kinds of observations can be done through filtering. We now show how this is relevant with respect to the program $\pi_6(D, O)$. Recall that $\pi_6(D, O)$ consists of four parts: π_2^{ef}, π_2^{in}, π_5^{obs}, and π_6^{en}. Since the rules π_2^{ef}, π_2^{in}, and π_6^{en} only depend on D, and π_5^{obs} only depends on O, let us refer to them as $\pi_6(D)$, and $\pi_6(O)$ respectively. Let us also denote π_4^{obs} by $Obs(O)$. Recall that if f **after** $a_1, \ldots, a_m$ is in O, then its translation in $Obs(O)$ will be $holds(f, [a_1, \ldots, a_m]) \leftarrow$. while its translation in $\pi_6(O)$ will be $\leftarrow$ **not** $holds(f, [a_1, \ldots, a_m])$. In the following proposition we show the connection between the abductive program $\langle \pi_6(D), Obs(O) \rangle$, and the filtering of $\pi_6(D)$ with $Obs(O)$.

Proposition 80 Let D be a consistent domain description, Abd be the set of ground literals about $holds$ in the situation s_0, and Obs be the set of ground atoms about $holds$. The AnsProlog$^{\neg, or}$ program $\pi_6(D)$ is filter-abducible with respect to Abd and Obs.   □

Proof: (sketch) We use the sufficiency conditions in Proposition 62. The sufficiency condition (i) can be shown to hold by the direct application of Proposition 71 and Lemma 5.1.6. It is straightforward to show that the other two conditions hold.   □

Since filtering $\pi_6(D)$ with $Obs(O)$ means adding $\pi_6(O)$ to $\pi_6(D)$ – as filtering in logic programs is done through adding constraints, the above proposition shows that the program $\pi_6(D, O)$ which is the union of $\pi_6(O)$ and $\pi_6(D)$ is equivalent to the abductive program $\langle \pi_6(D), Obs(O) \rangle$. In other words $\pi_6(D)$ is a 'good' program which allows easy assimilation of observations by just using them as filtering constraints. Although we cannot use the sufficiency conditions in Proposition 62 for showing filter-abducibility of π_5, a proposition similar to it can be proven and it can be shown that π_5 is also filter-abducible.

5.1.9 An alternative formulation of temporal projection in AnsProlog: $\pi_{2.nar}$

The formulation of temporal projection in the programs $\pi_1 - \pi_6$ in the previous sections closely follows situation calculus, where each situation is identified by a sequence of actions from the initial situation. These formulations are most appropriate for verifying the correctness of simple plans consisting of actions sequences, by checking if the program entails $holds(goal, action\_sequence)$. To do planning – where we are required to find a sequence of actions that lead to a situation where the goal conditions hold – with these formulations we either need interpreters that can do answer extraction, and then use such an interpreter to instantiate the variable $Plan$ in the query $holds(goal, Plan)$, or use a generate and test paradigm where possible action sequences are generated and tested to find out if they form a plan.

An alternative approach to formulate temporal projection is to use a linear time line, record action occurrences in this time line, and reason about fluents at different time points. Such an approach is used in event calculus, and in reasoning with narratives. Planning with such a formulation can be done by enumerating different action occurrences in different answer sets and eliminating the ones where the goal is not true in the final time point. The action occurrences in each of the resulting answer sets will correspond to plans. This approach, which is referred to as 'answer set planning' in recent literature, is similar to the planning with satisfiability approach where propositional logic is used instead.

In this section we give such an alternative AnsProlog formulation of temporal projection in the presence of a complete initial state. In a subsequent section we will discuss how it can be easily modified to do planning. Our formulation in this section is based on the program π_2 from Section 5.1.3. Besides the change in the approach, we make one additional change in the notation by introducing new predicates such as not_holds to avoid using $\neg$ in our program. This is done to make the program acceptable to interpreters such as Smodels.

Given a domain description D and a set of observations O which is initial state complete, we construct an AnsProlog program $\pi_{2.nar}(D, O)$ consisting of three parts $\pi_{2.nar}^{ef}$, $\pi_{2.nar}^{obs}$, and $\pi_{2.nar}^{in}$ as defined below.

(1) Translating effect propositions: The effect propositions in D are translated as follows and are collectively referred to as $\pi_{2.nar}^{ef}$.

For every effect proposition of the form (5.1.1) if f is a fluent then $\pi_{2.nar}^{ef}$ contains the following rules:

$$holds(f, T + 1) \leftarrow occurs(a, T), holds(p_1, T), \ldots, holds(p_n, T),$$
$$not\_holds(q_1, T), \ldots, not\_holds(q_r, T).$$

$$ab(f, a, T) \leftarrow occurs(a, T), holds(p_1, T), \ldots, holds(p_n, T),$$
$$not\_holds(q_1, T), \ldots, not\_holds(q_r, T).$$

else, if f is the negative fluent literal $\neg g$ then π_2^{ef} contains the following rules:

$$not\_holds(g, T + 1) \leftarrow occurs(a, T), holds(p_1, T), \ldots, holds(p_n, T),$$
$$not\_holds(q_1, T), \ldots, not\_holds(q_r, T).$$

$ab(g, a, T) \leftarrow occurs(a, T), holds(p_1, T), \ldots, holds(p_n, T),$
$\quad\quad\quad not\_holds(q_1, T), \ldots, not\_holds(q_r, T).$

(2) Translating observations: The value propositions in O are translated as follows and are collectively referred to as $\pi_{2.nar}^{obs}$.

For every value proposition of the form (5.1.5) if f is a fluent then $\pi_{2.nar}^{obs}$ contains the following rule:

$holds(f, 1) \leftarrow.$

else, if f is the negative fluent literal $\neg g$ then π_2^{obs} contains the following rule:

$not\_holds(g, 1) \leftarrow.$

(3) Inertia rules: Besides the above we have the following inertia rules that are referred to as $\pi_{2.nar}^{in}$.

$holds(F, T + 1) \leftarrow occurs(A, T), holds(F, T), \textbf{not } ab(F, A, T).$

$not\_holds(F, T + 1) \leftarrow occurs(A, T), not\_holds(F, T), \textbf{not } ab(F, A, T).$

Lemma 5.1.12 Let D be a consistent domain description and O be an initial state complete set of observations. Then $\pi_{2.nar}(D, O) \cup \{occurs(a_1, 1), \ldots, occurs(a_n, n)\}$ is acyclic.   □

From the above lemma and Proposition 34 it follows that $\pi_{2.nar}(D, O) \cup \{occurs(a_1, 1), \ldots, occurs(a_n, n)\}$ has a unique answer set.

Lemma 5.1.13 Let D be a consistent domain description and O be an initial state complete set of observations. Let M be the answer set of $\pi_{2.nar}(D, O) \cup \{occurs(a_1, 1), \ldots, occurs(a_n, n)\}$.

For any fluent f, and $i \leq l$, at least one, but not both, of $holds(f, i)$ and $not\_holds(f, i)$ belongs to M.   □

Lemma 5.1.14 Let D be a consistent domain description and O be an initial state complete set of observations such that (D, O) is consistent. Let (σ_0, Φ_D) be the unique model of (D, O) and M be the answer set of $\pi_{2.nar}(D, O) \cup \{occurs(a_1, 1), \ldots, occurs(a_n, n)\}$. Let f be a fluent.

(i) $f \in \Phi_D(a_n, \ldots, \Phi_D(a_1, \sigma_0) \ldots)$ iff $holds(f, n + 1) \in M$.
(ii) $f \notin \Phi_D(a_n, \ldots, \Phi_D(a_1, \sigma_0) \ldots)$ iff $not\_holds(f, n + 1) \in M$.   □

The proofs of the above three lemmas are similar to the proof of the Lemmas 5.1.5, 5.1.6, and 5.1.7 respectively.

Proposition 81 Let D be a consistent domain description and O be an initial state complete set of observations such that (D, O) is consistent. Let f be a fluent.

(i) $D \models_O f$ **after** $a_1, \ldots, a_n$ iff $\pi_{2.nar}(D, O) \cup \{occurs(a_1, 1), \ldots, occurs(a_n, n)\} \models$ $holds(f, n + 1)$.

(ii) $D \models_O \neg f$ **after** $a_1, \ldots, a_n$ iff $\pi_{2.nar}(D, O) \cup \{occurs(a_1, 1), \ldots, occurs(a_n, n)\} \models$ $not\_holds(f, n + 1)$. $\qquad\square$

Proof: (sketch) Follows from the Lemmas 5.1.1 and 5.1.14. $\qquad\square$

Exercise 18 Consider $\pi_{2.nar'}$ which is obtained from $\pi_{2.nar}$ by removing the rules with ab in their head, and replacing the rules in $\pi_{2.nar}^{in}$ by the following two rules.

$holds(F, T + 1) \leftarrow occurs(A, T), holds(F, T), \textbf{not } not\_holds(F, T + 1).$

$not\_holds(F, T + 1) \leftarrow occurs(A, T), not\_holds(F, T), \textbf{not } holds(F, T + 1).$

Show one-to-one correspondence between the answer sets of $\pi_{2.nar}$ and $\pi_{2.nar'}$ when we only consider the *holds* and *not_holds* facts. $\qquad\square$

5.1.10 Modifying $\pi_{2.nar}$ for answer set planning: $\pi_{2.planning}$

We now show how the program $\pi_{2.nar}$ from the previous section which reasons about fluent values at different time points, given a set of consecutive action occurrences starting from time point 1, can be enhanced to perform planning. The basic idea is that we decide on a plan length l, enumerate action occurrences up to time points corresponding to that length, and encode goals as constraints about the time point $l + 1$, such that possible answer sets that encode action occurrences that do not satisfy the goal at time point $l + 1$ are eliminated. Thus each of the answer sets which survives the constraints encodes a plan. We now describe this modification to $\pi_{2.nar}$.

Given a domain description D, a set of observations O which is initial state complete, a plan length l, and a goal h, we construct the following AnsProlog program $\pi_{2.planning}(D, O, h, l)$ consisting of five parts: $\pi_{2.nar}^{ef}$, $\pi_{2.nar}^{obs}$, and $\pi_{2.nar}^{in}$, are from the previous section, and $\pi_{2.planning}^{choice}$ and $\pi_{2.planning}^{goal}$ are described below.

(1) Choice rules: We have the following choice rules that make sure that one and only one action occurs at each time point up to l. They are collectively referred to as $\pi_{2.planning}^{choice}$

$not\_occurs(A, T) \leftarrow occurs(B, T), A \neq B.$

$occurs(A, T) \leftarrow T \leq l, \textbf{not } not\_occurs(A, T).$

(2) Goal: Finally we have the following constraint, for our goal h. We refer to it as $\pi_{2.planning}^{goal}$.

$\leftarrow \textbf{not } holds(h, l + 1).$

Proposition 82 Let D be a consistent domain description, O be an initial state complete set of observations such that (D, O) is consistent, l be the length of the plan that we are looking for, and h be a fluent which is the goal.

(i) If there is a sequence of actions $a_1, \ldots, a_l$ such that $D \models_O h$ **after** $a_1, \ldots, a_l$ then there exists a consistent answer of $\pi_{2.planning}(D, O, h, l)$ containing $\{occurs(a_1, 1), \ldots, occurs(a_l, l)\}$ as the only facts about *occurs*.

(ii) If there exists a consistent answer of $\pi_{2.planning}(D, O, h, l)$ containing $\{occurs(a_1, 1), \ldots, occurs(a_l, l)\}$ as the facts about *occurs* then $D \models_O h$ **after** $a_1, \ldots, a_l$.   □

Proof: (sketch) Follows from splitting the program to three layers, with the bottom layer consisting of $\pi_{2.planning}^{choice}$, the middle layer consisting of $\pi_{2.nar}(D, O)$, and the top layer consisting of $\pi_{2.planning}^{goal}$. It is easy to see that $\{occurs(a_1, 1), \ldots, occurs(a_l, l)\}$ is the set of *occur* atoms in an answer set of $\pi_{2.planning}^{choice}$, and uniquely identifies that answer set. (That is, no two different answer sets of $\pi_{2.planning}^{choice}$ can have the same set of *occurs*.) Now we can use Proposition 81 to show the correspondence between $D \models_O h$ **after** $a_1, \ldots, a_l$ and $\pi_{2.nar}(D, O) \cup \{occurs(a_1, 1), \ldots, occurs(a_n, l)\}$ $\models holds(h, l + 1)$, and use that correspondence to complete our proof.   □

One of the drawbacks of the above formulation is that we need to give the exact plan length. One way to overcome this limitation is to have a 'no-op' action that has no effect on the world, and then have l as an upper bound. In a later section (Section 5.3.2) we discuss an alternative approach where l can be an upper bound and we do not need the 'no-op' action.

5.2 Reasoning about actions and plan verification in richer domains

In the previous section we considered the simple action description language $\mathcal{A}$ and showed how reasoning about actions in $\mathcal{A}$ can be formulated in AnsProlog*. In the process we applied many results and notions from Chapter 3, thus demonstrating their usefulness. That was the reason why we used the simple language $\mathcal{A}$. In this section we consider extensions of $\mathcal{A}$ and their formulation in AnsProlog* and state the correspondences.

5.2.1 Allowing executability conditions

Our first extension to $\mathcal{A}$, which we will refer to as $\mathcal{A}_{ex}$, allows executability conditions in the domain description part. An executability condition is of the following form:

$$\textbf{executable } a \textbf{ if } p_1, \ldots, p_n, \neg q_1, \ldots, \neg q_r \qquad (5.2.7)$$

where a is an action and, $p_1, \ldots, p_n, q_1, \ldots, q_r$ are fluents. Intuitively, the above executability condition means that if the fluent literals $p_1, \ldots, p_n, \neg q_1, \ldots, \neg q_r$ hold in the state σ of a situation s, then the action a is executable in s.

A domain description of $\mathcal{A}_{ex}$ consists of a set of effect propositions and executability conditions. The transition function Φ_D defined by a domain description in $\mathcal{A}_{ex}$ has one more condition than it had originally when defined for domain descriptions in $\mathcal{A}$. This condition is as follows:

Given a domain description D in $\mathcal{A}_{ex}$, for any action a, and any state σ, $\Phi_D(a, \sigma)$ is said to be *defined* if there is an executability condition of the form (5.2.7) such that $p_1, \ldots, p_n, \neg q_1, \ldots, \neg q_r$ hold in σ. Otherwise, it is said to be undefined. When $\Phi_D(a, \sigma)$ is defined, the value of $\Phi_D(a, \sigma)$ is the same as the value of $\Phi_{D'}(a, \sigma)$ in $\mathcal{A}$, where D' consists of only the effect propositions of D. To define models and the corresponding entailment relation, the only additional requirement is that we declare that no fluent literal holds in an undefined state and if $\Phi_D(a, \sigma)$ is undefined then $\Phi_D(a', \Phi_D(a, \sigma))$ is undefined.

Given a domain description D, and a set of observations O, and a model $M = (\sigma_0, \Phi_D)$ of (D, O), we say a sequence of actions $a_1, \ldots, a_n$ is executable in M iff $\Phi_D(a_n, \ldots, \Phi_D(a_1, \sigma_0) \ldots)$ is defined. We say $a_1, \ldots, a_n$ is executable in (D, O), iff it is executable in all models of (D, O).

Example 102 Consider the following domain description D in $\mathcal{A}_{ex}$.

drive_to_airport **causes** *at_airport*
executable *drive_to_airport* **if** *has_car*
rent_a_car **causes** *has_car*

Let $\sigma_1 = \{\}$ and $\sigma_2 = \{has\_car\}$. We have $\Phi_D(drive\_to\_airport, \sigma_1)$ as undefined, while $\Phi_D(drive\_to\_airport, \sigma_2) = \{has\_car, at\_airport\}$. □

To compute the entailment relation $\models_O$ using AnsProlog* we now describe the changes that need to be made to the various programs in the previous section.

(1) $\pi_{1.exec}(D, O)$: To allow executability conditions $\pi_1(D, O)$ is modified as follows.
   - We add the following rules which we will collectively refer to as $\pi_{1.exec}^{ex}$.
     For each executability condition of the form (5.2.7) $\pi_{1.exec}^{ex}$ contains the following rule:

$$executable(a, S) \leftarrow holds(p_1, S), \ldots, holds(p_n, S), \textbf{not } holds(q_1, S), \ldots,$$
$$\textbf{not } holds(q_r, S).$$

   - To the body of each of the rules in π_1^{ef} and π_1^{in}, we add the literals $executable(a, S)$ and $executable(A, S)$, respectively.
   - The rules in π_1^{obs} remain unchanged.

(2) $\pi_{2.exec}(D, O)$: To allow executability conditions $\pi_2(D, O)$ is modified as follows.
- We add the following rules which we will collectively refer to as $\pi_{2.exec}^{ex}$.

  For each executability condition of the form (5.2.7) $\pi_{2.exec}^{ex}$ contains the following rule:

$$executable(a, S) \leftarrow holds(p_1, S), \ldots, holds(p_n, S), \neg holds(q_1, S), \ldots,$$
$$\neg holds(q_r, S).$$

- To the body of each of the rules in π_2^{ef} and π_2^{in}, we add the literals $executable(a, S)$ and $executable(A, S)$, respectively.
- The rules in π_2^{obs} remain unchanged.

(3) $\pi_{3.exec}(D, O)$: To allow executability conditions $\pi_3(D, O)$ is modified as follows.
- We add $\pi_{2.exec}^{ex}$.
- To the body of each of the rules in π_3^{ef} and π_2^{in}, we add the literals $executable(a, S)$ and $executable(A, S)$, respectively.
- The rules in π_2^{obs} remain unchanged.

(4) $\pi_{4.exec}(D, O)$: To allow executability conditions $\pi_4(D, O)$ is modified as follows.
- We add the following rules which we will collectively refer to as $\pi_{4.exec}^{ex}$.

$$reachable(s_0) \leftarrow .$$

For each executability condition of the form (5.2.7) $\pi_{4.exec}^{ex}$ contains the following rule:

$$reachable(res(a, S)) \leftarrow reachable(S), holds(p_1, S), \ldots, holds(p_n, S),$$
$$\neg holds(q_1, S), \ldots, \neg holds(q_r, S).$$

- To the body of each of the rules in π_3^{ef} and π_2^{in}, we add the literals $reachable(res(a, S))$ and $reachable(res(A, S))$, respectively.
- To the body of each of the rules in π_4^{obs} we add the literal $reachable([a_m, \ldots, a_1])$.
- The rules in π_4^{-in} and π_4^{back} remain unchanged.

(5) $\pi_{5.exec}(D, O)$: To allow executability conditions $\pi_5(D, O)$ is modified as follows.
- We add $\pi_{2.exec}^{ex}$.
- To the body of each of the rules in π_2^{ef} and π_2^{in}, we add the literals $executable(a, S)$ and $executable(A, S)$, respectively.
- The rules in π_5^{en} and π_5^{obs} remain unchanged.

(6) $\pi_{6.exec}(D, O)$: To allow executability conditions $\pi_6(D, O)$ is modified as follows.
- We add $\pi_{2.exec}^{ex}$.
- To the body of each of the rules in π_2^{ef} and π_2^{in}, we add the literals $executable(a, S)$ and $executable(A, S)$, respectively.
- The rules in π_6^{en} and π_5^{obs} remain unchanged.

(7) $\pi_{2.n.exec}(D, O)$: To allow executability conditions $\pi_{2.nar}(D, O)$ is modified as follows.
- We add the following rules which we will collectively refer to as $\pi_{2.n.exec}^{ex}$.

For each executability condition of the form (5.2.7) $\pi_{2.n.exec}^{ex}$ contains the following rule:

$$executable(a, T) \leftarrow holds(p_1, T), \ldots, holds(p_n, T),$$
$$not\_holds(q_1, T), \ldots, not\_holds(q_r, T).$$

- The rules in $\pi_{2.nar}^{ef}$, $\pi_{2.nar}^{in}$, and $\pi_{2.nar}^{obs}$ remain unchanged.
- We add the following rule which we will refer to as $\pi_{2.n.exec}^{constr}$.

$$\leftarrow occurs(A, T), \textbf{not } executable(A, T).$$

(8) $\pi_{2.p.exec}(D, O, h, l)$: To allow executability conditions $\pi_{2.planning}(D, O, h, l)$ is modified as follows.
- We add the rules in $\pi_{2.n.exec}^{ex}$.
- The rules in $\pi_{2.nar}^{ef}$, $\pi_{2.nar}^{in}$, $\pi_{2.nar}^{obs}$, $\pi_{2.planning}^{choice}$, and $\pi_{2.planning}^{goal}$ remain unchanged.
- We add the rule $\pi_{2.n.exec}^{constr}$.

As in the previous sections we can now state the correspondences between the entailment relation $\models_O$ and the AnsProlog* programs. For brevity we state only one of them. Before that we would like to point out that the programs $\pi_{2.p.exec}(D, O, h, l)$ and $\pi_{2.n.exec}(D, O)$ differ from the other programs shown above in an important way. To incorporate the notions of executability $\pi_{2.p.exec}(D, O, h, l)$ and $\pi_{2.n.exec}(D, O)$ are obtained by only adding new rules – without 'making any surgery' on the original rules – to $\pi_{2.planning}(D, O, h, l)$ and $\pi_{2.nar}(D, O)$ respectively. This is not the case for the other programs, where some of the original rules are modified.

Proposition 83 Let D be a consistent domain description in $\mathcal{A}_{ex}$, O be an initial state complete set of observations such that (D, O) is consistent, l be the length of the plan that we are looking for, and h be a fluent which is the goal.

(i) If there is a sequence of actions $a_1, \ldots, a_l$ such that $D \models_O h$ **after** $a_1, \ldots, a_l$ then there exists a consistent answer of $\pi_{2.p.exec}(D, O, h, l)$ containing $\{occurs(a_1, 1), \ldots, occurs(a_l, l)\}$ as the only facts about $occurs$.

(ii) If there exists a consistent answer of $\pi_{2.p.exec}(D, O, h, l)$ containing $\{occurs(a_1, 1), \ldots, occurs(a_l, l)\}$ as the facts about $occurs$ then $D \models_O h$ **after** $a_1, \ldots, a_l$. $\qquad\square$

Exercise 19 Executability conditions of the form discussed in this section have the implicit assumption that normally actions are not executable in a state and the exceptions are listed as executability conditions. This assumption is also used in the STRIPS language.

But in some domains the opposite is true. That is, normally actions are executable and the few exceptions can be expressed as statements of the form:

impossible a **if** $p_1, \ldots, p_n, \neg q_1, \ldots, \neg q_r$

Define the semantics of an extension of $\mathcal{A}$ that allows such impossibility statements and list what changes need to be made to the various AnsProlog* formulations of the previous sections so as to reason and plan in this extended language.   □

5.2.2 Allowing static causal propositions

In the languages $\mathcal{A}$ and $\mathcal{A}_{ex}$ the transition between states due to actions is specified through effect axioms and executability conditions. The effect axioms explicitly state the transition while the executability conditions explicitly state the executability of an action in a state. It was recognized that we can often express knowledge about the states directly in terms of what are possible or valid states and this knowledge can be used to indirectly infer effects of actions, executability of actions, or both and thus result in a more succinct and elaboration tolerant representation.

An example of such a constraint is: "a person can be at one place at one time". This can be expressed in classical logic as $at(X) \wedge at(Y) \Rightarrow X = Y$. In the absence of such a constraint the effect propositions of an action $move\_to(Y)$ can be expressed as:

$move\_to(Y)$ **causes** $at(Y)$
$move\_to(Y)$ **causes** $\neg at(X), X \neq Y$

But in the presence of the constraint, we just need the first effect axiom, and $\neg at(X)$ can be indirectly derived from the constraint. At first glance this does not seem to be much of a reduction, as instead of two effect propositions we have one effect proposition and one constraint. But now if we consider a set of actions similar to $move\_to(Y)$ such as: $drive\_to(Y), fly\_to(Y), take\_a\_train\_to(Y), take\_a\_bus\_to(Y)$ we realize that for each of them we need only one effect proposition and overall we need one constraint. This supports our assertion about the advantage of using constraints. The indirect effects of an action due to constraints are referred to as *ramifications* due to the occurrence of that action. (Encoding this in a logical language is referred to as the ramification problem.)

Constraints can also indirectly force certain actions to be not executable in certain states. For example, consider the constraint that $married\_to(X) \wedge married\_to(Y) \Rightarrow X = Y$, which encodes the constraint: "a person cannot be married to two different persons." The effect of the action $marry(Y)$ can be expressed by the following effect proposition:

$marry(Y)$ **causes** $married\_to(Y)$

In the presence of a constraint about the impossibility of being married to two persons, we do not need an explicit executability condition saying that the action $marry(Y)$ is executable only when the person is not married to anyone else. This condition is indirectly enforced by the constraint, as otherwise there will be a violation of the constraint. Formalization of this indirect qualification of the executability of an action due to a constraint is referred to as the *qualification problem*.

An important point to note about the two constraints $at(X) \wedge at(Y) \Rightarrow X = Y$ and $married\_to(X) \wedge married\_to(Y) \Rightarrow X = Y$ is that they are syntactically similar; yet they have different purposes. The first results in ramifications while the second results in a qualification. This means the processing of these constraints by themselves cannot be automatic and for any automatic processing they will need additional annotation. This demonstrates the inability of classical logic for adequately expressing constraints. It is argued in the literature that a causal logic is more appropriate. In an $\mathcal{A}$-like syntax the above two constraints will be differently expressed as follows:

$at(X)$ **causes** $\neg at(Y)$ **if** $X \neq Y$, and
$married\_to(X) \wedge married\_to(Y) \wedge X \neq Y$ **causes** *false*

We now formally define the syntax and semantics of a causal logic that we will use to express which states are valid and that may result in ramifications, qualifications, or both.

A static causal proposition is of the form

$$p_1, \ldots, p_n, \neg q_1, \ldots, \neg q_r \textbf{ causes } f \qquad (5.2.8)$$

where $p_1, \ldots, p_n, q_1, \ldots, q_r$ are fluents and f is either fluent literal, or a special symbol *false*.

We say a state σ satisfies a static causal proposition of the form (5.2.8) if: (i) f is a literal and $p_1, \ldots, p_n, \neg q_1, \ldots, \neg q_r$ hold in σ implies that f holds in σ; or (ii) f is *false* and at least one of $p_1, \ldots, p_n, \neg q_1, \ldots, \neg q_r$ does not hold in σ. For a state σ, by $open(\sigma)$ we denote the set of fluent literals $\sigma \cup \{\neg f : f \text{ is a fluent and } f \notin \sigma\}$. We say a set s of fluent literals and possibly the symbol *false* satisfies a static causal proposition of the form (5.2.8) if $\{p_1, \ldots, p_n, \neg q_1, \ldots, \neg q_r\} \subseteq$ s implies that $f \in$ s.

Let s be a set of fluent literals and possibly the symbol *false* and Z be a set of static causal propositions. By $Cn_Z(\text{s})$ we denote the smallest set of fluent literals and possibly the symbol *false* that contains s and satisfies all propositions in Z. This set can be obtained by starting with s and repeatedly going over the static causal propositions in Z and adding the right hand side if the literals in the left hand side are already there, and repeating this until a fixpoint is reached.

Given a domain description D consisting of effect propositions, and static causal propositions, for an action a, and a state σ, we define $e_a(\sigma)$ as the set $\{f : \text{there exists an effect proposition of the form (5.1.1) such that } p_1, \ldots, p_n, \neg q_1, \ldots, \neg q_r \text{ hold in } \sigma\}$.

We say a state $\sigma' \in \Phi_D(a, \sigma)$ if $open(\sigma') = Cn_Z(e_a(\sigma) \cup (open(\sigma) \cap open(\sigma')))$.

Example 103 Consider the following domain description D of effect propositions and static causal propositions:

a **causes** c

$c, \neg f$ **causes** g

$c, \neg g$ **causes** f

Let $\sigma_0 = \{\}$. We will now illustrate that $\sigma_1 = \{c, f\}$ and $\sigma_2 = \{c, g\}$ are in $\Phi_D(a, \sigma_0)$, while $\sigma_3 = \{c, f, g\}$ is not in $\Phi_D(a, \sigma_0)$.

Let us refer to the set of static causal propositions in D as Z. Now, $open(\sigma_0) = \{\neg c, \neg f, \neg g\}$, $open(\sigma_1) = \{c, f, \neg g\}$, $open(\sigma_2) = \{c, \neg f, g\}$, and $open(\sigma_3) = \{c, f, g\}$.

$Cn_Z(e_a(\sigma_0) \cup (open(\sigma_0) \cap open(\sigma_1))) = Cn_Z(\{c\} \cup (\{\neg c, \neg f, \neg g\} \cap \{c, f, \neg g\}))$
$= Cn_Z(\{c\} \cup \{\neg g\}) = Cn_Z(\{c, \neg g\}) = \{c, f, \neg g\} = open(\sigma_1)$. Hence, $\sigma_1 \in \Phi_D(a, \sigma_0)$.

$Cn_Z(e_a(\sigma_0) \cup (open(\sigma_0) \cap open(\sigma_2))) = Cn_Z(\{c\} \cup (\{\neg c, \neg f, \neg g\} \cap \{c, \neg f, g\}))$
$= Cn_Z(\{c\} \cup \{\neg f\}) \; Cn_Z(\{c, \neg f\}) = \{c, \neg f, g\} = open(\sigma_2)$. Hence, $\sigma_2 \in \Phi_D(a, \sigma_0)$.

$Cn_Z(e_a(\sigma_0) \cup (open(\sigma_0) \cap open(\sigma_3))) = Cn_Z(\{c\} \cup (\{\neg c, \neg f, \neg g\}) \cap \{c, f, g\}))$
$= Cn_Z(\{c\} \cup \{\}) = Cn_Z(\{c\}) = \{c\} \neq open(\sigma_3)$. Hence, $\sigma_3 \notin \Phi_D(a, \sigma_0)$.   □

The above example shows that in the presence of static causal propositions, effects of actions could be nondeterministic. The following example illustrates that static causal propositions are not contrapositive. That is, the static causal proposition f **causes** g is not equivalent to $\neg g$ **causes** $\neg f$ and the direct effect of $\neg g$ does not indirectly cause $\neg f$.

Example 104 Consider the following domain description D:

shoot **causes** $\neg alive$

make_walk **causes** *walking*

$\neg alive$ **causes** $\neg walking$

Let us refer to the set of static causal constraints in D as Z, and let $\sigma_0 = \{alive, walking\}$, $\sigma_1 = \{\}$, $\sigma_2 = \{walking\}$.

Let us consider the effect of the action *shoot* in the state σ_0. We have $e_{shoot}(\sigma_0) = \{\neg alive\}$. Hence, $Cn_Z(e_{shoot}(\sigma_0) \cup (open(\sigma_0) \cap open(\sigma_1))) = Cn_Z(\{\neg alive\} \cup (\{alive, walking\} \cap \{\neg alive, \neg walking\})) = Cn_Z (\{\neg alive\} \cup$

$\{\}) = Cn_Z(\{\neg alive\}) = \{\neg alive, \neg walking\} = open(\sigma_1)$. Hence, $\sigma_1 \in \Phi_D(shoot, \sigma_0)$. We can similarly show that no other states belong to $\Phi_D(shoot, \sigma_0)$ and hence the set $\Phi_D(shoot, \sigma_0)$ is a singleton set implying that the effect of *shoot* in the state σ_0 is deterministic.

Now let us consider the effect of the action *make_walk* in the state σ_1. $e_{make\_walk}(\sigma_1) = \{walking\}$. $Cn_Z(e_{make\_walk}(\sigma_1) \cup (open(\sigma_1) \cap open(\sigma_2))) = Cn_Z(\{walking\} \cup (\{\neg alive, \neg walking\} \cap \{\neg alive, walking\})) = Cn_Z(\{walking\} \cup \{\neg alive\}) = Cn_Z(\{\neg alive, walking\}) = \{\neg alive, walking, \neg walking\} \neq open(\sigma_2)$. Hence, $\sigma_2 \notin \Phi_D(shoot, \sigma_0)$. We can similarly show that no other state belongs to $\Phi_D(make\_walk, \sigma_0)$ and hence the set $\Phi_D(shoot, \sigma_0)$ is an empty set implying that *make_walk* is not executable in the state σ_0. This means that the static causal proposition $\neg alive$ **causes** $\neg walking$ neither is equivalent nor does it encode its contrapositive *walking* **causes** *alive*. If it were, then the indirect effect of *make_walk* would be that the turkey becomes *alive*, which of course is not intuitive. We get the intuitive conclusion that if anyone who tries to make a dead turkey walk will fail in the attempt. Thus the static causal proposition results in a qualification when reasoning about the action *make_walk* in the state σ_1.   □

Exercise 20 Consider the *move_to* and *marry* domains represented using static causal propositions and compute the transition due to the actions *move_to(b)* and *marry(b)* on the states $\{at(a)\}$ and $\{married\_to(a)\}$ respectively.   □

Given a domain description D consisting of effect propositions, executability conditions, and static causal propositions, and a set of observations O about the initial situation we say σ_0 is an initial state corresponding to (D, O) if (i) for all the observations of the form **initially** f in O, f holds in σ_0, and (ii) σ_0 satisfies the static causal propositions in D. We say $\sigma_0, a_1, \sigma_1, a_2, \sigma_2, \ldots, a_n, \sigma_n$ is a valid trajectory of (D, O), if (a) σ_0 is an initial state corresponding to (D, O), (b) for $1 \leq i \leq n$, a_i is executable in σ_{i-1}, and (c) for $1 \leq i \leq n$, $\sigma_i \in \Phi_D(a_i, \sigma_{i-1})$.

We now present an AnsProlog$^\perp$ program $\pi_{7.n.causal}(D, O)$ whose answer sets correspond to the valid trajectories of (D, O). The program $\pi_{7.n.causal}(D, O)$ consists of the components $\pi_{7.n.causal}^{en}(D, O)$, $\pi_{7.n.causal}^{ef}(D, O)$, $\pi_{7.n.causal}^{st}(D, O)$, $\pi_{7.n.causal}^{obs}(D, O)$, $\pi_{7.n.causal}^{in}(D, O)$, $\pi_{7.n.causal}^{ex}(D, O)$, $\pi_{7.n.causal}^{constr}(D, O)$, and $\pi_{7.n.causal}^{choice}$ as described below.

(1) Enumeration in $\pi_{7.n.causal}(D, O)$: The enumeration rules in $\pi_{7.n.causal}(D, O)$ collectively denoted by $\pi_{7.n.causal}^{en}$ consist of the following rules:

$holds(F, s_0) \leftarrow \textbf{not } not\_holds(F, s_0)$.

$not\_holds(F, s_0) \leftarrow \textbf{not } holds(F, s_0)$.

(2) Translating effect propositions: The effect propositions in D are translated as follows and are collectively referred to as $\pi^{ef}_{7.n.causal}$.

For every effect proposition of the form (5.1.1) if f is a fluent then $\pi^{ef}_{7.n.causal}$ contains the following rule:

$$holds(f, T+1) \leftarrow occurs(a, T), holds(p_1, T), \ldots, holds(p_n, T),$$
$$not\_holds(q_1, T), \ldots, not\_holds(q_r, T).$$

else, if f is the negative fluent literal $\neg g$ then $\pi^{ef}_{7.n.causal}$ contains the following rule:

$$not\_holds(g, T+1) \leftarrow occurs(a, T), holds(p_1, T), \ldots, holds(p_n, T),$$
$$not\_holds(q_1, T), \ldots, not\_holds(q_r, T).$$

(3) Translating static causal propositions: The static causal propositions in D are translated as follows and are collectively referred to as $\pi^{st}_{7.n.causal}$.

For every static causal proposition of the form (5.2.8) if f is a fluent then $\pi^{st}_{7.n.causal}$ contains the following rule:

$$holds(f, T) \leftarrow holds(p_1, T), \ldots, holds(p_n, T), not\_holds(q_1, T), \ldots,$$
$$not\_holds(q_r, T).$$

else, if f is the negative fluent literal $\neg g$ then $\pi^{st}_{7.n.causal}$ contains the following rule:

$$not\_holds(g, T) \leftarrow holds(p_1, T), \ldots, holds(p_n, T), not\_holds(q_1, T), \ldots,$$
$$not\_holds(q_r, T).$$

else, if f is the symbol *false* then $\pi^{st}_{7.n.causal}$ contains the following rule:

$$\leftarrow holds(p_1, T), \ldots, holds(p_n, T), not\_holds(q_1, T), \ldots, not\_holds(q_r, T).$$

(4) Translating observations: The value propositions in O are translated as follows and are collectively referred to as $\pi^{obs}_{7.n.causal}$.

For every value proposition of the form (5.1.5) if f is a fluent then $\pi^{obs}_{7.n.causal}$ contains the following rule:

$$\leftarrow \textbf{not } holds(f, 1).$$

else, if f is the negative fluent literal $\neg g$ then $\pi^{obs}_{7.n.causal}$ contains the following rule:

$$\leftarrow \textbf{not } not\_holds(g, 1).$$

(5) Inertia rules: Besides the above we have the following inertia rules referred to as $\pi^{in}_{7.n.causal}$.

$$holds(F, T+1) \leftarrow occurs(A, T), holds(F, T), \textbf{not } not\_holds(F, T+1).$$

$$not\_holds(F, T+1) \leftarrow occurs(A, T), not\_holds(F, T), \textbf{not } holds(F, T+1).$$

(6) We add the following rules which we will collectively refer to as $\pi^{ex}_{7.n.causal}$.

For each executability condition of the form (5.2.7) $\pi^{ex}_{7.n.causal}$ contains the following rule:

$$executable(a, T) \leftarrow holds(p_1, T), \ldots, holds(p_n, T),$$
$$not\_holds(q_1, T), \ldots, not\_holds(q_r, T).$$

(7) We add the following rules which we will refer to as $\pi^{constr}_{7.n.causal}$.

$\leftarrow holds(F, 1), not\_holds(F, 1).$

$\leftarrow occurs(A, T), \textbf{not } executable(A, T).$

$\leftarrow occurs(A, T), holds(F, T + 1), not\_holds(F, T + 1).$

(8) Choice rules: We have the following choice rules that make sure that one and only one action occurs at each time point up to l. They are collectively referred to as $\pi^{choice}_{7.n.causal}$.

$not\_occurs(A, T) \leftarrow occurs(B, T), A \neq B.$

$occurs(A, T) \leftarrow \textbf{not } not\_occurs(A, T).$

We now formally relate valid trajectories of (D, O) and answer sets of $\pi_{7.n.causal}(D, O)$.

Proposition 84 Let D be a domain description of effect propositions, executability conditions, and static causal propositions. Let O be a set of observations about the initial state.

(i) $\sigma_0, a_1, \sigma_1, \ldots, a_n, \sigma_n$ is a valid trajectory of (D, O) implies that there exists an answer set A of $\pi_{7.n.causal}(D, O)$ containing $\{occurs(a_1, 1), \ldots, occurs(a_n, n)\}$ as the only facts about $occurs$ during the time points 1 to n and for $0 \leq i \leq n$, $\sigma_i = \{f : holds(f, i + 1) \in A\}$ and $\sigma_i \cap \{f : not\_holds(f, i + 1) \in A\} = \emptyset$.

(ii) Let A be an answer set of $\pi_{7.n.causal}(D, O)$ with $\{occurs(a_1, 1), \ldots, occurs(a_n, n)\}$ as the set of facts about $occurs$ during the time points 1 to n; then $\sigma_0, a_1, \sigma_1, \ldots, a_n, \sigma_n$ is a valid trajectory of D and O, where for $0 \leq i \leq n$, $\sigma_i = \{f : holds(f, i + 1) \in A\}$.   □

5.2.3 Reasoning about parallel execution of actions

So far in this chapter we have reasoned only about sequential occurrences of actions and planned with them. In a more realistic scenario actions may be executed in parallel. Reasoning about such executions is the goal of this sub-section. When actions that do not interfere, which is often the case, are executed in parallel their effect can be computed as the cumulative effect of the individual actions. In some cases though they may interfere with each other and the effect may be different from their cumulative effect. An example of the latter are the actions *left_lift* and *right_lift* with respect to a large bowl of soup. Individually each of these two actions will cause the bowl of soup to spill, while when done in parallel the effect is different;

instead of the soup being spilled the bowl is lifted. A straightforward approach of formalizing effects of parallel execution of actions would be to have effect propositions for each possible parallel execution of actions. But that would lead to explicitly representing the effect of 2^n action combinations, when our domain has n actions. This can be avoided by the use of normative statements and exceptions. The normative statement would be: Normally parallel execution of a set of actions inherits the individual effect of the actions in the set. We can then have exceptions to such inheritance, which encode the cases when inheritance should not be used, including when two actions interfere with each other, or complement each other resulting in a different effect.

To formulate the reasoning about such parallel actions in an $\mathcal{A}$-like language we minimally extend $\mathcal{A}$ and allow the actions in the effect propositions of the form (5.1.1) and observations of the form (5.1.4) to be compound actions, which we represent by a set of basic actions. We refer to this extension of $\mathcal{A}$ as $\mathcal{A}_c$.

Example 105 Consider the domain of lifting a bowl of soup. We can express the effect of the actions as follows:

{left_lift} **causes** *spilled*
{right_lift} **causes** *spilled*
{left_lift, right_lift} **causes** *lifted*

As in the case of $\mathcal{A}$ the role of the effect propositions is to define a transition function from states and actions – which now are compound actions represented by a set of basic actions, to states. We now define a transition function for domain descriptions in $\mathcal{A}_c$ which differs from the transition functions of domain descriptions in $\mathcal{A}$ in that when we have effect propositions a **causes** f **if** p and a **causes** $\neg f$ **if** p, we now treat it to mean a is not executable in a state where p is true, rather than interpreting it as the domain being inconsistent. This isolates the 'badness' of having the effect propositions a **causes** f **if** p and a **causes** $\neg f$ **if** p in a domain description.

We say that a fluent literal f is an immediate effect of an action a in a state σ, if there exists an effect proposition of the form (5.1.1) such that $p_1, \ldots, p_n, \neg q_1, \ldots, \neg q_r$ hold in σ. For a state σ and an action a, the set of positive (and respectively negative) fluent literals that are immediate effects of a on σ is denoted by $direct^+(a, \sigma)$ (and respectively $direct^-(a, \sigma)$). We say that a fluent literal f is an inherited effect of an action a in a state σ, if there exists $b \subset a$ such that f is an immediate effect of b and there is no $c, b \subset c \subseteq a$ such that the complement of f is an immediate effect of c. For a state σ and an action a, the set of positive (and respectively negative) fluent literals that are inherited effects of a on σ is denoted by $inherited^+(a, \sigma)$ (and respectively $inherited^-(a, \sigma)$). We say that a fluent literal f is an effect of an action a in a state σ, if f is either an immediate effect or an inherited effect of a in σ. We then define $E^+(a, \sigma)$ as the set of fluents that are effects of a in σ, and $E^-(a, \sigma)$ as the set of fluents f such that $\neg f$ is an effect of a in σ. In other words, $E^+(a, \sigma) = direct^+(a, \sigma) \cup inherited^+(a, \sigma)$ and $E^-(a, \sigma) = direct^-(a, \sigma) \cup inherited^-(a, \sigma)$. We say that $\Phi(a, \sigma)$ is undefined if $E^+(a, \sigma)$ and $E^-(a, \sigma)$ intersect; otherwise $\Phi(a, \sigma)$ is defined as the set $\sigma \cup E^+(a, \sigma) \setminus E^-(a, \sigma)$. Note that unlike domain descriptions in $\mathcal{A}$, a domain description D in $\mathcal{A}_c$ always has a transition function, and we denote it by Φ_D.

We say σ_0 is an initial state corresponding to a domain description D and a set of observations O, if for all observations of the form (5.1.4) in O, $[a_m, \ldots, a_1]\sigma_0$ is defined and the fluent literal f holds in it. We then say that (σ_0, Φ_D) *satisfies* O. Given a domain description D and a set of observations O, we refer to the pair (Φ_D, σ_0), where Φ_D is the transition function of D and σ_0 is an initial state corresponding to (D, O), as a *model* of (D, O). We say (D, O) is *consistent* if it has a model and is *complete* if it has a unique model.

Example 106 Let D_1 be the domain description $\{\{lift\} \textbf{ causes } lifted; \{open\} \textbf{ causes } opened\}$, and $O = \{\textbf{initially } \neg lifted; \textbf{initially } \neg opened\}$. The only model of D_1 and O is given by (σ_0, Φ), where $\sigma_0 = \emptyset$ and Φ is defined as follows:

$\Phi(open, \sigma) = \sigma \cup \{opened\}$
$\Phi(lift, \sigma) = \sigma \cup \{lifted\}$
$\Phi(\{open, lift\}, \sigma) = \sigma \cup \{opened, lifted\}$
$D_1 \models_O opened \textbf{ after } \{open, lift\}$ and $D_1 \models_O lifted\} \textbf{ after } \{open, lift\}$.   □

Example 107 Consider a domain containing three unit actions *paint*, *close*, and *open*, and two fluents, *opened* and *painted*. The effects of these actions are described by the following domain description D_3:

$\{close\} \textbf{ causes } \neg opened$
$\{open\} \textbf{ causes } opened$
$\{paint\} \textbf{ causes } painted$

Let O be the empty set. The transition function Φ of D_3 is defined as follows:

$\Phi(\emptyset, \sigma) = \sigma$
$\Phi(\{paint\}, \sigma) = \sigma \cup \{painted\}$
$\Phi(\{close\}, \sigma) = \sigma \setminus \{opened\}$
$\Phi(\{open\}, \sigma) = \sigma \cup \{opened\}$
$\Phi(\{paint, close\}, \sigma) = \sigma \cup \{painted\} \setminus \{opened\}$
$\Phi(\{paint, open\}, \sigma) = \sigma \cup \{painted\} \cup \{opened\}$
$\Phi(\{close, open\}, \sigma)$ and $\Phi(\{close, open, paint\}, \sigma)$ are undefined.

Then D_3 and O have four models, which are of the form (σ, Φ) where $\sigma \subseteq$ {*opened, painted*}. □

We now present an AnsProlog$^{\neg, \perp}$ formulation that computes the entailment relation $\models_O$, given a domain description D and a set of observations O. The program we present is also a sorted program like those in Section 5.1.1; the only small difference being in the sort action, which now refers to compound actions that represent parallel execution of a set of basic actions. We refer to the AnsProlog$^{\neg, \perp}$ of this section as $\pi_{5.compound}(D, O)$ implying that it is similar to $\pi_5(D, O)$ from Section 5.1.1 and it allows compound actions. The program $\pi_{5.compound}(D, O)$ consists of $\pi_{5.compound}^{ef.dep}$, $\pi_{5.compound}^{obs}$, $\pi_{5.compound}^{ef.indep}$, $\pi_{5.compound}^{in}$, $\pi_{5.compound}^{inh}$, $\pi_{5.compound}^{en}$, and $\pi_{5.compound}^{aux}$ as defined below.

(1) Translating effect propositions: The effect propositions in D are translated as follows and are collectively referred to as $\pi_{5.compound}^{ef.dep}$.

For every effect proposition of the form (5.1.1) if f is a fluent then $\pi_{5.compound}^{ef.dep}$ contains the following rule:

$$causes(a, f, S) \leftarrow holds(p_1, S), \ldots, holds(p_n, S), \neg holds(q_1, S), \ldots, \neg holds(q_r, S).$$

else, if f is the negative fluent literal $\neg g$ then $\pi_{5.compound}^{ef.dep}$ contains the following rule:

$$causes(a, neg(g), S) \leftarrow holds(p_1, S), \ldots, holds(p_n, S), \neg holds(q_1, S), \ldots, \neg holds(q_r, S).$$

(2) Observations as constraints: The value propositions in O are translated as follows and are collectively referred to as $\pi_{5.compound}^{obs}$.

For an observation of the form (5.1.4) if f is a fluent then $\pi_{5.compound}^{obs}$ contains the following rule:

$$\leftarrow \textbf{not } holds(f, [a_m, \ldots, a_1]).$$

else if f is the fluent literal $\neg g$, then $\pi_{5.compound}^{obs}$ contains the following rule:

$$\leftarrow \textbf{not } \neg holds(g, [a_m, \ldots, a_1]).$$

(3) Domain independent effect rules: The domain independent effect rules in $\pi_{5.compound}(D, O)$ collectively denoted by $\pi_{5.compound}^{ef.indep}$ contain the following rules:

$$holds(F, res(A, S)) \leftarrow causes(A, F, S), \textbf{not } undefined(A, S).$$
$$\neg holds(F, res(A, S)) \leftarrow causes(A, neg(F), S), \textbf{not } undefined(A, S).$$
$$undefined(A, S) \leftarrow causes(A, F, S), causes(A, neg(F), S).$$
$$undefined(A, res(B, S)) \leftarrow undefined(B, S).$$

(4) Inertia rules: The inertia rules in $\pi_{5.compound}(D, O)$ collectively denoted by $\pi_{5.compound}^{in}$ consist of the following:

$$holds(F, res(A, S)) \leftarrow holds(F, S), \textbf{not } causes(A, neg(F), S), singleton(A),$$
$$\textbf{not } undefined(A, S).$$
$$\neg holds(F, res(A, S)) \leftarrow \neg holds(F, S), \textbf{not } causes(A, F, S), singleton(A),$$
$$\textbf{not } undefined(A, S).$$

(5) Inheritance axioms: The inheritance rules in $\pi_{5.compound}(D, O)$ collectively denoted by $\pi_{5.compound}^{inh}$ consist of the following rules:

$$holds(F, res(A, S)) \leftarrow subset(B, A), holds(F, res(B, S)), \textbf{not } noninh(F, A, S),$$
$$\textbf{not } undefined(A, S).$$
$$\neg holds(F, res(A, S)) \leftarrow subset(B, A), \neg holds(F, res(B, S)),$$
$$\textbf{not } noninh(neg(F), A, S), \textbf{not } undefined(A, S).$$
$$cancels(X, Y, F, S) \leftarrow subset(X, Z), subseteq(Z, Y), cause(Z, neg(F), S).$$
$$cancels(X, Y, neg(F), S) \leftarrow subset(X, Z), subseteq(Z, Y), cause(Z, F, S).$$
$$noninh(F, A, S) \leftarrow subseteq(U, A), causes(U, neg(F), S),$$
$$\textbf{not } cancels(U, A, neg(F), S).$$
$$noninh(neg(F), A, S) \leftarrow subseteq(U, A), causes(U, F, S), \textbf{not } cancels(U, A, F, S).$$
$$undefined(A, S) \leftarrow noninh(F, A, S), noninh(neg(F), A, S).$$

(6) Enumeration about the initial situation in $\pi_{5.compound}(D, O)$: The enumeration rules in $\pi_{5.compound}(D, O)$ collectively denoted by $\pi_{5.compound}^{en}$ consist of the following rules:

$$holds(F, s_0) \leftarrow \textbf{not } \neg holds(F, s_0).$$
$$\neg holds(F, s_0) \leftarrow \textbf{not } holds(F, s_0).$$

(7) Auxiliary rules: The auxiliary rules in $\pi_{5.compound}(D, O)$ collectively denoted by $\pi_{5.compound}^{aux}$ consist of the following rules:

$$\neg subseteq(U, V) \leftarrow in(X, U), \textbf{not } in(X, V).$$
$$subseteq(U, V) \leftarrow \textbf{not } \neg subseteq(U, V).$$
$$eq(X, X) \leftarrow.$$
$$\neg singleton(X) \leftarrow in(Y, X), in(Z, X), \textbf{not } eq(Y, Z).$$
$$singleton(X) \leftarrow \textbf{not } \neg singleton(X).$$
$$subset(X, Y) \leftarrow subseteq(X, Y), \textbf{not } subseteq(Y, X).$$

We now analyze $\pi_{5.compound}(D, O)$ and relate entailments with respect to $\pi_{5.compound}(D, O)$ with queries entailed by D, O.

Lemma 5.2.1 [BG97] Let D be a domain description and O be a set of observations. A set S is a consistent answer set of $\pi_{5.compound}(D, O)$ iff S is the consistent answer set of $\pi_{5.compound}(D, O) \cup \{holds(f, s_0) : holds(f, s_0) \in S\} \cup \{\neg holds(f, s_0) : \neg holds(f, s_0) \in S\}$. $\square$

Lemma 5.2.2 [BG97] Let D be a domain description, and O be a set of observations. Then $M = (\sigma_0, \Phi)$ is a model of (D, O) iff M is the model of (D, O_M), where $O_M = O \cup \{\textbf{initially } f : f \in \sigma_0\} \cup \{\textbf{initially } \neg f : f \notin \sigma_0\}$. $\square$

In the following we denote the situation $[a_1, \ldots, a_n]$ by s_n, and the state $[a_m, \ldots, a_1]\sigma_0$ by σ_m.

Lemma 5.2.3 [BG97] **Models of D vs Answer sets of πD.** Let D be a domain description and O be a set of observations. Let $M = (\sigma_0, \Phi)$ be a model of (D, O) and A be a consistent answer set of $\pi_{5.compound}(D, O)$ such that $\sigma_0 = \{f : holds(f, s_0) \in A\}$.

(1) If $a_1, \ldots, a_n$ is executable in M then
    (a) $f \in direct^+(a_n, \sigma_{n-1})$ iff $causes(a_n, f, s_{n-1}) \in A$.
    (b) $f \in direct^-(a_n, \sigma_{n-1})$ iff $causes(a_n, neg(f), s_{n-1}) \in A$.
    (c) $f \in inherited^+(a_n, \sigma_{n-1})$ iff $noninh(neg(f), a_n, s_{n-1}) \in A$.
    (d) $f \in inherited^-(a_n, \sigma_{n-1})$ iff $noninh(f, a_n, s_{n-1}) \in A$.
    (e) $undefined(a_n, s_{n-1}) \notin A$.
    (f) $f \in \sigma_n \Leftrightarrow holds(f, s_n) \in A$
    (g) $f \notin \sigma_n \Leftrightarrow \neg holds(f, s_n) \in A$.
(2) If $a_1, \ldots, a_n$ is not executable in M then

    $holds(f, s_n) \notin A$ and $\neg holds(f, s_n) \notin A$ and $undefined(a_n, s_{n-1}) \in A$. $\square$

Lemma 5.2.4 [BG97] Let D be a domain description and O be a set of observations such that (D, O) is consistent. For every model $M = (\sigma_0, \Phi)$ of (D, O), there exists a consistent answer set A of $\pi_{5.compound}(D, O)$ such that $\sigma_0 = \{f : holds(f, s_0) \in A\}$. $\square$

Lemma 5.2.5 [BG97] Let D be a domain description and O be a set of observations such that (D, O) is consistent. For every consistent answer set A of $\pi_{5.compound}(D, O)$ there exists a model $M = (\sigma_0, \Phi)$ of (D, O) such that $\sigma_0 = \{f : holds(f, s_0) \in A\}$. $\square$

Theorem 5.2.6 Soundness and completeness of $\pi_{5.compound}$. Let D be a domain description, O be a set of observations, f be a fluent, and $a_1, \ldots, a_n$ be a sequence of actions that is executable in all models of (D, O). Then

(i) $\pi_{5.compound}(D, O) \models holds(f, [a_1, \ldots, a_n])$ iff $D \models f$ **after** $a_1, \ldots, a_n$.
(ii) $\pi_{5.compound}(D, O) \models \neg holds(f, [a_1, \ldots, a_n])$ iff $D \models \neg f$ **after** $a_1, \ldots, a_n$. $\square$

Proof: (sketch) Directly from Lemma 5.2.3, Lemma 5.2.4 and Lemma 5.2.5.

5.3 Answer set planning examples in extensions of $\mathcal{A}$ and STRIPS

In Sections 5.1.10 and 5.2.1 we discussed how to formulate planning using AnsProlog and in Section 5.1.9 we briefly mentioned the notion of 'answer set planning'. In this section we use the answer set planning methodology for planning with the blocks world example. We now further motivate answer set planning and our use of it in this section.

In answer set planning, each plan corresponds to an answer set of the program. In this program a linear time line is used and the initial situation corresponds to the time point 1. Action occurrences at different time points are enumerated using the notion of 'choice' and possible answer sets (and the actions occurrences encoded in them) that do not lead to the holding of the goal at a required time point – defined by a given plan length – are eliminated using constraints. Thus the answer sets each encode a plan that achieves the goal at the required time point. As before, given what holds in a time point, reasoning about what holds in the next time point is formulated using effect rules and inertia rules.

Recently, there has been a lot of attention given to answer set planning. Some of the main reasons behind this are:

- We now have the interpreters dlv and Smodels which can generate one or more answer sets of an AnsProlog program. These interpreters are different from the query answering type of interpreters such as PROLOG. The former is suitable for answer set planning, while the latter is more appropriate for planning using variable instantiation.
- Answer set planning is similar to the satisfiability based planning, while planning in PROLOG using variable instantiation is based on the principles of theorem proving. In the past a theorem proving approach to planning was tried and abandoned because of its failure to plan in large domains. On the other hand satisfiability based planning has enjoyed tremendous success [KS96] in recent years.

In this section we start with blocks world planning in STRIPS using the PDDL syntax [GHK$^+$98] that has been the standard in recent planning contests. We encode the blocks world example in AnsProlog and run it using smodels. The program that we present is an improvement over the program $\pi_{2.p.exec}$ from Section 5.2.1. The improvements allow the user to give an upper bound of the plan length rather than the exact plan length, and forbid further action occurrences in an answer set once the plan is found. Moreover we make additional modifications to reduce the number of predicates, and to make it easier to match with the PDDL syntax.

We then incorporate domain specific temporal constraints into the program so as to make the planning more efficient, and thus demonstrate the ease with which such constraints can be encoded in AnsProlog.

Finally, we consider richer action language features such as defined fluents, causal qualification and ramification constraints, and conditional effects, and show how they can be formulated in answer set planning. We also show that by allowing these features the programs become shorter and the execution time to find plans also reduces. We would like to point out here that it is not yet known how to incorporate causal constraints and the use of an upper bound of the plan length (instead of the plan length) in propositional logic formulations used in satisfiability based planning.

5.3.1 A blocks world example in PDDL

In this section we introduce PDDL by giving the specification of the blocks world domain in it. We first give the domain description part.

```
(define (domain BLOCKS)
  (:requirements :strips :typing)
  (:types block)
  (:predicates (on ?x - block ?y - block)
               (ontable ?x - block)
               (clear ?x - block)
               (handempty)
               (holding ?x - block)
               )

  (:action pick-up
            :parameters (?x - block)
            :precondition (and (clear ?x)
             (ontable ?x) (handempty))
            :effect
            (and (not (ontable ?x))
                  (not (clear ?x))
                  (not (handempty))
                  (holding ?x)))

  (:action put-down
            :parameters (?x - block)
            :precondition (holding ?x)
            :effect
            (and (not (holding ?x))
                  (clear ?x)
                  (handempty)
                  (ontable ?x)))
```

```
(:action stack
            :parameters (?x - block ?y - block)
            :precondition (and (holding ?x) (clear ?y))
            :effect
            (and (not (holding ?x))
                  (not (clear ?y))
                  (clear ?x)
                  (handempty)
                  (on ?x ?y)))
(:action unstack
            :parameters (?x - block ?y - block)
            :precondition (and (on ?x ?y) (clear ?x)
             (handempty))
            :effect
            (and (holding ?x)
                  (clear ?y)
                  (not (clear ?x))
                  (not (handempty))
                  (not (on ?x ?y)))))
```

The above PDDL description can be encoded in $\mathcal{A}$ as follows:

(1) Sort: $block(X)$. In the rest of the descriptions X and Y range over the sort $block$.
(2) Fluents: $on(X)$, $ontable(X)$, $clear(X)$, $handempty$, $holding(X)$.
(3) Executability conditions:

   executable $pick\_up(X)$ **if** $clear(X), ontable(X), handempty$
   executable $put\_down(X)$ **if** $holding(X)$
   executable $stack(X, Y)$ **if** $holding(X), clear(Y)$
   executable $unstack(X, Y)$ **if** $on(X, Y), clear(X), handempty$

(4) Effect propositions:

   $pick\_up(X)$ **causes** $\neg ontable(X), \neg clear(X), \neg handempty, holding(X)$
   $put\_down(X)$ **causes** $\neg holding(X), clear(X), handempty, ontable(X)$
   $stack(X, Y)$ **causes** $\neg holding(X), \neg clear(Y), clear(X), handempty, on(X, Y)$
   $unstack(X, Y)$ **causes** $holding(X), clear(Y), \neg clear(X), \neg handempty, \neg on(X, Y)$

We denote the above by D_{bw}. We now give a particular initial condition and a particular goal expressed in PDDL.

```
(define (problem BLOCKS-4-0)
(:domain BLOCKS)
(:objects D B A C - block)
(:INIT (CLEAR C) (CLEAR A) (ONTABLE C)
       (ONTABLE B) (ON A B) (HANDEMPTY))
(:goal (AND (ON A C) (ON C B) )) )
```

In the language of $\mathcal{A}$ the sort *block* has the extent $\{a, b, c, d\}$ and the initial conditions are described as:

initially *clear(c)*
initially *clear(a)*
initially *ontable(c)*
initially *ontable(b)*
initially *on(a, b)*
initially *handempty*

We denote such a set of initial conditions by O, and this particular set by $O_{bw.1}$. In STRIPS/PDDL the assumption is that only fluents that are true are specified and all other fluents are false. For our convenience by $Comp(O)$ we denote the set $O \cup \{$**initially** $\neg f : f$ is a fluent, and $f \notin O\}$. The goal is the set of literals $\{on(a, c), on(c, b)\}$. We denote such sets by G, and this particular one by $G_{bw.1}$.

5.3.2 Simple blocks world in AnsProlog: $\pi_{strips1}(D_{bw}, O_{bw}, G_{bw})$

In this subsection we show how to encode the simple blocks world planning problem described in Section 5.3.1. We divide our encoding into two parts: the domain dependent part and the domain independent part. The former is a direct translation of the domain description (whether in $\mathcal{A}$ or in PDDL). The latter is independent of the domain and may be used for planning with other domains.

(1) The domain dependent part $\pi_{strips1}^{dep}(D_{bw}, O_{bw}, G_{bw})$: This consists of five parts, defining the domain, the executability conditions, the dynamic causal laws, the initial state, and the goal conditions.

    (a) The domain $\pi_{strips1}^{dep.dom}(D_{bw})$: This part defines the objects in the world, the fluents, and the actions.

        block(a).
        block(b).
        block(c).
        block(d).

        fluent(on(X, Y)) $\leftarrow$ *block(X), block(Y).*
        fluent(ontable(X)) $\leftarrow$ *block(X).*
        fluent(clear(X)) $\leftarrow$ *block(X).*

$fluent(holding(X)) \leftarrow block(X).$
$fluent(handempty).$

$action(pick\_up(X)) \leftarrow block(X).$
$action(put\_down(X)) \leftarrow block(X).$
$action(stack(X, Y)) \leftarrow block(X), block(Y).$
$action(unstack(X, Y)) \leftarrow block(X), block(Y).$

(b) The executability conditions $\pi_{strips1}^{dep.exec}(D_{bw})$: This part states the executability conditions. Note that the simple form that is used here is only appropriate for STRIPS domains where the executability condition of an action is a conjunction of fluents. (In Sections 5.3.4 and 5.3.5 we consider blocks world encodings that use more general executability conditions such as the one given in Section 5.2.1.) Here, $exec(a, f)$ means that f is among the executability conditions of a, and intuitively, a is executable in a state if all its executability conditions hold in that state. The latter part will be encoded as a domain independent rule.

$exec(pick\_up(X), clear(X)).$
$exec(pick\_up(X), ontable(X)).$
$exec(pick\_up(X), handempty).$

$exec(put\_down(X), holding(X)).$

$exec(stack(X, Y), holding(X)).$
$exec(stack(X, Y), clear(Y)).$

$exec(unstack(X, Y), clear(X)).$
$exec(unstack(X, Y), on(X, Y)).$
$exec(unstack(X, Y), handempty).$

(c) The dynamic causal laws $\pi_{strips1}^{dep.dyn}(D_{bw})$: This part states the effects of the actions. Note that the simple form that is used here is only appropriate for STRIPS domains where the effects are not conditional. Blocks world planning using encodings that have conditional effects – as in $\mathcal{A}$ and ADL – will be discussed in Section 5.3.5.

$causes(pick\_up(X), neg(ontable(X))).$
$causes(pick\_up(X), neg(clear(X))).$
$causes(pick\_up(X), holding(X)).$
$causes(pick\_up(X), neg(handempty)).$

$causes(put\_down(X), ontable(X)).$
$causes(put\_down(X), clear(X)).$
$causes(put\_down(X), neg(holding(X))).$
$causes(put\_down(X), handempty).$

$causes(stack(X, Y), neg(holding(X))).$
$causes(stack(X, Y), neg(clear(Y))).$
$causes(stack(X, Y), clear(X)).$

causes(stack(X, Y), handempty).
causes(stack(X, Y), on(X, Y)).

causes(unstack(X, Y), holding(X)).
causes(unstack(X, Y), clear(Y)).
causes(unstack(X, Y), neg(clear(X))).
causes(unstack(X, Y), neg(handempty)).
causes(unstack(X, Y), neg(on(X, Y))).

(d) The initial state $\pi_{strips1}^{dep.init}(O_{bw.1})$: This part defines the initial state by explicitly listing which fluents are true in the initial state. It is assumed that the fluents not explicitly listed to be true are false in the initial state. Thus the knowledge about the initial state is assumed to be complete.

initially(handempty).
initially(clear(a)).
initially(clear(c)).
initially(ontable(c)).
initially(ontable(b)).
initially(on(a, b)).

(e) The goal conditions $\pi_{strips1}^{dep.goal}(G_{bw.1})$: This part lists the fluent literals that must hold in a goal state.

finally(on(a, c)).
finally(on(c, b)).

(2) The domain independent part $\pi_{strips1}^{indep}$: As mentioned before, this part is independent of the content of a particular domain. It does assume that the domain dependent part is expressible in STRIPS.

(a) Defining time: In answer set planning, we need to give either the exact bound or at least an upper bound of the plan lengths that we want to consider. This is what makes each answer set finite. The encoding $\pi_{strips1}^{indep}$ depends on a constant referred to as *length* which is the upper bound of the length of plans that we intend to consider. Using this *length* we define a predicate *time* which specifies the time points of our interest.

time(1).   . . .   *time(length).*

(b) Defining *goal(T)*: The following rules define when all the goal conditions are satisfied.

not_goal(T) ← *time(T), finally(X),* **not** *holds(X, T).*
goal(T) ← *time(T),* **not** *not_goal(T).*

(c) Eliminating possible answer sets which do not have a plan of the given length: The following constraint eliminates possible answer sets where the goal is not satisfied in the last time point of interest.

← **not** *goal(length).*

(d) Defining contrary: The following facts define when a fluent literal is the negation of the other.

$contrary(F, neg(F))$.
$contrary(neg(F), F)$.

(e) Defining executability: The following two rules use the executability conditions to define when an action A is executable in a time T. Note that we are only interested in times before the time point denoted by *length*, as no actions are supposed to occur after that.

$not\_executable(A, T) \leftarrow exec(A, F),$ **not** $holds(F, T)$.
$executable(A, T) \leftarrow T < length,$ **not** $not\_executable(A, T)$.

(f) Fluent values at time point 1:

$holds(F, 1) \leftarrow initially(F)$.

(g) Effect axiom: The following rule describes the change in fluent values due to the execution of an action.

$holds(F, T + 1) \leftarrow T < length, executable(A, T), occurs(A, T), causes(A, F)$.

(h) Inertia: The following rule describes the fluents which do not change their values after an action is executed. In the literature, this is referred to as the frame axiom.

$holds(F, T + 1) \leftarrow contrary(F, G), T < length, holds(F, T),$
$\qquad\qquad\qquad$ **not** $holds(G, T + 1)$.

(i) Occurrences of actions: The following rules enumerate action occurrences. They encode that in each answer set at each time point only one of the executable actions occurred. Also, for each action that is executable in an answer set at a time point, there is an answer set where this action occurs at that time point.

$occurs(A, T) \leftarrow action(A), time(T),$ **not** $goal(T),$ **not** $not\_occurs(A, T)$.$\qquad$ (*)
$not\_occurs(A, T) \leftarrow action(A), action(AA), time(T), occurs(AA, T), A \neq AA$.
$\leftarrow action(A), time(T), occurs(A, T),$ **not** $executable(A, T)$.

Notice that the rule (*) is different from the corresponding rule in Section 5.1.10. The main difference is the presence of the naf-literal **not** $goal(T)$ in the body of the rule. This prevents occurrence of actions once the goal is reached. By having that, we no longer have to decide on the exact goal length and can specify only an upper bound. The following proposition reflects this.

Proposition 85 Let D_{bw} be the consistent domain description obtained from the STRIPS/PDDL blocks world specification in Section 5.3.1. Let O_{bw} be a set of observations about the initial state obtained from a STRIPS/PDDL blocks world specification of the initial state, $G_{bw} = \{g_1, \ldots, g_m\}$ be the set of literals that are obtained from a STRIPS/PDDL blocks world specification of the goal, and *length* be a number denoting the upper bound of plan lengths that we are interested in. For any $n < length$,

for all $k.1 \leq k \leq m$ $(D_{bw} \models_{Comp(O_{bw})} g_k$ **after** $a_1, \ldots, a_n)$ and
for all $j < n$ (there exists $l.1 \leq l \leq m$ $D_{bw} \not\models_{Comp(O_{bw})} g_l$ **after** $a_1, \ldots, a_j)$ iff
$\pi_{strips1}(D_{bw}, O_{bw}, G_{bw})$ has an answer set A with $\{occurs(a_1, 1), \ldots, occurs(a_n, n)\}$ as the set of facts about *occurs* in it. □

Note that unlike the choice rules in $\pi_{2.planning}$ from Section 5.1.10 we cannot split $\pi_{strips1}(D_{bw}, O_{bw}, G_{bw})$ with the first two rules of (2) (i) at the bottom. This makes the proof of the above proposition harder.

Exercise 21 Replace (2)(i) in $\pi_{strips1}(D_{bw}, O_{bw}, G_{bw})$ so that the latter can be split with the rules defining *occurs* and *not_occurs* in the bottom part. □

5.3.3 Simple blocks world with domain constraints

Planning in the blocks world domain in the general case is known to be NP-complete. One way to do efficient blocks world planning is to use domain dependent knowledge about the blocks world to cut down on the search for the right action in each step. A particular set of such knowledge is based on defining the notion of good and bad towers and putting temporal constraints on the plans so that good towers are not destroyed, bad towers are not further built up, and blocks are not held if they have to be finally on top of another block and the latter block is not on top of a good tower yet.

A good tower is defined as a tower whose top block is not required to be held in the goal state and the tower below it is not a bad tower. The tower below a block (X) is said to be a bad tower if one of the following holds. (i) X is on the table and it is supposed to be on top of another block in the goal state; (ii) X is on top of block Y, and X is supposed to be on the table or supposed to be held in the goal state; (iii) X is on top of block Y, and Y is supposed to have nothing on top in the final state; (iv) X is on top of block Y, and X is supposed to be on top of some other block in the final state; (v) X is on top of block Y, and some other block is supposed to be on top of Y in the final state; (vi) X is on top of block Y, and there is a bad tower below Y.

We now first present the above knowledge about good towers and bad towers using AnsProlog rules; and then represent the temporal domain constraints as constraints with the intention of speeding up finding an answer set by eliminating non-answer sets earlier in the process of determining that it does not lead to a plan. We refer to the resulting program as $\pi_{strips.cons1}(D_{bw}, O_{bw}, G_{bw})$.

(1) Defining *bad_tower_below*

$holds(bad\_tower\_below(X), T) \leftarrow holds(ontable(X), T), finally(on(X, Y)).$
$holds(bad\_tower\_below(X), T) \leftarrow holds(on(X, Y), T), finally(ontable(X)).$
$holds(bad\_tower\_below(X), T) \leftarrow holds(on(X, Y), T), finally(holding(Y)).$
$holds(bad\_tower\_below(X), T) \leftarrow holds(on(X, Y), T), finally(clear(Y)).$
$holds(bad\_tower\_below(X), T) \leftarrow holds(on(X, Y), T), finally(on(X, Z)), Z \neq Y.$
$holds(bad\_tower\_below(X), T) \leftarrow holds(on(X, Y), T), finally(on(Z, Y)), Z \neq X.$
$holds(bad\_tower\_below(X), T) \leftarrow holds(on(X, Y), T), holds(bad\_tower\_below(Y), T).$

(2) Defining *goodtower*

$holds(goodtower(X), T) \leftarrow holds(clear(X), T), \textbf{not } finally(holding(X)),$
$\qquad\qquad\qquad\qquad\quad \textbf{not } holds(bad\_tower\_below(X), T).$

(3) Defining *badtower*

$holds(badtower(X), T) \leftarrow holds(clear(X), T), \textbf{not } holds(goodtower(X), T).$

(4) The temporal constraints.

$\leftarrow holds(goodtower(X), T), holds(on(Y, X), T + 1),$
$\quad \textbf{not } holds(goodtower(Y), T + 1).$
$\leftarrow holds(badtower(X), T), holds(on(Y, X), T + 1).$
$\leftarrow holds(ontable(X, T)), finally(on(X, Y)), \textbf{not } holds(goodtower(Y), T),$
$\quad holds(holding(X), T + 1).$

The temporal conditions in (4) above can be replaced by the following direct constraints on action occurrences. This further cuts down on the planning time.

$\leftarrow holds(goodtower(X), T), occurs(stack(Y, X), T),$
$\quad \textbf{not } holds(goodtower(Y), T + 1).$
$\leftarrow holds(badtower(X), T), occurs(stack(Y, X), T).$
$\leftarrow holds(ontable(X, T)), finally(on(X, Y)), \textbf{not } holds(goodtower(Y), T),$
$\quad occurs(pick\_up(X), T).$

5.3.4 Adding defined fluents, qualification, and ramification to STRIPS

In this section we consider representing the blocks world planning problem in a richer language that allows defined fluents, qualification, and ramification constraints. We separate the fluents to two categories: basic fluents, and defined fluents. Intuitively, the defined fluents are completely defined in terms of the basic fluents and thus if our formulation includes those definitions, then when expressing the effects of actions we need only to express the effect on the basic fluents. The qualification and ramification constraints (also referred to as static causal laws) state the causal relationship between the basic fluents and by having them we can further simplify the effect axioms and executability conditions.

In the blocks world domain of Section 5.3.1 the fluents $on(X)$, $ontable(X)$, and $holding(X)$ can be considered as basic fluents, while the fluents $clear(X)$ and *handempty* can be thought of as defined fluents. The intuition is that we can define the latter in terms of the former. For example, $clear(X)$ is true in a state iff there does not exist any block Y such that $on(Y, X)$ is true in that state. Similarly, *handempty* is true in a state iff there does not exist a block Y such that $holding(Y)$ is true in that state.

We refer to this richer language as ADL1, meaning 'action description language 1'. In this richer language the blocks world domain D_{bw1} can be described as follows:

(1) Sort: $block(X)$
(2) Basic fluents: $on(X)$, $ontable(X)$, $holding(X)$.
(3) Defined fluents: $clear(X)$, *handempty*.
(4) Definition of defined fluents.
   - $clear(X)$ iff $\not\exists Y : on(Y, X)$
   - *handempty* iff $\not\exists Y : holding(Y)$
(5) Executability conditions:

   executable $pick\_up(X)$ **if** $clear(X)$, $ontable(X)$, *handempty*
   executable $put\_down(X)$ **if** $holding(X)$
   executable $stack(X, Y)$ **if** $holding(X)$, $ontable(Y)$
   executable $stack(X, Y)$ **if** $holding(X)$, $on(Y, Z)$
   executable $unstack(X, Y)$ **if** $clear(X)$, $on(X, Y)$, *handempty*

   The difference between these and the executability conditions of Section 5.3.1 are that in the third and fourth conditions above, $clear(Y)$ is removed, and $ontable(Y) \vee on(Y, Z)$ is added. The condition $clear(Y)$ is removed to demonstrate the usefulness of *qualification* constraints. The rule is split into two and we add the conditions $ontable(Y)$ and $on(Y, Z)$ so as to prevent the block X from being stacked on a nonexisting block.

(6) Effect propositions:

   $pick\_up(X)$ **causes** $holding(X)$
   $put\_down(X)$ **causes** $ontable(X)$
   $stack(X, Y)$ **causes** $on(X, Y)$
   $unstack(X, Y)$ **causes** $holding(X)$

(7) Causal ramification constraints:

   $on(X, Y)$ **causes** $\neg holding(X)$
   $holding(X)$ **causes** $\neg on(X, Y)$
   $ontable(X)$ **causes** $\neg holding(X)$
   $holding(X)$ **causes** $\neg ontable(X)$

(8) Causal qualification constraint:

$on(X, Y), on(Z, Y), X \neq Z$ **causes** *false*

The representation of a set of initial conditions (O_{bw1}) and a goal (G_{bw1}) is similar to that of $O_{bw.1}$ and $G_{bw.1}$, respectively from Section 5.3.1.

We now describe how we can use AnsProlog to encode planning in an ADL1 domain. Given a domain D_{bw1}, a set of initial conditions O_{bw1}, and a goal G_{bw1}, our AnsProlog encoding will be referred to as $\pi_{adl1}(D_{bw1}, O_{bw1}, G_{bw1})$ and as in Section 5.3.2 our encoding will consist of two parts, the domain dependent part and the domain independent part.

(1) The domain dependent part $\pi_{adl1}^{dep}(D_{bw1}, O_{bw1}, G_{bw1})$:

(a) The domain $\pi_{adl1}^{dep.dom}(D_{bw1})$: This part defines the objects in the world, the basic fluents, the defined fluents and actions. The definitions for blocks and actions are as in $\pi_{strips}^{dep.dom}(D_{bw})$ of Section 5.3.2. We use the predicate *fluent* to denote the basic fluents, and the predicate *defined_fluent* to denote defined fluents.

fluent$(on(X, Y))$.
fluent$(ontable(X))$.
fluent$(holding(X))$.

defined_fluent$(clear(X))$.
defined_fluent$(handempty)$.

(b) The executability conditions $\pi_{adl1}^{dep.exec}(D_{bw1})$: The executability conditions in D_{bw1} are more general than in D_{bw} in the sense that in D_{bw1} the action $stack(X, Y)$ has two executability conditions while in D_{bw} each action has only one executability condition. In the following encoding instead of representing executability conditions as facts and then having domain independent rules to define when an action is executable, we directly translate the executability conditions to rules.

executable$(pick\_up(X), T) \leftarrow T < length, holds(clear(X), T),$
$\qquad\qquad\qquad\qquad holds(ontable(X), T), holds(handempty, T).$
executable$(put\_down(X), T) \leftarrow T < length, holds(holding(X), T).$
executable$(stack(X, Y), T) \leftarrow T < length, holds(holding(X), T),$
$\qquad\qquad\qquad\qquad holds(ontable(Y), T).$
executable$(stack(X, Y), T) \leftarrow T < length, holds(holding(X), T),$
$\qquad\qquad\qquad\qquad holds(on(Y, Z), T).$
executable$(unstack(X, Y), T) \leftarrow T < length, holds(clear(X), T),$
$\qquad\qquad\qquad\qquad holds(on(X, Y), T), holds(handempty, T).$

(c) The dynamic causal laws $\pi_{adl1}^{dep.dyn}(D_{bw1})$: The use of defined fluents and causal ramification constraints drastically cuts down on the number of dynamic causal laws. Instead of 18 of them, we now have only four.

causes$(pick\_up(X), holding(X))$.
causes$(put\_down(X), ontable(X))$.

$causes(stack(X, Y), on(X, Y))$.
$causes(unstack(X, Y), holding(X))$.

(d) Defined fluents $\pi_{adl1}^{dep.def}(D_{bw1})$: The following rules define the defined fluents in terms of the basic fluents.

$holds(neg(clear(X)), T) \leftarrow holds(holding(X), T)$.
$holds(neg(clear(X)), T) \leftarrow holds(on(Y, X), T)$.
$holds(clear(X), T) \leftarrow holds(ontable(X), T), \textbf{not } holds(neg(clear(X)), T)$.
$holds(clear(X), T) \leftarrow holds(on(X, Y), T), \textbf{not } holds(neg(clear(X)), T)$.
$holds(neg(handempty), T) \leftarrow holds(holding(X), T)$.
$holds(handempty, T) \leftarrow \textbf{not } holds(neg(handempty), T)$.

(e) Qualification constraints $\pi_{adl1}^{dep.qual}(D_{bw1})$:

$\leftarrow holds(on(X, Y), T), holds(on(Z, Y), T), neq(X, Z)$.

(f) Static ramification constraints $\pi_{adl1}^{dep.ram}(D_{bw1})$:

$static\_causes(on(X, Y), neg(holding(X)))$.
$static\_causes(holding(X), neg(on(X, Y)))$.
$static\_causes(ontable(X), neg(holding(X)))$.
$static\_causes(holding(X), neg(ontable(X)))$.

(g) The initial state $\pi_{adl1}^{dep.init}(O_{bw1})$: The initial state can be defined as in $\pi_{strips}^{dep.init}(O_{bw})$ of Section 5.3.2, or we may simplify it by only stating the truth about the basic fluents.

(h) The goal state $\pi_{adl1}^{dep.goal}(G_{bw1})$: The goal state is defined exactly as in $\pi_{strips}^{dep.init}(G_{bw}))$ of Section 5.3.2.

(2) The domain independent part π_{adl1}^{indep}:

  (a) Defining *time*: Same as in (2)(a) of Section 5.3.2.

  (b) Defining *goal(T)*: Same as in (2)(b) of Section 5.3.2.

  (c) Defining plan existence: Same as in (2)(c) of Section 5.3.2.

  (d) Defining contrary: Same as in (2)(d) of Section 5.3.2.

  (e) Fluent values at time point 1: Same as in (2)(f) of Section 5.3.2.

  (f) Defining literal: The following two rules define the predicate *literal* in terms of the predicate *fluent*. Thus *literal(F)* denotes that F is a literal made up of a basic fluent.

$literal(G) \leftarrow fluent(G)$.
$literal(neg(G)) \leftarrow fluent(G)$.

  (g) Effect axioms: Unlike in (2)(g) of Section 5.3.2 the effect axioms only define the effects of actions on literals made up of basic fluents.

$holds(F, T + 1) \leftarrow literal(F), T < length, executable(A, T), occurs(A, T),$
$\qquad\qquad\qquad causes(A, F)$.

(h) Inertia: Unlike in (2)(h) of Section 5.3.2 the inertia axioms are also defined only with respect to literals made up of basic fluents.

$$holds(F, T + 1) \leftarrow literal(F), contrary(F, G), T < length, holds(F, T),$$
$$\textbf{not } holds(G, T + 1).$$

(i) Effect axiom for static causal laws:

$$holds(F, T) \leftarrow T < length, holds(G, T), static\_causes(G, F).$$

(j) Occurrences of actions: Same as in (2)(i) of Section 5.3.2.

Proposition 86 Let D_{bw1} be the consistent domain description mentioned above. Let O_{bw1} be a set of observations about the initial state, $G_{bw1} = \{g_1, \ldots, g_m\}$ be a set of literals specifying the goal, and *length* be a number denoting the upper bound of plan lengths that we are interested in. For any $n < length$,

for all $k.1 \leq k \leq m$ $(D_{bw1} \models_{Comp(O_{bw1})} g_k$ **after** $a_1, \ldots, a_n)$ and
for all $j < n$ (there exists $l.1 \leq l \leq m D_{bw1} \not\models_{Comp(O_{bw1})} g_l$ **after** $a_1, \ldots, a_j)$ iff
$\pi_{adl1}(D_{bw1}, O_{bw1}, G_{bw1})$ has an answer set A with $\{occurs(a_1, 1), \ldots,$
$occurs(a_n, n)\}$ as the set of facts about *occurs* in it.   □

5.3.5 Blocks world with conditional effects

In this section we consider another dimension in enriching STRIPS. We allow conditional effects and refer to this language as ADL2. In the ADL2 representation of the blocks world problem instead of having four different actions we only need a single action $puton(X, Y)$. Intuitively, in the action $puton(X, Y)$, X is a block and Y can be either a block or the table, and $puton(X, Y)$ means that we put the block X on top of Y. The executability conditions and effects of this action can be described by the following domain description D_{bw2}.

executable $puton(X, Y)$ **if** $clear(X), clear(Y), X \neq Y \neq table$
executable $puton(X, table)$ **if** $clear(X), X \neq table$

$puton(X, Y)$ **causes** $on(X, Y)$ **if** $X \neq Y, X \neq table$
$puton(X, Y)$ **causes** $\neg on(X, Z)$ **if** $on(X, Z), X \neq Y \neq Z$
$puton(X, Y)$ **causes** $clear(Z)$ **if** $on(X, Z), X \neq Y \neq Z, X \neq table, Z \neq table$
$puton(X, Y)$ **causes** $\neg clear(Y)$ **if** $X \neq Y \neq table$

In the above description we have to take special care as Y in $puton(X, Y)$ can be either a block or the table, and we need to distinguish between $clear(X)$ when X is a block and *clear(table)*. In particular, we need to encode that putting a block on the table neither affects nor depends on *clear(table)*.

As before we can use AnsProlog to encode planning in ADL2. Given a domain D_{bw2}, a set of initial conditions O_{bw2}, and a goal G_{bw2}, our AnsProlog encoding will be referred to as $\pi_{adl2}(D_{bw2}, O_{bw2}, G_{bw2})$ and as in Section 5.3.2 our encoding will consist of two parts, the domain dependent part and the domain independent part.

(1) Domain dependent part $\pi_{adl2}^{dep}(D_{bw2}, O_{bw2}, G_{bw2})$:

    (a) The domain, initial state, and goal conditions are expressed as in 1(a), 1(d) and 1(e) of Section 5.3.2, respectively.

    (b) The executability conditions $\pi_{adl2}^{dep.exec}(D_{bw2})$:

        $exec(puton(X, Y), [clear(X), clear(Y)]) \leftarrow neq(X, Y), neq(X, table),$
          $neq(Y, table).$
        $exec(puton(X, Y), [clear(X)]) \leftarrow neq(X, Y), eq(Y, table).$

    (c) The dynamic causal laws $\pi_{adl2}^{dep.dyn}(D_{bw2})$:

        $causes(puton(X, Y), on(X, Y), []) \leftarrow neq(X, Y), neq(X, table).$
        $causes(puton(X, Y), neg(on(X, Z)), [on(X, Z)])$
           $\leftarrow neq(X, Y), neq(X, Z), neq(Z, Y).$
        $causes(puton(X, Y), clear(Z), [on(X, Z)]) \leftarrow neq(X, Y), neq(X, Z), neq(Z, Y),$
                                      $neq(Z, table), neq(X, table).$
        $causes(puton(X, Y), neg(clear(Y)), []) \leftarrow neq(X, Y), neq(Y, table), neq(X, table).$

(2) Domain independent part π_{adl2}^{indep}:

    The definition of time, the definition of $goal(T)$, the constraint that eliminates non-plans, the definition of contrary, the rule defining fluent values at time point 1, the inertia rule, and the rules that enumerate action ocurrences are exactly the same as in (2)(a), (2)(b), (2)(c), (2)(d), (2)(f), (2)(h) and (2)(i), of Section 5.3.2 respectively. The only changes are to 2(e) and (2)(g) that define executability and effects of actions. In addition we need to define when a set of fluent literals holds, at a time point.

    (a) Defining when a set of fluents holds at a time point:

        $not\_holds\_set(S, T) \leftarrow literal(L), in(L, S), notholds(L, T).$

        $holds\_set(S, T) \leftarrow notnot\_holds\_set(S, T).$

    (b) Defining executability:

        $executable(A, T) \leftarrow T < length, exec(A, S), holds\_set(S, T).$

    (c) Effect of actions:

        $holds(F, T + 1) \leftarrow T < length, action(A), executable(A, T), occurs(A, T),$
                    $causes(A, F, S), holds\_set(S, T).$

One of the plans generated by this AnsProlog program with $length = 5$ is as follows:

$occurs(puton(c, table), 1)$
$occurs(puton(b, c), 2)$
$occurs(puton(a, b), 3)$

Proposition 87 Let D_{bw2} be the consistent domain description in mentioned above. Let O_{bw2} be a set of observations about the initial state, $G_{bw2} = \{g_1, \ldots, g_m\}$ be a set of literals specifying the goal, and *length* be a number denoting the upper bound of plan lengths that we are interested in. For any $n < length$,

for all $k.1 \le k \le m$ $(D_{bw2} \models_{Comp(O_{bw2})} g_k$ **after** $a_1, \ldots, a_n)$ and
for all $j < n$ (there exists $l.1 \le l \le m$ $D_{bw2} \not\models_{Comp(O_{bw2})} g_l$ **after** $a_1, \ldots, a_j)$ iff
$\pi_{adl2}(D_{bw2}, O_{bw2}, G_{bw2})$ has an answer set A with $\{occurs(a_1, 1), \ldots, occurs(a_n, n)\}$
as the set of facts about *occurs* in it. $\square$

5.3.6 Navigating a downtown with one-way streets

In this section we consider another domain in a language similar to STRIPS, the only difference being that instead of describing when actions are executable, in this language conditions are given when actions are not executable. We refer to this language as STRIPS2. The domain we consider is the domain of navigating a downtown area with one-way streets in a vehicle. The only action in this domain is $move(V, L1, L2)$ and the the fluents are $at(V, L)$ and $edge(L1, L2)$. Given the domain (D_{nav}), the initial position of a vehicle and the one-way description (O_{nav}), and the final location of the vehicle (G_{nav}), we would like to find a plan to get to the final location from the initial location obeying the one-way descriptions. Here, we directly give the encoding $\pi_{strips2}(D_{nav}, O_{nav}, G_{nav})$.

(1) The domain dependent part: $\pi_{strips2}^{dep}(D_{nav}, O_{nav}, G_{nav})$

  (a) The domain $\pi_{strips2}^{dep.dom}(D_{nav})$:

  $vehicle(v) \leftarrow.$
  $location(l_1) \leftarrow \ldots. location(l_{12}) \leftarrow .$
  $fluent(at(V, L)) \leftarrow vehicle(V), location(L).$
  $action(move(V, L1, L2)) \leftarrow vehicle(V), location(L1), location(L2).$

  (b) When actions are not executable $\pi_{strips2}^{dep.exec}(D_{nav})$:

  $impossible\_if(move(V, L1, L2), neg(at(V, L1))).$
  $impossible\_if(move(V, L1, L2), neg(edge(L1, L2))).$

  It should be noted that unlike (1)(c) of Section 5.3.2, here we express when an action is impossible to execute instead of saying when it is executable.

  (c) The effects of actions $\pi_{strips2}^{dep.dyn}(D_{nav})$:

  $causes(move(V, L1, L2), at(V, L2)).$
  $causes(move(V, L1, L2), neg(at(V, L1))).$

  (d) The initial street description, and the initial position of the vehicle $\pi_{strips2}^{dep.init}(O_{nav})$:

  $initially(edge(l_1, l_2)).$
  $initially(edge(l_2, l_3)).$

$initially(edge(l_3, l_4))$.
$initially(edge(l_4, l_8))$.
$initially(edge(l_8, l_7))$.
$initially(edge(l_7, l_6))$.
$initially(edge(l_6, l_5))$.
$initially(edge(l_5, l_1))$.
$initially(edge(l_2, l_6))$.
$initially(edge(l_7, l_3))$.
$initially(edge(l_1, l_9))$.
$initially(edge(l_9, l_{10}))$.
$initially(edge(l_{10}, l_{11}))$.
$initially(edge(l_{11}, l_{12}))$.
$initially(edge(l_{12}, l_2))$.
$initially(edge(l_{12}, l_9))$.
$initially(at(v, l_3))$.

(e) The goal state $\pi_{strips2}^{dep.goal}(G_{nav})$:

$finally(at(v, l_2))$.

(2) The domain independent part $\pi_{strips2}^{indep}$:

   (a) The rules in (2)(a)(2)(d) and (2)(g)(2)(i) of Section 5.3.2 belong to the domain independent part.

   (b) Instead of (2)(e) of Section 5.3.2 we need new rules that define executability in terms of the *impossible_if* conditions given in the domain dependent part. These rules are:

$not\_executable(A, T) \leftarrow impossible\_if(A, B), holds(B, T)$.

$executable(A, T) \leftarrow \textbf{not } not\_executable(A, T)$.

   (c) In lieu of (2)(f) of Section 5.3.2 we have two rules defining both what holds and what does not hold in time point 1. Thus the following substitutes (2)(f) of Section 5.3.2.

$holds(F, 1) \leftarrow initially(F)$.
$holds(neg(F), 1) \leftarrow \textbf{not } holds(F, 1)$.

One of the plans generated by this AnsProlog program with *length* $= 9$ is as follows:

$occurs(move(v, l_3, l_4), 1)$.
$occurs(move(v, l_4, l_8), 2)$.
$occurs(move(v, l_8, l_7), 3)$.
$occurs(move(v, l_7, l_6), 4)$.
$occurs(move(v, l_6, l_5), 5)$.
$occurs(move(v, l_5, l_1), 6)$.
$occurs(move(v, l_1, l_2), 7)$.

5.3.7 Downtown navigation: planning while driving

Consider the case that an agent uses the planner in the previous section and makes
a plan. It now executes part of the plan, and hears on the radio that *an accident
occurred between point l_1 and l_2* and that section of the street is blocked. The agent
now has to make a new plan from where it is to its destination. To be able to encode
observations and make plans from the current situation we need to add the following
to our program in the previous section.

(1) The domain dependent part
  (a) The observations

$happened(move(v, l_3, l_4), 1).$
$happened(move(v, l_4, l_8), 2).$
$happened(acc(l_1, l_2), 3).$

  (b) Exogenous actions

$causes(acc(X, Y), neg(edge(X, Y)))$

(2) The domain independent part
  (a) Relating *happened* and *occurs*

$occurs(A, T) \leftarrow happened(A, T).$

With these additions one of the plans generated by this AnsProlog program with
$length = 13$ is as follows:

$occurs(move(v, l_8, l_7), 4).$
$occurs(move(v, l_7, l_6), 5).$
$occurs(move(v, l_6, l_5), 6).$
$occurs(move(v, l_5, l_1), 7).$
$occurs(move(v, l_1, l_9), 8).$
$occurs(move(v, l_9, l_{10}), 9).$
$occurs(move(v, l_{10}, l_{11}), 10).$
$occurs(move(v, l_{11}, l_{12}), 11).$
$occurs(move(v, l_{12}, l_2), 12).$

Although it does not matter in the particular example described above, we should
separate the set of actions into *agent_actions* and *exogenous_actions*, and in the
planning module require that while planning we only use *agent_actions*. This can
be achieved by replacing the first and third rule about *occurs* in (2)(i) of Section 5.3.2
by the following two rules.

(1) $occurs(A, T) \leftarrow time(T), happened(A, T).$
(2) $occurs(A, T) \leftarrow agent\_action(A), time(T), executable(A, T), \textbf{not } goal(T),$
$\qquad \qquad \textbf{not } not\_occurs(A, T).$

5.4 Approximate planning when initial state is incomplete

The planning encodings in Section 5.3 assume that the initial state is complete. When we remove this assumption those encodings are no longer appropriate. In fact since planning in this case belongs to a complexity class that is not expressible in AnsProlog, in general we cannot have a sound AnsProlog encoding that will give us all the plans. The best we can do is to have encodings that find at least some of the plans. We present such an encoding here and show that the encoding is sound in the sense that the set of *occurs* facts in any answer set of this encoding does indeed give us a plan. However, there may not be answer sets corresponding to some plans. In that sense they are not complete. We consider the language from Section 5.3.5 and remove the completeness assumption about the initial state, and allow fluents to be unknown in the goal state. We refer to this language as ADL3. Given a domain description D, a set of initial state observations O, and a set of 3-valued $(f, neg(f),$ and $unk(f))$ fluent literals G, our encoding $\pi_{adl3}(D, O, G)$ consists of the following:

(1) Domain dependent part $\pi_{adl3}^{dep}(D, O, G)$:
   (a) The domain is expressed similarly to (1)(a) of Section 5.3.5.
   (b) The executability conditions and dynamic causal laws are similar to (1)(b) and (1)(c) of Section 5.3.5.
   (c) The initial state $\pi_{adl3}^{dep.init}(O)$: There is no longer the assumption that the initial state is complete. Hence, the initial state is a set of atoms of the form $initially(l)$, where l is a fluent literal.
   (d) The goal state $\pi_{adl3}^{dep.goal}(G)$: In addition to specifying that certain fluents should be true, and certain others should be false in the final state, we may say that the truth values of certain fluents be *unknown* in the final state. In that case we say: $finally(unk(f))$.

(2) Domain independent part $\pi_{adl3}^{indep}(D, O, G)$:
   The definition of time, the definition of $goal(T)$, the constraint that eliminates nonplans, the definition of contrary, the rule defining fluent values at time point 1, and the rules that enumerate action occurrences are exactly the same as in (2)(a), (2)(b), (2)(c), (2)(d), (2)(f), and (2)(i) of Section 5.3.2 respectively.

   The definition of when a set of fluents holds at a time point, the definition of executability, and the effect axiom are exactly the same as in (2)(a), (2)(b) and (2)(c) of Section 5.3.5 respectively.

   The inertia rule is different, and we have additional rules for blocking inertia, rules that define when a set of fluent literals may hold at a time point, and rules that define when a fluent is unknown at a time point. These rules are given below:
   (a) Defining abnormality:

   $$ab(F, T + 1) \leftarrow T < length, action(A), executable(A, T), occurs(A, T),$$
   $$causes(A, F, S), m\_holds\_set(S, T).$$

(b) Inertia:

$$holds(F, T + 1) \leftarrow contrary(F, G), T < length, holds(F, T), \textbf{not } ab(G, T + 1).$$

The inertia and abnormality rules above are similar to the encoding in Section 5.1.4. The purpose is to be conservative in using the inertia rules. Thus, if we have an effect proposition a **causes** $\neg f$ **if** $p_1, \ldots, p_n$, and if there is a possibility that $p_1, \ldots, p_n$, may hold in time T, f is inferred to be abnormal in time T+1. This blocks the inference of f being true in time T+1 due to inertia.

(c) Defining when a set of fluents may hold:

$$m\_not\_holds\_set(S, T) \leftarrow in(L, S), contrary(L, LL), holds(LL, T).$$
$$m\_not\_holds\_set(S, T) \leftarrow \textbf{not } m\_not\_holds\_set(S, T).$$

(d) Defining when a fluent value is unknown:

$$holds(unk(F), T) \leftarrow \textbf{not } holds(F, T), contrary(F, G), \textbf{not } holds(G, T).$$

Proposition 88 Let D be a consistent domain description obtained from an ADL3 specification, Let O be a set of observations about the initial state, and $G = \{g_1, \ldots, g_m\}$ be a set of fluent literals, and *length* be a number denoting the upper bound of plan lengths that we are interested in. For any $n < length$,

$\pi_{adl3}(D, O, G)$ has an answer set A with $\{occurs(a_1, 1), \ldots, occurs(a_n, n)\}$ as the set of facts about *occurs* in it

implies for all $k.1 \leq k \leq m$ ($D \models_O g_k$ **after** $a_1, \ldots, a_n$). $\qquad\qquad \Box$

5.5 Planning with procedural constraints

In Section 5.3.3 we discussed the use of temporal constraints in planning in the blocks world domain. In this section we discuss planning in the presence of procedural constraints. An example of a simple procedural constraint is $a_1; a_2; (a_3|a_4|a_5); \neg f$. Intuitively, it means that the plan must have a_1 as the first action, a_2 as the second action, one of a_3, a_4 and a_5 as the third action, and $\neg f$ must be true after the third action. Such procedural constraints allow a domain expert to state a (non-deterministic) plan which is almost like a program in a procedural language except that it may have a few nondeterministic choices. The latter are to be explored by the interpreter so as to make the plan executable and make sure the fluent formulas in the procedural constraint are true at the appropriate moment. Our procedural constraints will have the following forms, where a is an action ϕ is a formula, and p and p_is are procedural constraints.

- a
- ϕ

- $p_1; \ldots; p_m$ (denoted using list notation)
- $(p_1| \ldots |p_n)$ (denoted using set notation)

In AnsProlog encodings we encode such a procedural constraint by giving it a name, say p; and have the following facts:

choice_st(p).
in(p_1, p).   . . .   *in*(p_n, p).

- *if*(ϕ, p_1, p_2)
- *while*(ϕ, p)
- *choice_arg*(ϕ, p)

Formulas are bounded classical formulas with each bound variable associated with a sort. They are defined as follows:

- a literal is a formula.
- negation of a formula is a formula.
- a finite conjunction of formulas is a formula.
- a finite disjunction of formulas is a formula.
- If $X_1, \ldots, X_n$ are variables that can have values from the sorts $s_1, \ldots, s_n$, and $f_1(X_1, \ldots, X_n)$ is a formula then $\forall X_1, \ldots, X_n.f_1(X_1, \ldots, X_n)$ is a formula.

In AnsProlog encodings we encode such a formula by giving it a name say f and have the following rule:

forall(f, $f_1(X_1, \ldots, X_n)$) $\leftarrow$ *in*(X_1, s_1), $\ldots$, *in*(X_n, s_n).

- If $X_1, \ldots, X_n$ are variables that can have values from the sorts $S_1, \ldots, S_n$, and $F_1(X_1, \ldots, X_n)$ is a formula then $\exists X_1, \ldots, X_n.F_1(X_1, \ldots, X_n)$ is a formula.

In AnsProlog encodings we encode such a formula by giving it a name, say f, and have the following rule:

exists(f, $f_1(X_1, \ldots, X_n)$) $\leftarrow$ *in*(X_1, s_1), $\ldots$, *in*(X_n, s_n).

Before we present an AnsProlog encoding that generates plans by exploiting procedural constraints we first give some examples.

Example 108 Consider the following domain description D:

a **causes** $p(f)$ **if** $\neg p(g)$
b **causes** $\neg p(g)$
c **causes** $\neg p(f)$
d **causes** $p(f)$, $p(g)$, $p(h)$
e_1 **causes** $p(g)$

e_2 **causes** $p(h)$

e_3 **causes** $p(f)$

executable $a, b, c, d, e_1, e_2, e_3$

Let the initial state specification O consist of the following:

initially $\neg p(f)$

initially $p(g)$

initially $\neg p(h)$

Consider the following five procedural constraints

(1) $p_1: b; (a|c|d); p(f)$

(2) $p_2: b; (a|c|d); \forall X.[X \in \{f, g, h\}]p(X)$

(3) $p_3: b; (a|c|d); \exists X.[X \in \{f, g, h\}]p(X)$

(4) $p_4: b; (a|c|d); \forall X.[X \in \{f, g, h\}]\neg p(X)$

(5) $p_5: while(\exists X.[X \in \{f, g, h\}]\neg p(X), (a|b|c|e_1|e_2))$

The plans generated using the procedural constraint p_1 are $b; a$ and $b; d$. The sequence $b; c$ is not a plan because it does not make $p(f)$ true, thus violating the procedural constraint that $p(f)$ must be true at the end. On the other hand $b; e_3$ is not a plan because e_3 does not agree with the given procedural constraint which requires that the second action must be one of a, c, and d.

Similarly, the plan generated using p_2 is $b; d$; the plans generated using p_3 are $b; a$ and $b; d$; and the plan generated using p_4 is $b; c$.

The procedural constraint p_5 can be simply considered as a planner for the goal $\exists X.[X \in \{f, g, h\}]\neg p(X)$ using only the actions a, b, c, e_1, and e_2. Thus procedural constraints can express classical planning. There are four plans (of length less than 5) that are generated using p_5. They are: (i) $e_2; b; a; e_1$, (ii) $b; e_2; a; e_1$, (iii) $b; a; e_2; e_1$, and (iv) $b; a; e_1; e_2$. The effects of actions are such that to achieve this goal any minimal plan must have b before a and a before e_1. Thus, e_2 can fit into four different slots resulting in four different plans.   □

We now present an AnsProlog encoding of planning with procedural constraints.

(1) The domain dependent part illustrating a particular domain: It consists of five parts: the domain, the executability conditions, the dynamic causal laws, the description of the initial state, and the procedural constraints. Among them, the domain, the description of the initial state, the executability conditions, and the dynamic causal laws are similar to those in the domain dependent part of Section 5.3.5. The only difference is that instead of goal conditions here we have the more general procedural constraints. We now encode

the domain dependent part of planning with respect to the procedural constraints in Example 108.

(a) The domain:

> *fluent*($p(f)$).
> *fluent*($p(g)$).
> *fluent*($p(h)$).

> *action*(a).
> *action*(b).
> *action*(c).
> *action*(d).
> *action*($e1$).
> *action*($e2$).

(b) The executability conditions:

> *exec*(a, []).
> *exec*(b, []).
> *exec*(c, []).
> *exec*(d, []).
> *exec*($e1$, []).
> *exec*($e2$, []).

(c) The dynamic causal laws:

> *causes*(a, $p(f)$, [*neg*($p(g)$)]).
> *causes*(b, *neg*($p(g)$), []).
> *causes*(c, *neg*($p(f)$), []).
> *causes*(d, $p(f)$, []).
> *causes*(d, $p(g)$, []).
> *causes*(d, $p(h)$, []).
> *causes*($e1$, $p(g)$, []).
> *causes*($e2$, $p(h)$, []).

(d) Description of the initial state:

> *initially*(*neg*($p(f)$)).
> *initially*($p(g)$).
> *initially*(*neg*($p(h)$)).

(e) Five particular procedural constraints: In the following we define five different procedural constraints. In each case they are identified through the predicate *main_cons*.

(i) Representing $b; (a|c|d); p(f)$

> *main_cons*([b, *choice*, $p(f)$]).
> *choice_st*(*choice*).

$in(a, choice)$.
$in(c, choice)$.
$in(d, choice)$.

(ii) Representing $b; (a|c|d); \forall X.[X \in \{f, g, h\}]p(X)$

$main\_cons([b, choice, rest3])$.
$choice\_st(choice)$.
$in(a, choice)$.
$in(c, choice)$.
$in(d, choice)$.
$forall(rest3, p(X)) \leftarrow in(X, \{f, g, h\})$.

(iii) Representing $b; (a|c|d); \exists X.[X \in \{f, g, h\}]p(X)$

$main\_cons([b, choice, rest4])$.
$choice\_st(choice)$.
$in(a, choice)$.
$in(c, choice)$.
$in(d, choice)$.
$exists(rest4, p(X)) \leftarrow in(X, \{f, g, h\})$.

(iv) Representing $b; (a|c|d); \forall X.[X \in \{f, g, h\}]\neg p(X)$

$main\_cons([b, choice, rest5])$.
$choice\_st(choice)$.
$in(a, choice)$.
$in(c, choice)$.
$in(d, choice)$.
$forall(rest5, neg(p(X))) \leftarrow in(X, \{f, g, h\})$.

(v) Representing $while(\exists X.[X \in \{f, g, h\}]\neg p(X), ch2)$

$main\_cons(while(rest6, ch2))$.
$exists(rest6, neg(p(X))) \leftarrow in(X, \{f, g, h\})$.
$choice\_st(ch2)$.
$in(a, ch2)$.
$in(b, ch2)$.
$in(c, ch2)$.
$in(e1, ch2)$.
$in(e2, ch2)$.

(2) Domain independent part: We now present the domain independent part of AnsProlog encodings that can plan using procedural constraints, and make comparison with the domain independent part of the previous encodings.

(a) Defining time: This is exactly the same as (2)(a) of Section 5.3.2.

$time(1)$. $\ldots$ $time(length)$.

(b) Defining if and when the procedural constraints are satisfied:

Unlike the goal conditions in Section 5.3.2, the notion of satisfiability of a procedural constraint is not about a particular time point; but about a time interval. Thus the first rule below says that the goal is reached at time point T if the main procedural constraint X is satisfied between 1 and T. The second rule says that if the goal is already reached by time T then it is also reached by time $T + 1$. We did not need such a rule in Section 5.3.2 as there the goal was about reaching a state where the goal conditions were satisfied and once such a state was reached, action executions were blocked and the goal remained satisfied in subsequent time points.

$goal(T) \leftarrow time(T), main\_cons(X), satisfied(X, 1, T).$
$goal(T + 1) \leftarrow time(T), T < length, goal(T).$

(c) Eliminating possible answer sets that do not satisfy the goal: This is exactly the same as (2)(c) of Section 5.3.2.

$\leftarrow \textbf{not } goal(length).$

(d) Auxiliary rules:

$literal(G) \leftarrow fluent(G).$
$literal(neg(G)) \leftarrow fluent(G).$
$contrary(F, neg(F)) \leftarrow fluent(F).$
$contrary(neg(F), F) \leftarrow fluent(F).$
$def\_literal(G) \leftarrow def\_fluent(G).$
$def\_literal(neg(G)) \leftarrow def\_fluent(G).$
$contrary(F, neg(F)) \leftarrow def\_fluent(F).$
$contrary(neg(F), F) \leftarrow def\_fluent(F).$
$leq(T, T) \leftarrow.$
$leq(Tb, Te) \leftarrow Tb < Te.$

(e) Defining executability: This is similar to the rule (2)(b) of Section 5.3.5.

$executable(A, T) \leftarrow action(A), set(S), T < length, exec(A, S), holds\_set(S, T).$

(f) Fluent values at time point 1: This is similar to the rule (2)(f) of Section 5.3.2.

$holds(F, 1) \leftarrow literal(F), initially(F).$

(g) Effect axiom: This is similar to the rule (2)(c) of Section 5.3.5.

$holds(F, T + 1) \leftarrow literal(F), set(S), T < length, action(A), executable(A, T),$
$occurs(A, T), causes(A, F, S), holds\_set(S, T).$

(h) Static causal laws: This is similar to the rule (2)(i) of Section 5.3.4.

$holds(F, T) \leftarrow literal(F), literal(G), T < length, holds(G, T),$
$static\_causes(G, F).$

(i) Inertia: This is exactly the same as the rule (2)(h) of Section 5.3.2 together with domain predicates in the body.

$$holds(F, T + 1) \leftarrow literal(F), literal(G), contrary(F, G), T < length,$$
$$holds(F,T),\textbf{not } holds(G, T + 1).$$

(j) Enumeration of action occurrences: This is similar to the rule (2)(i) of Section 5.3.2.

$$occurs(A, T) \leftarrow action(A), executable(A, T), \textbf{not } goal(T), \textbf{not } not\_occurs(A, T).$$
$$not\_occurs(A, T) \leftarrow action(A), action(AA), occurs(AA, T), neq(A, AA).$$

(k) Defining satisfaction of procedural constraints: The following rules define when a procedural constraint can be satisfied during the intervals Tb and Te. The intuitive meaning of the first rule is that the procedural constraint with the first part as P_1 and the rest as P_2 is satisfied during the intervals Tb and Te, if there exists a $Te1$, $Tb \leq Te1 \leq Te$ such that P_1 is satisfied in the intervals Tb and $Te1$, and P_2 is satisfied in the intervals $Te1$ and Te. Similarly, the second rule says that a procedural constraint consisting of only action A is satisfied during the intervals Tb and $Tb + 1$ if A occurs at time Tb. The intuitive meaning of the other rules is similar.

$$satisfied([P1|P2], Tb, Te) \leftarrow leq(Tb, Te), leq(Tb, Te1), leq(Te1, Te),$$
$$satisfied(P1, Tb, Te1), satisfied(P2, Te1, Te).$$
$$satisfied(A, Tb, Tb + 1) \leftarrow action(A), occurs(A, Tb).$$
$$satisfied([], Tb, Tb) \leftarrow$$
$$satisfied(N, Tb, Te) \leftarrow leq(Tb, Te), choice\_st(N), in(P1, N),$$
$$satisfied(P1, Tb, Te).$$
$$satisfied(F, Tb, Tb) \leftarrow formula(F), holds\_formula(F, Tb).$$
$$satisfied(F, Tb, Tb) \leftarrow literal(F), holds(F, Tb).$$
$$satisfied(if(F, P1, P2), Tb, Te) \leftarrow leq(Tb, Te), holds\_formula(F, Tb),$$
$$satisfied(P1, Tb, Te).$$
$$satisfied(if(F, P1, P2), Tb, Te) \leftarrow leq(Tb, Te), \textbf{not } holds\_formula(F, Tb),$$
$$satisfied(P2, Tb, Te).$$
$$satisfied(while(F, P), Tb, Te) \leftarrow leq(Tb, Te),$$
$$holds\_formula(F, Tb), leq(Tb, Te1),$$
$$leq(Te1, Te), satisfied(P, Tb, Te1),$$
$$satisfied(while(F, P), Te1, Te).$$
$$satisfied(while(F, P), Tb, Tb) \leftarrow \textbf{not } holds\_formula(F, Tb).$$
$$satisfied(choice\_arg(F, P), Tb, Te) \leftarrow leq(Tb, Te), holds(F, Tb),$$
$$satisfied(P, Tb, Te).$$

(l) Defining when a formula holds: The rules for satisfiability of the 'if' and 'while' procedural constraints need us to define when a formula holds at a time point. We do that using the following rules. Among these rules the nonobvious ones are the rules for formulas with a quantification. Let us consider formulas with an existential quantifier. In that case the existential formula F leads to a collection of ground facts of the form *exists*(*F*, *F*1). The variable instantiations are done in the domain dependent part (1)(e) through rules with *exists*(*F*, _) in the head. Thus formula *F* is said to hold in time *T*, if there exist an *F*1 such that *exist*(*F*, *F*1) is true and *F*1 holds in *T*. Similarly a universally quantified formula *F* is said to hold in time *T*, if for all *F*1 such that *forall*(*F*, *F*1) is true, and we have *F*1 holds in *T*.

holds_formula(*F*, *T*) ← *disj*(*F*), *in*(*F*1, *F*), *holds_formula*(*F*1, *T*).
not_holds_conj_formula(*F*, *T*) ← *time*(*T*), *conj*(*F*), *in*(*F*1, *F*),
                                  not *holds_formula*(*F*1, *T*).
holds_formula(*F*, *T*) ← *conj*(*F*), **not** *not_holds_conj_formula*(*F*).
holds_formula(*F*, *T*) ← *negation*(*F*, *F*1), **not** *holds_formula*(*F*1, *T*).
holds_formula(*F*, *T*) ← *literal*(*F*), *holds*(*F*, *T*).
holds_formula(*F*, *T*) ← *exists*(*F*, *F*1), *holds_formula*(*F*1, *T*).
not_holds_forall_formula(*F*, *T*) ← *forall*(*F*, *F*1), **not** *holds_formula*(*F*1, *T*).
holds_formula(*F*, *T*) ← *forall*(*F*, *F*1), **not** *not_holds_forall_formula*(*F*, *T*).

formula(*F*) ← *disj*(*F*).
formula(*F*) ← *conj*(*F*).
formula(*F*) ← *literal*(*F*).
formula(*F*) ← *negation*(*F*, *F*1).
formula(*F*1) ← *negation*(*F*, *F*1).
formula(*F*) ← *exists*(*F*, *F*1).
formula(*F*1) ← *exists*(*F*, *F*1).
formula(*F*) ← *forall*(*F*, *F*1).
formula(*F*1) ← *forall*(*F*, *F*1).

(m) Defining when a set of fluents holds: This is exactly same as the rule (2)(a) of Section 5.3.5.

not_holds_set(*S*, *T*) ← *set*(*S*), *in*(*L*, *S*), **not** *holds*(*L*, *T*).
holds_set(*S*, *T*) ← *set*(*S*), **not** *not_holds_set*(*S*, *T*).

As expected, the above encoding with *length* = 5 gives us answer sets that encode the corresponding plans from Example 108.

5.6 Explaining observations through action occurrences and application to diagnosis

In Section 5.1.9 we presented a narrative based approach to formulating the projection problem in AnsProlog and later in Section 5.1.10 we used it to describe answer set planning – a model enumeration approach to planning based on computing answer sets of a narrative based AnsProlog encoding of an action description. In Section 5.3.7 we gave an example of using answer set planning in a dynamic domain. We now generalize the encoding in that section to describe the reasoning component of a deliberative agent in a dynamic domain. After that we will formulate the notion of explaining observations and discuss its applicability to diagnosis of physical systems.

5.6.1 Specifying and reasoning with histories

In Sections 5.1.1 and 5.2.3 we presented the action description languages $\mathcal{A}$ and $\mathcal{A}_C$ and their semantics. In both those languages observations either were about the initial situation or were hypothetical statements. Such observations are adequate for applications such as planning in a static domain where the world only changes due to the agent's own actions. For agents in a dynamic world where exogenous actions may occur we need more expressive observations to adequately express the evolution of the world. In particular, we need to record and reason with our observations about actual (rather than hypothetical) action occurrences and fluent values at different time points (referred to as *fluent facts*) in the history. But since our observations may be incomplete, we will also need to reason about action occurrences and fluent facts that we did not explicitly observe. To achieve this we modify the observation language of $\mathcal{A}$ and $\mathcal{A}_C$. The modified observation language has a new sort *time* consisting of the set of nonnegative integers. Propositions in the modified observation language are of the following forms:

$$a \textbf{ occurs\_at } k \tag{5.6.9}$$

$$f \textbf{ at } k \tag{5.6.10}$$

The intuitive meaning of the proposition (5.6.9) is that the action a occurs at time point k, and the intuitive meaning of the proposition (5.6.10) is that the fluent literal f is observed to be true at time point k.

Given a domain description D in $\mathcal{A}$ or $\mathcal{A}_c$ and a set of observations O of the above kind, a model of (D, O) (also referred to as a *possible history* of (D, O)) is now a sequence $\langle \sigma_0, a_1, \sigma_1, \ldots, a_n, \sigma_n \rangle$ which satisfies the following:

(1) $\sigma_i = \Phi_D(a_i, \sigma_{i-1})$,
(2) $a_i = \{a : a \textbf{ occurs\_at } i\text{-}1 \in O\}$, and
(3) if $f \textbf{ at } k$ is in O then f holds in σ_k.

As before we say (D, O) is inconsistent if it does not have a model. According to the above notion of model, (D, O) is consistent if D is consistent (i.e., there is a Φ_D) and all essential action occurrences are observed. That is, we do not fail to observe an action occurrence but observe a change in fluent value due to that action. For consistent pairs of (D, O) even though there may be multiple models, all of the models are of the same length, and if this length is $(2 \times n) + 1$, then n is referred to as the *current moment of time* and denoted by $t_c^{D,O}$ or simply by t_c.

With the modified observation language we also have a modified query language. Queries are now of the following form.

$$f \textbf{ after } a'_1, \ldots, a'_m \textbf{ at } t \tag{5.6.11}$$

where f is a fluent literal, $a'_1, \ldots, a'_m$ are actions, and t is a time or t_c. We say a domain description D in the presence of a set of observations O entails a query of the form (5.6.11), denoted by $D \models_O f \textbf{ after } a'_1, \ldots, a'_m \textbf{ at } t$, if

- t is a time, and for all models $\langle \sigma_0, a_1, \sigma_1, \ldots, a_n, \sigma_n \rangle$ of (D, O), with $t \leq n$, the fluent literal f holds in $\Phi_D(a'_m, \ldots, \Phi_D(a'_1, \sigma_t) \ldots)$, or
- $t = t_c$ and for all models $\langle \sigma_0, a_1, \sigma_1, \ldots, a_n, \sigma_n \rangle$ of (D, O), the fluent literal f holds in $\Phi_D(a'_m, \ldots, \Phi_D(a'_1, \sigma_n) \ldots)$.

Exercise 22 In this section so far we have assumed Φ_D to map from action and states to states. Extend the formulation of models and the entailment relation $\models_O$ when Φ_D maps from action and states to a set of states. That is, Φ_D is a non-deterministic transition function. □

5.6.2 From reasoning with histories to agents in a dynamic domain

In most of this chapter so far we have focused on the planning that an agent in a static domain does. Such agents have information about the initial state and knowledge about its actions and given a goal, they generate a plan which is a sequence of actions and then sequentially execute the actions in the plan. In a dynamic domain this approach may not work as there may be other agents and their actions – referred to as exogenous actions – are beyond the control of the main agent. In that case the main agent has to record the happenings in the world and if necessary make new plans. These new plans are made with respect to the state of the world at that time, not with respect to the initial state. This leads to an architecture of agents in dynamic worlds, which consists of repeated execution of the following steps.

(1) Observe the world and add the observations to the agent's set of observations (O).
(2) Construct a plan from the current moment of time to achieve the goal.
(3) Execute the first action of the plan and add this execution as an observation to the set O.

In the above architecture we assume that in the first step the agent makes all the observations about action occurrences, both agent's actions and exogenous actions. The second step involves finding a sequence $a'_1, \ldots, a'_m$ such that $D \models_O goal \textbf{ after } a'_1, \ldots, a'_m \textbf{ at } t_c$. This can be implemented using AnsProlog and an illustration of this implementation for the navigation example was given earlier in Section 5.3.7.

Exercise 23 Given a domain description in the language $\mathcal{A}$, a set of observations O consisting of propositions of the form (5.6.9) and (5.6.10), and a goal g write an AnsProlog program whose answer sets will encode plans for g from the current moment of time.

5.6.3 Explaining observations

When we remove the assumption that the agent observes all the action occurrences in the first step, we need to modify the first step and instead of simply adding the observations we need to *incorporate* them. That is because if we missed observing a particular action occurrence a simple recording of the observations may lead to an inconsistent (D, O). In that case we need to find *explanations* for the unexplained observations in O and add them to the set of observations. (This is referred to as *incorporation*.) These explanations are exogenous action occurrences (as the agent always observes and records its own actions) that were not observed but that need to be added to O so as to make D and the modified observation set consistent. More formally,

Definition 79 Let FO be a set of observations of the form f **at** t, and O be a set of observations. An explanation of FO with respect to (D, O) is a set H of observations of the form a **occurs_at** t, where a is an exogenous action, such that $(D, O \cup FO \cup H)$ is consistent. $\qquad\square$

In the above definition explanations are action occurrences and we are explaining observations about fluent values at certain times.

In a formulation where we can explain observations, it is preferable to use an action description language such as $\mathcal{A}_c$ that allows parallel execution of actions. In that case the unobserved exogenous actions could be actions that occurred in parallel with some observed actions. If parallel execution of actions is not allowed then explanations become severely limited as in that case unobserved exogenous actions can only occur in time points where no action occurrences were previously observed.

We now discuss how to use AnsProlog in computing explanations of certain observations.

(1) We have the action description part as facts. That is for each proposition of the form
   a **causes** f **if** $p_1, \ldots, p_n, \neg q_1, \ldots, \neg q_n$ we have the fact:

   $causes(a, f, [p_1, \ldots, p_n, \neg q_1, \ldots, \neg q_n]) \leftarrow.$

   We have similar facts for executability conditions, if any are allowed.

(2) For each observation of the form a **occurs_at** k in O we have the fact

$happened(a, k) \leftarrow.$

and for each observation of the form f **at** k in O we have the fact

$observed(f, k) \leftarrow.$

(3) We have AnsProlog rules that encode projection from time T to time $T + 1$. In these rules we use the predicate $occurs$ for action occurrences and $holds$ for fluent values. These rules can either be generalizations of the rules in Section 5.1.9 to allow parallel action occurrences or modification of the rules in Section 5.2.3 to a narrative formulation.

(4) We have the following rules relating $happened$ and $observed$ with $occurs$ and $holds$.

$occurs(A, T) \leftarrow happened(A, T).$
$holds(L, T) \leftarrow observed(L, T).$

(5) We assume FO is a list of literals and we have rules defining when $member(l, FO)$ is true for a literal l.

(6) Finally if our focus is to find explanations within the last m time points then we need the following explanation module:

$unexplained \leftarrow member(L, FO), \textbf{not } holds(L, t_c).$
$\leftarrow unexplained.$
$occurs(A, T) \leftarrow t_c\text{-}m \leq T < t_c, exogenous\_action(A), \textbf{not } not\_occurs(A, T).$
$not\_occurs(A, T) \leftarrow t_c\text{-}m \leq T < t_c, exogenous\_action(A), \textbf{not } occurs(A, T).$

Explanations are now extracted from answer sets of the above program in the following way. For an answer set S of the above program, $E_S(m)$, the set $\{happened(a_i, t) : t_c\text{-}m \leq t < t_c, a_i$ is an exogenous action, $occurs(a_i, t) \in S$ and $happened(a_i, t) \notin S\}$ is an explanation. It consists of exogenous action occurrences which explain the observations but yet were not explicitly observed.

5.6.4 Application to diagnosis

Diagnosis of a physical system involves determining which components of the system are bad. To make such a determination a diagnostic program has a description of the system. This description has a special predicate ab where $ab(c)$ means that the component c is abnormal or bad. In addition it has (i) other fluents, (ii) static causal relations between the various fluents, (iii) actions that are done to the system such as pushing a lever, turning a switch on, etc., (iv) the executability conditions of these actions and their effect on the various fluents of the system, and (v) a distinction between exogenous actions and agent actions.

Together with such a description the diagnostic program records observations about action occurrences and fluent values. Periodically it checks if the action description (D) and set of observations (O) are consistent with the assumption that all components are normal. If they are not consistent, it then tries to explain the observations about the system. For this the formulation in the previous section (Section 5.6.3) is used. Once such an explanation is found then the explanation can be added to the observation set. Let $\langle \sigma_0, a_1, \sigma_1, \ldots, \sigma_n \rangle$ be a model of the resulting theory. Then $\Delta = \{c : ab(c) \in \sigma_n\}$ is a diagnosis that tells us which components may be bad at the current moment of time.

5.7 Case study: Planning and plan correctness in a space shuttle reaction control system

The reaction control system (RCS) of a space shuttle has the primary responsibility for maneuvering the shuttle while it is in space. It consists of fuel and oxidizer tanks, valves and other plumbing necessary for the transmission of the propellant to the maneuvering jets of the shuttle, and electronic circuits for controlling the valves and fuel lines, and also to prepare the jets to receive firing commands. The RCS is computer controlled during take-off and landing and the astronauts have the primary control during the rest of the flight. Normally the astronauts follow pre-scripted plans. But in the presence of failures, the astronauts often have to rely on the ground flight controllers, as the possible set of failures is too large for there to be scripts for all of them.

The United Space Alliance, a major NASA contractor, together with faculty and students from Texas Tech University and the University of Texas at El Paso, built an AnsProlog system to verify plans and to generate plans for the RCS. We will refer to this system as the RCS-AnsProlog system.

The RCS-AnsProlog systems has 3 modeling modules: (i) Plumbing module *PM*, that models the plumbing system of the RCS, (ii) Valve control module *VCM* that models the valves and the impact of their opening and closing, and (iii) Circuit theory module *CTM* that models the electrical circuit; and a planning module. We now describe each of these modules in greater detail.

The plumbing module *PM* has a description of the structure of the plumbing systems as a directed graph whose nodes represent tanks, jets, and pipe junctions and whose arcs are labeled by valves. Possible faults that may change the graph are leaky valves, damaged jets, and stuck valves. The *PM* encodes the condition of fluid flow from one node to another node of the graph, which is that there exists a path without leaks from the source to the destination, with all open valves along the path. More generally, the *PM* encodes a function from the given graph and the state of the valves and faulty components, to the pressures through the nodes in the graph, readiness of jets for firing, and executability of maneuvers that can be performed. The following is a simplified instance of an AnsProlog rule in the *TM*, which encodes the condition that a node $N1$ is pressurized by a tank Tk at time

T, if $N1$ is not leaking, and is connected by an open valve to a node $N2$ which is pressurized by Tk.

$$holds(pressurized\_by(N1, Tk), T) \leftarrow \textbf{not } holds(leaking(N1, T),$$
$$link(N2, N1, Valve),$$
$$holds(state\_of(Valve, open), T),$$
$$holds(pressurized\_by(N1, Tk), T).$$

The valve control module *VCM* is divided into two parts: the basic *VCM* and the extended *VCM*. The basic *VCM* assumes that all electrical circuits connecting switches and computer commands to the valves are working properly, and does not include them in the representation. The extended *VCM* includes information about the electrical circuits and is normally used when circuits malfunction. We now describe both parts in greater detail.

The basic *VCM* encodes a function from initial positions and faults of switches and valves, and the history of the actions and events that have taken place, to the position of valves at the current moment. The output of this function is used as an input to the plumbing module. The *VCM* encoding is similar to the encoding of effects of action and inertia rule described earlier in this chapter. Following are examples of two rules from the basic *VCM* module:

$$holds(state\_of(Sw, S), T + 1) \leftarrow occurs(flip(Sw, S), T),$$
$$\textbf{not } holds(state\_of(Sw, stuck), T).$$
$$holds(state\_of(V, S), T) \leftarrow controls(Sw, V), holds(state\_of(Sw, S), T),$$
$$\textbf{not } holds(ab\_input(V), T),$$
$$S \neq no\_con, \textbf{not } holds(state\_of(Sw, stuck), T),$$
$$\textbf{not } holds(bad\_circuitry(Sw, V), T).$$

The first rule encodes that a switch Sw is in the state S at time $T + 1$, if it is not stuck at time T, and the action of flipping it to state S occurs at time T. The second rule encodes that under normal conditions – i.e., the circuit connecting Sw and the valve V it controls is working properly, switch Sw is not stuck, and V does not have an abnormal input – if switch Sw that controls valve V is in some state S which is different from no_con then V is also in the same state. Here, a switch can be in one of three positions: open, closed, or no_con. When it is in the state no_con, it has no control over the state of the valve.

The extended *VCM* is similar to the basic *VCM* except that it allows additional information about electrical circuits, power and control buses, and the wiring connections among all the components of the system in its input. Part of this input information comes from the *CTM* which we will discuss later. The output is the same as in the basic *VCM*. The following is an example of a rule from the extended *VCM* which encodes the condition that the value of the output wire W_o of a switch

Sw is the same as the value of its input wire W_i if the switch is in a state that connects W_i and W_o.

$$holds(value(W_o, Val), T) \leftarrow holds(value(W_i, Val), T),$$
$$holds(state\_of(Sw, S), T), connects(S, S_w, W_i, W_o).$$

The circuit theory module *CTM* models the electrical circuits of the RCS, which are formed by the digital gates and other electrical components, connected by wires. The *CTM* describes the normal and faulty behavior of electrical circuits with possible propagation delays and 3-valued logic. It encodes a function from the description of a circuit, values of signals present on its input wires, and the set of faults affecting its gates, to the values on the output wires. The following is an example of a rule from the *CTM* which encodes the condition that the value of a wire W is X if W is the output of a gate G with delay D, whose inputs are $W1$ and $W2$, and $W1$ is stuck at X, $W2$ has the value 1, and W is not stuck.

$$holds(value(W, Val), T + D) \leftarrow delay(G, D), input(W2, G),$$
$$input(W1, G), output(W, G), W1 \neq W2,$$
$$holds(value(W2, 1), T),$$
$$holds(value(W1, Val), T),$$
$$holds(stuck(W1), T), \textbf{not } holds(stuck(W), T).$$

The planning module of RCS-AnsProlog is based on the answer set planning paradigm discussed earlier in this chapter where action occurrences encoding possible plans are enumerated, and enumerations that do not lead to the goal are eliminated resulting in answer sets each of which encodes a plan. In addition the planning module of RCS-AnsProlog encodes several domain independent and domain dependent heuristics that narrows the search. An example of a domain independent heuristics is: "Under normal conditions do not perform two different actions with the same effects." In RCS a valve V can be put into state S either by flipping the switch Sw that controls V or by issuing a command CC to the computer that can move V to state S. The following AnsProlog$^\perp$ rule encodes the above mentioned heuristics information.

$$\leftarrow occurs(flip(Sw, S), T), controls(Sw, V), occurs(CC, T),$$
$$commands(CC, V, S), \textbf{not } holds(bad\_circuit(V), T).$$

An example of a domain dependent heuristics is the notion that for a normally functioning valve connecting node $N1$ to $N2$, the valve should not be opened if $N1$ is not pressurized. This is indirectly encoded as follows:

$$\leftarrow link(N1, N2, V), holds(state\_of(V, open), T),$$
$$\textbf{not } holds(pressurized\_by(N1, Tk), T),$$
$$\textbf{not } holds(has\_leak(V), T), \textbf{not } holds(stuck(V), T).$$

5.8 Notes and references

The simple action description language $\mathcal{A}$ was proposed and a sound formulation of it in AnsProlog⁻ was presented in [GL92, GL93]. The relationship between the AnsProlog⁻ formulation and partial order planning was studied in [Bar97b]. The language $\mathcal{A}$ was extended to $\mathcal{A}_C$ to allow compound actions and sound and complete formulations of it in AnsProlog* were given in [BG93, BG97, BGW99]. It was extended to $\mathcal{L}$ in another dimension to allow interleaving of execution and planning (for agents in a dynamic domain) in [BGP97]. AnsProlog* encoding of static causal information and reasoning about them during action execution was carried out in [Bar95, MT95, Tur97], and Example 104 is from [MT95]. The representation in [Bar95] was inspired by the notion of revision programming [MT94a] and its encoding in AnsProlog [Bar94, Bar97a, PT95]. Reasoning about defeasible effects of actions was presented in [BL97]. Approximate reasoning about actions in the presence of incompleteness and sensing actions was formulated in [BS97]. The papers [LW92, LMT93] presented implementations of reasoning about actions using AnsProlog. The volume [Lif97] had several papers on reasoning about actions and logic programming. Transition systems are represented in logic programming in [LT99].

The generate and test approach to planning using answer sets (i.e., answer set planning) was first presented in [SZ95] and then taken up in [DNK97]. Recently it has been taken up with new vigor in [Lif99a, Lif99b, EL99]. In [TB01] the impact of knowledge representation aspects on answer set planning is studied and in [SBM01a] answer set planning is extended to allow procedural constraints. Reasoning about actions in a dynamic domain in a generate and test setting is studied in [BG00]. The methodology of planning using temporal constraints was championed by Bacchus and Kabanza in [BK00] and their TLPlan system is currently one of the fastest planning systems. Reasoning about complex plans consisting of hierarchical and procedural constructs is studied in [BS99]. This idea was expanded into the development of a planning system that exploits temporal, procedural, and hierarchical domain knowledge in [SBM01b]. The procedural constraints used in it are based on the language GOLOG [LRL⁺97]. Planning under incomplete knowledge using the dlv system is reported in [EFL⁺00].

The use of action languages in formulating diagnosis was first proposed in [Thi97] and also studied in [McI97, McI98]. The paper [BMS00] used reasoning with narratives and explanations of observations with respect to narratives in formulating diagnosis. An alternative formulation that leads to AnsProlog* implementations is proposed in [GBG01]. In Section 5.6 we presented the ideas from [GBG01].

The case study of the RCS-AnsProlog system is based on the reported work in [BW99, Wat99, BGN⁺01].

Chapter 6

Complexity, expressiveness, and other properties of AnsProlog* programs

Earlier in Chapter 3 we discussed several results and properties of AnsProlog* programs that are useful in analyzing and step-by-step building of these programs. In this chapter we consider some broader properties that help answer questions such as: (a) how difficult is it to compute answer sets of various sub-classes of AnsProlog*? (b) how expressive are the various sub-classes of AnsProlog*? (c) does the use of AnsProlog* lead to compact representation or can it be compiled to a more tractable representation? and (d) what is the relationship between AnsProlog* and other knowledge representation formalisms?

The answers to these questions are important in many ways. For example, if we know the complexity of a problem that we want to solve then the answer to (a) will tell us which particular subset of AnsProlog* will be most efficient, and the answer to (b) will tell us the most restricted subset that we can use to represent that problem. With respect to (c) we will discuss results that show that AnsProlog* leads to a compact representation. This clarifies the misconception that since many AnsProlog* classes belong to a higher complexity class, they are not very useful. For specifications where AnsProlog* leads to (exponentially) compact representation the fact that they are computationally harder is canceled out and they become preferable because compact representation means that the programmer has to write less. So the burden is shifted from the programmer to the computer, which is often desirable.

To make this chapter self-complete we start with the basic notions of complexity and expressiveness, and present definitions of the polynomial, arithmetic, and analytical hierarchy and their normal forms. We later use them in showing the complexity and expressiveness of AnsProlog* sub-classes.

6.1 Complexity and expressiveness

We start with a review of complexity classes starting from the polynomial hierarchy.

6.1.1 The polynomial hierarchy

A decision problem is a problem of deciding whether a given input w satisfies a certain property Q. That is, in set-theoretic terms, whether it belongs to the corresponding set $S = \{w \mid Q(w)\}$.

Definition 80 The basic complexity classes

- A decision problem is said to belong to the class **P** if there exists a deterministic Turing machine (DTM) that takes polynomial time in solving this problem.
- A decision problem is said to belong to the class **NP** if there exists a nondeterministic Turing machine (NDTM) that takes polynomial time in solving this problem.
- A decision problem is said to belong to the class **coNP** if the complement of the problem is in **NP**.
- A decision problem is said to belong to the class **PSPACE** if there exists a DTM that takes polynomial space in solving this problem.
- For any deterministic or nondeterministic complexity class C, the class C^A is defined to be the class of all languages decided by machines of the same sort and time bound as in C, except that the machine now has an oracle A.
- The Polynomial hierarchy is defined as follows:

    - $\Delta_0 \mathbf{P} = \Sigma_0 \mathbf{P} = \Pi_0 \mathbf{P} = \mathbf{P}$
    - $\Delta_{i+1} \mathbf{P} = \mathbf{P}^{\Sigma_i \mathbf{P}}$
    - $\Sigma_{i+1} \mathbf{P} = \mathbf{NP}^{\Sigma_i \mathbf{P}}$
    - $\Pi_{i+1} \mathbf{P} = \mathbf{coNP}^{\Sigma_i \mathbf{P}}$ □

In this book we will use the following alternative characterization of the polynomial hierarchy in our proofs. In these characterizations we will use the notions: *polynomially decidable* and *polynomially balanced*, which we define now. A (k+1)-ary relation P on strings is called polynomially decidable if there is a DTM deciding the language $\{u_1; \dots; u_k; w : (u_1, \dots, u_k, , w) \in P\}$. We say P is polynomially balanced if $(u_1, \dots, u_k, w) \in P$ implies that the size of u_is is bounded by a polynomial in the size of w.

Proposition 89 Alternative characterization of the polynomial hierarchy

- A problem belongs to the class **NP** iff the formula $w \in S$ (equivalently, $Q(w)$) can be represented as $\exists u P(u, w)$, where $P(u, w)$ is polynomially decidable and polynomially balanced. Note that the class **NP** is also denoted by $\Sigma_1 \mathbf{P}$ to indicate that formulas from this class can be defined by adding 1 existential quantifier (hence Σ and 1) to a polynomial (hence **P**) predicate.
- A problem belongs to the class **coNP** iff the formula $w \in S$ (equivalently, $Q(w)$) can be represented as $\forall u P(u, w)$, where $P(u, w)$ is polynomially decidable and polynomially balanced. The class **coNP** is also denoted by $\Pi_1 \mathbf{P}$ to indicate that formulas from this

class can be defined by adding 1 universal quantifier (hence Π and 1) to a polynomial predicate.

- For every positive integer k, a problem belongs to the class $\Sigma_k\mathbf{P}$ iff the formula $w \in S$ (equivalently, $Q(w)$) can be represented as $\exists u_1 \forall u_2 \ldots P(u_1, u_2, \ldots, u_k, w)$, where $P(u_1, \ldots, u_k, w)$ is polynomially decidable and polynomially balanced.
- Similarly, for every positive integer k, a problem belongs to the class $\Pi_k\mathbf{P}$ iff the formula $w \in S$ (equivalently, $Q(w)$) can be represented as $\forall u_1 \exists u_2 \ldots P(u_1, u_2, \ldots, u_k, w)$, where $P(u_1, \ldots, u_k, w)$ is polynomially decidable and polynomially balanced.
- A problem belongs to the class **PSPACE** iff the formula $w \in S$ (equivalently, $Q(w)$) can be represented as $\forall u_1 \exists u_2 \ldots P(u_1, u_2, \ldots, u_k, w)$, where the number of quantifiers k is bounded by a polynomial of the length of the input, and $P(u_1, \ldots, u_k, w)$ is polynomially decidable and polynomially balanced.   □

In this chapter we often use the above alternative characterizations of the polynomial hierarchy to show the membership of particular problems in classes in the polynomial hierarchy. The following example illustrates this approach.

Example 109 It is well known that the problem of satisfiability of a propositional formula is in **NP**, and that the problem of unsatisfiability of a propositional formula is in **coNP**. We will now use the above proposition in showing these.

(i) Let w be a propositional formula, and $Q(w)$ be true iff w is satisfiable. To show that the problem of satisfiability of a propositional formula is in **NP** we need to come up with a polynomially decidable and polynomially balanced property $P(u, w)$ such that w is satisfiable iff $\exists u\, P(u, w)$ is true.

Let u be an assignment of true or false to the propositions, and $P(u, w)$ be the evaluation of the formula w using the assignments in u. Obviously, $P(u, w)$ is polynomially decidable and polynomially balanced. Moreover, w is satisfiable iff $\exists u P(u, w)$ is true. Hence, the problem of satisfiability of a propositional formula is in **NP**.

(ii) Let w be a propositional formula, and $Q'(w)$ be true iff w is unsatisfiable. To show that the problem of unsatisfiability of a propositional formula is in **coNP** we need to come up with a polynomially decidable and polynomially balanced property $P'(u, w)$ such that w is unsatisfiable iff $\forall u P'(u, w)$ is true.

Let u be the assignment of true or false to the propositions, and $P'(u, w)$ be the complement of the evaluation of the formula w using the assignments in u. Obviously, $P'(u, w)$ is polynomially decidable and polynomially balanced. Moreover, w is unsatisfiable iff $\forall u P'(u, w)$ is true. Hence, the problem of unsatisfiability of a propositional formula is in **coNP**.   □

Definition 81 A problem is called *hard* in a class C of the polynomial hierarchy if any other problem from this class can be reduced to it by a logarithmic space reduction. It is called *complete* in a class C if it is in C and is hard in C. □

By 'logarithmic space reduction' of a problem P_1 to another problem P_2 we mean that there exists a DTM R such that for any input x of P_1, $R(x)$ can be computed using logarithmic space, and P_1's answer to x is yes iff P_2's answer to $R(x)$ is yes.

Often it suffices to use polynomial time reduction in the above definition. But when defining **P**-completeness we need to stick to logarithmic space reduction.

Proposition 89 also leads us to several basic problems that are complete with respect to the various classes in the polynomial hierarchy. We enumerate them in the following proposition and use them later in the chapter when showing that particular AnsProlog* sub-classes are data-complete with respect to complexity classes in the polynomial hierarchy.

Proposition 90 [Pap94] Given a boolean expression ϕ, with boolean variables partitioned into sets $X_1, \ldots, X_i$, let E_QSAT_i denote evaluating the satisfiability of the formula $\exists X_1, \forall X_2, \ldots, Q X_i \phi$, where Q is $\exists$ if i is odd and $\forall$ otherwise; and let F_QSAT_i denote evaluating the satisfiability of the formula $\forall X_1, \exists X_2, \ldots Q X_i \phi$, where Q is $\exists$ if i is even and $\forall$ otherwise.

(i) For all $i \geq 1$ E_QSAT_i is $\Sigma_i \mathbf{P}$ complete.
(ii) For all $i \geq 1$ F_QSAT_i is $\Pi_i \mathbf{P}$ complete. □

It should be noted that it is still not known whether we can solve any problem from the class **NP** in polynomial time (i.e., in precise terms, whether **NP** = **P**). However, it is widely believed that we cannot, i.e., **NP** ≠ **P**. It is also believed that to solve an **NP**-complete or a **coNP**-complete problem, we may need $O(2^n)$ time, and that solving a complete problem from one of the second-level classes $\Sigma_2 \mathbf{P}$ or $\Pi_2 \mathbf{P}$ requires more computation time than solving **NP**-complete problems and solving complete problems from the class **PSPACE** takes even longer.

6.1.2 Polynomial and exponential classes

Although earlier we defined the classes **P**, **NP**, and **PSPACE**, we now define them slightly differently and use that notation to define some complexity classes which are beyond the polynomial hierarchy, but are recursive. We start with the following:

$TIME(f(n)) = \{L \; : \; L \text{ is decided by some DTM in time } O(f(n))\}$,
$NTIME(f(n)) = \{L \; : \; L \text{ is decided by some NDTM in time } O(f(n))\}$,

$SPACE(f(n)) = \{L : L$ is decided by some DTM within space $O(f(n))\}$,
$NSPACE(f(n)) = \{L : L$ is decided by some NDTM within space $O(f(n))\}$.

Using the above notations we can now define the classes **P**, **NP**, EXPTIME, NEXPTIME, and PSPACE as follows:

$\mathbf{P} = \bigcup_{d>0} TIME(n^d)$
$\mathbf{NP} = \bigcup_{d>0} NTIME(n^d)$
$\text{EXPTIME} = \bigcup_{d>0} TIME(2^{n^d})$
$\text{NEXPTIME} = \bigcup_{d>0} NTIME(2^{n^d})$
$\mathbf{PSPACE} = \bigcup_{d>0} SPACE(n^d)$

Earlier we defined completeness with respect to the classes **P**, **NP**, and **PSPACE**. The notion of EXPTIME-complete and NEXPTIME-complete is defined in exactly the same way as in the Definition 81.

6.1.3 Arithmetical and analytical hierarchy

The arithmetical and analytical hierarchy are similar to the polynomial hierarchy. The starting point in the arithmetical hierarchy is the class of *recursive* problems – defined in Appendix B – instead of the class **P** in the polynomial hierarchy. The arithmetical hierarchy is denoted by Σ_i^0 and Π_i^0, where i is a nonnegative integer, while the analytical hierarchy is denoted by Σ_i^1 and Π_i^1. We first define the arithmetical hierarchy.

(1) A k-ary relation R is said to be recursive if the language $L_R = \{x_0; \ldots; x_{k-1} : (x_0, \ldots, x_{k-1}) \in R\}$ is recursive.
(2) We say a decision problem belongs to the class Σ_0^0 iff it is *recursive*.
(3) We say a decision problem belongs to the class Σ_1^0 iff it is *recursively enumerable*.
(4) Σ_{n+1}^0 denotes the class of all languages L for which there is a (n+2)-ary <u>recursive</u> relation R such that $L = \{y : \exists x_0 \forall x_1 \ldots Q_n x_n R(x_0, \ldots, x_n, y)\}$ where Q_k is $\forall$ if k is odd, and $\exists$ if k is even. Alternatively, Σ_{n+1}^0 denotes the relations over the natural numbers that are definable in arithmetic by means of a *first-order formula* $\Phi(\mathbf{Y}) = \exists \mathbf{X}_0 \forall \mathbf{X}_1 \ldots Q_k \mathbf{X}_n \psi(\mathbf{X}_0, \ldots, \mathbf{X}_n, \mathbf{Y})$ with free variables $\mathbf{Y}$, Q_k is as before, and ψ is quantifier free.
(5) $\Pi_{n+1}^0 = \mathbf{co}\Sigma_{n+1}^0$, that is, Π_{n+1}^0 is the set of all complements of languages in Σ_{n+1}^0. It can be easily shown that Π_{n+1}^0 denotes the class of all languages L for which there is a (n+2)-ary <u>recursive</u> relation R such that $L = \{y : \forall x_0 \exists x_1 \ldots Q_n x_n R(x_0, \ldots, x_n, y)\}$ where Q_k is $\exists$ if k is odd, and $\forall$ if k is even. Alternatively, Π_{n+1}^0 denotes the relations over the natural numbers that are definable in arithmetic by means of a *first-order formula* $\Phi(\mathbf{Y}) = \forall \mathbf{X}_0 \exists \mathbf{X}_1 \ldots Q_k \mathbf{X}_n \psi(\mathbf{X}_0, \ldots, \mathbf{X}_n, \mathbf{Y})$ with free variables $\mathbf{Y}$, and ψ is quantifier free.

Note that the difference between the classes $\Sigma_{n+1}\mathbf{P}$ and $\Pi_{n+1}\mathbf{P}$ from the polynomial hierarchy and the classes Σ_{n+1}^0 and Π_{n+1}^0 from the arithmetical hierarchy is that the relation ψ has to be decidable (i.e., we can determine if a tuple belongs to that relation or not) in polynomial time in the first case, while it must be recursive in the second case. We now define the analytical hierarchy.

(1) The class Σ_1^1 belongs to the *analytical hierarchy* (in a relational form) and contains those relations which are definable by a *second order formula* $\Phi(\mathbf{X}) = \exists \mathbf{P}\phi(\mathbf{P}; \mathbf{X})$, where $\mathbf{P}$ is a tuple of predicate variables and ϕ is a first order formula with free variables $\mathbf{X}$.

(2) The class Π_1^1 belongs to the *analytical hierarchy* (in a relational form) and contains those relations which are definable by a *second order formula* $\Phi(\mathbf{X}) = \forall \mathbf{P}\phi(\mathbf{P}; \mathbf{X})$, where $\mathbf{P}$ is a tuple of predicate variables and ϕ is a first order formula with free variables $\mathbf{X}$.

(3) Σ_{n+1}^1 denotes the set of relations which are definable by a *second-order formula* $\Phi(\mathbf{Y}) = \exists \mathbf{P}_0 \forall \mathbf{P}_1 \ldots Q_k \mathbf{P}_n \psi(\mathbf{P}_0, \ldots, \mathbf{P}_n, \mathbf{Y})$, where the $\mathbf{P}_i$ are tuples of predicate variables and ψ is a first order formula with free variables $\mathbf{Y}$.

(4) Π_{n+1}^1 denotes the set of relations which are definable by a *second-order formula* $\Phi(\mathbf{Y}) = \forall \mathbf{P}_0 \exists \mathbf{P}_1 \ldots Q_k \mathbf{P}_n \psi(\mathbf{P}_0, \ldots, \mathbf{P}_n, \mathbf{Y})$, where the $\mathbf{P}_i$ are tuples of predicate variables and ψ is a first order formula with free variables $\mathbf{Y}$.

Note that the difference between the classes Σ_{n+1}^0 and Π_{n+1}^0 from the arithmetical hierarchy and the classes Σ_{n+1}^1 and Π_{n+1}^1 from the analytical hierarchy is that Φ is a first-order formula in the first case, while it is a second-order formula in the second case; and the quantification is over variables in the first case and is over predicates in the second case.

Definition 82 A problem L_1 is called *complete* in a class C of the arithmetical or analytical hierarchy if, (i) L_1 is in C and (ii) any other problem L_2 from this class can be reduced to it (L_1) by Turing reduction.

By Turing reduction of L_2 to L_1 we mean that L_2 can be decided by a deterministic Turing machine with oracle L_1.   □

6.1.4 Complexity and expressiveness of languages

So far we have defined what it means for a decision problem to be in a complexity class, and defined and characterized various important complexity classes. Our interest in complexity in this chapter is mainly in regard to complexity and expressiveness of AnsProlog* sub-classes. We now proceed towards formally defining what that means.

Intuitively, the notion of complexity of an AnsProlog* sub-class characterizes how hard it is to compute an entailment with respect to programs in that sub-class and the notion of expressiveness characterizes all that can be expressed in that sub-class. Since AnsProlog* programs can also be viewed as a function, there are three different complexity measures associated with AnsProlog* sub-classes: data complexity, program complexity, and combined complexity. In the first two cases, the AnsProlog* program is considered to consist of two parts, a set of *facts* and a set of *rules* referred to as the program. In the case of data complexity the program part is fixed and the facts are varied and the complexity measure is with respect to the size of the facts, while in the case of program complexity the facts are fixed and the program is varied and the complexity measure is with respect to the size of the program. In the case of combined complexity, the complexity measure is with respect to both the program and the facts. The following example illustrates the difference.

Example 110 Consider Π consisting of a set of ground facts and a rule with a nonempty body:

$$p(a_1) \leftarrow. \quad \ldots \quad p(a_k) \leftarrow.$$
$$q(X_1, \ldots, X_l) \leftarrow p(X_1), \ldots, p(X_l).$$

It is easy to see that $ground(\Pi)$ consists of $k + k^l = k + 2^{lg_2(k) \times l}$ rules; the size of the ground facts in Π is $c_1 \times k$, for some positive constant c_1; and the size of the rules with nonempty body in Π is $c_2 \times l$, for some positive constant c_2.

Now, if we consider the facts part to be constant then the size of $ground(\Pi)$ is of the order of $O(2^{lg_2(k) \times n})$ where n is the size of the rule with nonempty body, and k is a constant. Similarly, if we consider the rule with nonempty body part to be constant then the size of $ground(\Pi)$ is of the order of $O(m^l)$ where m is the size of the facts, and l is a constant. Thus, if we keep the facts fixed then the size of $ground(\Pi)$ is exponential in terms of the size of the rest of Π and if we keep the rule with nonempty body part fixed then the size of $ground(\Pi)$ is polynomial in terms of the size of the facts in Π. □

We now formally define data complexity and program complexity of AnsProlog* sub-classes. Although in our definition below L is considered to be a sub-class of AnsProlog*, the definition holds if we generalize L to be any language like AnsProlog* which has two parts and has an entailment relation.

Definition 83 Let L be a sub-class of AnsProlog*, Π be a program in L, D_{in} be a set of ground facts in L, and A be a literal.

The *data complexity* of L is the complexity of checking $D_{in} \cup \Pi \models A$, in terms of the length of the input $\langle D_{in}, A \rangle$, given a fixed Π in L.

The *program complexity* of L is the complexity of checking $D_{in} \cup \Pi \models A$, in terms of the length of the input $\langle \Pi, A \rangle$, given a fixed D_{in} in L.

The *combined complexity* of L is the complexity of checking $D_{in} \cup \Pi \models A$, in terms of the length of the input $\langle \Pi, D_{in}, A \rangle$. □

One of our goals in this chapter is to associate complexity classes with the various AnsProlog* sub-classes. In this we are interested in both membership in the complexity classes, and completeness with respect to these complexity classes. Thus we extend the notion of data complexity and program complexity to notions of an AnsProlog* sub-class being *data-complete* or *program-complete* with respect to a complexity class C. In this we first start with the definitions for data-completeness. In general, our focus in this chapter will be more on data complexity than on program complexity for two reasons: (a) Often the size of data is much larger than the size of the program. (b) For the applications that we focus on throughout the book the more appropriate measure is data complexity. For example, suppose we want to measure the complexity of our AnsProlog* encodings of planning problems. For them the variable part is the description of the domain which can be encoded by facts. Similarly, for the graph domains, the complexity of the graph problems corresponds to the data complexity of their AnsProlog* encodings; this is because when the graph is changed, the facts in the program change, and the rules remain the same.

Definition 84 Given an AnsProlog* program Π the recognition problem associated with it is to determine if $\Pi \cup I \models A$, given some facts I and a ground literal A. Alternatively, the recognition problem of Π is to determine membership in the set $\{\langle I, A \rangle : \Pi \cup I \models A\}$. □

Definition 85 An AnsProlog* program Π is said to be in complexity class C if the recognition problem associated with Π is in C. □

It should be noted that in the above definitions, our focus is on data complexity, as we are keeping the program fixed and varying the facts.

Definition 86 (Data-complete) An AnsProlog* sub-class L is *data-complete for complexity class C* (or equivalently, the data complexity class of L is C-complete) if

(i) *(membership)*: each program in L is in C, and
(ii) *(hardness)*: there exists a program in L for which the associated recognition problem is complete with respect to the class C. □

We now define the notion of program-completeness in a slightly different manner. In this definition and henceforth when we say that a decision problem P can be expressed by a program Π in L, we mean that the answer to the decision problem can be expressed using the entailment with respect to Π. That is, if P involves deciding if an input w satisfies a certain property Q then $Q(w)$ iff Π together with w entails 'accept'.

Definition 87 (Program-complete) An AnsProlog* sub-class L is *program-complete for complexity class C* (or equivalently, the program complexity class of L is C complete) if

 (i) *(membership)*: the program complexity of L is C, and
(ii) *(hardness)*: there is a complete problem P in class C, which can be expressed by a program in L, over a fixed set of facts.   □

For example, we can use the above definition to show that AnsDatalog$^{-\mathbf{not}}$ is program-complete for EXPTIME, by showing that (i) the program complexity of AnsDatalog$^{-\mathbf{not}}$ is EXPTIME and (ii) if a deterministic Turing machine (DTM) M halts in less than $N = 2^{n^k}$ transitions on a given input I, where $|I| = n$, then we can construct an AnsDatalog$^{-\mathbf{not}}$ program $\pi(I)$ with a fixed set of ground facts F such that $\pi(I) \models accept$ iff M accepts the input I.

We now define the notion of expressiveness and explain how it differs from the notion of complexity.

Definition 88 (Expressiveness) An AnsProlog* sub-class L is said to *capture the complexity class C* if

 (i) each program in L is also in C, and
(ii) every problem of complexity C can be expressed in L.   □

Although the notions of being data-complete for complexity class C and capturing the class C are close, they are not equivalent. We elaborate on this now.

- L is data-complete in C does not imply that L captures C.

  This is because, even though there may exist queries in L for which the associated recognition problem is complete with respect to the class C, there may be problems in the class C which cannot be expressed in L.

  An example of this is the query classes *fixpoint* and *while* which are data-complete for *PTIME* and *PSPACE* respectively, but yet neither can express the simple query: .

  even(R) = true if $|R|$ is even, and false otherwise.

- L captures C does not imply that L is data-complete in C.

This is because even though L captures C there may not exist a problem that is C-complete. For example, as mentioned in [DEGV01] second-order logic over finite structures captures the polynomial hierarchy PH, for which no complete problem is known, and the existence of a complete problem of PH would imply that it collapses at some finite level, which is widely believed to be false.

To further explain the difference let us discuss the familiar definition of **NP**-completeness. The *definition* of **NP**-completeness is that a problem X is **NP**-complete if (i) it belongs to **NP**, and (ii) all problems in **NP** can be polynomially reduced to instances of X. This definition is close to the definition of *expressiveness* where we use the phrase *can be expressed* instead of the phrase *can be polynomially reduced*. Now let us consider how we normally prove that a problem X is **NP**-complete. We show it belongs to **NP** and then take a known **NP**-complete problem Y and give a polynomial time reduction of Y to X. This approach is close to the definition of data completeness above. Why then are the two notions of *expressiveness* and *complexity* different? One of the reasons is that data complexity of L being **NP**-complete does not imply L captures **NP**. This is because when we are dealing with query languages, there is no guarantee that the query language of our focus can express the polynomial reducibility that is used in the definition and proof strategy of **NP**-completeness.

6.1.5 Technique for proving expressiveness: general forms

To show that an AnsProlog* sub-class L captures the complexity class C, we need to show that (i) every program in L is in C, and (ii) every query of complexity C can be expressed in L. To show the first condition we consider arbitrary programs from L and show that entailment with respect to them can be computed as per C. To show the second condition, we will often use general (or normal) forms of complexity classes. A general form of a complexity class C, is a form in which all problems in class C can be expressed. All complexity classes may not have a general form. But when a complexity class has one, to show (ii) we only need to consider arbitrary expressions in a general form of C, and show how to express it in L. In the following proposition we list a few general forms that we will use in our proofs.

Proposition 91 General form of some complexity classes Consider a signature $\sigma = (O, F, P)$, where O is finite, and $F = \emptyset$ meaning that there are no function symbols. By a finite database over $\sigma = (O, F, P)$ we mean a finite subset of the Herbrand Base over σ.

(1) [Fag74, Sto77] A collection S of finite databases over the signature $\sigma = (O, \emptyset, P)$ is in $\Sigma_k \mathbf{P}$ iff there exists a $\Sigma_k^1(\sigma)$ sentence Ψ such that for any finite database w over σ, $w \in S$ iff w satisfies Ψ.

(2) [Fag74, KP88] A collection S of finite databases over the signature σ is in **NP** iff it is definable by an existential second order formula over σ, i.e., iff there is a formula of the form $\exists U_1, \ldots, U_m \forall \bar{x} \exists \bar{y} (\theta_1(\bar{x}, \bar{y}) \vee \cdots \vee \theta_k(\bar{x}, \bar{y}))$, where $\theta_i(\bar{x}, \bar{y})$s are conjunctions of literals involving the predicates in σ and $\{U_1, \ldots, U_m\}$ such that for any finite database w over σ $w \in S$ iff w satisfies $\exists U_1, \ldots, U_m \forall \bar{x} \exists \bar{y} (\theta_1(\bar{x}, \bar{y}) \vee \cdots \vee \theta_k(\bar{x}, \bar{y}))$.

(3) [EGM94, EGG96] Assume that *succ*, *first*, and *last* are predicates that do not occur in P. By an enumeration literal (or literal in an enumerated theory) we mean literals in $(O, \emptyset, \{succ, first, last\})$ with the following conditions:

- *succ* describes an enumeration of all elements in O, where $(x, y) \subset succ$ means that y is the successor of x,
- and the unary relations *first* and *last* contain the first and last elements in the enumeration respectively.

A collection S of finite databases over the signature $\sigma = (O, \emptyset, P)$ is in $\Sigma_2 \mathbf{P}$ iff there is a formula of the form $\exists U_1, \ldots, U_m \forall V_1, \ldots, V_n \exists \bar{x} (\theta_1(\bar{x}) \vee \cdots \vee \theta_k(\bar{x}))$, where $\theta_i(\bar{x})$ are conjunctions of enumeration literals or literals involving predicates in $P \cup \{U_1, \ldots, U_m, V_1, \ldots, V_n\}$ such that for any finite database w over σ, $w \in S$ iff w satisfies $\exists U_1, \ldots, U_m \forall V_1, \ldots, V_n \exists \bar{x} (\theta_1(\bar{x}) \vee \cdots \vee \theta_k(\bar{x}))$.   □

Once we have proved that a certain language L captures a complexity class C by showing that (i) every program in a language L is in class C, and (ii) the general form of a complexity class C is expressible in a language L, to show that L is C-complete the only additional result we need to show is that there exists a C-complete problem. This is because this C-complete problem, by definition, belongs to class C. Hence, it can be expressed in the general form, which we would have already shown to be expressible in L. Hence, we have a C-complete problem expressible in L. This together with (i) will prove that L is C-complete.

6.2 Complexity of AnsDatalog* sub-classes

In this section we consider several sub-classes of AnsDatalog* (AnsProlog* programs with no function symbols) and explore their data and program complexity classes. We start with propositional AnsDatalog programs.

6.2.1 Complexity of propositional AnsDatalog^{-not}

In the case of propositional programs our main interest lies in their combined complexity. We now state and prove the combined complexity of AnsDatalog^{-not} programs.

Theorem 6.2.1 Given a propositional AnsDatalog^{-not} program Π and a ground literal A the complexity of deciding $\Pi \models A$ is P-complete.   □

Proof:

Membership: The answer set of a propositional AnsDatalog$^{-\textbf{not}}$ program can be obtained by the iterated fixpoint approach. Each iteration step can be done in polynomial time. The total number of iterations is bound by the number of rules plus one. Hence, $\Pi \models A$ can be determined in polynomial time.

Hardness: Let L be a language in **P**. Thus L is decidable in $p(n)$ steps by a DTM M for some polynomial p. We now present a feasible transformation of each instance I of L into a propositional AnsDatalog$^{-\textbf{not}}$ program $\pi(M, I, p(|I|))$ such that $\pi(M, I, p(|I|)) \models accept$ iff M with input I reaches an accepting step within $N = p(|I|)$ steps.

(1) We first define the various propositions that we will use and their intuitive meaning.
  (a) $state_s[t]$ for $0 \le t \le N$: at time point t the state of the Turing machine is s.
  (b) $cursor[n, t]$ for $0 \le t \le N$ and $0 \le n \le N$: at time point t the cursor is at the cell number n (counted from the left).
  (c) $symbol_\alpha[n, t]$ for $0 \le t \le N$ and $0 \le n \le N$: at time point t, α is the symbol in cell number n (counted from the left) of the tape.
  (d) $accept$: the DTM M has reached state yes.
(2) We now present the part of $\pi(M, I, p(|I|))$ that describes the initial state, the initial cursor position, the input, and the transition dictated by the transition function δ of M.
  (a) $state_{s_0}[0] \leftarrow$.: at time point 0 the state of the Turing machine is s_0.
  (b) $cursor[0, 0] \leftarrow$.: at time point 0 the cursor is at the extreme left end of the tape.
  (c) If the input is $I = \alpha_1, \ldots, \alpha_{|I|}$, then we have the following:
$$symbol_{\alpha_1}[1, 0] \leftarrow. \qquad \cdots \qquad symbol_{\alpha_{|I|}}[|I|, 0] \leftarrow.$$
  (d) $symbol_>[0, 0] \leftarrow$. and $symbol_\sqcup[|I| + 1, 0] \leftarrow$.: beginning of the tape, and end of the input.
  (e) For each $\delta(s, \alpha) = (s', \beta, p)$, we have the following rules:
$$symbol_\beta[n, t + 1] \leftarrow symbol_\alpha[n, t], state_s[t], cursor[n, t].$$
$$state_{s'}[t + 1] \leftarrow symbol_\alpha[n, t], state_s[t], cursor[n, t].$$
$$cursor[X, t + 1] \leftarrow symbol_\alpha[n, t], state_s[t], cursor[n, t].$$
  where, X is $n + 1$ if p is $\rightarrow$, X is $n - 1$ if p is $\leftarrow$, and X is n if p is $-$.
(3) We also need inertia rules for the propositions $symbol_\beta[n, t]$ to describe which cell numbers keep their previous symbols after a transition. For $0 \le t < N$, $n \ne n'$, and $n, n' \le N$, we have the rules:
$$symbol_\alpha[n, t + 1] \leftarrow symbol_\alpha[n, t], cursor[n', t].$$
(4) Finally, we need a rule to derive $accept$, when an accepting state is reached.
$$accept \leftarrow state_{yes}[t], \quad \text{for } 0 \le t \le N.$$

The above program has $O(N^2)$ rules and thus is polynomial in the size of $|I|$. Hence, it can be constructed in polynomial time. Moreover, if we compute the answer set of the above program using the iterated fixpoint approach the computation mimics the transitions in the DTM, and the answer set contains *accept* iff an accepting configuration is reached by the DTM M with input I in at most N computation steps.   □

Exercise 24 Find the exact correspondence between the iterated fixpoint computation and the DTM configuration in the above proof.   □

The proof of the above theorem can also be directly used to show that entailment with respect to propositional AnsDatalog$^{-\mathbf{not}}$(3) programs is **P**-complete. This is because all the rules in $\pi(M, I, p(|I|))$ have at most 3 literals in their body.

6.2.2 Complexity of AnsDatalog$^{-\mathbf{not}}$

We start with the data complexity of AnsDatalog$^{-\mathbf{not}}$ programs.

Theorem 6.2.2 AnsDatalog$^{-\mathbf{not}}$ programs are data-complete for **P**.   □

Proof:

Membership: Following the computations in Example 110 it is clear that the Herbrand Base of a program is polynomial in the size of the input ground facts. Now, given a set of ground facts I and a ground literal A, we can determine if $\Pi \cup I \models A$ (where Π is an AnsDatalog$^{-\mathbf{not}}$ program) by computing the answer set of $\Pi \cup I$. We can obtain this answer set by the iterated fixpoint approach, and the maximum number of iterations that we may need is bounded by the size of the Herbrand Base, as in each iteration we must add at least one new atom for the iteration to continue. Each iteration takes a polynomial amount of time. Thus determining if $\Pi \cup I \models A$ can be done in time polynomial in the size of I.

Hardness: To show the hardness we use the result that entailment with respect to propositional AnsDatalog$^{-\mathbf{not}}$(3) programs is **P**-complete. Let us consider an arbitrary propositional AnsDatalog$^{-\mathbf{not}}$(3) program Π. We will represent this program as facts $D_{in}(\Pi)$ as follows:

For each rule $A_0 \leftarrow A_1, \ldots, A_i.$, $0 \leq i \leq 3$, we have the fact $R_i(A_0, A_1, \ldots, A_i) \leftarrow$.

Let us now consider the following AnsDatalog$^{-\mathbf{not}}$ program Π_{meta}:

$T(X_0) \leftarrow R_0(X_0).$
$T(X_0) \leftarrow T(X_1), R_1(X_0, X_1).$
$T(X_0) \leftarrow T(X_1), T(X_2), R_2(X_0, X_1, X_2).$
$T(X_0) \leftarrow T(X_1), T(X_2), T(X_3), R_3(X_0, X_1, X_2, X_3).$

It is easy to see that $\Pi \models A$ iff $D_{in}(\Pi) \cup \Pi_{meta} \models A$. Since the size of Π is of the same order as the size of $D_{in}(\Pi)$ and we keep Π_{meta} fixed, the data complexity of AnsDatalog^{-not} – to which Π_{meta} belongs – is the same as the complexity of entailment in propositional AnsDatalog^{-not}(3). Hence, AnsDatalog^{-not} is data-complete in **P**. □

Exercise 25 It is well known that AnsDatalog^{-not} cannot express the query which given a set of ground facts, determines if the number of facts are even or not. This obviously can be done in polynomial time. Explain why this does not contradict with our theorem above. □

We now state and prove the program complexity of AnsDatalog^{-not} programs.

Theorem 6.2.3 AnsDatalog^{-not} programs are program-complete for EXPTIME. □

Proof:
Membership: Recall from Example 110 that given a program Π, and a set of ground facts D, the size of $ground(\Pi)$ is exponential with respect to the size of Π. For an AnsDatalog^{-not} program Π, $ground(\Pi)$ is a propositional program and from Theorem 6.2.1 entailment with respect to $ground(\Pi) \cup D$ will be polynomial in the size of $ground(\Pi) \cup D$. Since we fix D, and the size of $ground(\Pi)$ is exponential with respect to the size of Π, program complexity of AnsDatalog^{-not} programs is in EXPTIME.
Hardness: Let L be a language in **EXPTIME**. Thus L is decidable in 2^{n^k} steps by a DTM M for some positive integer k. We now present a feasible transformation of each instance I of L into an AnsDatalog^{-not} program $\pi(M, I)$ with a fixed input database D, such that $\pi(M, I) \models accept$ iff M with input I reaches an accepting step within $N = 2^{|I|^k}$ steps. The fixed input database that we use is the empty database with the universe $U = \{0, 1\}$.

The AnsDatalog^{-not} program $\pi(M, I)$ is similar to the program in the hardness part of the proof of Theorem 6.2.1. But instead of the propositional symbols $state_s[t]$, $cursor[n, t]$, and $symbol_\alpha[n, t]$ used there, we now have predicates $state(s, t)$, $cursor(n, t)$, and $symbol(\alpha, n, t)$. The main difficulty now is to be able to define a predicate $succ(t, t')$ for $t' = t + 1$ without using function symbols. To achieve this we represent n and t as tuples of arity $m = |I|^k$, where each element of the tuple can take the value 0 or 1. Thus we can represent numbers from 0 to $2^m - 1$. Now we need to define a successor relationship between such binary representation of numbers. We achieve this by introducing predicates $succ^i$, for

$i = 1, \ldots, m$, which define the successor relationship between i-bit numbers. We also have predicates $first^i$, and $last^i$ to define the smallest and largest i-bit number. We now recursively define $succ^i$, $first^i$, and $last^i$ and define a predicate $less^m$ between m-bit numbers. (In the following, variables written in bold face represent m distinct variables, and constants written in bold face represent that number written in binary as m 0-1 constants.)

(1) The base case:

$succ^1(0, 1) \leftarrow.$
$first^1(0) \leftarrow.$
$last^1(1) \leftarrow.$

(2) Defining $first^i$ and $last^i$:

$first^{i+1}(0, \mathbf{X}) \leftarrow first^i(\mathbf{X}).$
$last^{i+1}(1, \mathbf{X}) \leftarrow last^i(\mathbf{X}).$

(3) Defining $succ^i$:

$succ^{i+1}(Z, \mathbf{X}, Z, \mathbf{Y}) \leftarrow succ^i(\mathbf{X}, \mathbf{Y}).$
$succ^{i+1}(Z, \mathbf{X}, Z', \mathbf{Y}) \leftarrow succ^1(Z, Z'), last^i(\mathbf{X}), first^i(\mathbf{Y}).$

(4) Defining $less^m$:

$less^m(\mathbf{X}, \mathbf{Y}) \leftarrow succ^m(\mathbf{X}, \mathbf{Y}).$
$less^m(\mathbf{X}, \mathbf{Y}) \leftarrow less^m(\mathbf{X}, \mathbf{Z}), succ^m(\mathbf{Z}, \mathbf{Y}).$

We now present the part of $\pi(M, I)$ that describes the initial state, the initial cursor position, the input, and the transition dictated by the transition function δ of M.

(1) $state(s_0, \mathbf{0}) \leftarrow.$: at time point $\mathbf{0}$ the state of the Turing machine is s_0.
(2) $cursor(\mathbf{0}, \mathbf{0}) \leftarrow.$: at time point $\mathbf{0}$ the cursor is at the extreme left end of the tape.
(3) If the input is $I = \alpha_1, \ldots, \alpha_r$, then we have the following:
$symbol(\alpha_1, \mathbf{1}, \mathbf{0}) \leftarrow.$ $\quad\quad \ldots \quad\quad$ $symbol(\alpha_r, \mathbf{r}, \mathbf{0}) \leftarrow.$
(4) $symbol(>, 0, 0) \leftarrow.$ and $symbol(\sqcup, \mathbf{r+1}, \mathbf{0}) \leftarrow.$: beginning of the tape, and end of the input.
(5) The transition function δ is specified as atoms of the form:
$trans(s, \alpha, s', \beta, p) \leftarrow.$
(6) We have the following rules that define the transition.
$symbol(B, \mathbf{N}, \mathbf{T'}) \leftarrow symbol(A, \mathbf{N}, \mathbf{T}), state(S, \mathbf{T}), cursor(\mathbf{N}, \mathbf{T}), succ^m(\mathbf{T}, \mathbf{T'}),$
$\quad\quad\quad trans(S, A, \_, B, \_).$
$state_{S'}(\mathbf{T'}) \leftarrow symbol(A, \mathbf{N}, \mathbf{T}), state(S, \mathbf{T}), cursor(\mathbf{N}, \mathbf{T}), succ^m(\mathbf{T}, \mathbf{T'}),$
$\quad\quad\quad trans(S, A, S', \_, \_).$
$cursor(\mathbf{N'}, \mathbf{T'}) \leftarrow symbol(A, \mathbf{N}, \mathbf{T}), state(S, \mathbf{T}), cursor(\mathbf{N}, \mathbf{T}), succ^m(\mathbf{T}, \mathbf{T'}),$
$\quad\quad\quad succ^m(\mathbf{N}, \mathbf{N'}), trans(S, A, \_, \_, \rightarrow).$
$cursor(\mathbf{N'}, \mathbf{T'}) \leftarrow symbol(A, \mathbf{N}, \mathbf{T}), state(S, \mathbf{T}), cursor(\mathbf{N}, \mathbf{T}), succ^m(\mathbf{T}, \mathbf{T'}),$
$\quad\quad\quad succ^m(\mathbf{N'}, \mathbf{N}), trans(S, A, \_, \_, \leftarrow).$

$cursor(\mathbf{N}, \mathbf{T'}) \leftarrow symbol(A, \mathbf{N}, \mathbf{T}), state(S, \mathbf{T}), cursor(\mathbf{N}, \mathbf{T}), succ^m(\mathbf{T}, \mathbf{T'}),$
$trans(S, A, \_, \_, -).$

We also need the following inertia rules to describe which cell numbers keep their previous symbols after a transition.

$symbol(A, \mathbf{N}, \mathbf{T'}) \leftarrow symbol(A, \mathbf{N}, \mathbf{T}), cursor(\mathbf{N'}, \mathbf{T}), less^m(\mathbf{N}, \mathbf{N'}).$

$symbol(A, \mathbf{N}, \mathbf{T'}) \leftarrow symbol(A, \mathbf{N}, \mathbf{T}), cursor(\mathbf{N'}, \mathbf{T}), less^m(\mathbf{N'}, \mathbf{N}).$

Finally, we need a rule to derive *accept*, when an accepting state is reached.

$accept \leftarrow state(yes, \mathbf{T}).$

The above program can be constructed in constant (hence, polynomial) time. Moreover, if we compute the answer set of the above program using the iterated fixpoint approach the computation mimics the transitions in the DTM, and the answer set contains *accept* iff an accepting configuration is reached by the DTM M with input I in at most N computation steps.   □

6.2.3 Complexity of AnsDatalog

Theorem 6.2.4 For any AnsDatalog program Π, and an input set of facts D, determining if $\Pi \cup D$ has an answer set is **NP**-complete. That is, determining if the set of answer sets of $\Pi \cup D$, denoted by $SM(\Pi \cup D)$ is $\neq \emptyset$, is **NP**-complete.   □

Proof:
Membership: Determining if $SM(\Pi \cup D) \neq \emptyset$ can be expressed as $\exists M. P_1(M, D)$, where $P_1(M, D)$ is true if the least model of $ground(\Pi \cup D)^M$ is equal to M. Since the size of the Herbrand Base of $\Pi \cup D$ is polynomial in the size of D, the size of M – a subset of the Herbrand Base, is polynomial in the size of D. Moreover, the size of $ground(\Pi \cup D)$ is also polynomial in the size of D. Hence, computing $ground(\Pi \cup D)^M$ is polynomial in the size of D and obtaining the least model through the iterated fixpoint approach of the AnsDatalog$^{-\mathbf{not}}$ program $ground(\Pi \cup D)^M$ is also polynomial time. Hence, P_1 is polynomially decidable, and polynomially balanced. Therefore, determining if $SM(\Pi \cup D) \neq \emptyset$ is in **NP**.

An informal way of showing the above is to say that after guessing an M, we can verify if M is an answer set or not in polynomial time.

Hardness: We show this by considering the well-known **NP**-complete problem 3-Sat. Let $\{a_1, \ldots, a_n\}$ be a set of propositions. Given any instance ϕ of 3-Sat consisting of propositions from $\{a_1, \ldots, a_n\}$ we construct an AnsDatalog program $\Pi_1 \cup D$, where D is dependent on ϕ, and Π is fixed, such that ϕ is satisfiable iff $\Pi_1 \cup D$ has an answer set.

Let ϕ be of the form $(l_{11} \vee l_{12} \vee l_{13}) \wedge \cdots \wedge (l_{m1} \vee l_{m2} \vee l_{m3})$, where the l_{ij} are literals made of the propositions $a_1, \ldots, a_n$.

D consists of the facts:

$$conj(l_{11}, l_{12}, l_{13}) \leftarrow. \quad \ldots \quad conj(l_{m1}, l_{12}, l_{m3}) \leftarrow.$$

The fixed program Π_1 consists of the following:

(1) It has rules of the following form – where $h(a)$ means a holds, or a is *true*, and $n\_h(a)$ means a does not hold, or a is *false* – to enumerate the truth of propositions in the language:

$h(a_i) \leftarrow \textbf{not } n\_h(a_i).$
$n\_h(a_i) \leftarrow \textbf{not } h(a_i).$
for $i = 1, \ldots, n.$

(2) It has the following rules which makes q true if one of the conjuncts is false:

$q \leftarrow conj(X, Y, Z), n\_h(X), n\_h(Y), n\_h(Z).$

(3) Finally we have the following rule which forbids any answer set where q may be true, thus making sure that if an assignment to the propositions does not make ϕ true then no answer set exists corresponding to that assignment.

$p \leftarrow \textbf{not } p, q.$

Now ϕ is satisfiable *implies* that there exists an assignment A of truth values for the a_is that makes ϕ true. This *implies* that $\{h(a_i) : A$ assigns a_i *true*$\} \cup \{n\_h(a_j) : A$ assigns a_j *false*$\}$ is an answer set of $\Pi_1 \cup D$.

ϕ is not satisfiable *implies* that there does not exist an assignment A of truth values for the a_is that makes ϕ true. This *implies* that there are no answer sets of Π_1. This is because if there was an answer set S of Π, in that answer set q would be true, which will then – because of the $p \leftarrow \textbf{not } p.$ construction – not be an answer set. $\square$

Theorem 6.2.5 AnsDatalog is data-complete for **coNP**. $\square$

Proof:
Membership: $\Pi \cup D \models A$ can be written as $\forall M.P_2(M, D, A)$, where $P_2(M, D, A)$ is true if the least model of $(\Pi \cup D)^M$ is equal to M implies $M \models A$. Computing $ground(\Pi \cup D)^M$ is polynomial time (in the size of D) and obtaining the least model through the iterated fixpoint approach of the AnsDatalog$^{-\textbf{not}}$ program $ground(\Pi \cup D)^M$ is also polynomial time (in the size of D). Determining if $M \models A$ is polynomial time (in the sizes of D and A). Hence, membership in P_2 is polynomially decidable. Since M is polynomial in the size of D, P_2 is also polynomially balanced. Thus the task of determining if $\Pi \cup D \models A$ is in $\Pi_1 P$, which is the same as **coNP**.

An equivalent way of showing the above is to show that the complement of the above problem is in **NP**. We can do that informally by guessing an M, and showing that M is an answer set of $\Pi \cup D$ and $M \not\models A$. The latter two can be done in polynomial time. Thus the complement of the above problem is in **NP**. Hence, the task of determining if $\Pi \cup D \models A$ is in **coNP**.

Hardness: Showing complexity of $\Pi \cup D \models A$ is **coNP**-complete, for AnsDatalog programs Π.

We show this by considering the well-known **coNP**-complete problem Unsatisfiability. Let $\{a_1, \ldots, a_n\}$ be a set of propositions. Given any instance ϕ of 3-Sat consisting of propositions from $\{a_1, \ldots, a_n\}$ we construct an AnsDatalog program $\Pi_2 \cup D$ – where D is dependent on ϕ and Π_2 is fixed, such that ϕ is unsatisfiable iff $\Pi_2 \cup D \models unsat$.

Let ϕ be of the form $(l_{11} \vee l_{12} \vee l_{13}) \wedge \cdots \wedge (l_{m1} \vee l_{m2} \vee l_{m3})$, where the l_{ij} are literals made of the propositions $a_1, \ldots, a_n$.

D consists of the facts:

$$conj(l_{11}, l_{12}, l_{13}) \leftarrow. \quad \ldots \quad conj(l_{m1}, l_{12}, l_{m3}) \leftarrow.$$

The fixed program Π_2 consists of the following:

(1) It has rules of the following form – where $h(a)$ means a holds, or a is *true*, and $n\_h(a)$ means a does not hold, or a is *false* – for enumerating truth of propositions in the language:

$$h(a_i) \leftarrow \textbf{not } n\_h(a_i).$$
$$n\_h(a_i) \leftarrow \textbf{not } h(a_i).$$
for $i = 1, \ldots, n$.

(2) It has the following rules which makes *unsat* true if one of the conjuncts is false:

$$unsat \leftarrow conj(X, Y, Z), n\_h(X), n\_h(Y), n\_h(Z). \qquad \square$$

Theorem 6.2.6 AnsDatalog is program-complete for coNEXPTIME. $\square$

Proof: (sketch)

Membership: For an AnsDatalog program Π the size of $ground(\Pi)$ is exponential with respect to the size of Π. Given an atom A, we will argue that determining if $\Pi \not\models A$ is in NEXPTIME. This means we need to find an answer set of Π where A is not true. To find an answer set we need to guess and check. Since the checking part involves computing an answer set of an AnsDatalog$^{-\textbf{not}}$ program, from Theorem 6.2.3 checking is exponential time. Hence, determining if $\Pi \not\models A$ is in NEXPTIME, and therefore determining if $\Pi \models A$ is in coNEXPTIME.

Hardness: The proof of hardness is similar to the proof of the hardness part in Theorem 6.2.3, except that we now need to simulate a nondeterministic Turing machine (NDTM). In an NDTM δ is a relation instead of a function. Thus in part (5) of the hardness proof of Theorem 6.2.3 we may have multiple facts of the form $trans(s, \alpha, s_1, \beta_1, p_1), \ldots, trans(s, \alpha, s_k, \beta_k, p_k)$. Thus the rules in part (6) of the hardness proof of Theorem 6.2.3 are no longer adequate. What we need to do is to simulate the multiple branches of computation that an NDTM can take. This is done by introducing a predicate *occurs* as follows and replacing *trans* in the bodies of the rules in part (6) of the hardness proof of Theorem 6.2.3 by *occurs*.

$other\_occurs(S, A, S_1, B_1, P_1, T) \leftarrow occurs(S, A, S_2, B_2, P_2, T), S_1 \neq S_2.$
$other\_occurs(S, A, S_1, B_1, P_1, T) \leftarrow occurs(S, A, S_2, B_2, P_2, T), B_1 \neq B_2.$
$other\_occurs(S, A, S_1, B_1, P_1, T) \leftarrow occurs(S, A, S_2, B_2, P_2, T), P_1 \neq P_2.$
$occurs(S, A, S_1, B_1, P_1, T) \leftarrow symbol(A, N, T), state(S, T), cursor(N, T),$
$$trans(S, A, S_1, B_1, P_1),$$
$$\textbf{not } other\_occurs(S, A, S_1, B_1, P_1, T).$$

The above rules ensure that at each time T there is exactly one answer set mimicking a possible transition. Thus the various computation paths have a one-to-one correspondence with the various answer sets.

Finally we replace the rule with *accept* in the head in the hardness proof of Theorem 6.2.3 by the following rules:

$reject \leftarrow state(no, T).$

Now *reject* is true in one of the answer sets of the above program iff the NDTM rejects the input. Thus, rejection will be in NEXPTIME and hence acceptance will be in coNEXPTIME. □

Theorem 6.2.7 Stratified AnsDatalog is data-complete for **P**. □

Proof: (sketch)
Membership: There are polynomial (in the size of the facts) numbers of strata. Iteration in each strata is polynomial time. So the unique answer set can be obtained in polynomial time.
Hardness: Same as the proof of the hardness part of Theorem 6.2.2. □

Theorem 6.2.8 Stratified AnsDatalog is program-complete for EXPTIME. □

Proof: (sketch)
Membership: There could be an exponential (in the size of the program) number of strata in the grounding of the program. Iteration in each strata is polynomial time. So the unique answer set can be obtained in exponential time.

Hardness: Same as the proof of the hardness part of Theorem 6.2.3.   □

The above results also hold for the well-founded semantics of AnsDatalog where instead of static stratas we have stratas that are determined dynamically.

Theorem 6.2.9 AnsDatalog with respect to well-founded semantics is data-complete for **P**.   □

Theorem 6.2.10 AnsDatalog with respect to well-founded semantics is program-complete for EXPTIME.   □

6.2.4 Complexity of AnsDatalog$^{or,-not}$

Unlike AnsDatalog^{-not} programs, AnsDatalog$^{or,-not}$ programs may have multiple answer sets. The multiplicity of the answer sets is due to the *or* connective that is now allowed in the head of rules. Moreover, as discussed in Example 30 a disjunctive fact of the form a *or* $b \leftarrow$. in a program cannot in general be replaced by the two AnsDatalog rules in $\{a \leftarrow \textbf{not } b., b \leftarrow \textbf{not } a\}$. In this section we formally show that entailment of negative literals with respect to AnsDatalog$^{or,-not}$ programs is more complex than with respect to AnsDatalog programs. This is due to the extra minimality condition in the definition of answer sets of AnsDatalog$^{or,-not}$ programs. Interestingly, this does not affect the complexity of entailment with respect to positive literals, as an AnsDatalog$^{or,-not}$ program entails a positive ground literal A iff all its answer sets entail A iff all its models entail A. The last 'iff' does not hold when A is a negative literal. We now formally state and prove the complexity results about entailment with respect to AnsDatalog$^{or,-not}$ programs. In this we only consider the data complexity.

Theorem 6.2.11 Given an AnsDatalog$^{or,-not}$ program Π, a set of facts D, and a positive ground literal A, determining $\Pi \cup D \models A$ is **coNP**-complete with respect to the size of D.   □

Proof:
Membership: $\Pi \cup D \models A$ can be written as $\forall M. P_3(M, D, A)$, where $P_3(M, D, A)$ is true if M is a model of $\Pi \cup D$ implies $M \models A$. Checking if M is a model of $ground(\Pi) \cup D$ and determining if $M \models A$ is polynomial in the size of D. Hence, membership in P_3 is polynomially decidable. Moreover, M is polynomial in the size of D, and hence P_3 is polynomially balanced. Thus the task of determining if $\Pi \models A$ is in $\Pi_1\textbf{P}$, which is the same as **coNP**.

An equivalent way of showing the above is to show that the complement of the above problem is in **NP**. For that we have to guess an M, show that M is a model of $\Pi \cup D$, and $M \not\models A$. The latter two can be done in polynomial time. Thus the complement of the above problem is in **NP**. Hence, the task of determining if $\Pi \cup D \models A$ is in **coNP**.

Hardness: We show this by considering the well-known **coNP**-complete problem unsatisfiability. Let $\{a_1, \ldots, a_n\}$ be a set of propositions. Given any instance ϕ of 3-Sat consisting of propositions from $\{a_1, \ldots, a_n\}$ we construct an AnsDatalog$^{or,-\textbf{not}}$ program $\Pi_3 \cup D$ – where D is dependent on ϕ and Π_3 is fixed, such that ϕ is unsatisfiable iff $\Pi_3 \cup D \models unsat$.

Let ϕ be of the form $(l_{11} \vee l_{12} \vee l_{13}) \wedge \cdots \wedge (l_{m1} \vee l_{m2} \vee l_{m3})$, where the l_{ij} are literals made of the propositions $a_1, \ldots, a_n$.
D consists of the facts:

$$conj(l_{11}, l_{12}, l_{13}) \leftarrow. \quad \cdots \quad conj(l_{m1}, l_{12}, l_{m3}) \leftarrow.$$

The fixed program Π_3 consists of the following:

(1) It has rules of the following form – where $h(a)$ means a holds, or a is *true*, and $n\_h(a)$ means a does not hold, or a is *false* – for enumerating the truth of propositions in the language:

$$h(a_i) \text{ or } n\_h(a_i) \leftarrow.$$

for $i = 1, \ldots, n$.

(2) It has the following rules which makes *unsat* true if one of the conjuncts is false:

$$unsat \leftarrow conj(X, Y, Z), n\_h(X), n\_h(Y), n\_h(Z). \qquad \square$$

Theorem 6.2.12 Given an AnsDatalog$^{or,-\textbf{not}}$ program Π, a set of facts D and a negative literal $\neg A$, determining $\Pi \cup D \models \neg A$ is $\Pi_2\textbf{P}$-complete with respect to the size of D. $\qquad \square$

Proof:
Membership: $\Pi \cup D \models \neg A$ can be written as $\forall M \exists M' P_4(M, M', D, A)$, where $P_4(M, M', D, A)$ is true if M is a model of $\Pi \cup D$ implies M' is a model of $\Pi \cup D$ and $M' \subseteq M$ and $M' \not\models A$. Checking if M and M' are models of $\Pi \cup D$ and determining if $M' \not\models A$ takes time polynomial in the size of D. Hence, P_4 is polynomially decidable. Moreover, since M and M' are polynomial in the size of D, P_4 is polynomially balanced. Thus determining if $\Pi \cup D \models \neg A$ is in $\Pi_2\textbf{P}$.
Hardness: We show this by considering the $\Pi_2 P$-complete problem, satisfiability of quantified boolean formulas ψ of the form $\forall x_1, \ldots, x_n \exists y_1, \ldots, y_m \phi$, where ϕ is a propositional formula made up of the propositions $x_1, \ldots, x_n, y_1, \ldots, y_m$. Given a formula ψ of the above form we construct an AnsDatalog$^{or,-\textbf{not}}$ program $\Pi_4 \cup D$ – where D is dependent on ψ and Π_4 is fixed, such that ψ is satisfiable iff $\Pi_4 \cup D \models \neg unsat$.

Let ϕ be of the form $(l_{11} \vee \cdots \vee l_{1k_1}) \wedge \cdots \wedge (l_{m1} \vee \cdots \vee l_{mk_m})$, where the l_{ij} are literals made of the propositions $x_1, \ldots, x_n, y_1, \ldots, y_m$.

D consists of the following facts:

(1) $conj(l_{11}, l_{12}, l_{13}) \leftarrow.$ .... $conj(l_{m1}, l_{12}, l_{m3}) \leftarrow.$
(2) $forall(x_1) \leftarrow..$ .... $forall(x_n) \leftarrow.$
(3) $exists(y_1) \leftarrow..$ .... $exists(y_m) \leftarrow.$

The fixed program Π_4 consists of the following:

(1) It has rules of the following form to enumerate the truth of propositions:

$h(X)$ *or* $n\_h(X) \leftarrow forall(X).$
$h(X)$ *or* $n\_h(X) \leftarrow exists(X).$

(2) It has the following rule which makes *unsat* true if one of the conjuncts is false:

$unsat \leftarrow conj(X, Y, Z), n\_h(X), n\_h(Y), n\_h(Z).$

(3) Rules of the form:

$h(X) \leftarrow exists(X), unsat.$
$n\_h(X) \leftarrow exists(X), unsat.$ $\square$

Exercise 26 Let Π be an AnsDatalog$^{or.-\textbf{not}}$ program. Show that $\Pi \models \neg A$ iff for all models M of Π there exists a model $M' \subseteq M$ of Π such that $M' \not\models A$. $\square$

6.2.5 Complexity of AnsDatalog^{or}

Theorem 6.2.13 AnsDatalog^{or} is data-complete for $\Pi_2 P$. $\square$

Proof:
Membership: Let Π be an AnsDatalog^{or} program and A be a ground atom. Then $\Pi \models A$ can be written as
$\forall M. \; M$ is an answer set of Π^M implies $M \models A$
$\equiv \forall M. \; [M$ is a model of Π^M and $\neg \; (\exists M', M' \subset M$ and M' is a model of $\Pi^M)]$
     implies $M \models A.$
$\equiv \forall M. \; [\neg \; (M$ is a model of $\Pi^M)$ or $(\exists M', M' \subset M$ and M' is a model of $\Pi^M)$ or
     $(M \models A).$
$\equiv \forall M. \; [\neg \; ((M$ is a model of $\Pi^M)$ and $\neg(M \models A))$ or $(\exists M', M' \subset M$ and M' is a
     model of $\Pi^M)]$
$\equiv \forall M. \; [(M$ is a model of $\Pi^M)$ and $(M \not\models A)]$ implies $(\exists M', M' \subset M$ and M' is a
     model of $\Pi^M).$
$\equiv \forall M. \; \exists M' \; (M$ is a model of Π^M and $M \not\models A)$ implies $(M' \subset M$ and M' is a
     model of $\Pi^M).$

Table 6.1. *Summary of the complexity results of AnsDatalog* sub-classes*

AnsDatalog* Class	Complexity Type	Complexity Class
AnsDatalog$^{-\textbf{not}}$	Data complexity	**P**-complete
AnsDatalog$^{-\textbf{not}}$	Program complexity	**EXPTIME**-complete
Stratified AnsDatalog	Data complexity	**P**-complete
Stratified AnsDatalog	Program complexity	**EXPTIME**-complete
AnsDatalog (under WFS)	Data complexity	**P**-complete
AnsDatalog (under WFS)	Program complexity	**EXPTIME**-complete
AnsDatalog (answer set existence)	Complexity of $SM(\Pi) \neq \emptyset$	**NP**-complete
AnsDatalog	Data complexity	**coNP**-complete
AnsDatalog	Program complexity	**coNEXPTIME** complete
AnsDatalog$^{\neg}$	Existence of answer set	**NP**-complete
AnsDatalog$^{\neg}$	Data complexity	**coNP**-complete
AnsDatalog$^{or,-\textbf{not}}$	Deciding $\Pi \models_{GCWA} A$	**coNP**-complete
AnsDatalog$^{or,-\textbf{not}}$	Deciding $\Pi \models_{GCWA} \neg A$	$\Pi_2\textbf{P}$-complete
AnsDatalog^{or}	Data complexity	$\Pi_2\textbf{P}$-complete
AnsDatalog^{or}	Program complexity	**coNEXPTIME$^{\textbf{NP}}$**-complete

Thus $\Pi \cup D \models A$ can be written as $\forall M \exists M' P_5(M, M', D, A)$, where $P_5(M, M', D, A)$ is true if $(M$ is a model of $\Pi^M \cup D$ and $M \not\models A)$ implies $(M' \subset M$ and M' is a model of $\Pi^M \cup D)$. It is easy to see that given M, M', and A, whether $P_5(M, M', D, A)$ holds or not can be determined in time polynomial in the size of D. Hence, P_5 is polynomially decidable. Moreover, since M and M' are polynomial in the size of D, P_5 is polynomially balanced. Hence for AnsDatalog^{or} programs $\Pi \cup D$ the task of determining if $\Pi \cup \models A$ is in $\Pi_2\textbf{P}$. In exactly the same way we can show that for AnsDatalog^{or} programs $\Pi \cup D$ the task of determining if $\Pi \cup D \models \neg A$ is in $\Pi_2\textbf{P}$.

Hardness: The hardness proof is the same as the proof of hardness for Theorem 6.2.12.   □

Theorem 6.2.14 AnsDatalog^{or} is program-complete for coNEXPTIME$^{\textbf{NP}}$.   □

The proof of the above theorem is similar to the proof of Theorem 6.2.6. The additional **NP** in the exponent of coNEXPTIME$^{\textbf{NP}}$ is due to the additional minimality necessary in AnsDatalog^{or} programs, and necessitates an NP oracle together with the NDTM when showing the hardness part.

We summarize in Table 6.1 the various complexity results for the different AnsDatalog* sub-classes.

6.3 Expressiveness of AnsDatalog* sub-classes

In this section we consider the expressiveness of AnsDatalog* sub-classes. In this we are interested in two kinds of results: When does a particular sub-class (completely) capture a complexity class or only express a strict subset of it; and how does a AnsDatalog* sub-class relate to other query languages such as First-order logic (FOL), fixpoint logic (FPL), relational algebra, and relational calculus? Note that FPL is an extension of first-order logic by a least fixpoint operator.

There are two mismatches between Turing machines and some of the AnsDatalog* sub-classes. These mismatches are: (i) the input in a Turing machine automatically encodes a linear order among the constituents of the input, while such an order between the constants in the AnsDatalog* program is not automatically given; and (ii) a Turing machine can check what is in its input and what is not, while certain sub-classes of AnsDatalog* do not have a way to find out if some atom is *false*.

The issue in (i) can be overcome in AnsDatalog* sub-classes that can encode nondeterminism. Then the program can have multiple answer sets each encoding a particular ordering. An example of such an encoding is given in Section 2.1.12, and we need the use of either '**not**' or '*or*' for encoding nondeterminism. In the absence of nondeterminism the only other option is to assume the presence of an ordering. The issue in (ii) can be overcome either by using '**not**' or some weaker negation.

Because of the above although AnsDatalog$^{-\textbf{not}}$ – known in the literature as Datalog – is data-complete in **P**, it cannot capture **P** and only captures a strict subset of **P**. In particular, it cannot express the query about whether the universe of the input database has an even number of elements. The book [AHV95] and the survey articles [DEGV97, DEGV01] discuss this and similar results in further detail. When Datalog is augmented with the assumption that the input predicates may appear negated in rule bodies then it still only captures a strict subset of **P**. This extension of Datalog is referred to as Datalog$^+$. It is known that Datalog$^+$ is equivalent in expressiveness to FPL$^+\exists$, a fragment of FPL where negation is restricted to the input relations and only existential quantifiers are allowed. On the other hand Datalog$^+$ together with the assumption that the input database is ordered captures **P**.

In Table 6.2 we summarize several of the expressiveness results. Among these results we present the proof of the expressiveness results about AnsDatalog and AnsDatalog^{or}. In those results by brave semantics we mean that $\Pi \models L$ iff there exists an answer set A of Π such that $A \models L$. Also, by AnsDatalog$^{or-\textbf{not}.\neq}$ we refer to the extension of AnsDatalog$^{or-\textbf{not}}$ with the $\neq$ predicate. The other results in the table, some with proofs, are discussed in greater detail in [AHV95, DEGV97, DEGV01].

Table 6.2. *Summary of expressiveness of AnsDatalog* sub-classes*

AnsDatalog* Sub-class	Relation	Complexity Class (or a non-AnsProlog* class)
Datalog$^+$	$\subseteq\neq$	**P**
Datalog$^+$ (on ordered databases)	captures	**P**
Datalog$^+$	equal	FPL$^+$(there exists)
Stratified AnsDatalog	$\subseteq\neq$	FPL
Non-recursive range restr AnsDatalog	equal	relational algebra
Non-recursive range restr AnsDatalog	equal	relational calculus
Non-recursive range restr AnsDatalog	equal	FOL (without function symbols)
AnsDatalog (under WFS)	equal	FPL
Stratified AnsDatalog (on ordered databases)	captures	**P**
AnsDatalog under WFS (on ordered databases)	captures	**P**
AnsDatalog under brave semantics	captures	**NP**
AnsDatalog	captures	**coNP**
AnsDatalog$^{or-\mathbf{not},\neq}$ (under brave semantics)	captures	$\Sigma_2\mathbf{P}$
AnsDatalog$^{or-\mathbf{not},\neq}$	captures	$\Pi_2\mathbf{P}$
AnsDatalog^{or} (under brave semantics)	captures	$\Sigma_2\mathbf{P}$
AnsDatalog^{or}	captures	$\Pi_2\mathbf{P}$

6.3.1 Expressiveness of AnsDatalog

Theorem 6.3.1 AnsDatalog under the brave semantics captures **NP**.   □

Proof:
Membership: Same as the membership part of the proof of Theorem 6.2.5.

Expresses all **NP** *relations*: To prove that every problem of complexity class **NP** can be expressed in AnsDatalog we demonstrate that the general form of a problem in the complexity class **NP** as shown in part (2) of Proposition 91 can be expressed in AnsDatalog. Thus, we construct an AnsDatalog program Π such that a finite database w satisfies $\exists U_1, \ldots, U_m \forall \bar{x} \exists \bar{y}(\theta_1(\bar{x}, \bar{y}) \vee \cdots \vee \theta_k(\bar{x}, \bar{y}))$ iff $\Pi \cup w$ has an answer set containing *yes*.

(1) For enumeration of the predicates $U_1, \ldots, U_m$, we have the rules:

$U_j(\bar{w}_j) \leftarrow \mathbf{not}\ U'_j(\bar{w}_j).$
$U'_j(\bar{w}_j) \leftarrow \mathbf{not}\ U_j(\bar{w}_j).$
for $j = 1, \ldots, m$

(2) For a given $\bar{x}$, we define $p(\bar{x})$ to hold when $\exists \bar{y}(\theta_1(\bar{x}, \bar{y}) \vee \cdots \vee \theta_k(\bar{x}, \bar{y}))$ holds by the following rules:

$p(\bar{x}) \leftarrow \theta_i(\bar{x}, \bar{y}).$
for $i = 1, \ldots, k$.

(3) To make q true if for some $\bar{x}$, $p(\bar{x})$ does not hold we have the rule:

$q \leftarrow \textbf{not } p(\bar{x})$.

(4) To eliminate answer sets where q may be true we have:

inconsistent $\leftarrow q$, **not** *inconsistent*.

(5) Finally to include *yes* in the answer sets which survive the elimination above we have:

yes $\leftarrow$. □

Corollary 5 AnsDatalog captures **coNP**. □

6.3.2 Expressiveness of AnsDatalog^{or}

Theorem 6.3.2 AnsDatalog^{or} under the brave semantics captures $\Sigma_2\textbf{P}$. □

Proof:
Membership: Same as the membership part of the proof in Theorem 6.2.13.

Expresses all $\Sigma_2\textbf{P}$ relations: Following part (3) of Proposition 91 we construct an AnsDatalog^{or} program Π such that a finite database w satisfies the formula $\exists U_1, \ldots, U_m \; \forall V_1, \ldots, V_n \exists \bar{x}(\theta_1(\bar{x}) \vee \cdots \vee \theta_k(\bar{x}))$, where $\theta_i(\bar{x})$s are of the form described in part (3) of Proposition 91, iff $\Pi \cup w$ has an answer set containing *sat*. This will prove that any problem in $\Sigma_2\textbf{P}$ can be expressed in AnsDatalog^{or} under the brave answer set semantics.

(1) For enumeration of the predicates $U_1, \ldots, U_m$, we have the rules:

$U_j(\bar{w}_j) \; or \; U'_j(\bar{w}_j) \leftarrow$.

for $j = 1, \ldots, m$

(2) For enumeration of the predicates $V_1, \ldots, V_n$, we have the rules:

$V_j(\bar{s}_j) \; or \; V'_j(\bar{s}_j) \leftarrow$.

for $j = 1, \ldots, n$

(3) Definition of linear ordering: Since $\theta_i(\bar{x})$s may include enumeration literals made up of predicates *succ*, *first*, and *last*, we need to define these predicates. The following rules achieve that. They are similar to the rules in Section 2.1.12, except that they use **not** in only one place, and use *or*.

$prec(X, Y) \; or \; prec(Y, X) \leftarrow \textbf{not } eq(X, Y)$.
$eq(X, X) \leftarrow$.
$prec(X, Z) \leftarrow prec(X, Y), prec(Y, Z)$.

$not\_succ(X, Z) \leftarrow prec(Z, X).$

$not\_succ(X, Z) \leftarrow prec(X, Y), prec(Y, Z).$

$not\_succ(X, X) \leftarrow.$

$succ(X, Y) \text{ or } not\_succ(X, Y) \leftarrow.$

$not\_first(X) \leftarrow prec(Y, X).$

$first(X) \text{ or } not\_first(X) \leftarrow.$

$not\_last(X) \leftarrow prec(X, Y).$

$last(X) \text{ or } not\_last(X) \leftarrow.$

$reachable(X) \leftarrow first(X).$

$reachable(Y) \leftarrow reachable(X), succ(X, Y).$

$linear \leftarrow last(X), reachable(X).$

(4) Definition of satisfiability

$sat \leftarrow \theta_i(\bar{x}), linear.$

for $i = 1, \ldots, k$.

Note that $\theta_i(\bar{x})$ may involve the use of '**not** $eq(X, Y)$'.

(5) To eliminate potential answer sets where for particular instances of the U_i not all interpretations of the V_j lead to *sat*, we add the following rules:

$V_j(\bar{s}_j) \leftarrow sat.$

$V_j'(\bar{s}_j) \leftarrow sat.$ □

for $j = 1, \ldots, n$.

Corollary 6 AnsDatalog^{or} captures $\Pi_2 P$.   □

Theorem 6.3.3 AnsDatalog$^{or, -\textbf{not}, \neq}$ under the brave semantics captures $\Sigma_2 P$.

    □

Proof: Almost the same as the proof of Theorem 6.3.2. The only changes that we need are (a) to replace the first two rules in the program constructed in the item (3) of the second part of the proof by the following rule:

$prec(X, Y) \text{ or } prec(Y, X) \leftarrow X \neq Y.$

and (b) replace occurrences of '**not** $eq(X, Y)$' in the body of item (4) by '$X \neq Y$'.

With this change the program constructed in the second part of the proof is an AnsDatalog$^{or, -\textbf{not}, \neq}$ program.

Corollary 7 AnsDatalog$^{or, -\textbf{not}, \neq}$ captures $\Pi_2 P$.   □

6.4 Complexity and expressiveness of AnsProlog* sub-classes

In this section we consider the complexity and expressiveness of AnsProlog* sub-classes when we allow function symbols. In this case, even for AnsProlog$^{-\textbf{not}}$

programs we may need infinite iterations of the iterative fixpoint operator to get to the answer set. Thus the set of answer sets of AnsProlog^{-not} programs is at best recursively enumerable. In general, when we allow function symbols the complexity and expressiveness classes of AnsProlog* sub-classes are no longer in the polynomial hierarchy; rather they are in the arithmetic and analytical hierarchy.

6.4.1 Complexity of AnsProlog* sub-classes

We start with the complexity of AnsProlog^{-not}.

Theorem 6.4.1 AnsProlog^{-not} is recursively enumerable complete. □

Proof: As before, to show AnsProlog^{-not} is recursively enumerable complete we will show that (a) membership: answer set of an AnsProlog^{-not} program is a recursively enumerable set; and (b) hardness: The recursively enumerable complete problem of Turing acceptability can be expressed in AnsProlog^{-not}.

Membership: Recall that AnsProlog^{-not} programs have unique answer sets that can be determined by iterative application of an operator until the least fixpoint is reached. Each application of the operator is computable, but the fixpoint may not be reached after a finite number of applications of the operator, although it is reached eventually. Thus in general the answer set of an AnsProlog^{-not} program is a recursively enumerable set.

Hardness: In the appendix we define a Turing machine M and when it accepts an input I. We now present a translation of an arbitrary Turing machine M and an arbitrary input I to an AnsProlog^{-not} program $\pi(M, I)$ and argue that $M(I) = $ 'yes' iff $\pi(M, I) \models accept$.

(1) We first define the various predicates that we will use and their intuitive meaning.
  (a) *state*(s, t): at time point t the state of the Turing machine is s.
  (b) *cursor*(n, t): at time point t the cursor is at the cell number n (counted from the left).
  (c) *symbol*(α, n, t): at time point t, α is the symbol in cell number n (counted from the left) of the tape.
  (d) *trans*$(s, \alpha, s', \beta, p)$: if s is the current state of the Turing machine, and α is the symbol pointed to by the cursor, then the new state should be s', α should be over-written by β, and the cursor should move as dictated by p.
(2) We now present the part of $\pi(M, I)$ that describes the initial state, the initial cursor position, the input, and the transition function δ of M.
  (a) *state*$(s_0, 0) \leftarrow .$: at time point 0 the state of the Turing machine is s_0.
  (b) *cursor*$(0, 0) \leftarrow .$: at time point 0 the cursor is at the extreme left end of the tape.
  (c) *symbol*$(\alpha_1, 1, 0) \leftarrow ..$ $\quad \ldots \quad$ *symbol*$(\alpha_k, k, 0) \leftarrow .$

if the input $I = \alpha_1, \ldots, \alpha_k$.

$symbol(>, 0, 0) \leftarrow.$
$symbol(\sqcup, k + 1, 0) \leftarrow.$

(d) $trans(s, \alpha, s', \beta, p).$: as specified by δ. Note that there are restrictions on this such as $\delta(S, >) = (S', >, \rightarrow)$.

(3) We now describe the remaining rules of $\pi(M, I)$ that describe how the states, the symbols in the tape, and the position of the cursor change.

(a) State change:

$$state(S, T + 1) \leftarrow state(S', T), cursor(N, T), symbol(A, N, T),$$
$$trans(S', A, S, \_, \_).$$

(b) Cursor location change:

$$cursor(N, T + 1) \leftarrow state(S', T), cursor(N, T), symbol(A, N, T),$$
$$trans(S', A, S, \_, -).$$
$$cursor(N - 1, T + 1) \leftarrow state(S', T), cursor(N, T), symbol(A, N, T),$$
$$trans(S', A, S, \_, \leftarrow).$$
$$cursor(N + 1, T + 1) \leftarrow state(S', T), cursor(N, T), symbol(A, N, T),$$
$$trans(S', A, S, \_, \rightarrow).$$

(c) Which symbols change and which do not:

$$symbol(B, N, T + 1) \leftarrow state(S', T), cursor(N, T), symbol(A, N, T),$$
$$trans(S', A, S, B, \_).$$
$$symbol(A, N, T + 1) \leftarrow cursor(N', T), symbol(A, N, T), less\_than(N, N').$$
$$symbol(A, N, T + 1) \leftarrow cursor(N', T), symbol(A, N, T), less\_than(N', N).$$

(d) Auxiliary predicates. (Note that we cannot define *eq* and then *neq* as the negation of *eq*, as we do not have **not** in our language.)

$less\_than(N, N + 1).$
$less\_than(X, Y) \leftarrow less\_than(X, Z), less\_than(Z, Y).$

$accept \leftarrow state(yes, T).$

The changes in the states, tape symbols, and position of the cursor as defined by the above rules mimic the corresponding changes in the Turing machines. Hence, $M(I) = $ 'yes' iff $\pi(M, I) \models accept$.

Note that the main difference between the above proof and that of Theorem 6.2.3 is that here we are allowed to use function symbols. Thus in the rules in (3)(a), (b) and (c), we have the term $T + 1$ which uses function symbols. In the proof of Theorem 6.2.3 we are dealing with AnsDatalog$^{-\textbf{not}}$ programs and hence are not allowed to use functions symbols.

We now consider the complexity of AnsProlog programs.

Theorem 6.4.2 AnsProlog is Π_1^1 complete. $\qquad\qquad\square$

Proof: (sketch) We show AnsProlog is Π_1^1 complete by first showing that entailment in AnsProlog is in Π_1^1.

Membership: Since AnsProlog programs are also AnsProlog^{or} programs, this follows from the membership proof of Theorem 6.4.4 below which is about AnsProlog^{or} programs.

Next we need to show that a Π_1^1 complete problem is expressible in AnsProlog. We do this by first pointing out that Presburger arithmetic with unary predicates is Π_1^1 complete [Hal91]. Next we point to our proof of Theorem 6.4.6 below where we will show that the general form of Π_1^1 problems is expressible in AnsProlog. Since Π_1^1 complete problems are also Π_1^1 problems, any Π_1^1 complete problem (and we have already mentioned the existence of one such) is expressible in AnsProlog. This completes our proof.

Theorem 6.4.3 AnsProlog under well-founded semantics is Π_1^1 complete.   □

Theorem 6.4.4 AnsProlog^{or} is Π_1^1 complete.   □

Proof: (sketch) We show AnsProlog *or* is Π_1^1 complete by first showing that entailment in AnsProlog is in Π_1^1.

Membership: We show that an AnsProlog^{or} program Π can be transformed to a formula Φ_Π of the form $\forall \mathbf{P} \phi(\mathbf{P}; \mathbf{X})$, such that $\Phi_\Pi(a)$ is *true* iff $\Pi \models R(a)$. The transformation is based on characterizing $\Pi \models R(a)$ in second order logic as $\forall S \exists S'$ (S is a model of Π) implies ($S \models R(a)$ or ($S' \subset S$ and S' is a model of Π^S)).

Without loss of generality let us assume that Π has two sets of predicates, EDBs and IDBs, with the restriction that EDBs do not appear in the head of rules. Let **P** be the set of IDB predicates in Π. Let us denote by $\phi_\Pi(\mathbf{S})$ the universal first-order formula obtained from Π, by treating $\leftarrow$ as classical reverse implication, by replacing each P_i from **P** by a new predicate variable S_i of the same arity, and then doing the conjunction of all the clauses obtained. Let us denote by $\psi_\Pi(\mathbf{S}, \mathbf{S'})$ the universal first-order formula obtained from Π, by treating $\leftarrow$ as classical reverse implication, by replacing each P_i from **P** by a new predicate variable S_i' of the same arity, for every naf-literal **not** $P_i(\mathbf{t})$, adding the literal $\neg S_i(\mathbf{t})$ to the body and then doing the conjunction of all the clauses obtained. The desired formula $\Phi_\Pi(\mathbf{x})$ is then given by the following formula that uses the formulas $\phi_\Pi(\mathbf{S})$ and $\psi_\Pi(\mathbf{S}, \mathbf{S'})$.

$$\forall S \exists S'. \phi_\Pi(\mathbf{S}) \Rightarrow [R(\mathbf{x}) \vee (\psi_\Pi(\mathbf{S}, \mathbf{S'}) \wedge (\mathbf{S'} < \mathbf{S}))]$$

where $(\mathbf{S'} < \mathbf{S})$ stands for $\bigwedge_i (\forall \mathbf{x}_i.(S_i'(\mathbf{x}_i) \Rightarrow S_i(\mathbf{x}_i))) \wedge \bigwedge_i \exists \mathbf{y}_i.(S_i(\mathbf{y}_i) \wedge \neg S_i'(\mathbf{y}_i))$.

     □

Note that the intuitive meanings of the formulas $\phi_\Pi(S)$ and $\psi_\Pi(S, S')$ are that S is a model of Π and S' is a model of Π^S respectively. More precisely, S' is a model of Π^S iff $S \cup S'$ with the transformation is a model of $\psi_\Pi(S, S')$. The Example 111 below illustrates this further.

Although, $\Phi_\Pi(a)$ is *true* iff $\Pi \cup A \models R(a)$ holds, $\Phi_\Pi(x)$ is not of the form $\forall P \phi(P; X)$, and hence not a Π_1^1 formula. Fortunately, it is a $\Pi_2^1(bool)$ formula, which is defined as a collection of Π_2^1 formulas whose first-order parts are boolean combinations of existential formulas. Eiter and Gottlob in [EG97] show that such formulas have equivalent Π_1^1 formulas. Hence there exists a Π_1^1 formula Ψ such that $\Psi(a)$ iff $\Pi \cup A \models R(a)$. This completes the membership part of our proof.

Next we need to show that a Π_1^1 complete problem is expressible in AnsProlog^{or}. Since AnsProlog is a sub-class of AnsProlog^{or}, our claim follows from the earlier result that a Π_1^1 complete problem is expressible in AnsProlog.   □

Example 111 Consider the following AnsProlog program Π:

$p_1(a) \leftarrow \mathbf{not}\ p_2(a).$
$p_2(a) \leftarrow \mathbf{not}\ p_1(a).$
$p_1(b) \leftarrow \mathbf{not}\ p_2(b).$
$p_2(b) \leftarrow \mathbf{not}\ p_1(b).$

Let $S = \{p_1(a), p_1(b), p_2(b)\}$ and $S' = \{p_1(a)\}$. It is easy to see that S' is a model of Π^S.

The formula $\psi_\Pi(S, S')$ is the conjunction of the following four:

$s_1'(a) \Leftarrow \neg s_2'(a), \neg s_2(a).$
$s_2'(a) \Leftarrow \neg s_1'(a), \neg s_1(a).$
$s_1'(b) \Leftarrow \neg s_2'(b), \neg s_2(b).$
$s_2'(b) \Leftarrow \neg s_1'(b), \neg s_1(b).$

It can now be easily shown that the transformation of $S \cup S'$ which is $\{s_1(a), s_1(b), s_2(b), s_1'(a)\}$ is a model of $\psi_\Pi(S, S')$.   □

We now discuss some decidable sub-classes of AnsProlog* that allow function symbols. In [Sha84] Shapiro uses alternating Turing machines to show that AnsProlog$^{-\mathbf{not}}$ programs which satisfy certain restrictions are PSPACE-complete.

Theorem 6.4.5 [Sha84] AnsProlog$^{-\mathbf{not}}$ is PSPACE-complete if each rule is restricted as follows: the body contains only one atom, the size of the head is greater than or equal to that of the body, and the number of occurrences of any variable in the body is less than or equal to the number of its occurrences in the head.   □

Dantsin and Voronkov [DV97] and Vorobyov and Voronkov [VV98] studied the complexity of nonrecursive AnsProlog. In [VV98] complexity of nonrecursive AnsProlog is classified based on the number of constants in the signature (k), number of unary functions (l), number of function symbols (m) of arity ≥ 2, presence of negation and range-restriction. We reproduce a summary of the classification from [DEGV01].

Signature	$(\geq 2, 0, 0)$	$(\_, 1, 0)$	$(\_, \geq 2, 0)$	$(\_, \_, \geq 1)$
			not range-restricted	
no negation	PSPACE	PSPACE	NEXPTIME	NEXPTIME
with negation	PSPACE	PSPACE	$TA(2^{O(n/\log n)},$ $O(n/\log n))$	NONELEMENTARY(n)
			range-restricted	
no negation	PSPACE	PSPACE	PSPACE	NEXPTIME
with negation	PSPACE	PSPACE	PSPACE	$TA(2^{n/\log n}, n/\log n)$

Exercise 27 Show that in the construction of $\psi_\Pi(\mathbf{S}, \mathbf{S}')$ in the proof of Theorem 6.4.4 the addition of the literals $\neg S_i(\mathbf{t})$ is redundant. $\square$

Table 6.3. *Summary of complexity results*

AnsProlog* Class (with Functions)	Complexity type	Complexity Class
AnsProlog$^{-\textbf{not}}$	complexity	recursively enumerable complete
AnsProlog$^{-\textbf{not}}$ (without recursion)	complexity	NEXPTIME-complete
AnsProlog$^{-\textbf{not}}$ (with restrictions[1])	complexity	PSPACE-complete
Stratified AnsProlog (n levels of stratification)	complexity	Σ_{n+1}^0-complete
Non-recursive AnsProlog	data complexity	**P**
AnsProlog (under WFS)	complexity	Π_1^1-complete
AnsProlog	complexity	Π_1^1-complete
AnsProlog$^{or,-\textbf{not}}$	under GCWA	Π_2^0-complete
AnsProlog^{or}	complexity	Π_1^1-complete

6.4.2 *Expressiveness of AnsProlog* sub-classes*

In this section we present the expressiveness of AnsProlog* sub-classes when they have function symbols.

---

[1] Each rule is restricted such that the body contains only one atom, the size of the head is greater than or equal to that of the body, and the number of occurrences of any variable in the body is less than or equal to the number of its occurrences in the head.

Theorem 6.4.6 AnsProlog captures Π_1^1.   □

Proof: To show AnsProlog captures Π_1^1 we have to show (i) (membership): any relation expressed using AnsProlog is in the class Π_1^1; and (ii) a general Π_1^1 relation can be expressed in AnsProlog.

Membership: Shown in the proof of Theorem 6.4.2.

Expresses all Π_1^1 relations: We present a transformation of general Π_1^1 relation Φ of the form $\forall \mathbf{P} \phi(\mathbf{P}; \mathbf{X})$ – where $\mathbf{P}$ is a tuple of predicate variables and ϕ is a first order formula with free variables $\mathbf{X}$, to an AnsProlog program $\Pi(\Phi)$ and show that $\Phi(a)$ is *true* iff $\Pi(\Phi) \models R(a)$. In this we will use the result from [vBD83] that states that using second order skolemization a general Π_1^1 relation Φ is equivalent to a formula of the form $\forall \mathbf{P} \exists \mathbf{y} \forall \mathbf{z}.\phi(\mathbf{x}, \mathbf{y}, \mathbf{z})$. Using this result, assuming that ϕ is of the form $\bigwedge_{1 \le j \le m} (l_{j1}(\mathbf{x}, \mathbf{y}, \mathbf{z}) \vee \cdots \vee l_{jk_j}(\mathbf{x}, \mathbf{y}, \mathbf{z}))$, and assuming that $\mathbf{P} = P_1, \ldots, P_n$, we construct the program $\Pi(\Phi)$ as follows:

(1) For enumerating the predicate P_is, we have the following rules for $1 \le i \le n$.

$P_i(\bar{X}) \leftarrow \mathbf{not}\ P_i'(\bar{X})$.
$P_i'(\bar{X}) \leftarrow \mathbf{not}\ P_i(\bar{X})$.

The above will guarantee that we will have different answer sets each expressing a particular interpretation of the P_i.

(2) For $j = 1, \ldots, m$, we have the following:

$s_j(X, Y, Z) \leftarrow l_{j1}'(X, Y, Z), l_{j2}'(X, Y, Z), \ldots, l_{jk_j}'(X, Y, Z)$.
$unsat(X, Y) \leftarrow s_j(X, Y, Z)$.

(3) $R(X) \leftarrow \mathbf{not}\ unsat(X, Y)$.

Now $\Phi(a)$ is *true* iff
$\forall \mathbf{P} \exists \mathbf{y} \forall \mathbf{z}.\phi(a, \mathbf{y}, \mathbf{z})$ is *true* iff
for all possible interpretations of $P_1, \ldots, P_n$, $\exists \mathbf{y} \forall \mathbf{z}.\phi(a, \mathbf{y}, \mathbf{z})$ is *true* iff
for all possible interpretations of $P_1, \ldots, P_n$, $\exists \mathbf{y} \neg (\exists \mathbf{z} \neg \phi(a, \mathbf{y}, \mathbf{z}))$ is *true* iff
in all answer sets of $\Pi(\Phi)$ for some Y, $unsat(a, Y)$ is *false* iff
$R(a)$ is *true* in all answer sets of $\Pi(\Phi)$ iff
$\Pi(\Phi) \models R(a)$.

Theorem 6.4.7 AnsProlog^{or} captures Π_1^1.   □

Proof:
Membership: Shown in the proof of Theorem 6.4.4.

Expresses all Π_1^1 relations: Since AnsProlog programs are also AnsProlog^{or} programs, and in the last theorem we proved that AnsProlog expresses all Π_1^1 relations, we have that AnsProlog^{or} expresses all Π_1^1 relations.

Theorem 6.4.8 AnsProlog (under well-founded semantics) captures Π_1^1. □

The following table summarizes the expressive power of AnsProlog* sub-classes.

AnsProlog* Class	Relation	Complexity Class
AnsProlog (under WFS)	captures	Π_1^1
AnsProlog	captures	Π_1^1
AnsProlog^{or}	captures	Π_1^1

6.5 Compact representation and compilability of AnsProlog

In this section we focus on the compactness properties of AnsProlog* as a knowl-edge representation language. In particular, given that entailment in function-free AnsProlog is **coNP**-complete, we would like to know if we can represent the same information in some other way with at most a polynomial increase in size so that inferences can be made in polynomial time with respect to this new representation. We will show that the answer to this question is negative, subject to the widely held belief that $\Sigma_2\mathbf{P} \neq \Pi_2\mathbf{P}$. This implies that for an alternative polynomial time inferencing it is very likely that there would be an exponential blow-up in the representation.

In the following we use the formulation from [CDS96, CDS94] to formalize the notion of compact representation and compilability. A problem P with fixed part F and varying part V will be denoted as $[P, F, V]$. Intuitively, a problem $[P, F, V]$ is compilable, if for each instance f of the fixed part F there is a data structure D_f of size polynomial in $|f|$ such that D_f can be used to solve the problem P in polynomial time. More formally,

Definition 89 A problem $[P, F, V]$ is compilable if there exists two polynomials p_1, p_2 and an algorithm ASK such that for each instance f of F there is a data structure D_f such that:

(1) $|D_f| \leq p_1(|f|)$;
(2) for each instance v of V the call $ASK(D_f, v)$ returns yes iff $\langle f, v \rangle$ is a 'yes' instance of P; and
(3) $ASK(D_f, v)$ requires time $\leq p_2(|v| + |D_f|)$. □

Example 112 Consider the problem $[T \models_{prop} q, T, q]$, where T is a propositional theory, $\models_{prop}$ is propositional entailment, and q is a literal. Determining $T \models_{prop} q$ is **coNP**-complete. But the problem $[T \models_{prop} q, T, q]$ is compilable, as we can compile it to a set of literals entailed by T. This set is polynomial in size of the theory T (which includes representation of the alphabet of T), and whether a literal belongs to this set can be determined in polynomial time. The same reasoning would apply to any knowledge representation language with an entailment relation $\models$ if the space of possible queries is polynomial in the size of T.

Now consider the case where q is a conjunction of literals. In that case the space of possible queries is exponential in the size of T. But even then $[T \models_{prop} q, T, q]$ is compilable, as we can compile it to a set S of literals entailed by T and to answer any query which is a conjunction of literals we just have to check if each of the literals in the query is in S. This, of course, can be done in polynomial time.

The above reasoning no longer applies if q can be an arbitrary propositional formula. In [CDS96] it is shown that if $[T \models_{prop} q, T, q]$, where q is an arbitrary propositional formula, is compilable then $\Sigma_2 \mathbf{P} = \Pi_2 \mathbf{P}$, which is believed to be false.   □

We now list similar results about AnsProlog.

Theorem 6.5.1 The problem $[\Pi \models q, \Pi, q]$, where Π is an AnsProlog program, and q is a conjunction of literals, is compilable.   □

Proof: (sketch) As in Example 112 we can compile the above problem $[\Pi \models q, \Pi, q]$ to a set S of literals entailed by Π. Here S is obviously polynomial in the size of Π and to answer any query which is a conjunction of literals we just have to check if each of the literals in the query is in S. This of course can be done in polynomial time.

Theorem 6.5.2 Unless $\Sigma_2 \mathbf{P} = \Pi_2 \mathbf{P}$, the problem $[\Pi \models q, \Pi, q]$, where Π is an AnsProlog program, and q is either a disjunction of positive literals or a disjunction of negative literals, is not compilable.   □

Theorem 6.5.3 The problem $[\Pi \models_{brave} q, \Pi, q]$, where Π is an AnsProlog program, and q is a disjunction of positive literals, is compilable.   □

Proof: (sketch) We can compile the above problem $[\Pi \models q, \Pi, q]$ to a set S of literals which is the union of all the answer sets of Π. Here S is obviously polynomial in the size of Π and to answer any query which is a disjunction of positive literals we just have to check if one of the literals in the query is in S. This of course can be done in polynomial time.

Theorem 6.5.4 Unless $\Sigma_2\mathbf{P} = \Pi_2\mathbf{P}$, the problem $[\Pi \models_{brave} q, \Pi, q]$, where Π is an AnsProlog program, and q is either a conjunction of positive literals or a disjunction of negative literals, is not compilable.   □

6.6 Relationship with other knowledge representation formalisms

In this section we relate AnsProlog* sub-classes with various other knowledge representation formalisms that have been proposed. In particular we consider classical logic formalisms, several nonmonotonic formalisms, and description logics. There are two directions in relating AnsProlog* with other formalisms: (i) Translating a program from a particular AnsProlog* sub-class to another formalism and showing the correspondence between answer sets of the original program and the 'models' of the translation. (ii) Translating a theory in another formalism to an AnsProlog* program and showing the correspondence between the 'models' of the original theory and the answer sets of the translation.

In both cases the expressiveness results about languages shed some light on the existence of such translations. For example, it was shown in [CEG97] that entailment in propositional default logic captures the class $\Pi_2\mathbf{P}$. Since AnsDatalog^{or} also captures $\Pi_2\mathbf{P}$, it means that any propositional default theory can be translated to an AnsDatalog^{or} program and vice-versa with a direct correspondence between their entailments. Similarly the result that AnsProlog captures the class Π_1^1 implies that the circumscriptive formalisms that are within Π_1^1 can be translated to an AnsProlog program and vice-versa with a direct correspondence between their entailments.

The important question about the translations is whether they are 'modular' or not. In Section 6.6.1 we formally define the notion of modular translation and show that there are no modular translations from AnsProlog to any monotonic logics, such as propositional and first order logic.

Because most of the other formalisms are syntactically more complex than AnsProlog* most of the results – in the literature – relating AnsProlog* with other nonmonotonic formalisms are of the type (i). Our focus in this section will also be on these types of result.

We now briefly discuss the implications of such results. These results will tell a practitioner of another logic how to interpret AnsProlog* rules without having to master the semantics of AnsProlog*. Thus they lead to alternative intuitions about AnsProlog* constructs and also suggest how notions of minimization, default reasoning, and knowledge modalities are expressed in AnsProlog*. In the past they have also led to transporting notions from AnsProlog* to the other logics. For example, the idea of stratification was transported to autoepistemic logic in [Gel87] and default logic in [Cho95], the idea of splitting was transported to default logic in [Tur96], default logic was extended with the AnsProlog* connective '*or*' in

[GLPT91], and well-founded semantics for default logic and autoepistemic logic were developed in [BS93].

6.6.1 Inexistence of modular translations from AnsProlog* to monotonic logics

We now formally define the notion of a modular translation from one language to another and show that there is no modular translation from propositional AnsProlog to propositional logic.

Definition 90 A mapping $T(.)$ from the language L_1 to L_2 is said to be *rule-modular* if for any theory (or program) Π in L_1, for each set (possibly empty) of atomic facts F, the 'models' of $\Pi \cup F$ and $T(\Pi) \cup F$ coincide.   □

Proposition 92 There is no rule-modular mapping from propositional AnsProlog to propositional logic.   □

Proof: Consider the AnsProlog program $\Pi = \{p \leftarrow \textbf{not } p.\}$. Suppose there exists a modular mapping T from AnsProlog to propositional logic. Since Π does not have an answer set $T(\Pi)$ is unsatisfiable. But $\Pi \cup \{p \leftarrow .\}$ has the answer set $\{p\}$ while because of monotonicity of propositional logic, $T(\Pi) \cup \{p \leftarrow .\}$ must remain unsatisfiable. Thus T cannot be a modular mapping from AnsProlog to propositional logic.   □

The above proof also suffices – with very little modification – to show that there cannot be any modular translation from AnsProlog to any monotonic logic.

6.6.2 Classical logic and AnsProlog*

In Section 2.1.6 we showed how propositional theories can be mapped to AnsProlog so that there is a one-to-one correspondence between the models of a propositional theory and the answer sets of the corresponding AnsProlog program. In Section 2.1.7 we discussed how to express the entailment of closed first-order queries from AnsProlog* programs. In this section our goal is slightly different. We would like to discuss translation of classical theories – first-order and beyond, to AnsProlog* theories and vice versa so that there is a one-to-one correspondence between the models of a classical theory and the answer sets of the corresponding AnsProlog* program.

In this quest the translations presented in the expressiveness and complexity results (in particular, in Theorems 6.4.2, 6.4.4, 6.4.6, and 6.4.7) are adequate if we only consider Herbrand models.

Example 113 Consider the first-order theory T given by $\exists X. p(X)$.

This can be translated to the following AnsProlog program Π with a one-to-one correspondence between the Herbrand models of T and the answer sets of Π.

$p(X) \leftarrow \textbf{not } n\_p(X)$.
$n\_p(X) \leftarrow \textbf{not } p(X)$.
$good\_model \leftarrow p(X)$.
$\leftarrow \textbf{not } good\_model$. $\qquad\qquad\qquad\qquad\qquad\qquad\qquad\qquad\qquad\qquad$ □

Since the semantics of AnsProlog* is based on the Herbrand Universe and answer sets of AnsProlog programs are Herbrand interpretations there is often a mismatch between classical theories and AnsProlog* programs if we do not restrict ourselves to Herbrand models. The following example illustrates this.

Example 114 Consider the first-order theory T_1 given by $ontable(a) \wedge ontable(b)$ and the AnsProlog* program Π_1 obtained by translating T_1 using the method suggested in the proof of Theorem 6.4.6 given as follows:

$ontable(X) \leftarrow \textbf{not } n\_ontable(X)$.
$n\_ontable(X) \leftarrow \textbf{not } ontable(X)$.
$good\_model \leftarrow ontable(a), ontable(b)$.
$\leftarrow \textbf{not } good\_model$.

Let us consider the query Q given by $\forall X.ontable(X)$. Since entailment in AnsProlog* is defined with respect to Herbrand models only we have[2] $\Pi_1 \models \forall X.ontable(X)$. But since the entailment with respect to first-order theories is not limited to Herbrand models we have $T_1 \not\models \forall X.ontable(X)$. For that reason while using resolution with respect to T_1 and Q, the clauses obtained from $T_1 \cup \{\neg Q\}$ is the set $\{ontable(a), ontable(b), \neg ontable(c)\}$ – where c is a Skolem constant, which does not lead to a contradiction. $\qquad\qquad\qquad\qquad\qquad\qquad$ □

Since in some cases it may be preferable to allow nonHerbrand models, one way to get around it while using AnsProlog* is to judiciously introduce Skolem constants, perhaps derived by transforming the query into a clausal form as is done during resolution.

Exercise 28 Explain why the transformations from AnsProlog and AnsProlog^{or} to classical theories given in Theorem 6.4.4 are not rule-modular. $\qquad\qquad$ □

---

[2] This is no longer true if we have other object constants besides a and b in the language of Π_1.

Exercise 29 Define a new entailment relation $\models_{nh}$ from AnsProlog* programs, where entailment is not restricted to Herbrand models.

Hint: Define $\Pi \models_{nh} Q$, by first transforming $\neg Q$ using the standard techniques in classical logic, to a clausal form possibly including Skolem constants. Use this transformed formula and the standard AnsProlog* entailment relation '$\models$' to define '$\models_{nh}$'. □

Before proceeding to the next section we would like to point out that the method suggested in the proof of Theorem 6.4.6 is one of the better ways to encode classical logic theories in AnsProlog*. Intuitively this method consists of enumerating each predicate in the language and then representing the classical theory as a constraint so as to eliminate any enumeration that does not satisfy the given classical theory. The answer sets of the resulting program all satisfy the classical theory, and there is an answer set corresponding to each Herbrand model of the classical theory as they are not eliminated by the constraints.

6.6.3 Circumscription and AnsProlog

Circumscription was proposed as a nonmonotonic reasoning methodology by Mc-Carthy [McC80]. True to its literal meaning, the idea behind circumscription is to circumscribe one or more predicates in a first-order theory. For example, if a first order theory T consists of the formula $ontable(a) \wedge ontable(b)$, then circumscribing the predicate $ontable$ in T would limit the extent of $ontable$ so that it is true only for those constants for which it needs to be true. In this case the circumscription of $ontable$ in T, denoted by $Circ(T; ontable)$, is equivalent to the formula $\forall X.ontable(X) \Longleftrightarrow (X = a) \vee (X = b)$. In general, circumscription of a predicate p in a theory A containing p, denoted by $Circ(A; p)$, is given by the second order sentence $A(p) \wedge \neg \exists P(A(P) \wedge P < p)$, where $P < p$ means that the extent of P is a strict subset of the extent of p. This can be expressed in classical logic as $(\forall X.P(X) \supset p(X)) \wedge \neg(\forall X.P(X) \equiv p(X))$.

The basic definition of circumscription, as in $Circ(A; p)$, minimizes the extent of p with the stipulation that the interpretation of other predicates, constants, and functions remains unchanged. Often we are willing to vary the interpretation of some of the other predicates, constants, and functions, in order to make the extent of p smaller. In that case we have the more general notion $Circ(A; p; z_1, \ldots, z_n)$, where we minimize p while varying $z_1, \ldots, z_n$. $Circ(A; p; z_1, \ldots, z_n)$ is then given by the second order sentence $A(p, z_1, \ldots, z_n) \wedge \neg \exists P, Z_1, \ldots, Z_n(A(P, Z_1, \ldots, Z_n) \wedge P < p)$.

A model theoretic characterization of $Circ(A; p; z_1, \ldots, z_n)$ is given by defining an ordering $\leq^{p;z}$ between structures, where a structure M is determined by its universe $|M|$ and by the interpretations $M[[c]]$ of all function and predicate constants c in the language. We then say that $M_1 \leq^{p;z} M_2$ holds if (i) $|M_1| = |M_2|$, (ii) $M_1[[c]] = M_2[[c]]$ for every constant c which is different from p and not in z, and (iii) $M_1[[p]] \subseteq M_2[[p]]$.

Proposition 93 [Lif85b] A structure M is a model of $Circ(A; p; z)$ iff M is minimal relative to $\leq^{p;z}$. □

The next generalization of circumscription is to minimize a set of predicates in a theory. We may then have priorities between these predicates. In the absence of priorities the second order definition of $Circ(A; p; z_1, \ldots, z_n)$ remains the same except that p now represents a tuple of predicates $p_1, \ldots, p_m$. In that case $p < P$, where P is a tuple of predicates $P_1, \ldots, P_m$, is defined as $p \leq P \wedge \neg(p = P)$ where $p \leq P$ stands for $p_1 \leq P_1 \wedge \cdots \wedge p_m \leq P_m$ and $p = P$ stands for $p_1 = P_1 \wedge \cdots \wedge p_m = P_m$. The notation $Circ(A; p_1, \ldots, p_m; z_1, \ldots, z_n)$ then denotes the parallel circumscription of $p_1, \ldots, p_m$ in theory A while varying $z_1, \ldots, z_n$. If $n = 0$, we simply write it as $Circ(A; p_1, \ldots, p_m)$.

Theorem 6.6.1 Let Π be an AnsProlog$^{-\textbf{not}}$ program and A_Π be the first order theory obtained from Π by replacing $\leftarrow$ by the classical connective $\Leftarrow$. Then M is an answer set of Π iff M is a Herbrand model of $Circ(A_\Pi; p_1, \ldots, p_m)$ where $p_1, \ldots, p_m$ are all the predicates in Π. □

The above theorem follows directly from Definition 8. It illustrates that, as in circumscription, the basic characterization of AnsProlog$^{-\textbf{not}}$ programs is based on minimality, whereby minimal (with respect to subset ordering) Herbrand models are selected. Selecting minimal models corresponds to parallel circumscription of all the predicates. In the case of AnsProlog programs, because of the **not** operator, simply selecting minimal models is not enough. This was illustrated in Example 13. But for stratified AnsProlog programs, a more restricted notion of minimality, referred to as perfect models in Section 3.2.4, is adequate. This notion of minimality corresponds to a form of circumscription referred to as prioritized circumscription.

In prioritized circumscription, there is a priority between the predicates that are to be circumscribed. Let us assume that the tuple of predicates p can be partitioned into smaller parts $p^1, \ldots, p^k$. Our goal is to circumscribe p, but with the predicates in p^1 being circumscribed at a higher priority than the predicates in p^2 and so on. This is denoted by $Circ(A; p^1 > \cdots > p^k; z_1, \ldots, z_n)$, and its definition, given by $A(p, z_1, \ldots, z_n) \wedge \neg \exists P, Z_1, \ldots, Z_n(A(P, Z_1, \ldots, Z_n) \wedge P \prec p)$, is quite similar to that before, except for the meaning of $\prec$. If q is a tuple of predicates of the same kind as p, and q is partitioned into smaller parts $q^1, \ldots, q^k$, then $p \preceq q$ denotes:

$$\bigwedge_{i=1}^{k} \left(\bigwedge_{j=1}^{i-1} p^j = q^j \supset p^i \leq q^i \right)$$

and $p \prec q$ denotes $p \preceq q \wedge \neg(p = q)$. We can now relate answer sets of stratified AnsProlog programs with prioritized circumscription of the transformation of the AnsProlog program into a first-order theory, where the priorities are based on the stratification. More formally,

Theorem 6.6.2 Let Π be a stratified AnsProlog program with the stratification $\pi_1, \ldots, \pi_k$. Let A_Π be the first-order theory obtained from Π by replacing **not** by $\neg$ and $\leftarrow$ by $\Leftarrow$. Then M is an answer set of Π iff M is a Herbrand model of $Circ(A_\Pi; \pi^1 > \cdots > \pi^k)$. $\square$

There are relatively fewer results that relate programs beyond stratified AnsProlog with circumscription. In [Prz89c] Przymusinski considers AnsProlog programs in general and relates the well-founded semantics with a 3-valued notion of circumscription. In [Lin91] Lin presents a translation from propositional AnsProlog theories to circumscription. Given a propositional AnsProlog program Π all of the atoms of which are from a set L, a propositional theory $prop\_circ_L(\Pi)$ is obtained from Π as follows:

- For each rule of the form '$L_0 \leftarrow L_1, \ldots, L_m, \textbf{not } L_{m+1}, \ldots, \textbf{not } L_n$.' in Π, the theory $prop\_circ_L(\Pi)$ consists of the following:

  $$L_1 \wedge \cdots \wedge L_m \wedge \neg L'_{m+1} \wedge \cdots \wedge \neg L'_n \supset L_0$$

  where the L_i are not in L.

Theorem 6.6.3 [Lin91] Let Π be a propositional AnsProlog program all of the atoms of which are from a set L, and let $prop\_circ_L(\Pi)$ be the propositional theory obtained as above. The answer sets of Π have a one-to-one correspondence with the models of $Circ(prop\_circ_L(\Pi); L) \cup \{p \equiv p' \mid p \in L\}$. $\square$

In the above results we discussed transforming AnsProlog programs to a circumscriptive formalism. In regard to the opposite, it must be noted that the second-order formulation of circumscription in general does not fall within the general form of the Π^1_1 complexity class. In particular, it was shown in [Sch87] that all Δ^1_2 sets of natural numbers are definable by means of circumscription. Hence, circumscription cannot in general be expressed in AnsProlog*. Nevertheless, several special cases have been identified in the literature [Lif94] where the circumscribed theory is equivalent to a first-order formalism. Those theories can then be expressed in AnsProlog*. Similarly, when the theory to be circumscribed is of the form A_Π in the Theorems 6.6.1 and 6.6.2, then of course those results give the relation between such a circumscriptive theory and the corresponding AnsProlog program. The identification of additional special cases where a circumscribed theory is equivalent to an AnsProlog program obtained by translating the former is still open.

6.6.4 Autoepistemic logic and AnsProlog*

Autoepistemic logic was proposed by Moore in [Moo85] to express nonmonotonic reasoning through introspection. Although syntactically a theory in autoepistemic logic is also a theory in (modal) nonmonotonic logics proposed by McDermott and Doyle in [MD80, McD82], Moore's autoepistemic logic avoids several pitfalls of the logics in [MD80, McD82]. Nevertheless, the ideas of McDermott and Doyle [MD80, McD82] were revived later and it was shown that the nonmonotonic version of certain modal logics also avoids the pitfall of the original logics proposed in [MD80, McD82]. This is detailed in the book [MT93]. In this section we focus on the relation between autoepistemic logic and AnsProlog* as this relationship is well studied compared to the other nonmonotonic modal logics.

To motivate autoepistemic logic and differentiate it from nonmonotonic logics based on default reasoning Moore wrote in [Moo85]:

> *Consider my reason for believing that I do not have an older brother. It is surely not that one of my parents casually remarked, 'You know, you don't have any older brothers', nor have I pieced it together by carefully sifting other evidence. I simply believe that if I did have an older brother I would know about it; therefore, since I don't know of any older brothers, I must not have any.*

The language $\mathcal{L}_B$ of an autoepistemic logic is defined – over a set of propositions S, as the least set $\mathcal{U}$ of strings such that:

(1) $S \subset \mathcal{U}$,
(2) if $\varphi \in \mathcal{U}$ then $\neg\varphi \in \mathcal{U}$,
(3) if $\varphi_1, \varphi_2 \in \mathcal{U}$ then $(\varphi_1 \vee \varphi_2) \in \mathcal{U}$, $(\varphi_1 \wedge \varphi_2) \in \mathcal{U}$, and
(4) if $\varphi \in \mathcal{U}$ then $B\varphi \in \mathcal{U}$.

Elements of $\mathcal{L}_B$ are called *formulas*, and formulas of the form $B\varphi$ are referred to as *modal atoms*. Intuitively, a modal atom $B\varphi$ means that the agent believes φ. Syntactically, an autoepistemic theory is a set of formulas constructed using propositions (in S) and modal atoms of $\mathcal{L}_B$ and propositional connectives $\neg, \vee, \wedge, \supset$, and $\equiv$. Thus an autoepistemic theory is like a propositional theory except that the 'propositions' in the autoepistemic theory can be either elements of S or modal atoms. (Often in writing an autoepistemic theory we will use predicates, but we will stay within languages with a finite Herbrand base and hence each atom can be thought of as a proposition.)

To define the meaning of autoepistemic theories we first define autoepistemic interpretations. An autoepistemic interpretation is similar to an interpretation of a propositional theory and maps each proposition and modal atom to either *true* or *false*. As in the case of propositional logic, an autoepistemic model M of an autoepistemic theory T must make T true. But there are two additional requirements that capture the notion that the reasoner has perfect introspection capability.

(1) If a formula φ evaluates to *true* with respect to M then $B\varphi$ must be mapped to *true* in M.

(2) If a formula φ evaluates to *false* with respect to M then $B\varphi$ must be mapped to *false* in M.

But as shown by the following example this is still not sufficient to capture the intuitions regarding nonmonotonicity.

Example 115 Consider the following autoepistemic theory which is suppose to capture the statement that if a is a bird and we do not believe that a does not fly then a flies.

$bird(a) \wedge \neg B\neg flies(a) \supset flies(a)$

The above theory has an autoepistemic model where $bird(a)$ is mapped to *true* and $flies(a)$ is mapped to false, which prevents us from concluding solely on the basis of autoepistemic models that a flies.   □

To overcome the above deficiency, autoepistemic theories (T) are characterized using the notion of *expansions* (E) which are a set of formulas such that (i) $T \subseteq E$, (ii) E incorporates perfect introspection, and (iii) all elements of E can be derived using T and the beliefs and nonbeliefs with respect to E. Condition (iii) is the one that was missing in the earlier notion of autoepistemic models. We now formally define the notion of expansions.

Definition 91 For any sets T and E of autoepistemic formulas, E is said to be an expansion of T iff $E = Cn(T \cup \{B\phi : \phi \in E\} \cup \{\neg B\psi : \psi \notin E\})$, where Cn is the propositional consequence operator.   □

A formula F is said to be autoepistemically entailed by T if F belongs to all expansions of T.

Example 116 Let us reconsider the following autoepistemic theory T from Example 115.

$$bird(a) \wedge \neg B\neg flies(a) \supset flies(a)$$

The above theory cannot have an expansion E containing $bird(a)$ and $\neg flies(a)$ as there is no way to derive $\neg flies(a)$ from T and $\{B\phi : \phi \in E\} \cup \{\neg B\psi : \psi \notin E\}$). On the other hand there is an expansion E' containing $bird(a)$ and $flies(a)$. In fact it can be shown that T autoepistemically entails $flies(a)$. $\square$

We now relate answer sets of AnsProlog programs and expansions of autoepistemic theories obtained by a particular transformation.

Theorem 6.6.4 [MT89] Let Π be a propositional AnsProlog program. Let $auto_1(\Pi)$ be an autoepistemic theory obtained by translating each rule in Π of the form

$$L_0 \leftarrow L_1, \ldots, L_m, \textbf{not } L_{m+1}, \ldots, \textbf{not } L_n.$$

to the autoepistemic formula

$$L_1 \wedge \cdots \wedge L_m \wedge \neg BL_{m+1} \wedge \cdots \wedge \neg BL_n \supset L_0.$$

Then M is an answer set of Π iff there is an expansion E of $auto_1(\Pi)$ such that $M = E \cap HB_\Pi$. $\square$

The above theorem suggests that the negation as failure operator in AnsProlog programs can be understood as an epistemic operator. In fact historically the definition of stable models in [GL88] was inspired by this transformation, which was earlier proposed in [Gel87] to show that the perfect models of stratified logic programs can be characterized in terms of expansions of the corresponding autoepistemic theory.

Theorem 6.6.5 [Lif93a, Che93] Let Π be a propositional AnsProlog^{or} program. Let $auto_2(\Pi)$ be an autoepistemic theory obtained by translating each rule in Π of the form

$$L_0 \text{ } or \cdots or \text{ } L_k \leftarrow L_{k+1}, \ldots, L_m, \textbf{not } L_{m+1}, \ldots, \textbf{not } L_n.$$

to an autoepistemic formula of the form

$$(L_{k+1} \wedge B\,L_{k+1}) \wedge \cdots \wedge (L_m \wedge B\,L_m) \wedge \neg B\,L_{m+1} \wedge \cdots \wedge \neg B\,L_n \supset$$
$$(L_0 \wedge B\,L_0) \vee \cdots \vee (B\,L_k \wedge L_k).$$

Then M is an answer set of Π iff there exists an expansion E of $auto_2(\Pi)$ such that $M = E \cap HB_\Pi$. $\square$

In the quest for a direct relationship between autoepistemic logic and Reiter's default theory, Marek and Truszczyński propose a more restricted notion of expansion, which they call *iterative expansion*. We now define iterative expansions of autoepistemic theories and relate them to answer sets.

Definition 92 For a set of formulas S, let $D(S) = Cn(S \cup \{B\varphi : \varphi \in S\})$.

Given sets E and A of formulas,

$D_0^E(A) = Cn(A \cup \{\neg B\varphi : \varphi \notin E\})$.
$D_{n+1}^E(A) = D(D_n^E(A))$.
$D^E(A) = \bigcup_{0 \le n \le \omega} D_n^E(A)$.

Then E is an iterative expansion of A iff $E = D^E(A)$. $\qquad \square$

Theorem 6.6.6 [MT91] Let Π be a propositional AnsProlog program. Let $auto_3(\Pi)$ be an autoepistemic theory obtained by translating each rule in Π of the form

$L_0 \leftarrow L_1, \ldots, L_m, \text{not } L_{m+1}, \ldots, \text{not } L_n$.

to the autoepistemic formula

$BL_1 \wedge \cdots \wedge BL_m \wedge \neg BBL_{m+1} \wedge \cdots \wedge \neg BBL_n \supset L_0$

Then M is an answer set of Π iff there is an iterative expansion E of $auto_3(\Pi)$ such that $M = E \cap HB_\Pi$. $\qquad \square$

6.6.5 *Default logic and AnsProlog**

The most widely studied default logic was proposed by Reiter in [Rei80]. Other default logics that have been put forward include [Luk84, Bre91, PP94]. In this section we focus on Reiter's default logic, which we will simply refer to as default logic and relate it to AnsProlog*. Reiter's default logic is similar to AnsProlog* in its use of variables as schema variables. Thus in this section we will focus on the default theories where the variables[3] have already been instantiated, resulting in a propositional default logic.

A default theory consists of two parts: a propositional theory, and a set of nonstandard inference rules referred to as *defaults*. The nonmonotonicity of default logic is due to the role defaults play. The normative statement 'normally birds fly' can be expressed as the default 'if X is a bird and it is consistent to assume that X flies then conclude that X flies'. Thus if we know tweety to be a bird and have no other information about tweety, then this default would lead us to make the conclusion

---

[3] A predicate default logic is proposed in [Lif90]. But its relationship with AnsProlog* is not well studied. Hence we do not discuss it here.

that tweety flies. On the other hand, if additional information about tweety being a penguin, and penguins inability to fly is added to our knowledge base then it is no longer consistent to assume that tweety flies. Hence the above default can no longer be used to conclude that tweety flies. This demonstrates the nonmonotonicity of reasoning with defaults.

Syntactically, given a propositional language L a *default* d is an expression of the form

$$\frac{p(d) : j(d)}{c(d)} \tag{6.6.1}$$

where $p(d)$ and $c(d)$ are propositional formulas in L and $j(d)$ is a set of propositional formulas in L. The notation $p(d)$ is called the *prerequisite* of d, $j(d)$ is called the *justification* of d and $c(d)$ is called the *consequent* or *conclusion* of d.

The normative statement 'normally birds fly' can then be expressed as the set of defaults given by the schema

$$\frac{bird(X) : fly(X)}{fly(X)}.$$

A default theory is a pair (D, W) where D is a set of defaults, and W is a set of propositional formulas in L. The semantics of default theories are defined in terms of sets of formulas called *extensions*. Extensions of a default theory (D, W) are defined as fixpoints of a function $\Gamma_{(D,W)}$ between sets of propositional formulas. The function $\Gamma_{(D,W)}$ associated with the default theory (D, W) is defined as follows:

Given a set E of propositional formulas $\Gamma_{(D,W)}(E)$ is the smallest set of sentences such that

(i) $W \subseteq \Gamma_{(D,W)}(E)$,
(ii) for any default of the form (6.6.1) from D, if $p(d) \in \Gamma_{(D,W)}(E)$ and $\neg j(d) \cap E = \emptyset$
    then $c(d) \in \Gamma_{(D,W)}(E)$, where $\neg j(d) = \{\neg \beta : \beta \in j(d)\}$, and
(iii) $\Gamma_{(D,W)}(E)$ is deductively closed.

A set of propositional formulas E is said to be an *extension* of a default theory (D, W) if $\Gamma_{(D,W)}(E) = E$. We now relate answer sets of AnsProlog* programs with the extensions of several translations of these programs to default theories.

Theorem 6.6.7 [GL90] Let Π be a propositional AnsProlog$^-$ program. Let $(D_1(\Pi), \emptyset)$ be a default theory obtained by translating each rule in Π of the form

$$L_0 \leftarrow L_1, \ldots, L_m, \textbf{not } L_{m+1}, \ldots, \textbf{not } L_n.$$

to the default

$$\frac{L_1 \wedge \cdots \wedge L_m : \bar{L}_{m+1}, \ldots, \bar{L}_n}{L_0}$$

where $\bar{L}$ denotes the literal complementary to L.

(i) A set M of literals is an answer set of Π iff $Cn(M)$ is an extension of $(D_1(\Pi), \emptyset)$.

(ii) A set of formulas E is an extension of $(D_1(\Pi), \emptyset)$ iff $E = Cn(E \cap Lit_\Pi)$ and $E \cap Lit_\Pi$ is an answer set of Π.

(iii) If E_1 and E_2 are two extensions of $(D_1(\Pi), \emptyset)$ and $E_1 \cap Lit_\Pi = E_2 \cap Lit_\Pi$, then $E_1 = E_2$. $\qquad\square$

The above result is a simple extension of results from [BF91], and [MT89].

The significance of the above result is that every AnsProlog$^\neg$ program can be identified with a particular default theory, and hence AnsProlog$^\neg$ programs can be considered as a special case of a default theory. On the other hand default theories all of whose defaults have justifications and consequents as literals, preconditions as conjunction of literals, and the W part as empty can be thought of as AnsProlog$^\neg$ programs. We now present some additional translations from AnsProlog programs to default theories and relate them.

Theorem 6.6.8 [MT89] Let Π be a propositional AnsProlog program. Let $(D_2(\Pi), \emptyset)$ be a default theory obtained by translating each rule in Π of the form

$$L_0 \leftarrow L_1, \ldots, L_m, \textbf{not } L_{m+1}, \ldots, \textbf{not } L_n.$$

to the default

$$\frac{: \neg L_{m+1}, \ldots, \neg L_n}{L_1 \wedge \cdots \wedge L_m \Rightarrow L_0}.$$

A set M of atoms is an answer set of Π iff there is an extension E of $(D_2(\Pi), \emptyset)$ such that $M = E \cap HB_\Pi$. $\qquad\square$

Theorem 6.6.9 [MT89] Let Π be a propositional AnsProlog program. Let $(D_3(\Pi), W_3(\Pi))$ be a default theory obtained by translating each rule in Π of the form

$$L_0 \leftarrow L_1, \ldots, L_m, \textbf{not } L_{m+1}, \ldots, \textbf{not } L_n.$$

to the default

$$\frac{L_1 \wedge \cdots \wedge L_m : \neg L_{m+1}, \ldots, \neg L_n}{L_0}$$

when $m \neq n$, and to the formula $L_1 \wedge \cdots \wedge L_m \Rightarrow L_0$ in $W_3(\Pi)$, when $m = n$.

(i) A set M of atoms is an answer set of Π iff there is an extension E of $(D_3(\Pi), W_3(\Pi))$ such that $M = E \cap HB_\Pi$.

(ii) A set of formulas E is an extension of $(D_3(\Pi), W_3(\Pi))$ iff $E = Cn(W_3(\Pi) \cup (E \cap HB_\Pi))$ and $E \cap HB_\Pi$ is an answer set of Π.

(iii) If E_1 and E_2 are extensions of $(D_3(\Pi), W_3(\Pi))$ and $(E_1 \cap HB_\Pi) = (E_2 \cap HB_\Pi)$, then $E_1 = E_2$. □

Somewhat surprisingly, the above results are not easily generalized to AnsProlog^{or}. One of the problems in finding a natural translation from AnsProlog^{or} programs to default theories is related to the inability to use defaults with empty justifications in reasoning by cases. The default theory $(D, W) = (\{\frac{q:}{p}, \frac{r:}{p}\}, \{q \vee r\})$ does not have an extension containing p and, therefore, does not entail p. It is easy to see that its AnsProlog^{or} counterpart entails p.

Two proposals have been made to overcome this. As pointed out in [Tur95], modifying (D, W) by adding $\{\frac{\neg q:}{\neg q}, \frac{q:}{q}, \frac{\neg r:}{\neg r}, \frac{r:}{r}\}$ to D will result in the intuitive conclusion of p.

In [GLPT91] a disjunctive default theory is proposed where disjunctions similar to the one in AnsProlog^{or} are added to default theory. In that formulation (D, W) would instead be written as $(\{\frac{q:}{p}, \frac{r:}{p}, \frac{:}{q|r}\}, \emptyset)$ and this theory would entail p.

6.6.6 Truth maintenance systems and AnsProlog*

In this section we will briefly discuss the relationship between AnsProlog programs and nonmonotonic truth maintenance systems (TMSs) [Doy79]. Systems of this sort, originally described by procedural (and sometimes rather complicated) means, have served as the inference engines of some AI reasoning systems. We will follow a comparatively simple description of TMSs from [Elk90]. We will need the following terminology: a *justification* is a set of directed propositional clauses of the form $\alpha \wedge \beta \supset c$ where c is an atom, α is a conjunction of atoms, and β is a conjunction of negated atoms. By an interpretation we will mean a set of atoms. The justification $\alpha \wedge \beta \supset c$ *supports* the atom c with respect to an interpretation M if $\alpha \wedge \beta$ is *true* in M. A model M of a set of justifications Π is *grounded* if it can be written as $M = \{c_1, \ldots, c_n\}$ such that each c_j has at least one justification $\alpha \wedge \beta \supset c_j$ that supports it where $\alpha \subseteq \{c_1, \ldots, c_{j-1}\}$. The task of a nonmonotonic TMS is to find a grounded model of a set of justifications Π.

The form of justifications suggests the obvious analogy with rules of AnsProlog programs where negated literals $\neg A$ from β are replaced by **not** A. For a nonmonotonic TMS Π let us denote the corresponding AnsProlog program by Π^*.

The following theorem establishes the relationship between TMSs and AnsProlog programs:

Theorem 6.6.10 [Elk90] An interpretation M is a grounded model of a collection of justifications Π iff it is an answer set of the program Π^*.   □

Similar results were obtained in [WB93], [GM90], [PC89], [RM89], and [FH89]. (The last two papers use autoepistemic logic instead of AnsProlog* programs.) They led to a better understanding of the semantics of nonmonotonic truth maintenance systems, to their use in computing answer sets [Esh90] and autoepistemic expansions [JK91], for doing abductive reasoning [IS91], [RP91], and to the development of variants of TMSs based on other semantics of logic programs. A good description of one such system, based on the well-founded semantics, together with the proof of its tractability can be found in [Wit91].

6.6.7 Description logics and AnsProlog*

One of the important sub-fields of knowledge representation and reasoning centers around *description logics*, also referred to as *concept languages* and *terminological systems* at different stages of its evolution. Its origin traces back to *frame based systems* and *semantic networks*, both early attempts to represent the classification of objects to a hierarchy of classes (with respect to the subset relationship), represent (mostly binary) relationships between classes, and reason with such information. A critical evolutionary step in this field, the KL-ONE system [BS85], formalized the main ideas in various frame based and semantic network based systems into a logical characterization of classes (or concepts), and relationships (or roles), and proposed a set of constructs to build new classes and relationships from these. Since then several different description logics have been proposed, each distinguished by the constructs and kinds of relationships allowed. Many of these have been implemented (for example, [BBMR89]), usually in sound but incomplete fashion. We now start with a small example of representation using description logic.

Example 117 Consider a simple hierarchy of concepts with *person* at the top (meaning every object in the world is a person) and beneath it the atomic concepts *male* and *female*. Also, let *childof* be an atomic relation. Using these we can define a new concept *child* consisting of elements x such that there exists a person y and (x, y) belongs to the relation *childof* (i.e., x is a child of y). In classical logic this is expressed as $child(x) \equiv \exists y \; childof(x, y) \land person(y)$. In description logic it is said that the concept *child* can be formed using the concept *person* and the role *childof* using the construct $\exists^{\geq n}$ as $\exists^{\geq 1} childof.person$. Since *person* is the top concept, it may be skipped and it is enough to write $\exists^{\geq 1} childof$ or simply $\exists childof$. Similarly, a concept *son* can be formed by *male* ⊓ *child* meaning that the concept *son* consists of elements who are both *male* and *child*. In Borgida's [Bor92] syntax, the above definitions of *child* and *son* are expressed as *child* = **at-least**[1, *childof*] and *son* = **and**[*male, child*].

□

Many consider description logic expressions to be easier to write and follow than the corresponding expression in classical logic, as in the former the variables are not explicitly specified. Some query languages for querying object oriented databases also have a similar syntax.

A knowledge base in a description logic consists of two parts traditionally referred to as the *TBox* (meaning 'Terminological Box') and the *ABox* (meaning 'Assertional Box'). The first consists of several assertions about concepts and roles, such as the definition of *child* and *son* in the above example, and the second consists of specific facts about a particular object belonging to a concept or a particular pair of objects belonging to a particular role, such as Jim being the child of Mary.

In the absence of an *ABox*, the questions of interest are whether two concepts are equivalent, whether one concept subsumes another, whether a concept is consistent (is nonempty), or whether a knowledge base as a whole is consistent. For example, from a knowledge base consisting of the *TBox* with the assertion *son* = **and**[*male, child*], we can conclude that the concepts *male* and *child* subsume the concept *son*. That is, every son is both a male and a child. At first glance it is often not clear why one should care about subsumption between concepts. This becomes clear when one considers reasoning in the presence of an *ABox*. Given a knowledge base with a nonempty *ABox*, the questions of interest are whether a particular object belongs to a particular concept or whether two objects have a particular role. To answer the first, concept subsumption is often an intermediate step. For example, given that *john* is a *son* we can easily conclude that *john* is a *male* if we are able to figure out that the concept *male* subsumes the concept *son*. Besides such reasoning, another important usefulness of description logic is that it can be used in expressing intensional answers to queries to a database. In other words instead of giving an answer as a set of objects, the answer can be expressed as a concept defined using description logic constructors in terms of other concepts and classes. Such answers are often more informative than the standard approach of listing individual objects.

Similarly to the origin of logic programming, where a subset of first-order formulas called Horn clauses were chosen for efficient reasoning, initial description logics focused on a select set of constructors that were expected to lead to efficient implementations. Many of the early implementations were subsequently found to be incomplete and since then expressiveness has also become an important issue in description logics and many new constructors have been proposed. Currently many people view descriptions logics to be useful in expressing *a particular part* of a knowledge base that is about concepts and roles and expect the complete knowledge base to consist of other parts in other knowledge representation languages.

Our main goal in this section is to show how reasoning in description logics can be done through a translation to AnsProlog. For this we consider the description logic language $\mathcal{ALCQI}$ [CDNL01]. We now start by formally defining this logic.

Concepts and roles in $\mathcal{ALCQI}$: syntax and semantics

Concepts and roles in $\mathcal{ALCQI}$ are formed using the following syntax:

$$C, C' \longrightarrow A \mid \neg C \mid C \sqcap C' \mid C \sqcup C' \mid \forall R.C \mid \exists R.C \mid \exists^{\geq n} R.C \mid \exists^{\leq n} R.C$$

$$R \longrightarrow P \mid P^-$$

where A and P are atomic concepts and atomic roles respectively, C and R denote arbitrary concepts and roles, and n denotes a positive integer. For readability, for any atomic concept A, $A \sqcap \neg A$ is abbreviated as $\bot$, and $A \sqcup \neg A$ is abbreviated as $\top$. Similarly, $\neg C \sqcup D$ is abbreviated as $C \Rightarrow D$, $\exists^{\geq n} R.C \sqcap \exists^{\leq n} R.C$ is abbreviated as $\exists^{=n} R.C$, and $R.\top$ is abbreviated as R.

Concepts are interpreted as subsets of a domain, and roles as binary relations over that domain. An interpretation $\mathcal{I} = (\Delta^{\mathcal{I}}, \cdot^{\mathcal{I}})$ over a set $\mathcal{I}$ of atomic concepts and a set $\mathcal{P}$ of atomic roles consists of a nonempty set $\Delta^{\mathcal{I}}$ (the domain of $\mathcal{I}$) and a function $\cdot^{\mathcal{I}}$ that maps every atomic concept $A \in \mathcal{I}$ to a subset of $\Delta^{\mathcal{I}}$ and every atomic role $P \in \mathcal{P}$ to a subset $P\mathcal{I}$ of $\Delta^{\mathcal{I}} \times \Delta^{\mathcal{I}}$. The interpretation function is extended to arbitrary concepts and roles as follows:

$(\neg C)^{\mathcal{I}} = \Delta^{\mathcal{I}} \setminus C^{\mathcal{I}}$.
$(C \sqcap C')^{\mathcal{I}} = C^{\mathcal{I}} \cap C'^{\mathcal{I}}$.
$(C \sqcup C')^{\mathcal{I}} = C^{\mathcal{I}} \cup C'^{\mathcal{I}}$.
$(\forall R.C)^{\mathcal{I}} = \{o \in \Delta^{\mathcal{I}} \mid \forall o'.(o, o') \in R^{\mathcal{I}} \rightarrow o' \in C^{\mathcal{I}}\}$.
$(\exists R.C)^{\mathcal{I}} = \{o \in \Delta^{\mathcal{I}} \mid \exists o'.(o, o') \in R^{\mathcal{I}} \wedge o' \in C^{\mathcal{I}}\}$.
$(\exists^{\geq n} R.C)^{\mathcal{I}} = \{o \in \Delta^{\mathcal{I}} : |\{o' \mid (o, o') \in R^{\mathcal{I}} \wedge o' \in C^{\mathcal{I}}\}| \geq n\}$.
$(\exists^{\leq n} R.C)^{\mathcal{I}} = \{o \in \Delta^{\mathcal{I}} : |\{o' \mid (o, o') \in R^{\mathcal{I}} \wedge o' \in C^{\mathcal{I}}\}| \leq n\}$.
$(R^-)^{\mathcal{I}} = \{(o, o') \in \Delta^{\mathcal{I}} \times \Delta^{\mathcal{I}} \mid (o', o) \in R^{\mathcal{I}}\}$.

Definition 93 A concept C is said to be *satisfiable* if it has a nonempty interpretation. Given two concepts C_1 and C_2, we say C_2 *subsumes* C_1 if $C_1^{\mathcal{I}} \subseteq C_2^{\mathcal{I}}$ holds in every interpretation. □

Knowledge bases in $\mathcal{ALCQI}$: TBox and ABox

A knowledge base (in $\mathcal{ALCQI}$) consists of two parts: a *TBox* and an *ABox*. The *TBox* consists of a finite set of *inclusion assertions* of the form:

$$C_1 \sqsubseteq C_2 \qquad (6.6.2)$$

where C_1 and C_2 are concepts. Often we will abbreviate the two assertions $C_1 \sqsubseteq C_2$ and $C_2 \sqsubseteq C_1$ by the single statement $C_1 \equiv C_2$.

If C_1 above is an atomic concept then it is referred to as a *primitive inclusion assertion* and statements of the form $C_1 \equiv C_2$ are then referred to as *equality assertions*.

An interpretation $\mathcal{I}$ is said to satisfy an assertion of the form $C_1 \sqsubseteq C_2$ if $C_1^{\mathcal{I}} \subseteq C_2^{\mathcal{I}}$. The *ABox* consists of *fact assertions* of the form:

$$C(a) \qquad \text{and} \qquad R(a, b) \qquad (6.6.3)$$

where C is a concept, R is a role, and a, b are elements of a new alphabet HB. In the presence of a nonempty *ABox* the interpretation function $\cdot^{\mathcal{I}}$ is extended to individuals in HB such that $a^{\mathcal{I}} \in \Delta^{\mathcal{I}}$ for each individual $a \in HB$ and $a^{\mathcal{I}} \neq b^{\mathcal{I}}$ if $a \neq b$.

A fact assertion $C(a)$ is said to be satisfied by an interpretation $\mathcal{I}$ if $a^{\mathcal{I}} \in C^{\mathcal{I}}$, and a fact assertion $R(a, b)$ is said to be satisfied by an interpretation $\mathcal{I}$ if $(a^{\mathcal{I}}, b^{\mathcal{I}}) \in C^{\mathcal{I}}$.

Definition 94 An interpretation is said to be a model of a knowledge base $\mathcal{K}$ if it satisfies all assertions in it; $\mathcal{K}$ is said to be *satisfiable* if it has a model; a concept C is said to be *consistent* in $\mathcal{K}$ if $\mathcal{K}$ has a model $\mathcal{I}$ such that $C^{\mathcal{I}} \neq \emptyset$; and for an assertion α, we say $\mathcal{K} \models^{dl} \alpha$, if α is satisfied by each model $\mathcal{I}$ of $\mathcal{K}$. $\square$

Since in AnsProlog* the semantics is defined with respect to a Herbrand Universe, we will define a restricted notion of interpretation, models, and entailment for description logics.

Definition 95 An *HB*-interpretation is an interpretation where the domain is *HB*. An *HB*-interpretation is said to be an *HB*-model of a knowledge base $\mathcal{K}$ if it satisfies all assertions in it; and $\mathcal{K} \models^{dl}_{HB} \alpha$, if α is satisfied by each *HB*-model $\mathcal{I}$ of $\mathcal{K}$. $\square$

Translating $\mathcal{ALCQI}$ to AnsProlog

Before we give a general translation from $\mathcal{ALCQI}$ to AnsProlog we will first illustrate the problem with a straightforward and simplistic translation. This translation was used in [Bor92] to demonstrate an inadequacy of logic programming in modeling such knowledge.

Example 118 A straightforward translation of the TBox assertions (from Example 117) *child* = there exists *childof* and *son* = *male* ⊓ *child* to declarative logic programming would be the following rules.

r_1: *child*(X) ← *childof*(X, Y).
r_2: *son*(X) ← *male*(X), *child*(X).

The above AnsProlog program is equivalent to the first-order formulas

(∀X.*child*(X) ⟷ ∃Y *childof*(X, Y))∧
(∀X.*son*(X) ⟺ *male*(X) ∧ *child*(X)).

The TBox assertions are also equivalent to the above formulas. Nevertheless, if we add the fact assertion *son*(a) to the description logic knowledge base then we will be able to infer *child*(a), while the same is not true for the logic program translation. That is, while {*child* = ∃ *childof*, *son* = *male* ⊓ *child*, *son*(a)} ⊨^{dl} *child*(a), {r_1, r_2, *son*(a)} ⊭ *child*(a).   □

The above illustrated inadequacy is now well understood in logic programming and proposals have been made to overcome it. In the following example, we use AnsProlog to enumerate the predicates *male* and *childof* and assimilate *son*(a) through filtering.

Example 119 Besides r_1 and r_2, the AnsProlog translation will consist of the following rules:

r_3: *male*(X) ← *top*(X), **not** *female*(X).
r_4: *female*(X) ← *top*(X), **not** *male*(X).
r_5: *childof*(X, Y) ← *top*(X), *top*(Y), X ≠ Y, **not** *not_childof*(X, Y).
r_6: *not_childof*(X, Y) ← *top*(X), *top*(Y), X ≠ Y, **not** *childof*(X, Y).
r_7:   ← *childof*(X, Y), *childof*(Y, X).

and facts about the predicate *top* listing all elements belonging to the concept ⊤.
    Now to assimilate the *son*(a) we need to add the following:

r_8:   ← **not** *son*(a).

whose effect is to eliminate all potential answer sets which do not contain *son*(a).
    Suppose the concept ⊤ consists of objects a and b. In that case the program

$P_1 = \{r_1, r_2, r_3, r_4, r_5, r_6, r_7, top(a), top(b)\}$ will have the following answer sets:
$A_1 = \{top(a), top(b), male(a), male(b), childof(a, b), n\_childof(b, a),$
          $child(a), son(a)\}$.
$A_2 = \{top(a), top(b), male(a), male(b), childof(b, a), n\_childof(a, b),$
          $child(b), son(b)\}$.

$A_3 = \{top(a), top(b), male(a), male(b), n\_childof(a, b), n\_childof(b, a)\}.$
$A_4 = \{top(a), top(b), male(a), female(b), childof(a, b), n\_childof(b, a),$
      $child(a), son(a)\}.$
$A_5 = \{top(a), top(b), male(a), female(b), childof(b, a), n\_childof(a, b), child(b)\}.$
$A_6 = \{top(a), top(b), male(a), female(b), n\_childof(a, b), n\_childof(b, a)\}.$
$A_7 = \{top(a), top(b), female(a), male(b), childof(a, b), n\_childof(b, a), child(a)\}.$
$A_8 = \{top(a), top(b), female(a), male(b), childof(b, a), n\_childof(a, b),$
      $child(b), son(b)\}.$
$A_9 = \{top(a), top(b), female(a), male(b), n\_childof(a, b), n\_childof(b, a)\}.$
$A_{10} = \{top(a), top(b), female(a), female(b), childof(a, b), n\_childof(b, a),$
      $child(a)\}.$
$A_{11} = \{top(a), top(b), female(a), female(b), childof(b, a), n\_childof(a, b),$
      $child(b)\}.$
$A_{12} = \{top(a), top(b), female(a), female(b), n\_childof(a, b), n\_childof(b, a)\}.$

The program P_2 obtained by adding r_8 to P_1 has only the answer sets A_1 and A_4, and since $child(a)$ belongs to both of them we have $P_2 \models^{dl} child(a)$. $\square$

We now give a general translation from $\mathcal{ALCQI}$ to AnsProlog, first focusing only on entailment of fact assertions.

Algorithm 3 $tr(\mathcal{K})$: a general translation to AnsProlog for entailing fact assertions

Notations: In the following if capital letter C is a concept and capital letter R is a role then the small letter c is a predicate that corresponds to C and the small letter r is a predicate that corresponds to R.

Step 1: For each element a of HB the translation contains the fact:

$top(a) \leftarrow.$

Step 2: For each atomic concept B the translation will have the rules:

$b(X) \leftarrow top(X), \textbf{not } not\_b(X).$
$not\_b(X) \leftarrow top(X), \textbf{not } b(X).$

Step 3: For each atomic role P the translation will have the rules:

$p(X, Y) \leftarrow top(X), top(Y), \textbf{not } not\_p(X, Y).$
$not\_p(X, Y) \leftarrow top(X), top(Y), \textbf{not } p(X, Y).$

Step 4: For each fact assertion of the form $C(a)$, the translation will have $tr(C)$ as described in Step 7 below and the following:

$\leftarrow \textbf{not } c(a).$

Step 5: For each fact assertion of the form $R(a, b)$, the translation will have $tr(R)$ as described in Step 8 below and the following:

$\leftarrow$ **not** $r(a, b)$.

Step 6: For each inclusion assertion of the form $C_1 \sqsubseteq C_2$, the translation will have rules defining predicates c_1 and c_2 as described in Step 7 below and the following (if C_1 and C_2 are nonatomic concepts then c_1 and c_2 will be new predicates):

$\leftarrow c_1(X),$ **not** $c_2(X).$

Step 7: For a concept expression C, its definition in terms of a predicate c denoted by $tr(C)$ is as follows:

(1) If C is of the form $\neg C'$, then $tr(C)$ contains the rule:

$c(X) \leftarrow top(X),$ **not** $c'(X).$

and the translation $tr(C')$.

(2) If C is of the form $C_1 \sqcap C_2$, then $tr(C)$ contains the rule:

$c(X) \leftarrow top(X), c_1(X), c_2(X).$

and the translations $tr(C_1)$, and $tr(C_2)$.

(3) If C is of the form $C_1 \sqcup C_2$, then $tr(C)$ contains the rules:

$c(X) \leftarrow top(X), c_1(X).$
$c(X) \leftarrow top(X), c_2(X).$

and the translations $tr(C_1)$, and $tr(C_2)$.

(4) If C is of the form $\forall R.C'$, then $tr(C)$ contains the rules:

$not\_c(X) \leftarrow r(X, Y),$ **not** $c'(Y).$
$c(X) \leftarrow top(X),$ **not** $not\_c(X).$

and the translations $tr(R)$ (to be defined in Step 8), and $tr(C')$.

(5) If C is of the form $\exists R.C'$, then $tr(C)$ contains the rule:

$c(X) \leftarrow r(X, Y), c'(Y).$

and the translations $tr(R)$ (to be defined in Step 8), and $tr(C')$.

(6) If C is of the form $\exists R^{\geq n}.C'$, then $tr(C)$ contains the rule:

$c(X) \leftarrow r(X, Y_1), \ldots, r(X, Y_n), c'(Y_1), \ldots, c'(Y_n),$
$\quad Y_1 \neq Y_2 \neq \cdots \neq Y_n.$

and the translations $tr(R)$ (to be defined in Step 8), and $tr(C')$.

(7) If C is of the form $\exists R^{\leq n}.C'$, then $tr(C)$ contains the rule:

$$not\_c(X) \leftarrow r(X, Y_1), \ldots, r(X, Y_{n+1}), c'(Y_1), \ldots, c'(Y_{n+1}),$$
$$Y_1 \neq Y_2 \neq \cdots \neq Y_{n+1}.$$
$$c(X) \leftarrow top(X), \textbf{not } not\_c(X).$$

and the translations $tr(R)$ (to be defined in Step 8), and $tr(C')$.

Step 8: For an arbitrary role R its definition in terms of a predicate r denoted by $tr(R)$ is as follows:

(1) If R is an atomic role P, then $tr(R)$ contains the rule:

$$r(X, Y) \leftarrow p(X, Y).$$

(2) If R is of the form P^-, where P is an atomic role, then $tr(R)$ contains the rule:

$$r(X, Y) \leftarrow p(Y, X). \qquad \qquad \square$$

Given a description logic knowledge base $\mathcal{K}$, we will denote the AnsProlog program obtained by the above algorithm by $tr(\mathcal{K})$.

Example 120 Let us now consider the example in the beginning of this section and translate it into AnsProlog using tr. The knowledge base consists of $\{child \equiv \exists childof.top, son \equiv male \sqcap child, son(a)\}$, with $HB = \{a, b\}$.

- Step 1.

$top(a) \leftarrow.$
$top(b) \leftarrow.$

- Step 2.

$child(X) \leftarrow top(X), \textbf{not } not\_child(X).$
$not\_child(X) \leftarrow top(X), \textbf{not } child(X).$
$male(X) \leftarrow top(X), \textbf{not } not\_male(X).$
$not\_male(X) \leftarrow top(X), \textbf{not } male(X).$
$son(X) \leftarrow top(X), \textbf{not } not\_son(X).$
$not\_son(X) \leftarrow top(X), \textbf{not } son(X).$

- Step 3.

$childof(X, Y) \leftarrow top(X), top(Y), \textbf{not } not\_childof(X, Y).$
$not\_childof(X, Y) \leftarrow top(X), top(Y), \textbf{not } childof(X, Y).$

- Step 4.

  ← **not** *son(a)*.

- Step 5 is not needed here.
- Step 6.

  ← *child(X)*, **not** *c(X)*.
  ← *c(X)*, **not** *child(X)*.
  ← *son(X)*, **not** *c'(X)*.
  ← *c'(X)*, **not** *son(X)*.

- Step 7.

  c(X) ← childof(X, Y), top(Y).
  c'(X) ← male(X), child(X).   □

Theorem 6.6.11 Let $\mathcal{K}$ be a description logic knowledge base in which C and R appear.

$\mathcal{K} \models^{dl}_{HB} C(a)$ iff $tr(\mathcal{K}) \models c(a)$ and
$\mathcal{K} \models^{dl}_{HB} R(a, b)$ iff and only if $tr(\mathcal{K}) \models r(a, b)$.   □

Note that the above theorem is not true for $\models^{dl}$ instead of $\models^{dl}_{HB}$. The discrepancy may arise when C is a concept using universal quantifiers. For example if $K = \{C(a), R(a, a)\}$ with $HB = \{a\}$ then $K \not\models^{dl} \forall R.C(a)$, while $K \models^{dl}_{HB} \forall R.C(a)$. In the logic programming literature this discrepancy is referred to as the universal query problem and several ways to overcome it are discussed in a later chapter (Section 9.5). We now use one such method.

We now discuss a translation with respect to $\models^{dl}$ (instead of $\models^{dl}_{HB}$) and consider reasoning tasks such as whether a description logic knowledge base $\mathcal{K}$ entails a inclusion assertion; or whether it is satisfiable; or whether a concept is consistent in it. We now give the translation tr'.

Algorithm 4 tr' and qtr: translations for entailing inclusion assertions and other reasoning tasks

Step 1': For each element a of HB the translation contains the fact:

   $top(a) ←.$

In addition, the translation contains the following:

   $top(a') ←.$
   $top(f(X)) ← top(X).$

where a' is an object constant that does not appear in $\mathcal{K}$, and f is a unary function symbol used to construct an infinite Herbrand Universe.

Steps 2–8 remain the same as in Algorithm 3. Given a description logic knowledge base $\mathcal{K}$, we will denote the AnsProlog program obtained by the above steps by $tr'(\mathcal{K})$.

Steps 9: For a query α given as $C_1 \sqsubseteq C_2$, the translation $qtr(\alpha)$ will have (a) rules defining two new predicates c_1 and c_2 as described in Step 7 and (b) the following.

> *violated* $\leftarrow c_1(X)$, **not** $c_2(X)$.
> *satisfied* $\leftarrow$ **not** *violated*. □

In cases where we are only concerned with finite domains the second rule in Step 1' of tr' can be omitted, making the translation simpler.

Theorem 6.6.12 Let $\mathcal{K}$ be a description logic knowledge base and α be an inclusion assertion such that the concepts in α appear in $\mathcal{K}$.

Then $\mathcal{K} \models^{dl} \alpha$ if and only if $tr'(\mathcal{K}) \cup qtr(\alpha) \models$ *satisfied*. □

Lemma 6.6.13 Let $\mathcal{K}$ be a description logic knowledge base. Then C_2 subsumes C_1 in $\mathcal{K}$ iff $\mathcal{K} \models^{dl} C_1 \sqsubseteq C_2$. □

Theorem 6.6.14 Let $\mathcal{K}$ be a description logic knowledge base in which C appears.

(i) $\mathcal{K}$ is satisfiable iff $tr'(\mathcal{K})$ has an answer set.
(ii) A concept C is consistent in $\mathcal{K}$ iff $tr'(\mathcal{K}) \cup \{non\_empty\_c \leftarrow c(X), top(X).\}$ has an answer set containing non_empty_c. □

A translation for description logic knowledge bases with noncyclic equality assertions

The translations in the previous two algorithms are general in the sense that they do not restrict the inclusion assertions. The program obtained by the translation enumerates all the atomic concepts and thus may result in a large search space while computing the answer sets. We now consider a restriction on the inclusion assertions and present a translation that cuts down on the enumeration and hence reduces the search space during answer set computation.

The restriction that we impose, which is also imposed in many early description logic systems, is that the TBox consist only of equality assertions with an atomic concept in the left hand side and that there be no cycles in the sense that no concept in the right hand side of an equality assertion refers (either directly or indirectly) to the atomic concept in the left part of the assertion.

Given such a TBox we refer to those atomic concepts that appear in the left hand side of an equality assertion as *derived atomic concepts* and all other atomic concepts as *nonderived atomic concepts*. We now describe the translation tr_n.

The translation tr_n has the same Steps 1, 3, 4, 5, 7 and 8 as tr. The Step 2 of tr_n enumerates only the *nonderived atomic concepts* other than *top*. In Step 6, for each equality assertion of the form $A \equiv C$, the translation has $tr(C)$ as described in Step 7 of tr and the rule:

$$a(X) \leftarrow c(X).$$

Example 121 Let us now consider our running example with the TBox = {*child* $\equiv$ $\exists$*childof.top*; *son* $\equiv$ *male* $\sqcap$ *child*} and ABox = {*son(a)*}. With respect to this TBox, *son* and *child* are derived atomic concepts while *male* and *top* are non-derived atomic concepts. We now show that the program obtained by tr_n for this description logic knowledge base is very close to the program

$$\{r_1, r_2, r_3, r_4, r_5, r_6, r_7, r_8, top(a) \leftarrow ., top(b) \leftarrow .\}$$

analyzed at the beginning of this section.

Step 1 of tr_n gives us $top(a)$ and $top(b)$. Step 2 of tr_n gives us r_3 and r_4 where we enumerate the nonderived concept *male*. Step 3 gives us r_5 and r_6. Step 4 gives us r_8. Step 6 gives us r_2 and a slight variant of r_1.   □

Theorem 6.6.15 Let $\mathcal{K}$ be a description logic knowledge base whose TBox consists of equality assertions and is noncyclic and in which C and R appear. Then

$\mathcal{K} \models_{HB}^{dl} C(a)$ if and only if $tr_n(\mathcal{K}) \models c(a)$ and
$\mathcal{K} \models_{HB}^{dl} R(a, b)$ if and only if $tr_n(\mathcal{K}) \models r(a, b)$.   □

If it is given that $\mathcal{K}$ is consistent and we are interested in finding out $\mathcal{K} \models_{HB}^{dl}$ $C(a)$ where C is a derived atomic concept then we can even avoid enumeration of nonderived atomic concepts.

6.6.8 Answer set entailment as a nonmonotonic entailment relation

In [KLM90] Kraus, Lehman, and Magidor proposed several intuitive properties that they suggested should be satisfied by nonmonotonic entailment relations. Dix [Dix95a, Dix95b] adapted these properties to the framework of logic programs (he referred to them as *structural properties*) and compared several semantics of logic programming with respect to them. In this section we list how the semantics of AnsProlog and the well-founded semantics fare with respect to these structural properties.

Kraus, Lehman, and Magidor considered an entailment relation ' $\mid\sim$ ' *between single propositional formulas* (α, β, and γ) and defined the following structural properties.

Right Weakening	$\models \alpha \to \beta$	and	$\gamma \mid\sim \alpha$	imply	$\gamma \mid\sim \beta$	
Reflexivity					$\alpha \mid\sim \alpha$	
And	$\alpha \mid\sim \beta$	and	$\alpha \mid\sim \gamma$	imply	$\alpha \mid\sim \beta \wedge \gamma$	
Or	$\alpha \mid\sim \gamma$	and	$\beta \mid\sim \gamma$	imply	$\alpha \vee \beta \mid\sim \gamma$	
Left Logical Equivalence	$\models \alpha \leftrightarrow \beta$	and	$\alpha \mid\sim \gamma$	imply	$\beta \mid\sim \gamma$	
Cautious Monotony	$\alpha \mid\sim \beta$	and	$\alpha \mid\sim \gamma$	imply	$\alpha \wedge \beta \mid\sim \gamma$	
Cut	$\alpha \mid\sim \beta$	and	$\alpha \wedge \beta \mid\sim \gamma$	imply	$\alpha \mid\sim \gamma$	
Rationality	not $(\alpha \mid\sim \neg\beta)$	and	$\alpha \mid\sim \gamma$	imply	$\alpha \wedge \beta \mid\sim \gamma$	
Negation Rationality	$\alpha \mid\sim \beta$	implies	$\alpha \wedge \gamma \mid\sim \beta$	or	$\alpha \wedge \neg\gamma \mid\sim \beta$	
Disjunctive Rationality	$\alpha \vee \beta \mid\sim \gamma$	implies	$\alpha \mid\sim \gamma$	or	$\beta \mid\sim \gamma$	

The above properties were defined for single formulas, but could be easily extended to a relation between *finite* sets of formulas using the connective $\wedge$. For infinite sets of formulas, Makinson [Mak94] used a *closure-operation Cn* to define several of the above mentioned properties and another property called *Cumulativity* which is defined as follows:

Cumulativity: $\Phi \subseteq \Psi \subseteq Cn(\Phi)$ implies $Cn(\Phi) = Cn(\Psi)$.

The following lemma relates Cn and $\mid\sim$ when dealing with finite sets.

Lemma 6.6.16 (Relating Cn and $\mid\sim$ for finite sets) If And holds, Cumulativity is equivalent to Cautious monotony and Cut. $\square$

The above structural properties are not directly applicable to our AnsProlog* as its entailment relation is between AnsProlog* programs and queries. To make it consistent with the notations of $\mid\sim$, we adapt $\mid\sim$ to AnsProlog* and define an entailment relation.

Definition 96 Let Π be an AnsProlog or AnsProlog^{or} program. Let $U = \{u_1, \ldots, u_n\}$ be a set of positive literals and $X = \{x_1, \ldots, x_m\}$ be a set of literals. We define:

$(u_1 \wedge \cdots \wedge u_n) \mid\sim_\Pi (x_1 \wedge \cdots \wedge x_m)$

iff $\Pi \cup \{u_1, \ldots, u_n\} \models x_1 \wedge \cdots \wedge x_m$ $\square$

This adaptation of $\mid\sim$ to $\mid\sim_\Pi$ results in one major difference between $\mid\sim$ and $\mid\sim_\Pi$. While $\mid\sim$ was a relation between propositional formulas, $\mid\sim_\Pi$ is a relation between conjunction of atoms and conjunction of literals. Because of this AnsProlog programs trivially satisfy the properties: Right weakening, Reflexivity, And, and Left logical equivalence. The only properties that remain to be considered are Cumulativity (i.e., Cautious monotony and Cut, since And is satisfied) and Rationality, which is considered as a strengthened form of Cautious monotony.

Theorem 6.6.17 [Dix95a] For stratified AnsProlog programs, its (answer set) semantics is *Cumulative* and *Rational*. □

Theorem 6.6.18 [Dix95a] For AnsProlog programs its (answer set) semantics satisfies Cut but not Cautious monotony. Hence it is not Cumulative. □

Example 122 Consider the following program Π_2:

$a \leftarrow \textbf{not } b.$
$b \leftarrow \textbf{not } a.$
$p \leftarrow \textbf{not } p.$
$p \leftarrow a.$

The above program has the unique answer set $\{p, a\}$. But the program $\Pi_1 \cup \{p\}$ has two answer sets $\{p, a\}$ and $\{p, b\}$, and thus a is not entailed by $\Pi_1 \cup \{p\}$. □

Theorem 6.6.19 [Dix95a] For AnsProlog programs, well-founded semantics is *cumulative* and *rational*. □

In the context of proof theory for their logical system **P** in [KLM90], Kraus, Lehman, and Magidor describe another property defined below which they call *Loop*.

$$\frac{\alpha_0 \mathrel{|\!\sim} \alpha_1, \; \alpha_1 \mathrel{|\!\sim} \alpha_2, \ldots, \alpha_{k-1} \mathrel{|\!\sim} \alpha_k, \; \alpha_k \mathrel{|\!\sim} \alpha_0}{\alpha_0 \mathrel{|\!\sim} \alpha_k} \qquad (Loop)$$

The following example taken from [Dix95a] shows that well-founded semantics does not satisfy *Loop*.

Example 123 Consider the following program Π:

$a_1 \leftarrow a_0, \textbf{not } a_2, \textbf{not } a_3.$
$a_2 \leftarrow a_1, \textbf{not } a_3, \textbf{not } a_0.$
$a_3 \leftarrow a_2, \textbf{not } a_0, \textbf{not } a_1.$
$a_0 \leftarrow a_3, \textbf{not } a_2, \textbf{not } a_1.$

$WFS(\Pi \cup \{a_0\}) = \{\neg a_2, \neg a_3, a_1\}$
$WFS(\Pi \cup \{a_1\}) = \{\neg a_0, \neg a_3, a_2\}$
$WFS(\Pi \cup \{a_2\}) = \{\neg a_1, \neg a_0, a_3\}$
$WFS(\Pi \cup \{a_3\}) = \{\neg a_2, \neg a_1, a_0\}$ □

The following theorem is due to Schlipf and points out another relationship between AnsProlog and the well-founded semantics.

Theorem 6.6.20 [Sch92] For an AnsProlog program Π if a is true in the well-founded semantics of Π then the answers sets of Π and $\Pi \cup \{a\}$ coincide. □

6.6.9 Answer sets as weakest characterizations with certain desirable properties

In this subsection we show that the semantics of AnsProlog programs and the approximation defined by the well-founded semantics (from Section 1.3.6) can be characterized using several principles. While in most of this chapter, and in Chapter 3, we present properties of AnsProlog* programs, in this section we take the opposite direction where we start with a set of properties (or principles) and the syntax of AnsProlog programs and show that its semantics and its well-founded characterization are unique with respect to that set of properties. To do that we start with a generic notion of semantics of programs with AnsProlog^{or} syntax. For that we need the notion of 3-valued interpretations and 3-valued models.

Recall that a Herbrand interpretation of a program Π is any subset I of its Herbrand Base HB_Π. Intuitively, all atoms in I are considered to be *true* with respect to I and all atoms in $HB_\Pi \setminus I$ are considered to be *false* with respect to I. Thus Herbrand interpretations are two-valued. In the case of 3-valued interpretations (also referred to as partial Herbrand interpretations in Section 1.3.3) a subset of the atoms of HB_Π are considered to be *true*, another disjoint subset of atoms of HB_Π are considered to be *false*, and the remaining are considered to be *unknown*. A naf-literal L is said to hold in a 3-valued interpretation if (i) L is a positive naf-literal and L is *true* in that interpretation, or (ii) L is a negative naf-literal **not** A and A is *false* in that interpretation.

Three valued models of AnsProlog programs are defined using Kleene's [Kle71] 3-valued logic. In it an ordering among truth values is defined: *false* < *unknown* < *true*; and **not** *true* is defined as *false*, **not** *false* is defined as *true*, and **not** *unknown* is defined as *unknown*. The truth value of a conjunction of naf-literals is defined as the minimum truth value among the conjuncts in the conjunction, and the truth value of a disjunction of naf-literals is defined as the maximum truth value among the disjuncts in the disjunction. The truth value of a rule $A \leftarrow B.$ is *true* if the truth value of A is greater than the truth value of B. The following truth table illustrates the above.

A	B	not A	A *or* B	A $\wedge$ B	B $\leftarrow$ A.
true	true	false	true	true	true
true	false	false	true	false	false
false	true	true	true	false	true
false	false	true	false	false	true
true	unknown	false	true	unknown	false
false	unknown	true	unknown	false	true
unknown	unknown	unknown	unknown	unknown	true
unknown	false	unknown	unknown	false	false
unknown	true	unknown	true	unknown	true

A 3-valued interpretation I is said to be a 3-valued model of an AnsProlog program if all rules in that program evaluate to *true* with respect to I. It should be noted that the notion of 3-valued models is different from the notion of partial Herbrand models in Chapter 1. For example in Section 1.3.3 partial Herbrand models are defined with respect to AnsProlog$^\neg$ programs. Here we are defining 3-valued models of AnsProlog programs. The 3-valued logic that we use here is different.

Definition 97 (**SEM**) A semantics SEM for a class of programs maps each program in that class to a set of 3-valued models of the program.

Given a program Π, a ground literal L, and a semantics *SEM*, we say $\Pi \models_{SEM} L$ if L holds in all the elements of $SEM(\Pi)$. □

Definition 98 We say a semantics SEM_1 is weaker than a semantics SEM_2, written as $SEM_1 \leq_k SEM_2$ if for all programs Π and all ground literals l the following holds:

$\Pi \models_{SEM_1} l$ implies $\Pi \models_{SEM_2} l$. That is, all atoms derivable from SEM_1 with respect to Π are also derivable from SEM_2. The notion $\leq_k$ refers to the knowledge ordering in three-valued logic. □

We now list five principles which it is desirable that a semantics has.

- **Principle 1: Elimination of tautologies**
  Suppose Π' is obtained from Π by using the transformation TAUT of Section 3.9.7. Then $SEM(\Pi) = SEM(\Pi')$.

- **Principle 2: Reduction**
  Suppose Π' is obtained from Π by using the transformations RED$^+$ and RED$^-$ of Section 3.9.7. Then $SEM(\Pi) = SEM(\Pi')$.
- **Principle 3: Generalized Principle of Partial Evaluation, GPPE**
  Let Π' be obtained from Π by the GPPE transformation of Section 3.9.7. Then $SEM(\Pi) = SEM(\Pi')$.
- **Principle 4: Subsumption**
  Let Π' be obtained from Π by the SUB transformation of Section 3.9.7. Then $SEM(\Pi) = SEM(\Pi')$.
- **Principle 5: Elimination of contradiction**
  Let Π' be obtained from Π by the CONTRA transformation of Section 3.9.7. Then $SEM(\Pi) = SEM(\Pi')$.

Theorem 6.6.21 [BD97] (i) A unique weakest semantics for AnsProlog programs that satisfies the Principles 1, 2, 3, 4, and 5 exists. (We will refer to it as SEM^{as}).

(ii) The entailment with respect to SEM^{as} coincides with the AnsProlog entailment $\models$. That is, for any AnsProlog program Π and ground literal L, $\Pi \models L$ iff $\Pi \models_{SEM^{as}} L$. $\qquad\square$

It has also been shown that any semantics satisfying Principles 1, 2, 3, 4, and 5 must select a subset of all answer sets [BD97]: no other 3-valued interpretations are possible.

Theorem 6.6.22 [BD99] (i) A unique weakest semantics for AnsProlog programs that satisfies the Principles 1, 2, 3, and 4 exists. (We will refer to it as SEM^{wf}).

(ii) For any AnsProlog program Π, SEM^{wf} is the singleton set consisting of the three-valued interpretation represented by $WFS(\Pi)$. $\qquad\square$

Note that the above principles cannot only be seen as declarative properties uniquely describing certain semantics, but as mentioned in Section 3.10 they can also be used as rewriting rules to actually compute semantics [BD98, BDFZ01, BDNP01, DFN01].

6.7 Notes and references

The complexity and expressiveness results in this chapter are based on the excellent articles [DEGV01, DEGV97] which survey the complexity and expressiveness results of various different logic programming semantics. The book [Pap94] is a very good resource on complexity classes and the book [AHV95] has several illuminating chapters on expressiveness of database query languages.

The **P**-completeness result about propositional AnsDatalog$^{-\text{not}}$ (Theorem 6.2.1) is implicit in [JL77, Var82, Imm86]. Moreover it is shown in [DG84, IM87] that using appropriate data structures, the answer set of a propositional AnsDatalog$^{-\text{not}}$ program can be obtained in linear time with respect to the size of the program. The **P**-data-completeness of AnsDatalog$^{-\text{not}}$ (Theorem 6.2.2) and EXPTIME-program-completeness (Theorem 6.2.3) is also implicit in [Var82, Imm86]. The complexity of existence of answer sets of AnsDatalog programs (Theorems 6.2.4) was shown in [MT91, BF91]. The **coNP**-data-completeness and coNEXPTIME-program-completeness of AnsDatalog (Theorems 6.2.5 and 6.2.6) was shown in [MT91, Sch95b, KP88, KP91]. The program and data complexity result about Stratified AnsDatalog (Theorems 6.2.7 and 6.2.8) is implicit in [ABW88]. Similar results about the well-founded semantics of AnsDatalog (Theorems 6.2.9 and 6.2.10) are implicit in [VGRS91]. The results about complexity of entailment in AnsDatalog$^{or,-\text{not}}$ programs (Theorem 6.2.11 and 6.2.12) are from [EG93a, EG93b, EG93c, EGM94]. The results about complexity of entailment in AnsDatalog^{or} programs (Theorems 6.2.13 and 6.2.14) are from [Got94, EG95, EGM94, EGM97].

The results about the general form of complexity classes in [Fag74, KP88, EGM94] form the basis of proving expressiveness results of various sub-classes of AnsProlog*. Expressiveness of AnsDatalog (Theorem 6.3.1) is from [Sch95b]. The expressiveness of locally stratified programs was first presented in [BMS95]. Expressiveness of AnsDatalog^{or} (Theorem 6.3.2) is from [EGM94, EGM97]. Related expressiveness results are presented in [GS97b, KV95, Sch90, Sac97, BE96].

The recursively enumerable-completeness of AnsProlog$^{-\text{not}}$ (Theorem 6.4.1) is from [AN78, Tar77]. The Π_1^1-completeness of AnsProlog (Theorem 6.4.2) is from [Sch95b, MNR94], and the same for the well-founded semantics is from [Sch95b]. The Π_1^1-completeness of AnsProlog^{or} (Theorem 6.4.4) is from [EG97]. The expressiveness results for AnsProlog and AnsProlog^{or} (Theorems 6.4.6 and 6.4.7) are from [Sch95b, EG97]. Additional complexity and decidability results are presented in [Sch95a].

Section 6.5 on compactness and compilability is based on [CDS96, CDS94].

The result about the lack of a modular translation from AnsProlog to propositional logic is from [Nie99]. The issue of capturing nonHerbrand models in AnsProlog* was first raised by Przymusinski in a technical report in 1987 and was later expanded by Ross in the appendix of [Ros89a]. Ross proposed a solution to this. Reiter in personal conversations also raised these issues. We discuss this issue further in Section 9.5.

Even though some affinity between logic programs and nonmonotonic logics was recognized rather early [Rei82, Lif85a], the intensive work in this direction started in 1987 after the discovery of model theoretic semantics for stratified logic programs

[Apt89]. Almost immediately after this notion was introduced, stratified logic programs were mapped into the three major nonmonotonic formalisms investigated at that time: circumscription [Lif88, Prz88a], autoepistemic logic [Gel87] and default theories [BF91, MT89]. Research in this area was stimulated by the workshop on *Foundations of Deductive Databases and Logic Programming* [Min88] and by the workshops on *Logic Programming and Nonmonotonic Reasoning* [NMS91, PN93]. A 1993 special issue of *Journal of Logic Programming* devoted to 'logic programming and nonmonotonic reasoning' includes an overview [Min93] on the relations between logic programming and nonmonotonic reasoning and an article [PAA93] on performing nonmonotonic reasoning with logic programming. Results relating logic programs with different semantics to various modifications of original nonmonotonic theories can be found in [PAA92a, Prz89c] among others.

The article [Lif94] is an excellent survey on circumscription and presents many results on special instances where a circumscribed theory can be equivalently expressed in first-order logic. The papers [GPP89, GL89] present additional relationships between circumscription and AnsProlog*. The result relating propositional AnsProlog and circumscription has remained largely unnoticed in [Lin91]. A recent paper [Lin02] by the author has revived interest in this result.

The book [MT93] gives a comprehensive exposition of default logic and autoepistemic logic. Its Chapter 6 is about logic programming and its Chapter 12 discusses relation between default and autoepistemic logics, other nonmonotonic modal logics, and AnsProlog*. Many of our results relating default logic, autoepistemic logic, and AnsProlog* are from [MS89, MT89, MT93]. Additional results relating autoepistemic logic and AnsProlog* are given in [Bon95].

There are similar results describing mappings from AnsProlog* to other logics that we did not discuss in this book such as reflexive autoepistemic logic [Sch91], and a logic of minimal belief and negation as failure called *MBNF* [LW92, LS92].

The lack of a modular translation from propositional default logic to AnsProlog* – even though they express the same complexity class – was first pointed out by Gottlob in an invited talk in KR 96. Gottlob elaborated on this in a recent letter as follows: 'Since there is a modular translation from AnsProlog to autoepistemic logic and it was shown in [Got95] that there does not exist a modular translation from default logic to autoepistemic logic, hence there cannot be a modular translation from propositional default logic to AnsProlog*.' The complexity and expressiveness of default logics is discussed in [CEG94, CEG97]. The survey article [CS92] and Chapter 13 of [MT93] has a compilation of complexity results about various nonmonotonic formalisms.

Among the impacts of logic programming on the development of nonmonotonic logic were identification of special classes of theories such as stratified autoepistemic theories and their variants, with comparatively good computational and other properties, and development of new versions of basic formalisms, such as 'default theories' [LY91, PP92], disjunctive defaults [GLPT91], reflexive autoepistemic logic [Sch91], introspective circumscription [Lif89], and MBNF [Lif91, LS90], to mention only a few.

The relationship between description logic and AnsProlog is from the preliminary work [AB01]. Two of the early description logic systems are the KL-ONE system [BS85] and CLASSIC [BBMR89]. In recent years several more expressive description logics have been proposed. For example, in [CDL01] identification constraints and functional dependencies are added to the description logic $\mathcal{DLR}$, which already includes n-ary relations. In [HM00], a description logic with number restrictions, role hierarchies and transitively closed rules is proposed. In [LR96, CPL97, DLNS98] description logics are augmented with Datalog constructs and hybrid languages are proposed. Although some of the initial description logics have been shown [Bor92] to be easily translatable to subsets of first-order logic, many of the recent and more expressive constructs, such as transitive closure of roles, are not amenable to a first-order translation. Besides [AB01], the other description logic papers related to AnsProlog [DLNS98, TW01, LR96, CPL97] have mostly concentrated on stratified function-free AnsProlog.

Dix studied the structural properties of various logic programming semantics in a series of papers [Dix91, Dix92b, Dix92a, Dix95a, Dix95b]. Our discussion in Section 6.6.8 is based on the papers [Dix95a, Dix95b]. The results in Section 6.6.9 are based on [BD97, BD99, BD98, BDFZ01, BDNP01, DFN01]. These papers contain additional results of similar kinds, in particular extensions of the weakest SEM characterization to AnsProlog^{or} programs.

Chapter 7

Answer set computing algorithms

In this chapter we discuss four algorithms for computing answer sets of ground AnsProlog* programs. The first three algorithms compute answer sets of ground AnsProlog programs while the fourth algorithm computes answer sets of ground AnsProlog^{or} programs. In Chapter 8 we will discuss several implemented systems that compute answer sets and use algorithms from this chapter.

Recall that for ground AnsProlog and AnsProlog^{or} programs Π answer sets are finite sets of atoms and are subsets of HB_Π. In other words answer sets are particular *(Herbrand) interpretations* of Π which satisfy additional properties. Intuitively, for an answer set A of Π all atoms in A are viewed as *true* with respect to A, and all atoms not in A are viewed as *false* with respect to A. Most answer set computing algorithms – including the algorithms in this chapter – search in the space of partial interpretations, where in a partial[1] interpretation some atoms have the truth value *true*, some others have the truth value *false* and the remaining are considered to be neither *true* nor *false*. In the first three algorithms in this chapter the partial interpretations are 3-valued and are referred to as *3-valued interpretations*, while in the fourth algorithm the partial interpretation that is used is 4-valued. Recall that we introduced 3-valued interpretations in Section 6.6.9, and that in 3-valued interpretations the atoms which are neither *true* nor *false* have the truth value *unknown*.

The common feature of the algorithms in this chapter is that given a partial interpretation they first try to *extend* them using some form or derivative of Propositions 20 and 22 from Chapter 3. If that fails they then arbitrarily select a naf-literal or use a heuristics to decide on a naf-literal to add to the current partial interpretation and then extend the resulting partial interpretation. These attempts to extend continue until an answer set is obtained or a contradiction is obtained.

---

[1] The notion of partial interpretation in this chapter is slightly different from the partial Herbrand interpretation in Chapter 1. Here partial interpretations could be 3-valued or 4-valued, while in Chapter 1 they were only 3-valued.

We now give some formal definitions and notations that we will use in the rest of the chapter. A 3-valued interpretation I is often represented as a pair $\langle T_I, F_I \rangle$, with $T_I \cap F_I = \emptyset$, where T_I is the set of atoms that has the truth value *true* and F_I is the set of atoms that has the truth value *false*. The atoms that are neither in T_I nor in F_I are said to have the truth value *unknown*. Sometimes a 3-valued interpretation is represented as a set S of naf-literals such that S does not contain both a and **not** a for any atom a. The two representations have a one-to-one correspondence. A 3-valued interpretation represented as a set S of naf-literals can be represented as the pair $\langle T_S, F_S \rangle$, where $T_S = \{a \ : \ a \in HB_\Pi \cap S\}$ and $F_S = \{a \ : \ \textbf{not} \ a \in S \text{ and } a \in HB_\Pi\}$. Similarly, a 3-valued interpretation I represented as a pair $\langle T_I, F_I \rangle$, can be represented by the set of naf-literals given by $T_I \cup \{\textbf{not} \ a \ : \ a \in F_I\}$. A 3-valued interpretation $\langle T_I, F_I \rangle$ is said to be 2-valued if $T_I \cup F_I = HB_\Pi$. In that case we say that the 3-valued interpretation $\langle T_I, F_I \rangle$ is equivalent to the interpretation T_I, and we often replace one by the other. A 3-valued interpretation $\langle T_I, F_I \rangle$ is said to *extend* (or *expand*) another 3-valued interpretation $\langle T_I', F_I' \rangle$ if $T_I' \subseteq T_I$ and $F_I' \subseteq F_I$. In that case we also say that $\langle T_I', F_I' \rangle$ *agrees with* $\langle T_I, F_I \rangle$.

Example 124 Let $HB_\Pi = \{a, b, c, d, e, f\}$. Let I be a 3-valued interpretation given by $\langle \{a, b\}, \{c, d\} \rangle$; it can alternatively be represented as $\{a, b, \textbf{not} \ c, \textbf{not} \ d\}$.

Similarly a 3-valued interpretation represented as $S = \{a, b, e, \textbf{not} \ c, \textbf{not} \ d\}$ can alternatively be represented as $\langle \{a, b, e\}, \{c, d\} \rangle$.

The 3-valued interpretation $\langle \{a, b, e\}, \{c, d\} \rangle$ extends I but the 3-valued interpretation $\langle \{b, e\}, \{c, d\} \rangle$ does not.

The 3-valued interpretation $S' = \{a, b, e, \textbf{not} \ c, \textbf{not} \ d, \textbf{not} \ f\}$ is equivalent to the interpretation $\{a, b, e\}$.

I and S agree with S'. We can also say that I and S agree with the interpretation $\{a, b, e\}$. But S does not agree with I. $\square$

7.1 Branch and bound with WFS: wfs-bb

The wfs-bb algorithm computes answer sets in two distinct phases. It first computes the well-founded semantics of the ground program. It exploits the fact that the well-founded semantics is sound with respect to the answer set semantics. This means that the 3-valued interpretation corresponding to the well-founded semantics of a program agrees with any answer set of the program. After computing the well-founded semantics it extends the corresponding 3-valued interpretation to answer sets by using branch and bound strategy together with recursive calls to the module that computes the well-founded semantics.

7.1.1 Computing the well-founded semantics

A comparatively straightforward way to compute the well-founded semantics of an AnsProlog program is to use the characterization in Section 1.3.6, where it is mentioned that the well-founded semantics of AnsProlog programs is given by $\{lfp(\Gamma_\Pi^2), gfp(\Gamma_\Pi^2)\}$. It is easy to show that Γ_Π is an anti-monotonic operator, and hence Γ_Π^2 is a monotonic operator. Thus the $lfp(\Gamma_\Pi^2)$ can be computed by iteratively applying Γ_Π^2 starting from the empty set; and $gfp(\Gamma_\Pi^2) = \Gamma_\Pi(lfp(\Gamma_\Pi^2))$.

The wfs-bb algorithm computes the well-founded semantics by improving on the above algorithm in two ways.

Improvement 1

We first compute a 3-valued interpretation through an iterative procedure based on an operator proposed by Fitting. The original operator of Fitting takes a program P and a three-valued interpretation $I = \langle I^+, I^- \rangle$ and extends I. In each iteration it adds atoms p to I^+ if there is a rule in P whose head is p and whose body evaluates to *true* with respect to I, and adds atoms q to I^- if for all rules in P whose head is q, their body evaluates to *false* with respect to I. The interpretation obtained by one iteration is denoted by *one_step*(P, I). Starting with an I where all atoms have the truth value *unknown* the *one_step* operator is iteratively applied until a fixpoint is reached.

This operator is monotonic and continuous with respect to I and the ordering $\preceq$ defined as $\langle T, F \rangle \preceq \langle T', F' \rangle$ iff $T \subseteq T'$ and $F \subseteq F'$. Hence if we start from $I_0 = \langle \emptyset, \emptyset \rangle$ and repeatedly apply *one_step* (keeping P constant) we reach the least fixpoint. Let us refer to this as $I_{Fitting}^P$. (Often if P is clear from the context we will just write $I_{Fitting}$.)

Proposition 94 Let P be an AnsDatalog program. $I_{Fitting}^P$ agrees with the well-founded semantics of P. $\qquad \square$

The following example illustrates the direct computation of $I_{Fitting}^P$, for a program P.

Example 125 Consider the following program P:

$r_1: a \leftarrow.$
$r_2: b \leftarrow a.$
$r_3: d \leftarrow \textbf{not } e.$
$r_4: e \leftarrow \textbf{not } d, c.$
$r_5: f \leftarrow g, a.$
$r_6: g \leftarrow f, d.$

$r_7: h \leftarrow \textbf{not } h, f.$
$r_8: i \leftarrow \textbf{not } j, b.$
$r_9: j \leftarrow \textbf{not } i, \textbf{not } c.$
$r_a: k \leftarrow \textbf{not } l, i.$
$r_b: l \leftarrow \textbf{not } k, j.$

Let us now compute $I^P_{Fitting}$.

Initially $I_0 = \langle \emptyset, \emptyset \rangle$.

$I_1 = one\_step(P, I_0) = \langle \{a\}, \{c\} \rangle$, as the body of r_1 is true with respect to I_0 and there is no rule in P with c in its head.

$I_2 = one\_step(P, I_1) = \langle \{a, b\}, \{c, e\} \rangle$, as the body of r_2 is true with respect to I_1 and r_4 is the only rule in P with e in its head and the body of r_4 is false with respect to I_1, since c is false in I_1.

$I_3 = one\_step(P, I_2) = \langle \{a, b, d\}, \{c, e\} \rangle$, as the body of r_3 is true with respect to I_2.

$I^P_{Fitting} = I_4 = I_3.$ □

The wfs-bb algorithm modifies the above steps to more efficiently compute $I^P_{Fitting}$. In the modified approach, after each iteration of *one_step* the program P undergoes a transformation so as to simplify it. The simplified program denoted by *modified*(P, I) is obtained from P by the following steps:

(1) All rules in P whose heads consists of an atom that has a truth value of *true* or *false* in I or whose bodies evaluate to *false* with respect to I are removed.
(2) From the remaining rules, naf-literals in the body that evaluates to *true* with respect to I are removed.

Note that none of the atoms that has the truth value *true* or *false* in I appears in the rules in *modified*(P, I).

The modified approach can now be described by the following iteration leading to a fixpoint.

I_0 has all atoms as *unknown*.

$P_0 = P.$
$I_{j+1} = one\_step(P_j, I_j).$
$P_{j+1} = modified(P_j, I_j).$

Proposition 95 [SNV95] The fixpoint interpretation obtained above is $I^P_{Fitting}$.
                                                                                              □

The simplified program that is obtained at the end of the fixpoint computation will be referred to as $P_{modified}$.

The following example illustrates the computation of $I_{Fitting}^P$ using the modified approach.

Example 126 Consider the program P from Example 125.

Let us now compute $I_{Fitting}^P$ using the modified algorithm.

Initially $I_0 = \langle \emptyset, \emptyset \rangle$, and $P_0 = P$.

$I_1 = one\_step(P_0, I_0) = \langle \{a\}, \{c\} \rangle$, as the body of r_1 is true with respect to I_0 and there is no rule in P with c in its head.

$P_1 = modified(P_0, I_0) = P_0 = P$.

$I_2 = one\_step(P_1, I_1) = \langle \{a, b\}, \{c, e\} \rangle$, as the body of r_2 is true with respect to I_1 and r_4 is the only rule in P with e in its head and the body of r_4 is false with respect to I_1, since c is false in I_1.

$P_2 = modified(P_1, I_1) = \{r_2', r_3, r_5', r_6, r_7, r_8, r_9', r_a, r_b\}$ as given below. The rule r_1 is not in P_2 as the head of r_1 is a, and a is *true* in I_1. The rule r_4 is not in P_2 as the body of r_4 has c, and c is *false* in I_1.

$r_2': b \leftarrow$.
$r_3: d \leftarrow$ **not** e.
$r_5': f \leftarrow g$.
$r_6: g \leftarrow f, d$.
$r_7: h \leftarrow$ **not** h, f.
$r_8: i \leftarrow$ **not** j, b.
$r_9': j \leftarrow$ **not** i.
$r_a: k \leftarrow$ **not** l, i.
$r_b: l \leftarrow$ **not** k, j.

$I_3 = one\_step(P_2, I_2) = \langle \{a, b, d\}, \{c, e\} \rangle$, as the body of r_3 is true with respect to I_2.

$P_3 = modified(P_2, I_2)$ is as given below.

$r_3': d \leftarrow$.
$r_5': f \leftarrow g$.
$r_6: g \leftarrow f, d$.
$r_7: h \leftarrow$ **not** h, f.
$r_8': i \leftarrow$ **not** j.
$r_9': j \leftarrow$ **not** i.

$r_a: k \leftarrow \textbf{not } l, i.$
$r_b: l \leftarrow \textbf{not } k, j.$

$I^P_{Fitting} = I_4 = I_3$, and $P_{modified} = P_4 = modified(P_3, I_3)$ is as given below.

$r'_5: f \leftarrow g.$
$r'_6: g \leftarrow f.$
$r_7: h \leftarrow \textbf{not } h, f.$
$r'_8: i \leftarrow \textbf{not } j.$
$r'_9: j \leftarrow \textbf{not } i.$
$r_a: k \leftarrow \textbf{not } l, i.$
$r_b: l \leftarrow \textbf{not } k, j.$ □

Improvement 2

The well-founded semantics of P can be directly obtained by computing the well-founded semantics of $P_{modified}$ and adding $I^P_{Fitting}$ to it.

Proposition 96 [SNV95] Let P be an AnsDatalog program. Let $P_{modified}$ and $I^P_{Fitting}$ be as defined earlier. The well-founded semantics of P is equal to the union of $I^P_{Fitting}$ and the well-founded semantics of $P_{modified}$.   □

The wfs-bb algorithm further optimizes in computing the well-founded semantics of $P_{modified}$. Let us refer to $P_{modified}$ by Π. Recall that the well-founded semantics of Π can be computed by starting from $\emptyset$ and repeatedly applying Γ^2_Π to it until a fixpoint is reached. This fixpoint is the $\mathrm{lfp}(\Gamma^2_\Pi)$ and applying Γ_Π to $\mathrm{lfp}(\Gamma^2_\Pi)$ gives us the $\mathrm{gfp}(\Gamma^2_\Pi)$. The well-founded semantics is then a characterization where all atoms in $\mathrm{lfp}(\Gamma^2_\Pi)$ are *true* and all atoms not it $\mathrm{gfp}(\Gamma^2_\Pi)$ are *false*. In other words we have the following two sequences:

$$\Gamma^0_\Pi(\emptyset) \subseteq \Gamma^2_\Pi(\emptyset) \subseteq \cdots \subseteq \Gamma^{2i}_\Pi(\emptyset) \subseteq \cdots \subseteq \mathrm{lfp}(\Gamma^2_\Pi);$$

and

$$HB_\Pi \backslash \Gamma^1_\Pi(\emptyset) \subseteq HB_\Pi \backslash \Gamma^3_\Pi(\emptyset) \subseteq \cdots \subseteq HB_\Pi \backslash \Gamma^{2i+1}_\Pi(\emptyset) \subseteq \cdots \subseteq HB_\Pi \backslash \mathrm{gfp}(\Gamma^2_\Pi)$$

the first giving us the set of atoms that are *true* in the well-founded semantics and the second giving us the set of atoms that are *false* in the well-founded semantics.

Example 127 Let us consider $\Pi = P_{modified}$ from Example 126 and compute its well-founded semantics using the above method.

$f \leftarrow g.$
$g \leftarrow f.$

$h \leftarrow \textbf{not } h, f.$
$i \leftarrow \textbf{not } j.$
$j \leftarrow \textbf{not } i.$
$k \leftarrow \textbf{not } l, i.$
$l \leftarrow \textbf{not } k, j.$

The Gelfond–Lifschitz transformation of Π with respect to $\emptyset$ is the following program which we will denote by Π_1:

$f \leftarrow g.$
$g \leftarrow f.$
$h \leftarrow f.$
$i \leftarrow.$
$j \leftarrow.$
$k \leftarrow i.$
$l \leftarrow j.$

The answer set of the above program is $\{i, j, k, l\}$. Hence, $\Gamma_\Pi(\emptyset) = \{i, j, k, l\}$. Let us denote this by I_1. Now let us compute $\Gamma_\Pi^2(\emptyset)$. To compute this we first need to compute the Gelfond–Lifschitz transformation of Π with respect to I_1. After the transformation we obtain the following program which we will denote by Π_2:

$f \leftarrow g.$
$g \leftarrow f.$
$h \leftarrow f.$

The answer set of the above program is $\emptyset$. Hence, $\Gamma_\Pi^2(\emptyset) = \emptyset$. Thus the least fixpoint of Γ_Π^2 is $\emptyset$ and the greatest fixpoint of Γ_Π^2 is $\{i, j, k, l\}$. Hence, the well-founded semantics of Π is $\langle \emptyset, \{f, g, h\}\rangle$. □

The slightly modified approach used in the wfs-bb algorithm to compute the well-founded semantics of $P_{modified}$ modifies the program each time the Γ operator is applied. The modification done is different in the odd and even iteration of the program. We refer to this modified method as the *pruning oscillation* method.

Initially, we have $I_0 = \emptyset$; $\Pi_0 = \Pi$; $T_0 = \emptyset$; and $F_0 = \emptyset$. This corresponds to $\Gamma_\Pi^0(\emptyset)$ of the first sequence above.

Similarly, $HB_\Pi \setminus \Gamma_\Pi^1(\emptyset)$ from the second sequence corresponds to $I_1 = \Gamma_{\Pi_0}(I_0)$; $T_1 = \emptyset$; and $F_1 = HB_\Pi \setminus I_1$. We need to define Π_1 such that $\Gamma_{\Pi_1}(I_1)$ together with T_0 will give us $\Gamma_\Pi^2(\emptyset)$.

Such a Π_1 is obtained by modifying Π_0 with respect to I_1. We refer to this modification as *modify*$^-(\Pi_0, I_1)$, where we modify Π_0 with the assumption that all atoms not in I_1 are false.

In general $modify^-(\Pi, I)$ is obtained from Π by removing all rules in Π whose head does not belong to I, or whose body contains an atom p, such that p does not belong to I. In addition naf-literals of the form **not** q in the body of the remaining rules are removed if q does not belong to I.

Similarly, $modify^+(\Pi, I)$ is obtained from Π by removing all rules in Π whose head belongs to I, or whose body contains a naf-literal **not** p, such that p belongs to I. In addition atoms of the form q in the body of the remaining rules are removed if q belongs to I.

We now define the rest of the sequence.

For even j, $j \geq 0$, $I_{j+2} = \Gamma_{\Pi_{j+1}}(I_{j+1})$; $\Pi_{j+2} = modify^+(\Pi_{j+1}, I_{j+2})$; $T_{j+2} = T_j \cup I_{j+2}$; and $F_{j+2} = F_j$.

For odd j, $j \geq 1$, $I_{j+2} = \Gamma_{\Pi_{j+1}}(I_{j+1})$; $\Pi_{j+2} = modify^-(\Pi_{j+1}, I_{j+2})$; $T_{j+2} = T_j$; and $F_{j+2} = F_j \cup (HB_{\Pi_{j+1}} \setminus I_{j+2})$.

Let $T_\Pi^{wfs} = T_n$ where n is the smallest integer such that $T_n = T_{n+2}$. Let $F_\Pi^{wfs} = F_{n+1}$. Let us denote Π_{n+1} by $P_{simplified}$. We now have the following proposition.

Proposition 97 [SNV95] Let T_Π^{wfs} and F_Π^{wfs} be as defined above. Then $T_\Pi^{wfs} = \text{lfp}(\Gamma_\Pi^2)$ and $F_\Pi^{wfs} = \text{gfp}(\Gamma_\Pi^2)$. $\square$

The well-founded semantics of $\Pi = P_{modified}$ as computed by $\langle T_\Pi^{wfs}, F_\Pi^{wfs} \rangle$ together with $I_{fitting}$ gives us the well-founded semantics of our original program P. We refer to it as $T_{wfs}(P)$ and $F_{wfs}(P)$. To find the answer sets of P we only need to find the answer sets of $P_{simplified}$ and add the well-founded semantics of P to it. More formally,

Proposition 98 [SNV95] Let P be a ground AnsProlog program, and $P_{simplified}$, $T_{wfs}(P)$, and $F_{wfs}(P)$ be as defined above. Then M is an answer set of P iff there is an answer set M' of $P_{simplified}$ such that $M = M' \cup T_{wfs}(P)$. $\square$

In the following example we illustrate the computation of $P_{simplified}$, T_Π^{wfs}, F_Π^{wfs}, $T_{wfs}(P)$ and $F_{wfs}(P)$, where $\Pi = P_{modified}$.

Example 128 Let us recompute the well-founded semantics of $\Pi = P_{modified}$ from Example 126 following the pruning oscillation method and contrast it with the computation in Example 127. Recall that $\Pi_0 = \Pi$ is as follows, $I_0 = \emptyset$, $T_0 = \emptyset$, and $F_0 = \emptyset$.

$f \leftarrow g.$
$g \leftarrow f.$
$h \leftarrow \textbf{not } h, f.$
$i \leftarrow \textbf{not } j.$

$j \leftarrow$ **not** i.
$k \leftarrow$ **not** l, i.
$l \leftarrow$ **not** k, j.

Now $I_1 = \Gamma_{\Pi_0}(I_0)$, $\Pi_1 = modify^-(\Pi_0, I_1)$, $T_1 = \emptyset$, and $F_1 = HB_\Pi \backslash I_1$. We compute them as follows:

- The Gelfond–Lifschitz transformation $\Pi_0^{I_0}$ is the following program:

$f \leftarrow g$.
$g \leftarrow f$.
$h \leftarrow f$.
$i \leftarrow$.
$j \leftarrow$.
$k \leftarrow i$.
$l \leftarrow j$.

Its unique answer set is $\{i, j, k, l\}$. Hence $I_1 = \{i, j, k, l\}$.

- $\Pi_1 = modify^-(\Pi_0, I_1)$ is the following program:

$i \leftarrow$ **not** j.
$j \leftarrow$ **not** i.
$k \leftarrow$ **not** l, i.
$l \leftarrow$ **not** k, j.

- $T_1 = \emptyset$.
- $F_1 = HB_\Pi \backslash I_1 = \{f, g, h\}$.

Now $I_2 = \Gamma_{\Pi_1}(I_1)$, $\Pi_2 = modify^+(\Pi_1, I_2)$, $T_2 = T_0 \cup I_2$, and $F_2 = F_0$. We compute them as follows:

- The Gelfond–Lifschitz transformation $\Pi_1^{I_1}$ is the empty program.
  Its unique answer set is $\{\}$. Hence $I_2 = \{\}$.
- $\Pi_2 = modify^+(\Pi_1, I_2)$ is the following program:

$i \leftarrow$ **not** j.
$j \leftarrow$ **not** i.
$k \leftarrow$ **not** l, i.
$l \leftarrow$ **not** k, j.

  which is the same as Π_1.
- $T_2 = T_0 \cup I_2 = \emptyset = T_0$.
- $F_2 = F_0 = \emptyset$.

Since $T_2 = T_0$ we have $T_\Pi^{wfs} = T_0$, and $F_\Pi^{wfs} = F_1$ and $P_{simplified} = \Pi_1$. Thus the well-founded semantics of $P_{modified}$ is $\langle \emptyset, \{f, g, h\} \rangle$.

Though we do not need to, for illustration purposes we compute I_3, Π_3, T_3, and F_3 and show that indeed they are equivalent to I_1, Π_1, T_1, and F_1 respectively. Recall that, $I_3 = \Gamma_{\Pi_2}(I_2)$, $\Pi_3 = modify^-(\Pi_2, I_3)$, $T_3 = T_1$, and $F_3 = F_1 \cup (HB_\Pi \setminus I_3)$. We compute them as follows:

- The Gelfond–Lifschitz transformation $\Pi_2^{I_2}$ is the following program:

$$i \leftarrow.$$
$$j \leftarrow.$$
$$k \leftarrow i.$$
$$l \leftarrow j.$$

  Its unique answer set is $\{i, j, k, l\}$. Hence $I_3 = \{i, j, k, l\}$.
- $\Pi_3 = modify^-(\Pi_2, I_3)$ is the following program:

$$i \leftarrow \textbf{not } j.$$
$$j \leftarrow \textbf{not } i.$$
$$k \leftarrow \textbf{not } l, i.$$
$$l \leftarrow \textbf{not } k, j.$$

  which is the same as Π_1.
- $T_3 = T_1 = \emptyset$.
- $F_3 = F_1 \cup (HB_\Pi \setminus I_3) = F_1$.

Recall that our goal is to compute the well-founded semantics of P, denoted by $\langle T_{wfs}(P), F_{wfs}(P) \rangle$, from Examples 125 and 126, which is obtained by adding $\langle T_\Pi^{wfs}, F_\Pi^{wfs} \rangle$ to $I_{fitting}^P$. From Example 126 we have $I_{fitting}^P = \langle \{a, b, d\}, \{c, e\} \rangle$. Hence, the well-founded semantics of P, denoted by $\langle T_{wfs}(P), F_{wfs}(P) \rangle$ is $\langle \{a, b, d\}, \{c, e, f, g, h\} \rangle$.   □

7.1.2 The branch and bound algorithm

The answer sets of $P_{simplified}$ are obtained by a straightforward branch and bound strategy where branching is done in terms of which atom to select next. After an atom is selected two branches arise, one where the selected atom is assumed to be *true* and the other where it is assumed to be *false*. We now present the branch and bound algorithm, whose input is a ground AnsProlog program P.

In this algorithm L is a list of triples, where in each triple the first element is a program, the second element is the set of atoms assigned the truth value *true*, and the third element is the set of atoms assigned the truth value *false*. The term *Ans_sets* denotes the set of answer sets. Initially it is assigned the empty set and its value is returned at the end of the algorithm. In the algorithm by $wfs(\pi)$ we denote the well-founded semantics of the fragment π computed with respect to the Herbrand Base of the initial program P. Finally, given a program Π and a naf-literal l, by $reduced(\Pi, l)$ we denote the program obtained from Π by removing any rule with the complement of l in its body and removing l from the bodies of the remaining rules.

Algorithm 5 procedure $bb(P)$

(01) $L := [(P, \emptyset, \emptyset)]$

(02) $Ans\_sets := \emptyset$

(03) **while** $L \neq \emptyset$ **do**

(04)   select the first node $Q = (\pi, T, F)$ from L;

(05)   remove Q from L;

(06)   **if** there is no $T_0 \in Ans\_sets$ such that $T_0 \subseteq T$ **then**

(07)   Select an atom A from $HB_P \setminus \{T \cup F\}$;

(08) $Q^- := (\pi^-, T^-, F^-)$ where

(09) $\pi^- := reduced(\pi, \mathbf{not}\ A)$.

(10) $T^- := T \cup$ the set of atoms true in $wfs(\pi^-)$, and

(11) $F^- := F \cup \{A\} \cup$ the set of atoms false in $wfs(\pi^-)$.

(12)   **if** T^- is not a superset of any $T_0 \in Ans\_sets$ **then**

(13)   **if** Q^- is consistent (i.e., $T^- \cap F^- = \emptyset$) **then**

(14)   **if** $T^- \cup F^- = HB_P$ **then**

(15) $Ans\_sets := Ans\_sets \cup T^-$

(16)   **else** append Q^- to the end of list L;

(17)   **endif**

(18)   **endif**

(19)   **endif**

(20) $Q^+ := (\pi^+, T^+, F^+)$ where

(21) $\pi^+ := reduced(\pi, A)$.

(22) $T^+ := T \cup \{A\} \cup$ the set of atoms true in $wfs(\pi^+)$, and

(23) $F^+ := F \cup$ the set of atoms false in $wfs(\pi^+)$.

(24)   **if** T^+ is not a superset of any $T_0 \in Ans\_sets$ **then**

(25)   **if** Q^+ (i.e., $T^+ \cap F^+ = \emptyset$) is consistent **then**

(26)   **if** $T^+ \cup F^+ = HB_P$ **then**

(27) $Ans\_sets := Ans\_sets \cup T^+$

(28)   **else** append Q^+ to the end of list L;

(29)   **endif**

(30)   **endif**

(31)   **endif**

(32)   **endif**

(33) **endwhile**

(34) return Ans_sets.

Algorithm 5 outputs the set of answer sets of programs P' if $P' = P_{simplified}$ for some ground AnsProlog program P. The algorithm does not work for arbitrary ground AnsProlog programs.

Proposition 99 Let P be a ground AnsProlog program, and $P' = P_{simplified}$ be the program obtained from P as described in this section. The set *Ans_sets* returned by $bb(P')$ is the set of all the answer sets of P'. □

Thus following Propositions 98 and 99 the answer sets of arbitrary ground AnsProlog programs are obtained by first computing $T_{wfs}(P)$ and $P_{simplified}$, then computing the answer sets of $P_{simplified}$, and then adding $T_{wfs}(P)$ to each of them.

In the following example we give a brief illustration of the working of the above algorithm:

Example 129 Let us apply $bb(P')$ where $P' = P_{simplified}$ from Example 128 given by

$i \leftarrow$ **not** j.
$j \leftarrow$ **not** i.
$k \leftarrow$ **not** l, i.
$l \leftarrow$ **not** k, j.

When $bb(P')$ is called in steps (01) and (02) L is initialized to $[(P', \emptyset, \emptyset)]$ and *Ans_sets* is initialized to $\emptyset$. In steps (04) and (05) the node $(P', \emptyset, \emptyset)$ is selected and removed from L. Suppose in step (07) the atom i is selected.

In that case π^- is the following program

$i \leftarrow$ **not** j.
$j \leftarrow$.
$l \leftarrow$ **not** k, j.

The well-founded semantics of π^- is $\langle\{j, l\}, \{i, k\}\rangle$. Hence $T^- = \{j, l\}$ and $F^- = \{i, k\}$. Since the conditions in steps (12), (13), and (14) are satisfied, we have *Ans_sets* $= \{\{j, l\}\}$ due to the assignment in step (15).

In step (21) π^+ is computed, which is the following program

$i \leftarrow$ **not** j.
$k \leftarrow$ **not** l.
$l \leftarrow$ **not** k, j.

The well-founded semantics of π^+ is $\langle\{i, k\}, \{j, l\}\rangle$. Hence $T^+ = \{i, k\}$ and $F^+ = \{j, l\}$. Since the conditions in steps (24), (25) and (26) are satisfied, we have *Ans_sets* $= \{\{j, l\}, \{i, k\}\}$ due to the assignment in step (27).

Since neither of steps (17) and (27) is used L remains empty and the while loop from (3)–(33) terminates. In step (34) $bb(P')$ returns the answer sets $\{\{j, l\}, \{i, k\}\}$.

Recall that the answer sets of P are obtained by adding $T_{wfs}(P)$ to each answer set of $P' = P_{simplified}$. Hence, the answer sets of P are:

$$\{\{j, l\} \cup \{a, b, d\}, \{i, k\} \cup \{a, b, d\}\} = \{\{a, b, d, j, l\}, \{a, b, d, i, k\}\}. \qquad \square$$

7.1.3 Heuristic for selecting atoms in wfs-bb

The wfs-bb algorithm is a modification of the branch and bound algorithm in the previous section. In wfs-bb the atoms selection step (07) of $bb(\Pi)$ is done using a heuristic function. We now describe that function.

The heuristic function is based on partitioning the set of atoms into several levels, and choosing an atom for branching from the lowest level. To partition the set of atoms a relation *depends on* between atoms is defined. An atom a is said to directly depend on an atom b if there is a rule with a in the head and either b or **not** b in the body, or if $b = a$. An atom a is said to depend on an atom b if it directly depends on b, or if there is an atom c such that a directly depends on c and c depends on b. Using the depends on relation, we define equivalent classes, where the equivalent class of an atom a, denoted by $||a||$ is the set of atoms b such that b depends on a and a depends on b. Next we define a partial ordering $\trianglelefteq$ between these equivalence classes as: $||a|| \trianglelefteq ||b||$ iff there exist an atom p in $||a||$ and an atom q in $||b||$ such that q depends on p. The equivalence classes are partitioned into layers $E_0, E_1, \ldots$ as follows: E_0 is the set of all $\trianglelefteq$ minimal equivalence classes and, for $i \geq 0$, E_{i+1} is the set of all $\trianglelefteq$ minimal members of the set of equivalence classes obtained after removing the ones in $\bigcup_{j \leq i} E_j$. Finally, the level of an atom a is given by the i, such that $||a|| \in E_i$. The following example illustrates this.

Example 130 Let us consider $\Pi = P_{simplified}$ from Example 128 given by

$i \leftarrow$ **not** j.
$j \leftarrow$ **not** i.
$k \leftarrow$ **not** l, i.
$l \leftarrow$ **not** k, j.

With respect to the above program Π, i depends on j, j depends on i, k depends on l and i, and l depends on k and j. Based on this dependency relation we have the following equivalence classes.

$||i|| = ||j|| = \{i, j\}$, and
$||k|| = ||l|| = \{k, l\}$.

Between these two equivalence classes we have $\{i, j\} \trianglelefteq \{k, l\}$. Thus we can partition the set of equivalence classes to layers E_0 and E_1, where $E_0 = \{\{i, j\}\}$ and $E_1 = \{\{k, l\}\}$. Based on this layering the levels of i and j are 0 and the levels of k and l are 1.

Hence in the selection step (07) the heuristics described in this section will lead us to choose either i or j in the first iteration of the while loop.   □

7.2 The assume-and-reduce algorithm of SLG

The assume-and-reduce algorithm (of the SLG system) to compute answer sets of ground AnsProlog programs exploits the *observation* that to find an answer set one only needs to guess the truth values of the naf-literals that appear in the program. Unlike the wfs-bb algorithm it does not compute the well-founded semantics on its way to compute the answer sets. But it does use concepts very similar to the notions *reduced*(P, L) and *one_step*, and the notion of *modified* from the previous section to simplify programs based on the truth value of the known atoms, and to infer the truth value of additional atoms.

7.2.1 The main observation

The earlier mentioned observation is formalized as follows:

Lemma 7.2.1 [CW96] Let P be a ground AnsProlog program, I be a 2-valued interpretation, and $N(P)$ be the set of ground atoms a, such that **not** a appears in a body of a rule in P. Then I is an answer set of P iff there is a 3-valued interpretation J that agrees with I such that $N(P) = \{ a : a$ is an atom and has a truth value of either *true* or *false* in $J\}$ and I is the unique minimal model of of the program P^J obtained from P and J by

(i) removing from P any rule that has a naf-literal **not** B in its body with B *true* in J, and
(ii) removing all naf-literals of the type **not** B in the bodies of the remaining rules if B is *false* in J.   □

The following example illustrates the application of the above lemma.

Example 131 Consider the following program P from Example 125:

r_1: $a \leftarrow$.
r_2: $b \leftarrow a$.
r_3: $d \leftarrow$ **not** e.
r_4: $e \leftarrow$ **not** d, c.
r_5: $f \leftarrow g, a$.

$r_6: g \leftarrow f, d.$
$r_7: h \leftarrow \mathbf{not}\ h, f.$
$r_8: i \leftarrow \mathbf{not}\ j, b.$
$r_9: j \leftarrow \mathbf{not}\ i, \mathbf{not}\ c.$
$r_a: k \leftarrow \mathbf{not}\ l, i.$
$r_b: l \leftarrow \mathbf{not}\ k, j.$

$N(P) = \{e, d, c, h, i, j, k, l\}.$

Recall that the answer sets of P are $I_1 = \{a, b, d, i, k\}$ and $I_2 = \{a, b, d, j, l\}$.

Let $J_1 = \langle\{d, i, k\}, \{e, c, h, j, l\}\rangle$ be a 3-valued interpretation where all the atoms in $N(P)$ are assigned a truth value of *true* or *false*. The program P^{J_1} is as follows:

$r_1: a \leftarrow.$
$r_2: b \leftarrow a.$
$r_3': d \leftarrow.$
$r_5: f \leftarrow g, a.$
$r_6: g \leftarrow f, d.$
$r_7': h \leftarrow f.$
$r_8': i \leftarrow b.$
$r_a': k \leftarrow i.$

The unique minimal model of P^{J_1} is $\{a, b, d, i, k\}$ which is equal to I_1 as dictated by the above lemma. We can similarly verify that I_2 is an answer set of P by having $J_2 = \langle\{d, j, l\}, \{e, c, h, i, k\}\rangle$. □

7.2.2 The SLG reduction: reduce$_{slg}$

The assume-and-reduce algorithm uses a slightly different reduction than the *reduced*(P, L) from the previous section in simplifying a program after making an assumption about an atom. We refer to this reduction as *reduced*$_{slg}$ and define it as follows:

Definition 99 Given a ground AnsProlog program P and a naf-literal L, the program *reduced*$_{slg}(P, L)$ is defined as the program obtained from P by deleting every rule in P, the body of which contains the complement of L, and removing every occurrence of L in P, if L is a negative naf-literal. □

Example 132 [CW96] Consider the following program P:

$p \leftarrow p.$
$r \leftarrow \mathbf{not}\ p.$

Let us now compute $reduced_{slg}(P, p)$. In that case we remove the second rule from P but do not remove p from the body of the first rule. Thus $reduced_{slg}(P, p) = \{p \leftarrow p.\}$.

On the other hand when we compute $reduced_{slg}(P, \textbf{not } p)$ we remove the first rule and also remove $\textbf{not } p$ from the body of the second rule. Hence, $reduced_{slg}(P, \textbf{not } p) = \{r \leftarrow .\}$. $\square$

Although the purpose of *reduced* in the previous section and the purpose of $reduced_{slg}$ are similar, the difference in them is due to the fact that *reduced* is applied to programs for which certain simplifications have already been done, while $reduced_{slg}$ is applied to arbitrary ground AnsProlog programs. The following lemma formalizes the impact of $reduced_{slg}$.

Lemma 7.2.2 [CW96] Let P be a ground AnsProlog program, I be a 2-valued interpretation, and A be a ground atom. Then I is an answer set of P iff either A is *true* in I and I is an answer set of $reduced_{slg}(P, A)$, or A is *false* in I and I is an answer set of $reduced_{slg}(P, \textbf{not } A)$. $\square$

Example 133 Consider the program P from Example 132. Its answer set is $I = \{r\}$.

The atom p is false in I. We will now show that I is an answer set of $reduced_{slg}(P, \textbf{not } p)$.

This is obvious as we recall that $reduced_{slg}(P, \textbf{not } p) = \{r \leftarrow .\}$. $\square$

7.2.3 The SLG modification

In the previous section we iterated *one_step* and *modified* to compute $I^P_{fitting}$ and $P_{modified}$ for a given program P. A similar computation is used by the assume-and-reduce algorithm. We now define this computation:

Let P be an AnsProlog program and U be the set of atoms that appear in P. By $one\_step_{slg}(P, U)$ we denote a 3-valued interpretation I, such that all atoms from U that appear as rules with empty body in P, are assigned *true* in I; and all atoms a in U, for which there is not a single rule in P with a in its head, are assigned *false* in I.

Let us consider the following sequence, where *modified* is as defined in Section 7.1.1.

$P_0 = P; U_0 = U$

$I_1 = one\_step_{slg}(P_0, U_0)$, $P_1 = modified(P_0, I_1)$, $U_1 = $ the set of atoms in P_1.

For $j \geq 1$, $I_{j+1} = one\_step_{slg}(P_j, U_j)$, $P_{j+1} = modified(P_j, I_{j+1})$, $U_{j+1} = $ the set of atoms in P_{j+1}.

The sequence stops when for some k, I_k does no assignment, and thus, $P_k = P_{k-1}$. We then say that P is *SLG-modified* to the interpretation $I' = \bigcup_{1 \leq r \leq k} I_r$, and the program $P' = P_k$.

Example 134 Consider the program P from Examples 125 and 126 and let us compute the interpretation and program by doing SLG-modification on P.

Initially $P_0 = P$, and $U_0 = \{a, b, c, d, e, f, g, h, i, j, k, l\}$.
$I_1 = one\_step_{slg}(P_0, U_0) = \langle \{a\}, \{c\} \rangle$, as the body of r_1 is empty and there is no rule in P with c in its head.
$P_1 = modified(P_0, I_1) = \{r'_2, r_3, r'_5, r_6, r_7, r_8, r'_9, r_a, r_b\}$ as given below. The rule r_1 is not in P_1 as the head of r_1 is a, and a is *true* in I_1. The rule r_4 is not in P_1 as the body of r_4 has c, and c is *false* in I_1.

$r'_2: b \leftarrow$.
$r_3: d \leftarrow \textbf{not } e$.
$r'_5: f \leftarrow g$.
$r_6: g \leftarrow f, d$.
$r_7: h \leftarrow \textbf{not } h, f$.
$r_8: i \leftarrow \textbf{not } j, b$.
$r'_9: j \leftarrow \textbf{not } i$.
$r_a: k \leftarrow \textbf{not } l, i$.
$r_b: l \leftarrow \textbf{not } k, j$.

$U_1 = \{b, d, e, f, g, h, i, j, k, l\}$.
$I_2 = one\_step_{slg}(P_1, I_1) = \langle \{b\}, \{e\} \rangle$, as the body of r_2 is empty and there is no rule with e in its head.
$P_2 = modified(P_1, I_2)$ as given below:

$r'_3: d \leftarrow$.
$r'_5: f \leftarrow g$.
$r_6: g \leftarrow f, d$.
$r_7: h \leftarrow \textbf{not } h, f$.
$r'_8: i \leftarrow \textbf{not } j$.
$r'_9: j \leftarrow \textbf{not } i$.
$r_a: k \leftarrow \textbf{not } l, i$.
$r_b: l \leftarrow \textbf{not } k, j$.

$U_2 = \{d, f, g, h, i, j, k, l\}$.
$I_3 = one\_step_{slg}(P_2, I_2) = \langle \{d\}, \{\} \rangle$, as the body of r'_3 is empty.
$P_3 = modified(P_2, I_3)$ is as given below.

$r'_5: f \leftarrow g$.
$r'_6: g \leftarrow f$.

$r_7: h \leftarrow \textbf{not } h, f.$
$r_8': i \leftarrow \textbf{not } j.$
$r_9': j \leftarrow \textbf{not } i.$
$r_a: k \leftarrow \textbf{not } l, i.$
$r_b: l \leftarrow \textbf{not } k, j.$

$U_3 = \{f, g, h, i, j, k, l\}.$
$I_4 = one\_step_{slg}(P_3, I_3) = \langle\{\}, \{\}\rangle.$ Hence, $P_4 = P_3$ and $U_4 = U_3.$

Thus P is SLG-modified to $I_1 \cup I_2 \cup I_3 = \langle\{a, b, d\}, \{c, e\}\rangle$ and $P_3.$ □

The following lemma states the properties of SLG-modification.

Lemma 7.2.3 [CW96] Let P be an AnsProlog program that is SLG-modified to the interpretations I' and P'. Then every answer set I of P is equal to $I' \cup J$, for some answer set J of P' and vice versa.   □

7.2.4 The assume-and-reduce nondeterministic algorithm

We now present the assume-and-reduce nondeterministic algorithm, which takes an AnsProlog program P as input and outputs an answer set of P, or reports failure. The nondeterministic algorithm can be easily converted to a backtracking algorithm which will result in the enumeration of all the answer sets.

Algorithm 6 procedure assume-and-reduce *(P)*
(01) Let P be SLG-modified to an interpretation I' and a program P'.
(02) *derived*:= I'; *program* := P'.
(03) *assigned*:= ∅; *assume_set* := $N(program)$;
(04) **while** *assume_set* ≠ ∅ **do**
(05)   Delete an arbitrary element A, from *assume_set*;
(06)   **if** $A \notin derived$ and **not** $A \notin derived$ **then**
(07)   *choice*(A, L) /* choice point: L can be either A or **not** A.
(08)   *assumed* := *assumed* $\cup \{L\}$;
(09)   Let *reduced_{slg}(program, L)* be SLG-modified to an interpretation I^*
(09)   and a program P^*;
(10)   *derived* := *derived* $\cup I^*$; *program* := P^*;
(11)   **if** *derived* $\cup$ *assumed* is inconsistent **then**
(12)   fail (and backtrack)
(13)   **endif**
(14)   **endif**
(15) **endwhile**
(16) **if** $A \in assumed$ and $A \notin derived$ for some atom A **then**

(17)   fail (and backtrack)

(18) **else**

(19)   return the set of positive naf-literals in *assumed* ∪ *derived* as an answer
set of *P*;

(20) **endif**

Theorem 7.2.4 [CW96] Let *P* be a ground AnsProlog program. If *P* has at least
one answer set then *assume-and-reduce(P)* will return an answer set of *P*.   □

7.2.5 *From assume-and-reduce to SLG*

SLG is a sound (but not complete in general) query evaluating system that answers
queries with respect to nonground programs. It uses some of the ideas from the
assume-and-reduce algorithm and two backward propagation rules described
below:

(1) If a ground atom *A* is assumed to be *true* and the program *P* contains exactly one rule
of the form $A \leftarrow L_1, \ldots, L_m.$, then every L_i $(1 \le i \le n)$ is assumed to be *true*.
(2) If a ground atom *A* is assumed to be *false*, then for every rule in *P* of the form $A \leftarrow L.$
with only one naf-literal in its body, *L* is assumed to be *false*.

Variants of the above backward propagation techniques are integrated into the next
two answer set computation algorithms.

7.3 The smodels algorithm

The main function of the smodels algorithm is *smodels* which takes as input a
ground AnsProlog program *P* and a set of naf-literals *A* and either returns *true*
if there is an answer set of Π that agrees with *A*, or if no such answer set exists
then it returns *false*. The *smodels* function calls three important functions: *expand*,
lookahead, and *heuristics*. Before describing the smodels function we first describe
these three functions and the functions called by them.

7.3.1 *The function* expand(P, A)

Given a ground AnsProlog program *P* and a set of naf-literals *A*, the goal of the
function *expand(P, A)* is to extend *A* as much as possible and as efficiently as possible so that all answer sets of *P* that agree with *A* also agree with *expand(P, A)*. It is
defined in terms of two other functions named *Atleast(P, A)* and *Atmost(P, A)*. The
function *Atleast(P, A)* uses Fitting's operator and two additional backward propagation rules to extend *A*. The function *Atmost(P, A)* gives an upper bound – referred
to as the upper-closure – on the set of atoms that can be true in any answer set that
extends *A*. Thus *A* can be extended with **not** *a* if *a* is not in *Atmost(P, A)*. We now

give algorithms for *expand*(P, A), *Atleast*(P, A), and *Atmost*(P, A), and describe their properties.

function *expand*(P, A)
   repeat
      $A' := A$
      $A := Atleast(P, A)$
      $A := A \cup \{\textbf{not } x \mid x \in Atoms(P) \text{ and } x \notin Atmost(P, A)\}$.
   until $A = A'$
   return A.

The function *Atleast*(P, A) is defined as the least fixpoint of the operator F_A^P defined as follows:

$$F_A^P(X) = A \cup X$$

  $\cup \{a \in Atoms(P) \mid$ there is a rule r in P with a in its head and whose body is *true* with respect to $X\}$
  $\cup \{\textbf{not } a \mid a \in Atoms(P)$ and for all rules r in P with a in its head, their body is *false* with respect to $X\}$
  $\cup \{x \mid$ there exists an $a \in B$ such that there is only one rule r in P with a in its head and whose body has x as a naf-literal, and the body is not *false* with respect to $X\}$
  $\cup \{not(x) \mid$ there exists $\textbf{not } a \in B$ such that there is a rule r in P with a in its head and whose body is true with respect to $X \cup \{x\}\}$.

Note that the first two sets constitute Fitting's operator and the other two are similar to the backward propagation rules of Section 7.2.5. The operator $F_A^P(X)$ is monotonic and continuous and hence its least fixpoint can be computed by the standard iteration method starting from the empty set. In fact it can be computed in linear time in the size of P. We discuss this later in Section 7.3.5.

    It should be noted that when A is the empty set, then during the fixpoint computation of F_A^P the backward propagation rules are not very relevant. This leads to the following proposition.

Proposition 100 [Sim00] Let P be a ground AnsProlog program. *Atleast*(P, $\emptyset$) is equal to $I_{Fitting}^P$.   ☐

But when A is not the empty set and includes naf-literals that are assumed (or chosen) during the computation of the answer sets then the backward propagation rules can be exploited to extend A sooner and with fewer new assumptions. The following example illustrates this.

Example 135 Consider the following program P:

$r_1: a \leftarrow \textbf{not } b.$
$r_2: b \leftarrow \textbf{not } a, c.$
$r_3: b \leftarrow \textbf{not } d.$
$r_4: c \leftarrow \textbf{not } d.$
$r_5: d \leftarrow \textbf{not } c.$

The well-founded semantics and $I^P_{Fitting}$ are both $\emptyset$ for this program. Thus both the *wfs-bb* and *assume-and-reduce* algorithms will get to the choice point where a naf-literal is assumed and further reasoning is done with respect to that assumption.

Suppose a is assumed and we have $A_1 = \{a\}$. In both *wfs-bb* and *assume-and-reduce* since only forward reasoning is done, A_1 cannot be extended further without making new assumptions. We will now show that the backward propagation steps in the computation of $Atleast(P, \{a\})$ are able to make additional conclusions.

We compute the least fixpoint of $F^P_{A_1}$ as follows:

$$F^P_{A_1} \uparrow 0 = F^P_{A_1}(\emptyset) = A_1 = \{a\}.$$
$$F^P_{A_1} \uparrow 1 = F^P_{A_1}(F^P_{A_1} \uparrow 0) = \{a\} \cup \{\textbf{not } b\}.$$

In the last computation there is only one rule r_1 with a in its head, and its body is not *false* with respect to $\{a\}$ and contains the naf-literal **not** b. Hence $\{\textbf{not } b\}$ was added.

$$F^P_{A_1} \uparrow 2 = F^P_{A_1}(F^P_{A_1} \uparrow 1) = F^P_{A_1} \uparrow 1 \text{ and we have the least fixpoint.}$$

Thus $Atleast(P, \{a\}) = \{a, \textbf{not } b\}$. The above illustrates the usefulness of one of the back propagation rules. We now illustrate the usefulness of the other back propagation rule.

Let us now assume **not** a instead of a and have $A_2 = \{\textbf{not } a\}$. As before, since in both *wfs-bb* and *assume-and-reduce* only forward reasoning is done, A_2 cannot be extended further without making new assumptions. We will now show that the backward propagation steps in the computation of $Atleast(P, \{\textbf{not } a\})$ is able to make additional conclusions.

We compute the least fixpoint of $F^P_{A_2}$ as follows:

$$F^P_{A_2} \uparrow 0 = F^P_{A_2}(\emptyset) = A_2 = \{\textbf{not } a\}.$$
$$F^P_{A_2} \uparrow 1 = F^P_{A_2}(F^P_{A_2} \uparrow 0) = \{\textbf{not } a\} \cup \{b\}.$$

In the last computation there is rule r_1 with a in its head, and its body is true with respect to $\{a\} \cup \{\textbf{not } b\}$. Hence $not(\textbf{not } b) = b$ was added.

$$F^P_{A_2} \uparrow 2 = F^P_{A_2}(F^P_{A_2} \uparrow 1) = F^P_{A_2} \uparrow 1 \text{ and we have the least fixpoint.}$$

Thus $Atleast(P, \{\textbf{not } a\}) = \{\textbf{not } a, b\}$. $\qquad\qquad\qquad\square$

The following proposition shows that the extension done by $Atleast(P, A)$ does not lose any answer sets.

Proposition 101 [Sim00] Let P be a ground AnsProlog program and A be a set of naf-literals. If S is an answer set of P such that S agrees with A then S agrees with $Atleast(P, A)$. □

Given a 3-valued interpretation $A = \langle A^+, A^- \rangle$ and a ground AnsProlog program P, the function $Atmost(P, A)$ is defined as the least fixpoint of the operator G_A^P defined as follows:

$$G_A^P(X) = \{a \in atoms(P) \mid \text{there is a rule } a \leftarrow b_1, \ldots, b_m, \textbf{not } c_1, \ldots, \textbf{not } c_n. \text{ such that } \{b_1, \ldots, b_m\} \subseteq X \setminus A^- \text{ and } \{c_1, \ldots, c_n\} \cap A^+ = \emptyset\} \setminus A^-.$$

The operator $G_A^P(X)$ is monotonic and continuous and hence its least fixpoint can be computed by the standard iteration method starting from the empty set. In fact it can also be computed in linear time. We discuss this later in Section 7.3.5. We now give an example that illustrates the computation of $Atmost(P, A)$.

Example 136 Consider the following program P:

$r_1: p \leftarrow p.$
$r_2: q \leftarrow \textbf{not } p.$
$r_3: r \leftarrow p.$

Let $A = \emptyset$. We compute the least fixpoint of G_A^P as follows:

$$G_A^P \uparrow 0 = G_A^P(\emptyset) = \{q\}.$$

The presence of q is explained by the fact that the q is in the head of r_2 and $\{p\} \cap A^+ = \emptyset$. On the other hand both p and r are absent because considering rules r_1 and r_3 respectively $\{p\} \not\subseteq \emptyset$.

$G_A^P \uparrow 1 = G_A^P(G_A^P \uparrow 0) = G_A^P \uparrow 0 = \{q\}$ and we have the least fixpoint. □

The following proposition characterizes the property of $Atmost(P, A)$.

Proposition 102 [Sim00] Let P be a ground AnsProlog program and A be a set of naf-literals. If A is 2-valued then $Atmost(P, A)$ is the same as $\Gamma_P(A)$. □

Proposition 103 [Sim00] Let P be a ground AnsProlog program and A be a set of naf-literals. If S is an answer set of P such that S agrees with A then $S \subseteq Atmost(P, A)$. □

We will now illustrate the computation of *expand*.

Example 137 Consider the P from Example 136 and let us compute $expand(P, A)$ where $A = \emptyset$.

In the first iteration of the computation of $expand(P, A)$ we have the following:

A is assigned the value $Atleast(P, A) = \emptyset$.

$Atmost(P, A) = \{q\}$.

Thus A gets the value $\emptyset \cup \{\textbf{not } p, \textbf{not } r\} = \{\textbf{not } p, \textbf{not } r\}$.

In the second iteration of the computation of $expand(P, A)$ we have the following:

A is assigned the value $Atleast(P, A) = \{q, \textbf{not } p, \textbf{not } r\}$.

$Atmost(P, A) = \{q, \textbf{not } p, \textbf{not } r\}$.

Thus A keeps the value $\{q, \textbf{not } p, \textbf{not } r\}$.

The next iteration has the value of A unchanged and thus we obtain $expand(P, A) = \{q, \textbf{not } p, \textbf{not } r\}$, which is also the well-founded semantics of P.   □

We now formally state the properties of the function $expand(\Pi, A)$. The first property states that $expand(\Pi, A)$ does not eliminate any answer set that agreed with A. The second property states that if $A = expand(\Pi, A)$ is a set of naf-literals that contain all the atoms of the program, then either A is inconsistent or A is an answer set. The third property states that $expand(\Pi, \emptyset)$ computes the well-founded semantics of Π.

Proposition 104 [Sim00] Let Π be a ground AnsProlog program and A be a set of naf-literals. Then, the following hold:

(1) $A \subseteq expand(\Pi, A)$, and
(2) every answer set of Π that agrees with A also agrees with $expand(\Pi, A)$.   □

Proposition 105 [Sim00] Let Π be a ground AnsProlog program and A be a set of naf-literals such that $A = expand(\Pi, A)$. Then, the following hold:

(1) if $atoms(A) = atoms(\Pi)$ and there is no answer set that agrees with A, then A is inconsistent, and
(2) if A is inconsistent, then there is no answer set of Π that agrees with A.   □

Proposition 106 [Sim00] Let Π be a ground AnsProlog program. The value of $expand(\Pi, \emptyset)$ is equal to the well-founded semantics of Π.   □

7.3.2 The function lookahead(P, A)

As we will see later the smodels function may call the *expand* function many times. For that reason *expand* is defined such that it can be computed efficiently. The smodels function has another function called *lookahead* which it calls less frequently and which also 'expands' a set of naf-literals. Although the function *lookahead* is less efficient than *expand*, it leads to early elimination of 3-valued interpretations that do not have any extensions which are answer sets. Thus the smodels function balances the more efficiently implementable but less aggressive in expanding function *expand*, with the less efficiently implementable but more aggressive in expanding function *lookahead* by calling the former more frequently and the latter·much less frequently.

The basic idea behind the function *lookahead* is as follows. To extend A with respect to P, beyond computing $expand(P, A)$, we can compute $expand(P, A \cup \{x\})$ for some naf-literal x and if we find that $expand(P, A \cup \{x\})$ is inconsistent then we can extend A by adding $not(x)$. This idea is supported by the following formal result.

Lemma 7.3.1 [Sim00] Let Π be a ground AnsProlog program and A be a set of naf-literals. Let y be a naf-literal such that $expand(P, A \cup \{y\})$ is inconsistent. Then, every answer set of Π that agrees with A also agrees with $expand(P, A \cup \{not(y)\})$. □

We now describe the function *lookahead*.

Algorithm 7 (lookahead(P, A) and lookahead_once(P, A))
function *lookahead (P, A)*
  repeat
    $A' := A$
    $A := lookahead\_once(P, A)$
  until $A = A'$
  return A.

function *lookahead_once(P, A)*
  $B := Atoms(P) \setminus Atoms(A)$
  $B := B \cup not(B)$
while $B \neq \emptyset$ **do**
    Select a literal x from B
    $A' := expand(P, A \cup \{x\})$
    $B := B \setminus A'$
    if A' is inconsistent **then**
      return $expand(P, A \cup \{not(x)\})$

endif
endwhile
return A.

The following example illustrates the computation of *lookahead* and its usefulness.

Example 138 Consider the following program P:

$p \leftarrow \textbf{not } p$.

The well-founded semantics of P is $\langle \emptyset, \emptyset \rangle$, and *expand*$(P, \emptyset)$ will also give us the same value. Now let us compute *lookahead*$(P, \emptyset)$.

When *lookahead_once*$(P, \emptyset)$ is called, we have B as $\{p, \textbf{not } p\}$. Let us first *select* p from B and compute *expand*$(P, \{p\})$. Since *atleast*$(P, \{p\}) = \{p, \textbf{not } p\}$ we have *expand*$(P, \{p\}) = \{p, \textbf{not } p\}$ which is inconsistent. Thus *lookahead_once*$(P, \emptyset)$ returns *expand*$(P, \{\textbf{not } p\})$ which is $\{p, \textbf{not } p\}$. Another call to *lookahead_once* does not change this and hence we have *lookahead*$(P, \emptyset) = \{p, \textbf{not } p\}$. The same would have happened if, **not** p had been *selected* instead.

The importance and usefulness of *lookahead* is that it spots inconsistencies like the one above early in its computation, thus avoiding exploration of large branches each ultimately ending in inconsistencies. ☐

The function *lookahead* also satisfies the main property of *expansions* in that it does not lose any answer sets. More formally,

Proposition 107 [Sim00] Let Π be a ground AnsProlog program and A be a set of naf-literals. Then, the following hold:

(1) $A \subseteq lookahead(\Pi, A)$, and
(2) every answer set of Π that agrees with A also agrees with *lookahead*(Π, A). ☐

7.3.3 The function heuristic(P, A)

In our effort to extend A after we have called *expand* and *lookahead* the next step is to assume the truth of one of the remaining literals. The smodels algorithm uses a function called *heuristic*(P, A) to make this choice. The basic idea behind the heuristic is to choose an atom which will lead to a bigger expansion. Since once an atom x is chosen there may be two paths, one where x is assumed to be *true* and another where x is assumed to be *false*, the function *heuristic*(P, A) takes into account the size of both *expand*$(P, A \cup \{x\})$ and *expand*$(P, A \cup \{\textbf{not } x\})$.

Thus the function *heuristic*(P, A) first selects an atom x from *atoms*$(P) \setminus atoms(A)$ such that it has the maximum value of $min(|expand(P, A \cup \{x\}) \setminus A|,$ $|expand(P, A \cup \{\textbf{not } x\}) \setminus A|)$. If there are more than one such x, then it selects the one with the greater $max(|expand(P, A \cup \{x\}) \setminus A|, |expand(P, A \cup \{\textbf{not } x\}) \setminus A|)$. Once x is selected, $heuristic(P, A)$ returns x if $|expand(P, A \cup \{x\}) \setminus A| \geq |expand(P, A \cup \{\textbf{not } x\}) \setminus A|$, otherwise it returns $\textbf{not } x$.

7.3.4 The main function: smodels(P, A)

We are now ready to describe the main function $smodels(P, A)$ in terms of $expand$, $lookahead$, and $heuristic$.

Algorithm 8 function $smodels(P, A)$
(01) $A := expand(P, A)$
(02) $A := lookahead(P, A)$
(03) **if** A is inconsistent **then** return $false$
(04) **elseif** $atoms(A) = atoms(P)$
(05)   **then** return $true$
(06)   **else**
(07) $x := heuristic(P, A)$
(08)   **if** $smodels(P, A \cup \{x\})$ **then** return $true$
(09)   **else** return $smodels(P, A \cup \{not(x)\})$
(10)   **endif**
(11)   **endelse**
(12) **endif**

It should be noted that if the above function returns $true$, then the set of atoms in the then value of A is an answer set of P. Normally the initial call to the above function is made by having $A = \emptyset$. To compute more than one answer set, instead of returning $true$ in step (5), the algorithm can print the answer set $atoms(A)$, and return $false$ to force the searching of additional answer sets.

We now present a lemma that justifies steps (08) and (09) of the algorithm.

Lemma 7.3.2 [Sim00] Let Π be an AnsProlog program, S be an answer set of Π and A be a set of naf-literals. If S agrees with A but not with $A \cup \{x\}$, for some naf-literal x, then S agrees with $A \cup \{not(x)\}$. $\square$

The following theorem states the correctness of the smodels function. It can be proved using the above lemma and the properties of the functions $expand$ and $lookahead$.

Theorem 7.3.3 [Sim00] Let Π be a ground AnsProlog program and A be a set of naf-literals. Then, there is an answer set of Π agreeing with A iff $smodels(\Pi, A)$ returns $true$. $\square$

7.3.5 Strategies and tricks for efficient implementation

In [Sim00] a detailed efficient implementation of the smodels function is described. In this section we very briefly mention some of the strategies and tricks discussed there.

During the computation of *Atleast* and *Atmost* a variant of the Dowling–Galier algorithm is used for linear time computation. Recall that during the computation of *Atleast*(P, A) an atom x is added to A if there exists a rule in P whose body holds with respect to A. This is efficiently implemented by using a counter for each rule in P. Initially the counter corresponding to a rule r, referred to as $r.literal$, has the value equal to the number of naf-literals in the body of r that are not true with respect to A. Every time a new naf-literal is added to A the counter corresponding to any rule whose body contains this literal is decremented by one. When the counter corresponding to a rule has the value 0, the head of that rule is added to A. Similarly, corresponding to each rule r, there is an inactivity counter $r.inactive$, whose value is the number of naf-literals in the body of r that are *false* with respect to A. When $r.inactive > 0$ it means that the body of r is *false* with respect to A, and we say r is inactive; otherwise r is said to be active. For each atom a, we have a counter $a.headof$ whose value indicates the number of active rules with head a. The naf-literal **not** a is added to A when the value of $a.headof$ becomes 0. The other two sets in the definition of F_A^P are similarly accounted for by the following:

(a) When $a.headof$ becomes 1, and $a \in A$, then every naf-literal in the body of the only active rule with a in its head is added to A.
(b) For an active rule r with a in its head, if **not** $a \in A$, and $r.literal$ becomes 1, then for the only naf-literal x in the body of r which is not in A, $not(x)$ is added to A.

Similar techniques are used in computing *atmost* in linear time. The computation of *atmost* is further expedited by recognizing that it is in fragments (of programs) of the kind in Example 138 or in the more general case of the kind below where *atmost* is useful.

$p_1 \leftarrow p_2.$
$p_2 \leftarrow p_3.$
$\vdots$
$p_{n-1} \leftarrow p_n.$
$p_n \leftarrow p_1.$

This observation is formalized and exploited by identifying strongly connected components of the atom-dependency-graph of a program without its negative naf-literals and localizing the computation of *atmost* with respect to the strongly connected components before moving on to the rest of the graph.

Another optimization step is to reduce the branching due to lines (07)–(09) of Algorithm 8 by taking advantage of the observations in Section 7.2.1. In that case the function *heuristics* only considers a selected subset of atoms in a program P, not the whole set $Atoms(P)$.

7.4 The dlv algorithm

The dlv algorithm is similar to the smodels algorithm of Section 7.3 with the main difference being that it is targeted[2] towards AnsProlog$^{\perp, or}$ programs (while the smodels algorithm is only for AnsProlog programs). Thus the expand function of dlv has to be able to reason about empty heads in rules and disjunctions in the head of the rules. Another distinguishing feature of dlv is that it uses a new truth value *mbt* (or simply M), meaning *must be true*, to – among other things – do backward propagation using constraints. For example, if an AnsProlog$^{\perp, or}$ program contains the constraint '$\leftarrow$ **not** p.', then p must be true in any answer set of Π. In that case, dlv will initially assign the truth value M to p. In this particular case, the truth value of M for p can be thought of as being that p has been 'observed' to be true, and we need to find 'explanations' for that observation. In general, the truth value of M for any atom p can be thought of as that there is some reason to assume that p is true, but there is no foundation yet to confirm the assumption. The dlv algorithm also uses backward propagation similar to the kind described in Section 7.2.5 to make additional conclusions. For example, if dlv has assigned p the truth value of M and there is only one rule '$p \leftarrow q, r$.' with p in its head in our program, then it assigns q and r with the truth value M.

To be able to reason with this extra truth value M we use some different notations in the rest of this subsection. An interpretation I, which we will refer to as a *dlv-interpretation*, is a mapping from HB_Π to $\{T, M, U, F\}$. Thus, p has the truth value of M in an interpretation I is represented as $I(p) = M$. The truth values of naf-literals, and heads and bodies of rules with respect to an interpretation I, are expressed using the function val_I. To define val_I we use the following: **not** $T = F$, **not** $M = F$, **not** $U = U$, and **not** $F = T$; and $T > M > U > F$. Now, for an atom p, $val_I(\textbf{not } p) = \textbf{not } I(p)$; $val_I(q_1, \ldots, q_n) = min_{1 \leq i \leq n}\{val_I(q_i)\}$, where q_is are naf-literals; and $val_I(p_1 \text{ or } \cdots \text{ or } p_m) = max_{1 \leq i \leq m}\{val_I(p_i)\}$, where p_is are atoms. For a rule r of the form '$p_1 \text{ or } \cdots \text{ or } p_m \leftarrow q_1, \ldots, q_n$.', by $val_I(head(r))$ and $val_I(body(r))$ we refer to $val_I(p_1 \text{ or } \cdots \text{ or } p_m)$ and $val_I(q_1, \ldots, q_n)$ respectively; and by $val_I(head(r) \setminus \{p_i\})$ we refer to $val_I(p_1 \text{ or } \cdots p_{i-1} \text{ or } p_{i+1} \text{ or } p_m)$. If r is a constraint (i.e., has an empty head) then $val_I(head(r))$ is defined as F.

---

[2] The dlv system accepts AnsProlog$^{\perp, or, \neg}$ programs, but while computing answer sets it makes a simple transformation to an AnsProlog$^{\perp, or}$ program and computes the answer sets of the transformed program.

For a dlv-interpretation I, by I^T (respectively I^M) we denote the set of atoms that have the truth value T (respectively M) in the interpretation I. Also, by $I \diamond x : r$ we mean the dlv-interpretation obtained by assigning x the truth value r and making no other changes to I.

We have three additional definitions. For an atom p, $support(p)$ (with respect to an interpretation I) is the set of rules in the ground program such that $val_I(head(r) \setminus \{p\}) < M$ and $val_I(body(r)) > F$. Intuitively, $support(p)$ consists of the set of rules in the ground program that *may* eventually force p to become *true*. We say a rule r is *satisfied* (with respect to an interpretation I) if $val_I(head(r)) \geq val_I(body(r))$. Intuitively, a rule r is *not satisfied* (with respect to an interpretation I) if eventually its body may become true and its head may become false. Given dlv-interpretations I and I', we say I' extends I if for all atoms p, $I(p) \preceq I'(p)$, where $U \preceq F, U \preceq M, U \preceq T$, and $M \preceq T$. Intuitively, $X \preceq Y$ means that Y is more concrete in knowledge terms than X and I' extends I means that I' represents more concrete knowledge than I.

The following example illustrates the above definitions.

Example 139 Consider an AnsProlog$^{\perp, or}$ program consisting of the following rules:

$r_1: a \text{ or } b \leftarrow c, d, \textbf{not } e.$
$r_2: \leftarrow d, e.$

Let I be a dlv-interpretation given as: $I(a) = M, I(b) = F, I(c) = M, I(d) = M$, and $I(e) = F$.

$val_I(head(r_1)) = max\{M, F\} = M, val_I(body(r_1)) = min\{M, M, T\} = M,$
$val_I(head(r_2)) = F, val_I(body(r_2)) = min\{M, F\} = F.$

With respect to I, we have $support(a) = \{r_1\}$, as $val_I(head(r_1) \setminus \{a\}) = val_I(b) = F < M$, and $val_I(body(r_1)) = M > F$. But $support(b) = \{\}$.

The rule r_1 is satisfied with respect to I as $val_I(head(r_1)) = M \geq val_I(body(r_1)) = M$. The rule r_2 is also satisfied with respect to I as $val_I(head(r_2)) = F \geq val_I(body(r_2)) = F$.

Now consider I' given as: $I(a) = T, I(b) = F, I(c) = M, I(d) = M$, and $I(e) = F$. I' extends I, as $I(a) = M \preceq I'(a) = T$, and I and I' have the identical mapping for the other atoms. □

As mentioned earlier, the dlv algorithm is similar to the smodels algorithm. Its main function *dlv* takes a ground AnsProlog$^{\perp, or}$ program Π and a dlv-interpretation I and prints all the answer sets of Π that extend I. During its execution it calls three other functions: $expand_{dlv}$, $heuristics_{dlv}$, and *isAnswerSet*. We first describe these functions and then given the main *dlv* function.

7.4.1 The function $expand_{dlv}(P, I)$

The function $expand_{dlv}(P, I)$ is similar to the *Atleast* function of Smodels and takes into account rules with disjunctions and empty heads that are not accounted for in the *Atleast* function of Smodels. It expands the dlv-interpretation I by adding deterministic consequences of I with respect to P. It can assign F, M, or T to any atom that was previously assigned to U, and can assign T or F to atoms that were previously assigned M. In the last case – when an atom assigned M is re-assigned as F – we say an inconsistency is detected.

The $expand_{dlv}(P, I)$ function iteratively extends I using the following rules. Each iteration is a monotonic operator, and is repeated until a fixpoint is reached. Each iteration step does the following:

(1) Each rule in P is considered one by one and I is expanded using the following:
  (a) If the head of a rule is *false* and its body is either *true* or *mbt*, then the function exits by returning $I = Lit$, which means that there is a contradiction.
  (b) If there is a rule r such that $val_I(body(r))$ is either M or T, and every atom in the head of r is *false* except for one atom p, then $val_I(p)$ is assigned the value $val_I(body(r))$.
  (c) If there is a rule r such that $val_I(head(r))$ is F, and every naf-literal in the body except one (l) is either T or M, then $val_I(l)$ is made false by (i) either assigning l the value *false*, when l is an atom, or (ii) when l is a naf-literal **not** a, then assigning a the value M.
(2) Each atom is considered one by one, its support is analyzed, and I is expanded based on that using the following guidelines.
  (a) If an atom p with truth value T or M has no support (i.e., $support(p) = \emptyset$) then the function exits by returning $I = Lit$, which means that there is a contradiction.
  (b) If an atom p with truth value U has no support (i.e., $support(p) = \emptyset$) then $I(p)$ is assigned the value F.
  (c) If an atom p with truth value T or M has exactly one supporting rule (i.e., $support(p) = \{r\}$) then,
    (i) if an atom q different from p is in $head(r)$, and q has the truth value U then q is assigned the value F.
    (ii) if an atom a with truth value U is in $body(r)$ then a is assigned the value M; and
    (iii) if a naf-literal **not** a with truth value U is in $body(r)$ then a is assigned the value F.

We now briefly relate the above steps to the steps in the *expand* function of Section 7.3.1 and the back propagation steps of Section 7.2.5. Step (1)(a) is new to this algorithm. Step (1)(b) is similar to the first constituent of F_A^P of the *Atleast*(P, A) function of Section 7.3.1. Step (1)(c) is a generalization of the second idea in Section 7.2.5 and is similar to the fourth constituent of F_A^P. Step (2)(a) is new to this algorithm. Step (2)(b) is similar to the second constituent of F_A^P. Step (2)(c) is similar to the third constituent of F_A^P and generalizes it to account for disjunctions in the heads of rules. The following proposition characterizes *expand*$_{dlv}$.

Proposition 108 [FLP99] Let P be a ground AnsProlog$^{\perp, or}$ program and I be a dlv-interpretation.

(1) If *expand*$_{dlv}(P, I) = Lit$ then no answer set of P extends I.
(2) Otherwise, *expand*$_{dlv}(P, I)$ extends I; and every answer set S of P that extends I also extends *expand*$_{dlv}(P, I)$. □

7.4.2 The function heuristic$_{dlv}(P, I)$

The function *heuristic*$_{dlv}(P, I)$ is different from the function *heuristic* used in the smodels algorithm. It uses a notion of *possibly-true* (PT) naf-literals and analyzes the impact of *expand*$_{dlv}$ if I was to be updated by making one of the PT naf-literals *true*. Based on this analysis it defines an ordering $\geq$ on PT naf-literals. It then selects one of the PT naf-literals which is maximal with respect to $\geq$.

We now define PT naf-literals, and the ordering $\geq$.

PT naf-literals: A *positive PT literal* is an atom p with truth value U or M such that there exists a ground rule r with $p \in head(r)$, the head is not true with respect to I, and the body is true with respect to I. A *negative PT literal* is a naf-literal **not** q with truth value U such that there exists a ground rule r with **not** q in the body, the head is not true with respect to I, all the atoms in the body are true with respect to I, and no negative naf-literal in the body is false with respect to I. A *PT naf-literal* is either a positive PT literal or a negative PT literal. The set of all PT naf-literals of a program P with respect to I is denoted by $PT_P(I)$.

Ordering between PT naf-literals based on their impact: The impact of a PT naf-literal p is comparatively defined based on analyzing the set of literals that become M or lose their truth value of M, when p is assumed to be true.

An atom p with truth value M *(called an mbt atom)* is said to be of level n if $|support(p)| = n$. For a PT naf-literal p, $mbt^-(p)$ is the overall number of *mbt* atoms which become true (using *expand*$_{dlv}$) by assuming p to be true; $mbt^+(p)$ is the overall number of *undefined* atoms which become M (using *expand*$_{dlv}$) by assuming p to be true; $mbt_i^-(p)$ is the number of *mbt* atoms of level i which become true (using *expand*$_{dlv}$) by assuming p to be true; $mbt_i^+(p)$ is the number of *undefined* atoms of level i which become M (using *expand$_{dlv}$*) by assuming p to be true; $\Delta_{mbt}(p) = mbt^-(p) - mbt^+(p)$; $\Delta_{mbt2}(p) = mbt_2^-(p) - mbt_2^+(p)$; and $\Delta_{mbt3}(p) = mbt_3^-(p) - mbt_3^+(p)$.

Given two PT naf-literals a and b:

- If $(mbt^-(a) = 0 \wedge mbt^-(b) > 0) \vee (mbt^-(a) > 0 \wedge mbt^-(b) = 0)$ then

  $a > b$ if $mbt^-(a) > mbt^-(b)$;

- Otherwise $a > b$ if

  (i) $\Delta_{mbt}(a) > \Delta_{mbt}(b)$; or
  (ii) $\Delta_{mbt2}(a) > \Delta_{mbt2}(b)$ and $\Delta_{mbt}(a) = \Delta_{mbt}(b)$; or
  (iii) $\Delta_{mbt3}(a) > \Delta_{mbt3}(b)$ and $\Delta_{mbt2}(a) = \Delta_{mbt2}(b)$ and $\Delta_{mbt}(a) = \Delta_{mbt}(b)$.

- If $a \not> b \wedge b \not> a$ then $a = b$.

One of the intuitions behind the above ordering is that the *mbt* atoms can be thought of as constraints that need to be satisfied. Thus a smaller number of *mbt* atoms are preferable to a larger number of *mbt* atoms as the former suggests that to find an answer set a lesser number of constraints need to be satisfied. Another intuition is to prefer some elimination of *mbt* atoms over no elimination.

Example 140 [FLP99] Consider the ground version of the following program which we will refer to as P.

node(a) ←.
node(b) ←.
node(c) ←.
node(d) ←.
node(e) ←.

arc(a, b) ←.
arc(a, c) ←.
arc(a, d) ←.
arc(a, e) ←.
arc(b, c) ←.
arc(c, d) ←.
arc(d, b) ←.
arc(d, e) ←.

start(a) ←.

r_1: *inpath(X, Y) or outpath(X, Y)* ← *arc(X, Y)*.

r_2: *reached(X)* ← *start(X)*.

r_3: *reached*$(X) \leftarrow$ *reached*(Y), *inpath*(Y, X).

r_4: $\leftarrow$ *inpath*(X, Y), *inpath*$(X, Y1)$, $Y \neq Y1$.

r_5: $\leftarrow$ *inpath*(X, Y), *inpath*$(X1, Y)$, $X \neq X1$.

r_6: $\leftarrow$ *node*(X), **not** *reached*(X).

Let I_0 be the dlv-interpretation which assigns the truth value U to all atoms. The call *expand*$_{dlv}(P, I_0)$ returns a dlv-interpretation with the *node*, *arc* and *start* facts assigned T; *reached*(a) assigned T (because of a ground instance of r_2); and *reached*(b), *reached*(c), *reached*(d), and *reached*(e) assigned to M (because of ground instances of r_6). Let us refer to this resulting dlv-interpretation as I_1 and consider the computation of *heuristic*$_{dlv}(P, I_1)$.

One of the PT-literals is *inpath*(a, b). Let us assume it is *true* and illustrate the computation of $mbt^-($*inpath*$(a, b))$, and $mbt^+($*inpath*$(a, b))$.

Using r_3 we can derive *reached*(b) to be T. Using r_4 and r_5 we can derive *inpath*(a, c), *inpath*(a, d), *inpath*(a, e), *inpath*(d, b) to be F. For further analysis let us consider the following ground instantiations of r_2 and r_3:

reached$(a) \leftarrow$ *start*(a).

reached$(b) \leftarrow$ *reached*(a), *inpath*(a, b).
reached$(b) \leftarrow$ *reached*(d), *inpath*(d, b).   (*)

reached$(c) \leftarrow$ *reached*(a), *inpath*(a, c).   (*)
reached$(c) \leftarrow$ *reached*(b), *inpath*(b, c).

reached$(d) \leftarrow$ *reached*(a), *inpath*(a, d).   (*)
reached$(d) \leftarrow$ *reached*(c), *inpath*(c, d).

reached$(e) \leftarrow$ *reached*(a), *inpath*(a, e).   (*)
reached$(e) \leftarrow$ *reached*(d), *inpath*(d, e).

Among the above rules, the bodies of ones marked by (*) evaluate to *false*. Hence for *reached*(c), *reached*(d), and *reached*(e) there is only one supporting rule. Thus using step (2)(c)(ii) of *expand*$_{dlv}$ we assign M to *inpath*(b, c), *inpath*(c, d), and *inpath*(d, e).

Now *inpath*(b, c), *inpath*(c, d), and *inpath*(d, e) occur in the head of exactly one rule (the corresponding instantiation of r_1) and the body of these rules is true. Thus using (2)(c)(i) of *expand*$_{dlv}$ we assign F to *outpath*(b, c), *outpath*(c, d), and *outpath*(d, e) and then using (1)(b) of *expand*$_{dlv}$ we assign T to *inpath*(b, c), *inpath*(c, d), and *inpath*(d, e).

In the subsequent iteration *reached*(c), *reached*(d), and *reached*(e) are assigned T.

In summary, the changes from I_1 to $expand_{dlv}(I_1 \diamond inpath(a, b) : T)$ are as follows:

$reached(b), reached(c), reached(d)$, and $reached(e)$: From M to T.

$inpath(a, c), inpath(a, d), inpath(a, e)$, and $inpath(d, b)$: From U to F.

$inpath(b, c), inpath(c, d)$, and $inpath(d, e)$: From U to M and then to T.

$outpath(b, c), outpath(c, d)$, and $outpath(d, e)$: From U to to F.

Thus $mbt^-(inpath(a, b)) = 7$ and $mbt^+(inpath(a, b)) = 3$.　　　　　　$\square$

7.4.3 The function isAnswerSet(P, S)

It should be noted that a proposition similar to Proposition 105 does not hold for $expand_{dlv}$. Hence, if $expand_{dlv}$ results in a dlv-interpretation I that is 2-valued (i.e., none of the atoms is mapped to U or M) it is not guaranteed that I would be an answer set. Thus the need for the function $isAnswerSet(P, S)$.

The function $isAnswerSet(P, S)$, where S is a set of atoms, and P is an AnsProlog$^{\perp, or}$ program, returns the value *true* if S is an answer set of P; otherwise it returns the value *false*. This can be verified by constructing the AnsProlog$^{\perp, or, -\textbf{not}}$ program P^S and checking if S is a minimal model of P^S.

7.4.4 The main dlv function

We now present the main dlv algorithm that uses $expand_{dlv}(P, I)$ and $heuristic_{dlv}(P, I)$, and prints the answer sets of an AnsProlog$^{\perp, or}$ program.

Intuitively, the function $dlv(P, I)$ takes a ground AnsProlog$^{\perp, or}$ program P and an interpretation I, and first computes the function $expand_{dlv}(P, I)$. If it returns Lit meaning a contradiction then the function dlv returns *false*. Otherwise it checks if $expand_{dlv}(P, I)$ encodes an answer set of P. If that is the case the answer set is printed, and the function dlv returns *false* so as to facilitate the generation of the other answer sets. If $I' = expand_{dlv}(P, I)$ does not encode an answer set of P then $heuristic_{dlv}(P, I')$ is used to pick a naf-literal x and dlv is called with two different updates of I', one where the truth value of x is T, and another where it is F, so as to print answers sets (if any) that can be reached from both interpretations.

Algorithm 9 function $dlv(P, I)$

(01) $I := expand_{dlv}(P, I)$.

(02) **if** $I = Lit$ **then** return *false*.

(03) **elseif** $PT_P(I) = \emptyset$

(04)   **then if** $I^M = \emptyset$ and *isAnswerSet*(P, I^T) **then** print(I^T), return(*false*).

(05)   **else**

(06) $x := heuristic_{dlv}(P, I)$.

(07)   **if** x is an atom **then**

(08)   **if** $dlv(P, I \diamond x : T)$ **then** return *true*.

(09)   **else** return $dlv(P, I \diamond x : F)$.

(10)   **end if**

(11)   **elseif** x is an naf-literal **not** p **then**

(12)   **if** $dlv(P, I \diamond p : M)$ **then** return *true*.

(13)   **else** return $dlv(P, I \diamond p : F)$.

(14)   **end if**

(15)   **end if**

(16)   **end if**

(17) **end if**

The function $dlv(P, I)$ is initially called with an I where all atoms are assigned the truth value U, and a P which is a ground AnsProlog$^{\perp, or}$ program. It always returns the value *false*, but prints all the answer sets (if any) of P. More formally,

Theorem 7.4.1 [FLP99] Let Π be a ground AnsProlog$^{\perp, or}$ program and I be a dlv-interpretation. The function $dlv(\Pi, I)$ prints all and only the answer sets of Π that extend I. $\qquad\qquad \Box$

7.4.5 Comparing dlv with Smodels

The dlv algorithm is applicable to the larger class AnsProlog$^{\perp, or}$ than the class of AnsProlog programs that is targeted by the smodels algorithm. This leads to one of the main differences between *expand*$_{dlv}$ and *expand*. In addition, while *expand* uses the upper-closure idea *expand*$_{dlv}$ does not. Thus, while *expand* will infer p to be *false* given a program consisting of the single rule $p \leftarrow p$., *expand*$_{dlv}$ will not. The heuristics used by the two algorithms are quite different, and *dlv* does not have a *lookahead* similar to the one used by *smodels*.

7.5 Notes and references

The wfs-bb algorithm is from [SNV95]. The assume-and-reduce algorithm is from [CW96]. The smodels algorithm is used in the smodels system described in [NS97]. The algorithm is described in great detail in [Sim00] which also includes a lot of implementation detail. The dlv algorithm is used in the dlv system described in [CEF+97, EFG+00]. The algorithm that we present is described in [FLP99].

Both smodels and dlv are systems that are often being updated and upgraded. So the algorithms that we presented may not be the ones used in the latest version of both systems. In particular, the *heuristic*$_{dlv}$ function is quite different from the corresponding function in the latest dlv implementation. The new function is described in [FLP01a, FLP01b]. Also, in the latest dlv implementation the *expand*$_{dlv}$ algorithm is upgraded to use the upper closure idea.

An important aspect of computing answer sets of AnsDatalog* programs is the grounding phase where a program with variables is converted to a ground program. Although we did not cover this step in this chapter, it is a crucial step, as the size of the ground program strongly affects the time of computation of the answer sets. The grounding phase of dlv is described in the paper [LPS01]. The grounding of smodels is described in [Syr98].

7.5.1 *Other query answering approaches*

In this chapter we have described algorithms used to compute answer sets of ground AnsProlog* programs. There are several issues that are not addressed in this chapter. We now briefly mention them.

When dealing with AnsProlog* programs that may have function symbols the answer sets may not have a finite cardinality and hence we need a way to finitely express such answer sets. Such an attempt was made in [GMN⁺96]. Bonatti recently explored computation of answer sets of particular AnsProlog* programs with function symbols.

An alternative approach, which is also useful when we are only interested in computing entailment and not in computing one or all of the answer sets is to develop derivation methods that compute the entailment. Several such methods have been proposed which are sound for restricted cases and complete for even more restricted cases. Some of these are the SLDNF resolution method [AD94, Str93] used in PROLOG, the SLD and SLDNF calculus proposed in [Lif95, Lif96], and the integration of assume-and-reduce and SLG resolution in [CW96].

In the database community, there has been a lot of research on techniques to answer queries in a focused manner – as done in top-down query processing systems, but using the bottom-up approach thus avoiding the non-termination issues. The technique that is used is referred to as 'magic sets' or 'magic templates' [Ull88a, Ull88b, BR86, BR87]. The basic idea behind this is to take a query binding pattern and transform a given program so that the bottom-up query processing with respect to the transformed program and queries that follow the initial binding pattern is as focused as it would have been with respect to top-down query processing. Such techniques have only been explored with respect to stratified programs. How to extend it beyond stratified programs, in particular with respect to programs that have multiple answer sets, remains an open question.

Finally in recent years several very efficient propositional model generators [MMZ+01, Zha97, MSS99] have been developed. For AnsProlog* sub-classes that can be compiled to equivalent propositional theories, this suggests an alternative way to compute answer sets. Such an approach has recently been pursued by Lin and also by Lifschitz. Since model generation of propositional theories can be translated to a correspondisng integer linear programming problem, a further alternative is to use integer linear programming solvers such as CPLEX. Such an attempt is made in [BNNS94] and we discussed it earlier in Section 3.9.4.

Chapter 8

Query answering and answer set computing systems

In this chapter we discuss three query answering and answer set computing systems: Smodels, dlv and PROLOG. Both Smodels and dlv are answer set computing systems and allow an input language with features and constructs not in AnsProlog*. While the Smodels system extends AnsProlog$^\perp$ and AnsProlog$^{\perp,\neg}$, the dlv system extends AnsProlog$^{\perp,or}$ and AnsProlog$^{\perp,or,\neg}$. We describe the syntax and semantics of the input language of Smodels and dlv and present several programs in their syntax. This chapter can be thought of as a quick introduction to programming in Smodels and dlv, not a full-fledged manual. At the time of writing this, both Smodels and dlv were evolving systems and readers are recommended to visit their corresponding web sites for the latest features.

After describing the Smodels and dlv systems with several small example programs, we consider several medium and large size applications and encode them using one or the other. In particular, we consider encoding of combinatorial auctions together with logical preference criteria, planning with durative actions and resources, resource constraint project scheduling, and specification and verification of active databases.

Finally, we give a brief introduction to the PROLOG interpreter and its approach to answering queries with respect to AnsProlog programs. We present conditions for AnsProlog programs and queries for which the PROLOG interpreter is sound and complete. We illustrate these conditions through several examples.

8.1 Smodels

The Smodels system is meant for computing the answer sets of AnsProlog$^\perp$ and AnsProlog$^{\perp,\neg}$ programs[1] and allows certain extensions to them. We refer to the extended language allowed by the Smodels system as AnsProlog$_{sm}$. The Smodels system consists of two main modules: lparse and smodels. The lparse module takes

---

[1] The Smodels system has primitive functionality with respect to AnsProlog^{or} and we do not discuss it here.

an AnsProlog$_{sm}$ program Π and grounds the variables in Π to produce *ground*(Π), a grounded version of Π, and outputs a representation of *ground*(Π) that is readable by the smodels module. The smodels module then computes the answer sets of *ground*(Π). The Smodels system expects the user input to be in the language expected by the lparse module, and not in the format expected by the smodels module. Thus the input language of lparse is a PROLOG like programming language while the input language of smodels is like a machine language.

To make sure *ground*(Π) is of finite length and to achieve fast grounding by processing each rule only once the lparse program requires that its input satisfy the property of being *strongly range restricted*, according to which, in every rule in the input; any variable that appears in the rule must also appear in a domain literal in the body. A domain literal is made up of domain predicates. We give a formal definition of domain predicates in Section 8.1.2.

The rest of this section is structured as follows. In Section 8.1.1 we present the syntax and semantics of ground AnsProlog$_{sm}$ and other ground statements. In Section 8.1.2 we describe how AnsProlog$_{sm}$ programs and other statements are grounded. In Section 8.1.3 we briefly present some of the other constructs in the input language of lparse and smodels modules. In Section 8.1.4 we present command line options for the lparse and smodels modules. We then present several small AnsProlog$_{sm}$ programs showcasing the features of the Smodels system.

8.1.1 The ground subset of the input language of lparse

We first start with ground AnsProlog$_{sm}$ programs and describe their semantics. We will then allow variables and describe the semantics of the resulting programs by explaining the grounding procedure.

A ground program in the input language of lparse consists of a set of ground AnsProlog$_{sm}$ rules, a set of compute statements and a list of optimize statements. Ground AnsProlog$_{sm}$ rules are more general than ground AnsProlog rules in that they allow more than atoms and naf-literals in their head and body respectively. They allow two kinds of constraints; cardinality and weight constraints.

- Ground cardinality constraint: A ground cardinality constraint C is of the form

$$L \ \{a_1, \ldots, a_n, \textbf{not} \ b_1, \ldots, \textbf{not} \ b_m\} \ U \tag{8.1.1}$$

where the a_i and b_j are atoms and L and U are integers. Both L and U are allowed to be missing and in that case their value is understood as $-\infty$ and ∞ respectively. Given a set of atoms S, by the value of C with respect to S (denoted by $val(C,S)$) we refer to the number $|S \cap \{a_1, \ldots, a_n\}| + (m - |S \cap \{b_1, \ldots, b_m\}|)$. We say C holds in S if $L \le val(C, S) \le U$. We refer to $lower(C)$ and $upper(C)$ as L and U respectively.

- Ground weight constraint: A weight constraint C is of the form

$$L\ [a_1 = w_{a_1}, \ldots, a_n = w_{a_n}, \textbf{not}\ b_1 = w_{b_1}, \ldots, \textbf{not}\ b_m = w_{b_m}]\ U \qquad (8.1.2)$$

where the a_i and b_j are atoms, and the w', L and U are integers[2]. The weight w_{a_i} denotes the weight of a_i being true in a set and the weight w_{b_j} denotes the weight of **not** b being true in a set. If the weight of a naf-literal is 1 then its explicit specification may be omitted. As before, both L and U are allowed to be missing and in that case their value is understood to be $-\infty$ and ∞ respectively. Given a set of atoms S, by the value of C with respect to S (denoted by $val(C,S)$) we refer to the number

$$\sum_{a_i \in S, 1 \le i \le n} w_{a_i} + \sum_{b_j \notin S, 1 \le j \le m} w_{b_j}.$$

We say C holds in S if $L \le val(C, S) \le U$. We refer to $lower(C)$ and $upper(C)$ as L and U respectively.

Exercise 30 Let $S_1 = \{a, b, c, d\}$, and $S_2 = \{b, c, e, f\}$. Consider the following ground cardinality and weight constraints.

$C_1 = 1 \{a, b, \textbf{not}\ d\}\ 3.$
$C_2 = 2 \{a, e, \textbf{not}\ d\}\ 4.$
$C_3 = 1 \{c, \textbf{not}\ d, e\}\ 1.$
$C_4 = 2 [a = 2, b = 3, \textbf{not}\ d = 2]\ 8.$
$C_5 = 6 [a = 3, d = 2, \textbf{not}\ e = 1]\ 10.$
$C_6 = 1 [a, b, \textbf{not}\ d]\ 3.$

Which of the above C_i hold with respect to S_1 and which of the C_i hold with respect to S_2?   □

For a ground constraint C (of either kind), by $atoms(C)$ we denote the set $\{a_1, \ldots, a_n\}$.

A ground AnsProlog$_{sm}$ rule is of the form:

$$C_0 :\text{-}\ C_1, \ldots, C_k.$$

where C_0 is either a ground atom, or a ground weight constraint, or a ground cardinality constraint, and C_i, $1 \le i \le k$, is either a ground literal, a ground weight constraint, or a ground cardinality constraint. If $k = 0$ then the above rule is written simply as:

$$C_0.$$

Consider the following ground AnsProlog$_{sm}$ rule

$$1 \{a, b, c\}\ 2 :\text{-}\ p.$$

---

[2] The restriction to integers is limited to the current implementation of the Smodels system. From the semantical point of view real numbers are acceptable.

Intuitively, the meaning of the above rule is that if p is true in any answer set of a program containing this rule then at least 1 and at most 2 among the set $\{a, b, c\}$ must be true in that answer set. In general, the truth of a cardinality constraint C with respect to a set of atoms S is defined by counting the number of naf-literals in C that evaluate to true with respect to S. If this number is (inclusively) in between the lower and upper bounds of C, then we say that C holds in S.

Example 141 Consider the following ground AnsProlog$_{sm}$ program.

1 $\{a, b, c\}$ 2 :- p.

p.

While $\{a, p\}$, and $\{a, b, p\}$ are among the answer sets of this program $\{a, b, c, p\}$ is not an answer set. Notice that unlike in AnsProlog here we can have answer sets which are proper subsets of other answer sets.   □

We now give the semantics of ground AnsProlog$_{sm}$ programs which have only nonnegative weights and whose rules do not have any naf-literals. The former restriction is for simplifying the definitions, and because negative weights can be eliminated through some transformations without changing the meaning of the program. Similarly, a positive literal a can be replaced by 1 $\{a\}$ 1 and a negative literal **not** a can be replaced by 1 $\{$**not** $a\}$ 1, without changing the meaning of the program.

The semantics is defined in a style similar to the definition of answer sets for AnsProlog programs by first defining the notion of reduct and then using the notion of deductive closure of a simpler class of programs. First we define reducts of constraints. Let S be a set of atoms, and C be a ground constraint. The reduct of C with respect to S denoted by C^S is defined as follows:

- When C is a ground cardinality constraint of the form (8.1.1), C^S is the constraint

L' $\{a_1, \ldots, a_n\}$

where $L' = L - (m - |S \cap \{b_1, \ldots, b_m\}|)$
- When C is a ground weight constraint of the form (8.1.2), C^S is the constraint

L' $[a_1 = w_{a_1}, \ldots, a_n = w_{a_n}]$

$$\text{where } L' = L - \sum_{b_j \notin S, 1 \leq j \leq m} w_{b_j}$$

Definition 100 Let Π be a set of ground AnsProlog$_{sm}$ rules and S be a set of ground atoms. The reduct Π^S of Π with respect to S is the set given by:

$\{p \leftarrow C_1^S, \ldots, C_k^S. \; : \; C_0 :\text{-} C_1, \ldots, C_k. \in \Pi, p \in atoms(C_0) \cap S$, and for each of the C_i, $1 \leq i \leq k$, $val(C_i, S) \leq upper(C_i)\}$.   □

Example 142 Consider a ground AnsProlog$_{sm}$ Π consisting of the following rule:

1 $\{a, b, c\}$ 2 :- 1 $\{a, c, \textbf{not } d\}$ 2, 3 $\{b = 2, c = 1, \textbf{not } e = 2\}$ 6.

Let $S = \{a, b\}$.

The reduct Π^S consists of the following rules:

a :- 0 $\{a, c\}$, 1 $\{b = 2, c = 1\}$.

b :- 0 $\{a, c\}$, 1 $\{b = 2, c = 1\}$. □

Notice that the constraints in the rules of the reduct do not have negative naf-literals and have only lower bounds, and the heads of the rules are only atoms. Such rules are monotonic in the sense that if the body of the rule is satisfied by a set of atoms S, then it is satisfied by any superset of S. The *deductive closure* of such a program is defined as the unique smallest set of atoms S such that if for any of the rules all the constraints in the body hold with respect to S then the atom in the head also holds with respect to S. This deductive closure can be obtained by an iterative procedure that starts from the empty set of atoms and iteratively adds heads of rules to this set whose bodies are satisfied by the set until no unsatisfied rules are left. Using the notion of deductive closure we now define answer sets of ground AnsProlog$_{sm}$ programs.

Definition 101 A set of ground atoms S is an answer set of a set of ground AnsProlog$_{sm}$ rules Π iff the following two conditions hold,

(i) For each rule in Π if each of the C_is in the body holds with respect to S, then the head also holds with respect to S, and
(ii) S is equal to the deductive closure of Π^S. □

The definition of reduct in Definition 100 does not pay attention to the lower and upper bound in the head of the rules. This is taken care of by condition (i) of the Definition 101. The following examples illustrates this.

Example 143 Consider a ground AnsProlog$_{sm}$ program Π consisting of the following rule:

1 $\{a, b\}$ 1.

Let $S_1 = \{a\}$, $S_2 = \{b\}$, and $S_3 = \{a, b\}$.

The reduct of Π with respect to S_1 consists of the only rule:

a.

whose deductive closure is $\{a\} = S_1$. Since S_1 also satisfies the condition (i) of Definition 101, S_1 is an answer set of Π. Similarly, it can be shown that S_2 is an answer set of Π.

Now let us consider S_3. The reduct of Π with respect to S_3 consists of the following two rules:

a.
b.

whose deductive closure is $\{a, b\} = S_3$. So although S_3 is equal to the deductive closure of Π^{S_3} (thus satisfying condition (ii) of Definition 101), it is not an answer set of Π as it does not satisfy condition (i) of Definition 101. $\quad\square$

Exercise 31 Extend the definition of answer sets to ground AnsProlog$_{sm}$ programs whose rules allow constraints with negative weights and give a transformation *tr* which eliminates negative weights, such that for any ground AnsProlog$_{sm}$ program π, the answer sets of π and $tr(\pi)$ coincide. (Hint: See page 9 of [NS97].) $\quad\square$

Recall that besides AnsProlog$_{sm}$ rules an input to lparse may also contain compute and optimize statements. The ground versions of these statements are of the following forms.

- Compute statement:

compute *number* $\{a_1, a_2, \ldots, a_n, \textbf{not } b_1, \textbf{not } b_2, \ldots, \textbf{not } b_m\}$.

A compute statement is a filter (with a role similar to integrity constraint but with a different interpretation of the set of literals) on the answer sets. It eliminates all answer sets that are missing one of the a_i or includes one of the b_j. In its presence the total number of answer sets that are generated is dictated by *number*. If *number* = 0 or *all* then all answer sets are generated. If *number* is absent then by default a single answer set is generated.
- Optimize statements: They are of the following four kinds.

$$\text{maximize } \{a_1, \ldots, a_n, \textbf{not } b_1, \ldots, \textbf{not } b_m\}. \tag{8.1.3}$$

$$\text{minimize } \{a_1, \ldots, a_n, \textbf{not } b_1, \ldots, \textbf{not } b_m\}. \tag{8.1.4}$$

$$\text{maximize } [a_1 = w_{a_1}, \ldots, a_n = w_{a_n}, \textbf{not } b_1 = w_{b_1}, \ldots, \textbf{not } b_m = w_{b_m}]. \tag{8.1.5}$$

$$\text{minimize } [a_1 = w_{a_1}, \ldots, a_n = w_{a_n}, \textbf{not } b_1 = w_{b_1}, \ldots, \textbf{not } b_m = w_{b_m}]. \tag{8.1.6}$$

If the program contains a single weight optimization statement, then it returns the answer sets that have the optimum (minimum or maximum as the case may be) value of $[a_1 = w_{a_1}, \ldots, a_n = w_{a_n}, \text{not } b_1 = w_{b_1}, \ldots, \text{not } b_m = w_{b_m}]$. With respect to an arbitrary set of atoms S this value is

$$\sum_{a_i \in S, 1 \le i \le n} w_{a_i} + \sum_{b_j \notin S, 1 \le j \le m} w_{b_j}.$$

If the program contains a list of optimization statements, then the optimality is determined by a multi-criteria ordering where the first optimization statement is most significant and the last optimization statement is the least significant.

Note that any maximize statement of the form (8.1.5) can be converted to a minimize statement of the following form:

minimize $\left[\text{not } a_1 = w_{a_1}, \ldots, \text{not } a_n = w_{a_n}, b_1 = w_{b_1}, \ldots, b_m = w_{b_m}\right]$.

Example 144 Consider a ground AnsProlog$_{sm}$ program Π consisting of the following rule:

1 $\{a, b, c, d\}$ 4.

This program will have 15 answer sets, each of the nonempty subsets of $\{a, b, c, d\}$.

Now suppose we have the following statement:

minimize $\{a, b, c, d\}$.

In that case only four answer sets, each of cardinality 1, will be returned.

Now if in addition we have the following statement:

maximize $[a = 2, b = 1, c = 2, d = 1]$.

Then the two answer sets that will be returned are $\{a\}$ and $\{c\}$.   □

8.1.2 *Variables and conditional literals and their grounding*

For programming convenience and to enable writing of smaller programs the input language of lparse allows variables and conditional literals which are of the form:

$$p(X_1, \ldots, X_n) : p_1(X_{i_1}) : \ldots : p_m(X_{i_m})$$

where $\{i_1, \ldots, i_m\} \subseteq \{1, \ldots, n\}$. The predicate p is referred to as the *enumerated predicate* and p_is are referred to as *conditions of p*. It should be noted that in a conditional literal a condition of the enumerating predicate could be the predicate itself. In other words $p(X) : p(X)$ is a syntactically correct conditional literal.

To make the grounding procedure – where variables and conditional literals are eliminated – efficient, lparse puts certain restrictions on the variables and the conditional literals.

Grounding of AnsProlog$_{sm}$ programs without constraints

Let us first consider the subset of AnsProlog$_{sm}$ programs where we only have atoms and naf-literals in the rules and no constraints. Intuitively, the main restriction in this case is that any variable that appears in a rule must appear in another atom in the rule whose predicate is a 'domain' or 'sort' predicate. This 'domain' or 'sort' predicate describes the range of values the variable can take. Thus during grounding variables are replaced only by the values defined by their corresponding sort predicate. To make grounding efficient the Smodels system requires that the 'domain' predicates be defined such that their extent can be computed efficiently.

Formally, a predicate 'p' of an AnsProlog$_{sm}$ program Π is a *domain predicate* iff in the predicate dependency graph of Π every path starting from 'p' is free of cycles that pass through a negative edge. Following Section 3.2.1 this means that the sub-program of Π that consists of rules with p or any predicate that can be reached from p – in the predicate dependency graph – in its head is stratified.

An AnsProlog$_{sm}$ rule is *strongly range restricted* if for every variable that appears in that rule, it also appears in a positive domain literal in the body of the rule. An AnsProlog$_{sm}$ program is *strongly range restricted* if all its rules are strongly range restricted.

The grounding of the rules is done by first computing the extent of the domain predicates and then grounding the rest of the rules by using the computed extent of the domain predicates. Since the definition of domain predicates does not involve recursion through **not**, their extent can be efficiently computed using the iteration method to compute answer sets of stratified programs.

Grounding of AnsProlog$_{sm}$ programs

In addition to variables, lparse allows the additional construct of 'conditional literals' to help in compactly writing constraints. For example, given that the extent of a domain predicate *col* is $\{c_1, c_2, \ldots, c_k\}$, the sequence $color(v, c_1), \ldots, color(v, c_k)$ can be succinctly represented by the conditional literal $color(v, C) : col(C)$. For this conditional literal *col* is the condition of the enumerated predicate *color*. With variables these literals allow great compactness in writing rules.

We now formally define weight and cardinality constraints that allow variable and conditional literals.

Cardinality and weight constraints are either in the form of ground cardinality and weight constraints or of the following forms:

$$L \ \{Cond\_Lit\} \ U \tag{8.1.7}$$

$$L \ [Cond\_Lit] \ U \tag{8.1.8}$$

respectively, where L and U are either integers or variables, and *Cond_Lit* is a conditional literal. For weight constraints of the form (8.1.8) the weights of naf-literals that may be generated in the grounding process may be explicitly given using weight definitions. The syntax of weight definitions is given in the next section.

Continuing with our example, consider the fact that we have a graph with n vertices $v_1, \ldots, v_n$ and we would like to test the k-colorability of this graph. To express this as an AnsProlog$_{sm}$ program we would first like to enumerate all possible colorings. With conditional literals and variables the enumeration part can be expressed by the single rule:

1 $\{color(X, C) : col(C)\}$ 1 :- $vertex(X)$.

and the facts

$\{col(c_1), \ldots, col(c_k), vertex(v_1), \ldots, vertex(v_n)\}$.

The grounding of the above rule would produce the following n ground rules whose heads will have k atoms.

1 $\{color(v_1, c_1), \ldots, color(v_1, c_k)\}$ 1 :- $vertex(v_1)$.

$\vdots$

1 $\{color(v_n, c_1), \ldots, color(v_n, c_k)\}$ 1 :- $vertex(v_n)$.

The lparse module requires that its input rules with conditional literals be *domain restricted* in the sense that each variable in the rules appears in a domain predicate or in the condition part of some conditional literal in the rule. Grounding of such AnsProlog$_{sm}$ rules is then done as follows:

(1) The variables in an AnsProlog$_{sm}$ rule are first divided into two categories: *local* and *global*. Those variables that appear only in a particular conditional literal, and nowhere else in the rule, are labeled as local with respect to that literal and all other variables in the rule are labeled as global. The grounding of the rules is now done in two steps.

(2) First, all global variables are eliminated by substituting them with ground terms as dictated by domain predicates corresponding to that variable.

(3) Second, conditional literals in constraints are eliminated by replacing a conditional literal say of the form $l(c_1, \ldots, c_n, X) : d(X)$ by $l(c_1, \ldots, c_n, d_1), \ldots, l(c_1, \ldots, c_n, d_k)$, where the extent of d is $\{d_1, \ldots, d_k\}$. (This is generalized to multiple conditions in the obvious way.)

8.1.3 Other constructs of the lparse language

The input language of lparse allows many additional constructs which facilitate programming using the Smodels system. We list some of them below and explain how they are processed.

- Range:
  A range is of the form

  start .. end

  where *start* and *end* are constant valued expressions.
  The range construct can be used for compact representation in certain cases. For example, instead of writing

  $p(5)$.
  $p(6)$.
  $p(7)$.
  $p(8)$

  we may simply write $p(5..8)$.
  Similarly, instead of writing

  $a :\text{-} p(3), p(4), p(5)$.

  we may simply write

  $a :\text{-} p(3..5)$.

- Multiple arguments:

  These are lists of arguments separated by semicolons and can be used for compact representation. For example,

  $p(5..8)$.

  can also be written as

  $p(5; 6; 7; 8)$.

  Similarly, instead of writing

  $a :\text{-} p(3), p(4), p(5)$.

we may write

$a :- p(3; 4; 5)$.

- Declarations
  - Function declaration: function f.
  This statement declares that f will be used as a numeric function throughout the program.
  Constant declaration: const *ident* $=$ *expr*.
  This statement declares that the identifier *ident* is a numeric constant with value *expr*, which may be any constant valued mathematical expression.
  - Weight definition: There are two kind of weight definitions.

  $$\text{weight } literal = expr.$$
  $$\text{weight } literal_1 = literal_2.$$

  The first declares that the default weight of the literal *literal* is given by a mathematical expression *expr*, which may include variables that appear in *literal*. The second declares the weight of $literal_1$ to be the same as the weight of $literal_2$ which may be defined in another part of the program. If the weight of a literal is defined more than once, only the latest one is used.

  Now suppose we have a predicate *value(Item, V)* that uniquely defines the value of an item. We can use the declaration

  $$\text{weight } value(Item, V) = 2 * V.$$

  to assign weights to *value* atoms based on the value of the particular item. This will allow the programmer to use the value of items in weight constraints or optimization statements.
  - Hide declaration: hide $p(X_1, \ldots, X_n)$.
  This statement tells the smodels program to not display atoms of the n-ary predicate p when displaying the answer sets.

  Alternatively, when the set of predicates to hide is large, then the statements

  $$\text{hide. show } p(X_1, \ldots, X_n).$$

  will only show the atoms of the predicate p when displaying the answer sets.
- Functions

  The lparse module has 18 different built-in functions: *plus, minus, times, div, mod, lt, gt, le, ge, eq, neq, assign, abs, and, or, xor, not*, and *weight*. Among these only the comparison functions and the weight function allow symbolic constants. The weight function takes a naf-literal as its only argument and returns its weight.

  The lparse module also allows user-defined C or C++ functions. But in comparison to the role of functions in classical logic or in PROLOG it has a very restricted view and usage. It distinguishes between *numerical* functions and *symbolic functions*. While numerical functions are used to compute something, symbolic functions are used to define new terms.

Numerical functions can occur either in a term or as a literal and in each case they are eliminated in the grounding phase. The role of symbolic functions is severely limited. Basically, if f is a symbolic function, then $f(a)$ defines a new constant that is given the name $f(a)$. Thus symbolic functions are not used to build lists. But we can have simple uses such as:

holds(*neg*(F), T) :- fluent(F), time(T), not *holds*(F, T).

where, *neg*(f) is a term defined using the symbolic function *neg*.
- Comments: % a comment.
  The symbol % indicates that any text following it and until the end of the line is a comment.
- Declaration identifier: # a declaration.
  Version 1.0.3 and later of lparse allow (and recommend) the symbol # before declarations.

Exercise 32 Convert the codes in Section 4.1 to AnsProlog$_{sm}$ and run them in the Smodels system. □

8.1.4 Invoking lparse and smodels

Given a program Π acceptable to lparse written in the file *file.sm*, answer sets of it are obtained by the following command:

lparse *file.sm* | smodels

When the above command is given in the command line prompt, if *file.sm* has one or more answer sets then one them is displayed in the terminal. To display 5 answer sets, we need to type:

lparse *file.sm* | smodels 5

in the command line. Replacing 5 by 0 results in the display of all the answer sets. To store the answer sets in a file we can use the standard UNIX output notation and need to type:

lparse *file.sm* | smodels 5 > *output_file*

We now give some of the options available with lparse and smodels and their meaning. The reader is advised to follow the lparse manual for the updated and extended information on the options. The general usage using those options is as follows:

lparse list_of_lparse_options *file1* ... *filen* | smodels list_of_smodels_options

(1) Important lparse options
   (a) −g *file*
   Reads previously grounded *file* to memory before grounding the program.
   (b) −v
   Prints the lparse version information.
   (c) −−true-negation[0 | 1]
   Enables the classical negation extension.
   (d) −t
   Prints the ground program in a human readable form.
(2) Important smodels options
   (a) −nolookahead
   Commands not to use lookahead during answer set computation.
   (b) −backjump
   Commands not to backtrack chronologically.
   (c) −sloppy_heuristic
   Commands not to compute the full heuristic after lookahead.
   (d) −randomize
   Does a randomized but complete search.
   (e) −w
   Displays the well-founded model.
   (f) −tries *number*
   Tries to find a model stochastically a *number* of times.
   (g) −seed *number*
   Uses *number* as seed for random parts of the computation.

8.1.5 Programming in Smodels: Graph colorability

Consider a program that can determine if a given graph is colorable by a given set of colors. The graph is described by the facts with respect to predicates *vertex* and *edge* and the given set of colors is expressed using the predicate *col*. In the following AnsProlog$_{sm}$ program the only rule with a cardinality constraint in its head assigns a unique color to each vertex. The same can be achieved through the following set of AnsProlog rules:

$other\_color(X, Y) \leftarrow vertex(X), color(X, Z), Y \neq Z.$
$color(X, Y) \leftarrow vertex(X), col(Y), \textbf{not } other\_color(X, Y).$

But the AnsProlog$_{sm}$ rule is more succinct and intuitive and also leads to better timings.

```
vertex(1..4).

edge(1,2).
edge(1,3).
edge(2,3).

edge(1,4).
edge(2,4).
% edge(3,4).

col(a;b;c).

1 { color(X,C) : col(C) } 1 :- vertex(X).
:- edge(X,Y), col(C), color(X,C), color(Y,C).

:- edge(Y,X), col(C), color(X,C), color(Y,C).

hide col(X).
hide vertex(Y).
hide edge(X,Y).
```

When we run the above program we get six answer sets, and in each of them the color assigned to nodes 3 and 4 is the same. But if we remove the % before edge(3,4) and run the resulting program then we do not get any answer set as the resulting graph is not colorable using three colors.

8.1.6 Programming in Smodels: Round-robin tournament scheduling

Consider scheduling a tournament with 10 teams that play in a round-robin schedule, where each team plays the other team exactly once. This obviously takes nine weeks. We have five stadiums where these games are played and each team plays every week. Besides obvious restrictions, such as only two teams can play at a time in a stadium, we have the restriction that no team plays more than twice in the same field over the course of the nine weeks. The following is an AnsProlog$_{sm}$ program that finds schedules for such a tournament. We use comments to give the intuitive meaning of some of the rules.

```
team(1..10).
week(1..9).
field(1..5).

%schedule(X,Y,Z) means that Z is a team that plays in field X
%in   week Y.

1 { schedule(X,Y,Z) : field(X) } 1 :- week(Y), team(Z).

% The schedule should be such that for a given week, a team is
% scheduled in only one field.

2 { schedule(X,Y,Z) : team(Z) } 2 :- week(Y), field(X).

%The schedule should be such that for a given week, and a given
%field exactly two teams are scheduled. In other words, 3
%different teams cannot be scheduled in the same field on the
%same week, and at least 2 teams are scheduled in the same
%field on the same  week.

1 { schedule(X,Y,Z) : week(Y) } 2 :- field(X), team(Z).

%The schedule should be such that no team plays more than
%twice in the same field over the course of the season; and
%every team plays at least once in each field.

hide week(X).
hide team(X).
hide field(X).
```

8.1.7 Programming in Smodels: Mini-ACC tournament scheduling

ACC is the Atlantic Coast Conference, a group of nine universities on the east coast of the USA that play various inter-collegiate games among themselves and share the revenue. The basketball teams of these universities are quite famous and they use a specific set of guidelines to schedule their games. Based on these guidelines an operational research based solution package has been developed [Hen01] and used. In this section we give an Smodels solution for a simplified version of the problem.

Although a couple of my students have come up with a reasonable solution that calls Smodels multiple times and follows some of the ideas from [Hen01],we have not been able to devise a direct formulation in Smodels that can produce a schedule in 24 hours. We now describe the simplified version, which we will refer to as the mini-ACC tournament scheduling.

There are five teams: duke, fsu, umd, unc, uva; duke and unc are considered rivals and also umd and uva. They play 10 dates over five weeks. In each week there is a weekday game and a weekend game. Besides the obvious restrictions such as a team cannot play itself, we have the following restrictions.

Two teams play exactly twice over the season. Over the season a team may play another team at home exactly once. No team may have more than two home matches in a row. No team can play away in both of the last two dates. No team may have more than 3 away matches or byes in a row. At the weekends, each team plays 2 at home, 2 away, and one bye. In the last date, every team, except fsu, plays against its rival, unless it plays against fsu or has a bye. No team plays on two consecutive days away against duke and unc. The following is an AnsProlog$_{sm}$ program whose answer sets encode schedules agreeing with the above restrictions and a few additional specific restrictions about particular teams.

```
date(1..10).
team(duke;fsu;umd;unc;uva).

rival(duke,unc).
rival(umd,uva).

rival(X,Y) :- team(X), team(Y), rival(Y,X).

weekday(X) :- date(X), not weekend(X).
weekend(X) :- date(X), not weekday(X).

weekday(X+1) :- date(X), weekend(X).
weekend(X+1) :- date(X), weekday(X).

%sch(X,Y,D) means that Teams X and Y are scheduled to plays
%on date D at the home court of X.

plays(X,Y,D) :- team(X), team(Y), date(D), sch(X,Y,D).

plays(X,Y,D) :- team(X), team(Y), date(D), sch(Y,X,D).

plays(X,D) :- team(X), team(Y), date(D), plays(X,Y,D).
```

```
plays_at_home(X,D) :- team(X), team(Y), date(D), sch(X,Y,D).

plays_away(X,D) :- team(X), team(Y), date(D), sch(Y,X,D).

has_bye(X,D) :- team(X), date(D), not plays(X,D).

0 { sch(X,Y,D) : team(Y) } 1 :- date(D), team(X).
```

%The schedule should be such that for a particular date a team
%may only play at most one other team at home.

```
:- team(X), team(Y), team(Z), date(D), not eq(Z,Y),
   plays(X,Y,D), plays(X,Z,D).
```

%The schedule should be such that for a particular date a team
%can not play more than one other team.

```
:- team(X), team(Y), date(D), sch(X,Y,D), sch(Y,X,D).
```

%The schedule should be such that for a particular date a team
%cannot play both at home and away.

```
:- team(X), team(Y), date(D), sch(X,Y,D), eq(X,Y).
```

%The schedule should be such that a team cannot play itself.

```
1 { sch(X,Y,D) : date(D) } 1 :- team(X), team(Y), not eq(X,Y).
```

%The schedule should be such that over the season a team plays
%another team at home exactly once; and thus two teams play
%each other exactly twice over the season.

```
:- team(X), plays_away(X,9), plays_away(X,10).
```

%No team plays away on both of the last two dates.

```
:- team(X), date(T), date(T+1), date(T+2), plays_at_home(X,T),
   plays_at_home(X,T+1), plays_at_home(X,T+2).
```

%No team may have more than two home matches in a row.

```
away_or_bye(X,D) :- team(X), date(D), plays_away(X,D).
away_or_bye(X,D) :- team(X), date(D), has_bye(X,D).

:- team(X), date(T), date(T+1), date(T+2), date(T+3),
   away_or_bye(X,T), away_or_bye(X,T+1),
   away_or_bye(X,T+2), away_or_bye(X,T+3).
```

%No team may have more than 3 away matches or byes in a row.

```
plays_at_home_weekend(X,D) :- team(X), date(D), weekend(D),
                             plays_at_home(X,D).
plays_away_weekend(X,D) :- team(X), date(D), weekend(D),
                           plays_away(X,D).

has_bye_weekend(X,D) :- team(X), date(D), weekend(D),
                        has_bye(X,D).

cond1(X) :- 2 {plays_at_home_weekend(X,D) : date(D)} 2,
team(X).

:- team(X), not cond1(X).

cond2(X) :- 2 {plays_away_weekend(X,D) : date(D)} 2, team(X).

:- team(X), not cond2(X).

cond3(X) :- 1 {has_bye_weekend(X,D) : date(D)} 1, team(X).

:- team(X), not cond3(X).
```

%The above set of rules enforce the condition that on the
%(five) weekends, each team plays 2 games at home, 2 away,
%and has one bye.

```
:- team(X), team(Y), plays(X,Y,10), not rival(X,Y),
   not eq(X,fsu), not eq(Y,fsu).
```

% On the last date, every team, except fsu, plays against its
% rival, unless it plays against fsu or has a bye.

```
plays_duke_unc(X,D) :- team(X), date(D),~sch(unc,X,D).
plays_duke_unc(X,D) :- team(X), date(D), sch(duke,X,D).

:- team(X), date(T), date(T+1), plays_duke_unc(T),
   plays_duke_unc(T+1).
```

%No team plays on two consecutive days away against duke and
%unc.

```
:- not plays(unc,duke,10).      %unc must play duke on date 10.
:- not has_bye(duke,7).         %duke has a bye on date 7.
:- plays_away(umd,10).          %umd does not play away on
                                %date 10.

:- has_bye(fsu,10).             %fsu does not have a bye on
                                %date 10.

:- has_bye(umd,8).              %umd does not have a bye on
                                %date 8.

:- plays(umd,uva,6).            %uva does not play at umd on
                                %date 6.

:- not plays_away(uva, 7).      %uva plays away in week 7.
:- not plays_at_home(unc,3).    %unc plays at home in week 6.
```

%%

```
hide team(X).
hide date(X).
hide rival(X,Y).
hide weekday(X).
hide plays(X,Y).
hide plays(X,Y,Z).
hide has_bye(X,Y).
hide plays_at_home(X,D).
hide plays_away(X,D).
hide away_or_bye(X,D).
hide home_or_bye(X,D).
hide plays_at_home_weekend(X,D).
hide plays_away_weekend(X,D).
hide has_bye_weekend(X,D).
hide plays_duke_unc(X,T).
```

```
hide plays_duke_unc_wfu(X,D).
hide cond1(X).
hide cond2(X).
hide cond3(X).
```

8.1.8 Programming in Smodels: Knapsack problem

We now give an example of encoding with Smodels that uses optimize statements. We consider a simple knapsack problem where we have five items (1–5) and each item has a cost (or size) and value associated with it. We have a sack with a given capacity (12) and the goal is to select a subset of the items which can fit into the sack while maximizing the total value. This can be encoded in Smodels as follows:

```
item(1..5).

weight val(1) = 5.
weight val(2) = 6.
weight val(3) = 3.
weight val(4) = 8.
weight val(5) = 2.


weight cost(1) = 4.
weight cost(2) = 5.
weight cost(3) = 6.
weight cost(4) = 5.
weight cost(5) = 3.


in_sack(X) :-  item(X), not not_in_sack(X).

not_in_sack(X) :- item(X), not in_sack(X).

val(X) :-  item(X), in_sack(X).

cost(X) :- item(X), in_sack(X).

cond1 :- [ cost(X) : item(X) ] 12.

:- not cond1.
```

```
maximize { val(X) : item(X) }.


hide item(X).
hide not_in_sack(X).
hide cost(X).
hide val(X).
```

8.1.9 Programming in Smodels: Single unit combinatorial auction

In a combinatorial auction problem bidders are allowed to bid on a bundle of items. The auctioneer has to select a subset of the bids so as to maximize the price it gets, and making sure that it does not accept multiple bids that have the same item as each item can be sold only once. Following is an example of a single unit combinatorial auction problem. The auctioneer has the set of items $\{1, 2, 3, 4\}$, and the buyers submit bids $\{a, b, c, d, e\}$ where a constitutes $\langle\{1, 2, 3\}, 24\rangle$, meaning that the bid a is for the bundle $\{1, 2, 3\}$ and its price is \$24. Similarly b constitutes $\langle\{2, 3\}, 9\rangle$, c constitutes $\langle\{3, 4\}, 8\rangle$, d constitutes $\langle\{2, 3, 4\}, 25\rangle$, and e constitutes $\langle\{1, 4\}, 15\rangle$. The *winner determination* problem is to accept a subset of the bids with the stipulation that no two bids containing the same item can be accepted, so as to maximize the total price fetched. We now present an AnsProlog$_{sm}$ encoding of this example.

```
bid(a;b;c;d;e).

item(1..4).

in(1,a).
in(2,a).
in(3,a).

in(2,b).
in(3,b).

in(3,c).
in(4,c).

in(2,d).
in(3,d).
in(4,d).
```

```
in(1,e).
in(4,e).
weight sel(a) = 24.
weight sel(b) = 9.
weight sel(c) = 8.
weight sel(d) = 25.
weight sel(e) = 15.


sel(X) :- bid(X), not not_sel(X).


not_sel(X) :- bid(X), not sel(X).


:- bid(X), bid(Y), sel(X), sel(Y), not eq(X,Y), item(I), in
   (I,X), in(I,Y).


maximize [ sel(X) : bid(X) ].


hide bid(X).
hide not_sel(X).
hide item(X).
hide in(X,Y).
```

8.2 The dlv system

The dlv system is meant for computing answer sets of AnsProlog$^{\perp,or}$ programs and offers several front-ends for knowledge representation tasks such as query answering in the brave and cautious modes, diagnosis, planning, and answering a subset of SQL3 queries.

When the dlv system is invoked with an input AnsProlog$^{\perp,or}$ program it processes it in several steps. First it converts the input to an internal representation. Then it converts the program to an equivalent program without variables. In the next step it generates possible answer sets and checks their validity. Finally the answer sets (or an answer set) go through post-processing as dictated by the front-end.

The main difference between the Smodels system of Section 8.1 and the dlv system is that the latter is centered around AnsProlog$^{\perp,or}$ programs, while the former has only primitive functionality with respect to disjunction. Among the other differences between these two systems, dlv allows the specification of queries in the program and supports both brave and cautious reasoning modes. The following table elaborates the differences between Smodels and dlv.

Issues	Smodels system	dlv system
Main focus	AnsProlog$^\perp$	AnsProlog$^{\perp, \, or}$
Notation for disjunction		3 alternative notations (v, |, ;)
Query specification	indirectly using constraints	allows direct specification
Notation for queries	or compute statements.	$p_1, \ldots, p_m,$ **not**
		$q_1, \ldots,$ **not** q_m?
		(where p_is and q_js are literals)
Query answering modes		brave, cautious
Beyond AnsProlog*	weight constraints, cardinality constraints, optimization statements	weak constraints, several front-ends (diagnosis, planning, SQL3)
Using arithmetic in rules	$p(T + 1) :\text{-} \operatorname{dom}_1(T), p(T).$	the one on the left is not acceptable;
	domain predicate is required	$p(TT) :\text{-} p(T), TT = T + 1.$ is. #maxint needs to be defined, no need of domain predicate
Function symbols	allowed with limitations	not allowed
Explicit negation	allowed *Lit* could be an answer set. (computes all answer sets)	allowed, uses the symbol '-' . *Lit* cannot be an answer set. (computes only consistent answer sets)
Anonymous variables	not allowed	can be specified using '_' as in *student*$(X) : -.$ *takes_class*$(X, \_).$
Restriction on rules	strongly range restricted	range restricted
Input interface		Oracle, Objectivity (both experimental)
API	user defined C/C++ functions	
Aggregation	can be simulated using weight constraints	under development

8.2.1 Some distinguishing features of dlv

In this section we discuss some of the distinguishing features of the dlv system in greater detail. Often we will refer to the extended language allowed by the dlv system as AnsProlog$_{dlv}$.

The dlv system requires that each rule in the input program be range restricted. Recall from Section 1.2.2 that a rule is said to be range-restricted if each variable occurring in the rule occurs in at least one of the nonbuilt-in comparative positive literals in the body of the rule. Note that this restriction on rules is weaker than the restriction of 'strong range-restrictedness' imposed by the Smodels system.

There are two exceptions to the range restricted requirement in rules: use of anonymous variables, and use of global #maxint definition that makes it unnecessary for variables in arithmetic built-in predicates to be range-restricted. *Anonymous variables* in dlv are denoted by _ (an underscore). For example, if we want to write a rule saying that X is a student if he or she is taking some class Y. We can write a rule using the anonymous variable notation in the following way.

student(X) :- *takes_class*$(X, \_)$.

The dlv system allows the usage of classical negation. Thus it accepts AnsProlog$^{\neg,\perp,or}$ programs. In its characterization of AnsProlog$^{\neg,\perp,or}$ programs it assumes it only needs to compute consistent answer sets. In other words if *Lit* is the answer set of a program then dlv will not report it. For example, although the following program

p.
q.
$\neg q$.

has $Lit = \{p, q, \neg q, \neg p\}$ as its answer set, the dlv system will not report it. This is a minor drawback of the dlv system as it does not allow us to distinguish between programs that do not have answer sets and programs that have only *Lit* as an answer set. In contrast in the Smodels system there is an option to specify whether to consider *Lit* as an answer set or not.

The dlv system allows the specification of queries. A query is of the form:

$$p_1, \ldots, p_m, \textbf{not } q_1, \ldots, \textbf{not } q_n? \tag{8.2.9}$$

where p_i and q_j are literals. The dlv system allows two modes of querying: brave and cautious, which are specified by the command line options $-FB$ and $-FC$ respectively. A query of the form (8.2.9) is true in the brave mode if the conjunctions of the p_is and **not** q_js are satisfied in at least one answer set of the program. A query is true in the cautious mode if it is satisfied in all answer sets of the program.

In the brave mode of reasoning, a query of the form (8.2.9) can alternatively be encoded by the following set of constraints:

:- **not** p_1.
$\vdots$

:- **not** p_m.
:- q_1.
$\vdots$

:- q_n.

which will eliminate answer sets that do not satisfy the query.

The dlv system allows four arithmetic predicates: #int, #succ, +, and *. When one or more of these predicates are used then dlv must be invoked with the option '-N = int-value'. For example, when dlv is invoked with '-N = 20' it means that the system only considers integers between 0 and 20. Intuitively, #int(X) is true if X is an integer less than or equal to int-value; #succ(X, Y) is true if $X + 1 = Y$; +(X, Y, Z) is true if $Z = X + Y$; and *(X, Y, Z) is true if $Z = X*Y$. The dlv system does allow writing $Z = X + Y$ instead of +(X, Y, Z) and $Z = X * Y$ instead of *(X, Y, Z). However, it should be noted that unlike in Smodels, + and * cannot be used as function symbols. Thus, the rule

$p(T + 1) :- p(T)$.

is not acceptable to dlv. An equivalent rule acceptable to dlv would be:

$p(TT) :- p(T), TT = T + 1$.

One of the other novel features of dlv is the notion of *weak constraints*. We discuss this further in the next section.

8.2.2 *Weak constraints in dlv vs optimization statements in Smodels*

Weak constraints in dlv are of the form

$$:\sim p_1, \ldots, p_m, \textbf{not } q_1, \ldots, \textbf{not } q_n.[weight:level] \qquad (8.2.10)$$

where p_is and q_js are literals, and weight and level are integers or integer variables that appear in the p_is.

Given a program with weak constraints its *best* answer sets are obtained by first obtaining the answer sets without considering the weak constraints and ordering each of them based on the weight and priority level of the set of weak constraints they violate, and then selecting the ones that violate the minimum. In the presence of both weight and priority level information, the minimization is done with respect to the weight of the constraints of the highest priority, then the next highest priority, and so on. Note that the weak constraints may contain none, or one, or both of the weight and priority information, but it is required that all the weak constraints have the same syntactic form. That is, if one of them has only weight information then all of them can have only weight information, and so on. If both the weight and level information are omitted then they are set to the value 1 by default.

Consider the following program with weak constraints.

$a \lor b$.
$-a \lor c$.
$:\sim a$.
$:\sim b, c$.

The *best* answer set of the above program is $\{-a, b\}$, which does not violate any of the weak constraints, while the other two answer sets $\{a, c\}$ and $\{b, c\}$, each violate one weak constraint.

Weak constraints in dlv serve a similar purpose to optimization statements in dlv. For example, the following optimizations statement in Smodels

$$\text{minimize } \{a_1 = w_{a_1}, \ldots, a_n = w_{a_n}, \textbf{not } b_1 = w_{b_1}, \ldots, \textbf{not } b_m = w_{b_m}\}.$$

can be expressed by the following set of weak constraints in dlv.

$$:\sim a_1.[w_{a_1} : 1]$$
$$\vdots$$
$$:\sim a_n.[w_{a_n} : 1]$$
$$:\sim \textbf{not } b_1.[w_{b_1} : 1]$$
$$\vdots$$
$$:\sim \textbf{not } b_m.[w_{b_m} : 1]$$

Similarly, a set of weak constraints specifying the same priority level can be replaced by a minimize statement with some additional rules to link conjunctions in the weak constraints to individual atoms that are included in the minimize statement.

8.2.3 Invoking dlv

To process a program using dlv, it is invoked by the following command

dlv [front-end-options] [general-options] [file1, . . . ,filen]

Earlier we mentioned two of the front-end-options (-FB and -FC resp.) for brave and cautious reasoning. In addition to those front-end options the following are some useful general options in dlv. The dlv manual has the exhaustive list of front-end options and general options.

(1) −filter = p

This option specifies that the literals made up of predicate p are not to be displayed. This option may be used multiple times to specify a set of predicates.

(2) −n = number

This option specifies the upper bound on the number of answer sets that will be displayed. If 'number' is 0 or 'all', then all answer sets are displayed.

(3) −N = number

This specifies the maximum value of integers that the program should consider. It assigns a built-in constant '#maxint' the value given by number. This assignment can also be done inside the program by writing

```
#maxint=15.
```

Once #maxint is defined either directly or in the command line then range-restrictedness is not necessary for variables that appear in arithmetic built-in predicates. For example, the following is a syntactically correct dlv program.

```
#maxint=15.
plus(X,Y,Z)  :-  Z = X + Y.
```

(4) −OH−

This option disables heuristics in the model generator. When this option is absent, by default, heuristics are used in the model generator.

(5) −instantiate

This option only performs the grounding and prints the instantiation.

(6) −silent

This option skips showing the status line and various informational output and blank lines.

(7) −−

This option tells dlv to read input from the stdin.

Exercise 33 Convert the codes in Section 4.1 to AnsProlog$_{dlv}$ and run them in the dlv system.   □

8.2.4 Single unit combinatorial auction using weak constraints

In Section 8.1.9 we showed how to encode the single unit combinatorial auction problem using AnsProlog$_{sm}$. Here we encode it in AnsProlog$_{dlv}$. The main differences in the two encodings are that here we use a rule with disjunction in the head for enumeration, and use weak constraints instead of the optimization statement in the AnsProlog$_{sm}$ encoding.

```
bid(a).
bid(b).
bid(c).
bid(d).
bid(e).

in(1,a).
in(2,a).
in(3,a).

in(2,b).
in(3,b).
```

```
in(3,c).
in(4,c).

in(2,d).
in(3,d).
in(4,d).

in(1,e).
in(4,e).


sel(X) v not_sel(X) :- bid(X).


:-  sel(X), sel(Y), X != Y, in(I,X), in(I,Y).


:~ not sel(a). [24:1]
:~ not sel(b). [9:1]
:~ not sel(c). [8:1]
:~ not sel(d). [25:1]
:~ not sel(e). [15:1]
```

8.2.5 *Conformant planning using dlv*

In Chapter 5 we discussed the issue of planning in great detail. But with the exception of Section 5.4 we assumed that the planning agent has complete information about the initial state. In Section 5.4 we relaxed this assumption and introduced a notion of approximate planning whose complexity is **NP**-complete. In this section we consider the more general notion of conformant planning, but whose complexity is $\Sigma_2\mathbf{P}$-complete. In conformant planning, we look for a sequence of actions which is a plan for all possible complete initial states that agree with the (incomplete) knowledge that the agent has about the initial state. Conformant planning is not expressible in AnsProlog, but is expressible in AnsProlog^{or}, the focus of the dlv system. We illustrate how to encode conformant planning problems in AnsProlog$_{dlv}$, through a simple example.

Consider a domain with actions a and b and fluents p and f, where the effects of the actions are described by the following propositions in the language $\mathcal{A}$ (from Chapter 5).

a **causes** f **if** p
a **causes** f **if** $\neg p$
b **causes** f **if** p

The (incomplete) information about the initial state is given by the following.

initially $\neg f$

The goal of the agent is to make f *true*.

Intuitively the only conformant plan of length 1 is the single action a. The following encoding has one answer set which encodes this plan. This encoding is similar to the encoding of existential-universal QBFs in Section 2.1.11, as a conformant plan can be characterized as 'there exists a sequence of actions (α) such that for all possible initial states (σ), execution of α in σ will take us to a goal state.'

```
time(1).

action(a).
action(b).

fluent(f).
fluent(p).
fluent(ff).
fluent(pp).

initially(ff).

holds(F,1) :- fluent(F), initially(F).

opp(f,ff).
opp(ff,f).
opp(p,pp).
opp(pp,p).

holds(F, TT) :- opp(F,FF), TT = T + 1, holds(F,T),
not holds (FF, TT).

holds(f, TT) :-   TT = T + 1, occurs(a,T), holds(p,T).
holds(f, TT) :-   TT = T + 1, occurs(a,T), holds(pp,T).
holds(f, TT) :-   TT = T + 1, occurs(b,T), holds(p,T).

not_occurs(A,T) :- action(A), A != B, occurs(B,T).

occurs(A,T) :- action(A), time(T), not not_occurs(A,T).
```

```
holds(p,1) } holds(pp, 1).

goal_sat :- holds(f,2).

holds(f,1)        :-   goal_sat.
holds(ff,1)       :-        goal_sat.
holds(p,1)        :-        goal_sat.
holds(pp,1)       :-   goal_sat.

holds(f,2)        :- goal_sat.
holds(ff,2)       :- goal_sat.
holds(p,2)        :- goal_sat.
holds(pp,2)       :- goal_sat.


:- not goal_sat.
```

We now show the output obtained by running the above program using dlv. We run two versions of the above program: planning10.dl and planning11.dl. The only difference between the two is that in the second one the constraint ':- not goal_sat' is commented out.

(1) dlv −N = 5 planning10.dl

```
dlv [build DEV/Nov  7 2000    gcc egcs-2.91.57 19980901
(egcs-1.1 release)]
{time(1), action(a), action(b), fluent(f), fluent(p),
fluent(ff), fluent(pp), initially(ff), opp(f,ff), opp(p,pp),
opp(ff, f), opp(pp,p), holds(ff,1), occurs(a,1),
not_occurs(b,1), holds(p,1), holds(pp,1), holds(ff,2),
holds(f,2), holds(p,2), holds(pp,2), goal_sat, holds(f,1)}
```

The reason we do not have answer sets with *occurs*(b, 1) and *goal_sat* is that even though there seems to be an enumeration where p is *true* at time point 1, this enumeration is not minimal, as it leads to *goal_sat* which makes all fluent literals *true* at time points 1–2, and there is another enumeration where pp – the inverse of p – is *true* at time point 1 which is a subset of the previous enumeration. Thus the first enumeration does not lead to an answer set. The second one is eliminated as it does not have *goal_sat*. As evident from the next item, when we remove the constraint ← *goal_sat*., we do have an answer set with *occurs*(b, 1) and *holds*(pp, 1) but without *goal_sat*.

In the case where we have *occurs*(*a*, 1), both possibilities, with *p* true at time point 1, and its inverse *pp* true at time point 1, lead to *goal_sat* which makes all fluent literals *true* at time points 1 and 2, leading to a single answer set.

(2) dlv −*N* = 5 planning11.dl

```
dlv [build DEV/Nov 7 2000 gcc egcs-2.91.57 19980901 (egcs-1.1
release)]

{time(1), action(a), action(b), fluent(f), fluent(p),
fluent(ff),  fluent(pp), initially(ff), opp(f,ff), opp(p,pp),
opp(ff,f), opp(pp,p), holds(ff,1), not_occurs(a,1),
occurs(b,1), holds(pp,1), holds(ff,2), holds(pp,2)}

{time(1), action(a), action(b), fluent(f), fluent(p),
fluent(ff), fluent(pp), initially(ff), opp(f,ff), opp(p,pp),
opp(ff,f), opp(pp,p), holds(ff,1), occurs(a,1),
not_occurs(b,1), holds(p,1), holds(pp,1), holds(ff,2),
holds(f,2), holds(p,2), holds(pp,2) goal_sat, holds(f,1)}
```

8.3 Applications of answer set computing systems

In this section we formulate several problem solving domains using AnsProlog$_{sm}$ and AnsProlog$_{dlv}$. These formulations use features that are not in AnsProlog*, but are in AnsProlog$_{sm}$ or AnsProlog$_{dlv}$. The domains we consider are: more complex combinatorial domains, planning using durative actions and resources, scheduling, and specification and verification of active databases. Our presentation in this section will be in most cases similar to our presentation in Chapter 4 and unlike in the earlier two sections of this chapter we will not always present the exact AnsProlog$_{sm}$ or AnsProlog$_{dlv}$ code. (The exact code is available at the supplementary web site of this book.) We start with some simple programming tricks which are useful when programming in AnsProlog$_{sm}$ or AnsProlog$_{dlv}$.

8.3.1 Some AnsProlog$_{sm}$ and AnsProlog$_{dlv}$ programming tricks

In this subsection we present some AnsProlog$_{sm}$ and AnsProlog$_{dlv}$ programming tricks and show how certain programming constructs and data structures can be encoded using these tricks. The programs we present are in AnsProlog$_{sm}$ and need very little modification to run in the dlv system.

(**I**) **Aggregation**: Weight constraints and cardinality constraints in AnsProlog$_{sm}$ can be used to encode certain aggregations such as *count* and *sum*. Consider the following example from Section 2.1.14, where *sold*(*a*, 10, *Jan*1) means that 10 units of item *a* were sold on January 1.

```
sold(a, 10, jan1).
sold(a, 21, jan5).
sold(a, 15, jan16).
sold(b, 16, jan4).
sold(b, 31, jan21).
sold(b, 15, jan26).
sold(c, 24, jan8).
```

We now show how to use weight constraints to compute the total units sold and total number of selling transactions for each of the items.

```
item(a;b;c).
number(1..100).
date(jan1;jan5;jan16;jan4;jan21;jan26;jan8).
weight sold(X,Y,Z) = Y.


total_sold(I, N)  :- item(I), number(N),
                  N [ sold(I, X, D) : number(X)
                      : date(D)   ] N.


total_sell_transactions(I, N)  :- item(I), number(N),
                  N { sold(I, X, D) : number(X)
                      : date(D)   } N.
```

(II) Sets and Lists: Since Smodels has very limited facility for expressing symbolic functions and dlv does not allow function symbols, we cannot use symbolic functions – as in PROLOG – to express lists. Nevertheless, we can explicitly express lists and process them. In the following we show some of the techniques.

(1) In representing effects of actions often the atom *causes*$(a, l_0, [l_1, \ldots, l_n])$ is used to express that the execution of action *a* will make l_0 true if $l_1, \ldots, l_n$ are initially *true*. In the absence of the [ ] notation (which is a short form of a term built using symbolic functions), we can express the above atom in AnsProlog$_{sm}$ or AnsProlog$_{dlv}$ in the following way:

```
causes(a, 10, s).

set(s).

in(l1, s).
...
in(ln, s).
```

(2) Now suppose we want to verify that every element of the set (S) holds at time T. This can be expressed in AnsProlog$_{sm}$ as follows:

```
not_holds(S, T) :- set(S), time(T), in(I,S), not holds(I,T).

holds(S,T) :- set(S), time(T), not not_holds(S, T).
```

(3) Now instead of sets, suppose we would like to deal with linear lists. For example, we may want to verify if l will be true after executing the sequence of actions $a_1, \ldots, a_n$ in time t. In other words we want to find out if *holds_after*($l, [a_1, \ldots, a_n], t$) is true or not. In AnsProlog$_{sm}$ we can express this as

```
holds_after(l, list, t).

action(1, list, a1).
...
action(n, list, a_n).
```

and will have the following AnsProlog$_{sm}$ rules to reason with it.

```
not_holds_set(Set, N, List, T) :- in(L, Set),
                                   not holds_after(L, N,
                                   List, T).
holds_set(Set, N, List, T) :- not not_holds_set(Set, N,
                                  List, T).

not_last(List, N) :- action(M, List, A), N < M.
last(List, N) :- not  not_last(List, N).

holds_after(L, List, T) :- holds_after(L, N, List, T),
                               last(List, N).
holds_after(L, 0, List, T) :- holds(L, T).
holds_after(L, N, List, T) :- holds_after(L, N-1, List,T),
                               action(N, List, A),
                               not ab.(L, N, List,T).
holds_after(L, N, List, T) :- action(N, List, A),
                               causes(A, L, Set),
                               holds_set(Set, N-1, List, T).

ab(LL, N, List, T) :-  action(N, List, A),
                       causes(A, L, Set),
                       holds_set(Set, N-1, List; T).
```

(4) Finally lists of arbitrary depth such as in the following atom $p([a, [b, [c, d]])$ can be expressed as follows:

```
p(1).

head(1,a).
body(1, 11).

head(11, b).
body(11, 12).

head(12, c).
body(12, 13).

head(13, d).
body(13, nil).
```

In Section 5.5 we used this notation in processing procedural constraints.

8.3.2 Combinatorial auctions

Earlier in Sections 8.1.9 and 8.2.4 we considered the case of single unit combinatorial auctions. In this section we consider combinatorial auctions in more generalized settings: when the bids are in conjunctive normal form, when we have multiple units, when we have a combinatorial exchange, and when there are many additional constraints.

(I) Combinatorial auction with CNF bids

We start by showing how the single unit combinatorial auction specification can be generalized such that a bidder can specify some options between bids. For example a bidder may want to specify that only one of the bids g and h be accepted, but not both. This can be generalized further such that a bidder can specify a CNF bid [HB00] which is a conjunction of (ex-or) disjunction of items such that one item from each of the conjuncts is awarded to the bidder. We show our encoding with respect to an example.

(I.a) Specifying the domain

(1) We will have the bid names and their values as follows:

$bid(a). weight sel(a) = 24.$ $bid(b). weight sel(b) = 9.$ $bid(c). weight sel(c) = 8.$
$bid(d). weight sel(d) = 25.$ $bid(e). weight sel(e) = 15.$

(2) We will specify the items as follows:

$item(1..4)$.

(3) We now need to specify the composition of each bid. Recall that a CNF bid is not a bundle of items, rather it could be of the following form:

$$a = (g1 \oplus h1) \wedge (g2 \oplus h2) \wedge (g3 \oplus h3)$$

which means that the bid a can be satisfied by granting one of the items $g1$ and $h1$, one of the items $g2$ and $h2$, and one of the items $g3$ and $h3$. We can represent this in AnsProlog$_{sm}$ as follows:

$conj(c1, a).\ disj(g1, c1).\ disj(h1, c1).$
$conj(c2, a).\ disj(g2, c2).\ disj(h2, c2).$
$conj(c3, a).\ disj(g3, c3).\ disj(h3, c3).$

(I.b) The general rules

(1) The following two rules label each bid as either selected or not selected.

$sel(X) \leftarrow bid(X), \textbf{not } not\_sel(X).$
$not\_sel(X) \leftarrow bid(X), \textbf{not } sel(X).$

They can be replaced by the following single AnsProlog$_{sm}$ rule:

$\{sel(X)\} \leftarrow bid(X).$

(2) Now it is not enough to just label bids as selected or unselected. After labeling a bid as selected we must identify which items are granted as part of that selected bid. We encode that using the following rules.

$other\_granted(X, C, G) \leftarrow granted(X, C, G'), G' \neq G.$
$granted(X, C, G) \leftarrow sel(X), conj(C, X), disj(G, C), \textbf{not } other\_granted(X, C, G).$

Intuitively, $granted(X, C, G)$ means that as part of the selection of bid X, to satisfy the conjunct C, item G is granted; and $other\_granted(X, C, G)$ means that some item other than G has been granted. The above two rules ensure that for any selected bid X, and its conjunct C exactly one item in that conjunct is granted in each answer set.

(3) To enforce the condition that we should not select two bids and grant the same item with respect to both, we need the following:

$\leftarrow bid(X), bid(Y), granted(X, C, G), granted(Y, C', G), X \neq Y.$

(4) The following optimization statement specifies that we must select bids such that their total price is maximized.

$maximize\ [sel(X) : bid(X)].$

(II) Multi-unit combinatorial auction

Multi-unit combinatorial auction is a generalization of the single unit case, where the auctioneer may have multiple identical copies of each item and the bids may specify multiple units of each item. The goal here is the same as before: to maximize the total price that is fetched; but the condition is that the bids should be selected such that for any item the total number that is asked by the selected bids should not be more than the number that is originally available for that item. As before, we describe our AnsProlog$_{sm}$ encoding with respect to an example: first the specification for a particular domain, and then a set of general rules.

(II.a) Specifying the domain

(1) The bid names and their values are specified as in part (1) of (I.a).

bid(a). weight sel(a) = 23.
bid(b). weight sel(b) = 9.
bid(c). weight sel(c) = 8.
bid(d). weight sel(d) = 25.
bid(e). weight sel(e) = 15.

(2) We specify the items and their initial quantities as follows:

item(i). item(j). item(k). item(l).
limit(i, 8). limit(j, 10). limit(k, 6). limit(l, 12).

(3) We specify the composition of each bid as follows:

in(i, a, 6). in(j, a, 4). in(k, a, 4).

Intuitively, the above means that, bid '*a*' is for 6 units of item '*i*', 4 units of item '*j*', and 4 units of item '*k*'.

in(j, b, 6). in(k, b, 4).

in(k, c, 2). in(l, c, 10).

in(j, d, 4). in(k, d, 2).in(l, d, 4).

in(i, e, 6). in(l, e, 6).

(II.b) The general rules

We have the following general rules which together with the domain specific rules of the previous subsection, when run in the Smodels system will give us the winning bids.

(1) The following two rules label each bid as either selected or not selected.

sel(X) ← *bid(X),* **not** *not_sel(X).*
not_sel(X) ← *bid(X),* **not** *sel(X).*

(2) The following rule defines $sel\_in(I, X, Z)$, which intuitively means that bid X is selected, and Z units of item I are in bid X.

$sel\_in(I, X, Z) \leftarrow item(I), bid(X), sel(X), in(I, X, Z).$

(3) The following weight declaration assigns the weight Z to the atom $sel\_in(X, Y, Z)$.

weight $sel\_in(X, Y, Z) = Z.$

The above weight assignment is used in the next step to compute the total quantity of
each item in the selected bids.

(4) The following rule enforces the constraint that for each item, the total quantity that is
to be encumbered towards the selected bids must be less than or equal to the initial
available quantity of that item.

$\leftarrow Y'[sel\_in(I, X, Z) : bid(X) : num(Z)], item(I), limit(I, Y), Y' = Y + 1.$

(5) As before we have the following optimization statement.

maximize $[sel(X) : bid(X)].$ —

When the above program is run through Smodels using the command

lparse file.sm | smodels 0

the system first outputs the answer set $\{sel(d), sel(a)\}$, and then outputs another
answer set $\{sel(e), sel(d), sel(b)\}$ and mentions that the latter one is optimal.

(III) Combinatorial exchanges

A combinatorial exchange is a further generalization, where we have buyers and
sellers. The buyers bid as before, while the sellers offer their items for a price.
The job of the exchange is to accept a subset of the bids of the buyers and sellers such that it maximizes the surplus (the amount it obtains from the buyers
minus the amount it has to pay to the sellers), subject to the condition that for
each item, the total number it obtains from the selected seller bids is more than
what it has to give in lieu of the selected buyer bids. Note that the maximization
condition guarantees that the exchange does not lose money outright. This is because by not accepting any bids the surplus will be zero. So when the exchange
accepts some bids its surplus would have to be positive. We now describe our
AnsProlog$_{sm}$ encoding for multi-unit combinatorial exchanges through a slight
modification of the example in (II). The modification is that instead of specifying
the initial quantity of each item, we create a seller f, who offers those quantities for
a price.

(1) We have part (1) and part (3) of (II.a) and only the items listing of part (2) of (II.a). We
do not have the description of the initial quantity for the items. Instead the bid for the

seller f is specified as follows:

$bid(f).\ weight\ sel(f) = -50.$

$in(i, f, -8).\ in(j, f, -10).\ in(k, f, -6).\ in(l, f, -12).$

A seller's bid is distinguished from a buyer's bid by having a negative price for the whole bid (meaning the seller wants money for those items, instead of being ready to give a certain amount of money), and similarly the atom $in(i, f, -8)$ means that the seller f has 8 units of item i to *sell*, while $in(i, a, 6)$ would mean that the buyer a wants to *buy* 6 units of item i.

(2) We have parts (1), (2), (3), and (5) of Section (II.b) and we replace part (4) by the following rule.

$\quad \leftarrow Y\ [sel\_in(I, X, Z) : bid(X) : num(Z)]\ Y, item(I), Y > 0.$

The above rule enforces the constraint that for each item (I), the *total number* encumbered with respect to the selected buyer bids should be less than or equal to the sum that is available from the selected seller bids. Note that the use of the same variable Y as the upper and lower bound of the weight constraint serves the purpose of computing the aggregate[3].

(3) Although the following rule is normally not necessary, as it is taken care of by the maximize statement, it helps to eliminate selections, where the exchange may lose money, earlier in the process.

$\quad \leftarrow Y[sel(X) : bid(X)]Y, Y < 0.$

When we run the above program through Smodels it tells us to not select any bids. This is expected because the maximum amount that can be obtained from the buyers is \$49 by selecting $b, d,$ and e; but to satisfy that we have to select f, which costs \$50, resulting in a net loss to the exchange. On the other hand if we change our example, and assign -45 as the weight of $sel(f)$, then the Smodels output is indeed to select $b, d, e,$ and f.

(IV) Expressing additional constraints

We now show how further generalizations and additional constraints can be easily expressed in AnsProlog$_{sm}$.

(1) Suppose we would like to express the constraint that item 1 must be sold. We can achieve this by adding the following rules:

$\quad sold(X) \leftarrow item(X), bid(Y), sel(Y), in(X, Y).$
$\quad \leftarrow \textbf{not } sold(1).$

---

[3] But the Smodels requirement of having a domain variable for Y (not shown in the above rule) makes it an inefficient way to compute aggregation. Having an efficient computation of aggregates together with the answer set semantics remains a challenge.

(2) Suppose we would like to have reserve prices[4] in the single unit combinatorial auction. This can be encoded by the following modification of the program in Section 8.1.9. The main change is that we replace $bid(X)$ by $bid(X, Y)$ where Y was originally the weight of $bid(X)$. This change allows us to compare the sum of the reserve prices of the items in a bid with the bid price, which now is the parameter Y instead of the weight of $bid(X)$.

As regards the specification of the domain, the bids are specified as follows:

$bid(a, 24)$. $bid(b, 9)$. $bid(c, 8)$. $bid(d, 25)$. $bid(e, 15)$.

The composition of items and bids are the same as the facts about the predicates *in* and *item* in Section 8.1.9. The general rules, as described below are different from the ones in Section 8.1.9.

(a) The following two rules label each bid as either selected or not selected. The third rule assigns a weight to $sel(X, Y)$.

$sel(X, Y) \leftarrow bid(X, Y), \textbf{not } not\_sel(X, Y)$.
$not\_sel(X, Y) \leftarrow bid(X, Y), \textbf{not } sel(X, Y)$.

$weight\ sel(X, Y) = Y$.

(b) The following enforces the constraint that two different bids with the same items cannot both be selected.

$\leftarrow sel(X, N), sel(Y, N'), X \neq Y, item(I), in(I, X), in(I, Y)$.

(c) We have the following optimization statement.

$maximize\ [sel(X, Y) : bid(X, Y)]$.

(d) We express the reserve price of each item by the following:

$rp(1, 2)$. $rp(2, 8)$. $rp(3, 8)$. $rp(4, 12)$.

(e) The following rules compute the sum of the reserve prices of bids and compare them with the bid price and eliminate possible answer sets where the bid price of a selected bid is less than the sum of the reserve prices of items in that bid.

$in\_rp(Item, Bid, Res\_pr) \leftarrow in(Item, Bid), rp(Item, Res\_pr)$.

$weight\ in\_rp(Item, Bid, Res\_pr) = Res\_pr$.

$item\_num(X, Y) \leftarrow item(X), num(Y)$.

$\leftarrow C\ [in\_rp(Item, Bid, Res\_pr) : item\_num(Item, Res\_pr)]\ C,$
$\qquad bid(Bid, Bid\_pr), sel(Bid, Bid\_pr), Bid\_pr < C$.

---

[4] In simple auctions the reserve price of an item is the minimum price a seller would accept for that item. Its extension [SS00] to combinatorial auctions will become clear as we proceed with this example.

(3) Suppose we would like to have a constraint that items (1) and (3) must not go to the same bidder. In the simple case if we assume that each bid is by a different bidder we can encode this by the following rule.

$\leftarrow bid(X, Y), sel(X, Y), in(1, X), in(3, X).$

(4) In the more general case where each bid has an associated bidder we first need to express this association as follows:

bidder(a, john). bidder(b, mary). bidder(c, john).
bidder(d,mary). bidder(e, peter).

Next we need the following rules:

goes_to(Item, Bidder) $\leftarrow$ *in(Item, X), bidder(X, Bidder), sel(X,Y).*

$\leftarrow$ *goes_to(1, B), goes_to(3, B).*

Similarly, if we want to specify that the items (1) and (3) must go to the same bidder, then the last rule can be replaced by the following rules.

$\leftarrow$ *goes_to(1, B),* **not** *goes_to(3, B).*
$\leftarrow$ *goes_to(3, B),* **not** *goes_to(1, B).*

(5) Suppose we would like to represent the constraint that every bidder must return happy, that is, at least one of his or her bids must be satisfied. This can be expressed by the following:

happy(Bidder) $\leftarrow$ *bidder(X, Bidder), bid(X, Y), sel(X, Y).*
$\leftarrow$ *bidder(Bid, Bidder),* **not** *happy(Bidder).*

(6) Suppose the seller wants to deal with only whole-sellers. That is, it wants to have the constraint that it only selects bids of a bidder if the total money to be obtained from that bidder is more than \$100. This can be achieved by adding the following rules.

sel(Bid, Value, Bidder) $\leftarrow$ *bid(Bid, Value),sel(Bid, Value),bidder(Bid, Bidder).*

weight sel(Bid, Value, Bidder) $=$ *Value.*

total(Bidder, C) $\leftarrow$ *C [sel(Bid, Value, Bidder) : bid(Bid, Value)] C.*

$\leftarrow$ *total(Bidder, C), C* $<$ 100.

(7) Suppose the seller wants to avoid bid '*a*' as it came late, unless it includes an item that is not included in any other bids. This can be expressed by the following rules.

ow_covered(Bid, Item) $\leftarrow$ *in(Item, Bid'), Bid* $\neq$ *Bid'.*
not_ow_covered(Bid) $\leftarrow$ *in(Item, Bid),* **not** *ow_covered(Bid, Item).*

$\leftarrow$ *sel(a, Value),* **not** *not_ow_covered(a).*

(8) To check inventory costs the seller may require that no more than five unsold items should be left after the selection. This can be expressed by the following rules.

$sold(I) \leftarrow item(I), bid(X, Y), sel(X, Y), in(I, X).$
$unsold(I) \leftarrow item(I), \textbf{not} \ sold(I).$

$\leftarrow C \ \{unsold(I) : item(I)\} \ C, C > 5.$

(9) To contain shipping and handling costs the seller may require that bids should be accepted such that at least five items go to each bidder. This can be expressed by the following rules.

$count(Bidder, C) \leftarrow C \ \{goes\_to(Item, Bidder) : item(Item)\} \ C, bidder(B, Bidder).$

$\leftarrow bidder(B, Bidder), count(Bidder, C), C < 5.$

(10) If item 'a' is a family treasure the seller may require that it can only be sold to bidder john or mary, who are relatives. This can be expressed by the following rule.

$\leftarrow goes\_to(a, X), X \neq john, X \neq mary.$

The above shows how additional constraints and generalizations can be easily expressed as new AnsProlog$_{sm}$ rules and often we do not have to change the original program, but just have to add new rules. The ability of AnsProlog$_{sm}$ to express both optimization criteria and logical constraints makes it a powerful language to serve as an engine for combinatorial auctions and engines. But we need a better implementation of the aggregation functions so as to make an AnsProlog* based combinatorial auction system competitive – in terms of running time – with respect to special purpose systems.

8.3.3 Planning with durative actions and resources using AnsProlog$_{sm}$

In Chapter 5 we explored reasoning about actions and planning using AnsProlog*. There we assumed actions were either instantaneous or of unit duration and considered only simple fluents. In this section we consider a more general framework with features such as: the executability of actions may depend on machines which may not be shared, and actions may have duration. We will exploit some of the features in AnsProlog$_{sm}$ to encode a planner for this general framework in it. Our encoding can reason about consumable and producible resources, can account for non-sharable machines, allows actions with durations, and produces plans with overlapping actions. We also discuss how AnsProlog$_{sm}$ allows us to express optimization criteria and alternative resource consumption and machine usage for the same action. We will illustrate our encoding through an example domain consisting of four actions: a1, a2, a3, and a4; four fluents: p1, p2, p3, and p4; two resources: r1 and r2; and one machine: m.

(1) The executability conditions of the actions are described by the following facts.

exec(a1, *true*).
exec(a2, *true*).
exec(a3, s1).
exec(a4, s2).

in(p2, s1).
in(p1, s2).
in(p3, s2).

Intuitively, the above means that *a*1 and *a*2 are always executable and *a*3 is executable at a time point if *p*2 is true at that time point and *a*4 is executable at a time point if *p*1 and *p*3 are true at that time point.

(2) The effect of the actions on the fluents is described by the following facts.

causes(a1, p1).
causes(a2, p2).
causes(a3, p3).
causes(a4, p4).

In a simple domain with durationless (instantaneous) actions *causes*(a1, p1) means that after the execution of *a*1, p1 will be true. When *a*1 is not instantaneous the meaning is a little different. In that case *p*1 becomes true as soon as *a*1 is finished, and *moreover if p*1 *was false before a*1 *was started then during the execution of a*1 *the value of p*1 *is 'unknown' or 'in-flux'*. This is to model the fact that we do not know when exactly during the execution of *a*1, p1 becomes true. To stay within the the the **NP**-complete class while planning we do not do case analysis with respect to the truth value 'in-flux' (or 'unknown').

   Here, we assume actions do not have conditional effects. This can be modeled by having *causes*(a, p, s) and *in*(p1, s), . . . , *in*(pk, s) to express the conditional effect *a* **causes** *p* **if** *p*1, . . . , *pk* and making appropriate changes in the frame axiom and effect axioms.

(3) The effect of actions on the resources is described by the following facts.

consumes(a1, r1, 1).
consumes(a2, r1, 1).
consumes(a3, r1, 1).
consumes(a4, r1, 1).

produces(a1, r2, 1).
produces(a2, r2, 1).

produces(*a*3, *r*2, 1).
produces(*a*4, *r*2, 1).

Intuitively, *consumes*(*a*1, *r*1, 1) means that as soon as the execution of *a*1 starts there is a reduction of the resource *r*1 by 1 unit. It does not mean that one unit of *r*1 is immediately consumed by *a*1, rather it encodes the conservative reasoning that one less unit of *r*1 is available for other actions. Similarly, *produces*(*a*1, *r*2, 1) means that at the end of execution of *a*1, there is an increase of *r*2 by one unit.

(4) The needs of the actions in terms of the machines is described by the following facts.

needs(*a*1, *m*, 3).
needs(*a*2, *m*, 2).

Machines are different from consumable and producible resources in that they only become temporarily unavailable by a particular amount during the execution of particular actions.

(5) The duration of the actions is described by the following facts.

duration(*a*1, 3).
duration(*a*2, 2).
duration(*a*3, 3).
duration(*a*4, 4).

(6) The capacity of the machines, the initial situation and the conditions in the final state are described by the following facts.

capacity(*m*, 4).

initially(*neg*(*p*1)).
initially(*neg*(*p*2)).
initially(*neg*(*p*3)).
initially(*neg*(*p*4)).

initially(*r*1, 5).
initially(*r*2, 1).

finally(*p*4).
finally(*r*2, 5).

Given the above facts describing the action domain, we will need the following domain independent rules. The rules we will present are simplified for presentation and brevity purposes from the actual AnsProlog$_{sm}$ code. As in Chapter 5 these domain independent rules can be added to *any* example domain – that conforms with the syntax given above, to construct plans for it by finding an answer set of the resulting program.

(1) The following rules encode when the goal – as described by the *finally* facts – is satisfied at a time point T.

$not\_goal(T) \leftarrow finally(X), \textbf{not } holds(X, T).$

$not\_goal(T) \leftarrow finally(R, N), \textbf{not } holds(R, N, T).$

$goal(T) \leftarrow time(T), \textbf{not } not\_goal(T).$

(2) The following constraint eliminates otherwise possible answer sets where the goal is not satisfied at the time point *plan_size*.

$\leftarrow \textbf{not } goal(plan\_size).$

(3) The following rules define when an action is executable at a time point, based only on the truth of fluents.

$executable(A, T) \leftarrow \textbf{not } not\_executable(A, T).$

$not\_executable(A, T) \leftarrow exec(A, S), in(F, S), \textbf{not } holds(F, T).$

(4) The following rules define when an action ends and when it is under execution.

$ends(A, T + D) \leftarrow initiated(A, T), duration(A, D).$

$in\_exec(A, T) \leftarrow initiated(A, T'), duration(A, D), T' < T \leq T + D.$

(5) The following rules reason about the truth value of fluents at different time points. The second rule encodes the delayed effect of an action taking into account the duration of the action. The third and fourth rules encode the frame axiom. They are slightly different from the standard encoding of the frame axiom (in Chapter 5) so as to take into account action duration and its impact as presented earlier in item (2) of the description of the domain.

$holds(F, 1) \leftarrow initially(F).$

$holds(F, TD) \leftarrow TD < plan\_size, ends(A, TD), causes(A, F).$

$ab(F, T + 1) \leftarrow T < plan\_size, initiated(A, T), causes(A, F).$

$holds(F, T + 1) \leftarrow contrary(F, G), T < plan\_size, holds(F, T), \textbf{not } ab(G, T + 1).$

(6) The following rules encode the change in the quantity of consumable and producible resources due to action executions.

$holds(R, N, 1) \leftarrow initially(R, N).$

$decrease(A, R, N, T) \leftarrow initiated(A, T), consumes(A, R, N).$

Intuitively, $decrease(A, R, N, T)$ means that there is a decrease of N units of resource R at time point T due to action A. Note that if A consumes N units of R then the decrease is immediate.

$weight \ decrease(A, R, N, T) = N.$ $(^{*}1)$

$increase(A, R, N, T) \leftarrow ends(A, T), produces(A, R, N).$

Intuitively, *increase*(A, R, N, T) means that there is an increase of N units of resource R at time point T due to action A. Note that if A produces N units of R then the increase in R does not happen immediately after A is initiated. It happens when the execution of A ends.

$$weight\ increase(A, R, N, T) = N. \tag{*2}$$

$$tot\_decrease(R, C, T) \leftarrow resource(R), time(T),$$
$$C[decrease(A, R, N, T) : action(A) : int(N)]C.$$

$$tot\_increase(R, C, T) \leftarrow resource(R), time(T),$$
$$C[increase(A, R, N, T) : action(A) : int(N)]C.$$

The last two rules aggregate the total decrease and increase of each resource R at each time point T. The aggregation is done using the weight constraint expressions $C[decrease(A, R, N, T) : action(A) : int(N)]C$ and $C[increase(A, R, N, T) : action(A) : int(N)]C$. To be able to evaluate these weight expressions the weight declarations (*1) and (*2) are used to assign weights to each atom *decrease*(A, R, N, T) and *increase*(A, R, N, T).

$$holds(R, N, T + 1) \leftarrow holds(R, NN, T), tot\_decrease(R, C, T),$$
$$tot\_increase(R, CC, T + 1), N = NN + CC - C.$$

The last rule takes into account the decrease and increase of resources to define how many units of each resource is available at each time point. The asymmetry in the time parameter in *tot_decrease*(R, C, T) and *tot_increase*$(R, C, T + 1)$ is because, when an action starts in time T, the decrease in resource due to that action takes effect from time $T + 1$, while when an action ends at time $T + 1$, the increase in resource due to that action takes effect from time $T + 1$.

$$\leftarrow holds(R, NN, T), tot\_decrease(R, C, T),$$
$$tot\_increase(R, CC, T + 1), NN + CC < C.$$

The last rule is a constraint that prevents particular action executions, in the absence of adequate resources.

(7) The following rules enumerate action initiations. To decrease the number of answer sets we have made the assumption that two action instantiations corresponding to the same action cannot overlap each other. This need not be the case in general.

$$has\_occurred\_before(A, T) \leftarrow initiated(A, TT), duration(A, D),$$
$$TT < T < TT + D.$$

$$initiated(A, T) \leftarrow executable(A, T), \textbf{not } has\_occurred\_before(A, T),$$
$$\textbf{not } not\_initiated(A, T).$$

$$not\_initiated(A, T) \leftarrow \textbf{not } initiated(A, T).$$

(8) The following rules are used to make sure that the various actions occurring at each of the time points do not overuse the machine resources. In case of overuse the corresponding answer sets are eliminated.

in_use(A, M, N, T) ← *in_exec(A, T), needs(A, M, N).*

Intuitively, *in_use(A, M, N, T)* means that *N* units of machine-resource *M* are being used at time point *T* because of action *A*.

weight in_use(A, M, N, T) = *N.*

resource_constraint_violated ← *time(T), capacity(M, C), CC* = *C* + 1,
$$CC[in\_use(A, M, N, T) : action(A) : int(N)].$$

Intuitively, the above rule says that for any resource *M*, and at any time *T*, if the total number of the *M* that are being used is more than the capacity *C* (i.e., greater than or equal to *C* +1) of that resource, then *resource_constraint_violated* is true.

← *resource_constraint_violated.*

When we run this program – with small changes, we obtain an answer set containing the following action initiations: {*initiated(a2, 1), initiated(a1, 3),* *initiated(a3, 3), initiated(a4, 6)*}, and the goal is satisfied at the time point 10. The truth values of the fluents at the different time points are as follows: *p1* is *false* from 1–3, *in-flux* at 4 and 5, and *true* at 6 and beyond; *p2* is *false* at 1, *in-flux* at 2, and *true* at 3 and beyond; *p3* is *false* from 1–3, *in-flux* at 4 and 5, and *true* at 6 and beyond; and *p4* is *false* from 1–6, *in-flux* from 7–9, and *true* at 10 and beyond.

AnsProlog$_{sm}$ allows us to easily express various kinds of optimizations. For example, minimization of the total number of action initiations can be achieved by the following two rules:

action_pair(A, T) ← *action(A), time(T).*

minimize {*initiated(A, T)* : *action_pair(A, T)*}.

We can also assign cost to each action by the expression *weight initiated(A, T)* = *w* and then the above minimization statement will give us the plan with minimal total cost. We can also easily express additional optimization conditions such as maximizing a particular resource at the end, minimizing inventory, etc. The main advantage of AnsProlog$_{sm}$ over ILP (Integer Linear Programming) for such planning is that it can easily mix logical (including temporal) conditions with the optimizations. For example, we can express minimization of inventory of those resources that are not touched for a given time period. Another feature that trips

ILP formulations is the presence of alternative ways to do the same action. For example, suppose a particular action $a1$ can be done in 3 ways: using 3 units of $m1$, 2 units of $m2$, and 2 units of $m3$; or using 2 units of $m4$ and 6 units of $m5$; or using 3 units of $m2$, 1 unit of $m3$, and 2 units of $m5$. This can be represented by replacing *needs* facts by the following *needs_bag* facts.

$needs\_bag(a1, s1).$
$in(m1, 3, s1).$
$in(m2, 2, s1).$
$in(m3, 2, s1).$

$needs\_bag(a1, s2).$
$in(m4, 2, s2).$
$in(m5, 6, s1).$

$needs\_bag(a1, s3).$
$in(m2, 3, s3).$
$in(m3, 1, s3).$
$in(m5, 2, s3).$

In addition we need the following change in the domain independent rules.

(1) When actions are initiated, we need the following rules which enumerate the different *needs_bag* facts that are selected.

$other\_initiated(A, S, T) \leftarrow initiated(A, S', T), S \neq S'$
$initiated(A, S, T) \leftarrow initiated(A, T), needs\_bag(A, S), \mathbf{not}\ other\_initiated(A, S, T).$

Intuitively, *initiated*(A, S, T) means that action A is initiated at time point T and S is the *needs_bag* that is selected.

(2) We now have to redefine *in_use* so that it takes into account the needs_bag that is selected.

$in\_use(A, M, N, T) \leftarrow initiated(A, S, T'), in(M, N, S), duration(A, D),$
$$T' < T < T' + D + 1.$$

Exercise 34 Fill in the missing facts and rules to make the program in this section run under the Smodels system.   □

8.3.4 Scheduling using AnsProlog$_{sm}$

In this section we show how RCPS (Resource Constraint Project Scheduling) can easily be done using an AnsProlog$_{sm}$ encoding similar to the previous section. In RCPS, we are given a set of jobs, a set of resources, and a fixed deadline. Each job has a set of tasks (operations) and each task operates uninterruptedly on a resource in a given period of time. Each task may consume some units of an assigned resource. Each resource has a capacity and may accommodate several tasks simultaneously. There are different constraints, namely precedence, resource, and deadline constraints. The precedence constraint is to enforce tasks occurrence in some predefined order. The resource constraint is to prevent all tasks operating on a single resource from over-using that resource. The deadline constraint is to enforce that all the tasks end their operation by the deadline. *A schedule is a mapping from tasks to integral start times*. We need to find a schedule that satisfies these three constraints.

As in the previous section we will show the encoding with respect to an example domain. In our example RCPS domain the set of resources $\mathcal{R}$ is equal to $\{r_1, r_2\}$, where r_1 has a capacity of 2 units and r_2 has a capacity of 7 units. The set of tasks has six instances $\{j_{11}, j_{12}, j_{13}, j_{21}, j_{22}, j_{23}\}$. All tasks have the same duration of 3 time units. Task resource consumption is described as follows: j_{11} and j_{21} each consumes 2 units of r_1, j_{11} also requires 3 units of r_2. All other tasks, except j_{21}, each consumes 2 units of r_2. The set of precedence constraints is: $j_{11} \prec j_{12}$, $j_{11} \prec j_{13}$, $j_{21} \prec j_{23}$, and $j_{22} \prec j_{23}$. We are given a deadline of 15 time units. The goal of the AnsProlog$_{sm}$ encoding is to find schedules that satisfy all three types of constraints for this particular instance of the RCPS problem. This domain can be encoded by the following facts.

(1) The capacities of the various resources are expressed by the following:

> *capacity*($r1, 2$).
> *capacity*($r2, 7$).

(2) The various tasks, their needs, and their durations are expressed by the following:

> *task*($j11$).
> *needs*($j11, r1, 2$).
> *duration*($j11, 3$).
>
> *task*($j12$).
> *needs*($j12, r2, 2$).
> *duration*($j12, 3$).
>
> *task*($j13$).
> *needs*($j13, r2, 2$).
> *duration*($j13, 3$).
>
> *task*($j21$).
> *needs*($j21, r1, 2$).
> *duration*($j21, 3$).

$task(j22).$
$needs(j22, r2, 2).$
$duration(j22, 3).$

$task(j23).$
$needs(j23, r2, 2).$
$duration(j23, 3).$

(3) The precedence constraints are expressed by the following:

$\leftarrow$ **not** $precedes(j11, j12).$
$\leftarrow$ **not** $precedes(j11, j13).$
$\leftarrow$ **not** $precedes(j21, j23).$
$\leftarrow$ **not** $precedes(j22, j23).$

We now describe the domain independent rules which when added to the facts and constraints corresponding to particular domains will give us answer sets, each corresponding to a valid schedule.

(1) The following AnsProlog$_{sm}$ rule ensures that in an answer set each task is initiated at a unique time point, and enumerates the various possible initiations.

$1 \{initiated(O, T) : time(T)\} 1 \leftarrow task(O).$

(2) Enforcing constraints:
   (a) The following rule specifies that task $O1$ precedes task $O2$ if $O2$ starts after the finishing time of $O1$:

$precedes(O1, O2) \leftarrow task(O1), task(O2), neq(O1, O2), initiated(O1, T1),$
$duration(O1, D1), initiated(O2, T2), duration(O2, D2),$
$T1 + D1 \leq T2, T2 + D2 \leq deadline.$

   (b) To express the constraint that tasks cannot overuse resources at any time moment we need the rules from item (7), of the domain independent part of the previous section (Section 8.3.3).
   (c) The constraint that all tasks must finish before the deadline can be expressed by the following rule:

$\leftarrow task(O), time(T), initiated(O, T), duration(O, D), T + D > deadline.$

Exercise 35 Fill in the missing facts and rules to make the program in this section run under the Smodels system. $\square$

8.3.5 Specification and verification of active databases using AnsProlog$_{sm}$

Triggers are mechanisms that are awakened by particular updates to a database and cause additional changes to the database beyond what is directly specified by the triggering update. Triggers are an essential component of active database systems and are now part of the SQL3 database standard. After their implementation in several research prototypes – many of them discussed in [WC96, Pat98, CF97] – they are now incorporated in commercial database systems such as Oracle, Sybase, and IBM's DB2-V2 [Cha96]. Although there has been a lot of research on the syntax of triggers, how they are to be executed, their execution models, and their implementations, and some work on formal frameworks for active databases in regard to semantics and expressiveness [PV95], there has been very little work on methodologies to write triggers, specify what triggers are supposed to achieve, and verify their correctness with respect to a specification.

In this section we first give the simplified syntax and semantics of triggers given in [NB00] and present the notion of when a set of triggers is correct with respect to a given specification. We then use AnsProlog$_{sm}$ to simulate the effects of triggers, specify the purpose of triggers and verify the correctness of a set of triggers with respect to its purpose.

Specifying the purpose of triggers in an active database

The basic purpose of the active features of a database is to constrain the evolution of the database. In [NB00] four kind of constraints are identified for this purpose: *state invariance constraints; state maintenance constraints (or quiescent state constraints); trajectory invariance constraints;* and *trajectory maintenance constraints.*

In the above constraints there are two dimensions: (i) state vs trajectory (ii) invariance vs maintenance. Intuitively, in state constraints we are concerned about the integrity of particular states, while the trajectory constraints focus on the trajectory of evolution of the database. On the other hand, invariance constraints are concerned about all states of the database, while the maintenance constraints focus only on the quiescent states. State constraints and trajectory constraints are formally defined as follows:

Definition 102 (State Constraints) [ADA93] A *state constraint* γ_s on a database scheme R, is a function that associates with each database r of R a boolean value $\gamma_s(r)$. A database r of R is said to *satisfy* γ_s if $\gamma_s(r)$ is true and is said to *violate* γ_s if $\gamma_s(r)$ is false. In the former case, it is also said that γ_s holds in r. A database r is said to satisfy a set of state constraints if it satisfies each element of the set. □

Definition 103 (Trajectory Constraints) [NB00] A *trajectory constraint* γ_t on a database scheme R is a function that associates with each database sequence Υ

of R a boolean value $\gamma_t(\Upsilon)$. A database sequence Υ of R is said to *satisfy* γ_t if $\gamma_t(\Upsilon)$ is true and is said to *violate* γ_t if $\gamma_t(\Upsilon)$ is false. In the former case, it is also said that γ_t holds in Υ. A database sequence Υ is said to satisfy a set of trajectory constraints if it satisfies each element of the set. $\square$

Often state constraints are expressed through sentences in propositional logic or first-order predicate calculus while we need temporal operators to express trajectory constraints. In addition, as in our upcoming example, we often also need aggregation operators. The ability of AnsProlog$_{sm}$ to express both and the availability of an interpreter for it makes it a better choice (over directly using a temporal logic which usually does not come with aggregation operators) for our goal.

We now define when a set of triggers is correct with respect to a specification consisting of a set of state and maintenance constraints. Since there are a multitude of semantics of triggers, at this point we do not commit to any of them, and assume that for a set of triggers T we have a function Ψ_T from states and action sequences to a sequence of states. In other words, given a database state σ and a sequence of actions (which we will refer to as a transaction) α, $\Psi_T(\sigma, \alpha)$ is the sequence of database states (quiescent or otherwise) recording how the database would evolve when a sequence of actions α is executed in σ in the presence of the set of triggers T.

To account for maintenance trajectory constraints, in our formulation we consider a larger evolution window where the database evolves through several exogenous requests each consisting of a sequence of (exogenous) actions. For this we use the notation σ_α to denote the last state of the evolution given by $\Psi(\sigma, \alpha)$. We use the notation $\sigma_{(\alpha_1, \alpha_2)}$ to denote the last state of the evolution given by $\Psi(\sigma_{\alpha_1}, \alpha_2)$, and similarly define $\sigma_{(\alpha_1, \dots, \alpha_i)}$.

Finally in the formulation of correctness, we also consider what kind of exogenous updates the system can expect. This is because often interactions with the database only happen through particular interfaces and forms, and not all conceivable updates are allowed. Moreover, without such restrictions the number of triggers needed may become unwieldy. We now give the correctness definition.

Definition 104 [NB00] Let Γ_{si} be a set of state invariant constraints, Γ_{sm} be a set of state maintenance constraints, Γ_{ti} be a set of trajectory invariant constraints, Γ_{tm} be a set of trajectory maintenance constraints, A be a set of exogenous actions, and T be a set of Event-Condition-Action (ECA) rules. We say T is correct with respect to $\Gamma_{si} \cup \Gamma_{sm} \cup \Gamma_{ti} \cup \Gamma_{tm}$ and A, if for all database states σ where the constraints in

Γ_{si} and Γ_{sm} hold, and action sequences $\alpha_1, \ldots, \alpha_n$ consisting of exogenous actions from A,

- all the states in the sequences $\Psi(\sigma, \alpha_1)$, $\Psi(\sigma_{\alpha_1}, \alpha_2)$, $\ldots$, $\Psi(\sigma_{(\alpha_1, \ldots, \alpha_{n-1})}, \alpha_n)$ satisfy the constraints in Γ_{si};
- all the states $\sigma_{\alpha_1}, \ldots, \sigma_{(\alpha_1, \ldots, \alpha_n)}$ satisfy the constraints in Γ_{sm};
- the trajectory obtained by concatenating $\Psi(\sigma, \alpha_1)$ with
  $\Psi(\sigma_{\alpha_1}, \alpha_2)$, $\ldots$, $\Psi(\sigma_{(\alpha_1, \ldots, \alpha_{n-1})}, \alpha_n)$ satisfies the constraints in Γ_{ti}; and
- the trajectory $\sigma, \sigma_{\alpha_1}, \ldots, \sigma_{(\alpha_1, \ldots, \alpha_n)}$ satisfies the constraints in Γ_{tm}. □

An illustration using AnsProlog$_{sm}$

We now illustrate the specification and verification of the correctness of triggers using AnsProlog$_{sm}$ through an example. Consider a simple purchase-payment database consisting of the following three relations:

purchase(*purchaseid*, *client*, *amount*).
payment(*paymentid*, *client*, *amount*).
account(*client*, *credit*, *status*).

In the above schema, the underlined attributes are the primary keys and the attribute *client* in the relations *purchase* and *payment* is a foreign key with respect to the relation *account*. The relation *purchase* records the purchase history of clients and the relation *payment* records the payment history of clients. The relation *account* stores the available credit and credit status for each client.

Let us now consider the case when the external (or exogenous) updates that are allowed are[5] addition of tuples to the *purchase* and *payment* relations for existing clients. Suppose we have the following state maintenance constraints:

(1) For each client c which appears in a tuple a in the relation *account*: if $a.credit < 3K$ then $a.status = bad$, and if $a.credit \geq 3K$ then $a.status = good$.
(2) For each client c which appears in a tuple a in the relation *account*: $a.credit$ is $5K$ minus the sum of all the purchase amounts for c plus the sum of all the payment amounts for c.

We now give a set of triggers whose purpose is to satisfy the above state maintenance constraints, in the presence of the above mentioned external updates.

- Trigger 1: When a tuple p is added to the *purchase* relation, then the tuple a in the relation *account* such that $p.client = a.client$ is updated so that the updated $a.credit$ has the value obtained by subtracting $p.amount$ from the old $a.credit$.

---

[5] For simplicity we do not allow and do not consider other updates such as deletion to the relation *account*. Such an update would cause a violation of the foreign key constraints and would necessitate additional triggers.

- Trigger 2: When a tuple a in the relation *account* is updated such that $a.credit$ is less than 3K then a is further updated such that $a.status$ has the value "bad".
- Trigger 3: When a tuple p' is added to the *payment* relation, then the tuple a in the relation *account* such that $p'.client = a.client$ is updated so that the updated $a.credit$ has the value obtained by adding $p'.amount$ to the old $a.credit$.
- Trigger 4: When a tuple a in the relation *account* is updated such that $a.credit$ is more than or equal to 3K then a is further updated such that $a.status$ has the value "good".

Simulation of the impact of triggers with respect to a particular initial database

We now simulate the impact of the above triggers on a particular initial database using AnsProlog$_{sm}$. (This simulation could also have been done using AnsProlog$_{dlv}$.) In our formulation we use the notation from reasoning about actions (Chapter 5) and answer set planning and have predicates $hold(f, t)$ meaning the fact (or fluent) f is true at time point t, $occurs(ins/del, f, t)$ meaning that f is inserted/deleted at time point t, $executable(ins/del, f, t)$ meaning that the insertion/deletion of f is executable at time point t, and $ab(f, t)$ meaning that f is abnormal with respect to inertia (or f is not inertial) at time point t.

A particular initial state where we have three clients a, b, and c with accounts and purchase and payment histories is represented as follows:

$holds(purchase(1, a, 3), 1)$.
$holds(purchase(2, b, 5), 1)$.

$holds(payment(1, a, 1), 1)$.
$holds(payment(2, b, 1), 1)$.

$holds(account(a, 3, good), 1)$.
$holds(account(b, 1, bad), 1)$.
$holds(account(c, 5, good), 1)$.

We refer to the above set of facts as Π_{in}. Suppose now (at time point 1) c makes a purchase of \$5K, with a *purchaseid* 5. This is expressed as the following action occurrence *which we will refer to by* Π_{occ}:

$occurs(ins, purchase(5, c, 5), 1)$.

We will now write AnsProlog$_{sm}$ rules which will simulate the change in the database due to action occurrences of the above kind. Our rules can be grouped into four parts:

(1) Representing actions: effects, inertia, and executability

The main actions in an active database setting are insertion of tuples into a table, deletion of tuples from a table, and updating of a tuple in a table. The following rules – *which we will refer to as* Π_{ef} – encode the effect of these actions. The first rule encodes the effect of an insertion, the second rule encodes the effect of an update, the third and fourth rules define a fact to be abnormal if it is deleted or updated, and the fifth rule encodes inertia. Thus when the deletion of a fact happens, because of the third rule, it no longer holds in the next time point.

$holds(F, T + 1) \leftarrow occurs(ins, F, T), executable(ins, F, T).$
$holds(G, T + 1) \leftarrow occurs(upd, F, G, T), executable(upd, F, G, T).$

$ab(F, T + 1) \leftarrow occurs(del, F, T), executable(del, F, T).$
$ab(F, T + 1) \leftarrow occurs(upd, F, G, T), executable(upd, F, G, T).$

$holds(F, T + 1) \leftarrow holds(F, T), occurred(T),$ **not** $ab(F, T + 1).$

The following rules – *which we will refer to as* Π_{ex} – define when the insertion, deletion, and updating actions are executable.

$executable(ins, purchase(X, Y, W), T) \leftarrow.$
$executable(del, purchase(X, Y, W), T) \leftarrow holds(purchase(X, Y, W), T).$
$executable(ins, payment(X, Y, Z), T) \leftarrow.$
$executable(del, payment(X, Y, Z), T) \leftarrow holds(payment(X, Y, Z), T).$
$executable(ins, account(X, Y, Z), T) \leftarrow.$
$executable(del, account(X, Y, Z), T) \leftarrow holds(account(X, Y, Z), T).$
$executable(upd, account(X, Y, Z), account(X, Y, Z2), T) \leftarrow$
$\qquad holds(account(X, Y, Z), T).$
$executable(upd, account(X, Y, Z), account(X, Y2, Z), T) \leftarrow$
$\qquad holds(account(X, Y, Z), T).$

When each of the above rules is presented to the Smodels system we need to add domain predicates for the variables that appear, so as to make the program range-restricted. We remove the domain predicates in all our rules in this section, so as to make the rules simpler and less space consuming. The restrictions of the Smodels system also force us to write individual rules for insertion, deletion, and updating to each of the individual relations instead of a single rule of the form:

$executable(del, F, T) \leftarrow holds(F, T).$

(2) Representing triggers

The effect of the triggers is encoded through the following rules *which we will refer to as* Π_{tr}:

$occurs(del, account(Y, B, S), T + 1) \leftarrow holds(account(Y, B, S), T),$
$\qquad\qquad\qquad\qquad\qquad occurs(ins, purchase(X, Y, W), T).$

$occurs(ins, account(Y, B - W, S), T + 1) \leftarrow holds(account(Y, B, S), T),$
$\qquad\qquad\qquad\qquad\qquad\qquad occurs(ins, purchase(X, Y, W), T).$

$occurs(del, account(X, Y, S), T + 1) \leftarrow Y < 3, S = good,$
$\qquad\qquad\qquad\qquad\qquad\qquad occurs(ins, account(X, Y, S), T).$

$occurs(ins, account(X, Y, bad), T + 1) \leftarrow Y < 3, S = good,$
$\qquad\qquad\qquad\qquad\qquad\qquad occurs(ins, account(X, Y, S), T).$

$occurs(del, account(Y, B, S), T + 1) \leftarrow holds(account(Y, B, S), T),$
$\qquad\qquad\qquad\qquad\qquad\qquad occurs(ins, payment(X, Y, W), T).$

$occurs(ins, account(Y, B + W, S), T + 1) \leftarrow holds(account(Y, B, S), T),$
$\qquad\qquad\qquad\qquad\qquad\qquad occurs(ins, payment(X, Y, W), T).$

$occurs(del, account(X, Y, S), T + 1) \leftarrow Y \geq 3, S = bad,$
$\qquad\qquad\qquad\qquad\qquad\qquad occurs(ins, account(X, Y, S), T).$

$occurs(ins, account(X, Y, good), T + 1) \leftarrow Y \geq 3, S = bad,$
$\qquad\qquad\qquad\qquad\qquad\qquad occurs(ins, account(X, Y, S), T).$

In the above encoding we have replaced updates by a pair of insert and delete. This is done to make the number of ground instantiations smaller. Otherwise the first two rules can be replaced by the following rule:

$occurs(upd, account(Y, B, S), account(Y, B - W, S), T + 1)$
$\quad \leftarrow holds(account(Y, B, S), T), occurs(ins, purchase(X, Y, W), T).$

Similarly, the third and the fourth rules, the fifth and the sixth rules, and the seventh and the eighth rules can each be replaced by one rule.

(3) **Identifying quiescent states**

The following rules – *which we will refer to as* Π_{qu} – define the quiescent time point when the action executions (due to triggers) stop.

$occurred(T) \leftarrow occurs(ins, F, T).$
$occurred(T) \leftarrow occurs(del, F, T).$
$occurred(T) \leftarrow occurs(upd, F, G, T).$
$occurs\_after(T) \leftarrow occurred(TT), T < TT.$
$quiescent(T + 1) \leftarrow occurred(T), \textbf{not } occurs\_after(T).$

(4) **Defining domains**

In addition we need rules to define domain predicates for the various types. These include types of the various attributes in the relations *purchase*, *payment* and *account*, a predicate *time*, and the following rules defining the type fluent in terms of other domain predicates. (Note that the F in $holds(F, T)$ is of the type fluent.) *We refer to the above mentioned rules by* Π_{dom}.

$fluent(purchase(X, Y, W)) \leftarrow id\_dom(X), cname\_dom(Y), amount(W).$
$fluent(payment(X, Y, Z)) \leftarrow id\_dom(X), cname\_dom(Y), amount(Z).$
$fluent(account(X, Y, Z)) \leftarrow cname\_dom(X), amount(Y), status(Z).$

Database evolution for this case

Given the initial database state and action occurrence at time point 1 described at the beginning of this section, the database evolution due to triggers is simulated by running Smodels on those facts plus the rules presented earlier in the section. Of particular interest to us is what actions occur (or are triggered) at the different time points and the database states at the different time points. The following is an illustration of this evolution.

Example 145 At time 1, we have the following state:

holds(purchase(2,b,5),1). holds(payment(2,b,1),1). holds(account(b,1,bad),1).
holds(purchase(1,a,3),1). holds(payment(1,a,1),1). holds(account(c,5,good),1).
$\qquad\qquad\qquad\qquad\qquad\qquad\qquad\qquad\qquad$ *holds(account(a,3,good),1).*

The following exogenous update happens and is recorded as:

occurs(ins, purchase(5,c,5),1).

The above update modifies the database and at time point 2 the database state is:

holds(purchase(2,b,5),2). holds(payment(2,b,1),2). holds(account(b,1,bad),2).
holds(purchase(1,a,3),2). holds(payment(1,a,1),2). holds(account(c,5,good),2).
holds(purchase(5,c,5),2). $\qquad\qquad\qquad\qquad\qquad$ *holds(account(a,3,good),2).*

The update at time point 1 triggers the following two actions which occur at time point 2.

occurs(ins, account(c,0,good),2). occurs(del, account(c,5,good),2).

The above actions modify the database and at time point 3 the database state is:

holds(purchase(2,b,5), 3). holds(payment(2,b,1),3). holds(account(b,1,bad),3).
holds(purchase(1,a,3),3). holds(payment(1,a,1),3). holds(account(c,0,good),3).
holds(purchase(5,c,5),3). $\qquad\qquad\qquad\qquad\qquad$ *holds(account(a,3,good),3).*

The updates at time point 3 trigger the following two actions which occur at time point 3.

occurs(ins,account(c,0,bad),3). occurs(del,account(c,0,good),3).

The above actions modify the database and at time point 4 the database state is:

holds(purchase(2,b,5),4). holds(payment(2,b,1),4). holds(account(b,1,bad),4).
holds(purchase(1,a,3),4). holds(payment(1,a,1),4). holds(account(c,0,bad),4).
holds(purchase(5,c,5),4). $\qquad\qquad\qquad\qquad\qquad$ *holds(account(a,3,good),4).*

Moreover the answer set also contains the fact *quiescent*(4) which indicates that the database has reached a quiescent state at time point 4.   □

We can now easily verify that the state maintenance constraints are indeed satisfied in the quiescent state of the database at time point 4 for the particular initial state and action occurrence at the initial state that we considered.

Specifying maintenance constraints using AnsProlog$_{sm}$

Using AnsProlog$_{sm}$ we can express when the quiescent state satisfies the state maintenance constraints by the following rules, *which we will refer to as* Π_{cons}:

payment_total(*C*, *Sum*, *T*) ← *time*(*T*), *cname_dom*(*C*),
          Sum[*holds*(*payment*(*X*, *C*, *Y*), *T*) : *id_dom*(*X*) :
          amount(*Y*)]*Sum*.

purchase_total(*C*, *Sum*, *T*) ← *time*(*T*), *cname_dom*(*C*),
          Sum[*holds*(*purchase*(*X*, *C*, *Y*), *T*) : *id_dom*(*X*) :
          amount](*Y*)]*Sum*.

violated(*c2*, *T*) ← *cname_dom*(*C*), *payment_total*(*C*, *Sum1*, *T*),
          purchase_total(*C*, *Sum2*, *T*), *holds*(*account*(*C*, *Cr*, *Status*), *T*),
          Cr ≠ 5 − *Sum2* + *Sum1*.

violated(*c1*, *T*) ← *cname_dom*(*C*), *holds*(*account*(*C*, *Cr*, *good*), *T*), *Cr* < 3.

violated(*c1*, *T*) ← *cname_dom*(*C*), *holds*(*account*(*C*, *Cr*, *bad*), *T*), *Cr* ≥ 3.

not_correct ← *maint_constr*(*X*), *quiescent*(*T*), *violated*(*X*, *T*).

correct ← **not** *not_correct*.

The first two rules perform the aggregate computation using the notion of weight constraints in Smodels. For that purpose we need the following weight assignment rules.

weight   *holds*(*payment*(*X*, *C*, *Y*), *T*) = *Y*.
weight   *holds*(*purchase*(*X*, *C*, *Y*), *T*) = *Y*.

The third rule defines whether the constraint 1 is violated at a time point *T*. The fourth and the fifth rules define whether the constraint 2 is violated at a time point *T*. The sixth rule encodes that the triggers are not correct with respect to the specification if they do not satisfy a maintenance constraint *X* at a quiescent time point *T*. The last rule defines when the triggers are correct with respect to a given specification.

We can now add these rules to our earlier program, and ask Smodels to compute its answer set. If the answer set contains the fact *correct* then we know that this particular evolution does conform to the specified purpose of the triggers. This indeed happens.

So far we considered the database evolution and whether it conforms with a given specification of the purpose of triggers with respect to a particular initial database state and a particular exogenous update at time point 1. Our next step is to generalize it so that we can verify the correctness with respect to any arbitrary initial database that satisfies the state invariance and maintenance constraints.

Enumerating the possible initial states

For the database in the previous section we can enumerate the different initial states by the following rules:

$$holds(purchase(X, Y, Z), 1) \leftarrow id\_dom(X), cname\_dom(Y), amount(Z),$$
$$\textbf{not } n\_holds(purchase(X, Y, Z), 1).$$

$$n\_holds(purchase(X, Y, Z), 1) \leftarrow id\_dom(X), cname\_dom(Y), amount(Z),$$
$$\textbf{not } holds(purchase(X, Y, Z), 1).$$
$$holds(payment(X, Y, Z), 1) \leftarrow id\_dom(X), cname\_dom(Y), amount(Z),$$
$$\textbf{not } n\_holds(payment(X, Y, Z), 1).$$
$$n\_holds(payment(X, Y, Z), 1) \leftarrow id\_dom(X), cname\_dom(Y), amount(Z),$$
$$\textbf{not } holds(payment(X, Y, Z), 1).$$
$$holds(account(X, Y, Z), 1) \leftarrow cname\_dom(X), amount(Y), status(Z),$$
$$\textbf{not } n\_holds(account(X, Y, Z)).$$
$$n\_holds(account(X, Y, Z), 1) \leftarrow cname\_dom(X), amount(Y), status(Z),$$
$$\textbf{not } holds(account(X, Y, Z)).$$

In addition we need the following constraint to make sure the initial state satisfies the state invariance and state maintenance constraints.

$$\leftarrow maint\_constr(C), violated(C, 1).$$

We will refer to the above rules and constraint by Π_{in}^{enum}. Now if the overall program entails *correct* then we can conclude that the triggers are correct with respect to the given specification, for all possible initial states, and the given update at time point 1. To consider all possible updates at time point 1 we also need to enumerate that.

We can enumerate the various possible updates by first defining what updates are possible and then by having the following enumeration rules.

$$not\_initially(X, Y) \leftarrow initially(U, V), U \neq X.$$
$$not\_initially(X, Y) \leftarrow initially(U, V), \textbf{not } same(Y, V).$$
$$initially(X, Y) \leftarrow possible(X, Y), \textbf{not } not\_initially(X, Y).$$

$same(purchase(X, Y, Z), purchase(X, Y, Z)) \leftarrow id\_dom(X), cname\_dom(Y),$
$$amount(Z).$$
$same(payment(X, Y, Z), payment(X, Y, Z)) \leftarrow id\_dom(X), cname\_dom(Y),$
$$amount(Z).$$
$same(account(X, Y, Z), account(X, Y, Z)) \leftarrow cname\_dom(X),$
$$amount(Y), status(Z).$$

$occurs(X, Y, 1) \leftarrow initially(X, Y).$

We will refer to the above rules and constraint by Π_{occ}^{enum} . *Now if the overall program entails* correct *then we can conclude that the triggers are correct with respect to the given specification, for all possible initial states, and for all possible updates at time point 1.*

Exercise 36 Let $\models_{sm}$ denote the entailment of the AnsProlog$_{sm}$. Prove that $\Pi_{in}^{enum} \cup$ $\Pi_{ef} \cup \Pi_{occ}^{enum} \cup \Pi_{ex} \cup \Pi_{tr} \cup \Pi_{qu} \cup \Pi_{\text{dom}} \cup \Pi_{cons} \models_{sm}$ *correct*. $\square$

Exercise 37 Generalize the above theorem to the class of active databases where every action has a single trigger, only one exogenous update occurs at the initial state, and the trigger specification is done in a style similar to Π_{cons}. $\square$

8.4 Pure PROLOG

PROLOG is a programming language based on logic and the term PROLOG is a short form of **Prog**ramming in **log**ic. A PROLOG program consists of a set of rules similar to AnsProlog rules. Users interact with PROLOG programs by asking PROLOG queries with respect to the program, where a PROLOG query is a sequence of naf-literals. The answer with respect to ground queries is *true* or *false* if the query processing terminates. When the query has variables, along with the answer *true* the PROLOG interpreter returns an answer substitution for the variables in the query. The query answering approach of PROLOG is very different from the approach in Smodels and dlv. While both Smodels and dlv compute the answer sets first, in PROLOG query answering is driven by the query.

PROLOG rules are more general than AnsProlog rules and have built-in predicates and nonlogical features such as *cut*. In this section our focus is on the behavior of the PROLOG's execution mechanism on programs in AnsProlog syntax. This language with the syntax of AnsProlog and semantics of PROLOG is referred to as *Pure PROLOG*.

The semantics of Pure PROLOG is defined procedurally in terms of the SLDNF-resolution with the following restrictions and exceptions:

- the leftmost selection rule is used and the resulting resolution is referred to as the LDNF-resolution,

- with the exception that selection of nonground literals is allowed (that is, floundering is ignored),
- during resolution rules are tried from the beginning of the program to the end, and
- occur check is omitted during unification.

We will explain each of these terms in the rest of this section, and present sufficiency conditions when the semantics of Pure PROLOG agrees with the semantics of AnsProlog.

We start with examples illustrating the procedural semantics of Pure PROLOG and its deviation from the semantics of AnsProlog. The analysis of the deviations led to the development of the sufficiency conditions that guarantee conformity with AnsProlog.

In the rest of this section, by a query, we will mean a PROLOG query, a sequence of naf-literals.

Example 146 Consider the following Pure PROLOG program:

r_1: $anc(X, Y) \leftarrow par(X, Y)$.
r_2: $anc(X, Y) \leftarrow par(X, Z), anc(Z, Y)$.

f_1: $par(a, b)$.
f_2: $par(b, c)$.
f_3: $par(h, c)$.
f_4: $par(c, d)$.
f_5: $par(e, f)$.
f_6: $par(f, g)$.

If the query $anc(a, b)$ is asked with respect to this program, the interpreter looks for a rule with *anc* in its head and whose head unifies with $anc(a, b)$. (Recall that the notion of unification was defined in Section 3.9.1 and in this case it refers to substitution of variables by terms such that after the substitution we obtain the same atom.) It finds such a rule r_1, with the most general unifier (mgu) $\{X/a, Y/b\}$. The interpreter now replaces $anc(a, b)$ in the query by the body of the rule with the mgu applied to it. So the new query is $par(a, b)$. The above step is referred to as: 'The query $anc(a, b)$ resolves to the query $par(a, b)$ via $\{X/a, Y/b\}$ using r_1.'

It now looks for a rule with *par* in its head and whose head unifies with $par(a, b)$. It finds such a rule f_1, with the mgu $\{\}$. As before, the interpreter now replaces $par(a, b)$ in the query by the body of the rule with the mgu applied to it. Since the body of f_1 is empty, the new query is empty. With an empty query the interpreter returns the answer *true*. That is, the query *par(a, b)* resolves to the empty query via {} using f_1. Since the original query did not have any variables, the interpreter does not return any answer substitutions.

Now consider the query *anc(e, W)*. It resolves to *par(e, W)* via $\{X/e, Y/W\}$ using r_1. In the next step *par(e, W)* resolves to the empty query via $\{W/f\}$ using f_5. The interpreter then returns *true* and the answer substitution $\{W/f\}$ meaning that f is an ancestor of e. If the interpreter is asked for another answer it backtracks its steps and resolves the query *anc(e, W)* to the query *par(e, Z), anc(Z, W)* via $\{X/e, Y/W\}$ using r_2. In the next step the query *par(e, Z), anc(Z, W)* resolves to the query *anc(f, W)* via $\{Z/f\}$ using f_5. The query *anc(f, W)* then resolves to the query *par(f, W)* via $\{X/a, Y/W\}$ using r_1. The query *par(f, W)* then resolves to the empty query via $\{W/g\}$ using f_6. The interpreter then returns *true* and the answer substitution $\{W/g\}$ meaning that g is another ancestor of e. If the interpreter is asked for another answer it backtracks and looks for another answer and it fails in its attempts and returns *false*.   □

The above example illustrates some aspects of the execution mechanism of Pure PROLOG. One important point of this illustration is that because of the query driven approach the facts f_1–f_4 are not touched while answering the query *anc(e, W)*. This is not the case if Smodels or dlv is used. Both of them will compute the answer set of the program and in the process reason about f_1–f_4 even though they are not relevant to the query.

Now let us illustrate the Pure PROLOG execution mechanism with respect to a program that has **not**.

Example 147 Consider the following program:

$p \leftarrow q, \textbf{not } r.$
$q \leftarrow.$
$r \leftarrow s.$
$r \leftarrow t.$

Consider the query p. It resolves to q, **not** r which resolves to **not** r. The execution mechanism treats negative naf-literals in a query differently. In this case it does not look for a rule whose head unifies with **not** r, as Pure PROLOG rules do not have negative naf-literals in their head. Instead it attempts to answer a new query r with respect to the program.

The query r initially resolves to s and s does not resolve to anything else. This leads to a failure branch and the execution mechanism backtracks and now resolves *r* to *t*, which again does not resolve to anything else leading to another failure branch. Since no further backtracking is possible, the query *r* is said to *finitely fail*.

The finite failure of the query *r* is interpreted as a success in resolving the query **not** *r* to the empty query, and hence the answer to the original query *p* is given as *true*.   □

The top-down execution mechanism of Pure PROLOG does, however, come with a price. If the query *p* is asked with respect to the program consisting of the only rule *p* ← *p*. then the Pure PROLOG execution mechanism goes into an infinite loop. This can also happen if the literals in the body of certain rules are not ordered correctly, or if the rules themselves are not ordered correctly. The following examples illustrate this

Example 148 [SS86] Consider the following Pure PROLOG program that defines appending of lists.

$append([X|XL], YL, [X|ZL]) \leftarrow append(XL, YL, ZL).$
$append([], YL, YL).$

If the query $append(Xlist, [a, b, c], Zlist)$ is asked with respect to the above program then the Pure PROLOG execution mechanism will not return any answers (nor will it say *false*). On the other hand if the order of the two rules in the program is swapped and we have the following program:

$append([], YL, YL).$
$append([X|XL], YL, [X|ZL]) \leftarrow append(XL, YL, ZL).$

and the same query is asked then the Pure PROLOG execution mechanism will continually return answers, as there are indeed an infinite number of answers to this query.

In contrast, from the AnsProlog point of view both programs are identical, as an AnsProlog program is a *set* of rules, and there is no ordering of elements in a set.   □

Example 149 Consider a undirected graph whose edges are written using the predicated *edge*. Following is an encoding for a particular graph.

$edge(X, Y) \leftarrow edge(Y, X).$
$edge(a, b).$
$edge(b, c).$
$edge(d, e).$

Now if the query *edge(b, a)* is asked then the Pure PROLOG execution mechanism will get into an infinite loop. On the other hand, if we alter the program by putting the first rule at the end of the program resulting in the following program,

edge(a, b).
edge(b, c).
edge(d, e).
edge(X, Y) ← *edge(Y, X)*.

then the query *edge(b, a)* will be answered correctly by the Pure PROLOG execution mechanism.   □

To avoid the problem illustrated by the above example, we will present conditions – referred to as *termination conditions* – that guarantee that no matter how the rules are ordered inside the program, the query processing mechanism will terminate. We now illustrate some of the other aspects of the procedural semantics of Pure PROLOG and the problems that arise.

Example 150 Consider the following program.

p ← **not** *q(X)*.
q(1).
r(2).

When the query *p* is asked with respect to the above program, the Pure PROLOG answering mechanism resolves *p* to **not** *q(X)*. It then tries to answer the query *q(X)* which resolves to the empty query with the answer substitution {*X*/1}. Thus the answer to the query *q(X)* is *true* and hence the answer to **not** *q(X)* is considered to be *false*. Since *p* does not resolve to any other query, the answer to the query *p* (with respect to the Pure PROLOG semantics) is *false*.

This is unsound with respect to the AnsProlog semantics as the ground version of the above program as given below:

p ← **not** *q(1)*.
p ← **not** *q(2)*.
q(1).
r(2).

makes it clear that because of the second rule *p* should be *true*.   □

The analysis of what went wrong results in the observation that the handling of negative naf-literals with variables by Pure PROLOG is not right. The selection of negative naf-literals with variables is referred to as *floundering*. To eliminate floundering we will suggest conditions that will guarantee that during the LDNF-resolution any naf-literal that is picked does not have any variables.

The following two examples show that Pure PROLOG also cannot correctly handle many nonstratified programs.

Example 151 Consider the following program.

$p \leftarrow a$.
$p \leftarrow b$.
$a \leftarrow$ **not** b.
$b \leftarrow$ **not** a.

When the query p is asked with respect to the above program, the Pure PROLOG answering mechanism resolves p to a and then to **not** b. It then tries to answer the query b, and resolves b to **not** a. It then tries to answer the query a, and resolves a to **not** b. It gets stuck in this loop. □

Example 152 Consider the following program.

$p \leftarrow$ **not** p.
q.

When the query p is asked with respect to the above program, the Pure PROLOG answering mechanism resolves p to **not** p. It then tries to answer the query p, and resolves p to **not** p. It gets stuck in this loop.

When the query q is asked with respect to the above program, the Pure PROLOG answering mechanism resolves q to the empty query and returns *true*. But according to the AnsProlog semantics this program does not have any answer set. □

In the above examples we have illustrated some aspects of LDNF-resolution, the notion of floundering, and nontermination due to ordering of rules in the program. It should be noted that the latter two are not part of LDNF-resolution. They are used in the implementation of Pure PROLOG and although they are useful in certain circumstances and contribute to an efficient implementation they lead to problems that we described. Before we formally define SLDNF and LDNF resolution we present an algorithm for unification and identify the *occur check* step that is bypassed in the Pure PROLOG semantics for the sake of a simpler and efficient implementation, and illustrate the problem caused by it.

8.4.1 A unification algorithm and the occur-check step

In Section 3.9.1 we defined the notion of unification. In this subsection we give an algorithm for unifying two atoms. It is obvious that two atoms are unifiable only if they have the same predicate. While unifying two atoms $p(s_1, \ldots, s_n)$ and $p(t_1, \ldots, t_n)$, $\{s_1 = t_1, \ldots, s_n = t_n\}$ is referred to as the corresponding set of equations, and is often denoted by $p(s_1, \ldots, s_n) = p(t_1, \ldots, t_n)$. A substitution θ such that $s_1\theta = t_1\theta, \ldots, s_n\theta = t_n\theta$ is called a unifier of the set of equations $\{s_1 = t_1, \ldots, s_n = t_n\}$ and obviously this set of equations and the atoms $p(s_1, \ldots, s_n)$ and $p(t_1, \ldots, t_n)$ have the same unifiers. Two sets of equations are called equivalent if they have the same unifiers and a set of equations is said to be *solved* if it is of the form $\{x_1 = t_1, \ldots, x_n = t_n\}$ where the x_i are distinct variables and none of the x_i occurs in a term t_j. An mgu θ of a set of equations E is called *relevant* if the variables in θ are a subset of the variables in E.

Lemma 8.4.1 If $E = \{x_1 = t_1, \ldots, x_n = t_n\}$ is solved, then $\theta = \{x_1/t_1, \ldots, x_n/t_n\}$ is a relevant mgu of E.   □

The θ in the above lemma is referred to as the *unifier determined by E*. The following algorithm – due to Martelli and Montanari [MM82] – to determine the mgu of two atoms transforms the set of equations corresponding to the two atoms to an equivalent set which is solved, and thus obtains the mgu.

Algorithm 10 Nondeterministically choose from the set of equations an equation of a form below and perform the associated action. If the set of equations does not satisfy any of (1)–(6) then halt.

(1)	$f(s_1, \ldots, s_n) = f(t_1, \ldots, t_n)$	replace by the equations $s_1 = t_1, \ldots, s_n = t_n$
(2)	$f(s_1, \ldots, s_n) = f(t_1, \ldots, t_n)$ where $f \neq g$	halt with failure
(3)	$x = x$	delete the equation
(4)	$t = x$ where t is not a variable	replace by the equation $x = t$
(5)	$x = t$ where x is not the same as t, x does not occur in t, and x occurs elsewhere	perform the substitution $\{x/t\}$ in every other equation
(6)	$x = t$ where x is not the same as t, and x occurs in t	halt with failure

Theorem 8.4.2 [MM82] If $p(s_1, \ldots, s_n)$ and $p(t_1, \ldots, t_n)$ have a unifier then the above algorithm successfully terminates and produces a solved set of equations determining a relevant mgu; otherwise it terminates with failure.   □

The test 'x does not occur in t,' in step (5) of the above algorithm, which we have underlined, is refered to as *occur check* and most implementations of PROLOG omit this check and step (6). Although this omission results in constant time unification (as opposed to linear time) in certain cases, it may lead to incorrect results in other cases. The following is an example of the latter.

Example 153 Consider the attempt to unify the atoms $p(y)$ and $p(f(y))$ using the above algorithm minus the occur check. Due to the modified step (5) the modified algorithm will yield the substitution $\{y/f(y)\}$. This is incorrect as $p(y)$ and $p(f(y))$ are not unifiable. □

Since Pure PROLOG inherits this omission of occur check from PROLOG, to avoid problems due to occur check we will present sufficiency conditions in Section 8.4.3 that guarantee that unification is correctly done even in the absence of occur check.

8.4.2 SLDNF and LDNF resolution

We now present the definitions that lead to the formulation of SLDNF and LDNF resolution.

Definition 105 We say that the rule
$$p \leftarrow p_1, \ldots, p_k, \textbf{not } p_{k+1}, \ldots, \textbf{not } p_n.$$
is a variant of the rule
$$q \leftarrow q_1, \ldots, q_k, \textbf{not } q_{k+1}, \ldots, \textbf{not } q_n.$$
if there exist substitutions θ and σ such that $p = q\theta$, $q = p\sigma$, $\{p_1, \ldots, p_k\} = \{q_1\theta, \ldots, q_k\theta\}$, $\{p_{k+1}, \ldots, p_n\} = \{q_{k+1}\theta, \ldots, q_n\theta\}$, $\{q_1, \ldots, q_k\} = \{p_1\sigma, \ldots, p_k\sigma\}$, and $\{q_{k+1}, \ldots, q_n\} = \{p_{k+1}\sigma, \ldots, p_n\sigma\}$. □

Definition 106 A query Q *resolves* to another query Q' via substitution α with respect to Σ, denoted by $Q \stackrel{\alpha}{\Longrightarrow} Q'(\Sigma)$ (also referred to as (α, Q') is a resolvent of Q and Σ), if *either*: $\Sigma = (L, R)$, L is a positive literal in Q, R is a rule, and for some variant $A \leftarrow E$ (the *input rule*) of R, α is an mgu of L and A and $Q' = Q\alpha\{L\alpha/E\alpha\}$ is obtained from $Q\alpha$ by replacing $L\alpha$ by $E\alpha$,

or: Σ is a negative literal in Q, $\alpha = \epsilon$, and Q' is obtained by removing Σ from Q. □

Consider the program in Example 146. The query $anc(a, b)$ resolves to $par(a, Z), anc(Z, b)$ via substitution $\{X/a, Y/b\}$ with respect to $(anc(a, b), r_2)$.

Similarly consider the program in Example 147. The query q, **not** r resolves to q via substitution {} (also denoted by ϵ) with respect to **not** r.

Definition 107 A rule R is called *applicable* to an atom if the rule has a variant whose head unifies with the atom.   □

Definition 108 A (finite or infinite) sequence $Q_0 \overset{\alpha_1}{\Longrightarrow} \ldots \overset{\alpha_n}{\Longrightarrow} Q_n \overset{\alpha_{n+1}}{\Longrightarrow} Q_{n+1} \ldots$ of resolution steps is a *pseudo derivation* if for every step involving a rule:

- (standardization apart) the input rule employed does not contain a variable from the initial query Q_0 or from an input rule used at some earlier step, and
- (relevance) the mgu employed is relevant.   □

In the above definition the standardization apart condition is to avoid any confusion with respect to answer substitutions. Thus the input rule used in any step is obtained by using variants of a rule in the program so that the variable in the input rule is a new one.

The notion of pseudo derivation is used to define SLDNF-derivation. Intuitively, an SLDNF-derivation is a pseudo derivation in which the deletion of ground negative literals is justified through finitely failed SLDNF-forests. We now define the notion of finitely failed SLDNF-forests.

Definition 109 A tree is called *successful* if it contains a leaf marked as success, and is called *finitely failed* if it is finite and all its leaves are marked as *failed*.   □

Definition 110 A *forest* is a triple $(\mathcal{F}, T, subs)$ where $\mathcal{F}$ is a set of trees, $T \in \mathcal{F}$ and is called the *main* tree, and *subs* is a function assigning to some nodes of trees in $\mathcal{F}$ a tree from $\mathcal{F}$.

A path in $\mathcal{F}$ is a sequence of nodes $N_0, \ldots, N_i, \ldots$ such that for all i, N_{i+1} is either a child of N_i in some tree in $\mathcal{F}$ or the root of the tree $subs(N_i)$.   □

Definition 111 A *pre-SLDNF-forest* relative to an AnsProlog program P is a forest whose nodes are queries of literals. The queries may be marked as: *failed*, *success*, or *floundered*, and one literal in each query may be marked as *selected*. The function *subs* assigns to nodes containing a marked negative ground naf-literal **not** A a tree in $\mathcal{F}$ with root A.   □

Definition 112 An *extension* of a pre-SLDNF-forest $\mathcal{F}$ is a forest obtained by marking all empty queries as *success* and performing the following actions for every nonempty query C which is an unmarked leaf in some tree $T \in \mathcal{F}$.

First, if no literal in C is marked as selected, then one of them is marked as selected. Let L be the selected literal of C.

- If L is a positive naf-literal, and
  C has a resolvent with respect to L and some rules from P, then for every rule R from P which is applicable to L, choose one resolvent (α, D) of C with respect to L and R and add this as child of C in T. These resolvents are chosen in such a way that all branches of T remain pseudo derivations.
  otherwise (i.e., C has no resolvents with respect to L and a rule from P) C is marked as failed.
- If $L = \mathbf{not}\ A$ is a negative naf-literal, and
  A is nonground, then C is marked as floundered.
  A is ground, and
  * $subs(C)$ is undefined, then a new tree T' with a single node A is added to $\mathcal{F}$ and $subs(C)$ is set to T'.
  * $subs(C)$ is defined and successful, then C is marked as *failed*.
  * $subs(C)$ is defined and finitely failed, then the resolvent $(\epsilon, C - \{L\})$ of C is added as the only child of C in T. □

Definition 113 The set of pre-SLDNF-forests is defined inductively as follows:

(1) For every query C, the forest consisting of the main tree which has the single node C is a pre-SLDNF-forest, referred to as an *initial* pre-SLDNF-forest.
(2) If $\mathcal{F}$ is a pre-SLDNF-forest, then any extension of $\mathcal{F}$ is a pre-SLDNF-forest. □

Definition 114 SLDNF-forest

- An SLDNF-forest is a limit of a sequence $\mathcal{F}_0, \ldots, \mathcal{F}_i, \ldots$ such that $\mathcal{F}_0$ is an initial pre-SLDNF-forest, and for all i, $\mathcal{F}_{i+1}$ is an extension of $\mathcal{F}_i$.
- An SLDNF-forest for C is an SLDNF-forest $\mathcal{F}$ in which C is the root of the main tree of $\mathcal{F}$.
- A (pre-)SLDNF-forest $\mathcal{F}$ is called successful (respectively finitely failed) if the main tree of $\mathcal{F}$ is successful (respectively finitely failed).
- An SLDNF-forest is called *finite* if no infinite path exists in it. □

Definition 115 A (pre-)SLDNF-derivation for C is a branch in the main tree of a (pre-)SLDNF-forest $\mathcal{F}$ for C together with all trees in $\mathcal{F}$ whose roots can be reached from the nodes in this branch. It is called *successful* if it ends with the empty query. An SLDNF-derivation is called *finite* if all paths of $\mathcal{F}$ fully contained within this branch and these trees are finite. □

Definition 116 Consider a branch in the main tree of a (pre-)SLDNF-forest $\mathcal{F}$ for C which ends with the empty query. Let $\alpha_1, \ldots, \alpha_n$ be the consecutive substitutions along this branch. Then the restriction $(\alpha_1, \ldots, \alpha_n)|C$ of the composition $\alpha_1, \ldots, \alpha_n$ to the variables of C is called a *computed answer substitution* of C in $\mathcal{F}$. $\square$

Theorem 8.4.3 [AD94]

(1) Every pre-SLDNF-forest is finite.
(2) Every SLDNF-forest is the limit of a unique sequence of pre-SLDNF-forests.
(3) If the SLDNF-forest $\mathcal{F}$ is the limit of the sequence $\mathcal{F}_0, \ldots, \mathcal{F}_i, \ldots$, then for all τ
     (a) $\mathcal{F}$ is successful and yields τ as a computed answer substitution iff some $\mathcal{F}_i$ is successful and yields τ as a computed answer substitution, and
     (b) $\mathcal{F}$ is finitely failed iff some $\mathcal{F}_i$ is finitely failed. $\square$

Definition 117 SLDNF-resolution Let P be a Pure PROLOG program, and Q be a query.

$P \models_{SLDNF} \forall Q\theta$ if there exists a successful SLDNF-derivation for Q (with respect to P) with computed answer θ.

$P \models_{SLDNF} \forall \mathbf{not}\ Q$ if there exists a finitely failed SLDNF-forest for Q (with respect to P). $\square$

Definition 118 A query Q is said to flounder with respect to a program P if some SLDNF-forest for Q (with respect to P) contains a node consisting exclusively of nonground negative naf-literals. $\square$

Definition 119 A program is called *terminating* if all its SLDNF-forests for ground queries are finite. $\square$

8.4.3 Sufficiency conditions

We now present results that specify under what conditions the Pure PROLOG semantics agrees with the semantics of AnsProlog. This means that under those conditions we can use the PROLOG interpreter to correctly make conclusions about query entailment with respect to $\models$. Recall that Pure PROLOG semantics is based on (i) SLDNF resolution with the leftmost selection rule (i.e., LDNF resolution) whereby only the leftmost literal in each query is marked selected (in the definition of pre-SLDNF-forests in Definition 111 and its extension in Definition 112); (ii) but ignoring floundering; (iii) omitting occur check during unification; and (iv) selecting input rules during resolution from the beginning of the program to the end.

Before presenting results about sufficiency of Pure PROLOG let us first consider SLDNF with (ii), (iii), and (iv). In this we use the notion of acyclic programs from Section 3.2.5. We start with conditions that guarantee correctness of $\models_{SLDNF}$.

Proposition 109 [AB91] Let Π be an acyclic AnsProlog program and G be a variable free atom that does not flounder. Then, $\Pi \models G$ iff $\Pi \models_{SLDNF} G$. $\quad\Box$

To allow more general queries than ground queries, we have the following definition.

Definition 120 A literal L is called *bounded with respect to a level mapping* λ on ground literals, if λ is bounded on the set of ground instances $gr(L)$ of L.

A query is called *bounded with respect to a level mapping* λ, if all its literals are so. $\quad\Box$

Proposition 110 [AP91] Let Π be an acyclic AnsProlog program and G be a bounded query. Every SLDNF forest of G (with respect to Π) is finite. $\quad\Box$

Corollary 8 Every acyclic program is terminating. $\quad\Box$

The above result about termination takes care of SLDNF together with (iv) above. To account for the omission of occur-check – condition (iii) – and the ignoring of floundering – condition (ii), we need the notion of well-moded from Section 3.1.4.

Theorem 8.4.4 [AP94] If an AnsProlog program Π is well-moded for some input-output specification and there is no rule in Π whose head contains more than one occurrence of the same variable in its output positions then Π is occur check free with respect to any ground query. $\quad\Box$

Theorem 8.4.5 [AP94, Str93] If an AnsProlog program Π is well-moded for some input-output specification and all predicate symbols occurring under **not** are moded completely by input then a ground query to Π does not flounder. $\quad\Box$

We now consider Pure PROLOG. For termination of Pure PROLOG programs we can use a more general notion than acyclic programs, referred to as *acceptable programs*.

Definition 121 Let P be a program in AnsProlog syntax, λ a level mapping for P, and I be a model of P. Then P is called *acceptable with respect to λ and I* if for every rule $A \leftarrow B_1, \ldots, B_n$. in $ground(P)$ the following holds for $i = 1, \ldots, n$: if $I \models B_1, \ldots, B_{i-1}$ then $\lambda(A) > \lambda(B_i)$.

Then P is called *acceptable* if it is acceptable with respect to some level mapping and a model of P.   □

Example 154 Let us consider the following program π_{anc}.

$par(a, b)$.
$par(b, c)$.
$anc(X, Y) \leftarrow par(X, Y)$.
$anc(X, Y) \leftarrow par(X, Z), anc(Z, Y)$.

We will show that π_{anc} is an acceptable program but not an acyclic program.

Let us consider the following level assignment, where all *par* atoms are assigned the level 0, $\lambda(anc(c, a)) = \lambda(anc(c, b)) = \lambda(anc(c, c)) = 2$, $\lambda(anc(b, a)) = \lambda(anc(b, b)) = \lambda(anc(b, c)) = 3$, $\lambda(anc(a, a)) = \lambda(anc(a, b)) = \lambda(anc(a, c)) = 4$, and all other *anc* atoms are assigned the level 1.

It is easy to see that the ground rules corresponding to the first three rules of π_{anc} satisfy the conditions of acyclicity and acceptability. Now let us consider the ground rules corresponding to the fourth rule. They are given below. The first rule below violates the acyclicity condition. To verify the acceptability conditions let us choose $I = \{par(a, b), par(b, c), anc(a, b), anc(b, c), anc(a, c)\}$.

$anc(a, a) \leftarrow par(a, a), anc(a, a)$.
$anc(a, b) \leftarrow par(a, a), anc(a, b)$.
$anc(a, c) \leftarrow par(a, a), anc(a, c)$.
$anc(b, a) \leftarrow par(b, a), anc(a, a)$.
$anc(b, b) \leftarrow par(b, a), anc(a, b)$.
$anc(b, c) \leftarrow par(b, a), anc(a, c)$.
$anc(c, a) \leftarrow par(c, a), anc(a, a)$.
$anc(c, b) \leftarrow par(c, a), anc(a, b)$.
$anc(c, c) \leftarrow par(c, a), anc(a, c)$.

$anc(a, a) \leftarrow par(a, b), anc(b, a)$.   (*)
$anc(a, b) \leftarrow par(a, b), anc(b, b)$.   (*)
$anc(a, c) \leftarrow par(a, b), anc(b, c)$.   (*)
$anc(b, a) \leftarrow par(b, b), anc(b, a)$.
$anc(b, b) \leftarrow par(b, b), anc(b, b)$.
$anc(b, c) \leftarrow par(b, b), anc(b, c)$.
$anc(c, a) \leftarrow par(c, b), anc(b, a)$.

$anc(c, b) \leftarrow par(c, b), anc(b, b).$
$anc(c, c) \leftarrow par(c, b), anc(b, c).$

$anc(a, a) \leftarrow par(a, c), anc(c, a).$
$anc(a, b) \leftarrow par(a, c), anc(c, b).$
$anc(a, c) \leftarrow par(a, c), anc(c, c).$
$anc(b, a) \leftarrow par(b, c), anc(c, a).$ (*)
$anc(b, b) \leftarrow par(b, c), anc(c, b).$ (*)
$anc(b, c) \leftarrow par(b, c), anc(c, c).$ (*)
$anc(c, a) \leftarrow par(c, c), anc(c, a).$
$anc(c, b) \leftarrow par(c, c), anc(c, b).$
$anc(c, c) \leftarrow par(c, c), anc(c, c).$

In the above rules, only in the ones marked with (*) is the *par* atom in the body entailed by I, and since $\lambda(anc(a, a)) > \lambda(anc(b, a)) > \lambda(anc(c, a))$, $\lambda(anc(a, b)) > \lambda(anc(b, b)) > \lambda(anc(c, b))$, and $\lambda(anc(a, c)) > \lambda(anc(b, c)) > \lambda(anc(c, c))$, the acceptability conditions are satisfied. Hence this program is acceptable.

It should be noted that if we change the ordering of literals in the fourth rule of π_{anc} to the following,

$anc(X, Y) \leftarrow anc(Z, Y), par(X, Z).$

the program is no longer acceptable; and indeed PROLOG gets into an infinite loop when trying to answer a query (about *anc*) with respect to this program.   □

Exercise 38 Generalize the π_{anc} program with respect to arbitrary sets of *par* atoms that do not have a cycle and show that such programs are acceptable.   □

We now have the following result about termination of programs with respect to the Pure PROLOG interpreter.

Proposition 111 [AP91] If Π is an acceptable AnsProlog program and Q is a ground query then all SLDNF derivations – with left most selection – of Q (with respect to Π) are finite and therefore the Pure PROLOG interpreter terminates on Q.
   □

The earlier result accounting for the omission of occur-check in Theorem 8.4.4 and ignoring of floundering in Theorem 8.4.5 are also applicable to the execution mechanism of Pure PROLOG. *In summary, one way to show that the Pure PROLOG semantics of a program agrees with the AnsProlog semantics is by showing that the conditions in Theorems 8.4.4 and 8.4.5 and Proposition 111 are satisfied.* In the next section we illustrate this.

8.4.4 Examples of applying Pure PROLOG sufficiency
conditions to programs

Let us consider the programs in Sections 5.1.2–5.1.6. We start with program π_1 from Section 5.1.2. As shown there, this program is acyclic and hence is an acceptable program. We now need to check if the conditions in Theorems 8.4.4 and 8.4.5 are satisfied or not.

For this let us consider the mode assignment in Section 5.1.7, which is

$$holds(-, +)$$
$$ab(+, +, +)$$

With respect to this mode assignment π_1 is well-moded and it also satisfies the other condition of Theorems 8.4.4. But it does not satisfy the condition 'all predicate symbols occurring under **not** are moded completely by input' of Theorem 8.4.5 as the body of the rules in π_1^{ef} has **not** *holds*.

Let us now consider the program π_2^+ from Section 5.1.3. As shown there, this program is also acyclic and hence is an acceptable program. Now let us consider the mode assignment in Section 5.1.7, which is

$$holds(-, +)$$
$$holds'(-, +)$$
$$ab(+, +, +)$$

With respect to this mode assignment π_2^+ is well-moded and it also satisfies the other conditions of Theorems 8.4.4 and 8.4.5. *Hence, the Pure Prolog semantics of π_2^+ agrees with its AnsProlog semantics.*

Since unlike Smodels and dlv, PROLOG can easily manipulate lists, we now consider a list based formulation of π_2, which we will refer to as $\pi_{2.lis}$, and analyze its Pure PROLOG characterization vis-a-vis its AnsProlog semantics. The program $\pi_{2.list}$ then consists of the following rules.

(1) For every effect proposition of the form (5.1.1) $\pi_{2.list}$ contains the following rule:

$$causes(a, f, [p_1, \ldots, p_n, not(q_1), \ldots, not(q_r)]).$$

(2) For every value proposition of the form (5.1.5) if f is a fluent then $\pi_{2.list}$ contains the following rule:

$$holds(f, []).$$

else, if f is the negative fluent literal $\neg g$ then $\pi_{2.list}$ contains the following rule:

$$holds(not(g), []).$$

(3) $\pi_{2.list}$ has the following rules to reason about effects and abnormality:

$holds(F, [A|S]) \leftarrow causes(A, F, L), holds\_list(L, S).$

$ab(F, A, S) \leftarrow causes(A, F, L), holds\_list(L, S).$
$ab(F, A, S) \leftarrow causes(A, not(F), L), holds\_list(L, S).$

(4) $\pi_{2.list}$ has the following inertia rule:

$holds(F, [A|S]) \leftarrow holds(F, S), \textbf{not } ab(F, A, S).$

(5) $\pi_{2.list}$ has the following rules for reasoning about lists of fluents.

$holds\_list([], S).$
$holds\_list([F|L], S) \leftarrow holds(F, S), holds\_list(L, S).$

Let us consider the following mode assignment for $\pi_{2.list}$:

$holds(-, +)$
$holds\_list(-, +)$
$ab(+, +, +)$
$causes(+, -, -)$

With respect to this mode assignment $\pi_{2.list}$ is well-moded and it also satisfies the other conditions of Theorems 8.4.4 and 8.4.5.

Now we will show that $\pi_{2.list}$ is acyclic through the following level mapping.

Let c be the number of fluents in the language plus 1, p be a list of fluent literals, f be a fluent literal, and s be a sequence of actions.

For any action a, $\lambda(a) = 1$, $\lambda([]) = 1$, and for any list $[a|r]$ of actions, $\lambda([a|r]) = \lambda(r) + 1$. For any fluent literal f, $\lambda(f) = 1$, $\lambda([]) = 1$, and for any list $[f|p]$ of fluent literals, $\lambda([f|p]) = \lambda(p) + 1$.

$\lambda(holds\_list(p, s)) = 4c * \lambda(s) + \lambda(p) + 3;$
$\lambda(holds(f, s)) = 4c * \lambda(s) + 3;$
$\lambda(ab(f, a, s)) = 4c * \lambda(s) + 3c + 2;$

and all other literals are mapped to 0.

Now let us consider the rules which have nonempty bodies. These appear in (3), (4) and (5) above.

- For a ground instance of the first rule in (3):

$\lambda(holds(f, [a|s])) == 4c * \lambda(s) + 4c + 3.$

The maximum value of $\lambda(holds\_list(p, s))$ will be $4c * \lambda(s) + max(\lambda(p)) + 3 = 4c * \lambda(s) + c - 1 + 3$

Obviously, $4c * \lambda(s) + 4c + 3 > 4c * \lambda(s) + c + 2$. Hence, this rule satisfies the acyclicity condition.

- For a ground instance of the second rule in (3):

$$\lambda(ab(f, a, s)) = 4c * \lambda(s) + 3c + 2.$$

Since $c > 1$, $4c * \lambda(s) + 3c + 2 > 4c * \lambda(s) + c + 2$. Hence, this rule satisfies the acyclicity condition.

- For a ground instance of the rule in (4):

$$\lambda(holds(f, [a|s])) = 4c * \lambda(s) + 4c + 3 > \lambda(ab(f, a, s)) = 4c * \lambda(s) + 3c + 2.$$ Hence, this rule satisfies the acyclicity condition.

- For a ground instance of the second rule in (5):

$$\lambda(holds\_list([f|p], s)) = 4c * \lambda(s) + \lambda(p) + 1 + 3.$$

$$\lambda(holds\_list(p, s)) = 4c * \lambda(s) + \lambda(p) + 3.$$

$$\lambda(holds(f, s)) = 4c * \lambda(s) + 3.$$

Hence, $\lambda(holds\_list([f|p], s)) > \lambda(holds\_list(p, s))$ and $\lambda(holds\_list([f|p], s)) > \lambda(holds(f, s))$; and therefore this rule satisfies the acyclicity condition.

Hence, the Pure PROLOG semantics of $\pi_{2.list}$ agrees with its AnsProlog semantics.

8.5 Notes and references

The Smodels system developed at Helsinki University of Technology is described in [NS96, NS97] and the Smodels web pages. Our presentation in this chapter is based on the lparse manual, [Sim00], and our experience with Smodels. The dlv system developed at TU Vienna is described in [EFG$^+$00, KL99, LRS96a, LRS96b] and the dlv manuals and tutorials are available in the dlv web pages.

Combinatorial auctions using AnsProlog$_{sm}$ and AnsProlog$_{dlv}$ are studied in [BU01]. Planning with durative actions and resources and resource project constraint scheduling using AnsProlog$_{sm}$ is studied in [BST01]. Specification and verification of active databases using AnsProlog$_{sm}$ is studied in [NE01]. Since the development of the Smodels and dlv systems, several other applications using them have been developed. We only mentioned a few in this chapter. Many others can be found in the Smodels and dlv web pages. An incomplete list of applications that we did not discuss in this book includes planning under incomplete knowledge using AnsProlog$_{dlv}$ [EFL$^+$00], product configuration using AnsProlog$_{sm}$ [SN99, NS98], deadlock and reachability in Petri nets using AnsProlog$_{sm}$ [Hel99], and wire routing and satisfiability planning [ELW00, ET01].

Starting from [CM81], there are several good books such as [SS86, O'K90, Ste90] on the Prolog programming language and its applications. The notion of Pure

PROLOG that we use here is from [SS86]. The definition of SLDNF resolution that we presented is from [AB94, AD94], where it is also pointed out that most earlier definitions of SLDNF resolution do not allow correct reasoning about termination. The sufficiency conditions for correctness of Pure PROLOG are from [AP94, AP93]. Our example in Section 8.4.4 is based on [BGP97].

Among the other systems that have similarity with the ones we presented in this chapter are DeRes [Tru99, CMT96, CMMT95], Ccalc [Lif95], XSB [CSW95] and LDL^{++} [WZ00a, Zan88]. The DeRes system generates extensions of Reiter's default theories. The Ccalc system implements a causal logic by translating it to propositional logic and then using propositional solvers. The XSB system is a top down system like PROLOG but it uses tabling mechanism to correctly handle some of the queries that send PROLOG interpreters to infinite loops. It also has options to compute the well-founded semantics and answer set semantics. The LDL^{++} system has an efficient implementation of a database query language that extends AnsDatalog with aggregate operators. Two new systems that use propositional solvers have been recently developed by the groups of Lin and Lifschitz.

Earlier in Section 7.5.1 we mentioned the relevance of research in magic sets to query answering and also mentioned using of propositional model generators in computing answer sets. We are told that dlv is in the process of incorporating them.

Chapter 9

Further extensions of and alternatives to AnsProlog*

So far in the book we have considered sub-classes of AnsProlog* which have been well-studied in the literature and two additional extensions AnsProlog$_{sm}$ and AnsProlog$_{dlv}$ which are the input language of the answer set computing systems Smodels and dlv. There have been several additional proposals for extending AnsProlog*, which are not that well-studied. Also, there have been many alternative proposals to characterize programs in the syntax of AnsProlog* and its sub-classes. In this chapter we give a brief overview of the above two aspects.

Some of the extensions that we consider are: (i) enriching the rules by allowing **not** in the head of rules, (ii) allowing nesting in the head and body of rules; (iii) allowing additional operators such as knowledge and belief operators; (iv) enriching the framework by allowing abduction; (v) allowing explicit specification of intent to use domain closure and its impact on the universal query problem; (vi) allowing set constructs; and (vii) allowing specification preferences between rules of a program.

In regard to alternative characterizations of programs in the syntax of AnsProlog* and its sub-classes, we focus mostly on AnsProlog and AnsProlog$^-$ syntax, and the well-founded semantics. In the process we define notions such as the 3-valued stable models, and stable classes which are related to both the well-founded characterization and the answer sets. We also briefly discuss the framework of argumentation which can be used in defining both answer sets and the well-founded characterization of programs in AnsProlog syntax.

9.1 AnsProlog$^{not,or,\ \neg,\bot}$: allowing not in the head

The AnsProlog* programs do not allow **not** in their head, although they do allow $\neg$ in the head. But the AnsProlog$_{sm}$ programs allow cardinality and weight constraints in their head, and these constraints may contain **not**. In this section we consider

458

extending AnsProlog* programs that allow **not** in their head. Such programs will be referred to as AnsProlog$^{\mathbf{not},or,\neg,\perp}$ programs. These programs will form a first step in analyzing strong equivalence of AnsProlog$_{sm}$ programs which we will discuss in a later section.

An AnsProlog$^{\mathbf{not},or,\neg,\perp}$ rule is of the form

$$L_0 \; or \cdots or \; L_k \; or \; \mathbf{not} \; L_{k+1} \; or \cdots or \; \mathbf{not} \; L_l \leftarrow L_{l+1}, \ldots, L_m,$$
$$\mathbf{not} \; L_{m+1}, \ldots, \mathbf{not} \; L_n. \quad (9.1.1)$$

where L_is are literals or when $l = k = 0$, L_0 may be the symbol $\perp$, and $n \geq m \geq l \geq k \geq 0$. It differs from an AnsProlog* rule by allowing **not** in the head of the rules. An AnsProlog$^{\mathbf{not},or,\neg,\perp}$ program is a collection of AnsProlog$^{\mathbf{not},or,\neg,\perp}$ rules.

Let Π be an AnsProlog$^{\mathbf{not},or,\neg,\perp}$ program and S be a set of literals. The reduct Π^S of Π by S is an AnsProlog$^{-\mathbf{not},\neg,or}$ program obtained as follows: A rule

$$L_0 \; or \cdots or \; L_k \leftarrow L_{l+1}, \ldots, L_m.$$

is in Π^S iff there is a ground rule of the form (9.1.1) in Π such that $\{L_{k+1}, \ldots, L_l\} \subseteq S$ and $\{L_{m+1}, \ldots, L_n\} \cap S = \emptyset$.

The intuition behind this construction is as follows: *First*, rules of the form (9.1.1) in Π are not considered for Π^S if either (i) at least one of $\{L_{m+1}, \ldots, L_n\}$ is in S, or (ii) at least one of $\{L_{k+1}, \ldots, L_l\}$ is not in S. In the first case the body of that rule will evaluate to false and hence that rule will not make any contribution to the answer set. In the second case one of the disjuncts in the head is already true with respect to S, so no new disjuncts in the head need to be made true. *Next*, we remove literals following **not** in the body and head of the remaining rules in Π and put them in Π^S. This is because the ones in the body are already true with respect to S and the ones in the head are already false with respect to S.

To define answer sets of AnsProlog$^{\mathbf{not},or,\neg,\perp}$ programs, recall that we have already defined – in Section 1.3.4 – answer sets of AnsProlog$^{or,\neg,\perp}$ programs and Π^S is such a program. We now say S is an answer set of an AnsProlog$^{\mathbf{not},or,\neg,\perp}$ program Π iff S is an answer set of the AnsProlog$^{or,\neg,\perp}$ program Π^S.

Example 155 [IS98] Consider the following AnsProlog$^{\mathbf{not},or,\neg,\perp}$ program π:

$r \leftarrow p.$
$p \; or \; \mathbf{not} \; p \leftarrow.$

We will show that $S_1 = \emptyset$ and $S_2 = \{p, r\}$ are two answer sets of this program.

$\pi^{S_1} = \{r \leftarrow p.\}$, and the answer set of π^{S_1} is $\emptyset$.
$\pi^{S_2} = \{r \leftarrow p.; p \leftarrow .\}$, and the answer set of π^{S_2} is $\{p, r\}$.   □

One important feature of answer sets of AnsProlog$^{not,or,\neg,\perp}$ programs that is evident from the above example is that they no longer have to be minimal. This is a departure from the answer sets of AnsProlog* programs.

There exists a mapping that can translate AnsProlog$^{not,or,\neg,\perp}$ programs to AnsProlog* programs so that there is a one-to-one correspondence between their answer sets. But the answer sets are not exactly the same, as they may contain some additional literals that are introduced during the translation process. The translation is as follows:

For every rule of the form (9.1.1) in the AnsProlog$^{not,or,\neg,\perp}$ program π, the translated program $tr(\pi)$ contains the following rules.

(1) r_0 or $\cdots$ or r_k or r_{k+1} or $\cdots$ or $r_l \leftarrow L_{l+1}, \ldots, L_m,$ **not** $L_{m+1}, \ldots,$ **not** L_n.
(2) $L_i \leftarrow r_i$.   for $i = 0, \ldots, k$
(3) $r_i \leftarrow L_i, L_{k+1}, \ldots, L_l$.   for $i = 0, \ldots, k$
(4) $\perp \leftarrow r_i,$ **not** L_j.   for $i = 0, \ldots, k$ and $j = k+1, \ldots, l$.
(5) $\perp \leftarrow r_j, L_j$.   for $j = k+1, \ldots, l$

Proposition 112 [IS98] Let π be an AnsProlog$^{not,or,\neg,\perp}$ program and $tr(\pi)$ be its translation. A set S is an answer set of π iff S' is an answer set of $tr(\pi)$ such that $S = S' \cap Lit_\pi$.   □

Example 156 Consider the following AnsProlog$^{not,or,\neg,\perp}$ program π_1:

p *or* **not** $q \leftarrow$.
q *or* **not** $p \leftarrow$.

The answer sets of π_1 are $\{p, q\}$ and $\emptyset$.
      The translation of π_1 is as follows:

r_1 *or* $r_2 \leftarrow$.
r_3 *or* $r_4 \leftarrow$.
$p \leftarrow r_1$.
$r_1 \leftarrow p, q$.
$\perp \leftarrow r_1,$ **not** q.
$\perp \leftarrow r_2, q$.
$q \leftarrow r_3$.
$r_3 \leftarrow q, p$.
$\perp \leftarrow r_3,$ **not** p.
$\perp \leftarrow r_4, p$.

It has the answer sets $\{r_1, r_3, p, q\}$ and $\{r_2, r_4\}$.   □

We now define a special class of AnsProlog$^{not,or ,¬,⊥}$ programs for which we can do a simpler translation such that the answer sets of the two programs coincide.

An AnsProlog$^{not,or ,¬,⊥}$ program is negative acyclic if there is a level mapping l for Π such that:

(i) for every $i = 0, \ldots, k$, and $j = k+1, \ldots, l, l(L_i) > l(L_j)$; and
(i) for every $i = 0, \ldots, k$, and $j = l+1, \ldots, m, l(L_i) \geq l(L_j)$.

Proposition 113 [IS98] Let π be a negative acyclic AnsProlog$^{not,or ,¬,⊥}$ program. Let $tr_2(\pi)$ be the AnsProlog program obtained from π by replacing every rule of the form (9.1.1) by the rule:

$$L_0 \text{ or } \cdots \text{ or } L_k \leftarrow L_{k+1}, \ldots, L_l, L_{l+1}, \ldots, L_m, \text{ not } L_{m+1}, \ldots, \text{ not } L_n.$$

Both π and $tr_2(\pi)$ have exactly the same answer sets.   □

9.2 AnsProlog$^{\{not,or ,¬,⊥\}^*}$: allowing nested expressions

The nesting of operators in a logic programming setting started off with certain PROLOG implementations where rules of the form

$$s \leftarrow (p \rightarrow q;r), t.$$

were allowed. There the construct $(p \rightarrow q;r)$ represents the 'if-then-else' construct and means *if p then q else r*. Using the operators in our language this rule will be expressed as

$$s \leftarrow ((p, q) \text{ or } (\textbf{not } p, r)), t.$$

which has the equivalent (intuitive) meaning as the following two rules:

$$s \leftarrow p, q, t.$$
$$s \leftarrow \textbf{not } p, r, t.$$

The PROLOG implementation is more efficient with respect to the nested rule than with respect to the above two rules as in the former case it evaluates p only once. Another motivation behind allowing nesting is the resulting compactness in representation, and a notion of equivalence that makes it easier to reason about strong equivalence of AnsProlog$_{sm}$ programs. In this section we will introduce the language AnsProlog$^{\{not,or ,¬,⊥\}^*}$ that allows nesting, give its semantics, discuss its usefulness, and present a translation from AnsProlog$^{\{not,or ,¬,⊥\}^*}$ to AnsProlog$^{not,or ,¬,⊥}$. We will focus on the propositional case, as the programs with variables can be grounded to eliminate the variables.

We now start with several notions that are specific to this section only. *Elementary formulas* are literals and the 0-place connectives $\perp$ and $\top$, represent *false* and *true* respectively. *Formulas* are built from elementary formulas using the unary connective **not**, and the binary connectives ',' (conjunction) and *or* (disjunction). Often we will use the symbol ';' for *or*. A *rule* is an expression of the form:

$$F \leftarrow G.$$

where F and G are formulas referred to as the *head* and *body* of the rule respectively. Often we will use the shorthand $F \rightarrow G; H$ for $(F, G); (\text{not } F, H)$. The rule $F \leftarrow \top.$ will often be written as $F \leftarrow.$ or simply F. Rules of the form $\perp \leftarrow G.$ will be referred to as *constraints* and written as $\leftarrow G$. An AnsProlog$^{\{\text{not}, or, \neg, \perp\}^*}$ program is a set of rules. An occurrence of a formula F in another formula or rule is said to be *singular* if the symbol before F in this occurrence is $\neg$; otherwise the occurrence is referred to as *regular*. It should be noted that in formulas the statuses of **not** and $\neg$ are different in the sense that $\neg$ can only precede an atom, while **not** can precede an arbitrary formula.

Formulas, rules, and programs that do not contain **not** will be called *basic*. A consistent set X of literals is said to satisfy a basic formula F denoted by $X \models_{form} F$ if:

- F is an elementary formula, and $F \in X$ or $F = \top$.
- F is the formula (G, H), and $X \models_{form} G$ and $X \models_{form} H$.
- F is the formula $(G; H)$, and $X \models_{form} G$ or $X \models_{form} H$.

A consistent set X of literals is said to be *closed* under a basic program Π if, for every rule $F \leftarrow G.$ in Π, $X \models_{form} F$ whenever $X \models_{form} G$. We say X is an answer set of Π if X is minimal among the consistent set of literals closed under Π.

Definition 122 The *reduct* of a formula, rule, or program relative to a consistent set X of literals, denoted by putting X as a superscript, is recursively defined as follows:

- If F is an elementary formula then $F^X = F$.
- $(F, G)^X = (F^X, G^X)$.
- $(F; G)^X = (F^X; G^X)$.
- $(\text{not } F)^X$ is equal to $\perp$ if $X \models_{form} F^X$, and $\top$ otherwise.
- $(F \leftarrow G)^X = (F^X \leftarrow G^X)$.
- For a program Π, $\Pi^X = \{(F \leftarrow G)^X : F \leftarrow G \in \Pi\}$. $\square$

Notice that for a program Π and a consistent set X of literals, the program Π^X is *basic*.

Definition 123 A consistent set X of literals is an *answer set* for a program Π if X is an answer set of Π^X. $\square$

Proposition 114 [LTT99] Let Π be an AnsProlog$^{not, or, \neg, \perp}$ program. Its answer sets corresponding to Definition 123 are its consistent answer sets with respect to the definition in Section 9.1. $\square$

In contrast to the rest of the book, the definition of answer set in this section precludes the possibility of inconsistent answer sets.

Example 157 Consider the following AnsProlog$^{\neg}$ program:

$p \leftarrow .$
$\neg p \leftarrow .$
$q \leftarrow .$

This program has the unique answer set *Lit*. But according to Definition 123, the corresponding AnsProlog$^{\{not, or, \neg, \perp\}^*}$ program does not have any answer sets. $\square$

The notion of strong equivalence in Section 3.9.5 can be transported to AnsProlog$^{\{not, or, \neg, \perp\}^*}$ programs. We will discuss transformations that preserve strong equivalence of AnsProlog$^{\{not, or, \neg, \perp\}^*}$ programs. We first define equivalence of formulas and transformations that preserve their equivalence.

Definition 124 Two formulas F and G are said to be equivalent, denoted by $F \Leftrightarrow H$, if for any consistent sets of literals X and Y, $X \models_{form} F^Y$ iff $X \models_{form} G^Y$. $\square$

Proposition 115 [LTT99] For any formulas, F, G, and H,

(1) $F, G \Leftrightarrow G, F$ and $F; G \Leftrightarrow G; F$.
(2) $(F, G), H \Leftrightarrow F, (G, H)$ and $(F; G); H \Leftrightarrow F; (G; H)$.
(3) $F, (G; H) \Leftrightarrow (F, G); (F, H)$ and $F; (G, H) \Leftrightarrow (F; G), (F; H)$.
(4) **not** $(F, G) \Leftrightarrow$ **not** $F;$ **not** G and **not** $(F; G) \Leftrightarrow$ **not** $F,$ **not** G.
(5) **not not not** $F \Leftrightarrow$ **not** F.
(6) $F, \top \Leftrightarrow F$ and $F; \top \Leftrightarrow \top$.
(7) $F, \perp \Leftrightarrow \perp$ and $F; \perp \Leftrightarrow F$.
(8) If p is an atom then $p, \neg p \Leftrightarrow \perp$ and **not** $p;$ **not** $\neg p \Leftrightarrow \top$.
(9) **not** $\top \Leftrightarrow \perp$ and **not** $\perp \Leftrightarrow \top$. $\square$

The equivalence of formulas can be used to show the strong equivalence of programs. The following proposition states the necessary conditions.

Proposition 116 [LTT99] Let Π be an AnsProlog$^{\{\textbf{not},or,\neg,\perp\}^*}$ program, and let F and G be a pair of equivalent formulas. Any program obtained from Π by replacing some regular occurrences of F by G is strongly equivalent to Π.

□

The following are some additional strong equivalence conditions for AnsProlog$^{\{\textbf{not},\ or,\neg,\perp\}^*}$ programs.

Proposition 117 [LTT99]

(1) $F, G \leftarrow H$ is strongly equivalent to

   $F \leftarrow H$
   $G \leftarrow H$

(2) $F \leftarrow G; H$ is strongly equivalent to

   $F \leftarrow G$
   $F \leftarrow H$

(3) $F \leftarrow G, \textbf{not not } H$ is strongly equivalent to $F; \textbf{not } H \leftarrow G$.
(4) $F; \textbf{not not } G \leftarrow H$ is strongly equivalent to $F \leftarrow \textbf{not } G, H$.   □

Proposition 118 [LTT99] For every AnsProlog$^{\{\textbf{not},or,\neg,\perp\}^*}$ program there is a strongly equivalent program consisting of rules in the syntax of AnsProlog$^{\textbf{not},or,\neg,\perp}$.   □

Note that in AnsProlog$^{\{\textbf{not},or,\neg,\perp\}^*}$ programs **not not** does not cancel out. For example the following two programs have different answer sets.

The program

$p \leftarrow \textbf{not not } p.$

has the two answer sets $\emptyset$ and $\{p\}$, while the program

$p \leftarrow p.$

has the single answer set $\emptyset$. This example also show that AnsProlog$^{\{\textbf{not},or,\neg,\perp\}^*}$ programs may have non-minimal answer sets.

We now present a translation from AnsProlog$_{sm}$ programs to AnsProlog$^{\{\textbf{not},or,\neg,\perp\}^*}$ programs so that they have the same answer sets. The transformation is as follows:

(1) The translation of a constraint of the form

   $L[c_1 = w_1, \ldots, c_n = w_n]$

is the nested expression

$$; \quad (\quad , \quad c_i)$$
$$X : \Sigma X \geq L \quad i \in X$$

where X ranges over the subsets of $\{1, \ldots, m\}$ and ΣX stands for $\Sigma_{i \in X} w_i$. The translation of LS is denoted by $[[LS]]$. In the above notation the empty conjunction is understood as $\top$ and the empty disjunction as $\perp$.

(2) The translation of a constraint of the form

$$[c_1 = w_1, \ldots, c_n = w_n]U$$

is the nested expression

$$, \quad (\quad ; \quad \textbf{not } c_i)$$
$$X : \Sigma X > U \quad i \in X$$

where ΣX is as defined before. The translation of SU is denoted by $[[SU]]$.

(3) The translation of a general weight constraint LSU denoted by $[[LSU]]$ is the nested expression $[[LS]], [[SU]]$.

(4) For any AnsProlog$_{sm}$ program Ω, its translation $[[\Omega]]$ is the AnsProlog$^{\{not, or, \neg, \perp\}^*}$ program obtained from Ω by replacing each AnsProlog$_{sm}$ rule of the form

$$L[l_1 = w_1, \ldots, l_m = w_m]U \leftarrow C_1, \ldots, C_m$$

by

$$(l_1; \textbf{not } l_1), \ldots, (l_m; \textbf{not } l_m), [[L[l_1 = w_1, \ldots, l_m = w_m]U]] \leftarrow [[C_1]], \ldots, [[C_m]].$$

The following example illustrates the above translation.

Example 158 Consider the AnsProlog$_{sm}$ program consisting of the following rule:

$$2[a = 1, b = 1, c = 1]2 \leftarrow p.$$

We translate the above program to an AnsProlog$^{\{not, or, \neg, \perp\}^*}$ program as follows:

$[[2[a = 1, b = 1, c = 1]]]$ is the nested expression
$(a, b); (b, c); (a, c); (a, b, c)$.
$[[[a = 1, b = 1, c = 1]2]]$ is the nested expression
$(\textbf{not } a; \textbf{not } b; \textbf{not } c)$.

Thus $[[2[a = 1, b = 1, c = 1]2 \leftarrow p.]]$ is the program consisting of the following rule:

$(a; \textbf{not } a), (b; \textbf{not } b), (c; \textbf{not } c), ((a, b); (b, c); (a, c); (a, b, c)), (\textbf{not } a; \textbf{not } b; \textbf{not } c) \leftarrow p.$ $\square$

Theorem 9.2.1 [FL01] For any AnsProlog$_{sm}$ program Ω, the programs Ω and $[[\Omega]]$ have the same answer sets. $\square$

It should be noted that the translation $[[\ ]]$ in general results in an exponential blow-up. Nevertheless, when L and U are either infinite or bounded by a fixed constant, which is often the case, the resulting translation is of reasonable size. One advantage of this translation over the translation in Section 2.1.18 is that in the case of the latter the correspondence between the answer sets is not one-to-one and onto, and new literals not in the language of the original program are introduced. On the other hand the translation in Section 2.1.18 is more succinct, in particular it is linear with respect to the size of the original program.

An important advantage of the translation mechanism of this section is that we can use the strong equivalence results of AnsProlog$^{\{not,\ or, \neg, \perp\}^*}$ programs to show the strong equivalence of AnsProlog$_{sm}$ programs.

9.3 AnsProlog$^{\neg, or, K, M}$: allowing knowledge and belief operators

Among the various AnsProlog* subsets and extensions that we have considered so far, there are only two forms of negation, the classical $\neg$, and the nonmonotonic **not**. Although the answer to a query with respect to an AnsProlog$^{\neg, or}$ program is *true* if it is *true* in all its answer sets, there is no way to reason within the language about a particular literal being *true* in all the (or some of the) answer sets.

The following example demonstrates the need for an extension of AnsProlog$^{\neg, or}$ that will allow such reasoning:

Example 159 Consider the following information. We know that (A) either 'john' or 'peter' is guilty (of murder), (B) 'a person is presumed innocent unless proven guilty', (C) 'a person can get a security clearance if we have no reason to suspect that he or she is guilty.'

Statement (A) can easily be written as an AnsProlog$^{\neg, or}$ rule:

$$A_1 : guilty(john) \ or \ guilty(peter) \leftarrow .$$

If we try to write statement (B) as an AnsProlog$^{\neg, or}$ rule, we have:

$$B_1 : presumed\_innocent(X) \leftarrow \textbf{not} \ guilty(X).$$

This, however, is not appropriate because the program consisting of A_1 and B_1 has two answer sets $\{guilty(john), presumed\_innocent(peter)\}$ and $\{guilty(peter), presumed\_innocent(john)\}$, and therefore $presumed\_innocent(john)$ is inferred to be *unknown*. Intuitively, we should be able to infer that $presumed\_innocent(john)$ is *true*. Hence, the operator **not** in the body of B_1 is not the one we want.

Similarly, if we consider representing statement C in the language of AnsProlog$^{\neg, or}$ programs, we have :

$$C_1 : \; cleared(X) \leftarrow \textbf{not} \; guilty(X).$$

But, C_1 is not appropriate because the program consisting of A_1 and C_1 has two answer sets: $\{guilty(john), cleared(peter)\}$ and $\{guilty(peter), cleared(john)\}$, and we infer $cleared(john)$ to be $unknown$. Intuitively, we would like to infer that $cleared(john)$ is $false$.

Our goal is to expand the language and redefine answer sets in such a way that:

(B_2) We would infer $presumed\_innocent(a)$ iff there is at least one answer set that does not contain $guilty(a)$.

(C_2) We would infer $cleared(a)$ iff none of the answer sets contains $guilty(a)$.   □

To capture the intuition in (B_2) and (C_2) in the above example, we use two unary operators K and M [Gel91b] and add them to our language. Intuitively, KL stands for L is $known$ and ML stands for L may be believed. For a literal L, and a collection of sets of literals S, we say that KL is $true$ with respect to S (denoted by $S \models KL$) iff L is $true$ in all sets in S. ML is $true$ with respect to S (denoted by $S \models ML$) iff l is $true$ in at $least$ one set in S. We say $S \models \neg KL$ iff $S \not\models KL$ and we say $S \models \neg ML$ iff $S \not\models ML$. This means $\neg KL$ is $true$ with respect to S iff there is at least one set in S where L is not $true$, and $\neg ML$ is $true$ with respect to S iff there is no set in S where L is $true$.

Using K and M we can represent the statements (B) and (C) in the above example by the rules:

$$innocent(X) \leftarrow \neg K \, guilty(X).$$

and

$$cleared(X) \leftarrow \neg M \, guilty(X).$$

We now define the syntax and semantics of AnsProlog$^{\neg, or, K, M}$ programs which are obtained by adding K and M to AnsProlog$^{\neg, or}$. We refer to a literal L without K or M as an $objective$ literal, and we refer to formulas of the form $KL, ML, \neg KL$, and $\neg ML$ as $subjective$ literals.

An AnsProlog$^{\neg, or, K, M}$ logic program is a collection of rules of the form:

$$L_1 \; or \; \cdots \; or \; L_k \leftarrow G_{k+1}, \ldots, G_m, \textbf{not} \; L_{m+1}, \ldots, \textbf{not} \; L_n. \quad\quad (9.3.2)$$

where the Ls are objective literals and the Gs are subjective or objective literals.

Let T be an AnsProlog$^{\neg, or, K, M}$ program and S be a collection of sets of literals in the language of T. By T^S we will denote the AnsProlog$^{\neg, or}$ program obtained from T by:

(1) removing from T all rules containing subjective literals G such that $S \not\models G$,
(2) removing from rules in T all other occurrences of subjective literals.

Definition 125 A set S will be called a *world view* of T if S is the collection of all answer sets of T^S. Elements of S will be called *belief sets* of T. The program T^S will be called the *reduct* of T with respect to S. □

An objective literal is said to be *true*(*false*) with respect to an AnsProlog$^{\neg, or, K, M}$ program if it is *true*(*false*) in all elements of its world view; otherwise it is said to be unknown. A subjective literal is said to be *true*(*false*) with respect to an AnsProlog$^{\neg, or, K, M}$ program if it is *true*(*false*) in its world view. Notice that subjective literals cannot be unknown.

Example 160 Consider the AnsProlog$^{\neg, or, K, M}$ program T_1:

(1) *guilty(john) or guilty(peter)* ←.
(2) *presumed_innocent(X)* ← ¬*K guilty(X)*.
(3) *cleared(X)* ← ¬*M guilty(X)*.
(4) ¬*presumed_innocent(X)* ← **not** *presumed_innocent(X)*.
(5) ¬*cleared(X)* ← **not** *cleared(X)*.

Let $S_1 = \{guilty(john), presumed\_innocent(john), presumed\_innocent(peter),$
$\qquad\qquad \neg cleared(john), \neg cleared(peter)\}$

and $S_2 = \{guilty(peter), presumed\_innocent(john), presumed\_innocent(peter),$
$\qquad\qquad \neg cleared(john), \neg cleared(peter)\}$

and $S = \{S_1, S_2\}$

Since, M *guilty(john)* and M *guilty(peter)* are both *true* with respect to S,

$S \not\models \neg M guilty(john)$ and $S \not\models \neg M$ *guilty(peter)*, and therefore, T_1^S does not contain any ground instance of rule (3). Similarly, $S \models \neg K guilty(john)$ and $S \models \neg K guilty(peter)$ and hence T_1^S consists of the rules:

guilty(john) or guilty(peter) ←.
presumed_innocent(john) ←.
presumed_innocent(peter) ←.
¬*presumed_innocent(X)* ← **not** *presumed_innocent(X)*.
¬ *cleared(X)* ← **not** *cleared(X)*.

The answer sets of T_1^S are S_1 and S_2. Hence, S is a world view of T_1. It is possible to show that S is the only world view of T_1 [GP91] and therefore $T_1 \models$ *presumed_innocent(john)*, $T_1 \models$ *presumed_innocent(peter)*, $T_1 \models \neg cleared(john)$ and $T_1 \models \neg cleared(peter)$ which corresponds to our specification.   □

Example 161 [Representing Unknown] Consider the AnsProlog¬, or program from Section 2.2.4. Recall that it consists of rules used by a certain college for awarding scholarships to its students, and a rule saying 'if the three rules do not determine the eligibility of a student then the student should be interviewed.'

In the formulation in Section 2.2.4 the above is encoded using the following rule:

$interview(X) \leftarrow$ **not** $eligible(X)$, **not** $\neg eligible(X)$.

We now argue that in the presence of multiple answer sets the above rule is not appropriate. Assume that, in addition to the earlier formulation, we have the following additional disjunctive information.

(5') *fairGPA(mike) or highGPA(mike)* ←.

The AnsProlog¬, or,K,M program $\pi_{gpa.1}$ consisting of (1)–(4) from π_{gpa} and (5'), has two answer sets: $A_1 = \{highGPA(mike), eligible(mike)\}$ and $A_2 = \{fairGPA(mike), interview(mike)\}$, and therefore the reasoner modeled by $\pi_{gpa.1}$ does not have enough information to establish Mike's eligibility for the scholarship (i.e. answer to *eligible(mike)* is *unknown*). Hence, intuitively the reasoner should answer *yes* to the query *interview(mike)*. But this is not achieved by the above representation.

The intended effect is achieved by replacing (4) by the following rule:

(4') $interview(X) \leftarrow \neg K eligible(X)$, $\neg K \neg eligible(X)$.

The AnsProlog¬, or,K,M program, $\pi_{gpa.epi}$, obtained by replacing (4) in $\pi_{gpa.1}$ by (4') has the world view $A = \{A_1, A_2\}$ where $A_1 = \{highGPA(mike), eligible (mike), interview(mike)\}$, and $A_2 = \{fairGPA(mike), interview(mike)\}$. Hence, $\pi_{gpa.epi}$ answers *unknown* to the query *eligible(mike)* and *yes* to the query *interview(mike)*, which is the intended behavior of the system.   □

Hence, in general (for theories with multiple answer sets), the statement 'the truth of an atomic statement P is *unknown*' is appropriately represented by

$$\textbf{not } K P, \textbf{not } \neg K P. \qquad (9.3.3)$$

So far we have only considered AnsProlog¬, or,K,M programs with a unique world view. The following example shows that AnsProlog¬, or,K,M programs may have multiple world views.

Example 162 Let T_2 consist of the rules

(1) $p(a)$ *or* $p(b)$ ←.
(2) $p(c)$ ←.
(3) $q(d)$ ←.
(4) $\neg p(X) \leftarrow \neg M p(X)$.

The specification T_2 has three world views:

$A_1 = \{\{q(d),\ p(c),\ p(a),\ \neg p(b),\ \neg p(d)\}\}$,

$A_2 = \{\{q(d),\ p(c),\ p(b),\ \neg p(a),\ \neg p(d)\}\}$, and

$A_3 = \{\{q(d),\ p(a),\ p(c),\neg p(d)\},\ \{q(d),\ p(b),\ p(c),\neg p(d)\}\}$.

Intuitively A_3 is preferred to the other two world views of T_2 as it treats $p(a)$ and $p(b)$ in the same manner (unlike A_1 and A_2) and can be used to answer queries with respect to T_2.   □

Exercise 39 Formulate a preference relation between world views of AnsProlog$^{\neg,\ or,K,M}$ programs, and develop conditions on the programs that guarantee unique preferred world views. (Hint: [Gel91b].)   □

9.4 Abductive reasoning with AnsProlog: AnsProlog^{abd}

Earlier in Section 3.8 we discussed a simple form of abduction using AnsProlog*. In this section we mention a notion of abductive logic programming which is more general than our earlier formulation in some aspects and less general in certain others. In this formulation a subset of the predicates in the language is referred to as the *abducible* predicates or *open predicates*. An AnsProlog^{abd} program is defined as a triple $\langle \Pi, A, O \rangle$, where A is the set of open predicates, Π is an AnsProlog program with only atoms of nonopen predicates in its heads, and O is a set of first order formulas. O is used to express *observations* and *constraints* in an abductive logic program. Abductive logic programs are characterized as follows:

Definition 126 Let $\langle \Pi, A, O \rangle$ be an abductive logic program. A set M of ground atoms is a *generalized stable model* of $\langle \Pi, A, O \rangle$ if there is a $\Delta \subset atoms(A)$ such that M is an answer set of $\Pi \cup \Delta$ and M satisfies O.

For an atom f, we say $\langle \Pi, A, O \rangle \models_{abd} f$, if f belongs to all generalized stable models of $\langle \Pi, A, O \rangle$. For a negative literal $\neg f$, we say $\langle \Pi, A, O \rangle \models_{abd} \neg f$, if f does not belong to any of the generalized stable models of $\langle \Pi, A, O \rangle$.   □

9.5 Domain closure and the universal query problem

Consider the AnsProlog program Π consisting of the following rule:

$p(a) \leftarrow .$

Suppose we would like to ask if $\Pi \models \forall X . p(X)$. Since this query is not part of our query language presented in Section 1.3.5, let us use the technique in Section 2.1.7 and modify the program Π to Π^* which consists of the following rules:

$p(a) \leftarrow .$
$not\_all\_p \leftarrow \textbf{not } p(X).$
$all\_p \leftarrow \textbf{not } not\_all\_p.$

and ask if $\Pi^* \models all\_p$. Since, when the language of a program is not explicitly stated, its language is inferred from the program itself, for this program the Herbrand Universe is $\{a\}$. Hence, we have $\Pi^* \models all\_p$. To many this answer is unintuitive, and they point to the fact that adding an unrelated $r(b) \leftarrow .$ to Π^* result in the retraction of all_p. That is, $\Pi^* \cup \{r(b) \leftarrow .\} \not\models all\_p$. Although we discussed this aspect in Section 3.5 and also briefly in Section 6.6.2 we consider a different angle here. Unlike Section 3.5 where we presented sufficiency conditions that guarantee language independence and tolerance, in this section we propose alternative semantics and alternative ways to characterize entailment.

There are four main proposals to handle this problem, referred to in the literature as the 'Universal Query Problem'.

(i) One proposal, advocated in [Ros92], is to add to every program a fact $q(f(c))$, where q, f, and c do not occur in the original program. Here the basic idea is to introduce an infinite number of terms to the Herbrand Universe. Following this approach, we have that $\Pi^* \cup \{q(f(c)) \leftarrow .\} \not\models all\_p$.

(ii) The second proposal advocated in [Kun89] is to have a universal language with an infinite number of terms in the Herbrand Universe in which all programs are expressed. In this case, $\Pi^* \not\models all\_p$, but $\Pi^* \models \neg all\_p$.

(iii) The third proposal advocated in [Kun87, Prz89b] is to consider arbitrary models instead of Herbrand models. In this case, $\Pi^* \not\models all\_p$, and $\Pi^* \not\models \neg all\_p$.

(iv) The fourth proposal by Gelfond articulated in [BG94], is to neither blindly assume a closed domain (as is done by using Herbrand models), nor blindly assume an infinite domain (as is done by arbitrarily enlarging the Herbrand Universe), but have a characterization with open domain – as is also done in (iii), and in addition have a way to selectively specify if we want closed domain. With respect to this proposal Π^*'s answer to all_p will be 'unknown' and the reasoning is that we do not know if a is the only object or not. Both assuming it to be the only object and answering 'yes' and assuming the presence of infinite other objects and answering 'no' amounts to preferring one assumption over another in terms of whether the domain is closed or infinite. We now present this characterization.

9.5.1 Parameterized answer sets and $\models_{open}$

Let Π be an AnsProlog$^\neg$ program over the language $\mathcal{L}_0$. To give the semantics of Π, we will first expand the alphabet of $\mathcal{L}_0$ by an infinite sequence of new constants $c_1, \ldots, c_k, \ldots$. We will call these new constants *generic*. The resulting language will be denoted by $\mathcal{L}_\infty$. By $\mathcal{L}_k$ we will denote the expansion of $\mathcal{L}_0$ by constants $c_1, \ldots, c_k$, and by Π_k, where $0 \le k \le \infty$, we mean the set of all ground instances of Π in the language $\mathcal{L}_k$. The entailment relation with respect to the language $\mathcal{L}_k$ will be denoted by $\models_k$.

Definition 127 Let Π be an AnsProlog or an AnsProlog$^\neg$ program. By k-*answer set* of Π we will mean a pair $\langle k, B \rangle$, where B is an answer set of Π in the language $\mathcal{L}_k$. For a query q, we say $\Pi \models_{open} q$, if q is true in all consistent k-answer sets of Π, for all k. $\qquad\Box$

We will refer to the collection of all consistent k-answer sets as *parameterized* answer sets.

Example 163 Consider a language $\mathcal{L}_0$ over the alphabet $\{a\}$ and an AnsProlog program Π^* consisting of the rules

$p(a) \leftarrow .$
$not\_all\_p \leftarrow \mathbf{not}\ p(X).$
$all\_p \leftarrow \mathbf{not}\ not\_all\_p.$

The following are parameterized answer sets of Π:

$\{\langle 0, \{p(a), all\_p\}\rangle\}, \{\langle 1, \{p(a), not\_all\_p\}\rangle\}, \{\langle 2, \{p(a), not\_all\_p\}\rangle\}, \ldots.$

Thus all_p is *true* in the first answer set as the only constant in the language $\mathcal{L}_0$ is a while it is not *true* in all other answer sets as the the corresponding languages contain constants other than a. Hence, as intended, Π's answer to the query all_p is *unknown*. That is, $\Pi \not\models_{open} all\_p$, and $\Pi \not\models_{open} \neg all\_p$. $\qquad\Box$

9.5.2 Applications of $\models_{open}$

We first show that the $\models_{open}$ characterization allows the explicit specification – when desired – of domain-closure assumption.

Let Π be an arbitrary AnsProlog$^\neg$ program in a language $\mathcal{L}_0$. We expand $\mathcal{L}_0$ by the unary predicate symbol h which stands for *named elements of the domain*. The following rules can be viewed as the definition of h:

$H_1.\ h(t) \leftarrow .$ (for every ground term t from $\mathcal{L}_0$)
$H_2.\ \neg h(X) \leftarrow \mathbf{not}\ h(X).$

The domain-closure assumption is then expressed by the rule:

$DCA. \leftarrow \neg h(X).$

The following example illustrates the role of DCA.

Example 164 Let Π be an AnsProlog$^\neg$ program consisting of H_1, H_2, and the following rules:

$p(a) \leftarrow.$
$q(a) \leftarrow \mathbf{not}\ p(X).$

$\neg p(X) \leftarrow \mathbf{not}\ p(X).$
$\neg q(X) \leftarrow \mathbf{not}\ q(X).$

The k-answer sets of Π are

$\{\langle 0, \{h(a), p(a), \neg q(a)\}\rangle\}$, if $k = 0$, and

$\{\langle k, \{h(a), \neg h(c_1), \ldots, \neg h(c_k), p(a), q(a), \neg p(c_1), \neg q(c_1), \ldots, \neg p(c_k), \neg q(c_k), \}\rangle\}$, if $k > 0$,

and, therefore, Π's answer to the query $q(a)$ with respect to $\models_{open}$ is *unknown*. That is, $\Pi \not\models_{open} q(a)$, and $\Pi \not\models_{open} \neg q(a)$. The answer changes if Π is expanded by the domain closure assumption (DCA). The resulting program, Π_C, has the unique answer set $\{< 0, \{h(a), p(a), \neg q(a)\} >\}$ and, therefore, Π_C's answer to $q(a)$ with respect to $\models_{open}$ is *no*, exactly the answer produced by the program $\{p(a) \leftarrow .; q(a) \leftarrow \mathbf{not}\ p(X).\}$ with respect to $\models$, which has the domain closure assumption built-in. □

Exercise 40 Show that for any AnsProlog$^\neg$ program Π, its answer to any query with respect to $\models$ is the same as $\Pi \cup \{H_1, H_2, DCA\}$'s answer with respect to $\models_{open}$. □

Now we will briefly discuss an example that shows the use of domain assumptions and of the concept of named objects.

Example 165 Consider a departmental database containing the list of courses which will be offered by a department next year, and the list of professors who will be working for the department at that time. Let us assume that the database knows the names of all the courses which may be taught by the department but, since the hiring process is not yet over, it does not know the names of all of the professors. This information can be expressed as follows:

$course(a) \leftarrow.$
$course(b) \leftarrow.$

$prof(m) \leftarrow.$
$prof(n) \leftarrow$

$\neg \, course(X) \leftarrow \neg h(X).$

The k-answer set of this program is

$\langle k, course(a), course(b), \neg \, course(c_1), \ldots, \neg course(c_k), prof(m), prof(n),$
$\quad h(a), h(b), h(m), h(n), \neg h(c_1), \ldots, \neg h(c_k)\}\rangle$

and, therefore, the above program answers *no* to the query

$\exists X \, (course(X) \wedge \neg h(X))$

and *unknown* to the query

$\exists X \, (prof(X) \wedge \neg h(X))$

with respect to $\models_{open}$. Notice that in this example, it is essential to allow for the possibility of unknown objects.

Let us now expand the informal specification of our database by the closed world assumptions for predicates *course* and *prof*. The closed world assumption for *course* says that there are no other courses except those mentioned in the database and can be formalized by the standard rule

$\neg course(X) \leftarrow \mathbf{not} \;\; course(X).$

Using this assumption, we will be able to prove that a and b are the only courses taught in our department. In the case of predicate *prof*, however, this (informal) assumption is too strong – there may, after all, be some unknown professor not mentioned in the list. However, we want to be able to allow our database to conclude that *no one known to the database is a professor unless so stated*. For that we need a weaker form of the closed world assumption, which will not be applicable to generic elements. This can easily be accomplished by the following rule:

$\neg prof(X) \leftarrow h(X), \mathbf{not} \;\; prof(X).$

The k-answer set of the resulting program Π is as follows:

$\langle k, \{c(a), c(b), \neg c(m), \neg c(n), \neg c(c_1), \ldots, \neg c(c_k), p(m), p(n), \neg p(a), \neg p(b),$
$\quad h(a), h(b), h(m), h(n), \neg h(c_1), \ldots, \neg h(c_k)\}\rangle,$

where c stands for *course* and p stands for *prof*. This allows us to conclude, say, that a is not a professor without concluding that there are no professors except m and n. $\square$

9.6 AnsProlog_set: adding set constructs to AnsProlog

Recently an extension to AnsProlog with a goal of making it easier to reason with sets has been proposed [BGN00, Gel01]. It introduces two new constructs called *s-atom* and *f-atom* .

(1) An *s*-atom is of the form:

$$\{X_1, \ldots, X_k \ : \ p(X_1, \ldots, X_k, \ldots)\} \subseteq \{X_1, \ldots, X_k \ : \ q(X_1, \ldots, X_k, \ldots)\}. \quad (9.6.4)$$

(2) An *f*-atom is either of the form:

$$|\{X_1, \ldots, X_k \ : \ p(X_1, \ldots, X_k, \ldots)\}| \leq r \quad (9.6.5)$$

or of the form

$$|\{X_1, \ldots, X_k \ : \ p(X_1, \ldots, X_k, \ldots)\}| = r \quad (9.6.6)$$

In the above, the variables $X_1, \ldots, X_n$ are referred to as bound variables. Intuitively, the meaning of an *s*-atom of the form (9.6.4) is that the set of tuples of X_is (together with the rest) satisfying p is a subset of the set of tuples of X_is (together with the rest) satisfying q. The meaning of an *f*-atom of the form (9.6.5) is that the number of tuples of X_is (together with the rest) satisfying p is less than or equal to r. The meaning of *f*-atoms of the form (9.6.6) is similar.

An AnsProlog_set program is now a collection of rules of the form

$$L_0 \leftarrow L_1, \ldots, L_m, \textbf{not } L_{m+1}, \ldots, \textbf{not } L_n. \quad (9.6.7)$$

where L_0 is an atom or an *s*-atom, and each L_i, $1 \leq i \leq n$, is an atom, an *s*-atom, or an *f*-atom.

Before defining the semantics of AnsProlog_set programs we need to define the truth of atoms, *s*-atoms, and *f*-atoms with respect to a set of ground atoms. Let S be a set of ground atoms. An atom l is true in S if $l \in S$. An *s*-atom (9.6.4) is true in S if for any tuple $(t_1, \ldots, t_k)$ either $p(t_1, \ldots, t_k, \ldots) \notin S$ or $q(t_1, \ldots, t_k, \ldots) \in S$. An *f*-atom (9.6.5) is true in S if the number of tuples of X_is (together with the rest) that satisfy p is less than or equal to r. An *f*-atom (9.6.6) is true in S if the number of tuples of X_is (together with the rest) that satisfy p is equal to r. For an atom, *s*-atom, or *f*-atom l, l is satisfied by S is denoted by $S \models_{set} l$ and we say **not** l is satisfied by S if $S \not\models_{set} l$.

Besides the bound variables in its *s*-atoms and *f*-atoms, an AnsProlog_set program allows other variables. These other variables are similar to variables in AnsProlog programs and are treated as schema variables. The grounding of these variables results in a ground AnsProlog_set program. Note that unlike a ground AnsProlog program, a ground AnsProlog_set program may have variables, but these variables are the bound variables in its *s*-atoms and *f*-atoms.

Given a set S of ground atoms and a ground AnsProlog$_{set}$ program Π we now define a transformed program $se(\Pi, S)$ (read as 'the set elimination of Π with respect to S') as follows:

(1) remove from Π all rules whose bodies contain s-atoms or f-atoms not satisfied by S;
(2) remove s-atoms and f-atoms from the body of all remaining rules;
(3) replace rules of the form $l \leftarrow \Gamma.$, by the rule $\leftarrow \Gamma.$ if l is an s-atom not satisfied by S; and
(4) replace the remaining rules of the form

$$\{X_1, \ldots, X_k \ : \ p(X_1, \ldots, X_k, a_1, \ldots, a_l)\} \subseteq \{X_1, \ldots, X_k \ : \ q(X_1, \ldots, X_k,$$
$$b_1, \ldots, b_l)\} \text{ by the rules } p(t_1, \ldots, t_k, a_1, \ldots, a_l) \leftarrow \Gamma. \text{ for each } p(t_1, \ldots, t_k, a_1, \ldots, a_l)$$
in S.

We say that a set S of ground atoms is an answer set of an AnsProlog$_{set}$ program Π if S is an answer set of the AnsProlog program $se(\Pi, S)$.

We now give an example illustrating the above definition and the various notations.

Example 166 Suppose we have a list of professor names and their areas of interest given as facts. Let us assume this list consists of the following:

prof(john, ai).
prof(mary, databases).
prof(sandy, systems).
prof(tom, systems).

We can use the following AnsProlog$_{set}$ rules to count the number of professors in each research area.

count$(N, A) \leftarrow |\{X \ : \ prof(X, A)\}| = N.$

The grounding of the above AnsProlog$_{set}$ rule results in the rules of the form,

count$(i, ai) \leftarrow |\{X \ : \ prof(X, ai)\}| = i.$
count$(i, databases) \leftarrow |\{X \ : \ prof(X, databases)\}| = i.$
count$(i, systems) \leftarrow |\{X \ : \ prof(X, systems)\}| = i.$

where i ranges from 0 to some maximum integer m. Note that unlike the grounding of rules with cardinality and weight constraints in AnsProlog$_{sm}$ which do not contain any variables at all, the above rules contain the bound variable X.

The above program has exactly one answer set with the facts about professors and the atoms *count*$(1, ai)$, *count*$(1, databases)$, and *count*$(2, systems)$. □

In the following example we show how the graph colorability problem from Section 8.1.5 can be encoded using AnsProlog$_{set}$.

Example 167 As in the program in Section 8.1.5 we will have the following facts describing the graph, and listing the available colors.

vertex(1).
vertex(2).
vertex(3).
vertex(4).

edge(1,2).
edge(1,3).
edge(2,3).
edge(1,4).
edge(2,4).

col(*a*).
col(*b*).
col(*c*).

$\{C : color(X, C)\} \subseteq \{C : col(C)\} \leftarrow vertex(X).$

$\leftarrow |\{C : color(X, C)\}| = N, N \neq 1.$

The above two rules make sure that each vertex is assigned a unique color from the set of colors defined by the predicate *col*.

$\leftarrow edge(X, Y), col(C), color(X, C), color(Y, C).$

Finally, the above constraint eliminates selections where two adjacent nodes are assigned the same color.   □

It has been conjectured that AnsProlog$_{set}$ has the same complexity and expressiveness as AnsProlog. Formal proofs of this are yet to appear in print.

Exercise 41 The new constructs in AnsProlog$_{set}$ provide an alternative way to express cardinality constraints of Section 8.1. Suggest a way to translate rules with cardinality constraints to rules in AnsProlog$_{set}$.   □

9.7 AnsProlog-<⁻ programs: AnsProlog⁻ programs with ordering

In Section 4.5 we discussed expressing normative statements, exceptions, and preferences as AnsProlog* facts of the form $rule(r, l_0, [l_1, \ldots, l_m])$, $default(d, l_0, [l_1, \ldots, l_m])$, $conflict(d_1, d_2)$, and $prefer(d_1, d_2)$, and reasoning with those facts through AnsProlog* rules. The kind of prioritized defaults that can be expressed using such facts is somewhat limited and a further generalization is to express the rules and defaults as AnsProlog⁻ rules. For that purpose there have been several proposals to develop languages that allow expression of preferences among rules in an AnsProlog⁻ program. In this section we discuss some of those proposals using a uniform framework which was suggested in [SW01].

An AnsProlog-<⁻ program is a pair $(\Pi, <)$, where Π is an AnsProlog⁻ program and $< \subseteq \Pi \times \Pi$ is an irreflexive and transitive relation between the rules of Π. Intuitively, $r_1 < r_2$ means that r_2 has *higher priority* than r_1. If $<$ is a total ordering, we say $(\Pi, <)$ is totally ordered. In the literature AnsProlog-<⁻ programs are referred to by many different terms such as, ordered logic programs, prioritized logic programs, and logic programs with preferences.

Recall that answer sets of AnsProlog⁻ programs are defined as the fixpoints of an operator. We use a similar methodology to define answer sets of AnsProlog-<⁻ programs. Since there are several proposals in the literature, we defined three different notions: w-answer sets, d-answer sets, and b-answer sets. We start with the notion of w-answer sets.

9.7.1 The w-answer sets of AnsProlog-<⁻ programs

The fixpoint operator for w-answer sets [SW01] takes into account the priorities between the rules. We will define the fixpoint operator through an iterated fixpoint of another operator.

Definition 128 Let $(\Pi, <)$ be an AnsProlog-<⁻ program and let X and Y be sets of literals. We define the set of immediate consequences of Y with respect to $(\Pi, <)$ and X as

$$\mathcal{T}_{(\Pi,<),X}(Y) \;=\; \left\{ head(r) \;\middle|\; \begin{array}{l} \text{I. } r \in \Pi \text{ is active with respect to } (Y, X) \text{ and} \\ \text{II. there is no rule } r' \in \Pi \text{ with } r < r' \\ \quad\;\; \text{such that} \\ \quad\;\; (a) \; r' \text{ is active with respect to } (X, Y) \text{ and} \\ \quad\;\; (b) \; head(r') \notin Y. \end{array} \right\}$$

if it is consistent, and $\mathcal{T}_{(\Pi,<),X} Y = Lit$ otherwise. □

The idea in the above operator is to apply a rule r only if the 'question of applicability' has been settled for all higher-ranked rules r'. The above definition allows us to define a counterpart of the standard consequence operator in the setting of AnsProlog-<⁻ programs:

Definition 129 Let $(\Pi, <)$ be an AnsProlog-<⁻ program and let X be a set of literals. We define $\mathcal{C}_{(\Pi,<)}(X) = \bigcup_{i \geq 0} \mathcal{T}_{(\Pi,<),X} \uparrow i$, where $\mathcal{T}_{(\Pi,<),X} \uparrow 0 = \emptyset$, and $\mathcal{T}_{(\Pi,<),X} \uparrow (i+1) = \mathcal{T}_{(\Pi,<),X}(\mathcal{T}_{(\Pi,<),X} \uparrow i)$ □

Note that the operator $C_{(\Pi, <)}$ also enjoys *anti-monotonicity*, i.e. $X_1 \subseteq X_2$, implies $C_{(\Pi, <)}(X_2) \subseteq C_{(\Pi, <)}(X_1)$.

Definition 130 Let $(\Pi, <)$ be an AnsProlog-<¬ program and let X be a set of literals. We define X as a w-answer set of $(\Pi, <)$ if $C_{(\Pi, <)}(X) = X$. □

For illustration, consider the following AnsProlog-<¬ program.

Example 168

$$
\begin{aligned}
&r_1: \neg f \leftarrow p, \textbf{not } f. \qquad &&\text{with } r_2 < r_1 \\
&r_2: \quad w \leftarrow b, \textbf{not } \neg w. \\
&r_3: \quad f \leftarrow w, \textbf{not } \neg f. \\
&r_4: \quad b \leftarrow p. \\
&r_5: \quad p \leftarrow .
\end{aligned}
$$

The program $\Pi = \{r_1, r_2, r_3, r_4, r_5\}$ admits two answer sets: $X = \{p, b, \neg f, w\}$ and $X' = \{p, b, f, w\}$ but only X is the w-answer set of $(\Pi, <)$. □

Proposition 119 [SW01] Let $(\Pi, <)$ be an AnsProlog-<¬ program and X be a set of literals. If X is a w-answer set of $(\Pi, <)$, then X is an answer set of Π. In particular, the w-answer sets of $(\Pi, \emptyset)$ are all answer sets of Π. □

This confirms that the preference strategy of Definition 128 implements a selection function among the answer sets of the underlying program. In addition we have the following two results.

Proposition 120 [SW01] Let Π be an AnsProlog¬ program and X be an answer set of Π. Then, there is a partial order $<$ such that X is the unique w-answer set of the AnsProlog-<¬ program $(\Pi, <)$. □

Proposition 121 [SW01] A totally ordered program has at most one w-answer set. □

Other preference strategies can now be embedded into the above framework by adjusting the operator $C_{(\Pi, <)}$. We will now formulate two other approaches to characterize AnsProlog-<¬ programs using this framework.

9.7.2 The d-answer sets of AnsProlog-<¬ programs

In [DST00] d-answer sets of AnsProlog-<¬ programs are defined using a notion of *order preservation*. We first give an independent definition of d-answer sets of

AnsProlog-$<^\neg$ programs using a notion of '$<^d$-preserving' and then cast d-answer sets as fixpoints of a fixpoint operator similar to $\mathcal{C}_{(\Pi, <)}$. For this we need the following notation:

The set $\Gamma_\Pi(X)$ of all *generating rules* of a set X of literals from program Π is given by

$$\Gamma_\Pi(X) = \{r \in \Pi \mid body^+(r) \subseteq X \text{ and } body^-(r) \cap X = \emptyset\}.$$

Definition 131 Let $(\Pi, <)$ be an AnsProlog-$<^\neg$ program and let X be an answer set of Π. Then, X is called $<^d$-preserving, if there exists an enumeration $\langle r_i \rangle_{i \in I}$ of $\Gamma_\Pi(X)$ such that for every $i, j \in I$ we have that:

(1) $body^+(r_i) \subseteq \{head(r_j) \mid j < i\}$;
(2) if $r_i < r_j$, then $j < i$; and
(3) if $r_i < r'$ and $r' \in \Pi \setminus \Gamma_\Pi(X)$, then $body^+(r') \not\subseteq X$ or $body^-(r') \cap \{head(r_j) \mid j < i\} \neq \emptyset$.

The d-answer sets of $(\Pi, <)$ are the $<^d$-preserving answer sets of Π.   □

In the above definition, by enumerating a set of rules, we assign a unique index r_i to each rule. The enumeration is said to be according to an ordering $<$ if between two rules (say, r_i and r_j) the one which is preferred (i.e., suppose $r_i < r_j$) has a lower index (i.e., $j < i$).

While d-preservation requires that a higher-ranked rule has been effectively applied, w-answer sets are satisfied with the presence of a head of the rule, no matter whether it was supplied by the rule itself or not. This difference is illustrated in the following example.

Example 169

$$\begin{aligned} r_1 &= a \leftarrow b. & \text{with} & & r_2 < r_1 \\ r_2 &= b \leftarrow . \\ r_3 &= a \leftarrow . \end{aligned}$$

The unique answer set of the program $\Pi = \{r_1, r_2, r_3\}$ is also the w-answer set of $(\Pi, <)$, but it is not a d-answer set of $(\Pi, <)$.   □

For providing a fixpoint definition for d-answer sets, we assume a bijective mapping *rule* among rule heads and rules, that is, $rule(head(r)) = r$, and $rule(\{head(r) \mid r \in R\}) = R$. Such mappings can be defined in a bijective way by distinguishing different occurrences of literals. Given this, we define a consequence operator $\mathcal{C}^d_{(\Pi,<)}$ by replacing $head(r') \notin X$ in Definition 128 with $r' \notin rule(X)$. More formally,

Proposition 122 [SW01] Let $(\Pi, <)$ be an AnsProlog-<¬ program and let X be a consistent set of literals. Then X is a d-answer set of $(\Pi, <)$ if and only if $\mathcal{C}^d_{(\Pi,<)}(X) = X$. ☐

9.7.3 The b-answer sets of AnsProlog-<¬ programs

We now define another characterization of AnsProlog-<¬ programs proposed in [BE99]. The approach here differs in two significant ways from the previous ones. First, the construction of answer sets is separated from verifying whether they respect the given preferences. Second, rules that putatively lead to counter-intuitive results are explicitly removed from the inference process.

This removal is defined using an operator $\mathcal{E}_X$ given below:

$$\mathcal{E}_X(\Pi) = \Pi \setminus \{r \in \Pi \mid head(r) \in X, body^- \cap X \neq \emptyset\}$$

Accordingly, we define $\mathcal{E}_X(\Pi, <) = (\mathcal{E}_X(\Pi), < \cap (\mathcal{E}_X(\Pi) \times \mathcal{E}_X(\Pi)))$.

In the rest of this section we assume that the above transformation has already taken place and consider only the programs obtained after this transformation. For those programs, $\mathcal{E}_X(\Pi) = \Pi$.

A b-answer set of an AnsProlog-<¬ program $(\Pi, <)$ is defined as a b-answer set of a fully ordered program where $\ll$ extends $<$. Moreover, an AnsProlog<¬ program is further reduced to a *prerequisite-free program* by (1) deleting any rule r with $body^+ \not\subseteq X$ and (2) deleting $body^+$ for any remaining rule r.

Definition 132 Let $(\Pi, \ll)$ be a fully ordered prerequisite-free AnsProlog-<¬ program, let $\langle r_i \rangle_{i \in I}$ be an enumeration of Π according to the ordering $\ll$, and let X be a set of literals. Then, $\mathcal{B}_{(\Pi,\ll)}(X)$ is the smallest logically closed set of literals containing $\bigcup_{i \in I} X_i$, where $X_j = \emptyset$ for $j \notin I$ and

$$X_i = \begin{cases} X_{i-1} & \text{if } body^- r_i \cap X_{i-1} \neq \emptyset \\ X_{i-1} \cup \{head(r_i)\} & \text{otherwise.} \end{cases}$$

Then X is a b-answer set of $(\Pi, \ll)$ if X is an answer set of Π and $X = \mathcal{B}_{(\Pi,\ll)}(X)$. ☐

In the above definition the role of the 'logical closed set' is to make the set *Lit* if it has both l and $\neg l$ for an atom l.

Let us consider Example 168 again. It can be verified that both X and X' are b-answer sets while the d-answer sets and w-answer sets consist only of X.

If we replace the condition '$r \in \Pi$ is active with respect to (Y, X)' in Definition 128 with '$r \in \Pi$ is active with respect to (X, X)', then we can define a new consequence operator $\mathcal{C}^b_{(\Pi, <)}$ in a similar way as was done for $\mathcal{C}^d_{(\Pi, <)}$ and $\mathcal{C}_{(\Pi, <)}$. Note that, $\mathcal{C}^b_{(\Pi, <)}$ is not anti-monotonic. This is related to the fact that the 'answer set property' of a set is verified separately. This leads to the following theorem.

Proposition 123 [SW01] Let $(\Pi, <)$ be an AnsProlog-$<^\neg$ program and let X be an answer set of Π. Then, we have that X is a b-answer set of $(\Pi, <)$ if and only if $\mathcal{C}^b_{(\Pi, <)}(X) = X$. $\square$

9.8 Well-founded semantics of programs with AnsProlog syntax

In Section 1.3.6 we presented a definition of the well-founded semantics and in Chapter 7 we used the computation of the well-founded semantics as a first step in computing the answer sets. The well-founded semantics, which we treat in this book as an approximate semantics, takes the center stage in certain circles (such as databases) where efficiency is a bigger concern than expressiveness. Moreover the many equivalent characterizations of the well-founded semantics are based on many interesting mathematical and logical notions. These include the use of 3-valued stable models (based on Kleene's 3-valued logic), stable classes, argumentation, unfounded sets, and alternating fixpoints. Some of these characterizations lead to answer sets with slight changes in certain parameters.

This is the motivation behind our presentation of the different characterizations of the well-founded semantics of programs with AnsProlog syntax. In a subsequent section we discuss how one of the characterizations is extended to programs with AnsProlog$^\neg$ syntax.

9.8.1 Original characterization using unfounded sets

The initial characterization of the well-founded semantics was made using a notion of *unfounded sets*. In this characterization a partial (or 3-valued) interpretation I is viewed as a pair $\langle T, F \rangle$, where $T \cap F = \emptyset$, and $T, F \subseteq HB$.

Definition 133 (Unfounded sets and greatest unfounded sets) Let Π be a program in AnsProlog syntax and I be a partial interpretation. We say $A \subseteq HB_\Pi$ is an unfounded set of Π with respect to I if each atom $p \in A$ satisfies the following condition: For each rule r in $ground(\Pi)$ whose head is p, at least one of the following holds.

(1) q is a positive naf-literal in the body of r and $q \in F$; or **not** q is a negative naf-literal in the body of r and $q \in T$. (That is, a naf-literal in the body of r is inconsistent with I.)
(2) Some positive naf-literal of the body occurs in A.

The greatest unfounded set with respect to I is the union of all sets that are unfounded with respect to I. □

Definition 134 Let Π be a program in AnsProlog syntax and I be a partial interpretation.

$T_\Pi(I) = \{p : $ there is a rule r in $ground(\Pi)$ with p in the head such that the body of r evaluates to true with respect to $I\}$.

$F_\Pi(I)$ is the greatest unfounded set with respect to I. □

Definition 135 For all countable ordinals α we define I_α as follows:

- $I_0 = \emptyset$.
- If α is a successor ordinal $k + 1$ then $I_{k+1} = \langle T_\Pi(I_k), F_\Pi(I_k) \rangle$.
- If α is a limit ordinal then $I_\alpha = \bigcup_{\beta < \alpha} I_\beta$. □

Lemma 9.8.1 I_α is a monotonic sequence of partial interpretations. □

The above sequence reaches a limit $I^* = \langle T^*, F^* \rangle$ at some countable (possibly beyond the first limit ordinal ω) ordinal. The *well-founded* semantics of a program in AnsProlog syntax is defined as this limit I^*.

9.8.2 A slightly different iterated fixpoint characterization

We now present a slightly different fixpoint characterization where the notion of greatest unfounded set used in $F_\Pi(I)$ and $T_\Pi(I)$ from Definition 134 is replaced by a fixpoint computation.

Definition 136 Let I be a partial interpretation, Π be a program in AnsProlog syntax, and T' and F' be sets of ground atoms.

$\mathcal{T}_I(T') = \{p : p$ is not true in I and there is a rule r in Π with p in the head such that each literal in the body of r evaluates to true with respect to I or is in T'.$\}$

$\mathcal{F}_I(F') = \{p : p$ is not false in I and for every rule r in Π with p in the head there is at least one literal in the body of r that evaluates to false with respect to I or is in F'.$\}$ □

Lemma 9.8.2 The operators T_I and $\mathcal{F}_I$ are monotonic, i.e., $T' \subseteq T'' \Rightarrow T_I(T') \subseteq T_I(T'')$ and $F' \subseteq F'' \Rightarrow \mathcal{F}_I(F') \subseteq \mathcal{F}_I(F'')$ □

Definition 137 For a program Π and partial interpretation I,

$$T_I \uparrow 0 = \emptyset; \; T_I \uparrow n + 1 = T_I(T_I \uparrow n); \; T_I = \bigcup_{n < \omega} T_I \uparrow n$$

$$F_I \downarrow 0 = HB_\Pi; \; F_I \downarrow n + 1 = \mathcal{F}_I(F_I \downarrow n); \; F_I = \bigcap_{n < \omega} F_I \downarrow n \qquad \square$$

Lemma 9.8.3 The transfinite sequence $\{T_I \uparrow n\}$ is monotonically increasing and the transfinite sequence $\{F_I \uparrow n\}$ is monotonically decreasing.

T_I is the least fixpoint of the operator T_I and F_I is the greatest fixpoint of the operator $\mathcal{F}_I$. □

Definition 138 Let $\mathcal{I}$ be the operator assigning to every partial interpretation I of P a new interpretation $\mathcal{I}(I)$ defined by:

$$\mathcal{I}(I) = I \cup \langle T_I; F_I \rangle. \qquad \square$$

Lemma 9.8.4 The operator $\mathcal{I}$ is monotonic with respect to the ordering $\preceq$ defined as $\langle T, F \rangle \preceq \langle T', F' \rangle$ iff $T \subseteq T'$ and $F' \subseteq F$. □

Definition 139 Let $M_0 = \langle \emptyset, \emptyset \rangle$;

$$M_{\alpha+1} = \mathcal{I}(M_\alpha) = M_\alpha \cup \langle T_{M_\alpha}; F_{M_\alpha} \rangle;$$

$$M_\alpha = \bigcup_{\beta < \alpha} M_\beta, \; \textit{for limit ordinal } \alpha. \qquad \square$$

The sequence $\{M_\alpha\}$ of interpretations is monotonically increasing. Therefore there is a smallest ordinal δ such that M_δ is a fixpoint of the operator $\mathcal{I}$. Let us refer to this fixpoint as M_Π.

Theorem 9.8.5 [Prz89a] Given a program Π in AnsProlog syntax, M_Π is its well-founded semantics. □

9.8.3 Alternating fixpoint characterization

We now give yet another characterization of the well-founded semantics.

Definition 140 Suppose I is a Herbrand interpretation and Π is a program in AnsProlog syntax. Construct a program Π' as follows: If

$$A \leftarrow B_1, \ldots, B_n, \textbf{not } D_1, \ldots, \textbf{not } D_m.$$

is in Π, then

$$A \leftarrow B_1, \ldots, B_n, \tilde{D}_1, \ldots, \tilde{D}_m.$$

is in Π'. Here $\tilde{D}_i = \tilde{p}(\vec{t})$ iff $D_i = p(\vec{t})$. In addition, if $A \notin I$, then the unit clause $\tilde{A} \leftarrow$. is added to Π'.

Now define $S_\Pi(\bar{I}) = HB_\Pi \cap T_{\Pi'} \uparrow \omega$. $\quad\square$

Note that $T_{\Pi'} \uparrow \omega$ contains new atoms of the form $\tilde{p}(\vec{t})$ and that these atoms may be used in deriving atoms in $S_\Pi(\bar{I})$, but atoms of the form $\tilde{p}(\vec{t})$ are themselves not present in $S_\Pi(\bar{I})$.

Definition 141 Given a program Π in AnsProlog syntax, we associate an operator A_Π with Π as follows:

$A_\Pi(I) = \overline{S_\Pi(\overline{S_\Pi(I)})}$.
$A^* = \mathrm{lfp}(A_\Pi)$.
$A^+ = S_\Pi(A^*)$. $\quad\square$

Theorem 9.8.6 [Gel89] A^+ is the set of atoms true in the well-founded model of Π. Similarly A^* is the set of atoms false in the well-founded model of Π. $\quad\square$

We now use Van Gelder's alternating fixpoint characterization to show that well-founded semantics is equivalent to a particular stable class as defined in the next subsection.

9.8.4 Stable classes and well-founded semantics

Suppose, given a program Π, we associate an operator F_Π that maps Herbrand interpretations to Herbrand interpretations such that $F_\Pi(I) = M(\Pi^I)$. Answer sets are defined in terms of the fixed point of this operator, i.e., I is an answer set of P iff $F_\Pi(I) = M(\Pi^I) = I$. However, this operator may not always have fixed points.

Definition 142 Let $\mathcal{A}$ be a set of indices. Let $S = \{I_i \mid i \in \mathcal{A}\}$ be a finite set of interpretations. Then S is said to be a *stable class* of program Π iff $S = \{F_\Pi(I_i) \mid i \in \mathcal{A}\}$. $\quad\square$

Example 170 Consider the following program Π:

$a \leftarrow \textbf{not } a$.
$p \leftarrow$.

This program does not have any answer sets. But it has two stable classes: S_0 which is the empty collection of interpretations and $S_1 = \{I_1, I_2\}$ where:

$I_1 = \{p\}$
$I_2 = \{a, p\}$

Thus, Π has a unique nonempty stable class, viz. S_1, and p is *true* in all interpretations contained in S_1. $\square$

Lemma 9.8.7 $S_\Pi(\bar{I}) = F_\Pi(I)$ $\square$

Lemma 9.8.8 Let Π be a program in AnsProlog syntax. Then $F_\Pi(\text{lfp}(F_\Pi^2)) = \text{gfp}(F_\Pi^2)$ and $F_\Pi(\text{gfp}(F_\Pi^2)) = \text{lfp}(F_\Pi^2)$, i.e., $\{\text{lfp}(F_\Pi^2), \text{gfp}(F_\Pi^2)\}$ forms a stable class of Π. $\square$

Lemma 9.8.9 $\text{lfp}(F_\Pi^2) = A^+$

$\text{gfp}(F_\Pi^2) = \overline{A^*}$ $\square$

Lemmas 9.8.7, 9.8.8, 9.8.9 and Theorem 9.8.6 are needed to establish the following theorem.

Theorem 9.8.10 [BS91] Let Π be a program in AnsProlog syntax. The well-founded semantics of Π is characterized by a particular stable class C of Π, i.e., a ground atom is true in the well-founded semantics of Π iff A is true in all interpretations in C, and A is false according to the well-founded semantics of Π iff A is false in all interpretations in C. Moreover, $C = \{\text{lfp}(F_\Pi^2), \text{gfp}(F_\Pi^2)\}$. $\square$

Example 171 Consider the following program Π_1:

$$\left. \begin{array}{l} p \leftarrow \textbf{not } a. \\ p \leftarrow \textbf{not } b. \\ a \leftarrow \textbf{not } b. \\ b \leftarrow \textbf{not } a. \end{array} \right\} \Pi_1$$

The above program has two answer sets $\{p, a\}$ and $\{p, b\}$. It has three stable classes, $\{\{p, a\}\}$, $\{\{p, b\}\}$, and $\{\{\}, \{p, a, b\}\}$. The stable class $\{\{\}, \{p, a, b\}\}$ corresponds to the well-founded semantics of the above program. $\square$

Example 172 Consider the following program Π_2 [VG88]:

$$\left.\begin{array}{l} q \leftarrow \mathbf{not}\ r. \\ r \leftarrow \mathbf{not}\ q. \\ p \leftarrow \mathbf{not}\ p. \\ p \leftarrow \mathbf{not}\ r. \end{array}\right\}\ \Pi_2,$$

which has a unique answer set, viz. $\{p, q\}$, and three strict stable classes (stable classes which have no proper subset which is also a stable class), namely, $C_1, C_2,$ and C_3, where $C_1 = \{\{q, p\}\}, C_2 = \{\emptyset, \{p, q, r\}\}$, and $C_3 = \{\{r\}, \{r, p\}\}$. Of these, the class C_2 corresponds to the well-founded semantics which says that p, q, r are all *undefined*. Notice that even though p is the consequence of Π_2 in the answer set semantics, its addition to Π_2 alters the set of consequences of Π_5. In particular, we will no longer be able to conclude q. $\square$

9.8.5 Characterizing answer sets and well-founded semantics using argumentation

An alternative approach to characterize programs in AnsProlog syntax is to use the notion of argumentation, where notions of 'attack' and 'defends' are defined, and negative naf-literals are viewed as hypotheses which are acceptable if they could defend themselves against all attacks against them. The following example illustrates this idea.

Example 173 Consider the following program Π:

$a \leftarrow \mathbf{not}\ b.$
$b \leftarrow \mathbf{not}\ c.$
$c \leftarrow \mathbf{not}\ d.$

Our goal is to define whether the negative naf-literals $\mathbf{not}\ a$, $\mathbf{not}\ b$, $\mathbf{not}\ d$, and $\mathbf{not}\ c$ are acceptable hypotheses with respect to Π. To do that we convert Π to an AnsProlog$^{-\mathbf{not}}$ program by replacing each negative naf-literal $\mathbf{not}\ l$ by a new atom not_l. We refer to such atoms as *assumptions*. (In the following the relation $\models$ that we use is for AnsProlog$^{-\mathbf{not}}$ programs.)

The resulting AnsProlog$^{-\mathbf{not}}$ program $\hat{\Pi}$ is as follows:

$a \leftarrow not\_b.$
$b \leftarrow not\_c.$
$c \leftarrow not\_d.$

Consider the sets $S_1 = \{not\_c\}$ and $S_2 = \{not\_d\}$.

The set S_2 attacks S_1 since $S_2 \cup \hat{\Pi} \models c$. But $S_1 \cup \hat{\Pi} \not\models d$. Therefore S_1 does not attack S_2 and hence S_1 cannot defend itself against S_2's attack. Therefore if

S_1 and S_2 are our only choices then S_1 should not be accepted and S_2 should be accepted.   □

We now give general definitions of 'attack' and 'acceptability'.

Definition 143 Let S and R be sets of assumptions, and $\hat{\Pi}$ be an AnsProlog$^{-\mathbf{not}}$ program obtained after converting negative naf-literals to assumptions in a program Π in AnsProlog syntax.

(1) S is said to *attack* R (with respect to $\hat{\Pi}$) if there is an assumption $not\_a \in R$ such that $\hat{\Pi} \cup S \models a$. We say that S is an attack against R.
(2) S is said to be *acceptable* (with respect to $\hat{\Pi}$) if S attacks each attack against it.   □

We now define a notion of stable sets of assumptions using the notions of attack and acceptability.

Definition 144 A set S is *stable* (with respect to $\hat{\Pi}$) if it attacks each assumption not belonging to it, i.e., S is stable iff for each $not\_a \notin S$, $S \cup \hat{\Pi} \models a$.   □

The correspondence between a stable set of assumptions and an answer set is given by the following theorem

Theorem 9.8.11 [Dun91a] Let Π be a program in AnsProlog syntax.

(1) Let M be an answer set of Π. Then the set $\{not\_a \mid a \notin M\}$ is a stable set of assumptions with respect to $\hat{\Pi}$.
(2) Let S be a stable set of assumptions with respect to $\hat{\Pi}$. Then
    (a) the set $\{a \mid S \cup \hat{\Pi} \models a\}$ is an answer set of Π.
    (b) $\{a \mid S \cup \hat{\Pi} \models a\} = \{a \mid not\_a \notin S\}$ □

We now define a notion of 'defends' and use it to give the well-founded characterization of programs in AnsProlog syntax.

Definition 145 We say that a set S of assumptions defends an assumption not_a iff S attacks each attack against not_a.   □

Let A be the set of all assumptions. Let us define a function $\mu : 2^A \rightarrow 2^A$ as $\mu(S)$ is equal to the set of all assumptions defended by S. It is not difficult to see that μ is monotonic with respect to set inclusion. Furthermore, it is also easy to see that a set S of assumptions is acceptable iff $S \subseteq \mu(S)$. We will refer to the least fixpoint of μ as the *grounded semantics* of P.

The correspondence between the well-founded semantics and the grounded semantics is given by the following theorem where the well-founded semantics is represented by a pair $\langle T, F \rangle$ of atoms where T contains those atoms that are *true* and F those that are *false*.

Theorem 9.8.12 [Dun91a] Let Π be a program in AnsProlog syntax.

(1) Let $\langle T, F \rangle$ be the well-founded semantics of Π. Then the set $S = \{not\_a \mid a \in F\}$ is the grounded semantics of $\hat{\Pi}$. Furthermore, $T = \{a \mid S \cup \hat{\Pi} \models a\}$.
(2) Let S be the grounded semantics of $\hat{\Pi}$. Let $T \doteq \{a \mid S \cup \hat{\Pi} \models a\}$ and $F = \{a \mid not\_a \in S\}$. Then $\langle T, F \rangle$ is the well-founded semantics of Π. □

9.8.6 3-valued stable models and the well-founded semantics

In Section 6.6.9 we defined the notions of 3-valued models of programs in AnsProlog syntax. In this section we define a notion of 3-valued stable models (also referred to as partial stable models) and relate them to answer sets and well-founded characterization of programs in AnsProlog syntax.

Recall that 3-valued models (and interpretations) are often denoted by a pair $\langle T, F \rangle$ where T is the set of atoms that are *true* and F is the set of atoms that are *false*. An ordering between 3-valued models is defined as follows: $\langle T, F \rangle \leq \langle T', F' \rangle$ if $T \subseteq T'$ and $F' \subseteq F$.

3-valued stable models of programs in AnsProlog syntax are defined in a similar way to the definition of answer sets. Given a program Π in AnsProlog syntax and a 3-valued interpretation $I = \langle T, F \rangle$, a transformed program $\frac{\Pi}{I}$ is obtained by replacing every occurrence of **not** a in the body of any rule of Π by (i) *true* if $a \in F$, (ii) *false* if $a \in T$ and (iii) *unknown* otherwise.

Definition 146 Let Π be a program in AnsProlog syntax. A 3-valued interpretation I is said to be a 3-valued model of Π if I is the unique minimal 3-valued model of $\frac{\Pi}{I}$. □

Proposition 124 [Prz90a, Prz90c] Let Π be a program in AnsProlog syntax. Then,

(i) Π has at least one 3-valued stable model.
(ii) The least 3-valued stable model of Π coincides with its well-founded model.
(iii) Any answer set of Π is a 3-valued stable model of Π. □

There have been several alternative characterizations of 3-valued stable models. As summarized in [YY95], these characterizations include the three-valued grounded models [WB93], the P-stable models [SZ90], the complete scenarios [Dun91a], and the normal alternating fixpoints [YY95]. Alternative semantics for programs with AnsProlog syntax such as regular models [YY90, YY94] and preferred extensions [Dun91a] have been defined using 3-valued stable models. Some of these are further investigated in [ELS97]. 3-valued stable models have been mainly used in formulating abduction and computing explanations [EK89, LY01].

9.9 Well-founded semantics of programs with AnsProlog⁻ syntax

The stable class formulation of well-founded semantics of programs in AnsProlog syntax [BS91] can be extended to define the well-founded semantics of programs in AnsProlog⁻ syntax. More precisely, let us consider $G_\Pi(S) = \mathcal{M}^{\neg,\perp}(\Pi^S)$. Then for any program Π in AnsProlog⁻ syntax, the fixpoints of G_Π define the answer sets, and $\{\text{lfp}(G_\Pi^2), \text{gfp}(G_\Pi^2)\}$ defines the well-founded semantics. A literal l is *true* (respectively *false*) with respect to the well-founded semantics of a program Π in AnsProlog⁻ syntax if $l \in \text{lfp}(G_\Pi^2)$ (respectively $l \notin \text{gfp}(G_\Pi^2)$). Otherwise l is said to be *undefined*.

Pereira et al. [PAA92a] showed that this definition gives unintuitive characterizations for several programs.

Example 174 Consider the program Π_0

$a \leftarrow \mathbf{not}\ b.$
$b \leftarrow \mathbf{not}\ a.$
$\neg a \leftarrow.$

The well-founded semantics infers $\neg a$ to be *true* and a and b to be *unknown* with respect to the above program. Intuitively, b should be inferred *true* and a should be inferred *false*.   □

Example 175 Consider the program Π_1

$b \leftarrow \mathbf{not}\ \neg b.$

and the program Π_2

$a \leftarrow \mathbf{not}\ \neg a.$
$\neg a \leftarrow \mathbf{not}\ a.$

The well-founded semantics infers b to be *true* with respect to Π_1 and infers b to be *undefined* with respect to $\Pi_1 \cup \Pi_2$ even though Π_2 does not have b in its language.   □

To overcome the unintuitiveness of the well-founded semantics Pereira et al. [PAA92a] proposed an alternative semantics of programs in AnsProlog⁻ syntax which we refer to as the Ω-well-founded semantics. We now define the Ω-well-founded semantics.

Definition 147 [PAA92a] Let Π be a program in AnsProlog⁻ syntax. Then $S(\Pi)$, the semi-normal version of Π, is obtained by replacing each rule of the form $L_0 \leftarrow L_1, \dots, L_m, \textbf{not } L_{m+1}, \dots, \textbf{not } L_n.$ by the rule:

$$L_0 \leftarrow L_1, \dots, L_m, \textbf{not } L_{m+1}, \dots, \textbf{not } L_n, \textbf{not } \neg L_0. \qquad (9.9.8)$$

$\square$

Definition 148 For any program Π in AnsProlog⁻ syntax, the function Ω_Π is defined as

$$\Omega_\Pi(X) = G_\Pi(G_{S(\Pi)}(X))$$

$\square$

Definition 149 A set of literals E is said to be an Ω-extension of a program Π in AnsProlog⁻ syntax iff

(1) E is a fixpoint of Ω_Π.
(2) E is a subset of $(G_{S(\Pi)}(E))$

$\square$

Pereira *et al.* [PAA92a] showed that if a program in AnsProlog⁻ syntax has an Ω-extension then Ω_Π is a monotonic function and hence has a least fixpoint. The Ω-well-founded semantics is defined as $\{\text{lfp}(\Omega_\Pi), G_{S(\Pi)}(\text{lfp}(\Omega_\Pi))\}$. Entailment with respect to the Ω-well-founded semantics is defined as follows: A literal l is *true* (respectively *false*) with respect to the Ω-well-founded semantics of a program Π in AnsProlog⁻ syntax if $l \in \text{lfp}(\Omega_\Pi)$ (respectively $l \notin G_{S(\Pi)}(\text{lfp}(\Omega_\Pi))$). Otherwise l is *undefined*.

Example 176 [PAA92a] Consider the following program Π_3

$c \leftarrow \textbf{not } b.$
$b \leftarrow \textbf{not } a.$
$a \leftarrow \textbf{not } a.$
$\neg b.$

The above program has $\{c, \neg b\}$ as the only Ω-extension. The Ω-well-founded semantics is given by $\{\{c, \neg b\}, \{c, a, \neg b\}\}$.

$\square$

We now briefly mention another class of semantics of programs in AnsProlog⁻ syntax based on contradiction removal [Dun91b, Wag93, PAA91a, GM90].

To illustrate the usefulness (and perhaps necessity) of contradiction removal consider the program Π_4:

(1) $p \leftarrow \mathbf{not}\ q.$
(2) $\neg p \leftarrow.$
(3) $s \leftarrow.$

Obviously, under the answer set semantics this program is inconsistent. It is possible to argue however that inconsistency of Π_4 can be localized to the rules (1) and (2) and should not influence the behavior of the rest of the program, i.e., Π_4's answer to query s should be *yes* and the rules causing inconsistency should be neutralized. There are several approaches to doing that. One, suggested in [KS90], modifies the answer set semantics to give preference to rules with negative conclusions (viewed as exceptions to general rules). Under the corresponding entailment relation Π_4 concludes s and $\neg p$. Another possibility is to first identify literals responsible for contradiction, which in this case is q. After that q can be viewed as abducible and hence Π_4 will entail s, $\neg p$, and q. Another possibility arises when Ω-well-founded semantics is used as the underlying semantics of Π_4. In this case we may want to have both q and $\neg q$ undefined. This can be achieved by expanding Π_4 by new statements $q \leftarrow \mathbf{not}\ q.$ and $\neg q \leftarrow \mathbf{not}\ \neg q.$ The resulting program Π_5 entails (with respect to the Ω-well-founded semantics) $\neg p$ and s and infers p to be *false*. The last idea was developed to a considerable length in [PAA91a, PA93].

Note that the above forms the background and motivation for the approaches in Sections 4.5 and 9.7 where priorities between rules are used.

9.10 Notes and references

In this chapter we have presented only a small and incomplete set of extensions and alternatives to AnsProlog* based on our perception of its closeness to the rest of the content of this book.

The material on the extension of AnsProlog* that allows **not** in the head is from [IS98]. The extension that allows nested expressions is from [LTT99, FL01]. The extension of AnsProlog* to allow knowledge and belief operators was proposed in [Gel91b] and further developed in [GP91].

The notion of generalized stable models in Section 9.4 is from [KM90] and the definition of entailment using generalized stable models is from [BG94]. Recently, Lin and You [LY01] proposed an alternative definition of explanations with respect to AnsProlog programs. They also presented a rewriting system for answering queries and generating explanations.

The discussion regarding open domain and the universal query problem is based on the papers [Ros89a, Ros92, Kun89, Kun87, Prz89b, BG94, AB94]. Complexity of reasoning with open domains was explored in [Sch93]. Application of open domains was discussed in [GT93, GP93]. The paper [GT93] shows the usefulness of open domain semantics in representing certain types of null values in databases, while [GP93] discusses an application to formalization of anonymous exceptions to defaults. The material in Section 9.6 is based on [Gel01].

The material in Section 9.7 is based on [SW01]. This paper considered some of the earlier characterizations of AnsProlog-$<^\neg$ programs and presented a new fixpoint characterization for such programs. In addition it showed that their framework can capture the earlier characterizations. In particular, it gave alternative fixpoint characterizations of the semantics in [BE99] and [DST00]. There are several other results in [SW01] including a theory of alternating fixpoints for AnsProlog-$<^\neg$ programs. Some of the earlier papers on this topic that we did not fully explore in this chapter are [ZF97, Bre94, Bre96]. The fixpoint characterizations in [SW01], as presented in Section 9.7, have led to implementation via some compilation techniques introduced in [DST00]. The corresponding compiler, called plp, serves as a front end to dlv and smodels and is described in [DST01] and is available in a web site. Among the proposed extensions that we did not cover in this book are the use of modules [EGV97] in programs.

Well-founded semantics of programs in AnsProlog syntax was initially defined by Van Gelder, Ross, and Schlifp in [vGRS88]. Later Van Gelder [Gel89] gave a different characterization of the well-founded semantics based on an alternating fixpoint approach. Some of the alternative characterizations of the well-founded semantics that we have presented in this book are based on [Prz89a, Prz90c, BS92, BS91, Fit91, Dun91a, Dun93, Prz90c]. The well-founded characterization of programs in AnsProlog$^\neg$ syntax is discussed in [AP92, PAA91b, PAA92a, PAA92b, Prz90a, KS90, Dun91b, Wag93, PAA91a, GM90, PA93] We have presented some of those results.

In the late 1980s and early 1990s several other semantics for programs with AnsProlog syntax were proposed. Some of these were proposed and studied in [FBJ88, Fit85, Fit86, Kun87, Kun89, LM85, Myc83, ELS97, ELS98]. Similarly several alternative characterizations of programs in AnsProlog^{or} syntax were also developed. Some of those are [Bar92, LMR92, RM90, BLM92, BLM91, Ros89b, Prz90b, Sak89, Prz91]. Przymusiński considered several extensions of AnsProlog^{or} syntax [Prz95, BDP96, BDNP01] and proposed semantics for these languages which when restricted to AnsProlog syntax coincided with the well-founded semantics. Similar extensions were also studied by Minker and Ruiz in [MR93].

Among the major omissions in this chapter are meta-logic programming [Kow79] and constraint logic programming [Mah93a]. Some of the meta-logic programming languages and their analyses are given in [Kow90, AR89, Pet92, HL91, CKW93, CL89, MDS92a, MDS92b, Mil86, BM90, GO92, BMPT92, BK82].

Appendix A: Ordinals, lattices, and fixpoint theory

Ordinals

The finite ordinals are the nonnegative integers. The first ordinal 0 is defined by the empty set, $\emptyset$. The second ordinal $1 = \{0\} = \{\emptyset\}$. The third ordinal $2 = \{0, 1\} = \{\emptyset, \{\emptyset\}\}$. The fourth ordinal $3 = \{0, 1, 2\} = \{\emptyset, \{\emptyset\}, \{\emptyset, \{\emptyset\}\}\}$.

The first infinite ordinal is $\omega = \{0, 1, 2, \ldots\}$, the set of all nonnegative integers.

The successor of an ordinal α is $\alpha + 1 = \alpha \cup \{\alpha\}$. Any ordinal which is the successor of another ordinal is referred to as a successor ordinal .

A limit ordinal is an ordinal other than 0 which is not the successor of any other ordinal. The first limit ordinal is ω. The successor ordinal of ω is $\omega + 1 = \omega \cup \{\omega\}$. The second limit ordinal is $\omega 2$, which is the set $\omega \cup \{\omega + n \mid n \in \omega\}$. The successor ordinal of $\omega 2$ is $\omega 2 + 1 = \omega 2 \cup \{\omega 2\}$.

Fixpoint theory

Let S be a set. A *relation* R on S is a subset $S \times S$. A relation R on S is a *partial order* if R is *reflexive*, *antisymmetric*, and *transitive*. A binary relation (not necessarily a partial order) is *well-founded* if there is no infinite decreasing chain $x_0 \geq x_1 \geq \ldots$.

Let S be a set with partial order $\leq$. Then $a \in S$ is an *upper bound* of a subset X of S if $x \leq a$, for all $x \in X$. Similarly, $b \in S$ is a *lower bound* of X if $b \leq x$, for all $x \in X$. $a \in S$ is the *least upper bound* (lub) of a subset X of S if a is an upper bound of X and for all upper bounds a' of X we have $a \leq a'$. Similarly, $b \in S$ is the *greatest lower bound* (glb) of a subset X of S if b is a lower bound of X and for all lower bounds b' of X we have $b' \leq b$.

A partially ordered set L is a **complete lattice** if $\text{lub}(X)$ and $\text{glb}(X)$ exist for every subset X of L. The lub(L) is called the top element ($\top$) and the glb(L) is called the bottom element ($\bot$).

Example 177 For any set S, its power set 2^S under $\subseteq$ is a complete lattice with $\text{lub}(X)$ being the union of all elements of X and $\text{glb}(X)$ being the intersection of all elements of L. The top element is S and the bottom element is $\emptyset$. □

Monotonicity: Let L be a complete lattice and $T : L \to L$ be a mapping. We say T is monotonic if $T(x) \leq T(y)$, whenever $x \leq y$.

Let L be a complete lattice and $X \subseteq L$. We say X is **directed** if every finite subset of X has an upper bound in X.

494

Continuity: Let L be a complete lattice and $T : L \to L$ be a mapping. We say T is continuous if $T(\mathrm{lub}(X)) = \mathrm{lub}(T(X))$, for every directed subset X of L.

Fixpoint, least fixpoint : Let L be a complete lattice and $T : L \to L$ be a mapping. We say $a \in L$ is the least fixpoint (lfp) if a is a fixpoint of T (i.e., T(a) = a) and for all fixpoints b of T, we have $a \leq b$.

Theorem A.2.1 [Tar55] Let L be a complete lattice and $T : L \to L$ be a monotonic mapping. Then T has a least fixpoint, $\mathrm{lfp}(T)$, and furthermore $\mathrm{lfp}(T) = \mathrm{glb}\{x : T(x) = x\} = \mathrm{glb}\{x : T(x) \leq x\}$. $\qquad\square$

Definition 150 Let L be a complete lattice and $T : L \to L$ be a monotonic mapping. Then,

$T \uparrow o = \bot$
$T \uparrow \alpha = T(T \uparrow (\alpha - 1))$, if α is a successor ordinal.
$T \uparrow \alpha = \mathrm{lub}\{T \uparrow \beta : \beta < \alpha\}$ if α is a limit ordinal. $\qquad\square$

Theorem A.2.2 Let L be a complete lattice and $T : L \to L$ be monotonic. Then $\mathrm{lfp}(T) = T \uparrow \alpha$, where α is a limit ordinal. $\qquad\square$

Theorem A.2.3 [Tar55] Let L be a complete lattice and $T : L \to L$ be continuous. Then $\mathrm{lfp}(T) = T \uparrow \omega$, where ω is the first limit ordinal. $\qquad\square$

Transfinite sequences

A *(transfinite) sequence* is a family whose index set is an initial segment of ordinals, $\{\alpha : \alpha < \mu\}$, where the ordinal μ is the *length* of the sequence.

A sequence $\langle U_\alpha \rangle_{\alpha < \mu}$ is *monotone* if $U_\alpha \subseteq U_\beta$, whenever $\alpha < \beta$, and is *continuous* if, for each limit ordinal $\alpha < \mu$, $U_\alpha = \cup_{\eta < \alpha} U_\eta$.

Appendix B: Turing machines

Turing machines

This appendix is based on [Pap94] and it is recommended that the reader refer to that for detailed exposition on Turing machines, and computational complexity.

Intuitively, a **deterministic Turing machine** (DTM) is an automata bundled with a semi-infinite tape with a cursor to read from and write to. So, like an automata, there is a state and state transitions are based on the current state and what the cursor points to on the tape. But in addition to the state transition, there is an accompanying transition that dictates if the symbol in the tape location pointed to by the cursor should be overwritten and if the cursor should move to the left or right – by one cell – of its current position. Special symbols mark the beginning of the tape ($>$), the end of the input on the tape ($\sqcup$), and the output of the computation ('*halt*', '*yes*', '*no*'). We now give a formal definition of DTMs.

Definition 151 A DTM is a quadruple $M = (S, \Sigma, \delta, s_0)$ where S is a finite set of nonfinal states that includes s_0 the initial state, Σ is a finite alphabet of symbols including the special symbols $>$ and $\sqcup$, and δ is a transition function that maps $S \times \Sigma$ to $S \cup \{halt, yes, no\} \times \Sigma \times \{\leftarrow, \rightarrow, -\}$. □

Intuitively, δ is the control (or the program) of the machine that dictates how the machine behaves. If $\delta(s, \alpha) = (s', \beta, \leftarrow)$ then it means that if the current state is s and the cursor is pointed at the symbol α then the state should change to s', α should be overwritten by β, and the cursor should move to the left of its current position. If instead of $\leftarrow$ we had $\rightarrow$, then that would dictate that the cursor move right, and if we had '$-$' instead, then that would dictate that the cursor remain where it is. The special symbol $>$ is used as the left marker of the tape. Hence, for any state s, we require that $\delta(s, >) = (s', >, \rightarrow)$, for some s'. This forces the cursor, when it is at the left end of the tape, to move right without overwriting the $>$ symbol at the left end.

Initially, the state of the machine is required to be s_0, and the cursor is required to be at the left end of the tape pointing to $>$. Moreover, the string starting after the left marker $>$, up to the first $\sqcup$, is considered to be the *input I*. From this initial configuration the machine makes the transition dictated by its δ, until it reaches one of the final states $\{halt, yes, no\}$. If the final state is *yes*, that means the machine accepted the input (i.e., M(I) = 'yes'), if it is *no*, that means the machine rejected the input (i.e., M(I) = 'no') , and if it is *halt*, that

496

means the machine computed an output $M(I)$, which is defined as the string starting after the left end marker $>$ up to the first $\sqcup$.

Note that it is possible that the machine never reaches a final state and keeps on computing for ever.

A set S is said to be recursive if there is a DTM M such that given an input x, $M(x) =$ '*yes*' iff $x \in S$, and $M(x) =$ '*no*' iff $x \notin S$. S is said to be recursively enumerable if there is a Turing machine M such that given an input x, $M(x) =$ '*yes*' iff $x \in S$. Note that in this case if $x \notin S$ then either $M(x) \neq$ '*yes*' or the Turing machine never reaches the 'halt' state.

The time taken by a DTM M on an input I is defined as the number of transitions taken by M on I from the start until it stops. If it does not stop then the time is considered to be infinite. For a function f from positive integers to itself, we say that a DTM M takes $O(f(n))$ time, if there exist positive integers c and n_0 such that the time taken by M on any input of length n is not greater than $c \times f(n)$ for all $n \geq n_0$.

Nondeterministic Turing machines

A nondeterministic Turing machine (NDTM) is a quadruple (S, Σ, δ, s_0) like a DTM, except that δ is no longer a function; it is a relation given as a subset of $(S \times \Sigma) \times 2tt2(S \cup \{halt, yes, no\}) \times \Sigma \times \{\leftarrow, \rightarrow, -\}$. As in a DTM, the role of δ is to be the control of the machine. When the machine is in state s and the cursor is pointed at the symbol α then the control considers all quadruples from δ whose first element is (s, α), and non-deterministically chooses one quadruple $((s, \alpha), s', \beta, dir)$ from it, and changes the state to s', replaces α by β, and moves the cursor according to dir.

The notions of 'acceptance' and 'rejection' of inputs by NDTMs are slightly different from those of DTMs and unlike DTMs are asymmetric. If starting from the initial configuration an NDTM can make a series of transitions sanctioned by its δ which takes it to the final state *yes*, then we say that the NDTM accepts the input. On the other hand if no possible series of transitions sanctioned by δ takes it to the state *yes*, then we say that the NDTM rejects the input.

Oracle Turing machines

An Oracle DTM M^A, also referred to as a DTM M with an oracle A, can be thought of as a DTM with an additional write-only tape referred to as the query tape, and three special states $\{q, q_y, q_n\}$. When the state of M^A is different from $\{q, q_y, q_n\}$ the computation of the oracle DTM M^A is the same except that M^A can write on the query tape. When the state is q, M^A moves to the state q_y or q_n depending on whether the current query string in the query tape is in A or not, while instantly erasing the query tape.

Bibliography

[AB90]   K. Apt and M. Bezem. Acyclic programs. In D. Warren and Peter Szeredi, editors, *Logic Programming: Proc. of the Seventh Int'l Conf.*, pages 617–633, 1990.

[AB91]   K. Apt and M. Bezem. Acyclic programs. *New Generation Computing*, 9(3,4):335–365, 1991.

[AB94]   K. Apt and R. Bol. Logic programming and negation: a survey. *Journal of Logic Programming*, 19,20:9–71, 1994.

[AB01]   G. Alsac and C. Baral. Reasoning in description logics using declarative logic programming. Technical report, Arizona State University, 2001.

[ABW88]   K. Apt, H. Blair, and A. Walker. Towards a theory of declarative knowledge. In J. Minker, editor, *Foundations of Deductive Databases and Logic Programming*, pages 89–148. Morgan Kaufmann, San Mateo, CA., 1988.

[AD94]   K. Apt and K. Doets. A new definition of SLDNF resolution. *Journal of Logic Programming*, 18:177–190, 1994.

[AD95]   C. Aravindan and P. Dung. On the correctness of unfold/fold transformation of normal and extended logic programs. *Journal of Logic Programming*, pages 201–217, 1995.

[ADA93]   P. Atzeni and V. De Antonellis. *Relational database theory*. The Benjamin/Cummings publishing company, 1993.

[ADO99]   J. Arrazola, J. Dix, and M. Osorio. Confluent rewriting systems in nonmonotonic reasoning. *Computacion y Sistemas*, Volume II, No. 2–3: 104–123, 1999.

[AHV95]   S. Abiteboul, R. Hall, and V. Vianu. *Foundations of Databases*. Addison Wesley, 1995.

[AN78]   H. Andreka and I. Nemeti. The generalized completeness of Horn predicate logic as a programming language. *Acta Cybernetica*, 4:3–10, 1978.

[AP91]   K. Apt and D. Pedreschi. Proving termination in general prolog programs. In *Proc. of the Int'l Conf. on Theoretical Aspects of Computer Software (LNCS 526)*, pages 265–289. Springer Verlag, 1991.

[AP92]   J. Alferes and L. Pereira. On logic program semantics with two kinds of negation. In K. Apt, editor, *Proc. of the Joint International Conference and Symposium on Logic Programming, Washington DC*, pages 574–588. MIT Press, Nov 1992.

[AP93]   K. Apt and D. Pedreschi. Reasoning about termination of pure prolog programs. *Information and Computation*, 106(1):109–157, 1993.

[AP94]   K. Apt and A. Pellegrini. On the occur-check free logic programs. *ACM Transaction on Programming Languages and Systems*, 16(3):687–726, 1994.

[Apt89]   K.R. Apt. Introduction to Logic Programming. In J. van Leeuwen, editor, *Handbook of Theoretical Computer Science*. North Holland, 1989.

[AR89]   H. Abramson and M. Rogers, editors. *Meta-Programming in Logic Programming*. MIT Press, 1989.

[Bar92]   C. Baral. Generalized Negation As Failure and Semantics of Normal Disjunctive Logic Programs. In A Voronkov, editor, *Proceedings of International Conference on Logic Programming and Automated Reasoning, St. Petersburg*, pages 309–319, 1992.

[Bar94]   C. Baral. Rule based updates on simple knowledge bases. In *Proc. of AAAI'94, Seattle*, pages 136–141, August 1994.

[Bar95]   C. Baral. Reasoning about Actions : Non-deterministic effects, Constraints and Qualification. In C. Mellish, editor, *Proc. of IJCAI'95*, pages 2017–2023. Morgan Kaufmann, 1995.

[Bar97a]   C. Baral. Embedding revision programs in logic programming situation calculus. *Journal of Logic Programming*, 30(1):83–97, Jan 1997.

[Bar97b]   C. Baral. Relating logic programming theories of action and partial order planning. *Annals of Math and AI*, 21(2–4):131–153, 1997.

[Bar00]   C. Baral. Abductive reasoning through filtering. *Artificial Intelligence Journal*, 120(1):1–28, 2000.

[BBMR89]   A. Borgida, R. Brachman, D. McGuinness, and L. Resnick. CLASSIC: A structural data model for objects. In *Proc. SIGMOD'89*, pages 58–67, 1989.

[BD97]   S. Brass and J. Dix. Characterizations of the Disjunctive Stable Semantics by Partial Evaluation. *Journal of Logic Programming*, 32(3):207–228, 1997.

[BD98]   S. Brass and J. Dix. Characterizations of the Disjunctive Well-founded Semantics: Confluent Calculi and Iterated GCWA. *Journal of Automated Reasoning*, 20(1):143–165, 1998.

[BD99]   S. Brass and J. Dix. Semantics of (Disjunctive) Logic Programs Based on Partial Evaluation. *Journal of Logic Programming*, 38(3):167–213, 1999.

[BDFZ01]   S. Brass, J. Dix, B. Freitag, and U. Zukowski. Transformation-based bottom-up computation of the well-founded model. *Theory and Practice of Logic Programming*, 1(5):497–538, 2001.

[BDNP01]   S. Brass, J. Dix, I. Niemelä, and T. Przymusiński. On the Equivalence of the Static and Disjunctive Well-Founded Semantics and its Computation. *Theoretical Computer Science*, 258(1–2):523–553, 2001.

[BDP96]   S. Brass, J. Dix, and T. Przymusiński. Super logic programs. In *Proc. of KR'96*, pages 529–540, 1996.

[BE96]   P. Bonatti and T. Eiter. Querying Disjunctive Databases Through Nonmonotonic Logics. *Theoretical Computer Science*, 160:321–363, 1996.

[BE99]   G. Brewka and T. Eiter. Preferred answer sets for extended logic programs. *Artificial Intelligence*, 109(1–2):297–356, 1999.

[BED92]   R. Ben-Eliyahu and R. Dechter. Propositional semantics for disjunctive logic programs. In *Proceedings of the 1992 Joint International Conference and Symposium on Logic Programming*, pages 813–827, 1992.

[BEL00]   Y. Babovich, E. Erdem, and V. Lifschitz. Fages' theorem and answer set programming. In *Proc. International workshop on non-monotonic reasoning*, 2000.

[BF91]   N. Bidoit and C. Froidevaux. General logical databases and programs:
            Default logic semantics and stratification. *Journal of Information and
            Computation*, 91(1):15–54, 1991.

[BG93]   C. Baral and M. Gelfond. Representing concurrent actions in extended logic
            programming. In *Proc. of 13th International Joint Conference on Artificial
            Intelligence, Chambery, France*, pages 866–871, 1993.

[BG94]   C. Baral and M. Gelfond. Logic programming and knowledge
            representation. *Journal of Logic Programming*, 19,20:73–148,
            1994.

[BG97]   C. Baral and M. Gelfond. Reasoning about effects of concurrent actions.
            Journal of Logic Programming, 31(1–3):85–117, May 1997.

[BG00]   C. Baral and M. Gelfond. Reasoning agents in dynamic domains. In
            J Minker, editor, *Logic Based AI*, pages 257–279. Kluwer, 2000.

[BGK93]   C. Baral, M. Gelfond, and O. Kosheleva. Approximating general logic
            programs. In *Proceedings of International Logic Programming Symposium*,
            pages 181–198, 1993.

[BGK98]   C. Baral, M. Gelfond, and O. Kosheleva. Expanding queries to incomplete
            databases by interpolating general logic programs. *Journal of Logic
            Programming*, 35:195–230, 1998.

[BGN00]   M. Balduccini, M. Gelfond, and M. Nogueira. A-Prolog as a tool for
            declarative programming. In *Proceedings of the 12th International
            Conference on Software Engineering and Knowledge Engineering
            (SEKE'2000)*, 2000.

[BGN+01]   M. Balduccini, M. Gelfond, M. Nogueira, R. Watson, and M. Barry. An
            A-Prolog decision support system for the space shuttle, 2001. Submitted for
            publication.

[BGP97]   C. Baral, M. Gelfond, and A. Provetti. Representing Actions: Laws,
            Observations and Hypothesis. *Journal of Logic Programming*,
            31(1–3):201–243, May 1997.

[BGW99]   C. Baral, M. Gelfond, and R. Watson. Reasoning about actual and
            hypothetical occurrences of concurrent and non-deterministic actions. In
            B. Fronhofer and R. Pareschi, editors, *Theoretical approaches to dynamical
            worlds*, pages 73–110. Kluwer Academic, 1999.

[BK82]   K. Bowen and R. Kowalski. Amalgamating language and metalanguage in
            logic programming. In K. Clark and S.A. Tarnlund, editors, *Logic
            Programming*, pages 153–173. Academic Press, 1982.

[BK00]   F. Bacchus and F. Kabanza. Using temporal logics to express search
            control knowledge for planning. *Artificial Intelligence*, 16:123–191,
            2000.

[BL97]   C. Baral and J. Lobo. Defeasible specification in action theories. In *IJCAI
            97*, pages 1441–1446, 1997.

[BLM91]   C. Baral, J. Lobo, and J. Minker. $W F^3$: A Semantics for Negation in
            Normal Disjunctive Logic Programs with Equivalent Proof Methods.
            In *Proceedings of ISMIS 91*, pages 459–468, October 1991. Springer-
            Verlag.

[BLM92]   C. Baral, J. Lobo, and J. Minker. Generalized disjunctive well-founded
            semantics for logic programs. *Annals of Math and Artificial Intelligence*,
            5:89–132, 1992.

[BM90]   A. Bonner and L. McCarty. Adding negation as failure to intuitionistic logic
            programming. In S. Debray and M. Hermenegildo, editors, *Logic*

Programming: Proc. of the 1990 North American Conf., pages 681–703, 1990.

[BMPT92] A. Brogi, P. Mancarella, D. Pedreschi, and F. Turini. Meta for modularising logic programming. In *Proc. META'92*, pages 105–119, 1992.

[BMS95] H. Blair, W. Marek, and J. Schlipf. The expressiveness of locally stratified programs. *Annals of Mathematics and Artificial Intelligence*, 15(2): 209–229, 1995.

[BMS00] C. Baral, S. McIlraith, and T. Son. Formulating diagnostic problem solving using an action language with narratives and sensing. In *KR'2000*, pages 311–322, 2000.

[BNNS94] C. Bell, A. Nerode, R. Ng, and V.S. Subrahmanian. Mixed integer programming methods for computing non-monotonic deductive databases. *Journal of ACM*, 41(6):1178–1215, 1994.

[Bon95] P. Bonatti. Autoepistemic logics as a unifying framework for the semantics of logic programs. *Journal of Logic Programming*, 22(2):91–149, 1995.

[Bor92] A. Borgida. Description logics are not just for the flightless-birds: A new look at the utility and foundations of description logics. Technical report, Rutgers University, 1992.

[BR86] F. Bancilhon and R. Ramakrishnan. An amateur's introduction to recursive query processing strategies. *Proc. of ACM SIGMOD'86*, pages 16–52, May 28–30, 1986.

[BR87] C. Beeri and R. Ramakrishnan. On the power of magic. *Proc. Principles of Database Systems*, March 1987.

[Bre91] G. Brewka. Cumulative default logic: in defense of nonmonotonic inference rules. *Artificial Intelligence*, 50:183–205, 1991.

[Bre94] G. Brewka. Reasoning about priorities in default logic. In *AAAI'94*, 1994.

[Bre96] G. Brewka. Well-founded semantics for extended logic programs with dynamic preferences. *Journal of AI research*, 4:19–36, 1996.

[BS85] R. Brachman and J. Schmolze. An overview of the KLONE knowledge representation system. *Cognitive Science*, 9(2):171–216, 1985.

[BS91] C. Baral and V. S. Subrahmanian. Duality between alternative semantics of logic programs and nonmonotonic formalisms. In *Proc. of the International Workshop in logic programming and nonmonotonic reasoning*, pages 69–86, 1991.

[BS92] C. Baral and V. S. Subrahmanian. Stable and Extension Class Theory for Logic Programs and Default Logics. *Journal of Automated Reasoning*, 8:345–366, 1992.

[BS93] C. Baral and V. S. Subrahmanian. Duality between alternative semantics of logic programs and nonmonotonic formalisms. *Journal of Automated Reasoning*, 10:399–420, 1993.

[BS97] C. Baral and T. Son. Approximate reasoning about actions in presence of sensing and incomplete information. In *Proc. of International Logic Programming Symposium (ILPS 97)*, pages 387–401, 1997.

[BS99] C. Baral and T. Son. Adding hierarchical task networks to congolog. In *Proc. of Agent, theories and Languages (ATAL'99)*, 1999.

[BST01] C. Baral, T. Son, and L. Tuan. Reasoning about actions in presence of resources: applications to planning and scheduling. In *Proc. of International conference on Information Technology, Gopalpur, India*, pages 3–8. TataMcGraw Hill, 2001.

[BU01]   C. Baral and C. Uyan. Declarative specification and solution of
            combinatorial auctions using logic programming. In *Proc. of LPNMR'01*,
            pages 186–200, 2001.

[BW99]   M. Barry and R. Watson. Reasoning about actions for spacecraft
            redundancy management. In *Proceedings of the 1999 IEEE Aerospace
            conference*, volume 5, pages 101–112, 1999.

[Cav89]   L. Cavedon. Continuity, consistency, and completeness properties for logic
            programs. In G. Levi and M. Martelli, editors, *Logic Programming: Proc. of
            the Sixth Int'l Conf.*, pages 571–584, 1989.

[CDL01]   D. Calvanese, G. DeGiacomo, and M. Lenzerini. Identification constraints
            and functional dependencies in description logics. In *Proc. of IJCAI'2001*,
            pages 155–161, 2001.

[CDNL01]   D. Calvanese, G. DeGiacomo, D. Nardi, and M. Lenzerini. Reasoning in
            expressive description logics. In A. Robinson and A. Voronkov, editors,
            Handbook of automated reasoning. North Holland, 2001.

[CDS94]   M. Cadoli, F. Donini, and M. Schaerf. Is intractability of non-monotonic
            reasoning a real drawback. In *AAAI'94*, volume 2, pages 946–951, 1994.

[CDS96]   M. Cadoli, F. Donini, and M. Schaerf. Is intractability of non-monotonic
            reasoning a real drawback. *Artificial Intelligence*, 88(1–2):215–251,
            1996.

[CEF+97]   S. Citrigno, T. Eiter, W. Faber, G. Gottlob, C. Koch, N. Leone, C. Mateis,
            G. Pfeifer, and F. Scarcello. The dlv system: Model generator and
            application front ends. In *Proceedings of the 12th Workshop on Logic
            Programming*, pages 128–137, 1997.

[CEG94]   M. Cadoli, T. Eiter, and G. Gottlob. Default logic as a query language. In
            KR'94, pages 99–108, 1994.

[CEG97]   M. Cadoli, T. Eiter, and G. Gottlob. Default logic as a query language. *IEEE
            TKDE*, 9(3):448–463, 1997.

[CF90]   A. Cortesi and G. File. Graph properties for normal logic programs. In *Proc.
            of GULP 90*, 1990.

[CF97]   S. Ceri and P. Fraternali. *Designing database applications with objects and
            rules – the IDEA methodology*. Addison-Wesley, 1997.

[CH85]   A. Chandra and D. Harel. Horn clause queries and generalizations. *Journal
            of Logic Programming*, 2(1):1–5, 1985.

[Cha96]   D. Chamberlin. *Using the new DB2: IBM's Object-relational database
            system*. Morgan Kaufmann, 1996.

[Che93]   J. Chen. Minimal knowledge + negation as failure = only knowing
            (sometimes). In *Proceedings of the Second Int'l Workshop on Logic
            Programming and Non-monotonic Reasoning, Lisbon*, pages 132–150,
            1993.

[Cho95]   P. Cholewiński. Reasoning with stratified default theories. In *Proc. of
            LPNMR'95*, pages 273–286, 1995.

[CKW93]   W. Chen, M. Kifer, and D.S. Warren. A foundation for higher-order logic
            programming. *Journal of Logic Programming*, 15(3):187–230, 1993.

[CL89]   S. Costantini and G.A. Lanzarone. A metalogic programming language. In
            G. Levi and M. Martelli, editors, *Proc. ICLP'89*, pages 218–233, 1989.

[CM81]   W. Clockin and C. Mellish. *Programming in Prolog*. Springer, 1981.

[CMMT95]   P. Cholewiński, W. Marek, A. Mikitiuk, and M. Truszczyński.
            Experimenting with nonmonotonic reasoning. In *Proc. of ICLP'95*, pages
            267–281, 1995.

[CMT96]   P. Cholewiński, W. Marek, and M. Truszczyński. Default reasoning system DERES. In L. Aiello, J. Doyle, and S. Shapiro, editors, *Proc. of KR 96*, pages 518–528. Morgan Kaufmann, 1996.

[CPL97]   M. Cadoli, L. Palopoli, and M. Lenzerini. Datalog and description logics: expressive power. In *Proc. of DBPL'97*, pages 281–298, 1997.

[CS92]   M. Cadoli and M. Schaerf. A survey on complexity results for nonmonotonic logics. Technical report, University di Roma "La Sapienza", Dipartiment o di Informatica e sistemistica, Roma, Italy, 1992.

[CSW95]   W. Chen, T. Swift, and D. Warren. Efficient top-down computation of queries under the well-founded semantics. *Journal of Logic Programming*, 24(3):161–201, 1995.

[CW96]   W. Chen and D. Warren. Computation of stable models and its integration with logical query processing. *IEEE TKDE*, 8(5):742–757, 1996.

[DEGV97] E. Dantsin, T. Eiter, G. Gottlob, and A. Voronkov. Complexity and expressive power of logic programming. In *Proc. of 12th annual IEEE conference on Computational Complexity*, pages 82–101, 1997.

[DEGV01] E. Dantsin, T. Eiter, G. Gottlob, and A. Voronkov. Complexity and expressive power of logic programming. *ACM Computing Surveys*, 33(3):374–425, September 2001.

[DFN01]   J. Dix, U. Furbach, and I. Niemelä. Nonmonotonic Reasoning: Towards Efficient Calculi and Implementations. In A. Voronkov and A. Robinson, editors, *Handbook of Automated Reasoning, Volume 2, Chapter 18*, pages 1121–1234. Elsevier Science Press, 2001.

[DG84]   W. Dowling and H. Gallier. Linear time algorithms for testing the satisfiability of propositional Horn formulae. *Journal of Logic Programming*, 1:267–284, 1984.

[Dix91]   J. Dix. Classifying semantics of logic programs. In *Proceedings of International Workshop in logic programming and nonmonotonic reasoning, Washington D.C.*, pages 166–180, 1991.

[Dix92a] J. Dix. Classifying semantics of disjunctive logic programs. In *Proc. of JICSLP'92*, pages 798–812, 1992.

[Dix92b] J. Dix. A framework for representing and characterizing semantics of logic programs. In *Proc. of KR'92*, pages 591–602, 1992.

[Dix95a] J. Dix. A classification theory of semantics of normal logic programs: I. strong properties. *Fundamenta Informaticae*, 22(3):227–255, 1995.

[Dix95b] J. Dix. A classification theory of semantics of normal logic programs: II. weak properties. *Fundamenta Informaticae*, 22(3):257–288, 1995.

[DLNS98] F. Donini, M. Lenzerini, D. Nardi, and A. Schaerf. AL-log: Integrating datalog and description logics. *Journal of Intelligent Information Systems*, 10(3):227–252, 1998.

[DNK97]   Y. Dimopoulos, B. Nebel, and J. Koehler. Encoding planning problems in non-monotonic logic programs. In *Proc. of European conference on Planning*, pages 169–181, 1997.

[Doy79]   J. Doyle. A truth-maintenance system. *Artificial Intelligence*, 12:231–272, 1979.

[DOZ01]   J. Dix, M. Osorio, and C. Zepeda. A General Theory of Confluent Rewriting Systems for Logic Programming and its Applications. *Annals of Pure and Applied Logic*, 108(1–3): 153–188, 2001.

[DST00]   J. Delgrande, T. Schaub, and H. Tompits. Logic programs with compiled preferences. In W. Horn, editor, *European Coordinating Committee for Artificial Intelligence (ECCAI)*, pages 392–398. IOS Press, 2000.

[DST01]   J. Delgrande, T. Schaub, and H. Tompits. A generic compiler for ordered logic programs. In T. Eiter, W. Faber, and M. Truszczyński, editors, *Proceedings of the Sixth International Conference on Logic Programming and Nonmonotonic Reasoning*, pages 411–415, 2001.

[Dun91a] P. Dung. Negations as hypothesis: An abductive foundation for logic programming. In K. Furukawa, editor, *Proc. of 8th ICLP*. MIT press, pages 3–17, 1991.

[Dun91b] P. Dung. Well-founded reasoning with classical negation. In *Proc. of 1st international workshop on logic programming and non-monotonic reasoning*, 1991.

[Dun92]   P. Dung. On the relations between stable and well-founded semantics of logic programs. *Theoretical Computer Science*, 105:7–25, 1992.

[Dun93]   P. Dung. On the acceptability of arguments and its fundamental role in nonmonotonic reasoning and logic programming. In *Proc. of IJCAI'93*, pages 852–857, 1993.

[DV97]   E. Dantsin and A. Voronkov. Complexity of query answering in logic databases with complex values. In S. Adian and A. Nerode, editors, *Proc. of 4th International Symposium on logical foundations of computer science (LFCS'97)*, pages 56–66, 1997.

[EFG⁺00] T. Eiter, W. Faber, G. Gottlob, C. Koch, C. Mateis, N. Leone, G. Pfeifer, and F. Scarcello. The dlv system. In J. Minker, editor, *Pre-prints of Workshop on Logic-Based AI*, 2000.

[EFL⁺00] T. Eiter, W. Faber, N. Leone, G. Pfeifer, and A. Polleres. Planning under incomplete knowledge. In *Computational Logic - CL 2000, First International Conference, Proceedings*, number 1861 in LNAI, pages 807–821, London, UK, July 2000. Springer Verlag.

[EG93a]   T. Eiter and G. Gottlob. Complexity aspects of various semantics for disjunctive databases. In *Proc. of PODS'93*, pages 158–167, 1993.

[EG93b]   T. Eiter and G Gottlob. Complexity results for disjunctive logic programming and application to nonmonotonic logics. In D. Miller, editor, *Proceedings of the International Logic Programming Symposium (ILPS), Vancouver*, pages 266–178. MIT Press, 1993.

[EG93c]   T. Eiter and G. Gottlob. Propositional Circumscription and Extended Closed World Reasoning are Π_2^P-complete. *Theoretical Computer Science*, 114(2):231–245, 1993. Addendum 118:315.

[EG95]   T. Eiter and G. Gottlob. On the computational cost of disjunctive logic programming: propositional case. *Journal of Logic Programming*, 15(3–4):289–323, 1995.

[EG97]   T. Eiter and G. Gottlob. Expressiveness of stable model semantics for disjunctive logic programs with functions. *Journal of Logic Programming*, 33(2):167–178, 1997.

[EGG96]   T. Eiter, G. Gottlob, and Y. Gurevich. Normal Forms for Second-Order Logic over Finite Structures, and Classification of NP Optimization Problems. *Annals of Pure and Applied Logic*, 78:111–125, 1996.

[EGL97]   T. Eiter, G. Gottlob, and N. Leone. Semantics and complexity of abduction from default theories. *Artificial Intelligence*, 90:177–223, 1997.

[EGM94]   T. Eiter, G. Gottlob, and H. Mannila. Adding disjunction to datalog. In *Proc. of PODS*, pages 267–278, 1994.

[EGM97]   T. Eiter, G. Gottlob, and H. Mannila. Disjunctive datalog. *ACM TODS*, 22(3):364–418, 1997.

[EGV97]   T. Eiter, G. Gottlob, and H. Veith. Modular Logic Programming and Generalized Quantifiers. In J. Dix, U. Furbach, and A. Nerode, editors, *Proceedings of the 4th International Conference on Logic Programming and Nonmonotonic Reasoning (LPNMR-97)*, number 1265 in LNCS, pages 290–309. Springer, 1997. Extended paper CD-TR 97/111 (Preliminary Report), Institut für Informationssysteme, TU Wien, 1997.

[EK89]   K. Eshghi and R. Kowalski. Abduction compared with negation by failure. In *Proc. 6th Int'l Conference on Logic Programming*, pages 234–254. MIT Press, 1989.

[EL99]   E. Erdem and V. Lifschitz. Transformations of logic programs related to causality and planning. In *Proc. of LPNMR'99*, pages 107–116, 1999.

[Elk90]   C. Elkan. A rational reconstruction of non-monotonic truth maintenance systems. *Artificial Intelligence*, 43(2): 219–234, 1990.

[ELS97]   T. Eiter, N. Leone, and D. Saccà. On the partial semantics for disjunctive deductive databases. *Annals of Mathematics and Artificial Intelligence*, 19(1/2):59–96, 1997.

[ELS98]   T. Eiter, N. Leone, and D. Saccà. Expressive Power and Complexity of Partial Models for Disjunctive Deductive Databases. *Theoretical Computer Science*, 206(1–2):181–218, October 1998.

[ELW00]   E. Erdem, V. Lifschitz, and M. Wong. Wire routing and satisfiability planning. In *Proc. CL-2000*, pages 822–836, 2000.

[Esh90]   K. Eshghi. Computing Stable Models by Using the ATMS. In *Proc. AAAI-90*, pages 272–277, 1990.

[ET01]   D. East and M. Truszczyński. More on wire routing with answer set programming. In *Proc. of AAAI Spring symposium on Answer Set Programming*, 2001.

[Fag74]   R. Fagin. Generalized first-order spectra and polynomial-time recognizable sets. In R. Karp, editor, *Complexity of Computation*, pages 43–74. AMS, 1974.

[Fag90]   F. Fages. Consistency of Clark's completion and existence of stable models. Technical Report 90–15, Ecole Normale Supérieure, 1990.

[Fag94]   F. Fages. Consistency of Clark's completion and existence of stable models. *Journal of Methods of Logic in Computer Science*, 1:51–60, 1994.

[FBJ88]   M. Fitting and M. Ben-Jacob. Stratified and Three-Valued Logic programming Semantics. In R.A. Kowalski and K.A. Bowen, editors, *Proc. 5th International Conference and Symposium on Logic Programming*, pages 1054–1069, Seattle, Washington, August 15–19, 1988.

[FH89]   Y. Fujiwara and S. Honiden. Relating the TMS to autoepistemic logic. In *Proc. IJCAI'89*, pages 1199–1205, 1989.

[Fit85]   M. Fitting. A Kripke-Kleene semantics for logic programs. *Journal of Logic Programming*, 2(4):295–312, 1985.

[Fit86]   M. Fitting. Partial models and logic programming. *Theoretical Computer Science*, 48:229–255, 1986.

[Fit91]   M. Fitting. Well-founded semantics, generalized. In *Proceedings of International Symposium on Logic Programming, San Diego*, pages 71–84, 1991.

[FL01]   P. Ferraris and V. Lifschitz. Weight constraints as nested expressions, 2001. unpublished draft (http://www.cs.utexas.edu/users/vl/papers.html).

[FLMS93]   J. Fernandez, J. Lobo, J. Minker, and V. S. Subrahmanian. Disjunctive LP +
           integrity constraints = stable model semantics. *Annals of Mathematics and
           AI*, 18:449–479, 1993.

[FLP99]   W. Faber, N. Leone, and G. Pfeifer. Pushing goal derivation in DLP
           computations. In M. Gelfond, N. Leone, and G. Pfeifer, editors, *Proc. of
           LPNMR'99*, pages 177–191. Springer, 1999.

[FLP01a]   W. Faber, N. Leone, and G. Pfeifer. Experimenting with heuristics for
           answer set programming. In *Proc. of IJCAI'01*, pages 635–640, 2001.

[FLP01b]   W. Faber, N. Leone, and G. Pfeifer. Optimizing the computation of
           heuristics for answer set programming systems. In *Proc. of LPNMR'01*,
           pages 295–308, 2001.

[GBG01]   M. Gelfond, M. Balduccini, and J. Galloway. Diagnosing Physical Systems
           in A-Prolog. In T. Eiter, W. Faber, and M. Truszczyński, editors, *Proc. of the
           6th International Conference on Logic Programming and Nonmonotonic
           Reasoning*, pages 213–226, 2001.

[Gel87]   M. Gelfond. On stratified autoepistemic theories. In *Proc. of AAAI'87*,
           pages 207–211, 1987.

[Gel89]   A. Van Gelder. The alternating fixpoint of logic programs with negation.
           In *Proceedings of the Symposium on Principles of Database Systems*,
           pages 1–10, 1989.

[Gel90]   M. Gelfond. Belief sets, deductive databases and explanation based
           reasoning. Technical report, University of Texas at El Paso, 1990.

[Gel91a]   M. Gelfond. Epistemic semantics for disjunctive databases. Preprint, ILPS
           Workshop on Disjunctive Logic Programs, San Diego, Ca., 1991.

[Gel91b]   M. Gelfond. Strong introspection. In *Proc. of AAAI'91*, pages 386–391,
           1991.

[Gel94]   M. Gelfond. Logic programming and reasoning with incomplete
           information. *Annals of Mathematics and Artificial Intelligence*, 12:19–116,
           1994.

[Gel01]   M. Gelfond. Representing knowledge in A-Prolog. In *Computational Logic:
           from logic programming to the future, collection of papers in honour of
           R. Kowalski*. 2001.

[GG97]   M. Gelfond and A. Gabaldon. From functional specifications to logic
           programs. In J. Maluszyński, editor, *Proc. of International symposium on
           logic programming*, pages 355–370, 1997.

[GG99]   M. Gelfond and A. Gabaldon. Building a knowledge base: An example.
           Annals of Mathematics and Artificial Intelligence, 25(3–4):165–199, 1999.

[GHK+98]   M. Ghallab, A. Howe, C. Knoblock, D. McDermott, A. Ram, M. Veloso,
           D. Weld, and D. Wilkins. PDDL – the planning domain definition language,
           Yale University, March 1998.

[GL88]   M. Gelfond and V. Lifschitz. The stable model semantics for logic program-
           ming. In R. Kowalski and K. Bowen, editors, *Logic Programming: Proc. of
           the Fifth Int'l Conf. and Symp.*, pages 1070–1080. MIT Press, 1988.

[GL89]   M. Gelfond and V. Lifschitz. Compiling circumscriptive theories into logic
           programs. In M. Reinfrank, J. de Kleer, M. Ginsberg, and E. Sandewall,
           editors, *Non-Monotonic Reasoning: 2nd International Workshop (Lecture
           Notes in Artificial Intelligence 346)*, pages 74–99. Springer-Verlag, 1989.

[GL90]   M. Gelfond and V. Lifschitz. Logic programs with classical negation. In
           D. Warren and P. Szeredi, editors, *Logic Programming: Proc. of the Seventh
           Int'l Conf.*, pages 579–597, 1990.

[GL91]   M. Gelfond and V. Lifschitz. Classical negation in logic programs and disjunctive databases. *New Generation Computing*, 9:365–387, 1991.

[GL92]   M. Gelfond and V. Lifschitz. Representing actions in extended logic programs. In K. Apt, editor, *Joint International Conference and Symposium on Logic Programming.*, pages 559–573. MIT Press, 1992.

[GL93]   M. Gelfond and V. Lifschitz. Representing actions and change by logic programs. *Journal of Logic Programming*, 17(2,3,4):301–323, 1993.

[GLPT91]   M. Gelfond, V. Lifschitz, H. Przymusińska, and M. Truszczyński. Disjunctive defaults. In J. Allen, R. Fikes, and E. Sandewall, editors, *Principles of Knowledge Representation and Reasoning: Proc. of the Second Int'l Conf.*, pages 230–237, 1991.

[GM90]   L. Giordano and A. Martelli. Generalized stable models, truth maintainance and conflict resolution. In *Proc. of the Seventh International Conference on Logic Programming*, pages 427–441. The MIT Press, 1990.

[GMN+96]   G. Gottlob, S. Marcus, A. Nerode, G. Salzer, and V. S. Subrahmanian. A non-ground realization of the stable and well-founded semantics. *Theoretical Computer Science*, 166(1–2):221–262, 1996.

[GO92]   L. Giordano and N. Olivetti. Negation as failure in intuitionistic logic programming. In *Proc. of the Joint International Conference and Symposium on Logic Programming*, pages 430–445. The MIT Press, 1992.

[Got94]   G. Gottlob. Complexity and expressive power of disjunctive logic programming. In *Proc. of ILPS'94*, pages 23–42, 1994.

[Got95]   G. Gottlob. Translating default logic into standard autoepistemic logic. *JACM*, 42(4):711–740, 1995.

[GP91]   M. Gelfond and H. Przymusińska. Definitions in epistemic specifications. In A. Nerode, W. Marek, and V. S. Subrahmanian, editors, *Logic Programming and Non-monotonic Reasoning: Proc. of the First Int'l Workshop*, pages 245–259, 1991.

[GP93]   M. Gelfond and H. Przymusińska. Reasoning in open domains. In L. Pereira and A. Nerode, editors, *Proceedings of the Second International Workshop in Logic Programming and Nonmonotonic Reasoning*, pages 397–413, 1993.

[GP96]   M. Gelfond and H. Przymusińska. Towards a theory of elaboration tolerance: logic programming approach. *Journal of Software and Knowledge Engineering*, 6(1):89–112, 1996.

[GPP89]   M. Gelfond, H. Przymusińska, and T. Przymusiński. On the relationship between circumscription and negation as failure. *Artificial Intelligence*, 38(1):75–94, 1989.

[GS91]   P. Gardner and J. Shepherdson. Unfold/Fold transformation in logic programs. In J-L. Lassez and G. Plotkin, editors, *Computational Logic: Essays in honor of Alan Robinson*, pages 565–583. MIT press, 1991.

[GS97a]   M. Gelfond and T. Son. Reasoning with prioritized defaults. In J. Dix, L. Pereira, and T. Przymusiński, editors, *Proc. of the Workshop on Logic Programming and Knowledge Representation*, volume LNCS 1471, pages 89–109. Springer, 1997.

[GS97b]   S. Greco and D. Saccà. Deterministic semantics for Datalog⁻: Complexity and expressive power. In *Proc. of DOOD'97*, pages 337–350, 1997.

[GSZ93]   S. Greco, D. Saccà, and C. Zaniolo. Dynamic programming optimization for logic queries with aggregates. In *Proc. of ILPS'93*, pages 575–589, 1993.

[GT93]   M. Gelfond and B. Traylor. Representing null values in logic programs. In *Workshop on Logic Programming with incomplete information, Vancouver, BC.*, 1993.

[Hal91]   J. Halpern. Presburger arithmetic with unary predicates is π_1^1-complete. *Journal of Symbolic Logic*, 56, 1991.

[HB00]   H. Hoos and C. Boutilier. Solving combinatorial auctions using stochastic local search. In *Proc. of AAAI'00*, 2000.

[Hel99]   K. Heljanko. Using logic programs with stable model semantics to solve deadlock and reachability problems for 1-safe petri nets. *Fundamenta Informaticae*, 37(3):247–268, 1999.

[Hen01]   M. Henz. Scheduling a major college basketball conference – revisited, *Operation Research*, 49(1), 2001.

[HL91]   P. Hill and J. Lloyd. The Godel report. Technical Report TR-91-02, University of Bristol, 1991.

[HM00]   V. Haarslev and R. Moller. Expressive Abox reasoning with number restrictions, role hierarchies, and transitively closed roles. In *Proc. of KR'00*, pages 273–284, 2000.

[IM87]   A. Itai and J. Makowsky. Unification as a complexity measure for logic programming. *Journal of logic programming*, 4(105–117), 1987.

[Imm86]   N. Immerman. Relational queries computable in polynomial time. *Information and Control*, 68:86–104, 1986.

[Ino91]   K. Inoue. Extended logic programs with default assumptions. In *Proc. of ICLP'91*, 1991.

[IS91]   N. Iwayama and K. Satoh. Computing abduction using the TMS. In *Proc. of ICLP'91*, pages 505–518, 1991.

[IS98]   K. Inoue and C. Sakama. Negation as failure in the head. *Journal of Logic Programming*, 35(1):39–78, 1998.

[JK91]   U. Junker and K. Konolige. Computing the extensions of autoepistemic and default logics with a truth maintenance system. In *Proc. of AAAI'90*, pages 278–283, 1991.

[JL77]   N. Jones and W. Lasser. Complete problems in deterministic polynomial time. *Theoretical Computer Science*, 3:105–117, 1977.

[KL99]   C. Koch and N. Leone. Stable model checking made easy. In *IJCAI'99*, pages 70–75, 1999.

[Kle71]   S. Kleene. *Introduction to Metamathematics*. Wolters-Noordhoff publishing, 1971.

[KLM90]   S. Kraus, D. Lehman, and M. Magidor. Nonmonotonic reasoning, preferential models and cumulative logics. *Artificial Intelligence*, 44(1):167–207, 1990.

[KM90]   A. Kakas and P. Mancarella. Generalized stable models: a semantics for abduction. In *Proc. of ECAI'90*, pages 385–391, 1990.

[Kow79]   R. Kowalski. *Logic for Problem Solving*. North-Holland, 1979.

[Kow90]   R. Kowalski. Problems and promises of computational logic. In J. Lloyd, editor, *Computational Logic: Symposium Proceedings*, pages 80–95. Springer, 1990.

[KP88]   P. Kolaitis and C. Papadimitriou. Why not negation by fixpoint? In *Proc. of PODS'88*, pages 231–239, 1988.

[KP91]   P. Kolaitis and C. Papadimitriou. Why not negation by fixpoint? *Journal of Computer and System Sciences*, 43(1):125–144, 1991.

[KS90]   R. Kowalski and F. Sadri. Logic programs with exceptions. In D. Warren
           and P. Szeredi, editors, *Logic Programming: Proc. of the Seventh Int'l
           Conf.*, pages 598–613, 1990.

[KS92]   H. Kautz and B. Selman. Planning as satisfiability. In *Proc. of ECAI'92*,
           pages 359–363, 1992.

[KS96]   H. Kautz and B. Selman. Pushing the envelop: planning, propositional logic
           and stochastic search. In *Proc. of AAAI'96*, pages 1194–1201, 1996.

[Kun87]   K. Kunen. Negation in logic programming. *Journal of Logic Programming*,
           4(4):289–308, 1987.

[Kun89]   K. Kunen. Signed data dependencies in logic programs. *Journal of Logic
           Programming*, 7(3):231–245, 1989.

[KV95]   P. Kolaitis and M. Vardi. On the expressive power of Datalog: Tools and a
           case study. *Journal of Computer and System Sciences*, 51(1):110–134, 1995.

[Lif85a]   V. Lifschitz. Closed-world databases and circumscription. *Artificial
           Intelligence*, 27, 1985.

[Lif85b]   V. Lifschitz. Computing circumscription. In *Proc. of IJCAI'85*, pages
           121–127, 1985.

[Lif88]   V. Lifschitz. On the declarative semantics of logic programs with negation.
           In J. Minker, editor, *Foundations of Deductive Databases and Logic
           Programming*, pages 177–192. Morgan Kaufmann, San Mateo, CA., 1988.

[Lif89]   V. Lifschitz. Between circumscription and autoepistemic logic. In
           R. Brachman, H. Levesque, and R. Reiter, editors, *Proc. of the First Int'l
           Conf. on Principles of Knowledge Representation and Reasoning*, pages
           235–244, 1989.

[Lif90]   V. Lifschitz. On open defaults. In J. Lloyd, editor, *Computational Logic:
           Symposium Proceedings*, pages 80–95. Springer, 1990.

[Lif91]   V. Lifschitz. Nonmonotonic databases and epistemic queries: Preliminary
           report. In *Proceedings of International Joint Conference on Artificial
           Intelligence*, pages 381–386, Sydney, Australia, 1991.

[Lif93a]   V. Lifschitz. A language for representing actions. In *Working Papers of the
           Second Int'l Symp. on Logical Formalizations of Commonsense Knowledge*,
           1993.

[Lif93b]   V. Lifschitz. Restricted monotonicity. In *Proc. of AAAI'93*, pages 432–437,
           1993.

[Lif94]   V. Lifschitz. Circumscription. In D. Gabbay, C. Hogger, and J. Robinson,
           editors, *Handbook of Logic in AI and Logic Programming*, volume 3, pages
           298–352. Oxford University Press, 1994.

[Lif95]   V. Lifschitz. SLDNF, Constructive Negation and Grounding. In *Proc. of
           ICLP'95*, pages 581–595, 1995.

[Lif96]   V. Lifschitz. Foundations of declarative logic programming. In G. Brewka,
           editor, *Principles of Knowledge Representation*, pages 69–128. CSLI
           Publications, 1996.

[Lif97]   V. Lifschitz, editor. *Special issue of the Journal of Logic Programming on
           Reasoning about actions and change*, volume 31(1–3), May 1997.

[Lif99a]   V. Lifschitz. Action languages, answer sets and planning. In K. Apt,
           V. Marek, M. Truszczyński, and D. Warren, editors, *The Logic
           Programming Paradigm: a 25-Year perspective*, pages 357–373. Springer,
           1999.

[Lif99b]   V. Lifschitz. Answer set planning. In *Proc. International Conf. on Logic
           Programming*, pages 23–37, 1999.

[Lin91]   F. Lin. *A study of non-monotonic reasoning*. PhD thesis, Stanford
             University, 1991.

[Lin02]   F. Lin. Reducing strong equivalence of logic programs to entailment in
             classical propositional logic. In *Proc. of KR'02*, 2002.

[Llo84]   J. Lloyd. *Foundations of logic programming*. Springer, 1984.

[Llo87]   J. Lloyd. *Foundations of logic programming*. Springer, 1987. Second,
             extended edition.

[LM85]   J. Lassez and M. Maher. Optimal fixedpoints of logic programs. *Theoretical
             Computer Science*, 39:15–25, 1985.

[LMR92]   J. Lobo, J. Minker, and A. Rajasekar. *Foundations of disjunctive logic
             programming*. The MIT Press, 1992.

[LMT93]   V. Lifschitz, N. McCain, and H. Turner. Automation of reasoning about
             action: a logic programming approach. In *Posters of the International
             Symposium on Logic Programming*, 1993.

[LPS01]   N. Leone, S. Perri, and F. Scarcello. Improving ASP instantiators by
             join-ordering methods. In *Proc. of LPNMR'01*, pages 280–294, 2001.

[LPV01]   V. Lifschitz, D. Pearce, and A. Valverde. Strongly equivalent logic
             programs, *ACM Transactions on Computational Logic*, 2(4): 526–541,
             2001.

[LR96]   A. Levy and M. Rousset. CARIN: A representation language combining
             Horn rules and description logics. In *Proc. of ECAI'96*, pages 323–327,
             1996.

[LRL$^+$97] H. Levesque, R. Reiter, Y. Lesperance, F. Lin, and R. Scherl. GOLOG: A
             logic programming language for dynamic domains. *Journal of Logic
             Programming*, 31(1–3):59–84, April–June 1997.

[LRS96a]   N. Leone, P. Rullo, and F. Scarcello. On the computation of disjunctive
             stable models. In *Proc. of DEXA'96*, pages 654–666, 1996.

[LRS96b]   N. Leone, P. Rullo, and F. Scarcello. Stable model checking for disjunctive
             logic programs. In *Proc. of Logic in Databases (LID'96)*, pages 265–278,
             1996.

[LS90]   F. Lin and Y. Shoham. Epistemic semantics for fixed-points nonmonotonic
             logics. In R. Parikh, editor, *Theoretical Aspects of Reasoning and
             Knowledge: Proc. of the Third Conf.*, pages 111–120, Stanford University,
             Stanford, CA, 1990.

[LS92]   F. Lin and Y. Shoham. A logic of knowledge and justified assumptions.
             Artificial Intelligence, 57:271–290, 1992.

[LT94]   V. Lifschitz and H. Turner. Splitting a logic program. In Pascal
             Van Hentenryck, editor, *Proc. of the Eleventh Int'l Conf. on Logic
             Programming*, pages 23–38, 1994.

[LT95]   V. Lifschitz and H. Turner. From disjunctive programs to abduction. In
             Non-monotonic extensions of logic programming (Lecture notes in AI),
             pages 23–42, 1995.

[LT99]   V. Lifschitz and H. Turner. Representing transition systems by logic
             programs. In *Proc. of LPNMR'99*, pages 92–106, 1999.

[LTT99]   V. Lifschitz, L. Tang, and H. Turner. Nested expressions in logic programs.
             Annals of Mathematics and Artificial Intelligence, 25(3–4):369–389,
             1999.

[Luk84]   W. Lukaszewicz. Considerations on default logic. In R. Reiter, editor, *Proc.
             of the international workshop on non-monotonic reasoning*, pages 165–193,
             1984.

[LW92]   V. Lifschitz and T. Woo. Answer sets in general nonmonotonic reasoning. In
            *Proc. of the Third Int'l Conf. on Principles of Knowledge Representation
            and Reasoning*, pages 603–614, 1992.

[LY91]   L. Li and J. You. Making default inferences from logic programs. *Journal of
            Computational Intelligence*, 7:142–153, 1991.

[LY01]   F. Lin and J. You. Abduction in logic programming: a new definition and an
            abductive procedure based on rewriting. In *Proc. of IJCAI'01*, pages
            655–661, 2001.

[Mah87]   M. Maher. Correctness of a logic program transformation system. Technical
            report IBM Research Report RC 13496, IBM TJ Watson Research Center,
            1987.

[Mah88]   M. Maher. Equivalences of logic programs. In J. Minker, editor,
            Foundations of Deductive Databases and Logic Programming, pages
            627–658. Morgan Kaufmann, San Mateo, CA., 1988.

[Mah90]   M. Maher. Reasoning about stable models (and other unstable semantics).
            Technical report, IBM TJ Watson Research Center, 1990.

[Mah93a]   M. Maher. A logic programming view of CLP. In *Proc. of ICLP'93*, pages
            737–753, 1993.

[Mah93b]   M. Maher. A transformation system for deductive database modules with
            perfect model semantics. *Theoretical computer science*, 110:377–403, 1993.

[Mak94]   D. Makinson. General patterns in nonmonotonic reasoning. In D. Gabbay,
            C. Hogger, and J. Robinson, editors, *Handbook of Logic in AI and Logic
            Programming*, volume 3. Oxford University Press, 1994.

[McC80]   J. McCarthy. Circumscription – a form of non-monotonic reasoning.
            Artificial Intelligence, 13(1, 2):27–39,171–172, 1980.

[McD82]   D. McDermott. Nonmonotonic logic II: Nonmonotonic modal theories.
            Journal of the ACM., 29(1):33–57, 1982.

[McI97]   S. McIlraith. Representing actions and state constraints in model-based
            diagnosis. In *Proc. of AAAI'97*, pages 43–49, 1997.

[McI98]   S. McIlraith. Explanatory diagnosis: Conjecturing actions to explain
            observations. In *Proc. of KR'98*, 1998.

[MD80]   D. McDermott and J. Doyle. Nonmonotonic logic I. *Artificial Intelligence*,
            13(1,2):41–72, 1980.

[MDS92a]   B. Martens and D. De Schreye. A Perfect Herbrand Semantics for Untyped
            Vanilla Meta-Programming. In *Proc. of the Joint International Conference
            and Symposium on Logic Programming*. The MIT Press, 1992.

[MDS92b]   B. Martens and D. De Schreye. Why untyped non-ground meta-
            programming is not (much of) a problem. Technical report, Department of
            Comp. Science, Katholieke Universiteit Leuven, Belgium, 1992.

[Mil86]   D. Miller. A theory of modules in logic programming. In *Proc. of IEEE
            Symposium on Logic Programming*, pages 106–114, 1986.

[Min88]   J. Minker, editor. *Foundations of Deductive Databases and Logic
            Programming*. Morgan Kaufman, 1988.

[Min93]   J. Minker. An overview of nonmonotonic reasoning and logic programming.
            *Journal of Logic Programming (special issue on nonmonotonic reasoning
            and logic programming)*, 17(2–4), 1993.

[MM82]   A. Martelli and U. Montanari. An efficient unification algorithm. *ACM
            transaction on programming languages and systems*, 4:258–282, 1982.

[MMZ$^+$01] M. Moskewicz, C. Madigan, Y. Zhao, L. Zhang, and S. Malik. Chaff:
            Engineering an efficient sat solver. In *Design Automation Conference*, 2001.

[MNR94]   W. Marek, A. Nerode, and J. Remmel. The stable models of a predicate
           logic program. *Journal of Logic programming*, 21:129–153, 1994.

[Moo85]   R. Moore. Semantical considerations on nonmonotonic logic. *Artificial
           Intelligence*, 25(1):75–94, 1985.

[MR93]   J. Minker and C. Ruiz. On extended disjunctive logic programs. In *Proc. of
           ISMIS'93*, 1993. invited paper.

[MS89]   W. Marek and V. S. Subrahmanian. The relationship between logic program
           semantics and non–monotonic reasoning. In G. Levi and M. Martelli,
           editors, *Proc. of the Sixth Int'l Conf. on Logic Programming*, pages
           600–617, 1989.

[MSS99]   J. Marques-Silva and K. Sakallah. GRASP: a search algorithm for
           propositional satisfiability. *IEEE transactions on computers*, 48:506–521,
           1999.

[MT89]   W. Marek and M. Truszczyński. Stable semantics for logic programs and
           default reasoning. In E. Lusk and R. Overbeek, editors, *Proc. of the North
           American Conf. on Logic Programming*, pages 243–257. MIT Press,
           1989.

[MT91]   W. Marek and M. Truszczyński. Autoepistemic logic. *Journal of the ACM.*,
           3(38):588–619, 1991.

[MT93]   W. Marek and M. Truszczyński. *Nonmonotonic Logic: Context dependent
           reasoning*. Springer, 1993.

[MT94a]   W. Marek and M. Truszczyński. Revision programming, database updates
           and integrity constraints. In *Proc. of 5th International conference in
           Database theory, Prague*, 1994.

[MT94b]   N. McCain and H. Turner. Language independence and language tolerance
           in logic programs. In *Proc. of the Eleventh Int'l Conference on Logic
           Programming*, pages 38–57, 1994.

[MT95]   N. McCain and H. Turner. A causal theory of ramifications and
           qualifications. In *Proc. of IJCAI 95*, pages 1978–1984, 1995.

[MT99]   W. Marek and M Truszczyński. Stable models and an alternative logic
           programming paradigm. In Apt, K. and Marek, V. and Truszczyński, M. and
           Warren, D., editors, *The Logic Programming Paradigm: a 25-Year
           perspective*, pages 375–398. Springer, 1999.

[Myc83]   A. Mycroft. Logic programs and many valued logics. In *Proc. of the 1st
           STACS conference*, 1983.

[NB00]   M. Nakamura and C. Baral. Invariance, maintenance and other declarative
           objectives of triggers – a formal characterization of active databases. In
           *Proc. of First International Conference on Computational Logic (DOOD
           track) CL'2000*, pages 1210–1224, 2000.

[NE01]   M. Nakamura and R. Elmasri. Specifying and verifying correctness of
           triggers using declarative logic programming – a first step. In *Proc. of
           International conference on Information Technology, Gopalpur, India*,
           pages 129–137. TataMcGraw Hill, 2001.

[Nel49]   D. Nelson. Constructible falsity. *Journal of Symbolic Logic*, 14:16–26, 1949.

[Nie99]   I. Niemelä. Logic programs with stable model semantics as a constraint
           programming paradigm. *Annals of Mathematics and Artificial Intelligence*,
           25(3–4):241–271, 1999.

[NMS91]   A. Nerode, W. Marek, and V. S. Subrahamanian, editors. *Logic
           Programming and Non-monotonic Reasoning: Proceedings of the First
           International Workshop*. MIT Press, 1991.

[NS96]   I. Niemelä and P. Simons. Efficient implementation of the well-founded and
           stable model semantics. In *Proc. Joint international conference and
           symposium on Logic programming*, pages 289–303, 1996.

[NS97]   I. Niemelä and P. Simons. Smodels – an implementation of the stable model
           and well-founded semantics for normal logic programs. In J. Dix,
           U. Furbach, and A. Nerode, editors, *Proc. 4th international conference on
           Logic programming and non-monotonic reasoning*, pages 420–429.
           Springer, 1997.

[NS98]   I. Niemelä and T. Soininen. Formalizing configuration knowledge using
           rules with choices. In *Proc of workshop on Formal Aspects and Applications
           of Nonmonotonic Reasoning, Trento, Italy*, 1998.

[NSS99]   I. Niemelä, P. Simons, and T. Soininen. Stable model semantics of weight
           constraint rules. In *Proc. of LPNMR'99*, pages 317–331, 1999.

[O'K90]   R. O'Keefe. *The craft of Prolog*. MIT Press, 1990.

[ONA01]   M. Osorio, J. Navarro, and J. Arrazola. Equivalence in answer set
           programming. In *Proceedings of LOPSTR'01*, pages 18–28, 2001.

[ONG01]   M. Osorio, J. Nieves, and C. Giannella. Useful transformations in answer
           set programming. In A. Provetti and T. Son, editors, *Proceedings of the
           AAAI 2001 Spring Symposium Series*, pages 146–152. AAAI press,
           Stanford, 2001.

[PA93]   L. Pereira and J. Alferes. Optative reasoning with scenario semantics. In
           Proceedings of ICLP'93, Hungary, pages 601–619, 1993.

[PAA91a]   L. Pereira, J. Aparicio, and J. Alferes. Contradiction removal within
           well-founded semantics. In A. Nerode, V. Marek, and V. S. Subrahmanian,
           editors, *Logic Programming and Non-monotonic Reasoning: Proc. of the
           First Int'l Workshop*, pages 105–119. MIT Press, 1991.

[PAA91b]   L. Pereira, J. Aparicio, and J. Alferes. Non-monotonic reasoning with
           well-founded semantics. In *Proc. of the Eighth International Logic
           Programming Conference*, pages 475–489, 1991.

[PAA92a]   L. Pereira, J. Alferes, and J. Aparicio. Default theory for well founded
           semantics with explicit negation. In D. Pearce and G. Wagner, editors, *Logic
           in AI, Proc. of European Workshop JELIA'92 (LNAI, 633)*, pages 339–356,
           1992.

[PAA92b]   L. Pereira, J. Alferes, and J. Aparicio. Well founded semantics for logic
           programs with explicit negation. In *Proc. of European Conference on AI*,
           1992.

[PAA93]   L. Pereira, J. Alferes, and J. Aparicio. Nonmonotonic reasoning with logic
           programming. *Journal of Logic Programming (special issue on
           nonmonotonic reasoning and logic programming)*, 17(2–4):227–263, 1993.

[Pap94]   C. Papadimitriou. *Computational Complexity*. Addison-Wesley, 1994.

[Pat98]   N. Paton. *Active rules in database systems*. Springer-Verlag, 1998.

[PC89]   S. Pimental and J. Cuadrado. A truth maintainance system based on stable
           models. In *Proc. North American Conference on Logic Programming*, 1989.

[Pet92]   A. Pettorossi, editor. *Meta-programming in Logic*. Springer Verlag, June
           1992.

[PN93]   L. Pereira and A. Nerode, editors. *Logic Programming and Non-monotonic
           Reasoning: Proceedings of the Second International Workshop*. MIT Press,
           1993.

[PP90]   H. Przymusińska and T. Przymusiński. Weakly stratified logic programs.
           Fundamenta Informaticae, 13:51–65, 1990.

[PP92]   H. Przymusińska and T. Przymusiński. Stationary default extensions. In
           Proceedings of 4th International Workshop on Non-monotonic reasoning,
           pages 179–193, 1992.

[PP94]   H. Przymusińska and T. Przymusiński. Stationary default extensions.
           Fundamenta Informaticae, 21(1/2):67–87, 1994.

[Prz88a]   T. Przymusiński. On the declarative semantics of deductive databases and
           logic programs. In J. Minker, editor, *Foundations of Deductive Databases
           and Logic Programming*, pages 193–216. Morgan Kaufmann, San Mateo,
           CA., 1988.

[Prz88b]   T. Przymusiński. Perfect model semantics. In R. Kowalski and K. Bowen,
           editors, *Logic Programming: Proc. of the Fifth Int'l Conf. and Symp.*,
           pages 1081–1096, 1988.

[Prz89a]   T. Przymusiński. Every logic program has a natural stratification and an
           iterated least fixed point model. In *Proc. of Principles of Database Systems*,
           1989.

[Prz89b]   T. Przymusiński. On the declarative and procedural semantics of logic
           programs. *Journal of Automated Reasoning*, 5:167–205, 1989.

[Prz89c]   T. Przymusiński. Three-valued formalizations of non-monotonic reasoning
           and logic programming. In R. Brachman, H. Levesque, and R. Reiter,
           editors, *Proc. of the First Int'l Conf. on Principles of Knowledge
           Representation and Reasoning*, pages 341–348, 1989.

[Prz90a]   T. Przymusiński. Extended stable semantics for normal and disjunctive
           programs. In D. Warren and Peter Szeredi, editors, *Logic Programming:
           Proc. of the Seventh Int'l Conf.*, pages 459–477, MIT press, 1990.

[Prz90b]   T. Przymusiński. Stationary semantics for disjunctive logic programs and
           deductive databases. In *Proc. of NACLP'90*, pages 40–59, 1990.

[Prz90c]   T. Przymusiński. The well-founded semantics coincides with the
           three-valued stable semantics. *Fundamenta Informaticae*, 13(4):445–463,
           1990.

[Prz91]   T. Przymusiński. Stable semantics for disjunctive programs. *New generation
           computing*, 9(3,4):401–425, 1991.

[Prz95]   T. Przymusiński. Static semantics for normal and disjunctive logic programs.
           Annals of Mathematics and Artificial Intelligence, 14(2–4):323–357, 1995.

[PT95]   T. Przymusiński and H. Turner. Update by means of inference rules. In
           Proc. of Int'l Conf. on Logic Programming and non-monotonic reasoning,
           May–June 1995.

[PV95]   P. Picouet and V. Vianu. Semantics and expressive issues in active
           databases. In *Proc. of PODS'95*, pages 126–138, 1995.

[PW89]   D. Pearce and G. Wagner. Reasoning with negative information 1 – strong
           negation in logic programming. Technical report, Gruppe fur Logic,
           Wissentheorie and Information, Freie Universitat Berlin, 1989.

[Rei78]   R. Reiter. On closed world data bases. In H. Gallaire and J. Minker, editors,
           Logic and Data Bases, pages 119–140. Plenum Press, New York, 1978.

[Rei80]   R. Reiter. A logic for default reasoning. *Artificial Intelligence*,
           13(1,2):81–132, 1980.

[Rei82]   R. Reiter. Circumscription implies predicate completion (sometimes). In
           Proc. of IJCAI'82, pages 418–420, 1982.

[Rei87]   R. Reiter. A theory of diagnosis from first principles. *Artificial Intelligence*,
           32(1):57–95, 1987.

[RM89]   R. Reiter and A. Mackworth. A logical framework for depiction and image
           interpretation. *Artificial Intelligence*, 41(2):125–156, 1989.

[RM90]   A. Rajasekar and J. Minker. On stratified disjunctive programs. *Annals of Mathematics and Artificial Intelligence*, 1(1–4):339–357, 1990.

[Rob65]   J. Robinson. A machine-oriented logic based on the resolution principle. *JACM*, 12(1):23–41, 1965.

[Ros89a]   K. Ross. A procedural semantics for well founded negation in logic programming. In *Proc. of the eighth Symposium on Principles of Database Systems*, pages 22–34, 1989.

[Ros89b]   K. Ross. The well founded semantics for disjunctive logic programs. In *Proc. of DOOD'89*, pages 385–402, 1989.

[Ros92]   K. Ross. A procedural semantics for well-founded negation in logic Programs. *Journal of logic programming*, 13(1):1–22, 1992.

[RP91]   W. Rodi and S. Pimentel. A nonmonotonic assumption-based TMS using stable bases. In J. Allen, R. Fikes, and Erik Sandewall, editors, *Proc. of the Second Int'l Conf. on Principles of Knowledge Representation and Reasoning*, 1991.

[Sac93]   D. Saccà. Multiple stable models are needed to solve unique solution problems. In *Informal Proc. of the Second Compulog Net meeting on Knowledge Bases (CNKBS 93)*, 1993.

[Sac97]   D. Saccà. The expressive powers of stable models for bound and unbound datalog queries. *Journal of Computer and System Sciences*, 54(3):441–464, 1997.

[Sag88]   Y. Sagiv. Optimizing datalog programs. In J. Minker, editor, *Foundations of Deductive Databases and Logic Programming*, pages 659–698. Morgan Kaufmann, San Mateo, CA., 1988.

[Sak89]   C. Sakama. Possible model semantics for disjunctive databases. In *Proc. of the first international conference on deductive and object oriented databases*, pages 1055–1060, 1989.

[Sat87]   T. Sato. On the consistency of first-order logic programs. Technical report, ETL, TR-87-12, 1987.

[Sat90]   T. Sato. Completed logic programs and their consistency. *Journal of logic programming*, 9(1):33–44, 1990.

[SBM01a]   T. Son, C. Baral, and S. McIlraith. Extending answer set planning with sequence, conditional, loop, non-deterministic choice, and procedure constructs. In *Proc. of AAAI Spring symposium on Answer Set Programming*, 2001.

[SBM01b]   T. Son, C. Baral, and S. McIlraith. Planning with different forms of domain dependent control knowledge – an answer set programming approach. In *Proc. of LPNMR'01*, pages 226–239, 2001.

[Sch87]   J. Schlipf. Decidability and definability with circumscription. *Annals of pure and applied logic*, 35, 1987.

[Sch90]   J. Schlipf. The expressive powers of the logic programming semantics. In *Proc. of PODS'90*, pages 196–204, 1990.

[Sch91]   G. Schwarz. Autoepistemic logic of knowledge. In A. Nerode, V. Marek, and Subrahmanian V. S., editors, *Logic Programming and Non-monotonic Reasoning: Proc. of the First Int'l Workshop*, pages 260–274, 1991.

[Sch92]   J. Schlipf. Formalizing a logic for logic programming. *Annals of Mathematics and Artificial Intelligence*, 5:279–302, 1992.

[Sch93]   J. Schlipf. Some remarks on computability and open domain semantics, 1993. manuscript.

[Sch95a]   J. Schlipf. Complexity and undecidability results for logic programming. *Annals of Mathematics and Artificial Intelligence*, 15(3–4):257–288, 1995.

[Sch95b]   J. Schlipf. The expressive powers of the logic programming semantics. *Journal of computer and system sciences*, 51(1):64–86, 1995.

[Sek91]   H. Seki. Unfold/Fold transformation of stratified programs. *Theoretical Computer Science*, 86:107–139, 1991.

[Sek93]   H. Seki. Unfold/Fold transformation for the well-founded semantics. *Journal of Logic programming*, 16:5–23, 1993.

[SGN99]   T. Soininen, E. Gelle, and I. Niemelä. A fixpoint definition of dynamic constraint satisfaction. In *Proceedings of the Fifth International Conference on Principles and Practice of Constraint Programming, Alexandria, Virginia, USA.* Springer-Verlag, October 1999.

[Sha84]   E. Shapiro. Alternation and the computational complexity of logic programs. *Journal of Logic Programming*, 1:19–33, 1984.

[Sha97]   M. Shanahan. *Solving the frame problem: A mathematical investigation of the commonsense law of inertia.* MIT Press, 1997.

[Sim99]   P. Simons. Extending the stable model semantics with more expressive rules. In *Proc. of International Conference on Logic Programming and Nonmonotonic Reasoning, LPNMR'99*, 1999.

[Sim00]   P. Simons. *Extending and implementing the stable model semantics.* PhD thesis, Helsinki University of Technology, 2000.

[SN99]   T. Soininen and I. Niemelä. Developing a declarative rule language for applications in product configuration. In G. Gupta, editor, *Proc. of Practical Aspects of Declarative Languages '99*, volume 1551, pages 305–319. Springer, 1999.

[SNV95]   V. S. Subrahmanian, D. Nau, and C. Vago. WFS + branch and bound = stable models. *IEEE Transactions on Knowledge and Data Engineering*, 7(3):362–377, 1995.

[SS86]   L. Sterling and E. Shapiro. *The art of Prolog.* MIT press, 1986.

[SS00]   T. Sandholm and S. Suri. Improved algorithms for optimal winner determination in combinatorial auctions and generalizations. In *Proc. of AAAI'00*, 2000.

[Ste90]   L. Sterling. *The practice of Prolog.* MIT press, 1990.

[Sto77]   L. J. Stockmeyer. The Polynomial-Time Hierarchy. *Theoretical Computer Science*, 3:1–22, 1977.

[Str93]   K. Stroetman. A Completeness Result for SLDNF-Resolution. *Journal of Logic Programming*, 15:337–355, 1993.

[SW01]   T. Schaub and K. Wang. A comparative study of logic programs with preference. In B. Nebel, editor, *Proceedings of the International Joint Conference on Artificial Intelligence*, pages 597–602, 2001.

[Syr98]   T. Syrjänen. Implementation of local grounding for logic programs with stable model semantics. Technical Report B18, Digital Systems Laboratory, Helsinki University of Technology, October 1998.

[SZ90]   D. Saccà and C. Zaniolo. Stable models and non-determinism in logic programs with negation. In *Proc. of the Ninth Symp. on Principles of Database Systems*, 1990.

[SZ95]   V. S. Subrahmanian and C. Zaniolo. Relating stable models and AI planning domains. In L. Sterling, editor, *Proc. ICLP-95*, pages 233–247. MIT Press, 1995.

[Tar55]   A. Tarski. A lattice-theoretical fixpoint theorem and its applications. *Pacific Journal of Mathematics*, 5:285–309, 1955.

[Tar77]   S. Tarnlund. Horn clause computability. *BIT*, 17:215–216, 1977.

[TB01]   L. Tuan and C. Baral. Effect of knowledge representation on model based planning: experiments using logic programming encodings. In *Proc. of AAAI Spring symposium on Answer Set Programming*, 2001.

[Thi97]   M. Thielscher. A theory of dynamic diagnosis. *ETAI (http://www.ep.liu.se/ea/cis/1997/011)*, 2(11), 1997.

[Tru99]   M. Truszczyński. Computing large and small stable models. In *Proc. of ICLP'99*, pages 169–183, 1999.

[TS84]   H. Tamaki and T. Sato. Unfold/Fold transformation of logic programs. In *Proc. of 2nd International conference on logic programming*, pages 127–138, 1984.

[TS88]   R. Topor and L. Sonenberg. On domain independent databases. In J. Minker, editor, *Foundations of Deductive Databases and Logic Programming*, pages 217–240. Morgan Kaufmann, San Mateo, CA., 1988.

[Tur93]   H. Turner. A monotonicity theorem for extended logic programs. In D. S. Warren, editor, *Proc. of 10th International Conference on Logic Programming*, pages 567–585, 1993.

[Tur94]   H. Turner. Signed logic programs. In *Proc. of the 1994 International Symposium on Logic Programming*, pages 61–75, 1994.

[Tur95]   H. Turner. Representing actions in default logic: A situation calculus approach. In *Proceedings of the Symposium in honor of Michael Gelfond's 50th birthday*, 1995.

[Tur96]   H. Turner. Splitting a default theory. In *Proceedings of AAAI'96*, 1996.

[Tur97]   H. Turner. Representing actions in logic programs and default theories. *Journal of Logic Programming*, 31(1–3):245–298, May 1997.

[Tur01]   H. Turner. Strong equivalence for logic programs and default theories (made easy). In *Proc. of LPNMR'01*, pages 81–92, 2001.

[TW01]   D. Toman and G. Weddell. On attributes, roles and dependencies in description logics and the Ackermann case of the decision problem. In *Proc. of DL'01*, pages 76–85, 2001.

[Ull88a]   J. Ullman. *Principles of Database and Knowledge-base Systems, volume I*. Computer Science Press, 1988.

[Ull88b]   J. Ullman. *Principles of Database and Knowledge-base Systems, volume II*. Computer Science Press, 1988.

[Var82]   M. Vardi. The complexity of relational query languages. In *ACM symposium on theory of computing (STOC)*, pages 137–146, 1982.

[vBD83]   J. van Benthem and K. Doets Higher order logic. In D. Gabbay and F. Guenthner, editors, *Handbook of Philosophical Logic*, volume 1, pages 275–329. Reidel Publishing Company, 1983.

[VG88]   A. Van Gelder. Negation as failure using tight derivations for general logic programs. In J. Minker, editor, *Foundations of Deductive Databases and Logic Programming*, pages 149–176. Morgan Kaufmann, San Mateo, CA, 1988.

[VGRS88]   A. Van Gelder, K. Ross, and J. Schlpif. Unfounded Sets and Well-founded Semantics for General Logic Programs. In *Proc. 7th Symposium on Principles of Database Systems*, pages 221–230, 1988.

[VGRS91]   A. Van Gelder, K. Ross, and J. Schlipf. The well-founded semantics for general logic programs. *Journal of ACM*, 38(3):620–650, 1991.

[VV98]   S. Vorobyov and A. Voronkov. Complexity of nonrecursive logic programs with complex values. In *Proc. of PODS'98*, pages 244–253, 1998.

[Wag93]   G. Wagner. Reasoning with inconsistency in extended deductive databases. In *Proc. of 2nd International workshop on logic programming and non-monotonic reasoning*, 1993.

[Wat99]   R. Watson. An application of action theory to the space shuttle. In G. Gupta, editor, *Proc. of Practical Aspects of Declarative Languages '99*, volume 1551, pages 290–304. Springer, 1999.

[WB93]   C. Witteveen and G. Brewka. Skeptical reason maintainance and belief revision. *Artificial Intelligence*, 61:1–36, 1993.

[WBOL92]   L. Wos, J. Boyle, R. Overbeck, and E. Lusk. *Automated Reasoning: Introduction and Applications*. McGraw Hill, 2nd edition, 1992.

[WC96]   J. Widom and S. Ceri, editors. *Active Database Systems – Triggers and Rules for advanced database processing*. Morgan Kaufmann, 1996.

[Wit91]   C. Witteveen. Skeptical reason maintenance system is tractable. In J. Allen, R. Fikes, and E. Sandewall, editors, *Proc. of KR'91*, pages 570–581, 1991.

[WZ98]   H. Wang and C. Zaniolo. User defined aggregates for logical data languages. In *Proc. of DDLP'98*, pages 85–97, 1998.

[WZ00a]   H. Wang and C. Zaniolo. Nonmonotonic Reasoning in LDL++. In J. Minker, editor, *Logic-Based Artificial Intelligence*. Kluwer, 2000.

[WZ00b]   H. Wang and C. Zaniolo. User defined aggregates in object-relational systems. In *Proc. of ICDE'00*, pages 135–144, 2000.

[WZ00c]   H. Wang and C. Zaniolo. Using SQL to build new aggregates and extenders for object-relational systems. In *Proc. of VLDB'00*, 2000.

[YY90]   J. You and L. Yuan. Three-valued formalization of logic programming: is it needed? In *Proc. of PODS'90*, pages 172–182, 1990.

[YY94]   J. You and L. Yuan. A three-valued semantics for deductive databases and logic programs. *Journal of Computer and System Sciences*, 49(2):334–361, 1994.

[YY95]   J. You and L. Yuan. On the equivalence of semantics for normal logic programs. *Journal of Logic Programming*, 22:212–221, 1995.

[Zan88]   C. Zaniolo. Design and implementation of a logic based language for data intensive applications. In R. Kowalski and K. Bowen, editors, *Logic Programming: Proc. of the Fifth Int'l Conf. and Symp.*, pages 1666–1687, 1988.

[ZAO93]   C. Zaniolo, N. Arni, and K. Ong. Negation and aggregates in recursive rules: the LDL++ approach. In *Proc. of DOOD'93*, pages 204–221, 1993.

[Zha97]   H. Zhang. SATO: An efficient propositional prover. In *Proc. of CADE'97*, pages 272–275, 1997.

[ZF97]   Y. Zhang and N. Foo. Answer sets for prioritized logic programs. In *Proceedings of ILPS'97*, pages 69–83, 1997.

Index of notation

519

Index of terms